Letters
From The Attic

Also by Charles Young

The Last Man on Earth

Luck of the Draw

Clouds over Hydra (Greek)

Potassett

The Hydra Chronicle

Letters FROM THE ATTIC

Save the Last Dance for Me

CHARLES YOUNG

iUniverse LLC
Bloomington

LETTERS FROM THE ATTIC
SAVE THE LAST DANCE FOR ME

This is a work of fiction. All of the characters, names, incidents, organizations, and dialogue in this novel are either the products of the author's imagination or are used fictitiously.

iUniverse books may be ordered through booksellers or by contacting:

iUniverse LLC
1663 Liberty Drive
Bloomington, IN 47403
www.iuniverse.com
1-800-Authors (1-800-288-4677)

ISBN: 978-1-4759-7601-4 (sc)
ISBN: 978-1-4759-7602-1 (hc)
ISBN: 978-1-4759-7603-8 (ebk)

Library of Congress Control Number: 2013903315

Printed in the United States of America

iUniverse rev. date: 09/05/2013

Cover – author at Columbia 1947, Photo by David Manzella.

This novel is dedicated to the memory of my sister Betty who saved the last dance for me.

ITHACA

When you set out on your journey to Ithaca,
pray that the road is long,
full of adventure, full of knowledge.
The Lestrygonians and the Cyclops,
the angry Posidon—do not fear them:
You will never find such as these on your path,
if your thoughts remain lofty,
if a fine emotion touches your spirit and your body.
The Lestrygonians and the Cyclops,
the fierce Posidon you will never encounter,
if you do not carry them within your soul,
if your soul does not set them up before you.

Pray that the road is long.
That the summer mornings are many, when,
with such pleasure, with such joy
you will enter ports seen for the first time;
stop at Phoenician markets,
and purchase fine merchandise,
mother-of-pearl and coral, amber and ebony,
and sensual perfumes of all kinds,
as many sensual perfumes as you can;
visit many Egyptian cities,
to learn and learn from scholars.

Always keep Ithaca in your mind.
To arrive there is your ultimate goal.
But do not hurry the voyage at all.
It is better to let it last for many years:
and to anchor at the island when you are old,
rich with all you have gained on the way,
not expecting that Ithaca will offer you riches.

Ithaca has given you the beautiful voyage.
Without her you would have never set out on the road.
She has nothing more to give you.

And if you find her poor, Ithaca has not deceived you.
Wise as you have become, with so much experience,
you must have already understood what Ithaca means.

Constantine P. Cavafy (1915)

-ONE-

NEW BRITAIN, CONNECTICUT 2010

I AM HOME. LIKE the grizzled Odysseus, I have returned to spend my final years in my native land after a long absence abroad that began in 1967. At the time, the tapestry that was the United States had begun to unravel –Vietnam, the assassinations of the two Kennedys and Martin Luther King, Jr., and sex, drugs, and rock and roll all took their toll on the nation. To care for my wife, Marcie, who was recovering from a bout with thyroid cancer, and our three small children, I found myself working sixteen hours a day at two jobs, teaching and managing a general store. Fate then intervened. I spotted a notice for teaching positions abroad at the placement office of Central Connecticut University. Outlandish as it seemed, I filled out an initial application for Athens College in Athens, Greece. Over the next few months, more paperwork followed, I was interviewed in New York and finally signed a three-year contract. In the fall of 1967 I moved with my wife and our three kids to Marousi, a sleepy little hamlet north of Athens on the slopes of Pendeli that time had forgotten. Life was idyllic. We lived on a dirt street, dusty in summer, muddy in winter; goats grazed in shady olive groves; chickens roamed free. Gypsies wandered through, peddling their wares and offering to sharpen knives. At night revelers wending their way home from the local *taverna* were often heard singing. My wife's health, always precarious, vastly improved. The kids happily bonded with the family a few doors away and soon babbled in Greek. At the end of my contract, I signed on again at the college. Two years later tragedy struck. The cancer, which had been in remission, reared its ugly head. Marcie succumbed in 1975.

On my own with three rampant teenagers, I could not have coped without Mary, a classy Greek American guidance counselor at the college. Having recently lost her husband to the same insidious disease as my wife, Mary, who was childless, found herself suddenly besieged by a desperate widower and his three waifs. Because of her ability to charm the hellions and magically solve problems, I called her Circe, after the enchantress loved by Odysseus. It was she who suggested I look for an inexpensive piece of property on one of the nearby islands in the Saronic Gulf—a hangout for weekends and holidays would keep the kids away from the temptations and distractions of metropolitan Athens.

That fall we made several trips to look at real estate on the islands of Aegina, Poros, and Spetses. Everything was pricey, far out of my budget. About to give up, we made a final trip to Hydra, a small, rocky island four hours from the port of Piraeus. Ten miles long and two wide, the island had little going for it other than a picturesque, horseshoe shaped port. The prices looked right, but then we discovered that the island fell under the jurisdiction of the National Archaeological Society, whose policies mandated adherence to a strict building code.

"Which means?" I asked the realtor, a short, balding man in an ill-fitting three-piece suit.

"No worry," he quickly assured us, waving his arms about. "Start with ruin. Same footprint like old house. No wood, no brick, only stone. All the stones you want right here on island. White outside like everybody else, same kind tile roof. Just one bad thing. No automobile, no truck, no motorbike. All forbidden."

I looked at Circe, who was listening enthralled. "I can live with that. We know what cars are doing to Athens."

In its heyday during the eighteenth and nineteenth centuries, Hydra housed forty thousand inhabitants; in the 1970's it was down to two thousand. Abandoned dwellings in all stages of disrepair were everywhere. Locating the lawful owner and reaching an agreement, however, was no simple task. In property after property that we considered, the parties appeared prepared to sell until it came to the price, which often rose astronomically as we spoke. Multiple heirs were another ordeal. One family member had immigrated to Africa, another to Australia; they had been long out of touch. Two sisters, joint owners, had not spoken to each other in years. After a dozen or so of these frustrating episodes, we were about to give up when the agent mentioned a piece of property that had just come on the market. An American army officer serving in Greece had purchased the land on the island and started to build. He was transferred back to the States and was now anxious to sell.

I rolled my eyes. "Smells fishy, Circe. Something has to be wrong with the property if the guy wants to get rid of it."

"Not necessarily," she replied, excited at the prospect. "He could be having second thoughts now that he's back home. Maybe he's

3

got a wife who doesn't share his enthusiasm for the Mediterranean. What's important is that he began building. That means he has a proper deed. And a building permit. Since we're here, let's take a look at the property."

After lunch at a waterfront *taverna* in the port, we followed the huffing and puffing realtor up an endless flight of over three hundred steps and then wound our way through one sleepy neighborhood after another. We finally arrived at the crest of an empty hillside. On a site of about half an acre stood four stark, roofless stone walls with openings for windows and doors. A donkey stabled inside on a dirt floor littered with trash, straw and shit brayed a noisy greeting.

"Cheap, twenty thousand only," the agent offered, wiping the sweat from his brow. "You get papers of title, building permit, and plan for house. What more you want?"

I shrugged, feigning indifference. "We'll take a look around and think about it. I do like the view of the water down below and the mountains on the mainland across the way. And you say that the plans have been approved? Does that mean we have to follow them?"

"No, no, no," the realtor was quick to reply. "Only outside. Inside, do what you like. Take time, have good look. Come my office in port when you finished. You won't find no better property on island."

Over the next three or four hours, Circe and I checked out several nearby ruins. We also spoke to a number of friendly locals whose families went back for generations on the island. For an overview of the area, we carefully picked our way up a rocky path on the treacherous slope of a three hundred foot outcropping of cliff. I pointed out to Circe that this buffer would shield us from the north wind. At the top a pristine white chapel kept a lonely vigil over the vast scene below: on the inland side, a valley of scattered ruins amid red-tiled roofs of inhabited dwellings; on the seaside, three small islands dotted the body of blue water that stretched to the mainland some ten miles across the way. The chapel was dark and cool and smelled heavily of incense. We lit votive candles, and Circe crossed herself in front of an icon of Saint Thanasis, patron of the chapel. Back down at the site, we paced off the area that would eventually become our garden and inspected the original cistern. Although smelly and half filled with debris, it appeared to be in good shape structurally and needed only a thorough cleaning. We next measured the existing walls, finding there was more than ample room for a large living room with an inglenook, a dining room, kitchen, and bathroom. The bedrooms and a master bathroom would make up the second level. A terrace for the western view, Circe insisted, was a must.

I chuckled at her enthusiasm. "Talk about putting the cart before the horse. We don't even own the property, and you have us moving in. Twenty grand does seem a lot for four empty stone walls."

"But we'll be getting a clear title and the building permit. And no static from a dozen relatives spread all over the globe. Look, Charlie, you've still got royalties coming in from your last book. And I can loan you money if you get in a pinch. We don't have to do everything all at once. If we cover the existing walls, put in windows and doors, we can move into the first floor on weekends and save on hotel bills. Play Greek. Put in a bid of eighteen thousand."

Two weeks later our bid was accepted. We signed the papers on Hydra and the property was registered in the town hall. Throughout the following winter, rain or shine, we faithfully camped out in our ruin every weekend and holiday, moving rocks, shifting dirt, cleaning the cistern, whitewashing, and painting. During the week a pair of local stonemasons hauled up building materials from the port by horse and donkey –bags of cement, sand, gravel and slabs of slate and marble to complete the second floor and terraces. A local carpenter built and installed doors, windows, kitchen cabinets, bookcases, closets, and a magnificent bed. The final touch was the electricity – no more kerosene lamps. And plumbing. We called the first flush, "the flush heard round the world." In late spring, seven months after construction had begun, our villa was a home ready for occupancy. This was some kind of record according to our awed neighbors and the priest who officiated at the traditional house blessing and a feast of roast lamb.

Kids have a way of growing up. Before we knew it, all three had left the nest and returned to the States for schooling and careers. It was then 1978, and cars and pollution had exacted their toll on the capital. Sadly, our beloved Marousi had become a vast shopping center clogged with motor vehicles. Gone were the goats, gypsies, and olive trees. Our dirt street was paved.

On Hydra, I accepted a position in the English department at the National Maritime Academy and persuaded Circe to opt for early retirement. We then moved permanently to the island. For the next thirty years we lived our dream: I continued my teaching and wrote two bestsellers. During evenings on our terrace we witnessed spectacular sunsets over the mountains of the Peloponnese, wined and dined, and danced under the stars.

Those halcyon years fled all too quickly. Out of nowhere a myriad of health issues that accompany aging – arthritis, glaucoma, diabetes two, hearing loss – made it necessary for us to return to my family home in Connecticut. While I no longer drive , Circe, who is a few years younger, manages to see that we get from one appointment to the next with doctors, doctors, doctors, who prescribe pills, pills, pills for a host of pesky ailments.

We miss the island life, the friendly neighbors, our hilltop villa, evening sunsets, and glorious views of the sea and mountains, but the old family homestead in New Britain is comfortable enough and meets all of our needs. The town, though a ghost of what it once was, still has good doctors and a hospital. My sister is just a short fifteen-minute walk away. The house has a large garden and a patio off the kitchen. For company, we have rabbits, a clan of gray squirrels, and the occasional skunk or possum. Hummingbirds, woodpeckers, and doves keep me busy filling the feeders. My retreat on the third floor is an open studio lined with shelves overcrowded with books and old manuscripts. An oversized desk that once held my typewriter is now home to my computer. A trapdoor in the ceiling above the desk opens to an attic crammed with old furniture, steamer trunks, lamps, and boxes.

"You won't believe what I just found on the third floor," my wife announced, coming down the steps into the living room. "I was up there looking for some place to store my yarn, and there it was, this box. I know it wasn't there before."

"Had to be the carpenter installing insulation. He probably took it down from the attic and didn't put it back. A lot of that junk up there has to be pitched."

"No, no, not this box," Circe vigorously protested. "It's full of letters postmarked from the forties. Bundles of them, all neatly tied up. And photos and greeting cards. Family history. You've got to look at them."

"I will," I said, my curiosity aroused. "Could be letters I wrote home during the war. Sounds like something my mother would save. She was a real pack rat, never threw anything away."

The box was sturdy cardboard and packed with letters as my wife had said. I brought the box down from the third floor, set it on the kitchen table and handed Circe a loose bulky envelope off the top.

"Check this out, love." I said, and took up a slim packet of letters that had a small jeweler's box attached. The dried out rubber band broke and crumbled in my hand.

Launa Darcy. August 1940.

I caught my breath and stared at the name in disbelief. *Launa Darcy.* My first love. How … how … did these letters happen to turn up after all these years? Where was Launa today? Was she well? And her husband, who was older, was he still alive? Did she have the sons she often talked about and who would be the age of my kids? Had she read my books? The humiliation of our last meeting—the love, anger, jealousy, guilt, hate, regret, rage—rose in my psyche like a swarm of locusts that had lain dormant for the past sixty years.

Circe's scream snapped me back to the present. "A dead mouse!" she cried, wringing her hands. "Oh my God, Charlie, burn the lot!"

"Easy, easy, love," I cautioned. "Let me look at what we have here."

I picked up the envelope she had thrown down and drew out a thick lock of blonde silken curls. *"Donny's first haircut,"* I read aloud my mother's neat calligraphy. "My little brother. He was eight when I went into the service. Didn't I tell you that my mother saved everything?"

"I'll take your word for it," Circe replied skeptically, now more composed. Gingerly she picked up the little jeweler's box on the table. "What can this be? Gold, maybe?"

"Don't count on it," I said, uneasily eyeing Launa's letters in my hand. "Back then in the Depression no one had money for jewelry or anything else."

"Look, smarty, it is jewelry. A pair of something. Not earrings. Can't be cufflinks. Each has a chain with the number forty, the year ..." Circe paused and regarded me with concern. "Love, are you all right? You look like you've seen a ghost."

"I ... I ... I ..." Words failed me. I took the box from her. "Maybe I have. I didn't expect anything like this to turn up."

"You still haven't told me what they are."

I felt my heart quicken. "Lapel pins. Rings for junior high graduation were too expensive for most families during the hard times. Instead, we were given these little trinkets. Same idea. Kids going steady often exchanged them."

"But there are two here. One has your initials. The other is L. D."

I took a deep breath and swallowed hard. "Launa," I said, feeling myself break into a sweat. "Launa Darcy. We were kids. . . Nathan Hale. . . in the ninth grade."

Circe smiled coyly. "But you didn't return her pin. You kept it. Were you sweethearts? "

"I guess you could say that." Anxious to drop the subject, I put the pins back into the case and snapped it shut. "As far as love goes, it was on-again, off-again while we wrote during the war. I was pretty shaken when we finally broke up. To be honest, I ... I didn't expect it. But like the song says ,*It was just one of those things*. No one ever died of a broken heart. During the war some guy or other was always getting a Dear John letter from a spouse or girlfriend calling it quits. Some took it pretty hard, but it didn't kill them."

"Is that what you got? A letter?"

"No, no. The final break didn't come until I was enrolled at Columbia, about a year after the war was over. But that's an ugly story I don't want to go into."

"So what ever became of this Launa? Do you know where she is she today?"

"The last I heard, she was living in the West Hartford area. My sister might know. You know how Betty keeps tabs on the old New Britain crowd."

Circe smiled and gave me a playful slap on the wrist. "Yes, and I think I'm beginning to feel a little bit jealous. So, Mr. Romeo, how many of these letters were from Launa?"

"Who knows?" I said, still very uncomfortable and anxious to get off the topic. "I wrote to a number of guys and girl friends, sometimes two or three times a day. Everybody did. Letters were our phone, TV, and computer. Relationships were different back then. The church was everything and sex was taboo, out of the question. A guy fell in love, got engaged, and married. Today kids don't even talk about falling in love. They meet, sniff, and hook up like dogs. I don't know whether we were naïve back then, or just plain dumb."

Circe picked up one of Launa's letters and glanced through it. "I can see that you must have been very much in love. And all this happened in the ninth grade?"

"Our last year in junior high. Launa had been dropped off in New Britain to stay with her aunt, Miss O'Hare. The aunt was only about ten years older than Launa and also our science teacher. A real snob, she always referred to herself in the third-person. *Miss O'Hare wants this; Miss O'Hare wants that.* She didn't think I was good enough for her niece. I remember one day in the cloakroom. I said to my buddy Benny, 'Miss O'Hare can shit in her hat and pull it down over her ears.' The witch was standing right behind us. She had me expelled for two days."

Circe laughed. "Charlie, that sounds just like you. But I'm interested in Launa. Tell me more about her. You said she was left in the care of this aunt."

"Yes, but the two didn't get along. Launa was left on her own at an early age and had learned to fend for herself. No one was going to tell her what to do. I think that's what I loved most about her. She was a free spirit. No brothers or sisters. She referred to her parents as Phoebe and Marvin, never Mom and Dad, which I always thought kind of weird. Anyway, they were never around, and life would have been sheer bliss had it not been for Minnie O'Hare. But still we managed to outfox the ogre. Launa and I were inseparable. In school, I squired her between classes and walked her home every day. It was only a couple of miles, but it sometimes took us an hour or two, or even longer. But, love, you don't want to hear all this. I'm boring you".

"No, you aren't. Darling, I'm fascinated. I want to know everything about you."

9

I paused. "Fridays were really special," I continued. "We had a school dance from four to six. We paid a nickel—five cents—and there was a live band. I guess it was supposed to teach us social graces or something. No jumping about, no jitterbug or lindy. Not even a polka. Waltz or foxtrot, slow gliding about the floor to music like 'Night and Day.' We thought the song was written for us. On Saturday evenings we used to meet on the sly after confession and have a few hours before Miss O'Hare's curfew, something Launa always ignored." I chuckled at the recollection. "We would linger beneath the streetlamp outside the house, and her aunt would have a regal fit—turn the porch light on and off, raise and lower the window shades. To spite her we would then take another turn or two about the block. On snowy nights I remember following our own footprints. It was beautiful. But boy, did Minnie O'Hare ever have it in for me."

Circe smiled. "And not without good reason. But enough about Miss O'Hare. Tell me what Launa was like."

"Bright. She hardly ever opened a book and got all A's. In college she talked about becoming a doctor. She certainly had the brains."

"And she must have been very attractive, from what you say."

"I certainly thought so. In junior high girls develop faster than boys. Some of the kids going together looked more like mother and son. Launa was my height, five eight or so. She used to tease me about finding a taller guy so she could wear high heels. She didn't smile often, but when she did, her smile was dazzling. She had perfect teeth and lovely hazel green eyes." I paused, for a moment lost in the past. "She wore Blue Grass, but never any makeup, no lipstick, rouge, or even nail polish. Her chestnut hair was never up or set, always straight and shoulder length. I remember how I loved the feel of it when I helped her with her coat, a kind of cape she wore."

"And was this great love of yours reciprocal? You weren't being used or led on?"

"Not at all. Launa was too open, too honest. Today, I would say she didn't love me. Not in the way I loved her. But she trusted me, and there was no one else that she cared about and talked with the way we did. I truly believed it was just a matter of time and that she would come around one day. Like I said, Launa had an independent streak. I never knew what she would come up with next. Once when we were studying astronomy in science, she suggested we sneak out of our houses to view the moon that was supposed to be full. I thought she was kidding, but she was serious. That night at midnight—it had to be March, it was quite cold—we met on a little wooden bridge near the spillway in the nearby park . For the next two or three hours, hand in hand, we cavorted through an incredible lunar landscape: the park, college campus, golf course, backyards—all deserted. Just the two of us in that vast, silent world."

"Really. I can't imagine your parents condoning such behavior."

"What did they know? Like Miss O'Hare, they were sound asleep in bed. For us, it was no big deal. That spring we met in the park whenever the moon was full, right up to that last night in June when we got caught. We never figured out how, but Miss O'Hare discovered Launa was not in her room and called my parents. And the police. The woman wanted to have me arrested. I caught hell from my folks, but they took it in stride. 'Kids will be kids,' they said, and the police agreed. Miss O'Hare, however, was wild. The day after graduation, she shipped Launa off to her parents, who were working that summer up at Indian Lake in Maine."

"You must have been terribly disappointed."

"I wouldn't say so," I replied, after some reflection. "You have to remember this was 1940. Because of the war waging in Europe, the economy here was finally on the upswing. I had my own plans for camping out with the guys that summer. Come fall, Launa and I would link up at high school in dear old New Britain, which was nothing like the dead town it is today. Back then it had seventy-five thousand people and was known as the hardware center of the world. Irish, Poles, Italians, Swedes, Armenians, Lithuanians, Ukrainians, and Jews poured into the town to work in factories like Landers, Stanley Works, Corbin Lock, and Fafnir Bearing. These immigrants lived in two and three-story tenement houses in the south and east quarters of the town, each with its own church, elementary school, and junior high. The mayor and police and fire chiefs were Irish. A snooty bunch—we called them harps—they were the first to arrive and controlled city hall. A generation later many had moved into the posh west end alongside the factory owners and professionals. We lived in Belvedere, the recently developed north end also known as Stanley Quarter. Although largely residential, we had a state normal school, the municipal park I just told you about, a golf course, and an elementary school. A small commercial strip at the center contained an A & P, barber shop, meat market, gas station, and drug store, which was the local hangout."

"Sounds idyllic—a great place to grow up in."

"It was. My father served in the First World War. After his discharge he bought two lots on Anise Street, an undeveloped cul-de-sac in Belvedere, and put up this house. In those days it was all open lots, fields, and forest. Ours was the only house on this side of the street. Two houses were across the way and behind us was the hill, an outcropping of cliff in a forested area rich with a variety of wildflowers in the spring. About a mile away beneath a railroad trestle was our swimming hole. There on hot summer days we frolicked naked and waved greetings to passengers on overhead trains. Winters we set out trap lines for muskrats and skunks. The pelts were sold to a local furrier. Winter was also the time for my father's business, the Evergrip Manufacturing Company. Throughout the dark, snowy months, three or four neighbor ladies sat at a large square table next to an oil stove in our converted two-car garage and packed links, a device patented by my father to repair broken tire chains—ten in a box, twenty-four boxes in a carton, twelve cartons in a case. The links were shipped to outlets all over New England and New York state. The business flourished during the Depression. In 1932 my father bought a new Auburn and another new one in 1936. With the advent of the snow tire, chains became obsolete and the business folded. I was in high school at the time."

"Quite a background. And only one high school. That's hard to believe for such a big city."

"Not if you think of the school as a giant talent pool. Thousands of kids from all parts of the city gathered in a single three-story granite edifice in the heart of downtown. Year after year New Britain was able to field champion football, basketball, and baseball teams."

"And the girls? How did they fare?"

"They were our cheerleaders and members of the band. Every year the glee club walked off with all kinds of honors. Dance was the big coed activity. And dance we did to the music of the big bands—Glen Miller, the Dorsey Brothers, Gene Krupa, Lionel Hampton. In this department, I did have a leg up. My mother loved to dance and saw to it that I had tap and ballroom lessons when I was a kid. For dates I was seeing a girl called Cheryl French. She lived in Belvedere but had recently moved to the neighboring town of Oakwood. Cheryl introduced my buddy Benny to her cousin Helen, and the two hit it off.

"So there was someone else. A Cheryl in your life."

"Yes, but with these other girls it was just friendship and silly flirting. Launa was the real thing, my true love. None of the others measured up to her."

"And what happened when you and Launa finally got back together in the fall?"

"We didn't. Miss O'Hare persuaded Launa's parents to enroll her at Briarly Hall, a private school in Massachusetts, but we still wrote and saw each other when she came to New Britain for weekends and holidays. I also had a lot more to think about. At school we had a field day because of the war. Discipline went by the board—we cut classes or took the whole day off. The Depression was over, so money was no longer a problem—everyone worked part time in one of the factories. In my sophomore year Pearl Harbor was attacked, war was declared on the Axis forces, and I had the draft to worry about. My physics and biology teachers were both called up. In Europe the war was going badly. Every day the newspaper carried banner headlines of some new defeat or a ship sunk by German U-boats. Posters all over the place screamed for volunteers to enlist—Uncle Sam Wants You!"

"I missed all that," Circe said. "I was only nine or ten. I do remember collecting scrap metal, newspapers, and fat for the war effort. In school we used to buy war stamps for twenty-five cents. But weren't you too young for the draft?"

"Seventeen. I had a year to get my act together. College was out—I didn't have the grades. What I did have going for me was skiing. My buddy Benny and I had become regular ski bums. Every weekend we headed up to Litchfield or across the border into Massachusetts and Vermont to polish our skills. Then, after the first of the year, the Army, impressed by the defense the Finns had put up against the Russians, decided to form its own mountaineering division. Benny and I saw an opportunity to beat the draft and made preliminary inquiries. Prospects of enlisting in this elite organization were promising. But before we could follow up on our applications, disaster struck. During a weekend up at Stowe, Vermont, Benny plowed into a tree on an icy trail and fractured his leg. Making matters worse, the attending physician botched the cast. For the next year Benny was out of commission—and out of the draft. Call it fate if you like. But since I was on my own, Colorado lost all allure, and I never did apply to the ski patrol. Later in the war the entire force was wiped out on the slopes of Italy."

"My God!" Circe gasped. "That *was* fate. But weren't you then subject to the draft?"

"I was. But before that could happen, I teamed up with Dick Walton, a fellow classmate who had recently moved out to Belvedere. Dick was my height and build, but there any similarity ended. He had dark, wavy hair, which the girls loved. Dick was a real brain, and also president of the National Honor Society and student council. He was editor of the school newspaper and the yearbook. Into everything but skiing. Golf was his sport, and he played like a pro. Strange as it may seem, we clicked, and Dick had me thinking about college and beating the draft, which, like the old saw mill, kept drawing closer with each passing day. Dick planned to be deferred by entering college as a premed student. With his grades and track record, he was a shoo-in. My own case was quite to the contrary. Typical was a German class I took during my freshman year. I knocked myself out but learned I had absolutely no ear for languages. At the end of the course my teacher said that she'd give me a passing grade for effort, but only on the condition that I didn't take a second year. I licked her hand and promised. In biology, chemistry, and physics I managed to get by, but just. In history and English I was a top student. My mother always claimed I was born with a book in my hand. But that wasn't going to get me into college with a deferment like my new sidekick Dick—or so I thought until the navy announced its V12 program. Because of a shortage of doctors and engineers, the navy agreed to sponsor anyone in these fields who could pass their test. Dick was one of the first to sign up and urged me to do the same.

Engineering? Medicine? Me? Dick told me free tuition was nothing to sneeze at. The war wasn't going to last forever. By the time I was through premed, the fighting would be over and I could go into any field that I liked. I didn't think I stood a chance, but Dick convinced me. In March I wrote *medicine* on my application and we took the test."

"And?" my wife asked when I paused. "What next?"

I shook my head. "Nothing. Day after day through March, April, May, not a damn word.

Meanwhile, Dick had fallen head over heels in love with Meg, a live-wire blonde in her junior year. The feeling was mutual and the two became the poster sweethearts of the class. As a favor to Dick, I dated Mary Jo, a friend of Meg, and we often made it a foursome."

"So when did you finally get word from the navy?"

"Not till mid-June. By that time fellows like Joe Rizzo thought it was a scam and joined the army. Mick Leary and Jack Neuman opted for the regular navy. Finally the first results of the V12 test began to trickle in. To the shock of everyone, Dick flunked. But he had already been accepted into the premed program at Duke. Danny Bray got into Wesleyan. Joe Katz made Holy Cross, and Mike Pierson, Tufts. I heard nothing, turned eighteen, chewed my nails, and waited for the other shoe to drop. But still no word. Nothing. And then came that glorious day in June I'll never forget. A bunch of us decided to skip school and cycle out to the quarry in nearby Berlin for a swim. On our way home we stopped at a hot dog stand on the highway, and I called home, fully anticipating the usual nothing or even an outright rejection."

"And?" Circe asked, when I again paused in my narrative.

I chuckled. "Harvard. My mother read me the letter. I damn near passed out. The kids in the class couldn't believe it. Even my teachers were dumbfounded. Talk about ego. At the prom, class night, graduation, this kid walked on air. And that was it. On July 1, I bid my parents, my kid sister, and my little brother good-bye in downtown New Britain and boarded a bus for the trip to Cambridge."

"What a story. Is this where the letters start?"

I closed up the box. "The bulk of them, from what I can see. Just the few on top from Launa were written in 1940."

That night I had little sleep. Twisting and turning, racked with guilt, I thought of my wife sleeping trustfully at my side while I conjured up a teen-age love that took place over seventy years ago and that I believed was long dead. Where was Launa today? She had been so beautiful. I had loved her so much. Most vivid was the memory of our final parting, a humiliating experience that I found still painful. Rather than face that trauma again, and out of loyalty to my beloved wife, I decided the letters should be returned to the attic. Unread.

In keeping with my plan, the following morning I took the box of letters up to the third floor. But curiosity then got the best of me. I looked again at the lapel pins. Hesitantly, I picked up the first of the Launa letters.

PO Box 8
Pinewood, Maine
June 9, 1940

Dear Charlie,

How very formal that sounds. I would much rather say, Hi Stinky – but seeing as how you don't like it I won't, I'm a thoughtful soul.

I was out playing tennis with one of the kids when your letter came – gosh, I was glad to see it. I'm so darn lonely up here and so bored that it's pathetic. I swore I was going to learn how to play tennis this year or die in the attempt sooooo this girl that's here, her name is Alva, and her brother Mark are trying in vain to teach me. I can beat Alva but Mark – oh, gosh can he play. I was in the middle of losing a game to him when the old Prof. came down with your letter so I stopped in the middle of the game to read it – the kids told me I was crazy and I could read it later but gee, I was sooooo glad to see it I had to read it then. That was about twenty minutes ago – and then it started pouring rain so I never did finish the game but what's the use, he would have beat me anyway. I then came up to the house and read the letter over 13 times and then I decided to write you. I'm a horrible letter writer in the first place. And, if I did know what to write, I wouldn't know how to write it so you see my letters to you are going to be quite a mess.

I've only been here about 4 days and it seems more like 4 weeks – gosh am I lonesome and unhappy and miserable and everything. I wish I was back in good old New Britain going for a walk with Patty Lou, you and Danny instead of up here in the mountains with a lot of pine trees and water. Do you think it would be possible for Patty Lou, you, Danny and the drug store to sort of move up here? I suppose not but it's a swell idea, don't you think?

You'll never know how scared I was going into the house Friday night. I expected it to be about quarter of eleven and it was only 5 after ten. Gosh—was I happy. I came in and Min told me what time it was and I started dancing around the room – giggling (how do you spell that?) and she thought I was crazy and said she was glad I was going away if going out with you kids made me act like that. If she had given me heck for coming in late it sort of would have ruined the whole night but as it was it was perfect. It doesn't seem possible that your white shoes could have gone through all that and still not shrink or crack or something – I'm still awfully sorry about that.

Oh!!! The rain is raining and it's all wet and I feel like crying – I'm so awfully lonesome. I was sitting on the deck gazing at the water the other day and thinking of walks and drug stores and Alva asked me if I had lost my best friend or if I was sick or what. I told her I was missing a couple of people an awful lot and that I wished I was home and so she thought I was crazy and wanted to know how anybody could want to be home instead of here. I started to explain but she said I was just plain "nuts" and ended up by pushing me in the water.

It stopped raining now so I'm going out to finish that darn tennis game – wish me luck! I'll finish this letter later.

L.D.

P.O. Box 84
Pinewood, Maine
June 21,1940

Hello, Angel puss,

In spite of the fact that I am very, very lonely I'm slightly happy—guess what—I beat Mark twice – Gosh, do I feel swell. I may learn to play tennis yet although I doubt it. Mark told me yesterday I was a hopeless case.

Gee, am I bored. Both Alva and Mark are bores. I can't stand them, but seeing as how they're teaching me to play tennis I'm nice to them.

Charlie, I just remembered and I feel like blushing – do you realize I never thanked you for the swell time I had Thursday? I hate people who do things like that so thanks heaps. I did have a marvelous time. I would have remembered but I got mad before I left you – I didn't think of it after that.

In your letter you mentioned you and Danny coming up – well, don't you even think of doing it without writing and telling me. I don't believe you will come up but if you dared without telling me!!!!!? You just wouldn't live that's all.

Seeing as I'm all hot and everything I'm going to take a swim and cool off. Please write soon 'cause I love to read your letters. 'Cause nothing ever happens up here.

Love and stuff,
Launa

P.S. If you see Mick give him my love and give some to Danny. Gosh but I'm getting generous with my love (especially where Danny is concerned)

PO Box 84
Pinewood, Maine
July 18, 1940

Dear Charlie,

I can imagine the swell time you kids are having and gee! Am I jealous. Here I am stuck up in the mountains with a lot of water and pine trees while you and Danny and dear Merton are having a wonderful time in a canoe. Ah – hell, it's all right with me if both Danny and Merton drown but please don't you drown. Just think of all the mess you'd make – I'd have to come back – all the way back there just to go to your funeral. So please don't.

I was awfully glad to get your letter but it took you long enough to write. I wrote to you and Patty Lou and Joan all on the same day and I heard from Patty Lou and Joan— 2 days later I heard from you. I hope you didn't rush but I suppose you have other things to do.

Guess what?!! We're finally going to get a sailboat. Gosh, am I happy!! One of the boys over in Brunswick had one for rent, so Marvin rented it for the rest of the season. We're going down early tomorrow morning and sail it back from Brunswick to the Point. We're going to take our lunch because we won't be back until after supper. Some fun!!

I'm sitting here listening to Kay Kaiser and they just played "I'm Sorry Playmate" and it made me think of Mick. Do you ever see him? How is he? Say "hello" to him from me the next time you see him.

So you got your picture taken, did you? Well, if you don't send me one I promise I won't ever speak to you again and I do mean it. And I know it isn't as bad as you say it is. It can't be. And I do want one very badly so please send me one soon (and I do mean soon.)

Maybe it's just as well that I won't be seeing you this summer because if you could see me as I am now you'd just run – in the opposite direction. Oh –I'm a wreck. My hair is fuzzy and I'm getting fat. I only hope I don't get any taller. – I must be over six feet now (or almost), I expect you'll almost have forgotten me by Sept. but I'll be back in spite of the fact that my dear, dear parents think I am going south with them – the poor disillusioned people don't know I'm going to stay north and have heaps and heaps of fun (I hope.)

By the way, I just remembered and I hope you do – you did promise you wouldn't show my letters to anyone – well, please don't. And that includes dear Daniel (the fish!)

It's almost 12 o'clock and I'd better go to bed now before I fall asleep sitting here.

Heaps of love and stuff,
Launa

P.S. You mentioned typing your next letter, well, don't.

PO Box 84
Pinewood, Maine
July 18, 1940

Dear Charlie,

I swore I would never write to you again, but I just got your letter and I thought I'd better answer it. I read it over 5 times and I admit it sounds swell but hardly likely under the circumstances. You said you loved me – if you do how could you go and deliberately break a promise like you did? Before I left you promised you'd never show my letters to anyone and then you deliberately went and showed my last one to one of your "tippsy" friends. If you can't think of anything better to do with my letters I decided it would be better if I just didn't write at all. I'm furious with you – I wish you were here so I could tell you what I think of you. You're a - a - a – well, I can't say it because I'm a lady but that's what you are regardless. I can tell by your letter that Danny hasn't told you what I asked him to tell you or else the letter hasn't reached him yet – well, you can tell by that how very, very, very mad (and I do mean mad) I am at you.

Is it the remark that your "tippsy" made after reading my letter that made you decide to write and ask me – did I love you? (or about the same)? I suppose it was – well, I don't make a habit of telling boys I love them – if I do they usually know it. If I was crazy about a boy he'd be the last one I'd tell, and if he asked me I'd say "no" definitely. Sooooooo that's how it is, see?

19

I can certainly say though that none of the letters you have written to me or will write will sound silly to me and as I keep my promises no one else will ever see them – so suit yourself.

I hope that when that friend of yours reads this letter he will not make the same remark as before. I'm still mad and I shall never forgive you for what you did – but then - ?

It's 11 o'clock and have to go to bed before Phoebe has fits. Sooooooo, goodnight!

Have fun!!!
Launa

P.S. Give my love to the fish!
P.S. I'm so mad!!!!

PO Box 84
Pinewood, Maine
August 1, 1940

Dear Grumpy,

I got your affectionate (?) postcard this morning and I'm awfully sorry but I was mad at you and now you're mad at me – oh, well – it will all blow over – I hope. I wrote you last Friday – I suppose you have the letter by now. Well, hurry up and answer it. I'm sooooo bored – the only fun I have is reading letters (Patty Lou's and yours). Gosh – gee- am I lonesome and unhappy and everything. I can't wait till September and good old school. Not that I like school – but it's just that I'm so damned bored with life in general. There is absolutely no one here around my age except some gooney little (?) boy who goes sailing with us. He's a pest and I hate him – so I'm very rude to him and then Phoebe and Marvin get mad at me – oh well, I'm afraid this isn't a very cheerful letter but I'm in a morbid mood. I wish you and Patty Lou and Danny and Mick and the car and the drugstore could move up here – I'm lonesome and I don't care who knows it. Oh gee, I just think of you and Danny having so much fun and I turn green with envy. It isn't fair. Damn it all anyway.

We went for a moonlight swim the other night and it was swell. The moonlight on the water and the stars and everything – gee! I really would have been happy if I had been with anyone else but my damned family and that brat from next door. He's 16 I think but he's a goon. I can't stand him. (Don't say, "Well, sit down.")

By the way, Charlie, have you got one of those graduation pictures with you at the lake? If you have will you please, please, Pu – lease! Send me one – I do want one and I think you're perfectly horrid if you don't send one.

Seeing as how I have yet to write to Patty Lou and to Joan tonight and it is now 10:15. I'd better stop writing, I'm sorry (again) about this letter being so gloomy but I am and I can't write happy letters feeling like this. Please write soon and in the meantime –

Have Fun!!!

Launa

P.S. Give my love to the Fish and the jitterbug (dear Merton). I hear he is quite a dancer.

PO Box 84

Pinewood, Maine

August 2, 1940

Hello –

You said to write "quick" so here I am sitting with my hair soaking wet and all the water running down my back – writing. It's about 11 o'clock and we just came in from swimming about 10 minutes ago. I love to swim at night- don't you? Gosh – it's nice on the lake – the stars and moon and the lights on the lake – gee. I'm getting sooooo tan (it looks horrible) that I'm beginning to look like Virginia – remember that "dark cloud" Virginia in Min's home-room? Well, I'm just one big blister. My nose and face are red all the time – I look like a beet. I'll have to do something about it before I get home – you'll see me and won't recognize me. I'm a total wreck.!!!! Gosh!!! Am I hot – Uh huh!! It's too hot to do anything but swim and sail. We were out sailing tonight till about 10. Gosh – I'm glad we got the boat. I love it. When I make my million dollars I'm going to have lots 'n lots of sailboats. I've got to go and do the damn dishes now but I'll finish this later.

Love,

Launa

Hi!!

I'm mad – gr-r-r-r – I just had a fight with Phoebe and then Marvin butted in so I had a fight with him too and I'm mad. Oh! Hell! I wish I was home. Last year I didn't come home until the day before school began. – well, they can't do that to me again – I won't stand for it. Oh, well, it's too hot to get mad at anything. Patty Lou won't be coming to school till a week after school starts 'cause she's going away sometime in August. I'll die if she isn't there when I get home.

I just heard that song "Happy little motor —put-put-put" and it reminded me of the night we walked home through the cemetery. Gosh we did have fun and I was certainly surprised at dear Roger — I didn't know he had it in him. We had lots of fun last year. I know next year won't be anything like it and it worries me. Darn it!!!

Phoebe is having fits 'cause I'm not in bed and she's mad already so I'm going.

Have Fun!!! (And have some for me 'cause I'm not having any.)
Launa

P.S. When I get home we'll discuss who loves who and why — o.k.? That is if you feel the same —maybe you won't. Oh well — there's nothing I can do about it so why worry, huh?

PO Box 84
Pinewood, Maine
August 9, 1940

Dear Charlie,

I got your letter about three days ago but I waited to write to you 'cause I wanted to be sure you would be home when the letter got there. By the way, what's the number of Danny's house? I know the street but have no idea of the number.

It has been awfully hot yesterday and today but I'm cold right now. We've been out for a sail in the moonlight — gee, it was purty. You know if I lie across the front deck I can dangle my feet in the water and part of my chin goes in too. My family decided that's how I get so crazy— from dangling my head down in the water — either that or from the sun. Marvin is disgusted with me — he says all I do all day is giggle. This is a crazy letter but I'm feeling very silly (as per usual). Please pardon the writing but I'm lying down in front of the fireplace and it's rather hard to write but I'm not going to move 'cause if I do I'll get cold.

You said you thought I'd be changed. — well, I certainly am. Uh huh! Not inside I guess but in appearance — gosh!! I'm a wreck — a total wreck. In the first place I'm covered with freckles — I look like Mick — I've grown about 3 inches (almost) and I've gained about 20 pounds. I'm getting positively fat!!!

And I would certainly never think of promising you such a thing but by that time it won't make a bit of difference to you. After you see me you'll say "ugh" and wonder how you could ever, ever think you loved me. And I did mean what I said about discussing it when I got home although I hardly think that question needs answering. I know you won't feel the same way when you see me – you couldn't possibly.

I'm awfully sorry about this – it really is a mess but I started to say something and then changed my mind. I should copy it over but I have 6 other letters to write and I do think I should get started on them. I won't be home until the first of Sept. I don't think. Damn it all anyway – well, in the meantime –Have Fun! (Have some for me, too.)

Launa

PO Box 84
Pinewood, Maine
August 16, 1940

Hi!

Ugh! Do I feel awful – uh-huh! I have just eaten 19 ½ toasted marshmallows, 3 bottles of Coca Cola, and some pop corn – gee! –gosh!— wow! I'll never be the same never. It is pouring rain and Roseanne and her brother Rob had the rest of the kids (me included) over for a rummy game but of course we never did play – we ate instead. Oh –oh-oh-oh!!! The rest of the kids ate just as much if not more - gee can those kids eat. I'm still very bored and I wish I were home but these goons were here last year and they are a lot of fun. Well – how goes things with you? It sounds as though you were having a swell time in good old N.B. I envy you- and how! Oh! Bore – bore – bore –Ah me!

By the way – I got your picture and thanks heaps. It's a swell one. You look positively handsome (or something) anyhow it is an awfully good picture. I would love to see you – have you changed? I don't suppose so. And by the way (again?) I don't see why on earth I should write more often – I answer all your letters and if you want more letters from me you can just write more yourself – see? Listen, you lug – I don't see where you got any idea about any "mission bum" but may I remind you that Sam is a very nice man with a wife and 3 kids so you see it would be quite impossible for me to be "running around" with him – You are without doubt one of the most crude people I have ever met.

And furthermore all the fun you have next winter will have to exclude me – my dear (very dear?) parents think their darling little daughter (that's me – believe it or not) is going to go south with them next winter. I had a fight with both Phoebe and Marvin this morning and it ended up with them determined to take me and me determined not to go! Oh! Gosh! I'll

*die if I have to go! Oh woe is me 'n stuff. I suppose all I can do is wait and
see and chew my fingernails – PHOOIE!*

*It stopped raining and the sun is almost out and I'm sizzling so I'm
going for a swim and cool off – so good bye! Goon!*

Launa

P.S. Write soon!

PO Box 84
Pinewood, Maine
August 24, 1940

Listen You,

*In the first place I hate to be referred to as "Babe" and if you can't think
of anything else to write for a salutation then skip it.*

*And in the second place you made a remark to the fact that I should give
"guys" up here an "old Darcy come-hither look" or make Rob take me to a
dance. Well, I can tell you right now that I don't have to depend on any
boys to have fun. And I certainly don't go around giving every other boy I
meet a "come-hither." And furthermore I have no desire whatsoever to go
to a dance with Rob and I doubt if he could go 'cause his father wouldn't
let him take the car out that late at night and we certainly couldn't walk
all way – so you see I do not intend to take your suggestions. What were
you trying to do, stir me up a hot romance? Well, you needn't bother in the
future— I can stir up my own if I feel like it.*

*Are you mad or something? Your letter certainly sounds it. I've never read
such a hard letter in all my life. And I don't like to be referred to as "kid" either.*

*I loved the poem. It was the only part of the letter that you didn't
sound angry with me or trying to make me mad. What the heck's the idea
anyway? I haven't done anything to you.*

*And Cheryl has her nerve to give me her love when I know just as
well as she does that she doesn't mean a word of it – I hate people like that
anyway. Say "hello" to her for me when you see her again and also say
"hello" to dear Mick. Is he still having trouble with Danny? I imagine so.*

*I'll take you up on that sweet cider idea. I can't think of anything I'd
rather do than get good and sick from cider. I'll remind you about it when
I get home.*

Gee – I can't wait to get home and see everybody and everything.

*You know that Latin book I took out to study for the summer – well, I
haven't even looked at it except once – to tear a couple of more pages out of
it. Miss Gilmore will have a couple of fits when I bring it back – woe is me.*

Marvin and I are going out for a sail so I have to go but please write soon.
So long Kid,
Launa
P.S. Now you can see how bad it sounds when you write it to me
(terrible, isn't it?)

PO Box 84
Pinewood, Maine
August 27, 1940

Hello, Angel-face,

I'm sorry I'm such a terrible letter writer but I just don't seem to get around to writing but I do think of you even though you'd never know it. I really meant to write to you last night but I had Rosemary and Bob and Tony down to play Monopoly 'cause Rob and Roseanne went this morning and I thought we had better do something the night before they left. So I'm practically all alone now way up in the mountains and I can't wait to get home. I miss you and the rest of the kids terribly and I feel like a hermit right now.

I envy you – walking in the rain – I love to. Let's go for a walk when it's raining sometime – but not when you have a cold. Are you nuts? Haven't you any brains at all? You goon! If you don't know any better than to go out for a walk in the rain when you have a cold so that it gets worse than before –well––you ought to be put in Middletown. And I do mean it. Do you want to die of pneumonia?

This letter is a mess but I'm writing in front of the fireplace with all the lights off and I can just about see what I'm writing. Phoebe and Marvin went to the store so I'm sitting here seeing what I can do to go slowly blind.

We've been out in the sailboat all day – we went all the way to Hillsboro about 8 or 10 miles. Gosh, did I get a sunburn! This is the first warm day we've had – my tan had gone completely and I was that awful greenish gray color you get when your tan wears off. My nose is bright red right now and I look like a beet – And how!!!

Did you really mean it about going to the movies some night? I'd love to – if I can. If Phoebe won't let me there is going to be murder. She probably won't – it seems to me I can't do anything, darn it all! You'll probably change your mind about wanting to go when you see me – ugh! I'm a wreck!

Charlie, Please, Please Pu-lese tell me your middle name – don't be a goon – it can't be that funny. Is it Rudolf or Raymond or what? Please tell me now!

I've got to give this to the old Prof. now so he'll mail it tomorrow so I'll have to go. You won't have a chance to answer this but I intend to keep writing 'cause I owe you so many letters.

Love,

Launa

P.S. I can't wait to see you and I miss you heaps.

PO Box 84
Pinewood, Maine
August 29, 1940

Hello, Charlie—

I know you're mad – well, I don't blame you. I owe you 2 or 3 letters and I'm really terribly sorry – I'll try to improve in the near future. O.K.?

I was awfully glad to get your letter – I certainly didn't expect it. I was still fuming at the last one and by the way – just disregard my last letters – I was so mad and I always say things that I don't mean. You know me.

If ever I go into that darn orchard again I most certainly will not ride a bicycle. Not again!! I always completely ruin myself and the bicycle every time I go in there so we'll walk – at least I can do that without falling down – I hope. Remember I had a date to go for a ride up there with you when the apple blossoms were out last year? We never did go, darn it all. What happened? We should have gone.

The swing sounds swell! And the hot dog roast even better. We could have lots of fun if the right kids came. It's a wonderful way to begin the school year. Good old school – Ugh! How I don't love it. Next year is going to be soooo very different from last year – I just know it will be and it makes me mad. We did have lots of fun last year and we won't have half as much next year – darn it! And darn it some more.

The weather here has been just like winter. I expect to wake up any morning and find snow on the ground. We have the fireplace going all the time. Roseanne and Rob came down last night and we played Monopoly and ate toasted marshmallows and drank Coca Cola until I nearly passed out. Those kids bore me stiff and I can't wait to get home to the kids I can talk to at least.

This is a very boring letter but nothing ever happens that I can write and tell you about so I guess I'll just have to wait and see you again. I'll write again tomorrow (about nothing, as usual) and then I'll be all caught up in my letter writing. Write soon.

Love 'n stuff,

Launa

Charlie –

By the way what is your middle name? You never did tell me although I've asked you over and over – I know it begins with R. and it isn't Robert so write and tell me – please!

Launa

I read Launa's last letter from the summer of 1940 and was stunned, absolutely flabbergasted. And elated. I was fifteen again and had just graduated from Nathan Hale Junior High in New Britain. At certain passages I wanted to weep; at others, I laughed aloud. The letters could have been written yesterday. They held so many memories, so many names of kids that I had forgotten. Kids? What was I thinking? Today those kids would be in their eighties. They could be dead.

"Anything interesting?"

Startled, as though wakened from a dream, I looked at Circe, a stranger in my world of 1940, and felt guilty. Completely absorbed in the letters of my first love, I had been unaware of my wife's approach until I felt her hand on my shoulder.

Circe smiled. "So, my love, you've decided to peep into the record of your wild oats."

I took in a deep breath to clear my head "I ... I don't know what to say," I faltered. "These letters ... I started reading and was hooked. I couldn't put them down."

"Then upload everything you have on to your computer. You could have another book."

"Oh, God, no. Not another book. I'm too old for that."

"Then we could share the letters with Betty. If they are from the family, I'm sure she would be interested.

"You can't be serious. There must be hundreds. From what I can see, the bulk of the correspondence was written between July of '43, when I went into the service, and the fall of '45, when the war was over. There are even letters that I wrote to Launa. She could have sent them back after we broke up. I was at Columbia and would have pitched them. My mother must have put them in the box with the correspondence that she had saved over the years. The mere thought of uploading all that boggles my mind."

"I don't see why not. You have the time. You're not working on a book, and you complain about sitting around watching mindless television. Start with the letters—arrange them in chronological order and see what you have. Then consider putting them on the computer."

The first stage took me the next three weeks. As Circe suggested, I created a file for the years from 1943 to 1945 and did a rough sorting. These I broke down into months and then into periods of two weeks. The work was daunting. Many letters were undated and required guesswork; others were in the wrong envelopes. Postmarks were often illegible. Finally came the actual reading and transcribing. Once again I was totally captivated and fell into a daily routine. Each morning before dawn I would make my way up to the third floor and enter into a time warp, a bubble world into the past that I had forgotten existed. Magically conjured up, Launa, Danny, Joe, Dick, my family, and all those others who had lain dormant in my psyche over the years appeared to greet me. Those hours together flew by; before I knew it, I was being paged for dinner. I would then make a printout of my work for Circe, shut down the computer for the day, and reluctantly reenter the mundane world.

-TWO-

CAMBRIDGE, MASSACHUSETTS 1943

Donny

Betty and Charlie

Mom and Dad

Prince

AT HARVARD I WAS assigned to a suite in Kirkland House on the Charles River, a far cry from the crude barracks I had anticipated. I had a room of my own, and with four other guys I shared a kitchenette and large living room with a fireplace. Very little was military - no marching or drilling. Not even uniforms. For two months we wore our civilian clothes. It took no time to settle in. Because I had goofed off in high school, I had none of Dick Walton's study habits and spent little time with my books. Of greater attraction was the university pool and boathouse. I swam every morning. Afternoons I rowed on the Charles River and soon proudly became stroke man in an eight-oared shell. Classes were held up near the square on the campus that was known as the Yard. Because our suite was on the river half a dozen blocks away, restriction to quarters as a disciplinary measure was impossible to enforce. Free to come and go, I frequently visited my uncle's brother, Sam Cabelus, and his wife, Mae, who lived nearby. Sam and Mae took me into the family as one of their own. Their daughter Dottie and her boyfriend, Dick Dolloff, a serviceman stationed at MIT, introduced me to Revere Beach. Together we visited museums and historic places of interest around Boston. In September, the girls returned to Radcliff and Wellesley, and the real fun began. Mixers were held on both campuses. On Saturdays we danced to the big bands out at the celebrated Totem Pole, more commonly known as the Scrotum Pole. When I look back, the fact that I remained in the program for a full term seems to me some kind of a miracle.

The White Horse Inn
Old Lyme, Conn.
June 29, 1940

Dear Charlie,

Surprised? Well, that isn't the word for it. I recognized the handwriting but I couldn't quite believe it 'til I opened the letter.

I can't tell you how glad I am that you passed the V12's. I think its swell. The last thing I expected you'd be was a doctor. As usual, you surprised me. In my opinion, that is the best profession there is. And I wish you all the luck in the world.

I'm awfully sorry about the dance, Charlie, but you know the way things stand. They've stood that way for a long time now, and they won't ever change. I do appreciate your asking me but – well, you know. The girl situation can't be so bad that you can't find a cute little blond to go with. Now especially that you are a Navy man! What can be better?

Thanks again, Charlie, and before I forget, "congratulations" on graduating.

Love,
Launa

17 Anise Street
New Britain, Conn.
July 2, 1943

Dear "Harvard Man,"

We were glad to hear from you so soon. I waited for the mailman all morning (and I do mean the mailman).

I'm enclosing three of the pictures of you boys. The other film didn't come out. A few of them came out but they were blurry. Oh, I'll send them anyway.

I'm so glad that you like the place. It certainly sounds nice.

Mother said that she would call Mrs. Walton tomorrow and send you Dick's address.

This morning Mother, Lala, Aunt Anna, and Fanny went to the State to see "Yankee Doodle Dandy" and they said it was awful. Lala even fell asleep. I guess they don't know a good movie when they see one. You know Mother, "It was alright, nothing extra." Aunt Anna is down here now and Aunt Stella is coming down tonight. Aunt Anna sends her love.

I might go to the dance tonight at the "Youth Center." I'm not sure though. (I know darn well that I'm going.)

Princey is o.k. Even though he hasn't been fed for a month. Daddy said to wait 'til he can't stand up anymore then give him something to eat. Your dog Prince also said "hello" to you. He can talk pretty good now. Last night he slipped his collar over his head and went out all night. (The little devil.) He came back this morning all in the bag.

I got a new bathing suit. It's a nice one, too. Thanks to you for the money. Well, that's all for now and Mother will write tomorrow.

Be a good boy and take care of yourself.

Love,
Betty and the family,
Prince, Chickens

P.S. Here's some gum for you. It's awful stuff but have some fun with it.

31

17 Anise Street
New Britain, Conn.
July 5, 1943

Dear Brother,

How are you feeling?

I think I slept a little over today. I got up about 11:35 a.m. I was just wondering why you always write to Ma and Pa and never write to me. How do you like it where you are staying? Prince is all alright. Yesterday Nathan (Natie) Roger and I went to Oakwood. We left about 10:25 and got back about 11:00. Billy is down here over the weekend. They had another beer party.

Sincerely yours
Don- Don

11:30 Monday A.M.
17 Anise Street
New Britain, Conn.
July 5, 1943

Dear Brother,

Well, how are you feeling today? We're all fine here at home. It's been pouring cats and dogs all this morning. I hope it stops this afternoon. Audry and I are going to see "China" this afternoon maybe.

Yesterday didn't seem at all like Fourth of July. We had a little beer party here yesterday. There were only about seven or eight here so it was o.k. Daddy is making another chair today. He made one yesterday too. Oh, I guess you weren't home when he started making chairs for the lawn.

What did you do over the weekend?

Billy Cabelus has been here for a couple of days. He's playing the piano now and he's driving me crazy. He's worse than Irene when he gets going.

I called Mrs. Walton yesterday. She said she didn't receive any letters from Dickey yet but he called her up when he got in N.C. She gave me his address. I hope it's right.

How did you like the pictures? There really isn't much to say because there hasn't been anything doing. So Long For Now.

Love,
Betty

P.S. I hope you hurry up and send your sport shirts home. I've been wearing your yellow one. It just fits too.
P.S.S. When are you going to get your uniforms?

P.S.S.S. I noticed this picture in the paper of some V12 Navy boys and thought you might like to see it.

> *17 Anise Street*
> *New Britain, Conn.*
> *July 5, 1943*

Hi Chick,

How you doing? With those five little easy subjects you won't have anything to do. What's the idea of taking Spanish?

I bet you had a good time at Revere Beach with Dottie and her boyfriend. I heard that the water was so cold that you can't stay in for more than 10 minutes.

The reason Mother doesn't write yet is that she is so busy in the house and in the garden and going up to the hospital. Oh, Aunt Anna (Fred's mother) had some kind of attack so she was sent to the hospital. They took X-rays but haven't the results yet.

Freddie called his Mother Sunday and he said he liked it a lot and he'd perhaps be home in a few weeks. Of course, she said she was fine and working every day.

I almost died laughing when you said Autry was singing, "I heard the crash on the highway but didn't hear anybody pray." I never heard that one before.

Daddy made three Adirondack chairs and they look swell.

Billy is still here with Wart.

Donny is just opening your letter. He's so excited he's stumbling all over the thing.

Donny and I had an argument about who was going to cut the grass. I told him if he started he would have to do it all and he did. I almost died and I think he did, too. He did it so he could get an allowance. I think Dad is going to give him a penny or so. I am not sure.

I need a bathing cap awfully bad and you can't buy them in New Britain at all. If you ever see one when you're shopping get me one and send it or tell Dot to see if she can get one. Any color with a strap (except black).

I'd just love a Harvard shirt if you can get one. Make sure it's nice and big. Well, that's all for now.

> *Love,*
> *Betty*

> *51 Forest St.*
> *Oakwood, Conn.*

July 7, 1943

Dear Charlie,

I received your short letter and was rather surprised to hear from you—especially after the way you left – but from what Benny told Helen about your farewell party etc. I can see why you didn't even have a minute to call.

So you really like Harvard. From what you say it sounds as though you were going to have a wonderful time while you are there even though your studies might be quite difficult. Do you wear any type of special uniform or the regular sailor's uniform? I can't wait to see how you look with it on.

Well, Charlie (Harvard boy) everything is the same at home only things seem duller since you and Freddy have stopped coming over. I'll be so glad when you get some sort of a leave. Do you have any idea when that might be?

Joyce has gotten about 100 letters since Freddy has left, and in his last one he says he doubts whether or not he'll be home. If he has written to you he no doubt told you about the nice Coast Guard bracelet he sent Joyce, along with some C.G. stickers, which we both have pasted all around our rooms. And say, did he tell you about his cross and chain that he gave her up at the tower! I was awfully surprised when she showed it to me that night.

By the time you get this letter you will probably be knee-deep in studies, while all I have to do is read, that is, until August 30. Then I suppose I'll wish I could have a little spare time.

Helen rode over on her bike last Sun. and I nearly died to see her, she was so very tired.

Oh, yes, our graduation things finally came and I think they were really worth waiting for, but I wish I had had it sooner, because I doubt whether or not I can wear it when I am at the hospital.

In your letter you asked me to enclose a picture. Well, I don't have a good one, and even if I did I wouldn't give it to you until you give me the one you promised before you left. I was looking forward to seeing you that night, not only for the picture you were going to bring me, but also to straighten out all our little arguments we have had, but now I guess we will have to do that in our letters – that is, if you want to keep on writing. I hope you do. So long until next time.

Love,

Cheryl

191 Bristol St.
New Britain, Conn.

July 8, 1943

Hello, Clown,

How's everything? I'm sending this airmail because I was going to answer it yesterday and didn't have a minute. Thought you were smart putting M "Landers" Bolan didn't you? Well, you'll have to stick a "Parker" in the middle because I'm not working at Landers. The job at Landers was terrible. At a bench soldering and wiring or something. (I can't even spell them much less do them) – the job at Parkers is wonderful. I get a ride home at noon and at night with Mr. Parker. (not his son.)

I'm so glad you like school. The apartment sounds swell. (also the meals.) Have you started studies yet? Or haven't you had a chance to flunk out yet?

Dick likes school, as he has probably written to you. It really must be "hammy" with him there.

Things are horribly dull around here. (I don't mean that I am dull) but there's no one home now (no one to use the couch at the club). Don't you dare eat any spaghetti or beer until we go to our beer garden again, or anything we had there. (water – butter – bread, etc.) or I'll knock the shellac out of you.

I hope you didn't tell Rob Tyson about our dances or the couch or anything! He might be down.

Love,

Meg

The White Horse Inn
Old Lyme, Conn.
July 8, 1943

Hello, Charlie,

As you said, I knew you'd write, but I didn't expect a letter so soon. Well, I thought I'd surprise you too and answer it. Surprised?

I think it's swell that you're at Harvard, Charlie. It's the best thing that could have happened to you. Your letter sounds as if someday you'll feel about Harvard the way I do about Briarly. It's funny how a place can get you like that. You sound very happy there – I'm glad.

What ever happened to Danny? The last time I was home he told me he was going in the Army in April. Did he go? It's funny how things turn out. Practically all the fellows I know are in the service now. It gives you an awfully queer feeling to see them all go.

Did I tell you that I've got a job? I'm making like Rosie the Riveter in a radio factory. More fun! But I'm collecting 55 cents an hour – that isn't bad considering I don't know how to do anything (nothing they'd appreciate, that is – or would they?) 'Nuf said!

I haven't seen Patty Lou in ages – and of course I haven't written to her. The last time I saw her she was practically engaged. Sometimes I don't understand people. Why would anyone want to be engaged at 17? Girls is the funniest animals!

No, I'm not going to be a nurse anymore. I've gone back to where I started – I'm going to be a doctor. I don't think I'm the Florence Nightingale type, do you? I must be some type but I can't imagine what it is.

I guess you're really going to work now—your courses sound wonderful(?). But I wouldn't want to be having them. By the way, what marks did you get this year? I was surprised to hear that you graduated – nasty aren't I? I know it!

How did graduation go? I imagine your heart is broken at graduating from good old New Britain High School. Did you have a good time at the dance? Knowing you, I'd say yes. Well, I guess that's my quota of dirty cracks for one night. I just wanted to let you know it was me.

No kidding, I've never been in such a horrible little town in my life! I had fun last year but now – you have no idea how dead it is. All the fellows are gone and there are no decent girls. Oh what a life I lead – but I love it. I've gone up to Providence a couple of times to see some of the kids so that broke the monotony. I just got back last night – I stayed out of work for the day and went up to say goodbye to one of the fellows I met up at the school. He left today for the Army Air Corps. No kidding – you have no idea what it's like to just sit around doing nothing and watch all the fellows go. I'd rather be going too – do you think you could get me into Harvard? What a question!

I haven't been to New Britain since Spring vacation – in May sometime. And believe me I don't miss it. I hated that town. Min and Sharon are coming up this weekend I think – I'll be awfully glad to see them. They're going to bring the little percolator too – I miss that dog something terrible!! Here's the latest news – Min is flying out to California to see Walt (that's the one she's engaged to) the 29th of July. Love is wonderful?

Well, I guess I've said enough – I have to go and wash my hair so I'll be glamorous for all the 4F's down at the factory – are you kidding?!

Love and kisses,
Launa

17 Anise Street
New Britain, Conn.

July 8, 1943

Dear Brother,

How are you feeling?

I received your letter yesterday noon. In your letter it said what did you go to Oakwood for to see your girlfriend. No we went to Oakwood to see if we could buy some fireworks but no there weren't any in town. Yesterday I cut the grass and today I will get my allowance. Betty is up the hospital. And Billy is getting the eggs. The young chickens are beginning to lay. Next Wednesday I am going to the Dentist. Did you get your uniform yet? All you need now is a gun.

Your loving brother,
Donald

P.S. I an sending you a couple of clippings.

Mother wants to add something.

Dear Son,

How are you doing? So glad you like Harvard. By the paper there must be an awfully lot of Navy men there. Study hard so you make good. There isn't much news around here. So we all wouldn't know what to write. As long as Betty writes you will get all the news. Freddy is going to call Sunday. His mother doesn't want him to know that she is in the hospital. The Farmers are busy making chairs like ours. I see Nealons have a couple of chairs. Aldie must have made them.

The Hotchkiss kid got married. Probably you will run into him or else you can write to him and the two of you can get together for a chat. That's all for now.

Love,
Mother

Duke University
Sunday, June 11, 1943

Dear Charles,

I received your letter of July 7 last Friday. I'm sorry that I haven't written sooner but a few subjects otherwise known as Mathematics and Botany have kept me quite busy. At any length, I have completed my studying for the next two days and am free for this evening.

As you described Harvard, I could almost picture it. Yes, I agree with you, Harvard must really be nice. We should have a lot of fun if we were together. But that's too big an "if."

Duke, on the other hand, is my pick for the college of the country. It is indescribable. The Cathedral (pictured above) is the main attraction of the campus. The rest of the buildings are built in a quadrangle. The architecture is all Gothic. It is really a beautiful sight, at night, when the chapel is lit up and the carillon is playing some sentimental song. Here at Duke, I have all the conveniences of home: hospital, swimming pool, barber shop, post office, "Dope" Shop (Liggett's of the South) book store, clothing store, theater etc. The hospitality of the South is wonderful and it hasn't gotten hot, yet!

My course consists of Math, English, Chemistry, French & Biology(Zoology & Botany.) I've gotten full assignments in all five subjects, and I mean full. I'll have to work my you know what off if I am to get B grades(which will admit me to medical school.)From what I understand it's going to be a tough grind.

You say you aren't homesick. By gosh, Charlie, I've never missed anything so much in all my life. Perhaps it is the relative distance that we are away from New Britain, but I really miss the old homestead. The summer can't fly by quick enough for me.

Speaking of needles, that's all I've been getting down here. No, not the needles you're thinking of. Since I came down here I've gotten two typhoid needles (and one to come), a Tuberculin needle and a blood test for syphilis. My arms are sore as h- -l.

The girls down here are beautiful but they don't have the class that northern girls have. There's one thing though, they are much more sociable. (Off the record – I have heard that Durham is filled with "bad women"!! That doesn't bother me in the least!)

Judging from the way the V12's are being handled here, you must be going every minute. How do you like the 6:00 A.M. exercises every morning? The navy officers wake me up every morning with their, "Hup 2-3-4." Gosh, that drives me crazy!!

I have two room-mates from N.C. and N.J. respectively. They both are very nice. The southern fellow especially, is really one swell guy. I bust my sides laughing at him. He has some of the oddest expressions.

As I told Meg, I felt that I was picking up a southern accent. The trouble is there are too many of them and only one of me.

I think you'll enjoy what I am about to tell you. Last night, as I was doing some math, somebody threw some water through the open transom above our door. At first, I didn't know what to make of it. When I realized what happened all I could do was laugh. However, the best part is yet to come. The method employed by the fellow who threw the water was this: he had gotten a used rubber and had filled it with water to the size of a basketball. What a splash it made when it landed. My roommate from N.J. had to sleep on the floor because a lot of the water landed on his bed. What fun!!!

Did you see Meg before you left? She wrote me and said that you intended to go home for the weekend. (Lucky, boy). If you did go home, how are things in general? I'm anxious to know. Did Meg happen to say anything?

Well, you "ole turd" I'll have to close. I hope that you'll get along O.K. (as I know you will) and please write and keep me informed of your experiences. I'll do the same.

I think that we're still going to have time to finish that chapter. Let's leave it open O.K.??

As ever,
Dick

P.S. Don't you forget about the first time either.

17 Anise Street
New Britain, Conn.
July 11, 1943

Hi, Kid—

I've been reading your letters the past week and from what I gather you seem to like the life of a sailor quite well. Well, don't let the studies get you down, they will be hard but if you want to get anyplace these days or any other, you have to work hard and plenty of it.

Danny Bray was over to the house this morning. He's at Wesleyan and Ma gave him your address so you no doubt will get a letter from him in a few days. He makes a fine looking man in uniform. A sailor at that.

I don't know just what to write, you've been gone only a week and things haven't changed only that Donny cut the lawn this week and did a good job of it. He had Billy with him and now he is over at the Cabeluses for the week, Betty is the only one left now.

The garden is coming along in good shape, so are the chickens. We get a few eggs from the pullets now. The parties continue the same as ever, this afternoon we are going over to Plainville to visit the Carlsons.

This will be about all for the first letter. I hope you make the grade, it's a long climb up the ladder. Pay less attention to the women and you'll go places.

I have an idea that you will be home in a couple of weeks for a week end visit and in the meantime I'll try and get your mother to write to you, so in the meantime Adios in Spanish to you. It isn't as hard as you think to learn this language. Supposed to be the easiest of all languages to learn.

Pop

51 Forest St.
Oakwood, Conn.
July 11, 1943

Dear Charlie,

Did you ever try to write a letter on your lap? Well, that's what I'm doing now because the front steps seem to be the coolest spot. I suppose I could wait until it cools off a little, but the sooner you get my letter, the sooner you will answer it, and I really do look forward to your letters, only it seems as though they are weeks apart.

I'm sorry I seemed angry in my last letter. But after hearing a million different excuses, I couldn't help feel that way. Oh yes, Helen claims she knows everything. Benny was at the party. She informed me "that he wasn't sneaky, and that he told her everything." I guess she put me in my place. I didn't dare say another word after that.

From your letter it sounds as though all you do is study, but I'm sure you must have a little fun, don't you? Do you have any kind of military training, or is it just like an ordinary college?

So you're going to have sailors' uniforms. Well, won't I feel proud going to the movies (I hope) with you on one of your leaves.

I was very surprised to hear that Freddy hasn't written to you. His address is: F. Wunch, Manhattan Beach Training Station, Brooklyn, N. York. He said that he hadn't heard from you either, so I think he will be pleased if you do drop him a line.

Oh, Charlie, you would have died if you were with Joyce and me the other night. We went to the movies, and when we got out we decided that we would bring some weenies (I don't know how to spell it, but you know what I mean) home, so we walked down to Johnson's and bought four of them. Well, everything was fine until we got on the bus, which was carrying about 500 people. All of a sudden the worst smell came from the floor, and Joyce and I started to laugh, but then we discovered it was the bag of weenies and not the people around us. We nearly died! She was ready to heave them out the window but it was so crowded she couldn't find it, so she held on to them and made believe she couldn't imagine where that awful smell of onions etc. was coming from.

The only picture I have now is the enclosed one. I wasn't going to send that either, but because your last letter was so nice & long, I thought I would. Just as soon as I can though, I'm going down to the studio and have some taken for you, provided you do the same. I'm tired of being reminded of you by my "little white elephant," and my hurricane lamp. I'd much rather have your picture on my dresser, so please hurry and send one. Did you bring your elephant to Harvard?

Dad's really proud of his garden even though his cucumbers aren't fully grown. There's even a baby squash that he is saving for you to see.

Mother, Dad, Fluffy, Joyce and I are all fine, and they all send their love, too.

Well, I guess I have to stop my chatter until next time. Write just as soon as you can.

Love,

Cheryl

P.S. I don't know what I'd do if I lost your address. I'm sure I couldn't remember it!

191 Bristol St.
New Britain, Conn.
July 12, 1943

Hi, Darlin', (Dick would appreciate that. I write "Dear Dick" to him and sign it "sincerely" – al- most.

I'm just all broken up about your shots in the arm, but they will be better when you come home to throw me around, won't they? I hope so. I won't sleep tonight, thinking about it. We might not be able to go to the "Astor" if your arms are weak.

You, little devil, can take me home any night you want to, but I've still got a lot of life left in me, even after a busy day (at the store, you "crazy fool").

When do you think you'll be coming home?(to wifey). I looked for you last Saturday 'cause you said you might come home. Call me up if you do. I think Lucy is a jerk not to answer your letter, doesn't she know what a break she is getting? A letter from you, the best dancer and acrobat in the world? She must have gone mad. Crazy fool.

I hope you won't flunk out for quite a while yet. Do you think you will? How are the women around there? Nothing could compare with the New Britain stock, but are they almost as good?

41

Today was my day off. I spent the day washing the clothes, ironing them, cleaning the house etc. Boy what a vacation, it will be good to go back to work tomorrow. (Me and my dish-pan hands.)

Jerry (Black-boy to you) is leaving Friday for the army. I bet you wish him all the luck in the world. Everyone has left. The town's so dull I'm just about ready to jump off a cliff. (Don't say it's a good idea, I heard you!)

Have you written to many of the kids besides Lucy? They'd like to hear from you, but that doesn't mean you have to spend all your time writing to other girls, mostly me – see! (Lucy would appreciate that, don't you think?) I just gave her the camera a few days ago. She was mad about the film. The dry-ball, she had the silly idea that because the camera and film were hers, she should take the pictures. Dim-wit! All kidding aside, why don't you write her again and she'll write to you.

Mary Jo just came over in a rotten mood, so I thought your letter would be just the thing so we're reading it and laughing – what a clown you are. Please write soon. I nearly died with the heat today but I'll be alive to answer your lovely letters. Don't do anything I won't do.

All my Shellac,

Meg

P.S. I just gave Mary Jo your address so she'll write.

P.S. There's a Beta Mu formal next Sat. Come home and I'll take you.

The White Horse Inn.
Old Lyme, Conn.
July 12, 1943

Dear Charlie,

I just got home from Providence – what again?! I went up to see the girl that roomed with me at school. We fooled around all afternoon and had a heck of a time dodging the O.P.A. – more fun! But gee I'm tired. I was up a 5:45 – had to go down and make like Rosie the Riveter until 11 o'clock. Oh, how I love it!!

Congratulations! I think all of a sudden you've gotten smart – I'm really surprised, By the way, I don't mean your marks. Maybe you don't know what I mean but if you don't – well, then that makes you stupid. So there you are.

I do think the marks you got this year were swell. I didn't think you had it in you. Maybe someday you'll really be something – and won't I be surprised?! It wouldn't be me if I wasn't nasty, would it?

What do you mean about my getting a new set of values? What's the matter with the ones I had? I've still got them – but slightly changed.

About Patty Lou and Shep – that's on the level. But I still don't get it. And as to my engagement – what a laugh! That ended years ago. How the devil can you love someone you never see? I still write to Eddie and all that stuff but – well, I guess I never did love him. I've been in love a couple of time since but that didn't last either. I guess the only one I love is Launa Darcy – but I'm happy this way so that's all that counts.

When I said Old Lyme was dull I didn't mean for you to come down and liven it up. Don't let my patriotic letter writing disillusion you.

As you said, I imagine your courses are awful but it will do you good, Charlie. You're awfully lucky. You've got a wonderful chance – but I guess you know that.

I'm dead tired so I guess I'll go to bed. Goodnight, Jughead.

Love and kisses,

Launa

17 Anise Street
New Britain, Conn.
July 12, 1943

Dear Brother,

How are you feeling? I received the sweater you sent me today. I am down Billy's house on a vacation for a week. Today Billy, I and Uncle Pete went to the Cheshire reform school to see two bulls that weighed 2,400 pounds. Besides the two bulls we saw 20 or 30 prisoners. In the sign shop one of the officers gave Billy and I two markers. I went swimming today. I just got through listening to Lux Radio Theater. Well, it is about 10:00 now and I got to go to bed now well this is all I have to say now. With love from

Donny

P.S. Thanks for the sweater. Send this to 475 Glen St.

91 West Street
New Britain, Conn.
July 13, 1943

Hi, Honey!!!

Well, I hear you're being worked pretty darn hard at "Harvard". It's what I heard from others, not from you. Someone must have rolled your hand up the wringer, not your mother's.

I'm still struttin' to the dirty, stinky, smelly, icky shop every day. When I get through for the day I'm ready for bed at 5:15 There is absolutely nothing to do in this freaky boom town.

Oh, a little excitement! Beta Mu is giving a formal dance at the Y.W.C.A. this Sat. They're having Carl Mitchell for a change. I hope everybody has a nice time, but of course they won't (how could they) when I won't be attending it.

Last Saturday I saw Joe Green, he had just gotten into New Britsky to spend a most enjoyable and exciting weekend. Cripes! I was talking to him for about one minute when Mary Spooner dashes up. Foiled again! Some days you can't make a wooden nickel. The men are so few around here, when you get a chance to talk to one, his old steady has to run up. Oh, well, it can't go on forever(so they say). Anyway, you're only as far as Boston, Peaches, and that's some consolation.

For the past week, Meg has been having the time of her life peeling my nice sunburned back. Exciting, no? No – she really ruined me. I suppose she told you about our little week-end trip to the beach. We had a nifty time.

Well, my little bun, I think this is all for now. So write real soon, until we fall again at the Canteen, and guzzle beer at Beckley's.

I remain

Just plain
Honey

Wesleyan University
Middletown, Conn.
July 13, 1943

Dear Charlie,

Well, how do you like Harvard, is it all that you expected or don't you like calisthenics? We have to get up at 0500 and do calisthenics for half an hour, then we have them again at 1400, what a work out, I never sweat so much in all my life.

The food here is excellent, I really like it.

How many men are in the V12 unit up there, we only have 150 or less here but there are about 500 air corps cadets

We raise hell night and day. The other night one fellow threw a coca cola bottle at another from the third floor. It flew in a million pieces when it broke. Another time they were shooting fire extinguishers at each other. We have to be in bed by 2200 but that doesn't mean much. One guy got up at 3:45 one morning and went out to the coke machine to have a coke.

*Another guy left on leave Sat. afternoon and was supposed to be back by
2100 Sunday night and didn't come back until 1100 Monday morning.
He went to Ohio.*

Well, that's all for now. I'll write when I get a chance.

I see we have the same room number. It's your patriotic duty to write to me.

Love,

Danny

17 Anise Street
New Britain, Conn.
July 13, 1943

Dear Charlie,

*I just received your letter a while ago and I read it to Mother. The both
of us wet our pants. Mother said you're just a crazy fool.*

Mother and I are going to can some string beans this afternoon.

*I got down the little Vic. I looked all over for some kind of a needle. I
found one and tried to put it in the holder but it just don't seem to fit right.
It keeps snapping out. I don't know what's the matter. Besides you don't
need a Victrola. You have plenty of studying to do. And another thing, lay
off the girls.*

*I didn't say that Mother was going to stay in the hospital. She just went
up to see Aunt Anna. But Aunt Anna is home now anyhow.*

I bet the shots in your arm felt awful, but I hope you feel o.k. now.

*Audry and I went up to the Res. swimming yesterday (Sunday). We
had a swell time.*

What did you do over the weekend?

*Donny is over to Cabeluses for a few days. Uncle Pete took Donny
and Billy to the Cheshire reformatory this morning. He had to go up to see
something, I don't know .Donny called a little while ago and said he saw
some prisoners up there. It's too bad they didn't keep him there. He said he's
going swimming at Willow Brook today.*

My legs are so sore today that I can hardly stand up.

*Aud and I were swimming for about two hours last night over at the
park. Audry said if you can find time to drop her a few lines.*

How are you coming with your studies? Do you have to study very long?

*I wish you would hurry up and get your uniforms. What have you been
wearing to classes? Don't answer that.*

*Prince and everybody else is o.k. Well, that's all for now. Don't forget
to study hard.*

Love,

Sister Betty XXXX

P.S. Danny Bray was over here Sunday. I didn't see him but Ma said he looked swell. Just got my shirt. Thanks a lot. It's neat. I wore it with my white shorts and it looked swell. Don didn't get his yet.

91 West St.
New Britain, Conn.
July 14, 1943

Hi ya, Lamby Pie,

Well, your little mill rat is pretty good, and how in h—l are you, you crazy fool!!

What do you know! A little excitement this week-end. Last night Danny Lynch, Larie, Joe and I went to the crappy Beta Mu dance, I think there were 50 kids all together. The oldest kids from Beta Mu were Pat Cline and Betty Harriman. The dance was so good that we left at 11:00 and went to the Burritt. We met Joe Green and "Dry Ball," "Dead Head," "Kill Joy," "Long Puss," Grace Hudson.(outside of that she's a super-duper, proper kid). They came to the Burritt with us and had about 15 snorts each. (all of us). How jealous I bet you are. After Joe and Grace left, we went to the Terminal Diner. (big time, hot shellac, that's us) and filled our faces. After that we walked up to the monument. We really had a swell time.

Cripes sake!!! Last year I lent hot shellac Conway my library card and apparently she hasn't returned it yet, because I received 3 cards, one letter and one personal visit from the library informing me that I owe 85 cents. Ha-Ha Big Joke.

Yes, Joe did have his uniform on. I don't know why you didn't come home this weekend. I thought you said you got your underwear. What more do you want? What kind of a kid are you anyway? Gee! You won't come home in your underwear, you wouldn't get undressed with us that night to go swimming. What a Dry Ball!!! I think this is all for now, my pet.

Muches of anything you want,
Your one and only Mill Rat.

N.A.T.T. Center
Jacksonville, Fla.
July 14, 1943

Dear Charles,

I'm sorry that I couldn't write sooner but this is our last week and we are as busy as all hell trying to check out, a lot of us will have to take this last week over. I just hope I won't be one of them.

Did you have a good time at the prom? Who did you go with and where did you go? My mother sent me the class book and it's swell. Thanks for taking care of getting it for me.

What are you doing up there and how long do you have to stay? I don't know whether you realize it or not but you are living like a king up there compared to the rest of the Navy. I showed a few of the fellows what you get to eat up there and they said not to write letters like that anymore. We haven't seen anything but scrambled eggs since I have been in and we get one damn small spoon of sugar and a damn small cake of butter and all the beans and rice we want.

I will have you know that I do attend mass regularly. I have only missed twice in the last seven months and that was because I couldn't walk the next morning, something like that night I was home and we went to the Canteen only a little worse.

Well, I guess that's all for now write soon and don't work too hard.

Mick

17 Anise Street
New Britain, Conn.
July 15, 1943

Hi, Kid,

We just got your letter and I thought I'd answer it right away.

There isn't much excitement around here with you and Donny away. I'm all by my lonesome.

I think that Freddy is coming home Sunday.

I sent your sneaks and playsuit today so I hope you get them.

Gosh, I bet you're awfully busy with your work. It's hard to study in such hot weather too. How's your Spanish and trig coming? When you write tell us a little more about your studies and how you're coming along.

I know how hard it is for you to answer all the letters you receive and so don't try to. Just as long as you write one letter every day or every other day or so. You know what I mean.

Donny went to the dentist and had one of his teeth filled. He said he didn't mind it at all either.

Daddy didn't like the idea of you asking for some money. He can't understand how you went through $30.00 in two weeks. Mother said *you can't go running out every night, you know. You have to do a lot of studying. Remember that.*

I went downtown with Audry today and I got two new dresses.

I'm going over to Mr. Anderson's tonight for my drumming lessons. I'm coming along pretty good. We have a couple new street beats. When are you going to get those old uniforms anywho? I'd ask if they would hurry up with them.

Love and kisses,
Betty

P.S. Study hard.
P.S. Tessie just blew in. I can hear her shooting off her mouth.

Duke University
July 17, 1943
About 4:45 P.M.

Dar Charles,

Received your letter of the 13th in yesterday's mail. And listen here, Charl-ass, my name is spelled Richard (I think I have got the advantage on you there.)

I'm sorry to hear you are being kept busy with your work for so am I. The assignments have been fairly heavy but not so bad as I expected them to be. I enjoy every subject except English. We have to hand in a theme a week (impromptu) free from serious mistakes. They're very kind – two misspelled words fail you and one grammar (and I don't mean "grandpar") mistake gives you a D grade. Ouch! I handed my first manuscript in today. Here's hoping! All in all, however, I'm getting along fine. All of my profs are pretty nice and I'll have plenty to tell you when we see each other again. (???)

I'm glad you got a kick out of the little episode I wrote you about. However, a few other things have happened since then. One little freshman was fooling around too much, so a bunch of "fellahs" ganged up on him, stripped him of his clothes, shaved his testicler (my own word) region and painted "it" black with shoe polish. Was it a howl! They also did the same with another kid. After they got through with him they added a little shaving lotion. This made it worse for the kid, so they told him to put some water on it. You can imagine the result. Another thing happened. One of my roommates parents sent him some twenty melons to be eaten (You notice I say "to be eaten".) Well, seeing that the three of us couldn't eat all twenty of them, we distributed them throughout the dorm. However, it seemed that after everyone had eaten their melon they didn't know what to do with the uneaten portion. Then the fun

48

started. *Melons started to fly from all directions.!!! Some overripe ones were rolled town the hall like a bowling ball; others were "scaled" through the air like plates and still others were squashed on heads as one would hit somebody over the head with a pie. (Just call me melon head). As a result globes (from the lights) were broken. What a mess! What fun!!*

I enjoyed looking over this folder. The fella from Dartmouth reminds me of you.

Honest, Charlie, I haven't had a wet dream in such a long time that it isn't even funny. There just isn't anything that excites me down here.

Well, two weeks have passed and I hope the next fourteen go by faster!

The only rowing we do down here is up the creek without a paddle. (If you know what I mean.)

It's been very warm down here for the last 4 days. It averages about 95 degrees. I don't seem to mind it, though .Well, I'll close now, you old "turd." Write.

Always,
Dick

Wesleyan University
Middletown, Conn.
July 17, 1943

Dear, No Fuck.

I feel like hell, I got the jitters. They herded us into the sick-bay the other night and gave us our shots. I walked into the room and two guys jumped me, two bad they weren't girls I'd have jumped them back, but as it was they each picked an arm and shoved a needle into it. They asked me my name and by the time I said Bray, D. another guy had already finished vaccinating me and right now it itches like hell.

They are going to extend our liberty to 2300 every night and 2130 Sunday nights.

I haven't looked over the stock here yet but tonight is the night. I'm going to a U.S.O. dance and I'm out to get it, I don't care what she looks like.

We are getting plenty of Salt Peter here but I raised one for about five minutes last night so I think they don't feed it to us around weekends.

What makes you think you'll be thrown out in November?

Do they make you stand Captain's Inspections on Saturdays. What hell, I hate it.

Your pal,
Danny

108 Park Lane
New Britain, Conn.
Sunday morn
After a dead Sat.
July 18, 1943

Dear Charlie,

This is going to be short and not so sweet. I suppose you thought I'd forgotten you, well, I haven't, it's just that I've been so terribly busy lately that I haven't written to anyone. Boy, if it was up to me to keep up the moral of the boys by writing, there would be little or no moral.

Got a card from Dick. He sounded homesick. I'll bet he cries himself to sleep at night.

By the way stinky, how do you like the navy or vice versa, emphasis on the vice. When are you coming home? I'm dying to see you in your new zoot suit.

Of course you do know that I'm taking my college entrance exams next week and I'm petrified. Pray for me – please.

Just at present I'm over at Campbell's. We just got back from church, you know, Charlie, that place people go on Sundays. How long has it been since you've seen the inside of one? Last night Beta Mu gave a formal at the "Y". It reeked and that is putting it mildly. I didn't go but we stopped in for a few minutes, God, this place is really a ghost town now. I'm so tired of talking to strange men. No, it's not really that bad yet, but when more draft quotas are filled the girls will be able to go around nude and no one will be able to molest them. We'll all be rude, nude, lewd and in the mood with no one around to cooperate. And I was trying to reform you! See what working in a factory has done to me. I've got a cop on one side of me, a fireman on the other and two teachers in front of me so I can't go too far wrong. Well, this is all for now – please write soon and where the hell are my pictures? As ever,

Lucy

191 Bristol St.
New Britain, Conn.
July 18, 1943

Dear Clown,

I know now why you write to me quickly, that dollar bet! You really are money mad. I'd forgotten all about it until Joe Rizzo told me you wrote him about it, Friday night. What was the bet anyway?

LETTERS FROM THE ATTIC

I guess you didn't get your uniform by Saturday night, did you, baby. Well, some other time when you come home, I'll throw a party for you, I mean us. Glad to hear your arms are alright, So you can wrap them around me twice! I don't know though, I eat an awful lot now, what with nothing else to do and am getting pretty hefty. Here's hoping you can get them around me once.

Please excuse this writing but it's a hell of a hot day, and I haven't got much ambition. Mary's asleep on the couch and I'm answering a couple of letters, yours first of course. (Dick's last.) (By that time I'll probably have melted.)

There isn't a damn thing doing around here and what there is to do, I haven't the ambition to do it. A couple of kids called this afternoon and I had mother tell them I was out. Doesn't sound like me, does it?

I'm still working hard all day, and we just go to the movies or hang around at night. Friday night Betsy Conway took us out to Shuttle Meadow Club for supper. Of course, Mary and I had lobster, the most expensive thing on the menu! Well, it was Friday and boy, was it good. I ate more than you could ever dream of!

How is school, with you there? I bet they're thinking about closing it for the next couple of years. Can you come home any weekend? Well, try to come home soon.

What else did Dick have to say, besides the Southern Class? Well, I can't write any more because Mary is afraid I'll tell you all that's going on and then she won't have anything to write.

Your favorite dancing partner,

Meg

P.S. I'm going to send that picture to Dick — or did I tell you?

17 Anise Street
New Britain, Conn.
July 19, 1943

Dear Chick,

Sorry I didn't write sooner. Freddy came home Saturday. But he had to be back Sunday at eight. He looked swell in his uniform.

Yesterday we had a party out in the yard for Eddy Newbauer (his birthday).

Aunt Anna stayed here last night and she's writing a letter to Freddy.

I tried to get you an eversharp but I couldn't get any. Freddy said that he might be able to get one for you because they have lots of pens and pencils where he is.

I had to laugh when you said you were washing out your undies. Do you use Lux? I bet you just love ironing your clothes.

Did you get that darn uniform yet? I hope so.

I think it was last weekend that Rod Shay and Joe Green were home. They had their uniforms already.

Remember the negatives of the boys that I sent you? Well, when you get through with them, Aunt Anna wants them to send to Freddy. O.K.?

How are your studies coming? Pretty hard I bet. Did you use your playsuit and sneaks for crew work?

We're all fine at home, including Prince and the chickens and Butch. Lala has a new kitten. His name is Spranky. Prince was afraid of him at first.

Saturday Betty Lee and I went to see "Stage Door Canteen." It was pretty good.

Sunday Audry & Hank Rahon and Jackie Carroll and I went on a picnic.

Jeanne Douglas invited me down to Soundview with them August 15ᵗʰ if they can get the cottage. They're pretty sure of getting one though. So long for now.

Love,

Sister Betty

P.S. $5.00 enclosed. Buy yourself a cigar.

17 Anise Street
New Britain, Conn.
July 19, 1943

Hi, Kid,

Gee, I'm awfully sorry that you didn't have any money to go anywhere over the weekend. You poor kid.

Well, I got my drum sticks out and drummed up $20.00 more. How's that? (I got $5.00 this morning).

If Abe Lincoln read by candle light and wrote on a shovel, why can't you? I'm only kidding. This is the second letter I wrote to you today.

Mother said that you could get a desk lamp in one of the stores up there a lot cheaper. I know you can get them here for about $4.00, nice ones too. Well, do what you wish.

Well, I'm sending this by special delivery I think. Good bye for now and cheer up a little so you won't feel so bad.
Love,
Betty
P.S. I didn't realize you had to spend so much for all the things etc.

The White Horse Inn
Old Lyme, Conn.
July 20, 1943
Saturday night

Dear Charlie,

Here I am again – monotonous, ain't it?! I decided I'd give you a piece of my mind – what, the last piece!! Well, anywho, I may be kind of stupid and all that – beauty and brains never do go together – but I'm not off the beam. You said you didn't think you were lucky to be there anymore – you fool! This is one great chance in your life to make something of yourself – if you don't take it then you're just as stupid as I always told you, you were. Of course it's hard – did you think it would be easy? You know yourself that you never worked really hard for anything. Well, you have to work now – and hard. But, Charlie, you know as well as I do that it's worth it. Think what you'll have when you get through. You've got the brains – even though you never use them – and you can do it if you want to. If you do flunk out I won't be very surprised – I never did think you had the guts anyway. I guess that's enough preaching for one night, but you know I'm right. 'Nuf said!

I don't know what I'm going to do next year – you know me – always letting things go to the last minute. I think probably it will be Connecticut College – right near the Sub Base and Coast Guard Academy. That should give me a good education. There you go taking me the wrong way again.

Did you ever hear of the little moron who cut a hole in the rug to see the floor-show and then covered it up again 'cause he didn't like the dirty cracks? Isn't that awful? – but I have to fill up the page somehow.

I went down to the store the other night and picked up an adorable blonde. He wanted me to go fishing with him (fishing for what?) so I said sure. He was awfully cute and everything but for some reason when he came up to get me I told him I couldn't go. It must have been woman's intuition, I guess. I found out he'd been kicked out of every high school around here and finally went to reform school. I know the nicest people!!

The kids told me today that if I went out with him I should take my father along for protection. Let that be a lesson to me – keep away from blondes.

I'm listening to the Hit Parade – with Frank Sinatra. Don't you love him? Well, I do! Nobody agrees with me – my father thinks I'm nuts. But did you ever hear him sing, "Let's Get Lost"? He's singing it now – gee, he's wonderful.

What the devil am I doing on another page? This is terrible!! I'm starving – pardon me while I go and make myself an onion sandwich.

Well, I ate the onion sandwich – smell the onions? Nice, huh? Do you like onion sandwiches – I'll bet you never had one. I'll make you one sometime – it's a sure way to make friends and influence people.

I got paid yesterday—$25.00—that's after the government got through taking out all the taxes. I swear I think I'm supporting the war all by myself. I'm afraid I won't make my million this way – not at this rate.

I talk too much – why don't you shut me up? I know – you can't. But don't forget what I told you – if you don't do it now you never will.

Love,

Launa

P.S. Frank Sinatra just sang "All or Nothing at All" – you should listen to him. It's the only radio program I ever listen to. He's just about the best I've ever heard – I wonder what he looks like? But with a voice like that what difference does it make? Oh, here he goes again – "In the Blue of Evening," – I can't even write – I'd better stop Goodnight, Jerk! Not very nice, am I?

17 Anise Street

New Britain, Conn.

July 20. 1943

Hi, Kid….

What's cookin'? (answer on back).

I hope you received the money o.k. It took a damn lot of drumming to get it too.

There isn't much news but I want to write anywho.

It was Mrs. Schussler's birthday today so the ladies had a party for her out under the tree. They just left a few minutes ago.

I'm going to put it in the paper tomorrow that Mrs. Young entertained her neighbors in the yard etc. I want Nellie Nealon to see it.

Aunt Anna is still here and Donny is over to Billy's again.

Do you think that you'll be able to come home pretty soon over the weekend sometime?

I wanted to sleep on the couch hammock last night so I did and never again. The darn mosquito's sounded like dive bombers around my ears.

I hope your cold is better and that your arms are o.k. too.

Merton went up for his physical a few days ago and is going up for another on Wednesday. He is joining some branch, oh I can't think about it, but it has something to do with guns. His girl, Edna, is going to be a nurse for the government. She's going to have 24 months training first at the New Britain Hospital and then be sent some where. Old Mr. Swanson (my boyfriend) went up to Lala's a few minutes ago. He didn't know the sprinkler was on and he walked right into it. He got soaking wet. Did he look nice, like a drowned rat. He didn't even stay, but walked right home. So long for now,

Love,

Betty

P.S. Pa is mad because this morning Mother called him a humdinger and he thought she said honkey

What's cookin'? (answer) Beans, you old fart. Cute, eh?

P.S. By the way, can you hang pictures on your wall? If you can tell me, okay? I saw a cute picture in a cut rate store I think you'd like.

29 Park Road
New Britain, Conn.
July 20, 1943

Hi, Charlie,

In the letter you wrote me, you asked how I, the old civilian, was, well, I am not a civilian anymore. I was inducted and sworn in yesterday. I am now home on leave for 21 days.

I saw Meg the other day and she said you wanted me to write, that's why I'm writing now. I also saw Ginger Dillon and she said she wanted to hear from you. So write her. If you don't have her address I'll see if I can get it for you.

Def. of a quickie — A guy who double parks in front of a whore house.

I just happened to remember that one and had to get it written down before I forgot it.

My Aunt and Uncle took the car, the Packard, and drove out to Arizona. They left the Saturday after you and got back yesterday.

55

I have not seen Navickas since you left, I think he went down to the lake.

Benny and I and Betty were going to see Helen one night but he left before we had the chance.

You really have a bitch of a course but with your brain you should do alright, that is if the other boys know what they are doing.

I'll think of you on the 6th stroke and you think of me on the 7th if you get that far.

Joey

P.S. Let me know if you have been salted yet and if so how it feels?
P.S. again. How much money have you made at $2.00 per? Have you broken out much? Are there any nice girls up there where you can get at them? Write me again sometime when you get the chance. If I go in the Army before I hear from you I'll send you my address and I hope it isn't as long as yours.

191 Bristol St
New Britain. Conn.
July 22, 1943

Dear Dope,

Glad to hear you don't answer my letters first just because of the bet. What the hell do you mean it would cost you millions of dollars to get another dancing partner? It would cost you ten times that and a century of labor!

Yes, Mary has been going out with Joe again. He's down at the shore again for two weeks so Mary is hanging around with the girls for a while.

I wish you'd get your uniform. You must look awfully funny in a bathing suit, underwear and shoes – doesn't everyone stare at you? (Party sounds good.)

I hope that Mary and I haven't answered your letters on the same day, or you'll be a wreck. What does Dick have to say about the Southern B—s? He never writes to me about them. (I can't understand it.)

Of course, Betsy Conway really read your last letter (about her legs and a "swift kick"), I forgot it was in it and Mary was reading and Betsy asked if she could read it next. I grabbed it. We had a nutty time last night. Mary Jo, Betty Logan, Ruthie House, Betsy, Mary Jane and Barbara L. were all over here and there was a blackout. The siren is right outside and nearly blew us out of the house. Then all of a sudden Ruthie and I were in the "room off the kitchen" and someone locked us in, with the kids still in

56

the living room! Then someone shined a light down the stairs. Gee, I was never so scared in my life. There were five of us on the couch. (You would have liked it.) Mary and Betty were in the sun porch, so we thought. The warden blew his whistle three times at us for making too much noise. My mother and father were at the movies. I think my hair turned three shades lighter. This morning Mr. Shepherd, chief of the wardens or something, called up to see if anyone was hurt last night! Cute kids.

Your blind date sounds and looks neat. Lucy was with me when I got the letter and also saw the picture. She's pretty mad at you, or maybe she was complimented.

Guess what! Jerry got funny at the shore, (so his sister tells me) and dyed his hair blonde. His eyebrows are really blonde but his hair is kind of red! He must look smooth. I can hardly wait to see him. He isn't going until August – aren't you excited?

There isn't much more news. I saw Kyttle and Vance Parker a few nights ago. I'm going out with Danny, I guess. (Just to keep up his moral.) I didn't say morals. I got a letter from Donny Ryan the other day and was very surprised to hear from him after our little trouble. Did I ever tell you about that? Remind me to sometime. Jane Forbes wrote me today, and she sent me a check for $2.50, that she owed me. I was so glad. Just call me money-mad Bolan.

My dear (?) sister is at camp and this place is wonderfully peaceful. I have no more of this paper so I'd better hang up.(Lucy really did read that).

U – no- who,
Meg

Wesleyan University
Middletown, Conn.
July 22, 1943

Dear Charlie,

Well, I can't complain about the girls in Middletown, they are all friendly to sailors even if they don't all do it. Well, I went to the dance and flirted around with a few of the girls then after the Dance which was over at 12 o'clock we walked around, me and one of the other fellows when a car with two girls in the front seat pulled up and we just piled in, the two of us in the front seat, because in the back seat were two other girls with three air corps cadets, they were all a little plastered and feeling pretty good. We found a street to park on, right in front of the air corps cadet's bunking quarters and I got my loving in although I had to wrestle for it. She resisted

57

because it was 1:30 a.m. and they all wanted to go home. Well, we finally left about 2:30 and I haven't heard from them since.

We got our fourth and fifth shots last night in one shot, double typhoid. Here's a good one for you!

The next time a girls asks you, "Have you got the time?" You say, "I've got the time if you've got the nerve."

I get a letter from Mick about once a week and sometimes twice.

I'm going home today if I don't get restricted, scholastically or by demerits.

Love,

Daniel

17Anise St.
New Britain, Conn.
July 23, 1943

Hi, Jeeter,

Here's that gal again.

Gosh, I bet that "old Hagg" track meet was swell. Thanks for the clippings of the meet and also the pictures.

Mother and Lala just came home from down-street. They didn't buy much of anything.

Fanny is feeling a lot better now. She has kidney trouble.

I went swimming up the Stanley mud hole yesterday. I got a beaut of a sunburn.

My tooth ache is still aching me, but I'm going to the dentist this afternoon so I guess he'll fix it up. I hope so.

Don't forget to tell me about your studies.

The coop is almost all done. It has wood shingles on it. What makes you think we had the porch enclosed? Well, we didn't. Daddy said he's going to wait. You know as well as I what that means.

Donny is down to the Cabeluses again. He's always on the go. He's going on some kind of a hike with the kids down there today.

When you write you never hardly mention your work, perhaps you don't want to talk about it .I'll sign off now.

Love,

Sister Bess

P.S. Don't worry about the books. I made out a money order and sent it in. P.S.S. I'll tell Aunt Anna and everybody about Dot if you don't send me $20.00. (Just kidding).

Stamford, Conn.

July 23. 1943

Dear Charlie,

Even though I'm rather late in answering you, it isn't because I've forgotten you. You see, we've been to Candlewood Lake for this week, and it's a little difficult getting letters mailed out here.

So far the weather has been wonderful, but it does look a little like rain today. I hope it holds out until Sat. when we leave for home.

I've gotten a letter a day from Joyce since we've been here. She went out with Freddy – alone – last Sat. and from her letters I guess she had a wonderful time. She said that when they got in Gabbers, the kids were all so glad to see Freddy. Oh yes, they went over to see your Aunts on Collins St. too. Joyce said they were very nice.

You aren't the only one that does a lot of rowing. Since we've been here my father has had me row him all the lake while he treads, plays, or whatever he does.

Last year I met so many nice kids here at "Joyceland" which is a kind of open hall near the water where they dance, but because of the few people that are able to be here this year, the place is closed. As a result, I haven't seen anyone here my age. I guess they are all in the Army & Navy. Darn it.

How are your studies coming along? I hope they aren't getting any harder.

Are there any other boys with you from Hartford or New Britain? It would be nice for you if there were some. Then it just wouldn't seem so lonesome for you. You haven't mentioned being lonesome at all in your letters but tell me, aren't you – just a little? I know I am beginning to miss you a lot. At first, it wasn't so bad 'cause it seemed as though we'd just had another of our little spats, but gosh, they never lasted this long, did they? I do hope you'll find time to call me this time when you come home!

You must be kept quite busy writing letters. Have you been writing to Joan and those other girls that were at your farewell party as regular as you are writing to me?

I want to thank you for the snapshot you sent me. It was nice, but I feel just as you do– I'd still love to have a larger one of you in your uniform. You won't forget, will you?

Speaking of uniforms, have you gotten them yet? Freddy wore his dark one home, and Joyce said he looked wonderful.

Well, Charles, you'll soon be addressing my letters to 37 Jefferson St. Nurses Training School. You know, I leave Aug. 30th, and after that there won't be much time for anything except studying – so I do hope you'll be home before then.

Oh dear, Dad wants me to row for him again, so I guess I'll have to close for now.

Write again as soon as you can.

Love & kisses,

Cheryl

P.S. Mother and Dad send their love, too.

Duke University

Ceiling zero, visibility unlimited

July 24, 1943

Dear Churullz,

How's every little "ting?" Received your letter Sat. and was glad to hear from you. So glad to know you are doing so well in your subjects! When are they shipping you out to sea?

I have calisthenics every day too. Gosh, does it take it out on me. (But I put it back in.) I look like Chas. Adams and am gaining weight. (7 lbs. and & don't mean strokes.)

I haven't seen any fairies down here – as yet. Do they climb in bed with you or don't you sleep in the infirmary??

The fun still goes on and I've been called down to the rooming office as a result. Well, it won't be long now (no ideas) for I'll be thrown out for misbehavior.

My marks are very satisfactory and I am not putting very much work into it. Although, when I do apply myself, it is concentrated and not dilute.

I hope you won't pick up that Harvard accent! I don't believe I'll get any even though I'm surrounded by a bunch of rebels.

You know Chas. they must be feeding me saltpeter (or something) because I haven't had a wet dream or a "heart on." Have you had any results yet?

Have you had any blisters from rowing (oh, is that what they call it up there?) No wonder you enjoy it so much.

Gosh, in rereading this letter I haven't told you anything constructive. Maybe, I'll settle down in the next!!

Glad to year that Launa writes you regularly. (Is she married yet???) Have any of the Wahas written to you, yet? I haven't heard from Lucy. Have you?

Well, I've got about eight more letters to write so I'll close until I hear from you again.

As ever,
Dick

P.S. I can't think of you on the fifth anymore because it only takes me three now.

J. Rizzo
29 Park Road
New Britain, Conn.
July 24, 1943

Dear Charley,

I just received a letter from you and am writing this after reading it. I hope that is soon enough.

Are you really failing up there, I thought you would do all right. I guess you're just giving me a line.

I got some books from the Book League. One of them is a little hot and I have not read the other yet. The hot one is "Seven French Novels". There are some good bedroom scenes in it, when you come down here I'll let you read it. The other book is "The Last Of Summer." I have not read it yet. I hope it's hot but I don't think so.

My Uncle lets me take the car to Simsbury where I take flying lessons. I have had one hour in the air, more fun. Next week I am going up every day and take an hour. He said I could use the car for pleasure driving if I could get the gas, so when you come back bring some gas coupons.

You should talk about Benny (the shit) and the letter he (the prick) wrote you, you had a big blot of ink on yours (the letter I mean). That letter he sent you "is one hell of a mess." You ought to send it back to him to translate for you.

Thank God, you did not drop that load when you heard I was going, it would have made an awful mess to clean up. I will not write you anything like that any more. The reason they took me is that I had the balls of a bull grafted on. You should see me now – I can hardly go to town. We have a farm. My Uncle just bought it, so now I can be a playboy. If you know what I mean, you can too when you come to see me, 40 cows, 1 goat, 3 horses, more fun, enough for all.

Expectantly yours,
Joe

P.S. You better be here before August 9th or else.

17 Anise Street
New Britain, Conn.
July 25, 1943

Dear Chic,

We are all very glad to hear that you are happy again. Now try to stay that way. I guess that the money helped a little.

Aunt Anna and I went to Hartford yesterday. She had to go to the doctor. He said she was doing fine, but not to go to work until next Wednesday. Now that she is o.k. Fanny is sick with some kind of pain. Charlie F. is calling the doctor again now.

Donny called from Billy's a little while ago and was glad to get your letter.

It's good that you are getting some of your things. It's about time.

It's 3 o'clock now. Narcums just came down a little while ago. Irene, Aunt Anna and I just rode down to get some nails for Daddy. Mr. Peterson is shingling our garage roof. I bet you can't guess what Irene's doing right now?

Aunt Anna got a letter from Freddy. He's not coming home again until August 7th. He was supposed to come home this Saturday but he's going on some detail for so many days. He sent home Aunt Anna $40.00. She doesn't think he could have got paid so quick. He probably won it in a crap game.

There was a picture of you in the Stanley Works magazine. Boy, were you all smiles. It said something about you passing the V12, U.S.N.R. Narcums brought the book down and showed it to us.

Your books came. They are "The Last of Summer" and "Seven French Novels". They look pretty good. Well, I'll be hearing from you.

Your dearest and only sister,
Betty

P.S. Study hard and stay happy. Prince sends all his love. XXXX. He writes pretty good now.
Send the negatives back if you think of them. O.K?

17 Anise Street
New Britain, Conn.
July 26, 1943

Dear Chick,

I hope you're feeling o.k. How many of those darn needles do you have to get anywho? How do you do your school work when your arm is sore? Or are you dismissed for a few days (slight chance)

I just gave Donald and Charles F. one of those Kool-aid hats. Boy, are they excited. They went flying home to show them to Fan. I gave Donald the Hostess hat, he'll never know the diff.

Everybody seems to be on the warpath around here except me this morning. Daddy and Axel Peterson are starting to build on to the chicken coop. Of course Pa didn't say anything to us. Mother is mad and I ain't kidding. I think he is going to build on the side where the three windows are. I'm afraid to ask him.

Then they had another beer party here yesterday. It was a party for Shirley Allen (birthday). I didn't stay home, Audry and I went up to Batterson Park.

I've been trying to take Princey's picture, but he won't stand still in the right position. I'll try again today. He seems to be awfully afraid of the camera.

Yep, Swanee and I go pretty steady now. I go over the mountain every night. Well, that's all for now.

Love,

Betty

P.S. Betty Lee and I saw "Lilly Mars" Saturday. It was pretty good.
P.S.S. Dad said not to write on the envelope anymore. Swell!

17 Anise Street
New Britain, Conn.
July 27, 1943

Dear Charlie,

I haven't hardly anything to write but I thought you'd like to hear from me any who.

Donny is down the cellar washing bottles. We are going to make root-beer.

The chicken coop is coming pretty good. Here's how it's being added on to. Pa said he is going to have shingles on the new part. The garage roof is all shingled and it looks neat.

Mr. Neubauer brought Butch down to the Doctors to have some of his hair shaved off. Boy did he cut it short. You wouldn't know the dog. He looked like Pudgie when you use to cut his hair off, only all over not just the behind. Remember how I use to scream?

Danny Bray was home from Wesleyan Saturday and Sunday. He likes it a lot, too.

How are your studies coming? Write and tell me if they're awfully hard or not or how you like them. Did you go to the beach or somewhere over the weekend? Well, that's all for now.

Love,

Betty—Ma & Pa (& Prince)

P.S. Did you get your lamp yet?
P.S.S. I'm going to the dentist tomorrow and have a tooth out that's killing me.

191 Bristol St.
New Britain, Conn
July 28, 1943

Hello, Honey,

How the – are you? It seems like ages since I wrote to you, all of two days I guess.

Listen Dope, don't be silly. Mary isn't going steady or anywhere near it! She doesn't even like Joe any more but she just goes out with him 'cause he's going away. So don't start looking for a new beer garden partner! I wrote Dick to try and get it so that you both could come home in Oct. on the same week-end. Do you think you could? Then we could go out to the beer garden. O.K?

No, Ruthie House isn't about 12. She's 17 and really a dream! You really should meet her. (She hasn't a brother.)

Gee, I bet you were thrilled to hear from "Hot Shellac" – it's about time she wrote you. I haven't seen her since you went away, except once or twice. I asked Dick if she wrote to him, and how many times. (We'll check up on her.) You weren't kidding when you say I'd better burn the letters. You'd better burn mine!

I think you're mean about Jerry. Poor kid, his eyebrows are white now, and his hair is red! I'm dying mine red, slowly.

How in the world did you know about "Moe" and the first date etc? I nearly died when you said that. I never told you that, who did?

My sister is at "Aya Po" Smart Aleck! And I never went.

Didn't do much last week-end. Friday night the "girls" went to the movies and Sat. I had a date. Don't faint, there are still a few people left around here. Just 'cause you're away do you think the town shuts down! All kidding aside, the place seems like a morgue (without you of course). But Monday I went swimming at a private pool on the Farmington River. I bet you wish I drowned.)

64

By the way did you know that Danny Lynch and Lorraine are going steady? Well, anyway they are.

What's it to you where I swipe the stationary! (It's actually Scott Towels but I iron them flat and add a little dye to them.) Don't tell anyone though.

Please excuse this terrible scribbling but my arm is tired, Danny Kelly wrote me today, asking me to write 2 or 3 times a week, even though he didn't answer all of them! Gee – you'd think all I had to do all day was to write him. Well, enough of this cattiness. Hope you can read this.Your clownish dream girl,

Meg

P.S. Write— or I'll tell— (next letter.)

> *475 Glen Street*
> *New Britain, Conn.*
> *July 22, 1943*

Dear Charlie,

Can't call you Sonny anymore as you are a college man now. Well, Don got your letter yesterday and was he thrilled or were we thrilled for Don passed the letter on to Uncle Pete and etc. down the line. The two kids are having a grand time running back and forth to the park. They come home long enough for a bite to eat and then they are off again. Don says there's no fun at his house.

Well, I suppose you're very busy with your studies which no doubt are very hard. But don't get discouraged whatever you do as anything worthwhile is always hard. But it pays big dividends in the end. Tag got discouraged quite a few times before he finally made PhM 2/c. He studied all the while once he made up his mind and came through with flying colors. It should be easier for you as you just got there and are continuing while Tag was away from studies all of three years. Remember Tom Mix (Radio Program.) – Ralston Winner never quits and a quitter never wins – a pretty good quotation to follow, don't you think? We're all counting on you, so please don't let us down. Have you seen Dottie lately, and how do you like Boston? I got a letter from Tag yesterday saying he was sending home some gear – whatever that meant and wanted me to give Uncle Pete the honor of having it as he didn't want me scared out of a year's growth. Maybe a Jap to hang up as a souvenir. That would be something. Well, pal I'll bring this letter to a close hoping it finds you happy and "rarin'" to go. Love and best wishes from all of us.

> *As ever,*
> *Aunt Anna Cabelus*

P.S. I had to specify which one as you are with two. Write when you can. It's 8:15 a.m. and Don is still sleeping. I suppose he'll write his own letter sometime today.

> 17 Anise Street
> New Britain, Conn.
> July 30, 1943

Hi, Kid,

How ya doing? We're all fine down here on "Tobacco Road." Daddy had the other side of the coop shingled, too. It really looks pretty good. He's going to paint it sort of a dark red color and cream. Here's how it looks. Cute, no? After the war I'm going to live there with "Swanee."

A few days ago it was Donald Farmer's birthday and today it's Fanny's. I think she's 19.

I'm enclosing a clipping about Warren. Maybe you'll be able to hear the broadcast.

Vivian Alllen is awfully sick with pneumonia. It's some kind of a germ she has. She goes out to the pool a lot and I think that is what it's from. Quite a few people have gotten diseases and sicknesses from out there. I'm afraid to go over there now.

The Belvedere Youth Center is giving a play in September. I was asked to be in it. It's 118 pages long, some play. We're having our first rehearsal tonight.

How's your work coming? I suppose you got some more shots in the arm today. More fun?? That's all Kid.

> Love,
> Daisy June Young

P.S. If you can, send me some of those red Harvard stickers, o.k?
P.S.S. Send Vivian a get well card to make her feel good. 387 Main Street, City.

> Wesleyan University
> Middletown , Conn.
> July 30, 1943

Hi, bum,

I don't know what you don't like about bags, they are the only things you can have any fun with. If you think the uniform will attract the nice girls you are badly mistaken. One fellow was telling me how he was walking down some street in Hartford and some pig grabbed him by the arm and asked if she could go with him but he said he just pushed her away.

Tomorrow they have promised us those syphilis moving pictures and also told us that if we don't know anything about sex now we certainly will Saturday. I'll tell you all about it and prepare you for it because you'll see it too sooner or later.

I didn't know you didn't have your uniforms yet, it must be kind of rotten without them. We had to go about four days without ours and my clothes were beginning to stink. How do you guys get along, have you got a change of clothes or do you wear the same ones all the time?

As for flunking out, a bunch of the guys down here are beginning to and the restriction list get longer every week. I'm not yet although I've got the lowest possible marks on all of my tests but not quite flunking.

They tell us we will get paid around Aug. 5, I don't know how true it is but if they don't pay us pretty soon my father will be broke.

Last night some wise guy balanced a bucket of water on the top of the door to my room, but I spied it in time and ran into his room and locked the door after me. I drank a coke and ate a chocolate bar on him then when I got back to my room he was just beginning to burn my books which he had piled up under the desk. Well, I took the bucket down from the door and poured it all over the poor fellow and all over my books. That's all the shit for now.

Your pal,
Danny

Duke University
August 1, 1943
Saturday
U-bang-it time

Hello, Charles,

So you're getting Navy "E's" (and I don't mean pennants). Beside that, everything is o.k.??? Well, glad to hear it as things stand the same here only I'm just beginning the alphabet.

But seriously, Chas, I hope that this note finds you as drunk as ever and that you haven't become "slap-happy" – yet, you old fruit!!! Where the heck did they ever get the idea that "fairies" were called "fruits"? Maybe because they're both gullible(sp).

My dorm is in hot water again. A couple of nights ago some of the fellas started to burn some film and throw stink bombs around. This created quite an odor and plenty of smoke. It was reported to the dean and he sent the campus cop up to investigate. He took some names and we can expect a call down any day now. The cop said that in his 13 years at Duke he's never met up with Freshmen like us (That is our floor – G – 2nd floor). It's gotten so we're called the G-Gorillas. Just call me "Dickey the Terror."

With all of this fooling going on I still devote the necessary time to all of my studies. It's surprising how little time I have to put on them. Bonnie Baker and Tommy Reynolds and his band are down here over the weekend. That should be interesting. Say, I've met a couple of nice Southern girls. (No, no first time.)

You still haven't convinced me that it's "Goodbye forever etc." I still think that there are plenty of good times in store for us. Who do you include in your so called "unit"? I can better answer you if I know this.

I've been writing to Meg, Mary, Betty Logan, Larry, Benny Swetchnick etc, That's all I ever do over the weekend. I wrote 10 letters last weekend and left out quite a few that I wanted to write to. I haven't received word from Lucy yet! I sent her a card the first day I was down here asking her to write! No answer yet! She can pound sand!!

Mom sent down some film for my movie camera and my still camera. I should get some real shots.

I've gained seven pounds, you old "turd," but I'm carrying it well by remote control.

It's stroking time once more so I remain,

> *Strokingly yours,*
> *Dick*

P.S. Do you think we're becoming a little too vulgar?
Feeling something I don't know what it is though!!!

> 17 Anise Street
> New Britain, Conn.
> August 2, 1943

Hi, Sailor!

So you got your uniform. Goody, Goody Gumdrop!!! I bet it looks swell, like a potato sack. Did it fit right or did you have to have it altered? When Freddy got his they gave him a size 40 and it cost him $8.00 to have it fixed.

It's too bad they had to shorten your weekend. It's up to you whether or not you feel like coming home. Of course, we want you to. Why don't you try to get a little longer leave if you can.

I got four letters today. One from Barbara Kirby, another from Dale Bolton out in Colorado and a ration book holder (Dutch Cleanser) and from you. Of course, you're the first one I'm answering.

The coop is all done and looks pretty neat. I'm going to try and take Princey's picture today. I'll perhaps have to take him tied up because once he's loose nothing can stop him.

I hope you had a good time at the beach. How's Dick's sister?? About 10 years old maybe.

Audrey's birthday is August 22nd. Don't forget to send her a card. Remember now. I'm going down to the shore for sure the 15th – good, huh. So long for now, Sailor.

Love,

Sis

P.S. Thanks for the stickers. Ma's going to paste Donny's mouth up for swearing.

N.A.T. T. Center
Jacksonville, Fla.
August 2, 1943

Dear Charles,

This letter is kind of late but it couldn't be helped. This radar shit keeps us busy and trying to get my clothes all cleaned and rolled up I hadn't had time to do much writing. In radar we go to school eight hours and at night we have anywhere from two to three hours studying and we have to do this in the school so I can't sneak in a letter or two while we are studying.

Radar is the most secret thing I ever saw. We have to wear badges and show our i.d. card to get in and then after we get in they search us and when we are leaving it is the same way. Everyone in the place wears a gun (not the students) and you are scared shitless to move. Every two hours we can have a smoke so that means two smokes a period (four the period). The only time you can leave the building is to eat, they still let us do that.

Well, enough for that. Hotch is leaving for Norfolk tomorrow, he made his rate. I am leaving next Tues. or Wed. for gunnery school. I don't know where yet but it will probably be Yellow Water about twenty miles from here, and then it will probably be back to this station for a squadron. Once the bastards get you in Florida they don't want to let you out.

When I said that a lot of us would have to take the last week over, I meant that we had a lot of final exams the last day and if we flunked one we had to take eight hours a day at that subject and if you flunked more than one you got thrown out of school, and I flunked one, it was sending, and I took that for eight hours for a whole week so I am a week behind my old class. They are going out today. That's the way they get rid of a bunch of the fellows at the end of school.

I haven't heard from any of the girls in Burlington or Winsted. I guess the best reason for that is that I haven't written to them, but I still hear from good old Cheryl. Do you hear from the girls in N.B? Joan and Bud write once in a while but they don't exert themselves.

Have they told you anything about leaves yet? The way it looks now I am due for one in about six months. (I hope,) Something to look forward to.

We don't get salt peter down here, they trust us enough now to get a hard on.

Well, I guess that's all for now, you had better not answer this letter. I will write to you as soon as I get to gunnery school. Don't work too hard.

So long,
Mick

P.S. I came out seventh in the class and made Seaman first.
Neuman is cleaning out ice boxes on an aircraft carrier.

108 Park Lane
New Britain, Conn.
August 2, 1943

Dear Charlie,

So what the hell's a matter with you, are you mad at me or am I just on your black list? Are you trying to get even with me for not writing to you sooner? Tell me, Mr. Anthony, what did I do?

Of course, you know I broke down and wrote to Dick and all the others I avoid letters to. It's a good thing moral isn't left up to me. Jim Donnelly told me today that Dick is going to get his questionnaire. Jim said he saw it at the draft board. I hope they don't drag Dick out of college. Jim goes up for induction into the Air Corp tomorrow, he'll leave in four to twenty-one days. There goes another, soon N.B. will look like a girls' town.

By the way, Errol, when are you coming home, or are you? Meg told me you haven't gotten your uniform yet, just shoes. That's nice, but don't forget the password – "Are you 18? I'd hate like hell to have to go to court and swear and swear under oath that you were a good boy. Not that I dislike or disapprove of lying. It's just that it wouldn't look too good in the papers. Anyhow, I take an awful picture. If you can't read this damn thing take it to the nearest Arabic interpreter, and he'll help you decipher it.

I'm still doing my bit for defense and it's slowly killing me. But I don't mind. They can put on my tombstone – "She did it for her country." Callous, aren't I? Go on, look it up in the dictionary.

Congratulate me, darling, I was accepted by the Rhode Island School of Design. I took my exams about two weeks ago in Providence. God, is the Dean of Admissions cute. I think I shall like college very much. I'm not sure yet whether school starts Sept. 15th or Oct. 6th. I hope it's in September. The college is beautiful and the dorms are these great big, old mansions. It's really a grand place. If I don't see you before I go, you'll have to come up and see me sometime. Who does that sound like?

Letty Smith just called and wants me to come over, I guess I will if I can get my shoes on. I have poison ivy all over my toes . It's perfect, you really ought to catch some, especially on your feet. It's the easiest way I can think of to going stark, raving mad. This will have to be all for now, and if you don't answer by the end of the week, this will be all – forever.

Love,

Lucy

91 West St.

New Britain, Conn.

August 3, 1943

Hi, you bundle of stuff,

Well, your little mill rat is writing you straight from the factory. I'm terribly glad to hear that you've got your uniform. I imagine that you were getting a little chilly traipsing around in your underwear all this time. Of course I know you weren't in the least embarrassed.

I read your letter to Meg. I'm really not money mad. Cripes, I haven't any left. All I do is spend it on the 4-F's that are still in New Britain. I have a whole list of them. Of course, I have to feed them liquor, and you know me, the Booze Hound. I don't have money for anything else. But when you come home, darlin', I know you'll buy me all the liquor I want, won't you?

A week from this Sat. we'll be down at Point-O-Woods for two weeks or until Labor Day. If by any chance you can get a week-end during that time, please come down and see me. It will be so easy for us to get crocked down at the shore. All we'll have to do is run in the water to sober up and then start all over again. Smooth, no?

Warren Stanley was home a couple of weeks ago. Cripes, the Army has certainly changed him. He's so darn cocky we civilians can't even talk to him. He really does look good in his uniform though.

I think I'll go crazy in this mill if I don't do something pretty quick. Since last Friday I haven't done one thing, 'cause all the typewriters are taken.

71

Last Friday John Schmitz, Maureen and I went down to Point-O-Woods to see Joe. We really had a swell time, but I haven't got a case on him, as you put it. I'm all through with him.

John Schmitz leaves for the army next Tuesday.

This is about all the crap I have to swing at this time. Write soon, Sugar, I'll be tearing my hair out till I hear from you.

Love and stuff

"Ratzy" – Mary Jo

191 Bristol Street

New Britain, Conn.

August 3, 1943

Dear Dopey,

I hope I'm writing quickly enough. I don't think you'll look so sharp with your fingernails bitten down to the elbow! Glad to hear you finally received your uniform. I think it must be a great change to wear that, after the shoes. (Aren't you hot?")

Gosh, I don't think there's going to be another dance this summer. You know we're going to the shore, I wish to hell you could come down with someone Sat. night. If there's any chance of getting a long week-end or something, write to me. We could all have a simply super time!

Yes, I know Bob Roberts. He's a nice kid, isn't he? Tina Andrews used to be one of my friends in West Hartford. Thanks for not telling him of our secret marriage and my habit of getting 'stinko."

Never mind about the black-mail, I could do a pretty good job of it myself. We'll see who can make the most money!

Smart – I didn't go out with "Mac" – and if I did, nothing would have happened! How did you know about the first time? Please, tell me. I want to know if Dick knew about it. Speaking of Dick, I got a horrible letter from him today – asking if it wouldn't be too much trouble to write once in a while etc. I wrote a neat one back, I only hope he answers it. I probably won't hear from him for a long while. Now. of course. we're not going steady and we haven't "agreed to a temporary separation" – that sounds much too serious for me. Don't you think? I hope you kids do come home together. Dick said you would. That would be fun. The pleasure Ban will be off by then, and we could use a car, without having to push it out of the driveway – Remember?

72

Please do send a picture. (10 ft. x 10 ft.) −(Paper the whole place.) Why don't you have them taken as quickly as possible. I'm dying to see them. That Harvard sticker was cute. Have you got any big ones? Send me a couple, o.k?

I've gotten the most wonderful new records lately. The latest is "Paper Doll," by the Mills Brothers. It's simply solid. We could dance to it neat. Have you ever heard it by them? It's the best record I've ever heard.

None of us did much this week-end. We went out to dinner Friday night, and then went to the movies (free). We ate at the Burritt ((Ra-Ra). Monday I worked at my father's office. Instead of doing my washing! I don't know what I'll do for clothes this week. Next Monday I'll probably break my back over a wash board, and iron. (Don't look so hopeful!) − (I'll push your face in.) (gentle Meg.) Write − and send pictures and stickers—.

Love,

Meg

The White Horse Inn
Old Lyme, Conn.
August 3, 1943

Dear Charlie,

I just heard, "There's Danger in Your Eyes, Cherrie," and that reminded me of you − I wonder why? And then I remembered that I hadn't written to you − I'm afraid my patriotism is slipping.

Before we go any further − let me tell you, my dear little moron − Frank Sinatra is 5 ft. 11 − and very nice looking. Don't you dare make any cracks about him − you're talking about the man I love!

Our letters seem to get more and more nasty as time goes by − who started it anyway? Well, far be it from me to stop. I can see that you haven't changed − you're not as smart as you think you are − Sucker!! I know what I was wondering about before − but I guess I knew it anyway − gee, you're dumb, huh? I'm glad I'm not there, you'd probably throw something at me, but then I guess you wouldn't. See what I mean?

I'm still waiting to hear from Conn. College. I went up there last week for my interview − my marks were o.k. and the College Entrance exams were o.k. but I'm so late − oh, what a mess! But it seems I'm always in a mess − its fun though.

Do you ever hear from Mike Leary? Do you have any idea where he is?

I went up to Providence Saturday again. I had to work in the morning so I didn't get there till 2 o'clock but we "fruited around" until 10:30 that night. I went up to see Snit — she's the girl that roomed next to me at Briarly. We had a heck of a time — she's a riot.

I got a letter from Patty Lou last week. She's working for the New York, New Haven and Hartford Railroad now and she's going into Teacher's College in September.

Have you got your uniform yet? I suppose so. You could send me a picture — with uniform. Maybe I could use it to scare away June-bugs or something. I have to write three more letters so I won't waste any more time on you.

Not much love,
Launa

17 Anise Street
New Britain, Conn.
August 4, 1943

Hi, Kid,

I'm just writing a few lines because there hasn't been much doing lately.

Mother is shopping with Lala. Jeanne and I are supposed to go shopping this afternoon for some things for the shore. It's starting to sprinkle and I don't know whether I'm going now.

Ma and I cleaned out the closets yesterday and we're sending some of your things to the cleaners. Some of the moths began to raise hell with my gray skirt, I aired the thing out just in time.

Tulip and our street were tarred yesterday. Donny got tar all over his pants and himself. Ma keeps telling him to stop sitting in it but it doesn't do any good.

Freddy is coming home the 24th of August so why don't you try to come home then. (if you want to). So long for now.

Love,
Sis

P.S. Don't forget Audrey's birthday. It's not till the 22nd though.
P.S.S. We had another meeting of the Belvedere Youth Center Dramatic Guild last night. If we can get the play ready before September 7th we can have it in the Teacher's College. I don't think it's possible though. It's 118 pages long. Love,

Sis

17 Anise Street
New Britain, Conn.
August 6. 1943

Hi, Kid,

I'm enclosing a letter from Francis as you will notice. I guess he didn't know you went away. He's a Corporal already. Wow!

Last night the boys played the men in a game of baseball. It was a neat game. Daddy and Mr. Newbauer, Ziegler, Conlin, Keevers, Rawlings, Walker and all the men played. The men were winning so they let the boys get ahead in the last inning. The men bought two watermelons and we all had some. Daddy can really play pretty good, too.

Donny wrote you a letter a couple of days ago and when he went to mail it he couldn't find it. I told him he has to write another one. It takes that kid about an hour to write a letter.

Mr. Andrews came over this morning and told us to keep Prince tied up because he knocks all his plants in the garden over. We only let him loose at night for a while.

I hope that you're work is coming along alright. That's all for now.

Love,

Sis

P.S. Taggy's picture was in the July 5 issue of "Life." He was kneeling down near a man on a stretcher after the place was bombed.

91 West Street
New Britain, Conn.
August 6, 1943

Hello, my poor Peaches,

I heard that you had to take some Spanish exams instead of coming home to your little shuffle girl. Gosh! Meg and I were both disappointed not to have seen you. Will you have to wait until Oct. now to come home? You just better get home when Mr. Walton does, or I'll steal my brother's piggy bank and go up to Harvard and drag you home. Cripes, here I was resting up all week for that nite and you don't come home. I rested so much that I'm tired all over again from too much rest.

The latest news. FLASH. Donald Ramis broke up with Betty Logan while he was home on leave (and still is until Friday.) He claims that he has another girlfriend that he's been going steady with for a week in Battle Creek, Mich.

Well, honey, Lorraine Minton is having a hen party so I must "cluck" along. (Please laugh.) How's college life treating you? – often enough??

All my (anything you want, butch.)
"Shuffy"

CHARLES YOUNG

WRITE SOON!

191 Bristol Street
New Britain, Conn.
August 6, 1943
11:30 p.m.

Dear Charlie,

I hope you notice the time! I just got in from the movies and decided that if you think I only write about once a month I'd better dash off a note to you. Really, I write about 2 times a week. The beginning and the end. So – what's your trouble? I write Dick about once although it takes longer go get to N.C. Jay Brant (don't laugh) got off the bus with me. (He lives way before you get to the park) to walk me home. I guess he wanted or rather expected me to ask him in but I just said, "Thanks and good-night." He looked so surprised I nearly laughed. He must be thinking that I've changed. Well, enough of this silly chatter.

About the beach, I'll talk to Mary and write you when it would be a good time to come down. I'm awfully glad you can come. Bring someone. The Hennessey's are taking a cottage at Point O' Woods. We're going for two weeks so there'll be three weekends during that time so I should think there should be one you can come down. Mary will be really glad!

Please do send some pictures. I'd love to hand them out, what makes you think that there are still that many people in Liggetts? There aren't! There isn't anyone. Also the stickers, don't forget!!!!!

Gee, you're lucky to be going to the Cape this week-end! I wish I was! I'll have you know I'll be seventeen this week-end. You can send me some stickers for my birthday. I quit work next Thursday. Gosh, will I be glad. We're leaving for the beach next week-end. I'll write just as soon as I can talk to Mary, 'cause I couldn't see her today - or tonight. So, seeing my mother is beating me with a club, I'll hurry and end this messy message .Hope you can decode it!

Love,
Meg

17 Anise Street
New Britain, Conn.
August 6, 1943

Dear Son,

Just a couple of lines letting you know everything is o.k. Not much news. Betty and Don just got through having a battle. She keeps on teasing him.

76

Have you heard from Benjamin?. We don't see anything of him. I wonder if he went to College. How are you getting along in your studies, do you find them any easier? Do you have any drill work or is it just studying? It's too bad they don't lift the ban on driving. We could take a ride and see Sam & Mae and you at the same time. Did you meet any new pals yet? I mean some you like real well like Joe & Dick? That's all for now. I know Betty keeps you in touch with almost everything. The rock garden is pretty well dried up, the corn you planted is growing swell. We have a swell garden this year.

Lots of love,
Mother

Friday Noon

Dear Brother

I am sorry I did not write sooner but I was too busy playing. Last night the Boys played the Men in baseball for a water melon. The score was "17" to "18". Daddy played with the men. Tonight we are going to have corn on the cob for supper. We have a lot of ripe tomatoes in our garden. About two weeks ago Mother and I made 10 gallons of root beer and half of it is gone and we are going to make 5 gallons more. Charlie Farmer painted his house white. Betty is just as fresh as ever.

Your Brother
Donny

P.S. Please write.

17 Anise St.
New Britain, Conn.
August 7, 1943

Dear Charlie,

Well, tomorrow is the big day, school. Donny is so excited he's running around the house like a chicken with his head cut off?? I don't mind going back though. Today Jean Ziegler and I went shopping. I bought some new clothes for school and then we helped "Lil" do some errands.

We got your clothes today and Mother is going to have your trench mouth, I mean coat, cleaned before she sends it back. Mother said that you left a raincoat over to Sam's and you'd better see that you get it back.

Betty Lee went home yesterday. She wasn't any trouble and I didn't mind her staying here, at least she kept me company.

I tried to get some chocolate over the store for some cookies but they didn't have any but perhaps we'll be able to get some downtown. I hope so anyway.

Love from all,

Sister Bess

P.S. I hope that you make good in your Spanish Exams.

"Sis"

17 Anise Street

New Britain, Conn.

August 9, 1943

Hi, Kid,

I just got home from the dentist and I'm all finished up. I feel swell.

I hope that you had a good time over the weekend .Did it rain there? I rained here a little Saturday and Sunday.

Sam from Cambridge and the Cabeluses were here for supper yesterday. Sam was telling us about the good time you kids had over to his house. The way he talks, George must be like you. You know, sort of crazy, always making faces or something.

Donny and Charles dug some kind of a hole over in the lot. Mother tells Donny to stay away from there because he's always getting dirty.

We had a practice air raid yesterday for about 40 minutes. The kids were using the hole for an air raid shelter.

What do you mean you won't send Audrey a card? You send her one or else......... Remember Kid, the 22ⁿᵈ!!!

I saw Vivian Allen downtown this morning. She's all better now. She said she got your card.

I can't wait till Sunday rolls around. I'm leaving for the shore then. That's all for now.

Love,

Sis

Prince is fine.

P.S. Pa is painting the coop barnyard red and cream. It looks neat.

P.S.S. Lala's dog Butchie just came over to me and said to say hello to you. We're all fine and hope you're the same.

191 Bristol Street

New Britain, Conn.

August 11, 1943

Dear Charlie,

Don't be silly. Dick won't be angry about the beach. I've already told him. Of course, I haven't heard from him since but it couldn't be that, no,

78

but seriously, he won't be mad. After all you always did go around with Mary and me when you were home, too.

Red left yesterday and also John Schmitz. "Moe" left Monday. Jerry also left Monday. Aren't you glad? Red hair and all.

I'm glad to hear you had a good time at the Cape. It sounds as though you were flying too low instead of driving too fast. Glad to hear the waves didn't drown you. Yes, I used to always go sailing on the ocean, 2 years ago. We used to go out almost everyday. We (kid I used to go with) nearly tipped over in a squall. Of course, I rescued us. I used to crew for a guy in the races too, we always came in last. Except once, we came in second from last.(Everyone threw a party that night.) Glad to hear you want to go to Florida when we're married, but really, Charlie, I don't think that would be good. I'd rather go to the South Sea Islands, wouldn't you? I think it would be much more romantic.

You know I'm not sure if you kids could stay at Hennessey's because Mrs. Hennessey just found out her sister and their kids are coming down, I think, but you could find somewhere to stay if you could get down. If you couldn't get down for that long, come down on a Sat. night. We're going down this Sat. and I think we'll stay over Labor Day. I hope so. So you write me when and if you can come down and I'll tell you if it's o.k. Probably next week-end would be best.

Send the stickers if you already haven't. Yes, I'm quite glad to be finally 17. It seems quite different. My father said he couldn't remember when he was 17 or 27. He said if I was 27, I could have my license. Generous,

Please excuse this messy, horrible, dreadful letter! I really have a horrible headache. Reminds me of how I used to feel after you threw me around at Beckley's! Write soon, per usual

Love,

Meg

17 Anise St.
New Britain, Conn.
August 11, 1943

Dear Brother,

I received your letter yesterday noon. I am sorry you can't come home over the week end. We got two new black chickens from Mr. Peterson the builder over on Foxon Place. Something is wrong with our radio. So Mother called up some man from Sears and Roebuck. Billy gave me his turtle a few days ago. The other day I killed a snake in back of the garage, it was about 15 feet long.

Your loving Brother,
Donny

17 Anise Street
New Britain, Conn.
August 11, 1943

Hi, Kid,

Gee. I'm glad you got paid. Will you get $50.00 every month or will they take some out for bonds and things?

I bet you had a neat time at the Cape. That inn you went to looked pretty classy.

Freddy was supposed to come home the 14th but he can't now. Somebody stole his wallet and the whole group has to take punishment for it. They have to walk quite a few miles everyday and they can't come home.

I just noticed that Nealon's have a new red and white awning over their porch. Looks nice.

We had a rehearsal for our new play yesterday morning. It lasted from 10 o'clock to 12 o'clock. I got the part I wanted too. (I think.) Perhaps they will take it away when I go away for a week.

I haven't much more to write. No more in fact. I'm supposed to be cleaning the house so I'd better hurry up and start.

Love,
Sis

P.S. Prince and everyone else is o.k.

17 Anise Street
New Britain, Conn.
August 12, 1943

Hi, Kid,

I was sorry to hear that your work was so hard. If you have to have a tutor you might as well get one of them. Why didn't you take German? You had that before – or Latin. I thought you were taking a medical course???

Prince is an awful nuisance. He barks all day long. We can't let him loose so he might as well get used to being tied.

I'm going to a party tonight at Dick Peterson's house. It's a going away party for Joe Passcrini. He was the president of our school (Nathan Hale.) I hope I have a good time. {Smooch like hell then stop).

We had another rehearsal this morning. We never seem to get anywhere though.

I'm enclosing a card from Francis.

There was a picture & article about Harry Billings in the paper tonight. (Warren's brother). He is missing in action. Well, I'll sign off now.

Love from all,

Sis

P.S. I'll write to you from down the shore o.k?

17 Anise Street

New Britain, Conn.

August 13, 1943

Dear Chick,

How are you feeling today? Good I hope.

I had a visitor over the weekend. Betty Lee stayed here Friday and Saturday night. She's sitting here playing with my dy-dee doll now. She's going home in a little while. Her mother went to New York.

There was an article in the Courant this morning that the V12 boys at Trinity got their uniforms. Perhaps you'll be getting yours pretty soon. I bet when you do get them, you'll get sick and tired of wearing them.

Boy, did I have a time at the dentist. I have to have a couple nerves killed in my teeth. When he put the drill in my mouth, I jumped out of the seat onto the floor.

When we went to church this morning, I noticed your name on the service flag in back of the church.

We saw "Bombardier" yesterday. It was one of the neatest pictures I ever saw. Well, so long for now.

Love & Kisses,

Betty

P.S. Donny and Charles are upstairs playing with some kind of telephones . They belong to John Nixon. Donny wants to buy them for $1.75. I don't even think they work.

The White Horse Inn

Old Lyme, Conn.

August 13, 1943

Dear Jughead,

Let me tell you the most important news first – I finally got accepted at Conn. College! They had to send away to Briarly for my marks – that's what caused the delay. I was a nervous wreck – I was to go out and join

81

the WAVES if I didn't get in. So I guess that settles my life for the next couple of years. I was so happy when I got the letter that I had to sit down on the floor and cry – silly, huh?

I don't suppose I'll ever convince you how wonderful Frank Sinatra is, but you don't have to show your ignorance by saying you don't like him, And he is not a midget - 5 ft - 11 is tall enough for me when he has a voice like that. I'll admit that it's kind of hard on me knowing that he has a wife and child – but he can always divorce her and marry me, can't he? I know I'm nuts, but I can dream, can't I?

I'm sorry to hear that you're working so hard – but as I said before – it'll do you good. Personally, I think it's hopeless, though.

I do not want to hear from either Danny or Mick so don't write and tell them so. I just asked you where they were, and you still haven't told me.

It's really too bad that you can't get mad at me – but then, you never could. That only goes to prove that you haven't changed and that you are just as stupid now as ever. Too bad – you lose!

Well, I've only got two more weeks to work – thank heavens! Gee, how I hate it! I don't think I'm the type to work in a factory – but definitely! They've made me a supervisor now – I'm teaching all the new girls and inspecting the radios. But I'm afraid I haven't got the patience – as I said before – I'm not the type!

I just found out yesterday that one of the fellows from Briarly is up there, too. His name is Harry Harland – do you know him? He's a jerk too so maybe you'd make a good pair. I worked on the yearbook with him and I never could make out whether he was a genius or a moron.

Well, I have a couple of other letters to write so I guess I'd better stop. So long, Sucker!

Launa

P.S. Do I get that picture or don't I? I have to have something to scare these rats away!

Duke University
August 15, 1943

Dear Charles,

I agree with you that our letters have been rotten to the point. So, I think we had better "lay off" for awhile.

I'm in the same predicament you're in. I have so much to say and no way to say it in!! It'll take me more than a week to tell you everything that I want to tell you. Believe me, that's going to be some bull session when we meet in the fall. I'm going to be home on Oct. 23ʳᵈ. If I'm correct, I think I'll be home then. Won't you!???

You mentioned something about that last week in June. You're right, Charlie, that was my idea of heaven, too. Gosh, you really don't realize how wonderful it was, until you look back. Darn it all, what I wouldn't give to spend a week like that when I get home! However, I think that I'll have my "fill" (no ideas) before I leave here.

As for the draft board, I received my questionnaire a week ago Friday! Yes, sir, Uncle Sam is surely catching up on me. I may be home sooner than I think.

I've gained 8 lbs. since I got down here. I'm as brown as can be and getting along fine.

My averages are as follows (incidentally, mid-term marks go home Oct. 26). French – A, Math – A, Botany –A, Chemistry – B, English – B. Not bad – considering the amount of work I've just put in.

I agree with you that we won't get together as a unit. It's pretty tough to say this, but, nevertheless, it's true until after the war, at least.

I manage to write home 4 times a week. My mother writes every day and my father writes on Tuesday. Meg averages about 4 letters a week. Does she write often to you??

Meg's spending the next few weeks at the beach. She mentioned that you might take a run down over the weekend. I hope you have a good time.

I've met a few fellahs from Conn, the closest being from Hartford.

Well, Chas, another week is about to begin. So good luck, don't whack it too much, & write soon.

As always,
Dick

P.S. Down here they call "them," "homos" and "gumdrops."

17 Anise Street
New Britain, Conn.
August 18, 1943

Dear Son,

Well, here goes. Not much news to tell you. Betty wrote to you from the shore.

Donny is busy making an airplane model. It's especially quiet around here with Betty gone. I sure thought that the dog went on a vacation. I let him loose Mon. afternoon for the first time in a couple of weeks and

83

he didn't come back until the next day. I surely thought Rowski had him. How are you coming along with your Spanish? Dad didn't think it was so hard. Why didn't you take German or Latin. You had it at high school.

How about your other subjects? Are they any easier? You have to work pretty hard at college if you want to get anywhere.

Freddy was home Sun. He said he would be home Labor Day. He was all tired out, he said he worked a lot of hours doing patrol duty.

We had a swell garden this year. We are going to have a lot of tomatoes. I'm going to can some tomorrow.

Tommy is down in S. Carolina – he said what a small hick town and so Shirley is down there with him. But he thinks he will be shipped out the 1ˢᵗ but doesn't know where. Kenneth was up to be examined – he probably will get another deferment – maybe. Willie Westerman has to go, We haven't had a beer party in three weeks. We went over to Almas Sunday. I am going down town with Fannie this morning and Oneida was just here and she's going.

I do hope you will be able to come home over Labor Day. Fannie can't wait to see you in your uniform. She's having a vacation now with Chas. away.

Will close now with love,

Mother

I'll have Donny write to you. He can probably think of something to tell you.

17 Anise Street
New Britain, Conn.
August 19, 1943

Dear Son,

Rec'd your letter this morning and thought I would answer right away. I suppose you heard from Betty by now. We had a card from her yesterday. Donny went to the show but we made root beer first. He fills the bottles and caps them. He doesn't know what to do with himself anymore. His bike is broken but he's using Betty's this week. Glad you are coming along with your studies better. Do you really think you will be home Labor Day? Do any of the other boys get home or do you have to have good marks? Do you get enough sleep? I bet you can't go to bed in the afternoon like you did home. But that was just a habit.

The kids were chopping down trees again so Pa got after them. Pa is working alone this week. John doesn't show up at all. He is painting Ramages's house. We are going over to Kitty's house for supper. It's her birthday today. Irene is a pretty good piano player and singer. She sings

84

in church Sundays and all alone, too. She wants her mother to buy her a horse, but now she will settle for a dog. Dad wanted to give her Prince but she didn't want him. We told her she could ride him.

Poop Neubauer went up to be examined yesterday. I bet he can't wait to go (Oh, yeah). I heard from Tag and he said he was glad you picked the Navy. I guess I told you everything so will close.

With love,
Mother

Point O Woods
South Lyme, Conn.
August 19, 1943

Dear Dopey,

I was awfully glad to hear from you so soon, Dick hasn't written since last week sometime.

We were awfully disappointed to hear you couldn't come down! Will you still be able to get home when Dick does in Oct. or the first of Nov.? Cripes, I hope so. The Saturday when you are home the four of us will go to Beckley's, o.k? I think it would be loads of fun to go back there, although we probably would not go swimming, 'cause it will be too cold. (or are you still hot enough for both of us?)

Your marks were really super! I guess you were lucky when you went to the "Cape" when you did or you might not have been able to go. Say hello to your friend with the Cadillac for me. But still, if there's any chance of coming down, come on down, a rest will do you good, you sound as if you needed it. How is the girl situation up there? Things are really tough down here. The kids are from 4 – 40 omitting 16 -22. The war is really hitting us hard. Speaking of the war, Dick said something about getting his classification, do you know what it is yet, or if he can stay in college? I wouldn't know, not having heard from him in so long.

Ann wants to write something to you now, so be good and write soon.

Crazily yours,
Meg

Querido Charlie –

Como estas? No le gustaria venir aqui, para bailar, y nadar con las chicas? ((Meg and I don't know what it means, so all we can say is Poo - Poo for you!!!)

Adios,
Ann

VT 29 F.P.P
Jacksonville, Fla.
August 19, 1943

Dear Charles,

Well, how are you? It's been a long time since I wrote to you but I'm on the mess cooking now or have been for the last week. We get through tomorrow. This base isn't too bad, still a little chicken shit but not too bad. One of the cooks in the galley is from Conn. so I have a pretty soft job. Over at the other base you couldn't get anything to drink for love or money but over here it is all over the place. If you opened up all the lockers ,I bet 95% of them would have at least a pint in them and in the ice boxes in the mess hall there are pints, quarts and everything else around. We took the pressure chamber test last Friday, it wasn't too bad. They took us up to 10,000 feet without an oxygen mask and we had to stay there ten minutes, a few of the fellows passed out, then we put on oxygen masks and went up to forty thousand and then dove (fighting is starting) the radio on. Well, as I was saying we dove down to twenty-five thousand that's where most of the guys went out. I came out o.k. except for a hell of an earache when we were in the dive. Of course this is all done in a large tank. They gave us these tests to find out what kind of planes we will fly in. I'm going to put in for dive bomber. Well, I have to hit the sack, salty. 0500 comes around early, Before I close, how are you doing up there? In the last letter you seemed kind of worried. Well, so long and write soon.

Mick

Point O Woods Beach
South Lyme, Conn.
August 20, 1943

Hi, Peaches,

Just got back from a nice cold swim, I mean I just got my feet wet up to the knees. My cousin ran in the water but she discouraged me from going all the way in by coming out with her goose pimples having little goose pimples. Sure is funny water!!

I'm sorry I haven't written to you sooner, honey, but Meg wrote to you and I thought that she would probably have told you all there is to tell.

This week-end we're having so darn much company that Meg and I are being shipped over to Bolan's at Crescent Beach so as to make a little room. No cracks!

Speaking of "cracks" we certainly met a couple last night. We saw them again tonight but just couldn't stand them another minute. (Believe it or not, by Hennessey).

The swimming is really wonderful and at last we're finally getting a little color, especially my nose. No, not from liquor, I'm still waiting for you, to enjoy our beer together. I can hardly wait! You and Dick just have to get home at the same time you know.

Jim D. left for the Army Air Corps last Sunday. I didn't see him at all before he left. We had a little mix up. My brother Dick was also inducted into the Air Corps today, so he's on 24 hour notice.

What a house this is, the only thing it attracts are dogs, sand and brats 5 years and younger.

We thought we'd be here 'till after Labor Day but the cottage is rented so we'll be home the 28th. That's 10 days before we go back to school. More fun for the kiddies, not us. This is about all the crap I have to throw at this time.

> *All my love 'n lipstick,*
> *"Cream"*

P.S. Write to me down here.

> *17 Anise Street*
> *New Britain, Conn.*
> *August 23, 1943*

Dear Brother,

I'm awfully sorry I didn't write sooner.

We came home from the shore Saturday instead of Sunday because Mr. Douglas had to be at work for a trucking strike. We had a swell time anywho.

Remember that I told you that Vivian Allen and Maggie Yurko were down there, well, it was a sorority, the Gamma Kappa, I think. We were talking to the chaperone. She said she can't do a thing with them and they don't go to bed until 5 A.M. When Jeanne and I were at O'Conners one night the whole gang of them and their boyfriends got kicked out for drinking! The little Devils.

I got a beautiful tan but the darn thing is almost all peeled off.

Your books came. They are "Without Lawful Authority," a German story and the works of Ibsen. I'm going to send the money order out today.

I was reading one of your letters and was glad to know that your work is improving, especially your Spanish.

It was Audrey's birthday yesterday so we went to the movies and saw "Dubarry was a Lady" in Technicolor. Red Skelton was pretty good. I met loads of Seaweeds (sailors) down the shore and soldiers, too. Some of them are going to write to me. (They just said that.)Well, so long for now.

Love from all,
Sister

P.S. I hope you received my cards.
P.S.S. We even had a sailor in the car when we came home from Soundview. It was Marion's girlfriend's boyfriend. (Darn it!)

17 Anise Street
New Britain, Conn.
August 26, 1943

Dear Brother,

How are you today? We're all fine.

I'm enclosing three pictures of Prince. They didn't come out too good but I think they're o.k. If you don't want them all, send back the ones you don't want.

I went to the Carnival last night. Of course, it wasn't as big as last year 'cause they couldn't get the prizes and so much equipment. Father Brophy was there and asked me how you were and how you liked College.

Mother is making a cake for the carnival tonight.

There was an article in Saturday night paper how Mick Leary graduated from Radio School.

That Irene is a little devil. The other night she and her girlfriend went over to Neubauers when they weren't home. They took the sprayer and put it in the garage. Russell bought a second hand parlor set and had it in Lala's garage. When Lala got home she didn't see the sprayer and got the water all over her, and then when she saw the parlor set – Ohhhh!!! All soaking wet. She had to take all the coverings off and put them on the line. That kid certainly takes the cake.

Oh – Princey just started to bark and I just fed him about 15 minutes ago. He'll be the death of me yet. Oh me, oh my small fry. (Cute, eh) I'll close now.

Love from all,
Sister Betty

P.S. I hope you like the photo.

17 Anise Street
New Britain, Conn.
August 29, 1943

Dear Brother,

How are you? We got your letter about a half hour ago. Billy is down here over the week end. Last night Billy and I went down to the carnival and we went on the ponies. When we were on the Ferris Wheel it started to rain so we came home. But anyways I won 50 dollars. Freddy will be home over Labor Day. Spudy was down here. So that's all for now. I have to eat dinner now.

Love,
Donny

Duke University
August 29, 1943

Dear Commander Young,

Received your letter last Sun, and because of mid-terms, I had to wait till this weekend to write. My mid-semester averages went home as follows – Eng – 82, Chem – 85, French – 91, Botany -93, Math -95. I suppose if you flunk out, they'll put you on the Hudson Ferry (no, that is not spelled fairy.) Down here they have a variety of names for "fairies." They call them "homos", "gumdrops" and "queers." I'll have a dictionary full of names for fairies by the time I see you.

Do you remember Dick Farrell? Well, he's in England now. When I learned this, Charles, I took a walk for myself and thought "things" over. I swear, I feel cheap down here with a great number of my friends in the armed forces. I'll feel guilty from now until I get a uniform on my back.

Our freshmen class is going to have a big dance in a couple of weeks. That should prove interesting. Did I tell you that I took in a weekly dance on the Women's Campus? Well, I did. I met girls from Nevada, Ohio, Florida and N.C. Most of the girls down here now are immoral witches, but the girls I met were pretty nice.

The campus will be overflowing with females soon, for the girls start in another week. This, along with the football games that start Sept. 15, should keep me busy. Don't you think?

Received a letter from Lucy this week. I don't know about you, but my mail has dropped considerably in the last couple of weeks. I guess some of the people in N.B. have forgotten that I'm still living!

Here's a joke that I picked up this week. I think that you'll enjoy it.

89

A woman wanted to buy a phonograph record so she called Sears and Roebuck. The operator, however, connected her with the plumbing dept. instead of the record dept.

When the "fella" in the plumbing dept. answered, the woman said:

Have you got "Hot Lips on a Moonlight Night?"

The "fella" thought that she was kidding him along, so he – said:

No, lady, but I've got two balls and a nine inch pole.

She said: – Oh, is that a record?

He said:–I don't know, lady, but it's a damn good average!!!

That's all for now, Charlie. Expect to hear from you soon. Be good,

Your pal always,

Dick

17 Anise Street

New Britain, Conn.

August 29, 1943

Hi, Kid,

That's swell that you'll be able to come home. Freddy is home today and he's coming home next week, too, so you can see him (good eh.)

Here's some money for your train ticket. Don't forget to come home now.

I just got home from my drumming lesson. It didn't go too good either. Aud and I went to the Carnival last night. They are going to have it Monday night too 'cause it rained Friday.

Yesterday Mrs. Hagearty and I went around collecting the cakes for the Carnival. They raffle them off and make $1.50 for each cake. (pretty good).

What time do you think you'll get in New Britain? Prince and I will go down and wait for you. Bring your dirty clothes home with you.

Love from all,

Betty

P.S. How many lessons in Spanish tutoring did you have, sailor?

U.S. Coast Guard

Brooklyn, N.Y.

August 30, 1943

Dear Ensign S - - - -

Well, I finally got your address from Donny Sun. when I was home, and I hope that you're coming home Sat. so I'll be able to see you. I've been home 4 times already and I'll get home at least twice more before I ship out. I know you're busy but I think you can find time to drop me a line and tell me if you're coming home Sat. As far as the boys in the Navy and the men in the Coast Guard are concerned, an Ensign is the lowest thing on earth, and I agree with them. I'll tell you more about it when I see you Sat (or if I see you.) Well, I have to go now and besides there isn't anything to write about, so until Sat.

Freddy

17 Anise Street
New Britain, Conn.
August 31, 1943

Dear Brother,

Gosh, I was sorry that Mother and Dad and I weren't home when you called last night. I was working at the Carnival. They raffled off the $500.00 last night but the Donnelys were the only ones from the parish that won.

Donny said that you wanted some white underwear (size 32). Well, what kind do you want? You know you have lots of jerseys and panties here if that's what you want.

Mother is canning relish down the cellar and Donny is out in the yard with Charles F. Charles just got home from the shore yesterday. He was gone for two weeks. Boy, Fanny certainly had a vacation.

Yesterday Mother let Princey loose and he didn't come back yet. Gee, I hope he comes back today. He usually does though. Well, that's all for now.

Love from all,
Betty

P.S. The church made about 3 thousand 2 hundred dollars at the Carnival.

17 Anise Street
New Britain, Conn.
August 31, 1943

Dear Son,

I have been looking forward this week to seeing you home but today we got your letter addressed to Donny saying that you might not be able to make it on account of a Spanish exam you have next Wednesday.

I have received a copy of a report on your studies at the school and it is needless to say that it was far from satisfactory. Also that you were warned by the Prof. regarding these marks. I will not go into detail and bawl you out because it must be hard work and maybe you didn't catch on the first few weeks of school as you said in one of your letters that you didn't know

91

what it was all about. I believe however that if you try real hard and forget about home for a week or two you will show some improvement and that is what they want to see. If there is no improvement, well, I also received a copy of the letter you got dated Aug. 30.

The gas ban is now lifted and mother and I will come down to Cambridge to visit the Cabelus's and see you at the same time. I believe this will be the weekend after Labor Day. In the meantime, Sonny, do your damndest. If you don't make the grade in your studies you will lose a great opportunity, so buck up. If you can't come home and have to study, we will come down every week if you want us to.

Your Pop

P.S. Will expect a phone call on either Wed. or Thurs. nite. Make it around 8.00 if you can. Reverse the charge.

17 Anise Street
New Britain, Conn.
September 3, 1943

Dear Charlie,

Well, here's that gal again. I hope you are o.k.

Betty Lee's grandfather died (Mr. Donnelly) and she is staying here with me over the weekend.

Mother and Dad were talking to Kitty and Frank about going up to see you Sunday. I'm not positive though.

I hope your work is improving & you're studying hard.

Donny's got a stomach ache and is hollering he wants an enema. Not through the mouth though.

We couldn't get any white underwear like you wanted so you'll have to buy them up there. But will send the socks soon, o.k.?

If Ma & Pa come up to Cambridge they'll go to Sam & Mays first and get in touch with you.

Love from all,
Sister Betty

P.S. Prince is home safe & sound.

191 Bristol Street
New Britain, Conn.
September 10, 1943

Dear Charlie,

Gosh I'm sorry I haven't written sooner but I thought that if I wrote last week you might have been on your way home or something. I was awfully sorry that you couldn't get home. Someone called Mary Saturday when she was out and she thought it was you, so she called your home and your sister said that you stayed at school for an exam or something. I guess you were glad your parents came up to see you anyway. When are you coming home? Don't tell me you're not coming home before the 23rd of October or I'll hammer you!!

I'll have you know that Mary Jo and I stayed downtown all Sat. afternoon, hoping you'd get home. Kill –Joy!!

Not much has happened here this week, but it was better than most, seeing Mary and I had dates! Remarkable, isn't it? No, really a date is a very rare thing in this town now days. Francine had a party for the girls Thurs. We had fun, everyone was there. Tonight Laurie is having one. That's why I'm writing in such a hurry. I'm supposed to be all ready to go but I'm not even dressed. (I decided that it would be cooler this way.)We've been going to the movies and playing tennis whenever there isn't anything to do(most of the time.)

School starts in a day, I can hardly wait! ((Kidding, of course!) Don't you wish you were still plugging away at High School – or do you? I hope you can read this. Please write soon.

Loads of love,
Meg

Coast Guard Station
Brooklyn, N.Y.
September 10, 1943

Hello, again,

Well, I have got nothing to do or anyone else to write to so figured I'd drop you a few more lines as long as I have the time. (I just sharpened my pencil.) I think I told you I wasn't coming home Sat. because of machine-gun watch and I didn't get any money. That's the main reason. I hate like hell to ask my mother for anymore. I give her $10.00 every time I get paid and I chisel about $20.00 back. I don't know where all my money goes but it sure goes (by the way I'm writing this in class). Why can't you get into the Coast Guard and see "Coney Island" (from Miami Beach)? Haven't you been out at all since you left? If you haven't you must have a hard on up to your chin, either that or a sore hand. I've only got laid once since I've been in and that was last week. (but that made up for all the waiting). Have you been down to "Scully Square" yet? We have some boy in here from the "Hub" and they say that it is so easy to get laid in Boston it's not even funny. I wrote Joyce Mon. night, Every time I write to her I can't think

93

of anything to talk about. So I write and I beat around the bush and I get by. Some how I can't think of anything more to write about so I'll have to say so long for now, Write if you can. I'll write as often as I can. I had to quit writing because the class was over. I started this letter on Tues. and I'm finishing it on Fri. night.

Write if you can,
Freddy

Room 16
New Britain High School
September 10, 1943

Hi, Kid,

Well, here I am in school. It's the second day we've had classes and I can find myself around pretty well. I just came back from the Caf and I'm in Mrs. Hildebrandt's room for study. I also have her for College English. My Math teacher is Mr. Gilbert, Bookkeeping, Miss Baer and Type, Miss Heher. Bookkeeping isn't easy by any means but I think I'm going to like it. In English we have to subscribe to the "Times" magazine for 20 weeks so we can see them for topics and oral topics. They are just what I hate and once a week, too. I suppose you don't want to be hearing about my school work but that's really the only thing I'm going to have time for now. I won't have to work as hard as you but I'll have to work.

I hope you're o.k. and your work also.

Prince went out for another run but came back in about a day and a half. Well, I guess I'll close now.

Love,
Betty

P.S. Excuse all the talk about school.
P.S.S. (time flies). I'm in study now but went to Bookkeeping last period. This is 103 but I don't know the teacher's name.

I'll have to mail this letter when I get home. The next time I'll bring my stamps and envelopes with me.

Mother told me you could come home the last weekend in October. That's swell. It's not very far off either.

Love,
B

17 Anise Street
New Britain, Conn.
Sept. 13, 1943

Dear Charlie,

Thanks for your encouraging letter. Mr. Gilbert happens to be a swell teacher. Miss Baer talks with a Kosher accent but she's o.k. We had some bookkeeping homework making inventories and present worth. It takes quite a bit of time but I like it a lot. Yes, Miss Heher is a nice young lady. I almost take fits sitting there typing JKJ – JKJ – FDF – FDF. We have to start all over so that's just fine.

Mrs. Hildebrandt is the "Hot Sketch." She gives us too much homework for English. We're reading "Silas Marner" and learning about the life of George Eliot and also studying some crazy booklet. The name is "How to Study." (Did you have it?)

I haven't been doing any social climbing as yet. And I'll go out with the Hunkeys if I want to!! Oh Yeah!! You went out with Marcelli Colletti, remember??? I was asked to the Phi Sigma (I think that's it or something similar) Rush but I wasn't interested. They're mostly all a bunch of Swedes.

I'm sending some of the pictures. After you show them to Sam & May (if you want to) you can send them back. The one's taken on the grounds came out sort of gloomy so I didn't bother sending them. Well, that's all for now.

Your loving sister,
Betty

P.S. I just saw a strike or a flash go by the window. Mother just let Prince loose.

191 Bristol Street
New Britain, Conn.
September 14, 1943

Dear "Charles" – (Harvard?)

Gosh, Honey, I can't tell you how glad I was to hear from you, and also how much you like Mary Jo and me to write to you. It works both ways 'cause I love to get a letter from you. So keep it up "Hon" and write as often as possible.

What do you mean "Why do you want me to get home before Oct. 23"! 'Cause I'm dying to see you that's why and October 23 is an awfully long time. There is a dance coming up – so Mary Jo has probably written you. It was going to be Sept. 25 but now they've changed it to Oct. 2nd. I guess it would be kind of difficult for you to take both Mary and me but boy – would you be a popular guy! Just think the best two kids at N.B. H.S. and you. Wow – (am I excited?) – answer, yes.

Never you mind who Mary and I have been having dates with. They aren't much – just 4F's. Bob McCahill is home, I guess you know, so that makes things a little better. He just took the Army Air Corps test today and passed. He's so glad, and I'm glad for him.

I'm so glad you decided to marry both of us although it will be quite crowded in our house. We'll have to get a twenty room house for all the 'family' – o.k? (Hand me a shovel.) The only thing that bothers me about the whole thing is: What will the neighbors think? Oh well – the heck with them. I'll tell them to mind their own business and leave us alone (the three of us.)

School has started. So have all the headaches that go with it, but not all the fun. It's the deadest, dullest place you can imagine! I guess you see I don't like it any too well. My course is a snap. Inter. Dec. – type – Problems – Eng. & Algebra so that's not bad.

I'm a bad girl. (don't get excited!) I stayed up too late Friday night and now I have to stay in for ten nights. It's not bad all week, but that includes two weekends. We've been taking up Poker lately, "the girls" I mean. We try to play once every weekend. It's really neat the way they take all my money and about two days later they how they've been cheating, and everybody laughs. I have to too but I really feel like killing them.

How is everything up at Harvard? (or is it down) – I guess you were pleased when your parents came up to see you. I suppose you showed them all over the place and introduced all your girls to them. – and I'm going to sneak up there and just see what's keeping you so busy up there, besides your studies. I have a terrible feeling that you're cheating on us. You just better not let us catch you – that's all.

I suppose Dick wrote you about our little disagreement, Or has he? Anyway, I was writing to a friend of his down there, someone I don't know, and he didn't know about it. Well, to make a long story short, he found out about it and didn't write me for about ten days .Finally he wrote and said to forget it etc. but in the meantime I've been writing to another fellow down there that also wrote me. Well, Dick hasn't written for a few days, so I suppose we'll go through the same thing again. I still think he's wrong. I don't see anything wrong in what I did - bla–bla–bla–bla etc. (Just talking myself into thinking I'm right).

Boy, will we all have fun after Oct. 23rd when you kids are home, but I hope none of us have changed and that we still have such good times together.

I know Mary Jo and I haven't. How could we around this same old town, but I bet both you and Dick have. (Maybe you won't even remember how we used to dance – and cut-up etc). How could anyone forget?

Be good – write quickly (I decided that soon is too common for you).

Tons of love,

Meg D. Bolan of N.B.H.S.

91 West Street
New Britain, Conn.
September 15, 1943

Charlie, Darlin',

About time I heard from you.

School is simply – oh, just simply. It's really awful not seeing the same old kids, especially you, honey. This year I really have a tough course. Eng, Typing, Shorthand, FOODs! Just think, when we get married we'll be able to have stewed peaches. That's what we're doing now in Foods. More fun. Me cooking. Ha.

Boy, do I feel like the woman of the world. I'm sweet 17 and never been kissed. Hee –Haw. I got my license last week. Send me a nice big hug and a kiss in your next letter for my birthday.

Ahem!! T.S. is giving a dance Oct. 2. You'd certainly be smooth taking Meg and me.

Saw "Stormy Weather" today with Lenawayback. Was it ever wonderful! Was it?

No, my pet, I'm not in the mill anymore. Helen Phillips got her hooks in me the other day so I decided I'd join the old maids in their happy little bookstore. Cripes, I hate it. I am slowly turning into an old maid.

Next Sat. N.B. plays Bristol. Should prove to be an interesting game. If I can tear myself away from the store, I'll probably attend the grand opening of the football season.

Morry, my dear sir, has now a mouthful of teeth. They really look good. Bert James is now the toothless wonder. He had all his uppers pulled. Boy, is he the smoothie now. Ha-Ha

Well, Peaches, s'all for now. Write soon.

Love n' stuff

Miss Hennessey

P.S. Just don't disappoint us again on Oct. 23rd.

U.S. Coast Guard
Brooklyn, N.Y.
September 16, 1943

Hello, Kid,

Well, you're not making out too good in your classes. That's tough. I missed you Sat but there will be another time. I'm writing this letter from my C.O.T.P. classroom. I was in Sick Bay for 3 days with a cold or something. The wouldn't tell me what was wrong with me. They told me I was sick and that's all I had to know. So you don't think you'll make the grade in school? Keep trying because I know if I had the chance to go to O.C. School I would and so would everybody else here. I didn't think that I would get out Sat. but they let me out of Sick Bay Fri. afternoon and I got a slip from the Doc saying I was fit for liberty. The Doc I had comes from Hartford. His name is Juneray I think. I think that coming from Ct. helped get me out a little if you know what I mean.

I get my Seaman 2 stripe in two weeks and a four buck raise in pay. (big thing). How much do you get a month? When do you think you'll get out? I have had 5 liberties already and I expect another on the 18th of this month. I would get one this week (the 11th) but we have Machine Gun watch. I might get out but it's doubtful.

How did you feel when you saw your mother Sunday? I bet it hit you like a ton of bricks. I know I felt that way the first time I was home. We are due to ship out of this "hell hole" in two or three more weeks. I don't know where we are going but I don't give a good god damn as long as I just get out of here.

Did you get your uniform yet? I had all my blues cut skin tight and they fit me like a glove. I didn't go out with Joyce last Sun. Cheryl came home and so Joyce and Mr. and Mrs. French went to the movies and I went out and got layed. There is more ass than I can take care of in the old home town. Wait till you get home and you'll see what I mean We went down to the lake and got half in the bag and picked up three girls and I dropped off the other two couples. I took my car and we went out in the woods and did we have fuckin' good time, and believe it or not she was nice. I know what you'll say but never the less she was. I think I'll write Joyce a letter though and ask her if she had a good time Sat. night. I went out with her last time and what a time we had. We were out near Beckley until almost 1:30. Well, there isn't much more from here so I'll have to say so long for now but if I have a few spare minutes during the week I'll drop you a line and let you know what the better half of the Navy is doing. I have a lot of things to tell you but I can't put them all on paper. I'll try and see you next time you're home. Bye and drop me a few lines if you can. I'll write because you must know what it is to get a letter from home (although I'm not home and you didn't say you were glad to here from me). So write if you can and I'll do the same.

As always,

Freddy

P.S. Send me Joe's address and I'll try to write to him too.

17 Anise Street

New Britain, Conn.

September 16, 1943

Hi, Kid,

I just received your letter a few minutes ago.

It seems good to be getting out of school at 1:45 instead of 3:15.

Even if I did get a bid to the Beta Mu, I don't think I'd like to join. They are worse than the Phi Sigma.

I saw Benny in the South Wing today. I thought he graduated. Perhaps he came back to make up some work or something.

It was in Saturday's paper that Marcelle DiVito got married. I didn't know it when I mentioned her in my last letter. She's only about 17 or 18 isn't she?

I'm glad you liked the photos. They did come out awfully good though. I think that once I heard you mention Mary Jane Ryan. She's in my Gym class. She's a hot sketch alright.

How are you and your studies? Good I hope.

I don't have too much homework but enough to keep me busy. Well, that's all for now.

Love,

Betty

P.S. Prince says hello to you. He keeps asking when you're coming home.

191 Bristol St.

New Britain, Conn.

September 19, 1943

Dear Charlie,

I'm writing as soon as possible 'cause I know what a wreck you must be waiting for my letters! I'm sure you're a physical and mental wreck. I

99

hope my writing more often will help a little. Seriously though, your hours sound terrible. By the end of the week you must be ready for the undertaker.

No, I don't want to bring Bob along. We were seeing each other quite a bit, maybe too much, but we had a fight and at present aren't speaking. So don't worry about him coming.

I finally got a letter from Dick and I guess you must have by now too. I guess the opening of the Women's Campus, and football games etc. have made him slow in writing (Joe College!)

We'll be around all week (23ʳᵈ). We haven't been working anyway. We're just lazy bums.

Last night Morry called up and wanted to know what Mary Jo and I were doing – we weren't doing anything so he took both of us to the movies and Gabers. I guess you're not the only one that can take both of us out together.

We've been hanging around with Caroline Sharp and those kids lately 'cause all the other kids are away – Lucy is still home, she has a cigarette case of mine and won't give it back, I could kill her. She's mad at you 'cause you haven't written.

I'll tell Benny to write when I see him in school tomorrow. He is pretty good, he just limps a little.

Loads of love,
Meg

91 West Street
New Britain, Conn.
September 20, 1943

Dear Charlie,

This afternoon all we hens went to Barbara Donahue's. She's going to Marymount College tomorrow. We had a quick game of poker. That seems to be our favorite past time. Betty Logan is leaving Thursday for Storr's. It's not bad enough to have all the fellows go, but now the girls are going. Prissy Jones left at 2 o'clock for college. She's covered from head to foot with poison oak.

Now, Charlie, you belittle me by saying that I must have 15 minutes of homework. I have at the most 30 min. and it practically kills me.

Up until last Friday I was employed at Helen Phillip's. Now I am loafing. No, I wasn't fired. I quit before – I couldn't stand that awful hole another minute.

100

Tomorrow Ginger Dillon is having a hot-dog roast. The only trouble is that it's going to be at 5 P.M. and Meg and I have to be home early. That won't give us much time.

Dick Jackabowski, Buddy Searls and Larry Kearney were all home last week. Boy, does it seem good to see the old kids again. How long will you be home for?

Love,
Peaches

Duke University
October 2, 1943
Sunday

Dear Honey,

It sure was good to hear from you. I didn't expect to hear from you for quite a while since I hadn't written you in two weeks. Well, I guess everyone isn't like me. I do hope you'll forgive me "Sugar," it won't happen again. I promise.

Duke won its third straight game yesterday by the score of 42 – 0. I see where Ha-a-vad won its game also.

That tickled my testicles about "Volga Olga." Are you sure it was for a "hamburger" that the band leader took her out for? Oh yes, have you been 'robin' anything from "Robin Jones" yet? Look out, she'll set her "Little John" on you!!

I went to the football game with a girl from West Virginia. She was "hot stuff." In the evening we took in the movie "Stormy Weather" and a sport dance. Listen "honey," what could I do but "sip" her honey while it was sweet, when she was laying nature at my feet. No, it really didn't get very far (no hallucinations). I was just another date.

I think I'm starting to get sick of women. I just can't wait to see my little "blonde bombshell" back in dear old N.B. Tonight, however, I'm going out with a Georgia "Peach" – Sho' nuff.

Damn it all, exams are but two weeks away. We have 12 days of classes left. I'll be home on the 22nd and looking forward to your return on the 24th.

I'm thinking pretty seriously about joining a fraternity. In fact I almost pledged up to one! Have you done anything in regards to this yet?

I'm sure that I'd like to go down to the old cider mill and get filled up. We're still going to Beckley's, aren't we???

I don't spend much money. I get about $12.50 every two weeks. This usually lasts me. I could use a little more.

Heard from Joan Rollins. She wrote me a swell letter. Has she written to you?

I don't see why you haven't gone home. If I were as close to home as you, I'd be home every other week. I think that we'll appreciate it more though.

My damn draft board hasn't even classified me yet.

Take care "honey." No first time yet. Write.

Always,
Dick

17 Anise Street
New Britain, Conn
Oct. 4, 1943

Hi, Kid,

I'm glad you got your book and I hope you have your coat, too.

You shouldn't have said anything to Sara Preston. I didn't want to get in the Beta Mu anywho. Saturday after the football game I was introduced to Laura and Mary Dougherty (spelt wrong). The game was o.k. and of course New Britain won. The score was 24-0. Agawam wasn't so tough after all.

Be sure to study hard and get some good marks on your finals.

It's freezing cold out today. I'll be wearing my winter coat before I know it.

Prince did look nice but not so fluffy as "Pudgie. He hasn't got quite as much hair, you know.

Aunt Anna has a new job at Pratt and Whitney (Fred's mother.) She works from 3 P.M. till 12. She likes it a lot too.

Our English class has to read "The Mill on the Floss," or "Adam Bede." Do you know where I can get a hold of either one of them? They're all taken from the libraries. If you do let me know. O.K?

I bet you didn't have much fun over the weekend with 80 cents. That's all for now.

Love from all,
Betty

Harvard University
October 5, 1943

Dear Betty,

Well, I got the coat and underwear today. So I'm happy now.

How did you like Joan and Lidia Donahue? They're both nice girls.

Why did Aunt Anna quite her old job? It seems silly to me.

I don't know where you can get a hold of any of those English books. Now that you're in High School you might as well get a card for the

102

institute. My card may be in the upper right hand corner drawer of my desk. You can look if you haven't already.

I borrowed some money from one of the kids in the other house. Everyone in our house was either flat broke or just had enough to last them. I'll bet you couldn't get a dollar together out of the whole unit (900 sailors). Today is pay day and are we excited. Well, I've gotta go now.

Love,

Charlie

P.S. I think I'll be able to stay here if I pass all but the Spanish, so I'm working like hell on Math, Physics and Chem.

P.S.S. I passed my Chem test (not the final) last week. I got D-, E is flunking. I got C in the math test, which was 3rd highest in the class. Don't ask if there are 3 kids in the class, Smarty.

P.S.S. A week from Thursday finals start ooooooooooo!

91 West Street
New Britain, Conn.
October 5, 1943

Dearest one,

Glad you heard from Dick. I thought that you kids might not talk to each other when you came home. That wouldn't be very nice, would it?

Charlie, I think that you must be a booze hound. Do you dream about it at night? I haven't acquired a taste for it as yet. Hope that doesn't ruin your plans. Meg and I are looking forward to seeing you kids. Try to get home as soon as you can. Meg and I get out of school before 1:00 every day so we should be able to keep you kids company. I get out at 11:30 three days a week.

I went to the T.S. dance with Kyttle. Cripes, was I mad at him. About 11:30 he passed out like a light. Was I wild. Thank heavens Lolly was there or I would have been up the creek without a paddle. The dance wasn't as good as the dances last year. But I had a pretty good time.

My brother got his call to leave for the Air Corps this Monday. I'm sure going to hate to see him go.

This Friday Meg and I are going to see "The Patriots" at the Bushnell. It's supposed to be very entertaining.

H.S. Conway is leaving for school in a couple of weeks. I swear that kid is using scratchy john paper. Her disposition lately has been unbearable. Write soon.

Love,

Me (Mary Jo)

191 Bristol Street
New Britain, Conn.
October 5, 1943

Dear Charlie,

When are you coming home? The 23rd or the 24th? How long are you going to be home? I'm full of questions.

How did you do on the Chem. exam you had last Friday? I hope you passed.

Morry is deferred for at least three months because he has high blood-pressure or something. He really feels quite badly about it I guess.

Lucy is going away to school in a few days I think. Gosh does she hate me all of a sudden. I don't know why. There isn't any reason I can think of. She says the rottenest things to me. Boy, she's no one to have mad at you. I guess she is mad at you too because you didn't write. (Please don't go out and shoot yourself now.)

Saturday was the T.S. dance. I was supposed to go but at about 5:30 my father said I couldn't go. Boy, was I mad! I fell down Sat. too and nearly broke a leg, so I was in quite a mood all day.

I'm glad you heard from "Joe College" – I do, now and then. He must be having a neat time (Co-ed-) Be good, write soon. I have to eat now. I'll eat some for you, o.k?

Love,
Meg

17 Anise Street
New Britain, Conn.
October 7, 1943

Dear Charlie,

I'm awfully glad that you passed your Chemistry. Now try hard to pass all the finals.

I hope you got paid and you're happy too.

I bought a red & blue plaid skirt today. It comes down to my knees.

Annie Giedraitis (spelt wrong) got married in Florida last week.

Nellie's boarders moved (the twins). It was getting too cold to sleep in the attic for them. When they left I bet Nellie shoved Barbara and Madeline up there.

This week they're having the missions over at the church. I only went once so far.

Donald Farmer broke his arm. He claims that Bob Walker pushed him. Poor Fanny always has the trouble. That's all for now.

Love from all,

Betty

Coast Guard Barracks

Kenmore, Wash.

October 7, 1943

Dear Charlie,

So very glad to hear from my cousin. You wrote Tues. I got the letter 8 days later (that's good time). It was addressed to M.B. Well, I'm having the best time of my life . There are more girls here than we can handle. We are expecting reinforcements. We can take them on the golf course and play golf. (We don't play golf every day and we call it the intercourse course) and damned fun, you should be here. They sent me out to take care of the sheep – whoever thought that I would be a sheep herder. Talking about sheep (joke) "these two soldiers were standing in a desert and one fellow said to the other, what would you rather have a WAVE in a cave, a WAAC in a shack or a SPAR in a car? The other fellow said, Right now, I would settle for a sheep in a jeep."

That's all,

Freddy

PS Write soon. I would like to hear from you before I leave the country.

17 Anise Street

New Britain, Conn.

October 8, 1943

Hi, Kid,

I'm enclosing a photo of myself. Do you think I've changed since you were gone? Mother took it of me before I went to church.

Fanny and I are going to church for the 40 hours in a little while. I told Donny you had to sit in church for 40 hours.

I really don't know what to write 'cause I wrote yesterday.

Sears and Roebuck just brought down a chain for Donny's bike. Daddy was trying to get the bike fixed a little so he had to order a chain.

Prince has been on good behavior lately. He doesn't bark quite as much as usually.

105

I'm not going to the game Saturday because I think I'll have to take care of Betty Lee.

That's all for now. Love,
Sis

Coast Guard Barracks
Kenmore, Wash.
October 8, 1943

Dear "Grape Nuts,"

Where did you hear that? I almost shit when I read it. How did you make out with the pigs the other night? I was out with one the other night and was she cute. I didn't have the heart to fool around with her. I met her on the bus Mon. night and I walked her home and made a date for Wed. She lives near the Club so we took the long way home. Then we went in and were sitting in the front room until 1:30. Boy, didn't we have fun. Then I got lost coming back to the Club and I roamed around in the woods for an hour trying to find the short-cut. I got back to the Club, it was about 3:00 and I had to get up at 6:00. I'm almost dead. So you're going to Newport. What's the matter, too tough for you?

There are more girls out here. I can't get over it. I was walking in Seattle and two were following me (until I flipped my butt.) No kidding, Charlie, there are more girls than we can handle out here. Why don't you ask to be transferred out here (First have you head removed.)

Do you have many short-arm and Foxhole inspections there? We have one every week or 10 days. Well, there isn't much more to write about. I just ran out of ink and haven't got any more.

Love and kisses,
Freddy

I haven't got the money to send this airmail. I wrote to Aunt Stella and dropped her a hint.

91 West Street
New Britain, Conn.
October 10, 1943

Dear Charlie,

I hear from Meg that you might be home Sat. night. Try awfully hard, won't you, dear?

To-nite the Civic Forum is having a Rally Dance so they can send the band to Stamford for the game. I don't imagine that there will be too many *there. But I'm going to be there and that's all that counts, no? Meg and I are going to sell soda – so, there goes the profit.*

My brother left for the Air Corps last Monday. Instead of going to Camp Devens first he went straight down to Greensboro, North Carolina. They had to take turns sleeping on the floor. Nice trip!!

Guess what, I have another job. I'm working at the Red Cross from 2 to 5 in the afternoon as a typist. No, I'm not volunteering either. I've had enough of that.

Well, Honey, time to eat. Wrote soon.

Love & Stuff,
"Peaches"

We don't have school next Thurs. or Friday!

191 Bristol Street
New Britain, Conn.
Oct. 10, 1043

Dear "Joe College,"

Thanks for the stickers. I think you send them for me to put up in my bedroom so when you come home you can ask to see them!

Gosh, am I mad about when you're coming home! Are you sure you'll be able to get home by Monday? Maybe you won't be able to get home at all! Nothing works out right lately.

I hope you got good marks on your exams. I'm not doing so well in school. I never feel like studying. I'm so mad at everything. We went to a play at the Bushnell on Friday night and it stunk! Last night I was supposed to go to a party and I came home from the game and fell asleep at 6:30 and didn't wake up till 9 this morning. I was so mad no one woke me up. Please excuse this mess, I'm tired!

Has Dick written to you lately? Write Benny. He wants you to. Good luck on your exams.

Love,
Meg

Harvard University
October 11, 1943

Dear Betty,

Well, we don't have exercise anymore for this term and we can keep our lights on till one o'clock until after exams.

That chem. final is going to be the toughest exam I ever took.

I got paid Tuesday. I'm going to buy my train ticket tomorrow because I'll be broke in a week.

Who did Annie Giedraitis marry? Was he from New Britain?

My God, Fanny really has a lot of tough luck. I'll bet she felt like breaking Donald's other arm. Well, I've got to tear along now, so I'll see you soon.

Love,

Charlie

P.S. Our room is security watch over the weekend but I think I'll be home Monday morn, Oct 25th. I'll probably have to come back a day early to be security watch.

The White Horse Inn
Old Lyme, Conn.
October 11, 1943

Dear Charlie,

I just remembered I forgot to answer your last letter – tough! I've been awfully busy though. College isn't as easy as I thought it was going to be. They have some queer idea that I should study – funny – huh? I really love it though – it's an awful lot of fun. The Coast Guard Academy is almost right across the street – very interesting to say the least. We had a tea dance over at the Academy this afternoon – more fun!

How are you making out? Still working as hard as ever? Or maybe you've flunked out by this time. I hope not.

I still haven't got a room at Conn. yet but I'm waiting patiently. I hate this riding back and forth on the bus like the devil. I think I'm supporting the bus line.

Did I tell you I saw Patty Lou when I went to New Britain? Maybe I told you before – I can't remember. Well, anyway, I did. That town gets worse and worse. Have you been home lately? This is an awful letter and I know it but I have to dash – I'm going out to the movies.

Love,

Launa

P.S. Do I get that picture of you or don't I?

17 Anise Street
New Britain, Conn.
October 11, 1943

Dear Charlie,

I'm enclosing two articles from the Herald. One is a summary of the news of the week. If you want me to send it to you every week, I will.

Joe Rizzo came home on furlough Saturday. I was talking to him in front of Liggetts.

Donny had a new pigeon. He got it from Billy Coyle. His name is "Chic". He lets him fly all over the house.

New Britain won the game Saturday. It was certainly close, the score was N.B. 14 and Hamden 13. I didn't go but I wish now I had.

Jean Ziegler and I went to see "Claudia" Saturday. It was a swell picture, Why is it that you spend your money so quick? Do you eat it?

Jean and I dragged Mother to church Sunday afternoon. It was the closing of the "Mission."

Mother bought a new coat. It's a blue greenish Chesterfield something like mine.

Why can't you come home Saturday or Sunday? It would be better if you could.

Well, that's all for now.

Love,
Betty

17 Anise Street
New Britain, Conn.
October 13, 1943

Hi, Clown,

I'm glad you liked my picture. It was sort of put up though. Don't think that I go around dressed up like that.

You'd better let the "Hot Rocks" alone until after the exams. It's not that I don't want you to have any fun. That girl has a pretty name. Ask her if she knows the "Bat Man." You know, "Batman and Robin."

I guess I told you I had a chance to go to the Stamford game but the kid doesn't have a license. I know he's a good driver though. All the kids are saying if they had the chance to go they'd certainly take it, but I haven't made up my mind yet.

Well, your exams come tomorrow and by the time you get this letter you'll have had it already so I hope you passed it. I had a bookkeeping test today and got 42. 43 was100%. We're having another one tomorrow. I got a "B" on my Silas Marner test and I'm satisfied.

So long for now,
Betty

P.S. Dad went fishing at Simsbury Sunday. They caught about 5 good size fishes.

*P.S.S. I'm a press agent for the Red and Gold. (Big thrill.) The paper is
10 cents this year.*
P.S.S. Do you know Bob Joyce? Just wanted to know.

Harvard University
October 13, 1943

Dear Betty,

*Today is Columbus Day and we have no school. So everyone is studying
like the devil.*

Thanks for the newspaper clippings but I didn't know anyone in them.

*I don't know how I spend my money but when you live in a huge city
like Boston everything costs a lot. I have my train ticket so don't worry. I
won't need any cash until I get home. I don't think they want the V12 boys
to take the trains so that's why we have to stay until Monday morn. Well,
I have to start studying now.*

Love,
Chic

*P.S. I'm enclosing that wonderful picture of you. You can put it in
Prince's house. No, you'd better not.*

17 Anise Street
New Britain, Conn.
October 15, 1943

Hi, Kid,

Don't get excited 'cause I'm not going to Stamford.

That was some test you had. Three hours is a long time for a test.

*It's pouring cats and dogs here now but I hope it stops. I'm going to
the Stamford Rally Dance at the school tonight. Audrey Glabau and Jean
Ziegler are always skipping school. They want me to, but nothing doing.
Jean's father saw Jean downtown today. Good, huh?*

*Tessie got the shock of her life. Spudy wrote her a letter and told her he
had been married for five months. That almost killed her. Then a couple
days later Tessie got burnt at work. A stove exploded or something. Spud
married some girl from West Hartford. He's now going to be shipped to
England, quite soon too. Don't you try any tricks like that now.*

*We're having American Poetry in English now. The study of Poetry
is awfully complicated. Similes, metaphors, Iambic Pentameter and
everything. That's all for now.*

Love,

Betty

P.S. How long will your furlough last?

P.S.S. Don't say hell in your letters anymore.

Harvard University

October 16, 1943

Dear Betty,

Well, I'm glad you're not going to Stamford. I always knew you had a lot of brains anyway. Donny and I are the dumb ones in the family.

All our finals are three hour tests. They don't fool around up here.

I'm glad you're not skipping school. It doesn't pay. Mick Leary and Morry Blair used to skip and it certainly didn't do them any good. I didn't cut one class for two years in high school. In my senior year Dick W. and I went swimming a few times but we knew what we were doing. Jean Z. and Audrey are a little nuts anyway. They'll probably wind up selling candy in the Five & Ten.

Guess what? I'm married (no, I'm not, I'm just kidding.) No fooling, I almost fell over when I heard Spud was married. Spud undoubtedly knew what he was doing, he's pretty intelligent. I was sorry to hear that Tessie got burnt. Is it very bad?

"American Poetry" is tough. I never did understand Iambic Tetrameter etc. But you shouldn't have any trouble with it because of your Latin.

I think I'll be home Saturday night for one week.

Love,

Charlie

P.S. I'm sorry I shocked you by writing "hell."

P.S.S. I'm having my uniform dry cleaned and I have my train ticket, and I'm going to get my leave papers Tuesday. Boy am I excite

Coast Guard Barracks

Kenmore, Wash.

October 17, 1943

Dear Charlie,

Well, I'm going again. I don't know where but I'm going. Mon. morning I got your letter saying you were going home for 7 days. I'd give anything to be there with you but what can you do? My arm is so sore I can just about write. I just got finished writing five letters, one of them was 5 pages on both sides. It is to Ralph, he is down in Miss. and he is homesick. I

111

tried to cheer him up by telling him the longer he is in the more he will hate it and different pleasant things like that. You know me "Cheerful Freddy." Oh yeah, well, how are you doing in your classes, Boot? (if you will please note S 2/c after my name).

Well, I have a few more letters to write and I have wash my dirty feet, take a shit so I'll say so long for now. I'll write and let you know what my new address is.

Love and kisses,
Freddy

P.S. I forgot the number that goes after Kirkland. Sorry.

173 Stanley Street
New Britain, Conn.
October 17, 1943

Dear Charlie (not Charles),

You can imagine my surprise when I picked up your letter. I know how it is when you are back in your work. Ray was the same way.

Things have been too dull around here since you left. (you can give me my quarter when you get here).

Say! I didn't like your insult to my intelligence when you told me you didn't write because you lost my address.

I can't wait to hear about your experiences.

I think Meg has a crush on you. Whenever I see her all she talks about is you. You should have fun when you next see her.

Where did you ever get the preposterous idea that I am chasing Peggy?

I am on the same status with Helen that I have always been and I welcome competition.

I'm going up for my physical Tuesday.

I have been appointed the leader of a contingent of men, how do you like that boloney? I received an order from the board which said I was responsible for the good conduct, papers, meal tickets of the men. They said I was appointed because of my integrity etc.

Oh yes, I am still limping like an old man, I'm going to the hospital Wednesday to get something done about it.

I think I'll take V12 test Nov. 9.

Ben

P.S. As I am doing my homework I haven't reread this letter.

17 Anise Street
New Britain, Conn.
October 18, 1943

Dear Son,

Got 3 of your letters yesterday. We had quite a snow storm here so the mail man didn't come down Monday. The snow is melting so fast – won't be much left by tomorrow.

Pa went up to Holyoke, Mass yesterday to an auction sale. He bought up a lot of paint and varnish, He got a good buy so he went up again today, the auction was continued. He wants to buy up a lot of wall paper. He isn't home yet. He said he may stay over to hire a truck to bring the stuff home. The way he spends, he bought enough stuff to last 5 years. So you can imagine the garage and cellar being filled up. He said there were wonderful buys. It was a great big hardware store. He said he never saw so much paint of all kinds of hardware and plumbing, electrical stuff in all his life. Well, that's enough about the auction.

That picture Morgan's Creek is coming here Fri. so I think I'll see it.

Betty got your razor yesterday. Do you want us to send it to you or shall we wait to see if you stay? Pa and John painted the Lit church on John St. Pa, Don and Russell went clamming Sat. and got quite a few steamers. Donny still talks about that monkey. I really think he thought you were going to send him one. That's all we need. An awful lot of fellows left here Monday. I guess they'll all be going but Poop Neubauer. Well, that's all the news for now. Hope you make out all right in your exams. Well, good luck to you.

Love,
Mother

17 Anise Street
New Britain, Conn.
October 19, 1943

Hi, Kid,

I'm sorry I didn't write sooner but yesterday I was awfully sick. Sunday Mother and I went to the Lithuanian Banquet. They had a chicken dinner. I think I got sick from the stuffing. I didn't go to school yesterday but I did today.

Your books came yesterday. They're "Survival" and "The Best Known Works of Oscar Wilde."

Donny was very glad to receive your letter. He's glad to receive anything.

I don't think we go to school Thursday or Friday because of Rationing. It doesn't make much difference though whether we go or not.

Aunt Anna hasn't heard from Taggie since the last time the island was bombed. We all hope he's o.k.

Mother went up to see Tessie today. She's pretty good now. She had first degree burns. It could have been a lot worse .That's all for now.

Love,

Betty

17 Anise Street
New Britain, Conn.
October 20, 1945

Dear Brother,

Gee I'm so sorry that you feel so miserable. I'll try to write more often but you don't know how fast the days fly by. I hope you feel in a better mood when you receive this letter.

I saw the "Miracle of Morgan's Creek" this afternoon. I didn't care for it though. It was too silly. I did roll down the aisle laughing though. There lots of snowballs and cupcakes in the aisle. You see, I collected money for the Red Cross in the Strand this afternoon. We went in about 2 o'clock and we were suppose to collect at 2 and 5:30. But Audry and I collected at 2:00 and went out at 5:00. Mr. Mahler didn't see us((I hope.) We went out with the crowd.

Daddy went to a painter's auction Wednesday and Thursday in Massachusetts. He bought about three thousand dollars worth of stuff. He got it all at a very low price. (Say it again and you'll believe it yourself.)

Two big trucks unloaded yesterday afternoon. There isn't any room for the truck or the car in the garage.

I took my second baton lesson last night. My hands are sore all over and my arms are all black and blue. I get a kick out of it though. Jean couldn't come and she's all excited that I'm a little ahead of her. I'm keeping away from the Ziegler house though.

There's an A.A. dance tonight but somehow I just don't feel like going.

The last couple times I went to the movies I got an awful headache. Do you think I need glasses? I don't sit in the very front row like you do either. I sit in the second. Well, that's all for now.

Love from your

Sister Betty

P.S. I'm going to ride my bike over to the church now. I left my bandana and gloves there last nite.

Harmony Church Falls
Ft. Banning, GA
October 22. 1943
(Post Card)

Hi, Charlie,

How are you old boy, I hear you were home not so long ago.

I have finished my 13 weeks of basic and should be sent off to school this week—I hope.

Have you heard from our dear friend Benny? Has the army or navy gotten their hands on him yet?

The army finally got old 4-F Walker. I have not heard from him since he left.

Is Dickey still going to Duke?

How are all the girls – do you still write to Meg?

No more room so will stop now. Write – and soon.

Joe

Coast Guard Barracks
Kenmore, Wash.
October 23, 1943

Hello, Kid,

Well, I'm still in Kenmore. We were due to ship out last Wed. but one of the kids we were leaving with went AWOL and we are waiting for them to find him. Then we can ship out. I don't know how long we will stay here, but a few days more I think. How often do you get liberty? I get it every night and 48 hours on weekends. I think it's pretty good, how about you? How is the food there? Here we have our good and bad days but most of the time the food is swell. By the time you get this letter you will be getting ready to go home. Boy, I wish I was in your shoes. I haven't got a chance of getting home until after the war is over or if I can get sent back East I could get home but I could only spend a day there so it wouldn't even pay to go and it would cost me about $200 and that's too much money to spend. The most I can get is 10 days and I could get it today if I wanted it. I'm going to wait about 6 mos. and then ask for 15. I don't know if I'll get it but I can try. Well, don't forget to drop up and see my mother when you're home. Say hello to your father and mother for me and have fun and be good. Love and kisses,

Freddy

P.S. Write to this address. They will forward my mail.

R.I. School of Design
Providence, Rhode Island
October 24, 1943

Dear Charlie,

The only reason I'm writing to you is to send you my address in hopes that sometime before the year 2000 you might drop me a post card. Or is that asking too much?

I put your picture on my desk for the simple reason the girls in my dorm think you're cute. They should see you in real life. But anyhow photographically you made a hit. Though considering some of them, 'specially my roommate, that isn't saying much.

Say why don't you stop in Providence some week-end and see me. You'll only be one more sailor among thousands , but at least you'll be familiar. (not that some of them aren't damned familiar). Brown University had their graduation exercises yesterday. They were neat. All the cadets and V12's marched down the hill to the Baptist Church across from one of my classes so we all left class to watch. As it happened yesterday was freshman initiation day and I looked like the wrath of God. Don't say, as usual. Well, when the graduates were returning, class got out and we caused quite a commotion among the former cadets. They practically rolled in the streets. Just think hundreds of men and I had to look like hell. Well, that is the way it goes. That's life .I have to go to class now, so for God's sake, Young, remember I'm still living and write to me soon. Say hello to Dick Walton for me and tell him he owes me a letter also.

Love,
Lucy

P,S. It would scare him too.
P.S.S. I was going to send it to the "Red and Gold."

17 Anise Street
New Britain, Conn.
October 25, 1943

Dear Brother,

How are you? We got your letter today. I'm sorry that I didn't write. I don't know if Betty told you in one of her letters that I got a pigeon. His name is Chic.

I got an appointment at 10:00 tomorrow morning at the DENTIST. I hope he don't pull all my teeth out.

Prince is asking for you. And do I hate school .Monday morning we are going to have a play. I am going to be a peon. The play is about Mexico. Well, we have to eat supper now and that's all I have to say.

Love

Donny

P.S. Please write to me.

-THREE-

NEWPORT, RHODE ISLAND 1943

THOSE GOOD TIMES AT Harvard and in Boston ended on a bleak, rainy morning in late October. Mustered in front of the dining hall, we heard the two hundred or so names read out of those who had failed to make the grade and would be sent to Newport, Rhode Island, for basic training. Not surprisingly, my name was on the list. Early the next morning I boarded a bus for the two-hour trip to Newport. The ramshackle facility made up of long, clapboard, single-story buildings had been in service since World War I and was about to be demolished. That we were to be the last class to pass through the historic landmark was little consolation given the unheated, roach-infested barracks, lack of hot water, and miserable chow. Our instructors, apathetic now that they were about to be reassigned, huddled in a shack while we drilled to the commands of a blaring PA system alongside the angry, freezing North Atlantic. At night, sewer water from the head backed up and flooded the deck beneath our hammocks. Why we all didn't perish from the flu or pneumonia, I'll never know.

U.S. Naval Base
Newport, Rhode Island
Oct. 30, 1943

Dear Mother,

Well, I'm here. It isn't as bad as I thought it was going to be. The food is good and we are getting more sleep. All the V12's from Harvard, Dartmouth, Columbia, Wesleyan and all over are here.

In our barracks are just the fellows from Harvard though.

We are going to be here seven weeks and then we'll be sent to schools. We'll have a furlough after seven weeks (I hope).

I sent a pile of stuff home. When you get my duffle bag take good care of it because I may need it when I get home.

Nothing exciting has happened yet, and I don't think it will. There is no way to spend money so I'll undoubtedly be a millionaire soon. Well, we have to stencil our things now so I'll sign off.

Love,
Charlie

U.S. Naval Training Station
Newport, Rhode Island
November 1, 1943

Dear Ma & Pa,

OOOOOOOOO! What a day! The dentist filled two teeth this morning. They are the worst butchers I ever saw. Half the fellows had to have teeth pulled.

We had tests yesterday. I was above average on the arithmetic, reading and average on the mechanical tests. They told me that I would probably be sent to a radio school for four months. I told them that I wanted to be a pharmacist's mate and they said they would do what they could. They'll let us know definitely in about six weeks.

I'm on watch tonight from 8-10. Next week I'll have it from 10-12 and so on around the clock. We only have to stand watch about once a week so it's not so bad.

We still don't know when we are going to get our leave. I wish that they would tell us.

Did you hear from Pa yet? Did he get anything? I hope so because I'd like about 25 lbs. of deer steak when I get home. Well, that's all for now. Write soon.

Love,
Charlie

U.S. Naval Station
Newport, R.I.
November 1, 1943

Dear Betty,

I didn't get the cookies yet, but I ought to tomorrow. Right now I'm eating cheese tid-bits. That and candy is all you can get around here.

We are now allowed to wear our coats. They don't let you wear coats or turn the heat on until 37 guys die of the cold. Think I'm kidding?

Will you ask Aunt Anna to send me Freddy's address. I wrote to him at Kenmore but haven't heard from him yet.

This place sounds like a bird cage. All we do is sing all day and night.

I wrote to my ex-roommates about the suitcase. I'll let you know soon. So keep your teeth in. Speaking of teeth, mine are still sore. They are getting better now.

Now the gang is singing "I've been working on the railroad."

Did Pa get home yet? Let me know as soon as he does.

I suppose Mother is just as good as ever and that Donny is just as fresh as ever. Tell him that the first thing I'm going to do when I get home is to beat him up royal!

We paraded this morning. It was very cold but we had our winter underwear on and gloves and coats so it wasn't bad. The sea was very rough. We can see it from our windows. Ships of all kinds go in and out all day. Well, I've got to mail this before nine so I'll say good-night.

Love,

Charlie

P.S. I'm enclosing some postcards that I had lying around. I can't use them and there's no sense throwing them out.

U.S. Naval Training Station
Newport, Rhode Island
November 2, 1943

Dear Mother and Dad,

Well, I'm starting another week. I hope this week goes by as fast as all the rest here.

We're going out to the rifle range this week, I think. We hike out there, it's about eight miles and we'll sleep there. Everyone says it's a lot of fun.

I went to the dentist this morning. He said there was nothing wrong with my tooth. If you want one pulled they won't do it. If you don't, they pull them all.

We had our first liberty yesterday. Lucy and her girlfriend came up. We went to a movie in Newport. That's about all you can do. We saw the picture "Sweet Rosie O'Grady." It was a gay nineties movie with Betty Grable. I thought it was very good.

Did Pa get the pictures of the hunting trip yet, or didn't they come out good? I wish that you would send them down.

Boy, is it cold here today. This is the first cold day we've had. We had to get out and run around the drill field for twenty minutes without our pea coats on. The heat is on in the barracks all the time now so it's not too bad here.

I hope I get home for Christmas. Joe, Mick. and Dick Walton are going to be home. They won't tell us anything definite. Well, that's about all for now, I guess.

Love,

Charlie

Newport, Rhode Island
November 4, 1943

Dear Betty,

Those pictures were pretty good. Especially those of me. Of course I'm better looking than the pictures but the camera isn't very good. The picture of Joan, Pa and you was very good. I'm going to keep the one of you and me.

Send me some food. Anything, I'm starved. The only thing we can buy here is candy. Send me some hot-dogs, hamburgers etc. No kidding, send some cookies or something. I eat everything that they give me but I'm still starved.

I sleep swell in a hammock. I could sleep swell standing up on a two by four if I had to.

We had tests this morning. They weren't too easy. We're going to have more this afternoon.

Friday we saw "Princess O' Rourke." Yesterday we saw a musical show from Boston. Last night we saw "Doughboys in Ireland," and tonight we're going to see Walt Disney's "Victory Through Airpower." I never saw so many movies in my life. This place is a vacation for the V12 students.

In about two weeks we're going on K.P. Maybe then we'll get something to eat.

I don't want anyone to see the dozen pictures that you have made up because I want to give them out for Christmas presents. Savvy? Well, that's all the news for now. Write everyday.

Love,

Chic

P.S. That suitcase should arrive later than the rest of the crap.

U.S. Naval Base
Newport, Rhode Island
November 7, 1943

Dear Mother and Dad,

Well, I'm back from the range. It was nice out there. Our shoulders are pretty sore. The first day we fired fifty rounds of twenty-twos and fifty rounds of thirty o' sixes. The second day we fired a hundred rounds of thirty o' sixes. We used Remington rifles. I qualified as a Navy marksman, that doesn't mean much.

Half of the guys almost died walking back. Everyone has sore feet. These clod hoppers that we have to walk in aren't very good for hiking.

Well, we've got to get our hair cut again. I'll finish this later.

Sunday

Well, I just got back from church and am I dead. We had liberty last night until eleven-thirty. We went roller skating and then to a dance at the "Y". Our whole floor had to walk around the barracks from twelve last night until four in the morning because our barracks were dirty. I went to bed at four and then got up at six and I was on duty for two hours. What a night!

There are about eighty fellows left in the company. The rest have been transferred to sea or schools. It seems as if they just take you when they want you. I wish they'd tell us something about getting out of here .Well, I guess that's all for now. I am too tired to write anymore.

Love,

Charlie

U.S. Naval Base
Newport, Rhode Island
November 10, 1943

Dear Mother and Dad,

The patient is doing very well today. He just muckled a pint of ice cream and guzzled a pint of milk. His temperature is normal and after this letter he is going to play cards with some other patients and WAVES.

We fool around and listen to the radio and dance and then someone yells, 'The Doctor's coming." Then everyone runs like hell and jumps in the bed and moans away. Then when he goes we all jump around like hell and have fun again. There's a lot of good music on radio.

The food is good here and the WAVES bring it to our beds. I think I'll stay here for the duration. I have my books and I study once in a while so I won't forget what I've learned so far.

The kid next to me had measles three times since he's been in the Navy. He knows all the doctors and nurses, and do we kid the nurses. They get so mad they tell us they are going to give us needles for the fun of it. We both had a mouth full of ice cream when the nurse took our temp. this afternoon. She thought we had rigor mortis. Well, that's all folks.

Love,

Charlie

U.S. Naval Base
Newport, Rhode Island
November 12, 1943

Dear Sis,

Well, I'm glad you're feeling fine. How was the dance?

123

What a miserable place this is. Half the kids have a fever and the other half have colds or pneumonia. One of the fellows was burning with a fever so he went to the infirmary. They didn't even take his temp. They gave him an aspirin and told him to run along. But the Navy's alright. They give you a nice funeral.

We're going to see "Sahara" tonight. It ought to be good. Humphrey Bogart is in it.

Well, I've got to dash a letter off to Tony Di Angelo now. So I'll sign off. The next letter will be longer.

Love,

Chas.

U.S. Naval Base
Newport, Rhode Island
November 12, 1943

Dear Mother,

I got the cookies today. Boy, were they good. I'm so sick of candy and bought cookies. I have the cookies hidden in the bottom of my sea bag. My friend from Dartmouth and I eat them when no one's around. They are too good to feed to the wolves around here.

I didn't get any mail this morning or this afternoon. I was so mad that I wrote to everyone I know and told them to jump in the river.

We did some old things today. We drilled and went to classes. I wish that we would go out on the rifle range. I'm sick of drilling with dummy rifles.

I suppose Pa's home now. Tell him to write to me and tell me about the trip and the guns he took and how the car held out etc. etc. etc. I'm dying to know.

We are going to a movie tonight. We are going to see the news, sing for a while, then see "Corvette." It's a movie about a Canadian destroyer, I think. Randolph Scott is in it so it should be good. It's a new picture.

I'm on watch from 10-12 tomorrow night. I don't suppose it will kill me. It's not outside. I just have to walk around the building and see that no one falls out of their hammock.

Well, I've got to go now if I want to mail this before the movie.

Love,

Chas.

P.S. Thanks for the cookies again and don't forget to tell Pa to write.

U.S. Naval Base
Sampson, New York

November 13, 1943

My Dear Mr. and Mrs. Young,

We've been pretty busy for the past few months learning to march, handle a gun, wash clothes, make beds etc.

Things are going a little slower so I have the afternoon free, that is free from work only, we can't leave the unit.

If you have Charlie's new address I'd appreciate your sending it to me as soon as possible. I don't know though whether to believe it or not that Charlie has been transferred, he kids me so much half the time I'm in a daze. If he is still at Harvard he had me fooled, if not, where is he?

Sincerely yours,
Benjamin

17 Anise Street
New Britain, Conn.
November 13, 1943
Sunday night

Hi, Kid,

How you doing? Have you been doing more "dive bombing"?

Jean and I just got back from the movies. We saw "Phantom of the Opera" in Technicolor. It was perfect.

Donny and Mother are making fudge out in the kitchen. It smells good!

Ma and Pa went up to the Humane Society in Hartford yesterday to get Princey. He was there five days. Somebody told us that they saw an English Setter up there.

Prince is tied to the clothesline now. He can run all over heck now. If he barks tonight Pa's going to get rid of him so here's hoping he keeps his trap shut for once. That's all for now.

Love,
Betty

P.S. Excuse the writing. I have to get this out before 7 o'clock.
P.S. Did Lucy come up Sunday?

U.S. Naval Base
Newport, R.I.
November 14, 1943

Dear Betty,

It's about time you put the dog at the end of the clothesline. Now he can run around.

I haven't been doing my dive bombing lately. It's too cold.

You know, Ginnie C. went to the dance with Dougie Driscoll. Lucy told me all the dirt. I almost died laughing. Dougie and Ginnie make a nice couple. And YOU didn't tell me about Holy Cross.

Tell Mother to send down a small chocolate cake. I'm hungry. One of the kids got a big tongue and two loaves of Jewish rye bread. We ate it up. Kosher or no Kosher.

We were out in the row boats for two hours this morning. It was snowing and cold. We nearly froze to death. I'll never thaw out. Well, Kid, that's all I know for now. Write soon.

Love,
Chas.

U.S. Naval Base
Newport, Rhode Island
November 15, 1943

Dear Betty,

Am I full! I just ate about two dozen raw oysters, olives, crackers and cheese, cookies, cake and jelly. One of the fellows got a big box of food for his birthday and we gather oysters down by the shore.

Am I rich. We all got nine dollars today. That's taken out of our pay. I've got fourteen now. Wheeee! Are we going to have fun Sunday. Lucy is coming up with a girlfriend.

I heard that N.B. won the game. It must have been very good.

See if you can keep up the all A stuff. That's very good. I suppose Wart got all U's. I'm so mad at that crapper. I'm going to beat his roof in when I get my hands on him. It's a good thing he didn't write. Now I won't have to send him a present. Maybe if he writes I'll send him a card. But that's all.

Did you go to the dance? It's kind of late to be making up your mind, isn't it? You could wear that maroon gown of Mother's. On you it would look good. Let Barbara Nealon wear the black velvet.

It hasn't snowed at all here yet. It was so warm that another kid and I went "dive bombing" all day. "Dive bombing" is walking along with a stick with a nail in it. We pick up papers and butts (we pick up butts anyway).

Well, Sis, I've got to get ready for chow now. Thanks again for the money.

Love,
Chas

R.I. School of Design
Providence, R.I.

November 14, 1943

Dear Charlie,

 Upon receipt of your last letter I hesitated momentarily to answer, since my mental plane is far below yours. But since we are constantly told that mail helps the morale (not the morals) of the service man I shall do my best in my humble way to equal your letter. If I should fall short in any way, I pray you excuse me since I am a poor, illiterate, not fortunate enough to have gone to Harvard.

 There, does that satisfy your newly acquired mental attitude? You seem all hep about your friend Robert from Dartmouth. Is he really as nice as you say? I hope so. Oh here's something that should give your ego a lift. More than one girl in the dorm has fallen in love with your picture. I took you off my desk because one, in fact, caller kept bouncing into my room every two minutes when I was trying to study to gaze at you. But they raised such stink (to put it vulgarly) that you again hold first place. Every time I look up from this letter there you are not two inches away. It's most disconcerting.

 Say, by the way, what the hell is the matter with you? Do I really love Dick? Are you stark, raving mad? I never did, don't and never will. He's a marvelous kid, but that's all he is to me. I value his friendship, but he's hardly my type. But then you wouldn't know my type anyway because you've never met or know anyone I've ever liked. I don't know what gave you that idea but for God's sake remove it from your mind, for once and for all. Don't you know, dear, you are my only love? (God forgive me for lying but it sounds good). Well, now that that's straightened out. I think that Red and Meg going to the dance together is a howl. I wonder if Red likes Meg? I know Meg can't make up her mind between Red and Bob Dunhill. The last time I saw Meg, Dunhill was in the lead. I feel sorry for Dick, he's too nice a person to be hurt by her.

 Say, by the way, Charlie, from the tone of your last letter I gather you're in love. Who is it, that nurse in Hartford? I thought for a while it was Meg, but I suppose it's Sara Prestly.

 Oh, hell, am I nosey! But since you seem to be able to ask personal questions, why can't I?

 By the way, thanks for correcting my spelling of prostitute. I hope to God I'm red blooded but after last night I'm beginning to wonder. Someday I'll explain, suffice it to say for now, I met two ROTCs last night who at the present own the worst reps on the hill. They're so good they look on wolves as amateurs. Oh, well, that's the way it goes, if you get a man nowadays you can't expect decency also.

Darling, I'll have to let you know about November28ᵗʰ.That's Thanksgiving weekend, but if possible I'll see you. I'll probably come back to Providence Sunday morn. But I'll write later this week and be a little more definite. Be good and write to me.

Lucy

U.S. Naval Base
Newport, R.I.
November 15, 1943

Dear Betty,

So you're running around with college boys. Why didn't you tell me about him? Does he have one arm? Was he better looking than Jean's date. Cripes, Kid! Get on the ball.

I got a letter from you, Poopsie and Mick. today.

I'll bet you wish you had gone to the dance with Dougie or one of the Campus gang. You always did like "Shu La."

I'll bet you were jealous of Ginnie Campbell. Have you got a case on Sonny Dean? Come on, tell me. Ginnie undoubtedly liked him. Does that make you feel better?

I was caught with another kid hiding in the attic during the happy hour. The guy(chief) didn't report us. He just said that seeing we were so tired we could stand the 2 - 4 (morning) watch for the next three days. Hee-Hee, I nearly died laughing. G'wan. I can see me crawling out of bed at two tomorrow morning. I eat that up. I guess that ought to teach us not to skip athletics. Well, that's all for now. I'm going to bed at seven. I'll write to Donny tomorrow.

Love,
Charlie

P.S. I'm enclosing a picture someone sent me. I'm the one on the left. Don't let Donny take it to school.

Hartford Hospital
Hartford, Conn.
November 15, 1943

Dear Charlie,

I received two letters from you today and honestly they seemed to cheer my whole day up. I was especially in need of a little cheering up too, because we had our mid-term exam in nutrition today and of course I couldn't help *worrying about it until it was over. It really was a fair exam though and I think I made out alright on it. (I hope.)*

There is one thing that I would like to straighten out before I forget, and that is, please try and understand my not writing as often as you do. You should know by this time that it's not because I don't want to write, 'cause if I had more time I'd write twice a day, but with all the studying we have I just about have time to eat. Gosh, I thought I was doing good in writing as much as I have been, but if you insist I'll stay up all night and write. I only get five hours of sleep anyway, so a few hours less won't make any difference.

Another thing that has been puzzling me is your wishing I were in your hammock with you. Well, Charles, you know that wouldn't be ethical!!! What in the world ever gave you such an idea? We had to write a paper on our philosophy of life for profess. adjustments, and according to my philosophy such an idea shouldn't even exist. But then I don't always live up to these standards.

I don't know whether you are serious or not about being anxious to be with me when you are home. I wish you were though, 'cause it does seem good to know someone feels that way about you. I know we'll have a wonderful time together (providing I'm not on duty at night). I can think of a million things I like to do, one of which is to dance. I miss our dancing together terribly, even though we did argue a lot, we usually had fun in the end. I wish you could be a little more definite about letting me know when you will be at home, because if I take my vacation Christmas, you'll be home New Years, and if I take it New Years you'll be home Christmas. It would be just our luck to have it happen that way. I guess you are just as anxious. I mean as I am though I can imagine they don't tell you in the Navy until the last minute.

Did you know that Whipple has been home? He called me last Sun. and said he wanted to say hello before he went back again. He's going to Virginia and from there out to sea again, I guess. He sounded anxious to get back but I supposed that is because none of the kids are home.

Henry was home for the last time this weekend and Mavis settled everything between them. She says it's strictly on a friendly basis. Gosh, I don't envy her at all. I have so much to look forward to when you come home, where all she has is a strictly impersonal date.

Before I close I want to let you know that I also got your letter about Lucy Conway and her girl friends planning to visit you and your boy friends. *Now whatever made you think it would burn me up? Gee, as long as she's as gruesome as you say, I shouldn't mind her keeping up your morale, but tell her not to make a habit of it, or I might resort to one of the interns around here – not that it would bother you, or would it?*

Now that all our kidding is over, I guess I ought to close so I can get back to my organic chemistry! Write as often as you can because I look for a letter every day.

All my love,
Cheryl

P.S. *Don't forget, Sweet, that when I do write my letters are twice as long as yours, so I'm really not too bad.*

17 Anise Street
New Britain, Conn.
November 16, 1943
Thurs. Night

Dear Brother,

How are you? I'm sorry I didn't write sooner. Yesterday I went to the movies and this morning I went to the football game, of course N.B. won for a change 6-0.

We had a nice dinner today. It was a PIG.

Prince ran away Sunday and didn't come back yet.

Betty is getting ready to go to a formal. She is going with a fellow from Holy Cross, his name is Jack.

We got our report cards Monday and it wasn't so bad in arithmetic. Betty got all A's.

Mr. Swanson is eating supper here and he is chewing Daddy's ear off.

Daddy and I went to Almas and I was shooting the 22. Daddy put two bottles in the pond and I hit the both of them in two shots. They were about 35 feet away from me.

That just fits into what I am telling you. Mother just let two flickers and they knocked me out of the chair.

Old man Prentice died. He got killed in an auto accident.

Maybe Betty told you that we had a few inches of snow.

Well, Aunt Anna got to mail this letter on her way home so I'll sign off now.

Love,
Donny

Connecticut College
November 17, 1943
Sunday night

Dear Charlie,

There's nothing I can say to you about Harvard—you'd probably rather it wasn't said. I hope for you own sake that you can go back after the war.

This was about the queerest letter I ever got from you. I think you're a little off the beam. Listen to me, you nut – you're not in love. Or if you are you're in love with some dream of a girl in your imagination – and I'm not she. I wish I could make you see that I'm not what you think I am – you don't even know me anymore. This whole mess started when we were in the 8ᵗʰ grade – can't you see that it's ridiculous after all this time? We'd better skip it because you don't really mean what you're saying.

And how the devil can they ship you out when you've only been there for a couple of months? Are you kidding me—again?

I'll be home for Xmas the 15ᵗʰ of December. I'll see you then 'cause there seems to be a lot to talk over.

I've finally gotten a room at the college – I moved up yesterday. It's going to be so much more fun this way.

I'm in the middle of doing my Chaucer so I'd better get back. As they say in the old country though – you'd better "Slow Down!" Write when you get a chance.

                    Love,
                        Launa

U.S. Naval Base
Newport, R.I.
November 17, 1943

Dear Sis,

Well, it's a good thing I heard from you today. I was good and mad at you yesterday. I suppose that you and F.B. were out in the park all night smooching. I suppose you're up to your old tricks. There's no one to go looking for you now. You like that, don't you?

Don't let Miss Baer tell you what to do. Have some girl kneel down in back of her and give her a push.

No, Sala isn't a Jehovah Witness nut! Jehovah means God in certain parts of the Bible. Cripes, Kid, get in the ball game. Guess I told you. Hee Haw.

We have one four hour watch every five weeks and two hour watches every four days. We'll only have one or two four hour watches while I'm here.

The cookies came this morning. I eat them up. Give Ma a big kiss for making them.

Well, kid that's all the manure I have to shovel now so I'll shove off.

Love,
Charlie

Connecticut College
November 22, 1943

Dear Charlie,

I'm writing right away because you seem to be in a pretty sad state. You wanted me to tell you the truth—o.k.— this is going to hurt.

I think you're mad. Not really, but you're just a little swept away by the times. You're one of those fellows who are too young to be in the service because you don't know how to take it. You're dramatizing yourself — "big strong wonderful boy going off to war and seeing his love once more before he dies". Don't be an ass. For heavens sake, grow up! Not very pleasant is it – but I know I'm right and you probably don't believe me. Your letter sounds like a love-sick school boy. I used to think it was funny that you loved me – but I've grown out of that. You know of course that I don't love you – I never could. But I honestly think you enjoy believing you're in love with someone who doesn't love you. Don't be so childish. How old are you now – 18? You act like a little boy and I always think of you as a little boy. And all your craziness is not due to the fact that you have a soul – we all have 'em. It's because you've got an overactive imagination and you know that's the truth. Well, you wanted it and you got it. I have no more to say. What I've told you is the truth not just my opinion. Think it over and see if you can't grow up enough to realize it.

Love always,
Launa

R.I. School of Design
Providence, R.I.
November 23, 1943

Dear Charlie,

Please ignore the delay in answering your last two letters. I've been rather busy lately – day and night. For the last week I've been on the go constantly and as a result am on the point of exhaustion. But I guess I'll survive. I always have.

While I think of it, thank you for the pictures of your friend. He made a big hit with the girls. They couldn't decide whether he was good-looking or homely. He is vey unusual looking you know. They finally settled for interesting.

If you definitely want us to come to Newport I'll see you Sunday then. What time? And for how long? We have to know so we can sign out, so please write immediately and let me know. I'm leaving here Wednesday afternoon and will be back Sunday morning.

God, my mouth tastes like hell, we all just had hamburgers with onions and we stink. I wish I was out with a guy I didn't like right now.

Well, to continue from your last letter dear, I gather you are in a mental quandary. But don't let it throw you. You're attitude at present, in view of the fact that you are disappointed at flunking out of Harvard, is to be expected. Your moods vary from self-pity to the spiritual. Knowing you as I do, this last mood will not stay with you long. Everybody finds out some time or other that they have found God, so to speak. They get all hepped up about the finer life. With most people life passes and they return to their normal every day outlook on life, some, probably a selected few, don't recover and so we find sidewalk preachers preaching blood and thunder, hell and brimstone on street corners all over the world. You've seen them in Central Park and no doubt have laughed. This is a dull and boring sermon, I know, but I hope, dear, you understand what I've tried t tell you. And I hope also that when I see you, you'll be the same Charlie I went swimming with on graduation night. Remember?

I finally met a nice (?) ROTC. Of course, as usual, I was sarcastic to him the first night and so as a result he thinks I'm very bitter towards the whole world. I hope I change his mind about me, 'cause he is very interesting. He has quite a rep with the women so that's why I'd like to get my hands on him. Wish me luck.

Well, I've got to crawl into bed now, it's raining like fury outside and the damn cars keep roaring by, but I'm so tired Errol Flynn couldn't keep me awake. So good-night.

Love,
Lucy

51 Forest St.
Oakwood, Conn.
November 24, 1943

Dear Charlie,

Well, here I am writing to you at last. Honestly, if I had a hundred dollars for every time I thought about writing to you, I'd be a millionaire by now. We've had the most hectic week I've ever lived through due to a Chemistry mid-term on Tues. and one in Anatomy today. We all stayed up until 1:30 this morning studying for the Anatomy, and it's a good thing too because the exam consisted of 6 !!! pages – including drawings to label and blood routes to trace over the entire body. There was so much to it that I can't imagine what kind of a mark I will get, but all I ask is that I pass. Now that those exams are over, all we have to worry about is the one in Psychology and Nursing Arts next week sometime. Gee, it's getting so the kids refer to themselves as "a brain followed by a body" with all we've learned in the past few months.

Just think, tomorrow is Thanksgiving. Somehow it doesn't seem as though the holidays are going to mean as much this year as they have before. I really shouldn't complain though because I'm only on duty from 7 a.m. to 11 a.m. then I have the rest of the day off. Right now I don't think I can stay awake long enough to get home and have our turkey dinner, but by tomorrow I'll feel good again. That reminds me, how do you feel? You sounded terribly depressed in your last letter. I guess that's why I've been thinking of you so much – and especially because you haven't written. Couldn't you manage to write often even though I can't always? You well know how much I look forward to your letters, and how disappointed I am when I don't have one from you.

Oh boy, I nearly got myself in a mess on the ward yesterday. I'm on a men's ward now and most of them are alcoholics that are so jittery that they can't even hold a glass of water. Well, I was giving this man a bath and after I finished his back rub he asked if I could leave the alcohol so he could rub his "fanny" I guess. It's a good thing I read his chart because it said he was so eager for something to drink that he'd try most anything. So when I offered to rub it for him, he said it wasn't that bad. I guess he must have thought I'd leave the bottle with him. Wouldn't that have been something if I had? I'd probably be put in jail for killing a man.

I was talking to Helen Sun. and she said Benny is in the hospital because of his leg. I guess she's really crazy about B . She writes to him every day and he, in return, sends her little trinkets etc. She claims that his letters aren't very sentimental or rather not the way like she'd like them to be. I guess all he tells her is the weather. That must be very disappointing especially when you're wondering whether or not a boy really likes you, or whether he's just humoring you with his compliments.

*I had another shock last Sat. morning. After Nutrition we decided that
we ought to see the morgue before we have to take someone down there by
ourselves. Well, Mavis and I and a couple of other girls went down there
and jeepers I nearly froze in there. Besides the awful smell it's really not
too bad. Because the bodies are all covered in shrouds. We saw a still-born
baby whose face was all crushed in. I looked at it and before I knew it I
said, 'Oh, look, it's a little boy, too." Of course, I would have to come out
with a bright thing like that. I guess I felt like a real ninny!!*

*It's 11:30 now and the mail just came in, and no letter from you again.
Have you forgotten so soon? I'll bet that you are so taken up with your
letters to Lucy Conway that you don't have time for me. Am I right? I was
hoping we could stay on a friendly basis for a change this Christmas, so
that when you come home we can have all that fun we've been looking for
together. How about it, Love? When you get home I hope I can remember
all of the jokes that are going around here. Janet Prager comes down about
every night with a load of new ones. I guess you told her most of them.
She comes in and all we do is talk about the good times we used to have in
High School. She told me about the fun you two used to have in your classes
when you sat in back of her, and I tell her about all the fun you and I used
to have at Riverside in the house of fun. Remember yelling, "Here 'Tis?"
I wonder what the other people must have thought you found every time
you yelled that. It sounds bad.*

*Goodness, it's 12:00 and I have to eat, get dressed and be in class by 1
o'clock so I guess I'll have to close now – until next time.*

Love and kisses,

Cheryl

*P.S. Why sure you can call me, Charlie, if you want to. All the kids do
anyway.*

P.S.S. How much snow is there in Newport? We had about 2 inches.

Ozette Patrol Base
Clallam Bay, Wash.
November 25,1943

Dear Cousin,

*Well, I got your letter today and I finally found time to write. I knew
your address for almost a week but I just couldn't get around to writing.*

*I saw a picture of some of the boys there. I'm sending them to you, you'll
shit. I can see you now.*

135

What's new by you? I am spending Thanksgiving eating beans. I was coming in from the Cape today and I shot a deer, that's 5 in the past four weeks. Between the dogs and the 24 men on patrol a deer doesn't go very far. It was only a small one, I should guess about 150 pounds. I got a buck three weeks ago and I think he was close to 300.

When will you be home again? Do you have any liberties at all? I'm going to try to get home in Apr. if I can save that much money.

I wrote to about everyone I know since I've been here and I'm getting writers cramp. How do they treat you, like dogs I bet. I know, I went through it and lived. Only Moon Beach is worse than Newport ever dreamed of being.

So you're all hot for Cheryl's body. Are you going to get in when you are home next time? Well, I wish you luck. Well, I can't think of anything else to write about but I'll write when I'm out on patrol again.

Love and kisses,
Freddy

P.S. See you in front of the pawn shop.

Duke University
November 27, 1943
Sunday afternoon

Dear Charlie,

Well, ha-a-a-a-u-u- ""dawlin." Judging from your letters you must be having a "ducky" time. It was really good to hear from you again, Charlie. I'm also glad that you answered so soon.

The way you describe Newport, R.I. isn't even funny. I didn't think that "tings were dat tuff." I guess that you'll get used to it or have you done that already?. As for Harvard, I think that you will go back some day, as you say. I guess that through you I finally realized why Harvard is the number one college in the country.

Well, darlin', I'm going home for Christmas, believe it or not. Yes, I was fortunate to make reservations both ways. It sure will be swell to be home for Christmas. Thanksgiving, on the other hand, passed very quietly. I had classes from 8 to 5 and worked at nite from 7 to 11. The only thing that even resembled Thanksgiving was the evening meal. It consisted of turkey, dressing, sweet potatoes with pineapple, peas, cranberries, salad, bread, butter, milk, fruit cake, ice cream, apples and oranges. Not bad for a Thanksgiving dinner—no?

My subjects this semester are much more interesting than those of last semester. Zoology is really a lot of fun. So far, I've looked at so much

136

"crap" on slides that I'm beginning to smell from it. I've dissected worms, tapeworms, leaches and grasshoppers. Can you believe it, daddy, I actually saw the heart of a cockroach beating? No kidding (and that's not a measure for birth control) though, it is the most interesting as well as the most involved "stuff" I've had yet. I've pulled off some good grades in Math, Chem and English. I'm also getting by in French.

I went to a Cabin Party with that Salisbury job last Sunday. I've also got a date with her tonight. She really is hot stuff and I go for it in a big way (all x inches). (You asked me whether I had the situation well in hand – what a silly question to ask. You know that I always have it in hand.) Next Saturday I'm going out with a girl from Troy. No, not in New York—North Carolina. Damn! She is the nicest thing I've run into down here. You can imagine what she's like. I had to get a date with her three weeks ahead of time. I don't care though, I think I can make time with it. Also, next Sunday, I'm going to another Cabin Party. Hells fire – do I eat that stuff up!!

I'm sorry that you didn't get a chance to see Robin before you left. These Southern "gals" are very emotional and she might have layed it on the line. Damn, you must be really hard up. How was "Lay for nuthin" Lucy? I didn't receive any telegram. So I guess she must have been armed or "som thin."

Gosh, I heard that it was snowing over the holiday in New England. Damn, it's warm as ever down here.

It's beating time now darlin', so I guess I'll have to do my duty. You know, Union laws. Anyway take care, Charlie. I'll be expecting to hear from you soon, and don't forget to telegraph.

Your pal,
Dick

410 Carlton St.
New Britain, Conn.
November 27, 1943

Dear Charlie (Hot Shit)

So you changed your mind about the Navy, or did they censor my letter? Or are you writing these letters at a point of a gun?

I could choke you! You write to me and give some "queen" a big build up, and tell me how you want to get engaged. Then after all that bullshitting you don't even tell me her name. What the hell is the matter with you? I'm going nuts. Who is this clean pig?

Speaking of Benny's letters, I was just about to write to you and ask your aid in translating that Greek.

I heard a rumor today and I think I'll be here until Jan. 1ˢᵗ. Of course I'm not sure. So on your Xmas vacation (if I'm around) we'll raise the God damn roof.

So Freddy is in the Coast Guard. I don't think I'd mind those Eskimo girls. Remember that old saying: "A hole is a hole, even if it hangs on a door."

I haven't been out with a girl since you left. Shit, I can't go out alone or with H.S. kids. I saw Lucy last night in front of Liggetts. Well, darling, I'll be seeing you.

Love,

Tony

P.S. Don't forget to write back soon and give me her name.

232 Mountain Drive
West Hartford, Conn.
November 28, 1943

Dear Charlie,

Surprise! I'm answering and promptly, too! I shall be deeply indebted to Eric for the rest of my life for having submitted the classic work of art to the Navy although I must say the incentive that made you write was not very flattering.

Things here are very dull – almost disgustingly so. Once in a while someone gets a furlough, but that causes so much confusion so no one knows what is really going on. The poor fellow is probably glad to return to his station because his leave is just one mad whirl. We girls are so cooperative – we share and share alike!

I am working and studying with unexpected fervor! I'll be through school in March or April, I think, so we are spending all our time now on speed work. I type 48 words per minute (that's not satisfactory yet) and take shorthand at 80 – fast worker (no cracks, please). When I leave school I'll be typing 65 and taking shorthand at 110. I have a gay time at the office now. My boss gives me dictation every day and it's very nerve wracking – he hasn't got much of a lap and his office isn't private so you can see what a hectic time I'm having!

I know that you hear from Ben so I can't tell you anything about him. I'm looking forward to seeing him as you can probably imagine and I think

138

it would be wonderful if you could have a weekend off while he is home. If you don't though there won't be anything stopping you from coming down when you do have your leave. We can have another fireside chat – minus the fire. It makes me feel good to think that we have all grown up to the point where we enjoy discussion. Of course, we'll have "to do the town" when Ben is home and save discussion for a less thrilling occasion.

You no doubt heard that Nancy has been out with Morry. The situation is very complicated and very amusing. I really think that Morry's line is much too smooth to be taken in by any girl in her right mind unless she has one to equal it. Nancy is no fool though, and things are going to be different this time.

Did you know that Jackie Kincaid left college? I saw her about a week ago and she was on her way to Pratt and Whitney in East Hartford. They are offering a course in some kind of technical work and it is a great opportunity. They had their Junior Prom at the college last Saturday and I think the fellows from Wesleyan were invited. Jackie went with Morry and Danny Bray was asked too. Do you ever hear from him? Every time I think of him I remember the "barrel incident" at Riverside.

I hope I'm not telling you things you already know. Maybe I'd better ask you a few questions.

I'm very curious to know: 1. How you like Newport?

I know the answer to that, of course, but you could fill pages telling me what you dislike about it.

2. Are there any further developments concerning the "love of your life"?

You don't have to answer these but I'm quite interested in hearing about it – I was quite fascinated by your childhood romance.

This is an especially long letter but I find it very easy to write you. I could write still more, I think, but I'll save it for next time.

Write often—I try to be prompt in answering as a rule, although I can't always guarantee very long letters.

Affectionately,
Helen

Connecticut College
November 29, 1943
Saturday morning

Dear Charlie,

I honestly don't see any point in my writing. I told you how I feel the last time I wrote. I'm glad I amused you – aren't you big enough to admit

I was right – or don't you get it still? I wonder what the devil you'd think if I wrote and told you that "I wanted to walk on soft pine needles holding your hand." !! See what I mean. Nobody but a love-sick adolescent would write such a thing.

And I wasn't trying to hurt you. You asked me what I thought and I told you—and I still feel the same way. No matter how much you think you've changed, I still think of you as a little boy. No, I'm not being nasty. I just wish I could make you see what the story is. But evidently that's impossible.

I don't see any reason to keep on writing. I've said what I wanted to say and it doesn't seem to do any good anyway.

Love always,
Launa

By the way, I can't think of anything more revolting than a boy's eyes getting misty when he writes to me. If that doesn't prove my point, then you really are thick.

17 Anise Street
New Britain, Conn.
November 30, 1943

Dear Son,

Just received your letter and thought I would answer right away. I'm glad the dentist found your teeth o.k. Dad went up and had one filled yesterday. Now that you have your liberty you will be able to go into town once in a while. That picture Rosie O'Grady played here in the Strand and Betty saw it. Betty was home sick yesterday. She had dinner up at the Ziegler's Sunday and might have eaten something that didn't agree with her for she threw up most everything that she ate. She still has those stomach aches she used to have when we thought it was her appendix. I'm going to take her to the doctor next week and see what it is.

Well, we are getting ready for the big party Friday. Betty is going to do some shopping today for candy and prizes. Donny keeps counting the days. He's got about 13 kids invited. I'll be glad when it's all over. Then we have to think about Xmas. But I don't think we will have much of one. Everything is so high, even Xmas trees. They want about $5.00 so I guess we will get an apple tree.

Just got a notice that your pictures are ready, so will get them this week. Your books came and I think I am going to cancel them. By the time you get to reading them they will be old. We can always get them again.

140

Our dog just came home. I let him out this morning. I suppose Betty told you how he was gone a week. The Humane Society had him, we had to go to Hartford after him. He is a regular Bum. If he runs away again we won't even go looking for him.

Dad and John were just home for dinner. They are working over to Reynolds doing some papering.

Rose Allen's father died. I suppose Dad and I will go to the wake tonight. Where is Mick. stationed at? I haven't written to Benny yet. I hope you will be able to come home for Xmas. Don't forget to write and thank Millie and Stella for the candy. Anna heard from Freddy. He still wants his hunting knife. He said he shot a bear and a deer—he is having fun. I hope they don't send you too far away from home. But they have Radio Schools all over. Well, I guess I've told you all the news, can't think of anything else. So will close so Donny can mail this on his way to school

Love,

Mother and the rest of them.

17 Anise Street
New Britain, Conn.
December 1, 1943

Dear Brother,

I just got through with my homework and I thought I should write since I didn't Monday or Tuesday. Monday I was awfully sick and I stayed home from school. I think it was something that I ate. I'm pretty good now though.

There isn't much of anything to tell you about the Holy Cross boys. Ned brought home two boys for Thanksgiving. Nice ones too. Oh, Boy!! Their names were Jack and Larry. So they took us to the dance. I went with Jack. He was almost 6 ft. They were both swell dancers and nice fellows. Mr. Anderson's (our drum teacher) band played at the dance.

Irene Narcum is going to take vocal lessons. Before when she banged on the piano we thought it was bad, now she'll be singing, too

All the kids are hanging around Donny 'cause he's going to have a party. Just like Jean and I used to hang around Peggy Callahan.

Yesterday we received a letter from Taggy. Of course, he couldn't say much. He sent Donny 5 dollars for a birthday present. Donny certainly was tickled pink. Well, that's all for now.

Love from all,

Sister

P.S. So you're a "Kosher Monkey" now.

U.S. Naval Base
Sampson, New York
December 1, 1943

Dear Charlie,

So your company has KP duty this week, too? Our men are slaving at KP too, but not this goldbrick. I'm working at the foot clinic about 6 hours a day and help in the morning with barracks cleaning for my work week.

We probably didn't see the same VD movies you did because these weren't gruesome, just a few pimples and everyone washing his hobby and getting a blood test.

I was called for an interview concerning V12. They asked about my education, my preference (engineering, med, dent. tech etc.)and where I wanted to go to school. Of course, Yale was my first choice. I signed a paper saying I would have to give up my Seaman 2nd class if I was chosen. When I had my regular interview I applied for radio technician, sound man, radio man, fire control man. I'll probably go straight to sea the day I get in O.G.U.

Oh, heard a joke about a foot doctor if I can remember it I'll repeat it. This man wanted it and was a stranger in town so he asked a man he met where he could get it. The man said, "Go to the corner of 3rd Street and go past a foot doctor's office and the first door on the right will be the place." He started out on his way, saw a tavern, had a few too many and then he started off again. He got to the building all right but went into the foot doctor's waiting room. The nurse said, "Get ready, I'll be right back." So the drunk stripped. When the nurse came back she looked at him and said, "That's no foot." He said, "Why quibble over a few inches?" Well, enough of my demoralizing jokes. Be good.
Love,
Ben

P.S. Tell me about Lucy.

10 Benefit Street
Providence, R.I.
December 2, 1943

Dear Charlie,

I couldn't hear you very well as you may have noticed so I thought I'd better write and tell you a few things. First, no I didn't get the rum and have no intention of getting it. You didn't drink before you joined the Navy

142

and it's no time to start. Of course, if you want to drink it's up to you—I can't tell you what to do, but I'll be darned if I help you. Now get mad if you want to.

Secondly, don't ever tell me what and what not to do. If I want to smoke myself to death that's my business. I'll admit I smoke too much but that isn't what makes me shaky and nervous. I've been that way for a long time, ask my doctor. Also what made you think of that at this late date? I've been smoking for three years and you've never noticed it before. And I don't see any connection with my wanting to be an artist and smoking. You really burnt me up tonite. If there's one thing I hate it's being ordered around by a fellow. So watch it—.

Thirdly, after talking it over with Emily and Barbara (the other girl, she's very cute) we decided we can't afford to come to Newport Monday. Sorry, dear, but we are not made of money.

After reading this letter you will undoubtedly dislike me as much as you once did, but I'm in a rare mood and you'll have to take it or leave it. Just in case I don't see you again—be good.

Lucy

P.S. Tell Bob, Emily had nothing to do with this in case you happen to get angry.

Ozette Patrol Base
Clallam Bay, Wash.
December 3, 1943

Dear Cousin,

I received your cheerful letter today. So it's cold there, boy, you should be here. It's nice and warm but its been raining for the past 38 days, well, not all of it—we had two nice days.

So you're going on leave again, you lucky dog. I put in for the last part of April and I hope to be home for Easter.

So you're not going to bother with Cheryl anymore? Why, from what Joyce tells me she's all hot for the heat of your body. So why don't you see if you can get in this time home? I know I would if I were you. Joyce didn't say much while you were home.

I haven't seen a woman in a month. All the boys are afraid of me (I wonder why). I'm saving up some money for Christmas and my leave if I ever get it. When are you going to be home again?

I'm on watch now and I get off in a few minutes. I'm getting writers cramp answering all these letters, this is the 6th one tonight.

There isn't much more I can write about so I'll have to say so long for now. I'll write again when I'm out on patrol. Where do you think you'll be after you leave boot camp? How did you like the pictures I sent you?

Well, if you get near a good glass of beer have one for me. All they have out here is Army beer, that 3.2 stuff. Will see you in front of the pawn shop—.

Love and kisses,
Freddy

232 Mountain Drive
West Hartford, Conn.
December 3, 1943

Dear Charlie,

I got your letter this morning and I'm in a very rare mood – thus the prompt answer.

I've been on a tear all week and it's going to last through the weekend. Nancy has asked me to stay with her this weekend and there's a formal at the Coast Guard Academy Saturday night. I'm sure you will be disgusted at my even considering the Coast Guard but then a man is a man! And his uniform is the same.

I have spent every cent I saved buying a new wardrobe – same old line "I haven't a thing to wear!" You should see me – I've lost about eight pounds more and all of my clothes have to be pinned on me. I tried one of my old gowns on – a strapless model – and what do you know – nothing to hold it up!?!

You should consider yourself fortunate to get a 6 hour pass. I think Ben has had only one 10 hour pass, but from what he says he likes it at Sampson.

By the way, I think you must have misunderstood my invitation. Don't you know that you couldn't cut Benny out , although I don't think it matters much to him. That "bottle" idea sounds appealing, but I feel like being obstinate – let's leave the lights on.

Oh, yes, Cheryl is very occupied with her work. I write to her occasionally but she doesn't have time to answer. We telephone back and forth when she's home. There's a formal for the student nurses this Saturday with V12's from Trinity acting as dates. I had to work late Tuesday night – until 10 p.m. in fact!! The night work exhausts me – night work – not night life!

I must go do up my hair – I look like a Hottentot from Africa now – I just washed it and it stands up on end now that it's so short.

Affectionately,
Helen

Better be careful of that rum. You can get stewed on that stuff! Somebody warned me once and I didn't pay any attention.

Hartford Hospital
Hartford, Conn.
December 4, 1943

Dear Charlie,

 Don't be surprised to hear from me again. At last we've finished all our mid-term exams, what a relief! We're all just about dead from studying but Mavis, Ann, Joyce and I mustered up enough energy to go out to supper tonight, then to the State to see Tommy Tucker. We had to be in at ten o'clock because I want to save my late leaves up for the week I have to work. Right now, it doesn't look like I'm going to get New Year's week off, but Christmas week instead. I really doesn't make much difference because I'll have these late leaves the week that I work. I think I'd sort of like to be home Christmas anyway, with my Mother and Dad.

 When I got up this morning I swore I'd be in bed at 10:30 because we're having the dance tomorrow night. They've invited some of the boys from Trinity and Brainard Field up so I think I'll just go down and see what they look like – and maybe dance a little. Wish you were here 'cause my mother bought me a new white evening wrap and I'm so anxious to wear it out.

 Helen called the other day and she told me about your enlightening correspondence with each other. Guess that explains the decrease in my letters. Right? Have you heard when Benny is coming home? It would be nice if you both got the same time off then you could get together again.

 Janet Prager just left, and after I read her your note, she sent the enclosed in hopes that you won't be caught in an embarrassing situation.

 Agnes was home last weekend and she called and told me all about Boston U. It sounds like a wonderful place.

 I got another letter from Roger and I guess he's out to sea again. He wanted to be remembered to you, too.

 Oh yes, Joyce has been getting two letters a day from Freddy lately, and he told her that his mother is going to let you have the car when you come home. Isn't that wonderful? It will make it ever so much easier for you to get all your visiting done.

Well, Chas, it's 12:15 a.m. and the maid is on her way upstairs to make her rounds. (Incidentally, the lights should be out at 10:30. Do you think she'll holler? Guess I'd better make like I'm asleep if I don't want to have an appointment at the Student Nursing Office.)

Try and write once in a while to an old friend even though it is only a short letter. I still look forward to getting them. Goodnight –

Love,

Cheryl

U.S. Naval Station
Newport, R.I.
December 5, 1943

Dear Mother and Dad,

Well, it's Sunday morning now. I just got back from church. Everyone has to go to church whether they like it or not. Some of the fellows never went before in their lives.

I saw the movie "Corvette K 225" last night. I don't think that Mother would like it but I know that Dad would. There is a lot of action in it.

The fellow that sleeps next to me had a toothache last night so he went over to the dentists and had it pulled. I didn't even wake up once. The place could burn down and I wouldn't know it if I was sleeping.

You know what I would like. A portable radio that you can plug into the wall. That's the only luxury that you can have here. You can take a radio out to sea or to a service school. I don't know if you can get one or not, but if you can I wish you would.

We have to go to a USO show this afternoon and I'm on watch tonight. I still have half the box of cookies so I'm going to eat them on watch.

You ought to see how everyone scrubs their teeth around here. No one wants to go to the dentists office again. Once is enough.

Well, that's about all for now. I'll write again tomorrow. I'm going to read "The Blue Jacket's Manual" now. It's a book that we had to pay a dollar for. It has everything about the Navy in it.

Love,

Chas.

P.S. I just remembered something. Would you please send me a map of New England? No one seems to know where we are. (There's probably a map lying around the garage.)

Duke University
December 5, 1943

Hi, Charles,

How is the sexceptional kid? How about a "flesh session," honeh? You sound sexier than all hell. Are your ankles getting weak yet? Or is something else weak? After I get through with this damn oration you'd better burn it or somebody will think we're dirty.

Judging from your letters, you're in love with the Navy as much as ever. That is the way to be, darlin'. Give it your whole hearted support. Duke is as interesting as ever, as I'll explain in the latter part of this note.

Before I do this, how do you like my new dormitory? Convenient as all hell—no? You'd be surprised what goes on in his place. Everything from "blow jobs" to the real thing. One of my roommates (the one from New Jersey) jerks off for me every night, my Southern roommate cleans it up and I lap it up. (Don't take me too seriously).

As for making all the girls in old N.B. pregnant, I'd like to, but "daddy," I don't think that would be very nice. (Who's kidding who). I don't know that I believe in premarital intercourse, but time will tell. You can pick up a piece down here anytime you want it, but I'm not in the market at present. (In case you're interested.)

See right now, I'm not clowning. I hope that you'll be able to get home for Christmas. I'll arrive on the 24th and leave on the 26th. All I'm going to see are my parents. I'd stay down here if the women were going to be here, but their semester ends on the 21st and they won't be back until Jan. 5th.

As for Meg (hot pants to you) I had been writing to her quite regularly and she was doing the same. Then suddenly, I didn't hear from her for about a week and a half. Her excuse was that she had written a note and forgotten to mail it for three days. How the hell do you like that? Besides this, Sarah Highschool's letters haven't been very inspiring which all leads up to—you can guess. I think that Christmas will be the time I'll be on the "checking out" end.

I'm sorry to hear that Launa doesn't like the size of yours anymore. I guess that one sided love is o.k. when you're on the right side.

Oh, before I forget, I was rejected by the V12 again because of my mental exam. More damn fun!!

Now I want to tell you why Duke is sooooo interesting. Last week, I went out with that Salisbury number. We saw the movie "A Lady Takes A Chance." Sexy as all hell! It was about 9:30 when we got out of the movies and she had to be in at 11:30. That meant that I had two hours to get to know her better. Well, we went to the Ark Women's Campus Dance Hall, danced, had cokes etc. During our conversation there, she stated that she made up her mind to dislike every Yankee she went out with. Well, I asked her if I had made any progress. She said, "Well, I dated you a second time, didn't I?" I said, "You mean, I dated you a second time?" (I'm a credit to the North aren't I, daddy, cementing Northern and Southern relations). Well, about 10:30 we decided to take a stroll around the campus. It was then that I cracked every single joke and slang expression that I knew, and did she eat it up. She said that I was the most interesting Yankee she'd ever met. I said, "Listen, babe, I'm more than that." The result was that about 11:00 o'clock, SHE asked ME to kiss HER. How do you like that, darlin'? I said that I wasn't in the mood and made a date with her for next Sat. nite Dec, 11th. I played hard to get so that I could get my fill next Saturday. Damn, do I like that little darlin'. I'd let her warm my foxhole anytime. I'll let you know how things work out.

Tonite, I've got a date with that girl from Troy, N.C. She's the "Chick" I had to date three weeks in advance. Damn, do I go in for this stuff too. (I swear there are so many nice girls down here I don't know which ones to give the breaks to.) Did I ever tell you about this Troy "quail"? Well, I had a date with her three weeks ago. During the process of conversing with her, it ended up with my promising to write her a letter. (She said that she was lonesome.) Well, I did – and what a letter!! I didn't think she'd want to go out with me after that. Well, I called her up the early part of this week and damned if she didn't sound hot for my body. No kidding, boy, I'm having great times.

I'm now a member of Pi Kappa Phi, but I've yet to be initiated – ouch. Tomorrow I'm going on a fraternity Cabin Party. I'm going with a girl from Indiana.

I'm about all unwound "honeh," so I'll close much to your approval. Take care and remember if the front stairs are painted, go up the back way.

All my love
Completely yours
Your ardent admirer,
Dick

Gosh, aren't I emotional?

17 Anise Street
New Britain, Conn.
December 6, 1943

Dear Son,

Just rec'd your letter and will answer for Betty has a lot of homework and will write tomorrow. Well, Son, the party was a big success. Donny got your money and Tag sent him $5.00 and he got some from the kids. He had about $14.00 in all and now he wants to do his Xmas shopping. He got quite a few presents. He said he was going to write and tell you all about it but he just doesn't seem to get started.

We had an accident with our car last Thurs. Pa and I were coming home from Russells and were stopped for the sign on Hartford and Stanley Street and this car came along and ran right into us. The damage will be about $125.00 and the other driver has no insurance. He was pinched for drunkenness. I will send you the clipping. The front wheel was knocked right off, the fender smashed, the axel bent. Betty said I bet Sonny will say too bad it wasn't wrecked but don't let Pa hear you say that. He thinks there's no car like his.

Aunt Anna let us take her car yesterday and we took a ride to Forestville to see Bert Church and then we went to Bristol to see Bob. He's in the pony business, he has about 10 of them. The kids ride them. I guess he does quite a business. Donny rode them. He said it was a little too slow.

It looks like snow today. Pa is asleep on the couch and Betty is doing her homework. Pa got thru early today. John got pinched for being drunk so Pa had to bail him out.

The dog is up to Swansons with the Farmers pooch. He sticks close to home now. I guess he knows winter is coming. Donny caught a big rat in his trap down the cellar last night. So he is going to set it again tonight.

I didn't get your pictures yet. I must go up tomorrow. I haven't done any Xmas shopping. I don't know what to buy, everything is so high. I hope you get home so then we can do a little shopping .

Where were the other boys shipped? I hope they don't send them across yet. I thought they would send you to some Radio school. Well, so long and don't forget to keep your barracks clean. If you keep it like you did your room no wonder they keep you up all night.

> *Love from all,*
> *Mother*

> *210 Benefit Street*
> *Providence, R.I.*
> *December 6, 1943*

Dear Charlie,

Alright so I do act like a kid about somethings, and I do smoke too much, or did. No, I haven't given it up, but I have cut back to almost a pack a day. Last week I didn't smoke for six hours straight. Good for me, don't you think?

About Friday night, Emily and Barbara Garside think it's swell. That's a twelve-thirty night, so they'll be able to stay a bit later than Em and I could the last time. While I think of it, sorry about Saturday but I was campused. Also Emily had gone home for the weekend.

Tell me more about Frannie. He has a face, I hope. How tall is he etc. All the things you told me about Bob. Oh, yes, have to tell you now that you have good taste as far as friends are concerned. Emily likes him and from what I saw he looks like a nice kid.

The weekend was dull for the first time, the only thing I did was go for a ten mile walk. That was very enjoyable. I went to the canteen last Thursday and spent most of my time fighting with a guy, who like you, thinks I smoke too much. But he decided and told me that long before you did. In fact, that and my swearing have been his pet peeves since I met him. What's the matter with men lately, don't they believe in any vices? I'm glad you've given up drinking—I suppose it was Bob's good influence.

Did I tell you that I'm going home the seventeenth of December? They suddenly got generous and lengthened our Christmas vacation. Just think, in about two weeks it will be Christmas again. I'm dying to get home 'cause if there's one day I love it's Christmas day. The only day in the year, I love the world.

Got a letter from Ginnie this morning and she said that she'd heard from Benny. He may get into the V12. Good. Also she said he was enjoying the Navy very much. He is at present in a hospital lugging patients around. That's the way she expressed it. She asked for you and sends her love (?). That's all she said except T.S. and A.D.S. are running a dance soon and there is going to be a Fri. dance. I intend to go to that, never mind how or with whom. Well, I have a lots to do tonight, Mr. Authority, so I'll sign off now.

Love,

Lu

P.S. Enough sarcasm for a while, friend. Make the next letter nice. I'm out of my bad mood temporarily. Did Bob get Em's letter? She can't remember if she mailed it or not?

17 Anise Street
New Britain, Conn.
December 7, 1943

Hi, Kid,

Well, here I am again.

Mother went shopping today. I can hear her laughing up to Neubauer's now.

Speaking of shopping I haven't even started to buy any Christmas gifts yet. I don't know what to buy either. What do you want me to get you for Christmas? Mother forgot to send the clippings so here they are now. Mother said that a cake would get squashed or crumbled if she sent one, so is there anything else she can send?

There isn't any news that I can tell you about so I don't know what to write.

School is the same old thing, day in and day out.

I'm getting my wisdom teeth. And, boy, does my jaw feel awful!

I think that I heard Pa drive in so I have to set the table. So long for now.

Love,
Sister

Pvt. Joe Rizzo
Northeastern University
Boston, Mass.
December 7, 1943

Dear Hot Shit,

Why didn't you leave the song alone? The woman and liquor are o.k. but the song is what ruined you.

I'll be home for Xmas so let's get together for that ruinous liquor.

Too bad you are not still in Boston because we could have some good times in this town.

The school term at Northeastern starts Dec. 13. 12 weeks from then I expect to be on my way to Japan.

How many times have I been in hell in Georgia? All there is, is shit, and I just got to Boston so I have not had much time to look the crop over.

I nearly shit when I heard Benny (the shit) was in the Navy. Where is he? What is his address? They must be hard up to want him.

Give Lucy one for me, and make it good. Tells me if she reels when she sees the rod. Ask her if you can contribute to her community chest.

Well, chow time. Hope to see you at Xmas time.

Joe

17 Anise Street
New Britain, Conn.
December 8, 1943

Dear Son,

It's a long time since I wrote so I thought a few words added to what Mother wrote you yesterday wouldn't hurt any.

You mentioned being on the rifle range and qualifying as a "Marksman." What does that mean, a good score or just average? What range did you shoot from or was it machine gunning you were practicing? You ought to turn in some pretty good scores with the experience you've had with rifles.

You say some of the lads in your Company were already sent out. I don't believe they were sent to sea yet as you are just getting your basic or boot training. I really think you will get a leave for the holidays or before you are sent out. Also I don't think you will have anything to say regarding a choice until you are sent to some other training center.

Harold Russell, the guy I went hunting with and who took the pictures I told you about in my last letter, told me last Friday that the pictures were pretty dark but the first chance I get to go around to his house I will get a few of them. Maybe something in the pictures will be recognizable.

I've just been upstairs to your room, cleaned the Johnson as there was a trace of rust in the barrel. I'm out of Hoppe's so I told Donny we would get some tomorrow and start cleaning the rest of the guns, don't know when we will be able to use them again.

I hear Merton Savage got a flock of medals for accuracy in shooting, he ought to if anybody does. Do you ever hear from him? If you don't you ought to write to him. Right now I don't know his address.

I suppose Mother wrote and told you about the smashup we had with the car last week. The wheel that you smacked was the one completely knocked off. I sent for quite a list of new parts and it will be at least another week before we take the car out again. I have a hunch we'll be getting a new buggy before long. Something tells me the car will never be the same after it's fixed up.

Was supposed to look at a house that was for sale today, a three-decker on Hawkins Street. I forgot all about it so will have to wait until tomorrow (always tomorrow is bad business).

As for myself I've been working most every day. There is still plenty of work around town, today I worked in the Neri Block in Plainville, have a couple of jobs in that town that will keep me going for the rest of the week.

We sold all the chains we could make up, a couple of weeks ago we shipped out 1446 units which was practically the last, have a few odds and ends around yet. I think we will get rid of most of the links this winter, we have only 75 cases of Jiffy Links on hand. I'm getting fed up with the painting business and I really think that when the war is over we will have to get into some sort of manufacturing racket as this is about the only way money can be made. We'll need some dough if you're to go to school again when you get back for good. If half of what we read in the papers is true the war should be over anytime within the next six months in Europe and a year to lick the Japs. Well, this will be all for now. I hope you are getting along fine.

Your POP

232 Mountain Drive
West Hartford, Conn.
December 8, 1943

Dear Charlie,

I think I'll tell you about the weekend before I forget. I was quite disappointed, I must say, at not seeing the girl for whom you're carrying that oversized match, but I thought I'd be able to discuss mutual friends with "Pris" Jones until I was told she was thrilling the Dartmouth men. Nan lives in Thames Hall and I didn't have much time to meet many girls from other houses – the Coast Guard drew most of my attention.

You make me feel very low with your virtuous personality. I'm practically a "butt fiend" now, especially after the weekend. I arrived in New London around 2 p.m. Saturday and the minute I go to Thames everybody gathered in the lounge with their packs of cigarettes and we all began our own little system of smoke signals and screens.

The dance was nice, Christmas decorations, my date was nice, too, but the fact that we had to be in by 12 was almost too much for me. I think my Mother would have been shocked if I ever strolled in at 12 at home. Usually I fall in around 3:30 and then, I have to say good-night (well, all the fellows say I have to). We had a good "bull session" after we got home so it was about three when we went to sleep.

Sunday morning is a sketch – you don't wash or comb your hair or anything. You roll your pajamas up, put on a trench coat and kerchief and then go eat. If Ben could have seen me then! We just sat around on Sunday and I came home at 6 o'clock.

Nan starts her Christmas vacation on the 15ᵗʰ. It seems like everything is happening about that time. My brother starts his furlough and he will become a proud father around that date, and Ben will be home. Oh, yes, and don't you expect to be home soon after that? (sigh)

For God's sake let's settle this little matter of your coming to see me. Come! Come! I beg you and implore you on bended knee to honor me with your presence. Bring the bottle and I'll break every d– lamp in the place so you can have darkness. Call me unpatriotic, will you!

Joyce was over last night. We were going bowling but we couldn't get an alley so we just talked.

Do you know anything about Freddy? I know all about him so if you want any information just ask me anything! Joyce will know if I don't.

I'm still struggling away at school. Someday when I can't think of anything to tell you, I'll describe our teachers—couple of gay girls!

It's bedtime, now I can go and dream. It would be wonderful if I knew that everything I dream will come true.

Be good,
Helen

Mother sends her love.

U.S. Navy Training St.
Sampson, N.Y
December 9, 1943

Dear Charlie,

It sure feels good to be breaking, we graduate Saturday and leave Tuesday. Don't you know when you will break? If you don't break this week, write and let me know.

I know what you mean by a sore shoulder. My rifle sling was so tight. I struggled with it for a while then I broke the sling (pulled the hinge off. It was only a dummy so it didn't matter.) Every once in a while my legs would cramp on me but heels on the deck sure got to me. When we started shooting the instructor kept yelling "treat your rifle like you would your girl friend, grasp it gently but firmly and squeeze, don't jerk." I don't expect too much luck with Helen. You know how she is.

I was cold for the first 3 or 4 days I was here but now the weather is fine. It isn't even freezing today.

Speaking of skiing I've got to wait till I can walk first. It was the opinion of the doctor in charge when I arrived here that I was incurable. ("unresponsive to treatment") I'm trying a little running and rope jumping to strengthen it.

I've got to go for my "dog tag" now so keep the situation in hand and I won't have to worry about my Helen.

Love,

Ben

P.S. I wish I had a key to it. Who knows maybe I can force the lock.

17 Anise Street
New Britain, Conn.
December 9, 1943

Dear Brother (is that better?)

We just received your letter a few minutes ago.

Ma and I will try to cook something up to send to you.

My goodness, why don't you clean the barracks once in a while? Doesn't the Navy teach you to be neat and orderly? I shouldn't think that you would mind picking up your clothes and things.

There's going to be a play at school tomorrow. The name of it is "Happy is the Bride." We saw a few scenes in the auditorium this morning. It was swell. Doc Schroeder asked me to go with him. Some Bargain!! Oh, but you went out with Lucy Conway. No remarks, please.

Ma just said she'll send a cake or something Monday. If she sent it today it wouldn't get to you over the weekend anyway. Well, I can't think of anything else to tell you now. I'll write tomorrow.

Love to all the Sailors. Ha, Ha,

Betty

419 Carlton St.
New Britain, Conn.
December 9. 1943

Dear Charlie,

Don't say it. I am very, very sorry for not writing sooner. As a pal I ask your forgiveness.

News have been popping like hell since last you heard from me. As you know I made application for Coast Guard. Well, I am going to take a physical on Dec. 14 (Tuesday). I will also be inducted on the same day. But I don't expect to be going before Jan. 1.

When are you getting that leave? I haven't been going out lately. I'm saving my energy for the hell raising we're going to do. Any different news on the R.I. pigs? I'm still waiting for that telegram. A good Navy man would have gotten down to business a long time ago. (I thought C.Y. was a fast worker.) Oh, well, so much for the love life.

New Britain is the same fucking old hole as when you left. All we need around this place is a fence. All you see on the streets now are hard up dames and 4-F's. I am going to the Amphion play tomorrow night with Shirley M. I will simply have a gruesome time. The Virgin is also riding in my car. (see what I mean). Well, old pal, take care of yourself and please write soon – very soon.

Love,

Tony

P.S. I am getting impatient so hurry home.

R. I. School of Design
Providence, Rhode Island
December 11, 1943

Dear Charlie,

Well, I'm back in Providence again with only one mishap on the way. God it was funny. We got in about 11:45 and Emily as usual was hungry so we tried a few places but they were closing so the railroad station lunch seemed the only thing left. Right smack in the town, full of servicemen and civilians, we stopped at a crossing. I felt something at my ankle so I looked down and there loomed this dark figure, I thought was a drunken sailor, and he was grabbing my ankle so I let out the most ungodly scream ever heard in Providence since the last witch-burning. Sailors, soldiers, everybody stopped dead in their tracks and just stared and for an instant I felt almost sorry for the figure in front of me. Then everyone started to laugh as the figure straightened up, it was an old man and he was merely picking up a lady's hat that had blown away and happened to come to a stop against my ankle. Hell, was I embarrassed. But that's the way it goes. That's life.

I'm returning the joke you sent as you requested. I told you I'd heard it before, but some of the kids hadn't.

Say, Emily can't figure Bob out. She thinks he liked a girl once and got hurt. She even described the girl. Red fingernails, drank, swore and smoked. All the things Bob doesn't like. Oh, yes, Bob asked me if you had

156

told me anything when you called. I said no, because you didn't tell me much. Also what was the sign language you two were indulging in last night. Every time I looked at you two, you were nodding and grinning at each other. What's the story?

Well, I've got a helluva lot to do so—

Love,

Lucy or Stella (if you prefer)

17 Anise Street
New Britain, Conn.
December 11, 1943

Dear Brother,

I just came from school a little while ago. I was trying to do some shopping but I can't find anything to buy.

They are putting up poles over at the park so there will be skating tomorrow. I think there's skating today til dark.

Daddy received your card today. It was very nice.

Are you sure that you'll be able to come home for Christmas?

So you're going to be Seaman 2/c. That's swell. Before you know it you'll be a Lieutenant. So long for now.

Love,

Betty

Northeastern University
Boston, Mass.
December 11, 1943

Dear Sonny,

Fun is right. I was home last week and had the car and no doubt will get it for Xmas. In fact my Uncle asked me if I wanted to use it. When I was home , I mean not at Xmas. I'll get it. Well, that takes care of our transportation. Cash, I've got that too. Girls, you get them, liquor we'll get that. What more do we want?

So Dick W. is still in school. I thought the draft would have caught him by now. What does he think of Meg being, as you put it, engaged to so many?

T.S. Too bad you did not get in but better luck next time and remember me.

I haven't had time to get to the Old Howard yet. In fact I been drunk only once since I've been in the Army. When I was in Georgia I went into Columbus (15 miles) by bus. There are very few places that sell mixed drinks. You bring the stuff and they sell the mix. We had gin and then we took the bus back. *The fellow with me was sicker than a dog (the bus ride, very rough) he puked all over the bus inside and out. I thought I would anytime but I held out. I guess it kind of sobered me up. We never tried that again. I was thinking of you and that New Years Eve. Remember?*

I'll get home for Xmas late Friday night. I'll probably have to leave at 1400, 2p.m. Sunday to get back in time.

By the way have you heard this joke? A girl, the only one in the class on human anatomy, was asked this question by the prof, "What part of the human body can enlarge itself nine times?" She stammered a while and finally said, "I don't think it's fair to ask the only girl in the glass that question." The prof. looked at her and said, "You're answer tells me 3 things. 1. You did not study your lesson last night. 2. You have a dirty mind and 3, you will be very disappointed in married life. The answer is the pupil of the human eye."

Well, after that joke I can guess what she was thinking of. Tell that one to Lucy. I had better quit till next time.
Joey

17 Anise Street
New Britain, Conn.
December 12, 1943

Dear Charlie,

Aunt Anna just left for the Post Office. Mother and she packed two boxes, one for Freddy and the other for you. You should get it around Saturday. So you'll have to drool until then.

I'm not so sure about the Christmas tree. A tree about 7 feet cost $4.50. There's loads of trees around but they're awfully high. Donny just said that Billy Coyle and he are going to get a tree down by the "big woods" Saturday. Perhaps they're going to take them from the college.

How can Benny get into the V12? He's in the Navy already.

Billy Coyle just called Donny and said that he couldn't go after Christmas trees because if he got caught his father would have to pay!! So I guess that's settled.

Where did you get the oranges from? Well, so long for now.
Love,
Betty

17 Anise Street
New Britain, Conn.
December 13, 1943

Dear Brother,

I had to be sure that I wrote today so you wouldn't squawk and say you didn't get any letters Saturday.

Mothers going over to Stanley school tonight. The Saint Francis Guild is having a Christmas party. Their going to have a grab bag. Ma's going to see if she can grab something.

Donny wants to go to the show tonite with Joel and his grandfather. I think he wants to meet Charlotte there and wants an excuse. That's all for now.

Love,
Betty

Connecticut College
New London, Conn.
December 13, 1943

Dear Charlie,

I got your letter this morning and, honestly, it's the most sensible one you've written. Congratulations! Seriously though, I guess you're back on the ball and I'm glad.

You'd better take it easy there, Jasper – you'll be fat. Min said you looked taller and heavier than before. Could be maybe you're growing up?!

And just to enlighten you – I don't drink. Don't laugh, I'm not kidding. I've hit a lot of vices but I haven't come to that one yet – it doesn't appeal to me.

There's another fellow down there I know – Louie Gonsales. Maybe you'd like him but personally I can't stand the boy. He got kicked out of Tufts. Not really worth looking up though.

I get out of this hole on the 15th and I can't wait. I'm sick to death of studying and you know what!!! I have to be in a ten o'clock at night! Being a freshman is more fun! Don't let me kid you, I really like it a lot – but I'm just not the studious type.

By the way, I wasn't trying to be mean and laugh at you. I was just trying to prove my point – and I guess I did. Well, be a good little boy and take it easy on the rum. See you soon.

Love always,
Launa

17 Anise Street
New Britain, Conn.
January 6, 1944

Dear Brother,

I just came home from school and found a letter from you. I also received one yesterday. It was the letter with all that crazy stuff in it that you didn't think anyone should see. But when I got home my mail was all opened up already.

You certainly have a nerve asking mother if Jimmie is a light Italian. I don't know what he is but I'll fix your boat if you make any more remarks. (got it, kid).

New Years night was Jimmie's last night home so he had a few couples over for a gathering. (You know and not a smooching party.)He said he's not coming home till June but he'll be home before then. He's only in New London.

You certainly seemed to have a nice Christmas. It would be a good idea to write to Father Brophy and tell him about your Xmas mass etc. He'd appreciate it a lot to hear from you.

I'm now at Aunt Anna's house. I came down here for supper with her. Fred was suppose to go back today at 4:30 but he didn't go. He said he's leaving tomorrow morning.

There was skating yesterday and this morning, but the sun came out this afternoon and now the pond is ruined again.

Gosh, it seems awful to be back in school. Our next vacation is in February. Oh, well, I'll live through it.

Aunt Millie was wondering if you received her package yet.

Fanny was very glad to get the letter from you. She's o.k. now but still a little nervous as usual. That's all for now.

Love and Kisses, xxxxx
Sister

Connecticut College
New London, Conn.
January 6, 1944

Hello, Eager Beaver –

I love that name – it suits you perfectly, no? This has been a bad day all around – from beginning to end. I had to get up at 4:30 so I got only 4 hrs. sleep. I've felt like a wet dish rag all day. And to top it off it's Sat. night and I don't have a date. Does that make you happy? Ten girls out of the 72 in the house had dates tonight. Pretty poor average, hmmmm? Something should be done. Going out and getting mail is about the only kick I'm getting out of life lately. Sometimes I get so damned discouraged

160

and sick of college. It's just one long grind and I'm not even half through. I'm even beginning to wonder if I'm learning anything. Don't mind me. I have to gripe to someone and seeing as I tell you most everything you have to put up with the gripes too. You can stop chewing your fingernails – you didn't send that letter about chastity and marriage to your father. I got it today. I think it would have been a riot if you had though – but I don't suppose you'll agree with me. By the way – were you lecturing to me about chastity in your own subtle little way? Hey, remember me? I'd really be rather insulted if you thought I needed it. You know me as well as anyone on earth – if you think – well, I know you don't think it. You couldn't. Or maybe you were lecturing to yourself. Betty's man came home for Xmas from two years in the Pacific – I heard quite a few tales about these unusual native women. Enough, huh? I agree with you, however, on the whole idea. A very good point. (I sound like a school teacher again.)

I just spent the last half hour over a Ouija board – guess who I'm going to marry – yep – it's you. But not in seven years it said. So I'm afraid you'll have to slow down.

By the way – to get back to that serious business again. Stop worrying about when we're going to get married. If I decided I loved you, you don't think you could make me wait 10 years, do you? You ought to know me better than that. I ain't the waiting type, m' love. I'd marry you as soon as you graduated. You don't have to be pres. of the company—as I'd be working anyway. But I would never consider getting married when you come home. We're too young – and besides we both have things we want to do first. All this is just supposin'. 'Cause in spite of your threat about giving me the shakes I doubt if I'll be swept off my feet. I'm beginning to think I'm just not the loving type. I haven't been really in love since Mick. Now laugh – go ahead. Nobody even seems to come near to what I want. And to top it off – I'm not sure what I do want. What a damn fool, huh? But as I told you before there's no sense in either of us dwelling on the idea of marriage now. I've got 2 ½ lovely years of studying ahead of me. What a pleasant outlook. I guess I'd better do some work. Sorry I'm in such a foul mood – but I usually survive it. I'll write tomorrow.

As ever,

Launa

17 Anise Street
New Britain, Conn.
January 8, 1944

Dear Son,

I suppose you wonder what happened to me. When I stop writing I can't get started again. Betty got two letters yesterday and I was waiting for her to come home so I could use her pen but Vera just called and said she went to the show with Barbara. So I'll use another pen.

Well, there's not much news around here. Pa worked all week, last week he loafed. John his partner is leaving to work at Pearl Harbor and Pa will have no one. At least John worked once in a while. I met Mrs. Savage and she said Merton is with Gen Patton's army over in Germany. She is so worried about him. I met Mrs. Noonan and John is home from the Pacific for a few days. Joe Bradley is home, he was over in the So. Pacific for over two years. Tag was home again, he manages to get home every weekend. Yes, he is wearing his blue sailor uniform. He was married in it. Did Betty tell you a Mrs. Wheatley wrote to me and told me about you. She said her son was in the same outfit as you. Do you know him? I was so glad to hear, now I won't have to worry. If they ever move you just mention Irene Narcum's boyfriend and the paragraphs, then we will know.

Well, Xmas is almost here. I haven't bought a thing, everything is so expensive and made so cheap. But I suppose I'll have to buy Donny and Betty something. Well, we will have a tree anyway. It doesn't seem like Xmas at all. Freddy was shipped out last week, they were repairing boats.

Did you get Pa's letter and the five dollars? I hope you get a higher rating so that you can send some money home. You will need it when you get back. Kenneth is still working. I guess he likes his job. Well, I can't think of anything else to write so will close with love.

From Mother

Cheryl hasn't called me in quite a while. Did you tell her about the cake?

Connecticut College
January 8, 1944

Hello, Darling –

No letter today and yesterday was Sunday – T.S. – I lose. I tell you, you've got me completely spoiled – and how I love it.

I'm in a stinking mood again. I think I'm finally beginning to appreciate you, m' love. I spend 8 hours with that damn minister yesterday – he's burdening me with all the problems of the world. I feel so low a worm could crawl over me. Gee – I think you and I have fairly intelligent conversations without making ourselves as gloomy as a funeral parlor. He never laughs – please don't ever stop being crazy. There has to be somebody who understands me. Hell, why don't you come home? Now I'm being childish so I'll shut up.

I really haven't got a thing to tell you. Nothing much ever happens. Let's talk about the weather – it snowed all day yesterday. The nice snow that crunches. It made me want to go skiing. By the way, I finally talked quite a few kids into the idea of going to Great Barrington after exams. We've written to the inn up there so I guess we'll really make it. Have you been there? Tell me about it.

I spent all afternoon reading about the sex life of a spider – zoology is so fascinating. I'm beginning to think theirs is more exciting that mine. You think I'm kidding? Well, I ain't. Life is beginning to disgust me. I love the way I boost your morale. I'd better look out or you'll be divorcing me again. But please don't, Papa, the children would miss you. Seems to me you told me that one.

I'm writing this in an awful hurry 'cause I have to go to honor court for being a bad girl – again. Eleven of us are going – en masse. Now I'll probably have a week on campus or something. Life is so – oh gay!

Rose is getting ready to go so I'd better stop. I was going to end it but I'll wait and finish it. Be back, Launa

Hello,

It's now 11:45 and I'm trying to get to bed fairly early. Tomorrow's the day I have 8 hours of classes with no break. And two tests on top of it all. I've been studying like a fiend all day and at this point I'm seeing two of everything.

The way you talk it sounds as if you're going to move and I suppose I won't be hearing from you. But I'll write anyway and chew my fingernails on the side. I'm not worrying about you – but please take care of yourself, hmmmm? Somebody's got to take care of me – and you're the only one that seems able to. I'm dead – so I guess I'm not making much sense. Do I confuse you as much as I confuse me? Write when you can, Stinky.

My love always,
Launa

Connecticut College
January 10, 1944

Dear Charlie,

Well – I got the letter. Thanks again. So you're walking out – kind of a new twist to the story, isn't it? O.K. m' love, - have things as you want them. I'm afraid I won't lose any sleep over the matter.

It never would have worked out anyway. You're still trying to tell me what to do – you should know by now that it doesn't work. As I told you before – if you were my husband I wouldn't write every day. I write (or should I say wrote) when I had time – and when I didn't have it, I didn't. That's all you could ever expect. As I see it you're mad because 5 days elapsed without a letter from me and "you're not going to take that kind of stuff". Tell me, Charlie, just who do you think you are? I guess I made the mistake of letting you think you mean more to me than you do. Your assuming too much, my friend, if you think that you or anyone else can push me around like that. I'll do as I please come hell or high water and you know it. And it amuses me to see you get up the nerve to write things that you'd never dare to say if you were with me. So you're through – the hell you are! Don't disillusion yourself – you can't forget me and you know it.

But for the present the best I can say is – the hell with you. I'm sure I'll get along just fine without you. And I'll bet five dollars you're the first to write – sucker! Goodnight darling –.

My love always,
Launa

Connecticut College
January 12, 1944
Tues. night

Hello, Darling,

How's the blight of my life? I've written you two letters and torn them both up. I'm a little off the beam I'm afraid. I refuse to start another so you're going to get this no matter what.

I got your first letter yesterday and the other one today – that's the spirit I like to see. After all you have to keep up my morale –yours doesn't seem to need keeping up. By the way, I miss you – I told you I was off the beam. I guess it's like a bad case of poison ivy – when it's gone you're kind of lost without it.

I heard "Night and Day" this afternoon. I thought I'd fall through the floor. Do you realize that a week ago today I was wading through a Zombie? I'll never forgive you for that – as I recall I told you everything that ever happened to me. You know all the worst side of me, I guess. And I don't love Mick Leary – it must have been the Zombie. I won't go into a long discussion about it but I hope you give me credit for more brains than that. There's one thing I'm sorry about though – that was the Zombie. You'd better forget that.

My birthday's the 31ˢᵗ. Gee, you've got a wonderful memory. What month is yours in, Angelpuss? Honestly, you don't know how glad I was you called. I was feeling awful and I felt much better after talking to you. I think calling me is a very good way for you to spend your money. Then you can't spend it on the sweet little southern girls. You'd better keep away from them – they'll teach you the wrong things. Wait and I'll teach you –

The day after I came back I decided that I'd seen enough of men and I was really going to settle down and study. I haven't curled my hair once since I've been back and I've cut off all my fingernails – a good start, huh? But Saturday Paul Hansen called so now I'm going to the Coast Guard formal Saturday night with no fingernails. Did I tell you about him too that night? I'm going to wear that black dress again – you liked it so he probably will too Men are all alike!! But I won't have any pretty pink camellias this time – oh, gee. He'll probably bring me a gardenia – and I hate 'em. I don't know why I tell you all this, except that I tell you everything. Men – I hate 'em! Just a necessary evil – but why necessary? I can't figure that one out.

This letter is getting to be quite a manuscript – but I feel like talking to you and this is the best I can do. I have to stop and finish an English paper – it'll probably take me till 1 in the morning – Hell! I'll finish this later –

Well, I finished and it's only 12:30. Can you imagine a 7 page theme on "What I Got By Reading Hamlet"?! What a hell of a subject. I wonder why I don't go out and end it all!

"Talk to me." I know this is a horribly long letter but you can read it in installments. I heard a good expression yesterday – he loves her not for herself but for himself – do you get what I'm driving at? You always do. That's funny – do you know we're very much alike? We have the same reactions to a lot of things. You don't know how much alike we really are – you're like the half of me I try to cover up and get away from. Just ignore me – I'm tired and it's too late at night to make much sense. But that's one reason we could never get married – we'd bore each other to tears after the first year. Tough!

I'll send you a picture if I can find one. But please make me happy – tell me I don't look like that! Please!! I should think it would be very depressing to look at such a sad puss all the time.

Oh, you said you weren't going to go out. Don't be childish! I won't get angry, darling – honest. I'm willing to share you – aren't I sweet? And if you want to get over your inferiority complex you should be a regular wolf. No kidding, it's a sure cure

I'm tired – we almost had company over Xmas vacation. I got a letter from Dick McCarthy today. He was home on a five day pass and called the college but couldn't find me – just as well.

I don't write to you to boost your morale – I do it to boost mine, I think. Oh, hell, I don't understand me anymore. It's too late and I'm too tired. Guess I'll go to bed. Why don't you write to me, huh??

Love always,
Launa

P.S. Do you think you'll get home again after the six weeks? I might be coaxed to go to N.B. just to keep up your morale.

P.S.S. Some more. Why the hell did you ever tell Prissy Jones that I was engaged? You've got an awfully big mouth, you dope. By the way, did you ever go out with her?

P.S.S.S. I wish I could see you.

-FOUR-

PORTSMOUTH, VIRGINIA 1944

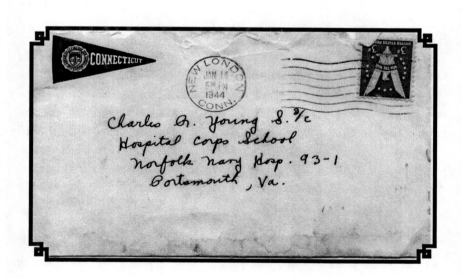

Charles D. Young S. ⅔c
Hospital Corps School
Norfolk Navy Hosp. 93-1
Portsmouth , Va.

IN JANUARY OUR DRAFT left wintry, dismal Newport for corps school in Portsmouth, Virginia, eagerly anticipating a warm and sunny southland. To our chagrin, we found the base under six inches of snow and ice. Portsmouth, a.k.a. Shit City, was a Jim Crow bastion with nothing to offer in the way of entertainment but a string of clap-ridden whorehouses in a seedy red-light district. The school, however, was new and squeaky clean, our quarters five-star, and the chow topnotch. With my recent failure at Harvard all too fresh in my mind, I hit the books hard. I was determined to be among the top 10 percent of the class who would receive a third-mate stripe upon graduation. The grind was relentless. Memorize, test—memorize, test. Twelve hours each day, seven days a week for eight weeks—*materia medica*, first aid and minor surgery, health and sanitation, anatomy, physiology, Latin, diagnosis, and prognosis. Memorize, test—memorize, test—memorize, test.

Connecticut College
January 13, 1944
Wednesday night

Hello, Darling,

That girl's here again. I got two letters from you today so I figured I'd better write one. It's now quarter of twelve – I seem to like late hours. I've just finished studying for five hours!! With only 15 minutes out for a butt – isn't that remarkable? I really can get on the ball when I want to – too bad I don't want to more often. Studying is a horrible thing, isn't it? I hate it!!

It sounds as if you can really go somewhere down there if you study. You can do it if you want to badly enough 'cause if there's one thing you don't lack it's brains. You seem to want so much out of life and you'll never get it if you don't make something of yourself. You know this as well as I do. But please study, huh?

'Nuff serious stuff!! You see, that's what I got from studying too much. I saw a movie the other day and they played "When The Lights Go On Again" and showed all the fellows coming home again. It got me to thinking about after the war – can you imagine how it will all be? It's sort of like a dream. I hope to hell it'll be soon – at least I'm praying that it will be. I can't seem to stop being serious – that's bad.

I wish I could talk to you. Do you think we could ever talk ourselves out? We never seem to reach a point where there's nothing to say.

Guess what, I'm going to be a W.A.N. – don't laugh!! That's a Women's Auxiliary Nursing Service – every Sunday morning. Wouldn't you like to wake up and find me pushing orange juice down your throat? God help the poor patients!!

If you tell me you aren't going out again, I'll go mad. Listen – you only live once. Go ahead and have a good time! You've got the wrong attitude.

I just washed my hair and have to stay up till it dries so I might just as well keep on writing. If I study anymore I'll go nuts! I think I've got a broken back—we had modern dancing today and I'm so stiff I can hardly move. Maybe I should have a picture taken in my little blue tights! That should keep up your morale – or something!! Do they teach you how to get rid of a broken back down there? You'd better let me know before I fold up and die. Well, I guess I'll go to bed—please study, huh? I want someone else to suffer too. Goodnight—.

Love always,
Launa

P.S. And don't try to tell me you never kissed anyone else like that – I know better. As I told you before, you'd better just forget that.

Connecticut College
January 14, 1944
Thursday night

Hello,

Say, I'm not going to be able to keep up with you on this writing business. Where do you get all the energy – and time? No kidding, I'm going crazy. We're having exams, mid-years the beginning of Feb. and if I don't pass I'll be out on my ear. That'll be one way of ending it all. I wouldn't mind all the work if I thought I was getting anywhere – but I can't see that I am. But I won't burden you with all my woe.

Haven't you gotten any of my letters yet? It seems I'm writing to you all the time – and you don't say anything about it. I hope you appreciate it – I haven't had a chance to write to anyone else since I've been back. What did you ever do to deserve all this attention?

I've lost 4 lbs. since I've been back – I'm just pining away without you. Tell me, darling, will you love me when I'm thin?

Paul Hansen called me this afternoon – he wanted me to go out. But I followed your policy – I had too much work to do. I guess you're a bad influence. Men bore me anyway.

I have to dash to supper – I'll finish this later.

Hello again –

Well, it's only 11 o'clock tonight. Some night I'm going to get to bed early—I suppose I won't be able to sleep then. You're in bed and fast asleep by now, I guess – you lucky dog. But then I don't get up till 8.

Did you see the moon? What a night to waste studying. But as they say, things are tough all over.

I'm dead – I guess I'll go to sleep. By the way, I dreamed about you last night – for about the first time in four years. I must have eaten too many pickles or something. Goodnight, Angelpuss—Write to me! And please study!

Love always,
Launa

Connecticut College
New London, Conn.
January 18, 1944

Dear Charles,

Please note the formal salutation—this letter is very serious business. I got five letters from you today and after reading them over a second time I've decided we'd better have a talk. I guess I've been off the beam – there's no doubt of that! But I'm back on it now. I must have been tight that night because I certainly don't remember telling you that I loved you – I'll never believe that. But no kidding, you know what the story is, don't you? I don't love you and I won't ever – oh, gee, do I have to go into that again? I must have been drunk but I still don't believe that I told you that. You and your damn Zombies!!! Let's just skip it – you know how I feel about this whole business.

It's 1 o'clock right on the nose and I've been going strong since 8 this morning. My brain is a little whoozy – so is my handwriting I guess. I'm in the middle of a source theme and the whole desk is covered with note cards. I'm dead – but after all those letters I at least have to write you one.

Stop fretting about the little C.G. boys and my black dress – I'm just amusing myself. I got roses – very pretty but I like camellias better. And the roses didn't give me a headache and I wasn't insulting and he asked me out again so there too! I've been going out with him since September – but he's just not my type. But neither are you, Jughead! Maybe I'd better be a nun.

And if you ever refer to me as "second hand" again, I'll kill you! Don' be old fashioned. And I've only kissed three fellows like that – Doc, Eddie and

170

you. Now are you satisfied? And I never would have started it with you only for that damn Zombie. I'll never touch another, so help me. Honestly, there isn't a damn thing you don't know about me!!

I went down to the hospital Sun. morning – very fascinating. I worked in the maternity ward – kind of gruesome. I was in a room next to the delivery room and some woman was having a baby – the sound effects weren't too good – maybe I'll only have three sons.

I waited on table today for two hours – gee what a madhouse. I get paid in war stamps - patriotic little devil, aren't I?

I'm glad you're studying – you better make the grade – or else!! You said something about helping other people for a change – honestly, it's the only thing worth while. Nothing on this earth is worse than thinking of yourself all of the time. Between us we'll make something of you, maybe, huh?

I haven't sent the picture yet but cheer up, I'll get around to it. You know what I look like anyway. I wish I could talk to you. You don't pay any attention to all the things I write, but I guess I can't. Tough, I lose. I'm falling asleep so goodnight, darling.

Love always,
Launa

Talk to me!
Stop dreaming about Joe. I never do. I didn't know you cared about him so much.

Connecticut College
January 19, 1944

Dear Jughead,

It seems that the only time I have to write to you is in the wee hours of the morning. It's 12:30 now and I'm so punchy I can't even see. This studying is beginning to get me down. But I have quite a few things to say so I'm going to get them off my chest. I've been doing a lot of thinking about us lately, Charlie. As a matter of fact it's taken up too much of my time. But I've finally seen the light and it's no go. As the kids say, "There's no future in it," as I told you before. I know you won't agree with me but at least try to understand. There's no sense in our writing – I get two letters a day telling me that you love me, and I write one a day telling you that I don't love you. As far as you're concerned matters are worse than they were before – and I know I got into it all by myself. I'm really sorry about that. But can't you see it's the sensible thing to do to quit now. I know you love me now but that isn't for always. You got along o.k. all these years without

171

hearing from me and the sooner you forget all about me the happier you'll be. It certainly isn't the easiest way out of it for either of us – I sort of like the letters – but it's the best way. Can't you see what I mean? I'm not trying to be dramatic about the whole thing but I'm not going to write anymore. And please don't write and try to talk me out of it. It's so much better this way. To tell you the truth I'm scared because I suddenly realized you were on the level – and I've only been fooling around – as usual. Things like that shouldn't be fooled around with so I'm quitting. Believe me when I say I am sorry for what happened over vacation – it was funny at the time. But I can't see it that way anymore. I can't stop you from writing but you must see that this is the right way out. I think an awful lot of you, Charlie, and I think I respect you more now than I ever have before. Please study and make something of yourself.

Love always,
Launa

Duke University
January 22, 1944

Dear Charles,

I received you note yesterday and was filled to ecstasy to hear from you. Judging from your letters , you seem to be enjoying yourself. At least, you never say anything to the contrary.

I'm sorry to hear that you haven't heard from Launa in three days. "TS darlin'." I guess that she is having exams for the Duke coeds are having their exams this week. Maybe that's a bit consoling to you, "darlin'." About that sour seminated slut Cheryl, I'm glad that you didn't "dip it," for I'd be terribly jealous, you know. You probably would have acquired a reputation anyhow for I think she'd be the type to talk.

As for my "ex-bag," (Hot Pants, to you) I finally gave her a break and wrote to her Thursday night. I wrote a long four page letter and told her exactly how I feel. I explained to her that what she did was about the lowest thing that's ever been done to me etc. and that we could never be anything but "old acquaintances." I said quite a few things that will probably hurt but that's the way they were meant to be. (I'm really very interested to find out what's going to happen. I can imagine!!)

Tonite is my "Hell nite." Monday I'll be officially initiated into the fraternity, but tonite is the big nite. Hell Nite starts about 12 midnight. The members toy with you and beat the hell out of you for about four hours and then take you out into the wilds of Carolina and drop you there. If I survive this nite, I'll survive anything.

This afternoon Duke has a swimming meet against Georgia Tech here at the pool. Alec Templeton is also coming here on January 31ˢᵗ.

I received a letter from Mary during the week and she told me about the riot you caused with your antics while you were home. She mentioned New Year's Eve and "The kiss of death."

From here on in, I'm going to have a fairly tough time. Exams start in four weeks and I'd better get prepared. I'm saying this now but I'll probably never do it. I've still got designs on the Salisbury slut and she's still putting out. Write soon.

Love and kisses,
Dick

17 Anise Street
New Britain, Conn.
February 16, 1944

Dear Charlie,

So you've got the measles. That beats everything. I bet that you sleep all day long. You always did get a kick out of sleeping.

Our drum corps is giving a supper at the Moose Hall February 9ᵗʰ. We should have a good time.

I hope it's o.k. with you that I brought the records down from upstairs. We have to play something now that the "Vic" is fixed. I borrowed about 9 or ten platters (slang for records) from Mrs. Domejan. So we have a little variety. I couldn't find By-u By-o or the La Conga. Do you know what happened to them? What were the records you brought over to Launa's that time?

I made a mistake – our reports don't come out till next Monday. Well, that's all for now.

Love,
Sis

P.S. How long will you have to stay in bed?
P.S.S. Keep away from those Waves and nurses. I bet you keep telling them you want a glass of water.

R. I. School of Design
Providence, R.I.
February 23, 1944

Charlie dear,

Son, you really outdid yourself in that last letter – Congrats. First I want to clear up a few things you mentioned in your letter – Milton's "Paradise Lost" is good, and now that you've finished that try "Paradise Regained" – also by Milton. Glad you've gone in for what is commonly termed 'better literature.' No, I haven't read "Jane Eyre" yet, but I shall soon. I have a copy somewhere. I'll get around to it some dull evening.

So you're confined to a prison bed for another week – you poor dear. Since when did you become so sexless that a beautiful nurse can't cheer your spirits? About marrying you at thirty-five, dear, if I'm not hitched by that age I shall quietly give up and depart for warmer climates.

That about takes care of your letter except for that crack about Trinidad, which I shall ignore. Personally, I would like to see some black woman make Red, red hot and blue – I always thought he was damn cold for an Irishman.

Frank Sinatra just went on and three gals fainted. Time out while I revive them.

They're okay now so I'll continue. I've come to the sad conclusion that I was born to be an illiterate s.o.b. To explain, I'll tell you, we got our marks today. Oh, well, that's the way it goes. Maybe I really don't want to be an artist. I think since I'm so lazy, I had rather be a kept woman. Forward any money you don't want to a trust in my bank.

Give my love to the 'Mole' and if she is being nice to you it's strictly from hunger, old boy. So don't go patting yourself on the back.

School starts tomorrow so I'll be bouncing off to a nightmare any time now. Bye for now, baby.

Love,

Lulu

Col. of the Ozarks
Clarksville, Ark.
February 24, 1944

Dear Charlie,

You can laugh all you want at Arkansas, for I'm laughing with you. Strange as it seems I'm having a swell time.

I've got something nice and clean I see every weekend. She's really very nice but I haven't fallen in love which makes me quite sad, as I've fallen in love every spring. It's nice and warm and sunny mostly every day.

Sometimes I wonder if I love Helen. I wish I got all gushed up every time I got a letter from her, but I don't.

Every Saturday afternoon we give the townspeople a thrill or something for everyone stands around and smiles. Can't you see the big brimmed hats and corncob pipes. They also get a kick out of our taking their women out. So do we as a matter of fact.

We've all got our troubles though, warding off shotgun weddings, etc.

This course is really fast. My roommate (a former Harvard V12 man) was really on the ball for the first 3–4 days here. Then he started talking to himself and giggling. We paid no attention, thinking him fooling. After that he kept insisting that he was a failure and a snafu and kept asking us to be friends with him. He sat down to chow one day but just stared at it for a while. My buddy asked him if he was hungry. He looked stunned and said, "Of course, I'm hungry" and started eating madly. Let me know if I told you about him in my last letter because I'm losing my memory. A few days ago he didn't come in for taps. Poor fellow!

I'm going to flunk I think because the shit they fling at us sounds like this: A D ground galvanometer whose resistance is 69352 deflects 20 cm with a current of 4.80 micro. Amp, watt potential difference etc.

You should become quite an interpreter after reading a few of my letters which are usually written in bed in the semi-darkness.

I hope you get your sick leave, you lucky stiff. Speaking of stiffs, take it easy.

Love,
Ben

P.S. Not yet.

Northeastern University
Boston, Mass.
February 24, 1944

Dear Sonny,

The shake-up in the A.S.T.P. will affect just about all of the fellows at N.U. We don't know yet what is going to happen to us but we will probably go back to the infantry. This weekend we are all taking the Army exam. The next weekend is the end of this term. We should get leaves about March 4th, unless something happens. We may get shipped out but I hope not. I hope to hell I get a letter and I also hope you do, maybe we could get together and get stewed or something. You know what I could get for 10 cents, maybe we could use some of them.

I want to tell you about the burlesque show I saw January 13. There was a nice stripper and she took it all off G-string and all. Well, never having been to a burlesque in Boston I thought it was o.k. here. Well, last Saturday I went to the same burlesque and it was about like the Hartford theater. I thought it was a lousy show. I expected to see something like I saw before. Well, anyway I bought a paper tonight and here was this babe who took it all off in court. I am sending you the article. So if you ever see her name go see the show.

The next time you write Helena tell her there is a lonesome soldier in Boston. He never hears from his former girl.

When I heard Benny is in the Ozarks, I laughed like hell, that is just the place for him. I hope he stays there.

I had no fun with the Bag. That did it, I don't think she loves me anymore. What I need is a nice girl like Helena- a nice (pat, pat) soldier like me.

I gather from your letters that you are up and around. So therefore you must be feeling better, that is if you ever felt bad.

I'll bet it was fun watching someone get slit open. Too bad it wasn't a woman, you might have learned something

Well, I guess that will be all for now. If I get home I'll call you, if you don't hear from me and you are home call my Aunt. Maybe she will know where I am. If you change your address and I mine write to me in care of my Aunt and write forward on it. She'll send it to me.

Love and kisses for the Waves,
Joe

U.S. Naval Station
Sampson, New York
February 29, 1944

Dear C H A S –

I am taking part in what is called "Sampson's physical fitness program for the outgoing unit." Unloading these fucking freight cars.

No kidding I was going to write sooner but I expected to be shipped out at any time. It is two weeks now and I am still here. Last weekend I went home on a 48 hour pass .It was a mad rush but it was worth it. Yesterday we changed barracks and have a new CPO. so I'll try again for a 48 hr.

I've asked for Quartermaster school but most likely I'll end up on some sea draft.

Oh, well, glassy, don't write to me until I get "put!" I'll drop you a card with my new address soon (I hope).

Love and stuff,
Tony

The moon may kiss the sun on high,
The sun may kiss the butterfly,
The sparkling rain may kiss the grass,
And you my friend farewell.

17 Anise Street
New Britain, Conn.
March 4 1944

Hi, Chick!

How are you? Hot as heck, I bet. I really haven't much to tell you but I thought I'd write anyway.

We had a man with a tractor come down and plow the lot and the garden in back. We have the part in back already planted. Narcums and Neubauers are going to use part of the lot for a garden, too.

Daddy painted the tables and chairs for under the apple tree. I suppose the "Beer Parties" will start pretty soon. I can't wait?? They had one over at Neubauer's Sunday.

Mother got her candy and card Saturday. The card was very pretty and Mother liked it a lot. The candy must have been in a very hot place because you could see it had melted a little and it was a funny color but it tasted o.k. None of us died yet anyway.

Jean and I were going to go to the Girls League Formal with two boys from Hartford but now I don't know. Everything is getting mixed up. (I'll tell you about it if I go.) Billy is going with Shirley James just in case he hasn't told you. She's some sketch.

Jean and I are going over to "Mazie" Domijans in a little while to see if we go to Hartford with her when she picks up her sister. We just love to ride in her car. (More darn fun.)

That's all for now.

Love and kisses and stuff,
Betty

P.S. Don't work too hard.

65 Arthur Street
New Britain, Conn.
March 9, 1944

Dear Charlesie,

How's my little "darlin?" Does you miss your Dickey-Wicky? (Aw right, ya clown, stop pulling my leg" you say).Glad to hear that you're recovering from the out-of-this-world fling in the "blood pit." I swear, "darlin," I feel as if I'm in the pit and this damned "burgh" is the "pendulum." I'm going "nuts" – but definitely. I take one look in the mirror – Scream!! Then I say to myself, "Damn it, Walton, but you're getting fat and ugly." I don't know what makes me say that but after this little soliloquy I beat my head (with the lead in it) with my fist, and then I proceed to smash my other head against the wall. (Doesn't it sound exciting?)

Since you left I've done nothing but rot and corrode. Monday I stayed in the house all day. Pardon! I took the garbage and papers out. Today I did something different for a change. I stayed home. What I need is something sensational to happen to me. I need a new love or some kind of inspiration. I'll go mad if something doesn't happen. Mother has made things interesting for me though. She's had me varnish a few things etc, Today I had to put in a new garbage pail (underground). The bottom fell out of the old one and froze. As a result I had to get down on my hands and knees and take the damned stuff out with my bare hands. All this meat and no potatoes! What fun!! Scre – ew- ew 'em. Mom has the crazy gleam in her eye. You know, she thinks I'm another Rembrandt.

Say, what in hell are you doing in the hospital? Is it your glands or just another attack of "Lackanookie?" I think that I feel the same as you, I doubt that I'll get my stuff until I take the fatal step. Talking about getting married, I was reading Guy de Maupassant book of short stories and came across the story "Wedding Night." Did you ever read it? What a sketch. I almost finished the book (reading only the hot stuff, of course) I've never become so passionate by reading a book in my life.

I mentioned that I went to Hartford Tues. I saw Lionel Hampton. What a jam session. The whole place was jumping. Oh, yes, do you know why the "Paper Doll" committed suicide? Well, "honeh" she found out that her mother was an old bag. Corn!! Reminds me of Meg.

Speaking of "Hot Pants," I haven't seen her nor heard from her since that Monday that we were out to her home. I'm definitely convinced that she'll never mean anything to me anymore.

I'll send that booklet back to you in the next letter, "darlin." This is your good friend and mine saying, "shake it easy!" Hear!! Write.

Hugs and kisses,
Dick

17 Anise Street
New Britain , Conn.
March 12, 1944

Dear Brother,

I guess it's about time one of us wrote.

I just got home from Drum Corps a while ago. We're getting our own drums pretty soon but I don't know whether we'll be able to bring them home or not. I hope so.

Everybody home is o.k. and I hope you are, too. Mother had the stitches taken out yesterday from her head. It certainly is a good thing she had them removed. (Bumps.)

It's just like spring today. Audry, Jean and I are going for a walk and are going to take some pictures.

I still don't know whether you're starting school over again.

New Britain lost the game last nite at New Haven. (Semi-Finals). They still have another chance at the championship though. The score was 27 – 36. The kids said that N.B. played an awful game. They didn't even have the Cheerleaders there. Some basketball team!!

Mother and Dad, Aunt Lena and Aunt Anna are going up to the farm this afternoon. Lena's come home and she wants to go up there to get some things. (gotta do the dishes).

Pa's calling me. The dishes are all done though.

Prince came to church this morning. He jumped on Fannys and Mothers back. It's a good thing he didn't see me. Two boys had to take him out. (Little Devil.)

So long for now.
Love,
Betty

U. S. Coast Guard
March 14, 1944

Dear Chas,

Received your letter yesterday. So – here I am today.

Did you have fun when you were home on leave? What were Joe and Dickey doing home? Did you get over to Cheryl's house and get your end in, or are you still a Virgin?

179

One of the boys got shot here about a week ago. One of the boys went out to the beach (open air) and some of the boys were going to have fun so they jumped him. Little did they know when they did that he had a 38. Oh, well, there are too many Coast Guardsmen anyway.

Are you still in Sick Bay? Write and tell me what you did on your leave. I'd like to know.

Well, there isn't anything else to write about so I'll close now and don't forget to tell me about your leave.

Freddy

17 Anise Street
New Britain, Conn.
March 15, 1944

Dear Son,

The days fly by so fast. Betty's been after me to write to you. You know how I like to write. There's not much to write about. Pa is working this week. Last week he loafed. But I guess from now on he will work steady.

We got two letters from you yesterday. Pa can't understand why you won't get a good mark. Is it going to be new work or is it much harder? Try hard anyway.

Pa just got home and we had supper. Betty and Donny aren't home yet. Betty must be down to the Jive Hive or else to the show, it's 5:30.

We took a ride up to Barty's Sunday. Aunt Lena, Aunt Anna, Billy and Donny. He is still up there living like a hermit. Where Lena lived it looks like gun molls live there. They have pigs, ducks, chickens, cows and everything else.

Betty just blew in, she was at the movies.

I haven't seen Dickey Walton around. I wonder if he joined up yet.

One of Nellie's boarders came back home. Nellie isn't working yet. I saw her over to Westermans. They were both sick in bed with the flu so I went down to see them. Everything is alright in the neighborhood. Well, I guess that's all for now.

Love from all,
Mother

Did the Dr. give you a good check-up when you went back? How is your ear?

232 Mountain Drive
West Hartford, Conn.
March 15, 1944

Dear Charlie,

This is the second letter I've started to you in two days. The minute I get something started the herd comes in from their class and I have to stop everything just for a little old shorthand. This is my very last day of school and I'm not going to do one blessed thing to exert myself. Yesterday I passed my 120 w.p.m. shorthand and I'll never miss what I would learn today.

Guess who was in yesterday? It was "Shep." – she came here to school, you know. What a knockout she is! I never got a real good look at her before, but now that I have – Wow! She even had me drooling.

I was terrifically sorry that you were late. Did they do anything to you or are you in the hospital for the heck of it? When I read your letter I burst out laughing and my mother was quite sure, even though you said it wasn't my fault, I was at the bottom of the whole thing. Oh, by the way, what are you trying to do, ruin my "rep" and break up my little romance? Gad! Ben will really think that I'm getting to be quite the gay girl instead of the virtuous angelic thing he once knew. Anyway I told Mom that it wasn't my fault because I was such an alluring creature that men couldn't bear to leave me. (cynical laugh)

I had a letter from my friend at Tufts yesterday. He said that he would have been down for the weekend, but, alas! Money was the cause of it all. He lost all his money and $25 of someone else's, probably in a crap game, he didn't say. I wrote and told him that as soon as he got paid he could run right down and see me and meanwhile I would devise ways for us to spend it. Just an unscrupulous gold-digger!

I got the earrings last Tuesday and they're the sweetest things. You're a darling to send them to me – I really didn't think you meant it when you said you would. All the girls at school wanted to know where I got them and where they could get a pair. You couldn't pick up a couple more for all of us, could you? (kidding, of course). Next time I bake cookies (Oh, pardon me, you know my secret) – next time my Mother bakes cookies I'll send you some.

We went over to Cheryl's last Sunday. She has a new dog. It's a red cocker spaniel and her name is Debbie – she jumps all over and is quite the lively little thing.

Cheryl doesn't think you will write to her anymore. She said she thinks you were quite annoyed, but I said, "Oh, sure, sure he'll write. He's not mad." She keeps asking me if you mentioned her and of course I always say no, you keep your love life to yourself – what love life?!

181

I went to see "Song of Russia" Saturday night. Robert Taylor isn't as good at Paul Henreid and I couldn't learn anything from him. Guess I'll have to see "In Our Time" again. Either that or learn from experience. Oh, boy!

Nancy is coming home this weekend. There's a dance Saturday night. Morry has been calling her quite often and is supposed to be on the water wagon for a time.

I haven't been reading very much lately either. Now that I'm out of school I won't have any homework so I can read all evening. That is if there isn't anything more exciting to do. I wish this damned war were over – I'm sick of going home and putting my hair up just because I know that no one will be over. Oh, well, things are rough all over—

Ben had his exams last week and said if he didn't pass them he'd be slapped back in boot camp. It would be swell to see him again, but not as a result of failing his exam. I hope you built up my cold to him – from what I said to him he had the idea that I had pneumonia, I guess.

Well, I really must be running now. I'm a full fledged "woiking goil" now and have to be punctual and efficient just like Rosalind Russell. Do you think I should wear a gardenia every day like the secretaries in the movies? On the money I'm getting, hankies would be cheaper and besides, I like orchids better.

Mary sends her regards—she feels good now—she just passed 50 w.p.m. in typing.

> *Affectionately,*
> *Helen*

> *17 Anise Street*
> *New Britain, Conn.*
> *March 15, 1944*

Dear Charlie,

Well, Kid, what's been the matter with you? Mother or I didn't get a letter from you in about 10 days. Mother's been sick all week too and that made it worse. You could have at least written a few lines to say that you were o.k. The next time you'll know better (I hope).

We've had a swell week for vacation and we go back to school Monday. Mother and I are house-cleaning this week.

Donny's been down to Cabeluses practically all week. He coming home this afternoon and he's going to get some shoes with Mother.

Jean and Margie Ziegler had their tonsils out Wednesday. They're almost all better now though.

The other night Mrs. Domejan and I went out to Roy's about 10:30. We had more fun. You see we didn't have enough money to pay the bill, but we explained to the waiter and he gave us coffee and ice cream for nothing. We just had enough for the sandwiches. After we went over to see a Navy plane that was in Hartford. The motor cut at about 2,000 feet but the pilot brought the plane down. He landed in sort of a swamp so the plane was all stuck in the mud. The pilot was an ensign and he was quite nervous about the whole thing. On the way home we almost froze, we couldn't get the top up on the car but we didn't care. That Mrs. D. certainly is a scream. That's all for now.

Love,

Betty

P.S. I see that you had enough time to write to Dickey.

Naval Keystone Schools
Bedford Springs, Pa.
March 16, 1944
(post card)

Dear Charlie –

As I think I have already told you I am still here at Bedford studying radio. Not a bad place after all. I've lost track of Benny. So when you answer this card, which I hope is soon, send me his address. So long, glassy.

Tony

Write soon.

65 Arthur Street
New Britain, Conn.
March 16, 1944

Dearest "Charlesie-warlsie,"

How is my little "eager-beaver? I'll wager that you, in the midst of all your "toidy-toid street" pals, are edging ahead with every opportunity that presents itself. That's why I love you so much, "happy head." Seriously though, Charlie, that was a tough break to be pushed ahead the way that you were. The nerve of them! Don't they realize whom they were dealing with? I'd quit if I were you. Tell them to keep their damn Navy. All right, "ya clown," you can dream, can't you?

I tried your cure for boredom, honey. It seemed to work perfectly up until the time where "it" gets hard. The damn varnish drips slimy – like from my tool while it (meaning my sex-stick) sticks up as big as life. Then what else have I to do but beat it. The next thing I know I'll be synthesized with a bottle of glue. Would you like to screeeew me then? What an experience that would be.

I meant to tell you about picking up some "stuff" in Hartford when I went up to see Hampton. I met her inside while I was at the ice cream bar. She was O.K. We sat together, and felt the same. Her turn, then my turn. It was something to talk about anyway. I had a couple of orgasms by just looking at her and then told her to screeeew. It happens all in a lifetime. Speaking of a lifetime, listen to this. I was sitting in the Drug Store Monday afternoon when a cute little brunette walks in. I looked at her a couple of times and "junior jumped." This meant something, so I thought I'd try to get acquainted. I asked about her and learned that she was going to the Teacher's College. So "Joe Gob to be" picked up the phone Mon. nite and got acquainted with the little woman. Everything was going fine (I'm coming!-) until I asked her for a date. Then she told me – she was engaged. I told her she was a "dead head" for being so situated. Oh, yes, I also asked her if that were a condition or a disease. I probably could have talked her into a date, but I want untouched stuff – you know.

Tomorrow nite I'm going to a "Shin-dig" at the College gym. I'm going with a girl by the name of Betty Rindge. I have been trying to meet her by going over to the Lounge for a while during the last couple of days. Yesterday Patty Lou asked me to enroll. This King stuff is supposed to be nice. Oh, yes, I met this Mary Ellen Bradley. She's O.K.! I discovered that I had known her all of my life. Well, at least through my Junior High School days. I'm a miserable wolf since I got home. I'm going to ask that blond in Hausman's Record Shop for a date. Do you know her? Her name probably ends in "ski" but this is war – you know.

I saw Mickey in the Drug Store Monday. He was home on a 10 hour pass.

I'd better finish this letter and get the hell out of here before Mother puts me to work. Take care now, and have fun.

Pounds of passion,
Tricky Dickey

P.S. Just call me Atlas.

17 Anise Street
New Britain, Conn.
March 17, 1944

Dear Brother,

I finally went to the dentist today. I went to Dr. Johnson. He's o.k

We got another war bond today. I just thought you wanted to know. Tonite I'm going over to the church for a meeting. I think we might elect a new twirler. Tomorrow were going to have a St. Patrick's Day party at Sodality.

Spuddy was wounded flying over some city in Germany. Dutchie and Spuddy's wife got a telegram but it said he wasn't wounded badly and he'll be flying in a few days. Tessie's on vacation out in California so I guess she doesn't know about it.

Didn't the needles hurt that you gave each other? Were they the kind with the square points?

I saw the "Cross of Lorraine" yesterday. It was perfect. It was about some French soldiers in a German concentration camp. Gene Kelly was in it.

Where do you think you'll go when you leave Virginia? Well, I guess that's all for now.

Love from all,
Betty

17 Anise Street
New Britain, Conn.
March 20, 1944

Dear Brother,

Well, today's the first day of spring and you should see the snow. It's been snowing since this morning and hasn't stopped yet. It's about 4 or 5 inches deep.

I went to the movies after school. I saw "A Guy Named Joe." It was perfect.

I went to the dentist again but he still didn't fill my tooth. He said he'd fill it Thursday. I hope so. He's slower than Dr. Zering.

Margie Ziegler has Scarlet Fever and Jean and June are quarantined for 10 days. Eddy Ziegler left for the Navy this morning but he was called back and he's also quarantined.

What d'ye think, Jean Z. and I are taking baton lessons. I'm going for my second lesson Thursday (Jean won't be able to) It's quite hard but it's fun. It certainly requires lots of practicing.

185

About 200 fellows left this morning for the Navy. Lennie Narcum left too. They gave a farewell party for him Saturday night. We all went except Donny. We had a swell time.

I hope your work is going o.k. Be a good boy and study hard.

I guess I'll go to bed early. I have a headache. Goodnight –

Love,

Sister

65 Arthur Street
New Britain, Conn.
March 21, 1944

Well, "ha–u–honeh"

In your last letter you wrote that you were writing with your pen in one hand and your dong in the other. Well, I've got something on you. I'm sitting here with my dong in both hands, and I'm still writing you. Figure that one out, "ya "clown!!! You really stimulate me!!!

Thanks for giving me the info about "Dirty Gerty." I haven't looked into this stuff yet, but I intend to do so for the weekend. Speaking of women (or bags, "soree,")I got a letter from Pat. What do you think – she loves me, so she says. Well, I guess I love her as far as letters go. Who gives a damn? I'm getting good experience writing to her. Maybe I love her – who the hell knows? I think I'll stick to my tool!

I've just got to tell you about my latest. No, not my monthly. I went out with that Betty Rindge I told you about in my last letter. What a time! What a woman! I haven't named "it" yet. Maybe it was just a first impression. I'll know Thurs. nite for I have a date with her then. I also have a "walking date" with her tomorrow eve. Wheeeee. Enough of dis luffink, Let's begin wid de -or- Dearest, darest I??? Yes? Will send official communiqué on progress in future correspondence.

Incidentally, have you seen the picture "Lifeboat?" If you haven't, you must see it!! Tallulah Bankhead has a prominent role in it. Well, Tallulah kisses (I mean bites) a fella in the pic – and what an embrace. I'm telling you "Humphy" has nothing on her. I'd love to see "Bogy" and her get together (Whose got the larger tonsils?). Incidentally, my motto is "I'll take Tallulah." Oh, yes, our man Bogart is coming (no not that "ya" clown – he's not as emotional as I am) in "Passage to Marseilles." That's a "must see" as far as I'm concerned.

This morning I went up to the Hospital to visit an intern and watch some operations. I saw an appendectomy and the birth of a child. I

186

remembered the latter, especially for you. I'm laughing my scrotum off thinking of what I'm going to say. Here's a description. The delivery was performed in a very small room – about the size of an average "head." Pardon, slightly bigger. I walked in and was told to stand in back of the Doctor where I had a ringside seat. Well, here was the woman, flat on her back , legs strapped at a 45 degree angle, and "box" painted in bright red (Oh, yes, it was shaven). Have you ever seen sap drooling from a pine tree? That is exactly the way her box looked (I'll take Tallulah). First, the Doc took some green stuff and greased her old box as if he were washing the sides of a kitchen pot, and then he washed it out with something that looked like a seltzer bottle. Can you just picture Mary or Meg lying on their backs, their legs up, having a doctor lubricating the old crack and using seltzer water for a chaser. Wheeeee! To continue – the "doc" then took two big prongs, - meat hooks, I guess – greased them up and stuck them up there to grab Junior. I thought he was going to pull her whole damn insides out – ovaries and all. The damn kid wouldn't stick his head out, so the "doc" calmly picked up a pair of scissors and made the driveway bigger. Could you just picture Meg when the "Doc" told her that he had cut her box? Wheeeee! Now the spook can get his in!!! Gosh, am I silly and "durdy." The kid finally poked his head out and came flyin' out with a "gush" of blood as if you were being thrown out of Josephine's Palace of Joy for taking the onions, vegetables etc away from the Madame, you know. The "doc' finally cut the umbilical chord and threw the kid on the "meat wagon". He then proceeded to pull the placenta and other membranes from the unpregnant darlin', sewed up "the old dirt road" and asked me if that were a good demonstration. He seemed to have enjoyed it. That was just a description from the comical point of view. From the practical side, it was really quite a thing to watch. Very revealing and I'm one that can be "revealed" or something. I hope you get to watch something like this someday.

Spring really came in with a bang yesterday. Ten "lousy" inches of snow. My damn back is broke. No, not from ploughin' – from shoveling.

I guess that Launa hasn't written, has she? Oh, Chop Fooey!!! Love is such a cheat – 'S wonderful tho!!!

Let's be bachelors, O.K.? That way we can cheat a woman out of a divorce and never make the same mistake once. You also know that married men have better halves, and single men have better quarters. Oh, have you heard? A hotel is a place where a guest often gives up good dollars for poor quarters. Wheeeee!

Well, my "blitzkrieg baby, I'm comin', so I'd better sign off before I spatter y'all. Take care and remember me on the fifth, or will it take that long?

I'll conclude this rehearsal with love by saying love me or leave me! Nite, love!!

Yours alone,
Padoodles of passion,
Dick

232 Mountain Drive
West Hartford, Conn.
March 21, 1944

Hello, my sweet,

Pretty good at reciprocation, don't you think? Pay no attention, it's just the thought of spring. Gad! You should see the snow we have here. I'd like to go on a sleigh ride – I don't know why – the same results could be produced at home on the divan. My mind's in the gutter, but I don't mind as long as I have your company.

Poor dear! – Did I get you all confused about whether I was through school or not? When I saw you I had about a week and a half more of school but I had already started my job – working part time. I finished school on the 15th and then started working full time on the 16th. Does that clear up the little mystery?

I'm sorry I can't type all my letters. I haven't got a typewriter at home. I think they look a lot neater (impersonal though), but I find it hard to type 'cause I can't get the words down fast enough.

I haven't written to Ben in a week and a half. I don't know what's the matter with me – I'm in a mood, I guess, and can't decide whether I want to write or not.

He passed his exams and now I suppose he'll be shipped again. You had yours today, didn't you? Let me know how you made out – I'm anxious to know if my prayers have any power.

You will probably be disappointed to know that you can't blame Cheryl for the dog's name. It came with the animal and I'd like to get a look at the person who did name her! It's certainly something that no one else could think of.

E'Gad! Do you realize the trouble you would be getting yourself into if I told Cheryl that you were all broken up, etc, etc? No doubt, she'd want to write you and beg your forgiveness. From the way she talks, she is sorry and admits she was quite snippy about the whole evening. I think I shall be the innocent bystander in this event.

Nancy was home for the weekend. Oh, that situation makes me shiver! As long as I've known Nan, I've never seen her like this. Is it love? I've been in and out of love so many times I don't recognize the symptoms anymore. It's great to be fickle!

This is a gay letter – I haven't told you one new thing. Maybe that's because nothing new happens. My next one will be better and longer, too.

Affectionately,
Helen

R.I. School of Design
March 22, 1944

Dear Charlie,

Been a long time since I've written to you, hasn't it? Did you think I'd fallen into the Providence River? Well, sometimes it's an idea. Thanks, dear, for the earrings. I like them very much and so do my roommates. It seems the Navy has done it again this season and the two of them took a fancy to my birthday present. It's really funny the attention they attract.

So, you were home and you didn't even call me – wanted to see me a lot, didn't you? Oh, well, never mind my father loves me. You said Dick was home – how is he? I haven't heard from him in yars & yars. Tell me, has Meg still got a priority on him? No, I'm not in love with him – but I am in love – damn it all. It's the most unsettled state to be in. It seems I fall out of love with one guy and I have to fall in love with another – so therefore I'm perpetually in love. Confused? So am I.

I've really been having some gay old times lately. Never drank so much as I have in the last two weeks. I'm getting to know every bartender in town. But I'm afraid I had better cut it out 'cause my friends are beginning to worry – they're sure I'll get in trouble sometime when I'm feeling gay – what kind of trouble they won't say – but trouble. Maybe you'd better start praying for my soul again.

It seems, honey, that the hospital is giving you the blues. Don't let it get you down. If you weren't there you'd be in some other hole – so why let it make that blonde hair white. Are you sure, dear, you had Scarlet Fever? Tell me, how's the Mole? And how are the rest of the patients? Any thing interesting? You know I'm always looking for new prospects – gotta keep

189

the business going. If people judged me from my letters they'd think I was another Joan Jones. Remember her – McEnerney's little friend.

Some fool has Guy Lombardo on, and it's driving me nuts. Say, are you going to be home for Easter? I've got three days and that's the last time I'll be home till almost July. From now on I'll spend my weekends in New York – I can hardly wait for the first one. We are going to cover the Waterfront so to speak. Emily and I have dates there. Since she lives just outside of New York there will be none of this curfew stuff that exists here at school. Emily, by the way, sends her love. Do you want it?

I'm so dead tired it isn't even funny. I've been going out too damn much – I'm going out tomorrow night again – I was out tonight. Last weekend was really a big one – I'm still recuperating. Rum is hell to drink straight, I know.

People are invading the privacy I've been enjoying till now, so I'll have to close – also have a date at 12:30 which is slightly against the rules. It's now 12:00, so I'll have to close. This damn fool is going to the South Pacific and it's the last time I'll be able to see him. So write to me soon, baby.

Love & stuff,
Lucy

17 Anise Street
New Britain, Conn.
March 28, 1944

Dear Brudder,

Yeah, heh, I usta go out wit dat kid you was talkin' about. I tink his name was Henry Siminski. Da boat of us always usta hang about da corner of Broad & Gold. We went to show once and he got mad on me and I ain't saw him since den. (I guess I told you)

Well, I went to the dentist again today. My tooth still isn't filled though.

We went to collect for the Red Cross in the Embassy today, but the manager said they had too many today but to come tomorrow. We had already been to the Strand so we didn't want to collect there again.

All the eight inches of snow are gone and it's raining like heck. (It's been raining cats and dogs all day and I just stepped on a poodle.) Ha, Ha!

I haven't hit anyone or thing with the baton yet. (I mean hard). I really haven't got a good place to practice though. The beams down the cellar are too low and I tried the dog house but it's too small. I'll be able to practice outside in a few weeks so I guess I'll manage.

Prince certainly is a little devil. Every time Dad goes out of he yard with the truck, he has to go too . If he doesn't let him go, Prince follows the truck all the way downtown. A couple of times on Main Street when Dad opened the door to get out, Prince jumped in. (He's a little devil)

Yesterday it was just like spring. (It is spring)Mary Willisel took a ride up to Roy's (new place). It's a nice place. Well, I'd better hang up now. I've got to practice a couple more movements on my "Shapleigh Stick."

Love,

Betty

P.S. Is your cold all gone and do you feel better now? I hope so.

65 Arthur Street
New Britain, Ct.
March 28, 1944

Dear "Bluebeard,"

How are ya' my lil' hunka temptation? We've had rain for the last few days, but as one says — after the rain comes the sunshine, so here it is as big as life and beatin' for the touch of your fairy-like hand. Dearest, darest we?? You're dangerous!! I'll be a friend "with pleasure."

O.K. now that the overture is over, over-sexed Walton will lightly and politely send some of the dirt etc. your way. Anything for you my, Blitzkrieg Baby. Love me or leave me, ya' clown.

I'm pleased to hear that you did so well on your finals. Does that 2/10ths of a point mean the difference between a rate, etc? If the Navy doesn't give it to you, tell 'em to pound sand, and tell them to rotate on this (midfinger) for a while and when they get up to the elbow whistle!! Wheeeee wouldn't that be a wonderful sensation? Oh, I'm in a lovable mood tonight!! Tell me with your kisses.

You say that we are two foolish virgins. True! True! But I love us, don't you? The feeling is mutual as far as liking each other. We had some great times together, 'darlin'" The more I see or hear of you, the more I like or respect you. I hope that nothing ever changes this. I'm in full approval of either type of trip. We would have a great time, I know. Somehow these thoughts seem so far away though. I only hope that these ideas will materialize some day. We'll probably do this by hobbling along on canes — old age.

I feel that we're being cheated out of so much, Charlie. I think that right now I'm at the most reckless point of my life. It seems that I'd do anything

191

– anything. Somehow I'm being held back. Enuf of dis luffink, let's fu–. Oh, well, I think too much anyway.

I just eat up that idea about tradin' wives. Wheeeee! Could we have fun! Just think we could become polygamists. Better than that we could travel. We could have a couple of wives in every port. Papa Divine would have nothing on us. "Screw 'em and leave." That would be our motto. We could have agents in all parts of the country who would make all of our bookings. We could call ourselves "The Passionate Polygamists." You really, really charge me – Katherine Hepburn style. Do you approve?

I went to the State Friday nite and literally urinated in my pants laughing at a comedian. Durdy and sexy as all hell!! Wheeeee! I only wish you were there. Boy! Could we quote and make hash of the stuff he flung us! Do you know that the taxi drivers in Boston are having a contest knocking down pedestrians? If you get knocked down in a Safety Zone there is no score registered. However, you get three points for women, four points for men, and when you hit one of those boogies the game is over!! I'd better watch out, huh? There were a number of cracks that he pulled, but they were too numerous to mention.

I haven't seen Ginger since that night that she had me in such an uproar. She's probably moved to "The House of the Good Shepherd." I hardly ever see "Hot Pants." She and Morry are always hibernating. I wouldn't be surprised if she's lost her cherry. He must have a long one!

I dated "dirty Gerty" last night. We had a very nice time. She was a lot of fun. I've got another date with her, but I don't think I could fall for her. This Rindge "stuff" is good "goods" too. Last week I took a walk with her Wed. nite, had a sexy time with her Thurs. afternoon and nite and almost started "doin' things" Friday nite. Gosh, does she love her lovin'. I also have it on good authority that she is as bad as the OPA as far as rationing that stuff goes. I've got so much of it that I'm almost sick of it. I've got a parlor date with her at her home tomorrow nite. I guess I'll have to wizz the wizz four or five times or I'll probably have an ejaculation.

By going out with Betty I've come to a few definite conclusions. To begin with, I'm positive I never liked or loved Meg the way that I thought. Betty is wonderful, probably the nicest girl I've met. She has plenty on the ball but I know I'd never get serious over her. What I'm trying to say is that I'm afraid I'll probably never really fall in love enough to get married. I'll do it because it's an old age custom and it's the proper thing to do — either that or a shotgun. I'm crazy talking like this, aren't I?? I wouldn't tell this to anyone else but you. I guess that you and I are the only ones that understand each other when we start talking like this. Furthermore, I've come to admire you a lot. That is, you're absolutely positive that Launa is what you want. No matter what happens that thought will remain foremost in your mind, and until you finally get her you'll never be satisfied. On the other hand, I'm living from fling to fling or flame to flame and getting nowhere. I only hope that someday I'll have the absolute determination that you have. Till then I'll be misbehavin' against myself. Oh, incidentally, Patty Lou is a very close friend of Betty's. Betty says that she knows Launa.

It's disheartening for me to hear that you may be sent out of the country. Nevertheless, if that's the way you feel you'll be satisfying yourself, that's best. Why don't you write Launa before you leave, or would she refuse to receive it? Damn that woman!!! But remember, my pet, they say that love makes time pass and time makes love pass!

I received word from Dick Farrell last week. He's still in the hospital. The letter was written on ordinary stationery, so he may even be in this country or nearer home than he was before. He seemed in good spirits.

It won't be long now and I'll be taking my physical. I only hope that I have nothing wrong with me. You can imagine how I feel.

In closing, my sweet, I'd like to leave you with a few words of wisdom. To begin with, I'm convinced that a little woman is a dangerous thing and that they are made to be loved and not understood. Finally, beware of the man who does not return your "blow", for he neither forgives you nor allows you to forgive yourself.

This letter has too much of a serious note to it to suit me. I hope that it suits the mood you're in when you read it.

I really enjoyed that joke of yours. I'll circulate it. Mary and Meg will appreciate it.

I'll bet that Lucy will want to join us! I'll just tell her that I'm a meteorologist and that I can look into her eyes and tell "weather." I'll make it a point to write to her when I get into the Navy. Take care and think of me, "darlin", you know when. I'm yours, "honeh" till the quail come back to San Quentin. Write when you can.

Love me!
Dick

-FIVE-

CAMP LEJEUNE, NORTH CAROLINA 1944

AFTER THE PITS OF Portsmouth, my hospital training at the Naval Hospital in Memphis turned out to be a pleasant break. Though the hospital was located on a barren scrub plain several miles out of town, the staff was congenial, the food and the living quarters, not half bad. Liberty was every other weekend; on one, I crossed the Mississippi River on a bus to Hot Springs, Arkansas, and I saw the great Bo Jangles tap dance.

The USO frequently held dances at the swank Hotel Peabody in downtown Memphis. It was there that I met Marietta Jones. The cute little brunette was a fabulous dancer. I did feel a little guilty but didn't consider dancing at the USO cheating on Launa. I felt otherwise, however, when after a second meeting with Marietta things warmed up.

Before anything serious could happen, the navy intervened. My medical training at the hospital was over. I was called down to the OD's office with half a dozen other guys. Fingers crossed, I hoped to receive orders to report for sea duty aboard a battlewagon or a cruiser, perhaps even one of the new super flattops.

"FMF," the Chief Petty Officer announced. There was a sadistic smirk on his face as he chomped on a cigar and shuffled through the stack of papers before him. "Fleet Marine Force," he continued. "You, shitbirds, forget the navy. From now on you're Gyrenes."

Stunned, I looked at the officer. Marines? Holy shit. He had to be kidding.

"The stupid jarheads don't have their own medical corps," the prick went on as I listened in disbelief. "We supply them with corpsmen. You'll get the full scoop once you get your asses to Lejeune."

Lejeune was sand flats and scrub pine—boot camp all over again. For eight weeks under the hot North Carolina sun we sweated out daily trips to the rifle range and dueled with fixed bayonets. We crawled on our bellies under barbed wire, tossed grenades, and waded through tropical swamps on night maneuvers. On one Saturday night liberty, I rode a rickety bus into nearby Jackson for two or three hours. The little hick town did not have a movie house, ice cream parlor, or bowling alley. At a hole-in-the-wall photo studio in a side alley, I had a picture taken in my marine uniform. Before leaving the town, I followed the example of my buddies and picked up a bottle of champagne, the only liquor available in the town that was supposed to be dry. Back at the base, I sat in the pine forest beside the river, champagne corks popping about me in the dark, and silently wondered how in hell I'd gotten here—and more importantly, where I was headed next.

17 Anise Street
New Britain, Conn.
March 29, 1944

Dear Son,

Just received your telegram saying you were in Tenn. I hope you will like it there – so glad to hear that you got a better rating. We received your other telegram yesterday and will get all of the papers out by tomorrow night.

Pa is working up in Hartford tonight. Mabel Ballard is opening a new store so John and him worked last night until 11 o'clock. I hope he finishes tonight for it's too much for hm. He's so tired when he gets home he can just about stand up. Just as soon as he has a nite off we have to straighten out the garage. We started Mon. nite but didn't get very far. Donny's getting to be quite a helper. He went down to the Boy Scout meeting to-nite and Betty is still juggling her baton.

I saw Merton today, he looked swell and got much fatter. He is going to be stationed in Indiana, I think this is his first furlough.

I'm glad you bought yourself a watch. I was thinking about getting you one but they are so expensive here. You can probably buy a better one reasonable. You didn't say whether you wanted your razor sent or not.

I didn't see that picture yet but if I don't see it I'll wait until it comes to the Palace. Freddy won't be home in April—all leaves were cancelled, I bet he's wild.

The guild had a cake sale today and I had to bake one for them. I called Father Brophy about a recommendation and he was very nice about it, he wanted to know how you were. He said to send Betty over after it today but he wasn't home. So Betty will have to go over tomorrow again.

I wonder if it will be as hot down there as in Va. I think Tommy was sent across. He came as far as New York. I think he will be sent to England. Aunt Anna said he was all banged up. He was riding a jeep down in California with a couple other fellows and they hit a tree. They thought he was killed.

Well, Son I guess I told you all the news and hope you will like your new place. So write and tell us all about it and the city of Tenn. It's raining cats and dogs and Betty said she stepped on a poodle. I guess it's mostly hail. I thought the winter was over but it's just beginning. Don just got home, he said that he got an awful sore throat. Well, that's all for now.

Love from all,
Mother

Torpedo Squadron 29
FPO New York, N.Y.
March 30, 1944

Dear Charles,

I got your letter yesterday and was glad to hear from you because I wasn't sure whether my letter would get to you or not. Excuse the pencil and the dirt marks on the paper but I am on watch now and I haven't any better implements.

I have this weekend off starting tomorrow when we get secured but we can never tell when that will be. Boy, I have never worked so hard since I have been in the Navy or, for that matter, never. We start out at 0700 and finish up at eleven or twelve at night. For the last two weeks I have flown at least eight hours and usually twelve or fourteen a day.

You asked about the old town. Well, it is the same as it was when you left. I haven't been home in a month. The last weekend I had I went to New York.

I took my second class tests Monday and I am now sweating it out hoping that it will come through and I will get it starting April 1st because otherwise I will have to wait until May 1st. Of course, that is if I passed the test.

So you are going to ship out soon. Well, I wish the hell we would pretty soon. We are supposed to go in about three months but I think it will be sooner than that.

Well, I think I will have to close now and take the jeep up to the canteen. We now have beer on the base. So long and write soon.

Mick

I hear that Launa is going to college here in New London. Is that right? Are you still carrying the torch?

232 Mountain Drive
West Hartford, Conn.
March 30, 1944

Hi, my pet!

You are truly a bete noir – getting me all excited with your line. Anyway, I'm glad I'm on your list of favorites. Now just close your eyes and imagine my eyelids fluttering while I say I like you, too. I don't think your method of classification is unique, though, for it is pretty general that we all like certain people for what they are; and put up with others for business or social reasons. It's the dislikes that really bring people out. Some people can hide their feelings and be as sweet as honey to those they dislike. But woe is me! I can't make like I love somebody when I really want to drive a blade in their back. Them's harsh words, I know, but when I dislike somebody I make them know it.

Lord, I must be off the beam – I miss all the good movies. Anyway I don't think I could get any thrill out of the biting technique. Wasn't there something in "Jane Eyre" about her drinking his life's blood? Gad, I always knew that love brings out the animal in you, but I've been taught a better way of satisfying the passionate desire. I have reserved the front seat of the early-bird show for Bogart's next picture and I'll bash anyone's head in who tries to keep me from seeing it.

I'm in the office with nothing to do and every time someone sallies forth to my desk I have to make like I'm doing important work on some government project. How do you like their stationary? I think, the texture is very nice but the letterhead seems to be missing something – my name, no doubt!!

Would you like to learn another French expression besides "Mon Dieu"? I think you could use this a lot. Whenever you want to say No?, Isn't it?, Don't you think so?, etc, anything like that, just say N'est-ce pas? (pronounced ness pa). Literally it means, "Is it not?" but it's used idiomatically for anything you want to say. You don't have to use this, you know, your letters are amusing anyway.

I must tell you about Bob Hope's program – I do hope you didn't hear it although it is funnier to hear Hope than to read about him. Well, anyway, they were comparing today's soldier with one from the Civil War, all of it taking place in the South. So he says to Frances Langford, "Gee, that's a pretty dress you have on, Francie." To which she returns, "Sho 'nuf?" Then Hope breaks out with, "I've got a line here but NBC won't let me read it!!" It is really funny – go back and read it again. Do you like "Blondie"?

The comic strip, of course. The enclosed was in the paper last night and I thought it was pretty good.

I've left fiction to its own devices for a while and am now reading "Only the Stars are Neutral." When you told me about it, I decided that I would have to be "in the know" so I could be on your intellectual level. I think it's quite good and the style in which it is written is easy to read for a brain as meager as mine. I would like to tackle "Journey Among Warriors," but it looks so long that I am prone to staying away from it. Did you say you liked it and do you think I would enjoy it?

March 31, 1944

Don't you feel like an executive having me use the real business form for a two-page letter? Note the date—this is my second day on your missile. A few other important matters came up and took my attention from you.

Last Sunday Mother and I went to see my little niece. Hazel (my sister-in-law) just returned from Florida, visiting my brother, and she is a nice cocoa brown color. My brother has been promoted to Staff Sergeant and he is waiting to bet sent to Texas to O.C.S. He has all the brains, ingenuity and all those accomplishments of the family and we are very proud of him. The baby is darling. She hasn't quite reached the age where she wants to be fussed with and she seems perfectly content to be left alone. I'm just dying to take her out for an airing and show her off to all my friends. I can just see myself if I ever have one of my own. I'm definitely one of those people who think a home isn't complete without the patter of little feet.

Maybe I'd better be an old maid and help you bring up your children to be bachelors. Don' dwell on being a bachelor too much – you know what God said, "It isn't good for man to be alone, so-o-o-o I will make him a mate". Your "Eve" must be floating around somewhere.

I haven't been smoking very much lately. A couple of weeks ago I had an unhappy experience with a match. The darn thing flared and singed my alluring curly eyelashes. On me it didn't look good so I gave up for a while.

I had a long conversation with Cheryl the other night. We didn't talk about anything important. Once in a while dragged you in and she is quite reconciled that she isn't going to hear from you. I didn't offer anything – it's sad but true.

Nancy is fine. She asks for you once in a while. Well, I can see this is getting boring, but you can't expect anything else. Look at the long letter I've written you!

> *Affectionately,*
> *Helen*

Afterthoughts –

I'm terribly sorry about your exams. You'll have a chance to try again soon, won't you?

What the devil does the "m" mean in S.W.A.M.K? I don't get around enough to know.

Oh, and if you address my letters "Miss Helena" anymore, I won't write to you for a month!

> 65 Arthur Street
> New Britain, Conn.
> April 3, 1944

Dear Charlesie (and gentlemen of the jury)

Get ready for some quack, Jack. Great news is in the making!! No, Not that!! I have my ideas about "that." I'll let you know about them later in the note. Yes, sir, my little chum, you're "gonna" laff your little ballsies off!! Wheeeee. Great news is in the making.!!

Now that I've got your "pugnacious pole of passion" poundin' passionately, I'll give ya' a bit of dirt here-a and there-a. You know – this loafin' isn't so bad! I'm enjoying myself now and then (mostly then). I've been studying in quite a bit abusing myself. Yessireee, I'm really getting to know that my parents are more than fixtures. I think that I'm wise by doing so, for these days may seem precious to both my parents and me when I am gone. Sounds as if I were going to beat myself into oblivion. The last time I wrote to you was last Tuesday. Since then, I've had a couple more dates with Betty Rindge. Wheeeee.!! Shall we call them "starchin' sessions"? I'm really becoming attached to that bag. I think that she really, really loves me. I know that she doesn't mean much to me, for I never yearn for her when I'm separated from her. But when we're together I have a great time and like her a lot. (You know what just struck me funny – I'll bet Hot Pants could eat apple pie through a picket fence. What a jaw – but you should see her offspring – brats to you.)As I was saying – oh, yes, I'm a second Humphrey Bogy. Last Friday nite I got sick and tired of dat conventional vacillating, so I said to her, Enough of dis loving, let's start lounging. I cautiously gave her larynx a sleigh ride with my tongue and almost choked her. I had her lying prostrate on the couch and I was kneeling at her side. I discovered that she hasn't any lack of emotion. The funny thing is that I don't think she knows whether I am serious or not. As I said before – she loves me. I'm pretty popular with myself, aren't you, Dick?? Ya clown! I hope that you get to meet "Bet" someday, Charlie. I'm sure that you'd like her. She's lovable and sociable! Yes, you're just the boy that would do it. What lips she has too – ya know that means tail, don't ya, darlin'??

Speaking of "tail" please don't get your piece while you're away from me. Someday we'll be together again and maybe we can both get it at the same time. Wouldn't we have a hell of a time?? Maybe we could both get into the same gal at the same time. That would be a circus!!! You'd probably take up most of the room and I'd have to be content on chewin' on her hairs. Who would you like to screw with me? Got any good suggestions??? Maybe we could run down and catch Eleanor in the White House someday even though she's always "on the run".

Oh, yes, great news is still in the making. Wait til you read it. I'm sorry to hear that you missed your rate. I guess that it is true—they must draw the line someplace. But what's this "1/c" on the envelope? That doesn't mean that you've lost your "2/c" because of missing your rate? Oh, what am I beating my gums for? "1/c" is higher than "2/c" rating. You see what I mean? Too much "tool" and you can't think straight.

Well, darlin', I'm 1-A with Uncle Sam. I went to the draft board today and asked that my deferment be cancelled, and that I be placed in 1-A. That I was – no doubt. What da ya tink, heh? I'm a volunteer now. Gee, "ain't I brave!!! Ya clown.

In that I'm listed as a volunteer, I'm granted my preference of any branch of service etc. so I'm fairly sure of getting into the Navy. I go up for my physical in New Haven on April 20ᵗʰ. Oh joy, all the fun I'm going to have. (I'll have a great description for you). I wonder if the doctor will be one of those booooys. Wheeeee. I'll bet they get hungry as hell looking at all those tools. After the 20ᵗʰ (if I pass my physical) I'll receive a 24 day furlough. That means I'll be leaving about the third week in May. All in all if everything goes "reet" I'll have about 38 more days to spend here at home.

Well, I might as well tell you what the great news is "honeh". Here it is!! I hope you laff. I did when I heard the news! No, I'd better wait till later in the note to tell you. I received a letter from "Cowboy Joe Donnelly" Friday. He's down in San Antonio, Texas. All the old guard is still in good ole New Britski. Morry is still here (with Elmer). Can you imagine Morry having to work in a war plant? That's what the latest fad from Washington is. All 4-F"s are going to be drafted onto industry. He'll probably lose his face and hair in a grinding machine. Wheeeee! Then he'll be like Elmer again. The gruesome twosome. I hope the hell I'm not 4-F. If I am, I think that I'll knock out my teeth and join Morry and Elmer. What a company – Morry, Elmer and Screwy (me).

Well, here's the big news!! Are you set? Seventeen girls in the high school are pregnant. (No, not me). Furthermore, all the girls in the school have to be examined. Gosh, would I love to be the examiner. I'll bet it was "The Spook." Wouldn't it be a howl if Meg or Mary were carrying something under their belts? I haven't got the full news on the "Sex fiend's" escapades but will try to keep you informed. Oh, "Screw Nuthin' Til Ya Hear From Me"! Did you like that bit of info? I think that I'll start a riot at this end of he town and rampage the Teacher's College. Balance things off, you know.

Oh, darlin, we do have fun, don't we? I also roar when I think of the fun we had and the views of life we have. I agree with your description of a woman, but doesn't she have two apertures at the bottom end? Or haven't you got that far?

I'm about all "writ" out until the next time. Hope that you are getting a great deal of enjoyment out of your new environment and all those Memphis Belles (in Sailor pants).

Take care, my li'l "Turtle". Don't forget to remember me. Hurry the whole process! Write as soon as you can. I love us, "Sugah."

Oodles of emotion,

Dick (the bull)

P.S. I'm very downhearted. I read last Thursday in a Medical Book that women are never sterile. How do you like that? Now they tell us!

232 Mountain Drive
West Hartford, Conn.
April 4, 1944

Dearest Charlie,

I just got back from seeing Mother off on a train to Canada and it is about 11:30 p.m. One of her sisters is ill so she tripped off for the weekend. You should have heard all the instructions I got about keeping the doors locked, and not speaking to strange men etc. I'd love to be going with her, but no can do and I'll probably have more fun at home. If this were pre-war I'd have a party.

I expect Nancy home this weekend. I stayed with her last weekend so maybe we can play turnabout this time. The kids in her dorm were caught smoking in their rooms so she is going to be confined for a month or so after this.

How's every little thing in Memphis? Tell me more about those Memphis Belles. You should know just how to treat possessive women. You know when I got your second letter with the surprise, for the first two paragraphs I expected that you were going to say that you had become engaged! Horror of all horrors!! Of course, after reading on I discovered that it was much better than that.

Since you mentioned my Easter array, I shall have to tell you about it. I decided on feminine clothes, but definitely, but I delayed so long in shopping that I didn't get exactly what I desired. Anyway, I appeared in low cut shoes with bows, a gay, light-hearted dress, and a dashing silly hat. The hat is really cute – it's a round affair that dips over one eye and has lots of veiling and stuff. Mother let me wear her mink furs, which were really smart and I felt like Lady Asterbilt though my wallet was flat.

Your schedule sounds pretty heavy. What do you do when you're on the job? I'm really interested more in what you do off the job, but I know that's none of my business.

You are now wearing your blue and whites, too. I'd like to see you. In fact, I'd like to see any man at this point!

I'm sorry you didn't like that French expression, but I'll try to think of something better.

Oh, I'm going to bed –– See you in the morning.

Sunday p.m.

This is the first chance I've had to get back to this. I've had a pretty good weekend, but I'm all by my lonesome tonight and I don't like it one bit. I'm dead tired and should go to bed. Friday night I reached slumberland at 4 a.m. only to be haunted by the alarm clock at 7:30. I stayed with Nancy and it was absolute agony to get up and go to bed while she stayed snuggled in blankets.

I had a permanent Saturday and so help me, I've been scalped. I haven't had my hair cut in so long that it frightens me to look at it. My hairdresser came in with a razor in her hand and I yelled, "Yipe! What are you going to do, shave me!!

I went to Cheryl's last night to stay, but that wasn't very exciting. Cheryl was in New Haven with the girls from the office so we just sat around and talked. I got to sleep around 2 a.m.

At your advice I don't think I'll read "Journey Among Warriors." I'm afraid I couldn't develop any desire to eat 100-year-old eggs and certainly

I couldn't derive anything from it if you couldn't. Hazel bought me "The Song of Bernadette" and I guess I could use a little religious reading.

Speaking of religion, I'd like to know if anyone else has the same feeling I have. Lately it seems as though I've been so completely indifferent about the whole thing. I go to church and all that, you know, but I am easily distracted. I think it must be a stage or phase, and I've had so much religion with Catholic schools that I am probably reveling in the fact that there's no compulsion behind me. I loathe discussing religion, but I just thought I'd mention it. I think I'll go take a nice hot bath.

Affectionately,

Helen

Maybe I'll let you call me Helena. There's a girl at work who is one of these "hep" kids, ah reet, all right, all root, and one day I walked in to be greeted by "Hi, Squash." After that anything sounds beautiful.

65 Arthur Street

New Britain, Conn.

April 4, 1944

Dear Charles, (formal as all hell, huh?)

Received your letter a few minutes ago and was as ever happy to hear from you! That goes without saying!! You know, it seems that either of us can write a letter tearing up Meg, Morry, the Spook etc. into insignificance, or suddenly become philosophical, but still we understand each other and enjoy our ignorance or "clownishness." I hope that this never changes, Charlie. I consider you as a real friend. Let's never do anything to break our bond of friendship.

You needn't apologize, as you did, for the way you wrote me in your last couple of notes. I really enjoy hearing you talk that way. I assure you I do not consider your remarks "the ravings of a mad man." On the contrary, I thought them perfectly natural, and I felt that I understood them quite well. I like your suggestion of "piling up some of the pleasantest memories imaginable when we are together again." I think that we've taken care of this quite well already. I know that I can't soon forget the many walks, graduation nite, our last date together (Ginger!!), Beckley's s quarry (bare-ass beach!) Wheeeee. Honestly, Charles, what memories!! Speaking of this word "memories" I can't soon forget Father Donavan's words ("King's Row") about life and memories. He philosophized on the past, present and future – saying that we live only in the past – on memories. His views impressed me so I took the time to write them out. Do you remember his remarks? Did they impress you as they did me?? When we meet again we'll have a chance to discuss this book more fully. I've marked and noted quite a few things.

Why you old "Sea Scout" ya,' floatin' around with the Waves, I see. More power to you (not that you need it), darlin'. As you say, perhaps it will do you good to have a fling. May I quote your note? You said – "I haven't had a fling in years and I'm almost tempted to try my hand," You coy boy!! It's a good thing that I'm broad minded.

In my last letter I moaned to you that you weren't writing enough! I'm just as bad as you I guess. It's been almost a week since I wrote you.

I've been fairly busy lately – V-garden, Golf Club, putting up screens – also, school is out this week and we have Patty and Connie coming down for the week. Patty keeps asking about you! I've also been playing golf during a few afternoons.

We had three or four days of wonderful weather. Today it is 80. Imagine how beautiful it will be tonight! Wouldn't it be swell if you were home and we could take a walk up to the Manor or something? Wishful thinking again. I had a date with Gertie tonite but I decided to break it. I may go to Compounce tonight tho. Enuff of dis luffink—.

Do you want to have a laugh? Well, do you know Dave Lennon – that stocky kid who lives here in Belvedere? I believe he stutters a little. Well, honeh, the boy is married. He's only 17 and his wife is only 15, He ploughed her four times, but on the fifth time he neglected to take advantage of that useful invention known as a rubber. Bang! Bang! Everyone claims that he has a marriage license. Everybody in Belvedere knows it except his parents. He seems to be proud of it though. He's acting just exactly the way I picture Morry would act – talking like that. It was funny! Last Sunday afternoon Lennon took his wife out for a walk. He went walking directly past the "Drug" with his "pregnant pussy" on his arm. Laugh, I thought my undies would never dry! I wonder how "The Spook" and "Hot Pants" would react if they were in that spot!! I'd love to see Pater and Meg walking down the street with Meg pregnant as all hell. Wheeeee.!!!

Well, darlin, I finally know when I'll be leaving the "unthriving" town of "New Britski." I'm in the Navy and will disembark on May 22. Sixteen fathers are leaving in the next bunch. There are only 13 other fellas leaving in the Navy with me. Gosh, you know, now that my thoughts have become a realization, I feel very queer about leaving—especially when it comes to Mother and Dad.

I received another letter from Joe Donnelly. He was at one time an ardent admirer of Hot Pants and confessed this to her at one time. I believe that it was while Meg and I had broken up last May. Well, he finally confessed that it was a rotten thing to do and that he wouldn't feel right until he apologized to me. I saw his sister yesterday, and she said that he washed out. Tough! But I'd never pictured him as a flyer.

What the hell is this world coming to? I've been asked to the Girl's League formal on May 19th by an eleventh grader I used to know. Who knows, I might give the kid a break!

This is your sex-box saying he'll be good because of you. "I knock the hell outta you." Take care now. Charles, and write when you get a chance. Make sure that your back is sore from working and not from "durking." Doodle – dee- do! Well, How – dee – doodie! I'll have you know, Charlie, that I have no cherry – my mother keeps telling me that!

Cherryly yours,
Dick

P.S. You know what just struck me funny – that episode at the Canteen with Mary and Meg. Remember when Mary dropped her fork and wiped it with her napkin. Then I made my remark, and "Hot Pants" and "Two Ton Tessie" became embarrassed. Just thought that the memory might give you a most needed laugh.

17 Anise Street
New Britain, Conn.
April 4, 1944

Dear Brother,

We received your letter yesterday. It takes quite a while for a letter to get here.

Well, I'm glad you liked your trip and I hope you'll continue liking it at Memphis.

Today's Good Friday and there isn't any school, but we go back Monday. Eddy Neubauer and Pa just got through burning the lot. I suppose they're having their eggnog now. They usually do. I got my powder blue coat for Easter and a yellow hat and gloves. Pretty snazzy, huh (and brown alligator shoes – dead ones.)

I was reading your letter yesterday and I was laughing like heck. You said you wanted some underwear and then I forgot to turn the page over *but went right over to the next page and it said something like this. "Will you send some underwear, mine are all flooded." Hah- Hah!!*

Jean just called me up. She wants me to show her some new lessons I learned last night. I don't want her to get ahead of me though. The baton lessons are getting quite a lot more complicated now. Mr. Walker and Father Brophy said that Gertie and I would make good partners for twirling, but now when Jean comes back she's going to put the Kibosh on everything.

The Glee Club is giving their Spring Concert next Wednesday &Friday. Audrey K. and I are going Friday. I'll love it???

You didn't even mention the articles we sent. Did you get them? That's all for now.

Love,

Betty

P.S. Have a nice Easter.

65 Arthur Street
New Britain, Conn.
April 7, 1944

"Fungus Face,"

How's my little "Fundle-bunny"? I'll bet you're surprised hearing from me again so soon. I believe that I wrote you Tuesday. I hope you got the letter. I wouldn't want my beautiful thoughts to fall into the wrong hands. You now — it just struck me funny! If someone accidentally picked up one of our letters , I bet they'd think that we were dirty! Well, it would be fun trying to dig up the money to pay off he blackmail threats.

It's a beautiful day here in the "blood pit" and I'm all in (up to the pelvis — toes and all). I haven't got to bed before 2 A.M. the last two nights and I had to get up early to go to church this morning. Last night Betty Rindge spent the night at my house. Wheeeee —with mother and me. What a gay time!! No, seriously though, mother wanted to meet her as I had been mentioning her name quite a few times since I started going out with her. (that can be taken two ways) I drove her home about 12:30 A.M. and didn't return until 2 A.M. I'll tell you something more of the time interval between 12:30 A.M. and 2:00 A.M. later in the note.

Oh, yes, I forgot to mention it in my last letter to you. Remember that record we made at my house one night with Edy P, Peggy Ericson, Clara Henry— etc.?? Well, I came across it last week, and I played it back! Laugh!!! O my stinkin' dear!!! Gosh, that sure did bring back the good old days – when you and I were foolish, Now – we're just foolish!!!! Some of the prominent tunes of that time were – "Sunuva Gun" "I'm going regular!" "Rollins, you're drunk" "Walton, get off of me" (Clara). Chas, remember it? Someday when we get together again we'll sit down and listen to the little bit of canned nonsense! Ya ol' turd!!

Speaking of Edy and Peg, I saw them both yesterday. Peg (along with most of the other Wahas) are home for the Easter holiday. Big thing!! I'd just as soon stay home and "toy with my tool."

I've been doing quite a bit of work around the house, namely, splicing movie film and painting screens. I haven't finished the latter. I still have 18 screens and four screen doors to paint. Wheeeee! Exciting, isn't it?

I'm sitting here on my "bi-lobed" rectum trying to think of someone to go out with tonite. Mother says that I've been staying in too much (How does she know?) and that I should start going out a little more! Well, let's see, I satisfied Cannibal Rindge last night—Dirty Gerty doesn't get through with work til seven – and that's too late. Most of the other women in town are having the monthlies, damn it!!! Who does that leave? Oh, hell, I suppose I'll have to give Rosie Rottencrotch a break again. If she's busy, Sophie Finger will surely go out with me!! How do you like the enclosed photo of Susie's kid? He looks exactly like exactly like the Spook!! Oh, but yu ain't seen "nuttin'" yet – you should see the other one – that one can scratch his larynx with her upper incisors— like his mother! No kidding (birth control measure) though, don't you think that the only progeny the "Spook" and the "Jaw" could ever hope to have – two kangaroos? I'd just like to see Meg nursing them by way of her breast. Pater would probably "scare" one of "them" away and start sucking!! Wheeeee! St. Vitas Dance Pater and "unemotional" Meg! Aw-right, Walton, enough of your clowning!!!

Oh, yes, about last night. "Bet" and I left here at 12;30 A.M. and reached her home about 12:45 A.M. Of course, the most natural thing to do was to start "luvin'." That we did!! I believe I told you in previous notes I was kissing her a la francais in a modified way. From the very first time I kissed her I noticed that she separated her "uppers and lowers" if you know what I mean, and I often wondered what she was doing with her tongue. Last night she finally brought this "organ" out of "hibernation" Well, you know what an extra thrill you got from Launa when you kissed her "that" way? Well, that's about the way I felt, I guess. You see, this was the first time that I had been really kissed like that! Need I say anymore? The trouble is that now I don't know whether she's kidding or not. Don't worry, darlin', I won't put the boxes to anyone until we're together to do it together. Reet! Or "somethin."

A fella just can't keep dating and necking a girl continually as I have with Betty and not make some sort of statement. So, last night after the first time she really "kissed" me, I told her that I couldn't tell her that I loved her because I didn't feel that I knew what "love" really was. I did tell her that I liked her very much. That's sort of putting myself on the safe side, and she seemed satisfied with having things that way. Before I left, she told me that she liked me ever so much and she was sorry that I was leaving soon. I agreed with her and told her we'd have a "lot" of "fun" before I leave. That's about all it'd be. The only thing is that I'm afraid she's going to be hurt in the long run. She's different from many girls, Charlie, for most of her ideas are settled. I just know (by her actions, words etc.) that she thinks more of me than she should. However, I'm going to be as "unserious" as possible with her and give both her and myself a good time when we are together. Enuff of dis luffink, let's start –! What comes after the latter? There's nothing to look forward to after that. Oh, but why be so pessimistic!! You and I can think of something interestin to follow, you know – trading wives, etc.

Oh, have you heard about the three unmarried Chinese maidens?

> *Tu Yung Tu*
> *Tu Dum Tu*
> *No Yen Tu*

You know, when I sat down to write, I didn't know what in the world I'd have to say. It's something hard to explain, but I think you're about the easiest person I know to write to. Perhaps it because we understand each other well. To tell the truth, I enjoy writing you a letter just as much as I do receiving a letter (from anyone but you). When I see the familiar handwriting of the old "turd" I know I'm in for a treat.

That's about all "fur" now, darlin'. I've got to get on the phone and give someone a break tonite. Take care and keep your "tool" clean.

Passionately yours (or anyone's.)
Love, Lustful Dick

P.S. Thanks for the card. That stuff is really wired.
P.S.S. If you haven't received my Tuesday letter yet, check on it. I sent it to Memphis

Memphis Naval Hospital.
Memphis, Tennessee

April 8, 1944

Dear Launa,

I'm fiercely in love with you tonight. I don't know whether it's the heat, spring or what – I'm writing this with firmness and conviction without the slightest trace of remorse or regret. It's no use, Launa, really. I've tried to forget but don't want to. Why should I? I wish that you'd write. If you do, you can ignore all things pertaining to us and be purely platonic. Come on, loosen up, you're not as cold as you think you are.

I'm working now and I like it a lot. I wish that you forget most everything that I wrote while I was in the hospital. My nerves were all shot then and I didn't know what to think or write. Too much thinking is very bad.

Memphis is a great town, in fact, I think it's the nicest city in the South. It's about twice the size of Hartford and what's more the people aren't allergic to sailors. By the way, Frankie is now singing, "I'll Get By," – the women are screaming.

The Southern women haven't the class of our Yankee women and they are more possessive. Joan Edwards is now singing, "I Didn't Sleep A Wink Last Night." Tough! You really brought me up right, Darlin' – if a girl smiles at me, I just know something is wrong and run. I'm just not used to being on the defensive, that's all. "Mares Eat Oats" is on now. I hate that damn song. You're probably listening to the same program but what the—.

I'll tell you about my new lady friend. Her name is Florence (can you picture me with a Florence?) No kidding, she is a nice girl. She is 5'8" tall, blond (you called it) a Norwegian and built. Yes, sir, I like women big and boney. She is from Lake Placid, New York, and she is a wonderful skier. We play tennis every afternoon and I'm getting so I can beat her now and then. I have no idea how old she is (and vice versa) but she's had a year and a half of chem. work at the Univ. Of Buffalo. (Frankie is now drooling out "Poinciana"). She isn't aggressive at all and blushes (with innocence, I hope) worse than Patty Lou. Oh, yes, she's a WAVE, and her barracks are right next to mine, which makes things very handy. There is only one hitch and that is her name isn't Launa. What a jerk I must be but I can't feed her a line for the life of me and I never think of kissing her. I'm a real jerk (don't agree with me!)

You know, Eddy and Doc and countless others are in love with you, and you can't love them all but you write to them. (Joan E. is now singing, "When They Ask About You" – irony). So why dontcha do right and write me a letter? Here I am miles from home all alone in the world just pining away. Speaking of pining away, I'm gaining weight by the ton. I weigh one hundred and fifty-five now and I'm gaining by the minute. The food is wonderful here and next to you I love food best. On second thought, I might like the food better. If I tried to live on your love, I'd have undoubtedly starved to death long ago.

By the way, I have a little pure unadulterated sarcasm for you. Mick is in New London. Did your heart skip a couple of beats or have you known it for weeks? I'm sorry I said that 'cause it isn't very nice and I'm trying to be a very honorable fellow. Don't you think I'm rather honorable? I do. Well, Whodinkie, I must bid you good night now. Be a good little girl now and write to me.

Love,
Charlie
P.S. I haven't time to read this over so forgive all errors etc.

91 West Street
New Britain, Conn.
April 8, 1944

Hi ya, "Stinky" –

I thought that you were going to write to your little bundle of joy as soon as you reached Portsmouth, untouched. I was waiting very impatiently to hear from you.

Well, only two days till Easter. I can hardly wait to wear my new attire this year. Guess what it is – a new veil – yes sir, that's the only thing I got new. Last night Francine, Meg, Martha B, Betty H, Loraine B, Betty S, Barbara D, H.S. Conway and I had a few snappy games of bridge. There's such a multiplicity of things to do around this boom town, you know. Nothing like spending a rough evening with the girls. The smoke hasn't cleared out of the rooms yet.

In two weeks Mary Jane Ryan and I are going down to the Great White Way, New York to you.

This time I'll really have to make it to Edgewood Park. That was my main reason for the trip last time when you were home.

Guess you know there's only 2 1/2 months afore graduation. I'll be the happiest kid on earth. It's been rumored that we may have the exercises at the Music Shell at Walnut Hill. There won't be any party after like last year. Gosh, I'd give anything if we could have one. It wouldn't be half as much fun though. Well, Peaches, this is all for now – and if you don't write soon, I'll never talk to you again - you lucky kid.

Love,

Mary Jo

17 Anise Street
New Britain, Conn.
April 10, 1944

Dear Charlie,

Thanks a lot for the flowers. They matched good too. I never expected to have a corsage this Easter (neither did Mother).

I just came from school a short while ago. I started to read your letter and when I saw what you had written about Julius Lewgeski I walked out of the room. You see Julius was sitting here. It certainly was a coincidence. He hasn't been here in a long time.

Today it's raining like heck, but yesterday it was swell out, nice and warm. It didn't seem like Easter though 'cause I didn't get a basket. Mother said I couldn't have one because you weren't home and you might be jealous. Donny got a mother rabbit from Violet.

Audrey and I went to the movies yesterday and saw "Around the World" with Kay Kyser, Joan Davis and Ishkabibble. (spelt wrong, I know!). That Joan Davis certainly is a "hot sketch." She reminds me of me.

I didn't understand what you said about Jack London being dead, but we'll skip it.

That wasn't very funny, "Sonny Young." Remember what you said about Julius Caesar. Speaking of English teachers, Miss Hildebrandt (now Mrs. Williams) came back today. We're starting to do more work already.

It just stopped sprinkling and the sun is out. It was just an "April Shower" I guess.

I just hinted around Pa for some money. He can only give you a finn because we're broke. We're starving and I haven't any clothes to wear. This is his last $5. But take it. You need it more than we do. (sob-sob), Ma has no cigarettes and Pa has no booze,

Well, I have to practice on my "Pogo" stick now and learn to throw it behind my back. It's all black and blue already. That's all for now.

Love from the Gang,

Sister

P.S. Thanks again for the posies.

212

65 Arthur Street
New Britain, Conn.
April 13, 1944

Hello, m' love,

Oh, honeh, you're so nice to me!! Gosh, I got three letters from you this week. Thanks a lot, Charlie, I really appreciate your taking time off to write. I really do look forward to receive your letters. They are just what the "doc" would order.

What a nite-club that hospital must be!! Your schedule in my estimation is very good — makes allowances for work and quite a bit of "free" time. As for the WAVEs! Wheeeee. I just can't wait till I get in to take a good healthy bite from a healthy, luscious, double-lipped crotch. Have you tried it yet? I am doing it every day. More fun!!!

As for "Sandy" — ask her why they call her that — she sounds as if she's in "shape for a rape" — oh, I forgot, she'll do it willingly. I don't like those kind. When Sandy is off restriction ask her if "she's handy with her candy?" Tell her also that you're an "all day sucker." If she asks you what flavor you like, tell her that you like "butterscotch in the crotch!" Wheeeee. If that doesn't make her "lollypop" hot for your "mop" tell her to screeeeeeeew. 'S'nuff said for Sandy.

Glad to hear that you've made other feminine connections. Have you really followed any of them up or are they strictly for the birds? If they are anything that answers the description of your "dream girl", I'd just as soon go out with Meg or her dog. That line about your being a "pasture playboy," surely tickled me. Speaking of the pasture, what do you know about birds? Well, how's this for a swallow?? Screeeeeeeew!!!

You know — I still urinate all over myself when I think of our last date together. I've seen Ginger a couple of times since then, and we only say "hello" and giggle at each other. More fun — if she ever knew!!!

Thanks ever so much for promising not to get your "nookie" till after the war!! I go in big for that idea about going down to the beach to turn all the lights off when they go on again. Wheeeee.! That sounds crazy and mixed up, just like us, I guess. I hope that we don't ever change.

Your remark about the possibility of the "Spook" not having a genital organ sent me rolling prostrate on the floor. He looks like the type that urinates through his ears. Maybe that is what fascinates Meg so much.

Morry (Whorey) and Elmer— the boys "who look like a booby trap went off in their in their yaps" are still around. I guess they're pretty worried about having to go into a factory in that they are both 4-F. Of course, you know Morry – his only remark is, "Huh, they'll never get me (with his uppers forgetting to go up)." I'd better keep quiet about being 4-F until I'm through my physical next week.

Oh, monkey piss!! Tomorrow nite I'm supposed to attend something for all prospective service men. This assembly is supposed to answer many questions about your entry into the service etc. I received my pre-induction notice to take my physical yesterday. How in the hell do you like it!! I have to be at the City Hall at 6 A.M. next Thursday. Who do they think they are? Oh, well, I guess that's life!!

I thought that you'd rather enjoy the news of the "pregnant pussies" in the ole "gloom town." I haven't heard or investigated any further. I have heard though that the girls are being carefully examined. I can just picture "Hot Pants" and Mary standing nakedly in the "meat line" with cigarettes hanging sloppily from the corner of their lips – the ascending smoke causing them to have to close their eyes. What a sight, what a spectacle!

I'm really flattered by being called a full-fledged Jack Rabbit – but, daddy, everyone calls me a "dumb bunny" – is that good? As for the V12, Charlie, I'm not at all sure about it myself. There are two sides to the story. You're getting an education for nothing, your duties are less on the fatiguing side shall we say, and of course you're not liable to be suddenly shipped out etc. Then again – you know the reputation that the V12 has etc. You may also feel that you are doing more for yourself and everyone else by staying where you are. Then again, in your case, you've already been taken out of the V12 (have you told them that?} Furthermore, you have had experience both in the V12 and the regular Navy. You should by all means be able to make up your mind. Finally, remember, Charlie, that after this war is over you may not have the opportunity to go to school again. If you get into the V12, you have a career and a commission to strive for; if you remain where you are, you have nothing to gain – have you? That's the way things appear to me.

Last Friday night when I wrote to you I had a date with Eileen Jensen. She's a good kid, but that's about all. Sat. and Sun were nights spent with my parents. Got to stay home once in awhile. Mon. Tues. and Wed. found me with a cold and sore throat, so last night I called off a date I had with "dirty Girtie."

I saw two great pictures the lass few days. Tues. nite I saw "Song of Russia." Gosh, that Susan Peters is "reet, pleet and indiscreet." I'd let her clean out my foxhole at any time. Yesterday I saw Miriam Hopkins and

Bette Davis in "Old Acquaintance." It was a great picture!! Tomorrow P.M. Betty Rindge and I are going to "splurge" and go to the Arch St. to see "Stormy Weather." Saw this film down at school, but it's worth a repeat.

Easter Sunday I went to St. Francis Church with Dad. The mass was very nice although it did seem rather strange. I'll probably do the same a couple of more times before I leave. As we were leaving I saw Launa. She looked very nice. Imagine that she was home for the Easter holiday. I guess your relations with her are very definite as they stand. Do you think that either of you will ever change?

Good to hear that you're enjoying the good weather of the Southland. You know how it is up here – it's as cold as Meg's box probably is.

I am lazy as all hell and getting worse. I started painting the screens last week and am only half way through. I've worked on them a grand total of two days (out of the last ten) – the eager beaver that I am. Wheeeee! Cripes, I hope I don't have to paint the damn kitchen before I leave.

By the way, have you heard the new needle song? (This is an original.) "Don't Get A Prick Much Anymore!"(Crude, ain't it?). From the picture of the same name. That's probably Meg's theme song, "No kidding." Morry says, "She'll go out with you!" – "Good ta hear it!"

Must eat now, my lil' Sea Scout!! "Screw nuttin' till you hear from me." (From a song by a different name.) Take it easy on those WAVEs, and please watch out for your cherry. Remember now!! "I'm saving myself for Dick." I'm one a thooooooose boooooooys. Take care now and have fun.

> *Tongues of Passion,*
> *Old Crotch Criminal 1265774*

> *R. I. School of Design*
> *Providence, R.I.*
> *April 15, 1944*

Dear Charlie,

The way you move about the country amazes me – When I was home last week, Mary Jo told me you were in Tenn. But I said she was crazy. But I guess she isn't. Oh, yes, I was in what you call the gloom town. Gloom is an understatement – that place is on the verge of a complete collapse. The only people I saw were "the girls" and Joe Green. God, how I hate to go home. Didn't see Walton. He must have known I was looking for him – 'cause why did everybody else see him but me? Oh, well, he goes into the Navy soon and maybe he'll be at Newport – just like you were.

215

I suppose that you've heard that Ginnie is going steady with a kid – and I mean a kid named Bob Joyce. He's nice but rather young. Oh, well, there's a shortage – or so they tell me.

Darling, this is going to be short and not too sweet I'm afraid – but I'm too confused to write anymore tonight. I've been this way two weeks – that's why you haven't heard from me. In fact every time I write to you I seem to be confused. It's getting to be a permanent state of mind. Maybe some day I'll come out of it and the sun will shine, but right now it's raining literally as well as figuratively. My ex-roommate and her date are having a cozy time right now so I'll close for now.

Love 'n stuff,
Lulu

17 Anise Street
New Britain, Conn.
April 17, 1944

Dear Son,

Betty said it was my turn to write so here goes. Nellie's father died so Oneida and I went to the funeral this morning, and then we went downtown shopping. Pa and John are working today. John's been pretty good lately. Pa's been busy almost every night working in the garage. He's been making shelves for his paint and wallpaper. He's got it pretty much cleaned up now. The junk man was down yesterday and he got rid of a lot of cartons and cases that were upstairs in the garage attic.

Pa will have to do a lot of work this year to use up the paint he bought.

Well, Donny is o.k. He just bought another rabbit. He is waiting for it to have little ones. Betty is coming along pretty well with her baton.

I saw Mick in church Sunday so he is still around. Freddy was shipped to California. That probably means that he will be sent across. He didn't get a furlough.

I raked the leaves out of your rock garden the other day. But it's so cold today we may have more snow. We are going to start cleaning up the yard this week. Pa's going to take the cans down to the dump. We had all our trees pruned so probably we will have more apples.

So glad you like Tenn. I hope they keep you there.

Was Betty surprised when she got the flowers, so was I. She couldn't imagine being all dressed up for Easter and no corsage. She came near buying herself one, a good thing she didn't. Betty sent the razor, hope you get it alright.

Well, I guess I've told you about everything. Oh, yes, I forgot to tell you Nellie's having an increase, that's why she's not working. We couldn't imagine her staying home for nothing. Well, I guess I'll close, hoping you write soon.

Love,

Mother

232 Mountain Drive

West Hartford, Conn.

April 17, 1944

Hello, you wonderful man!

I just knew that they couldn't keep a good man down! I've got butterflies in my stomach. I'm so thrilled for you. It's just impossible to tell you how glad I am by letter, but just try to imagine me all excited, and jumping up and down for joy (my rosary beads dangling from my fingers, of course).

I won't breathe a word of it, until you give me the signal. I suppose I have only a sleight idea of how your mother will feel and I know both Ben and Dick will be glad for you. Let me know as soon as you know what the story is, won't you?

Did you see Benny? I'm pleased that you could get together, but, oh darn, how I wish I could see you both. I comfort myself with the thought that 3's a crowd and you wouldn't have any fun with me around. I hate being so candid with myself, but since I'm a realist I simply have to face the truth.

I shall write you a real letter in a couple of days. I don't want to include any of my other silly prattle with my congratulations. I'm truly very happy and think the whole thing is marvelous. When you want me to go out and celebrate just tell me and I'll do anything short of getting soused.

Affectionately,

Helen

I love being your confidante. I always did delight in knowing secrets before anyone else did.

91 West Street

New Britain, Conn.

April 17, 1944

Dear Charlie,

For a while I thought you weren't going to write to me anymore. Notice that I am answering your letter the day that I got it.

217

Just because I go with Bob doesn't mean I can't keep up my correspondence with a dear, dear friend. We always have such good times together, don't we?

Memphis must be just like New Britsky. Movies are the only entertainment. I hope to heaven you will be able to get home for the school festivities. Class nite – June 16 – Prom 19 or 20 – Graduation 23. It seems wonderful to be planning for them. I hear Dick is leaving May 20 for the Navy, or was it April that he said?? I don't see him much now that he's all wrapped up with Betty. That's quite the little affair, no?

Now that I'm not working any more, I think I'm on the verge of a nervous breakdown. Honestly, I'm just a physical wreck. I smoke at least 1 pack of butts per day. No kidding – if something exciting doesn't happen pretty soon I'll lose my mind. I think I know the reason – no "MEN". I suppose I'm not the only one that feels this way.

Joe Donnelly is out In San Antonio, Texas – lucky stiff. I don't hear from him very much.

Well, Sweetie, s'all for now. So long, Slug – See ya in the slot machine.
Love,
Mary Jo
You betcha. Gundie still calls Googie Lolly.

Rhode Island School of Design
April 18, 1944

Dear Charlie,

If perchance this letter doesn't make sense the reason is – two damn fool lieutenants are clowning around the place and naturally I can't concentrate. As soon as they leave – and heaven help us that it's soon, I'll be able to think rationally again. They are definitely not my type. They seem to be slightly, oh so slightly conceited, self-centered and boresome – other than that, there's nothing wrong with them. You see, dear, I'm on hell call tonight. That in case you didn't know is when you answer the phone and doorbell and act as monitor for the night. It's really Emy's turn but since she is swamped with homework and I have none, I'm taking it for her. The house is now pretty quiet and it's only about 7:30.

So, I've been at school for almost three weeks and it has just flown by. My classes are very long but so darn interesting I don't mind it. Most days I go from 8:30 to 5:30 and that's a rough day – at school anyway. The nights are even rougher. I'm only kidding. I've only met four new fellows, none of whom I want to date. There is a boy here at school though that isn't bad. He reminds me of you for one reason in particular. His mouth and teeth look like yours. That's the only resemblance – he's good-looking, tall and an ex-Air Corps looie and is he smooth. Stop chewing your nails. As I was saying the night life isn't too gay so far. I've been to two formals but other than that...?

How's your night life, Charlie? You disappoint me – you're doing nothing to increase the birth rate in the South Pacific. That isn't living up to the best traditions and standards of the boys that went before you. Relax – I really wouldn't want you to have a harem.

I haven't heard from Dick in quite a while and so I guess I can cross him off my list. Did you have anything to do with that? I suppose that you still have a crazy notion that I'm attracted to Dick. I saw him during the summer and I'm afraid Dick is a little young – I suppose he has his opinions about me also. I'd rather not hear them.

My cellmates, as you so aptly put it, are Emily Johnson and Rita Brady known to all as "Neut" for Neuter – we decided she was neither male nor female, so consequently neuter. You know Emy and she of course is my best friend now – but don't tell B. Harriman. Rita's a swell gal. Crazy on the subject of jazz. She really goes all out for it. She's the type of gal that will do anything for fun – if someone else starts it. She's not the lone wolf type. In fact, she's not even a wolf. Right now she's got a crush on a fellow here at school who is one of my best friends. He looks like Sinatra, which almost kills him, and he's really a neat person. But Brady is scared to death to make a play for him. So when she wants to see him, I have to make a date with him. It's really rare – me playing cupid.

Incidentally, I have your picture here at school and more girls have asked me who you were and where you were. I told them that you were the great Young and also said that you were no where, where you could do any white woman any good. Complicated, isn't it? Ruth Howard is still around, also Jane Lidell (the hair episode). They send their love – take it or leave it. If you're as hard up as you seem, you'll take it.

Last week I got the old urge and bleached my hair again. This time it took so I'm definitely not a red head in front at least. The back is still brown. Do you like redheads? I do. I also like blondes and brunettes So that takes care of you and the rest of the male population. Well, dear, we are now going to have a surprise party – I just found out so—till later—.

Lots of love,
Lucy

P.S. What was that crack about loving you? Don't be silly, dear. I get that way over no one.

P.S.S. It says here in small print at the bottom of the page.

P.S.S.S. If I fall, and I won't unless it's mutual, I'll let you know – that guy at school is cute. – (Now I'm kidding)

17 Anise Street
New Britain, Conn.
April 20, 1944

Dear Son,

Having a few minutes to spare I thought I'd better write you a few lines. Dad went out to collect a bill. Betty is over to Dommijans and Donny is over to Dickey Coyles and I am home alone.

Pete just called and said how Tag is a 1/c Pharm. Mate and Tommy is over in England. We got a V-mail letter from him Tuesday. Freddy is in Alameda, California. Oneida and I went downtown today and I bought a new suit. I didn't tell Pa yet. Am I going to be dressed up.

Oneida, Kitty, Anna and I played bridge over at the school last night for the church. They made about $250.00 and they had a big crowd.

How are all your patients? You're not getting tired of taking temperatures yet? Do you have to clean any bed pans and what else do you have to do? Explain your work to us.

Pa just got back with a check so I have to hit him up for some money. By the way, we got a war bond of yours today. I don't know how many we've got. We will have to count them some day.

Pa just went out in the garage to mix some paint.

Eddie Newbauer is raising canaries. He's working in his garage building cages. He said he's going in the business. I guess that's all for now. Will write again in a few days. Probably Betty will write when she's over to Dommijans.

Love,
Mother

17 Everett St.
New Britain, Conn.
April 30, 1944

Dear Charlie:

I was very pleased to hear from you, and to know that all is going well with you in Uncle Sam's Navy. You are, no doubt, surprised to read this, to know that Uncle Sam caught up with me, and consequently, I too am in *the Navy. I received my "boot-training" at Sampson from March 21st until April 25th and am home on leave as I write this. They gave me a Ph.M 3/c rating when I was half through "boot." I return to Sampson tomorrow night and believe they will send me to a hospital for training , and then to some Naval Base for duty.*

Because my eyes are too poor, I can't go to officers' school, nor can I get sea duty for the same reason. So I'll have to be satisfied with being a dry-land sailor.

I doubt if you'd recognize me if you saw me, since I've lost nearly 20 pounds, and my waist-line is really quite trim.

I'm enclosing a letter of recommendation which, I trust, will be acceptable. If not, I'll be I'll be glad to try again. Who knows, but perhaps I'll need one from you some day?

So, best of luck to you, Charlie, and let's hear from you as to how you make out. As for my address, it would be better to write here to New Britain, until I get a more permanent address than my Sampson one.

Sincerely,

Jim Beach (biology teacher)

P.S. Forgive the stationery. I couldn't find any envelopes to fit the paper properly.

Regards to Ben Navikas when you run into him again.

R. I. School of Design
May 1, 1944

Charlie dear,

This is a hell of a time to be writing a letter – it's about 3 minutes before I have to go out. He' a beautiful ensign – Oh, yes, nothing like a Navy man. Really dear, I can't see you playing Florence Nightingale to a bunch of salts. But since the Navy seems to think it is your chosen role in life, dear, what can you do?

If you do go to Little Rock, don't you dare fall by the wayside – if I'm not there. You once mentioned you were wondering how it would feel to lose your virginity. Well, don't – if you already haven't.(Ha-Ha, Logan says nine out of ten boys have.) I don't want second hand material. After all you did ask me to marry you at thirty-five. You'd better not forget or I'll sue you for toying with my affections. Here I am so true to you – only go out seven out of eight nights of the week. Don't think I'm crazy, it's merely spring in Providence. And young men's fancies aren't the only ones that turn.

Here I am in the middle of a hectic love affair. Like the shower here in the dorm – sometimes hot and enjoyable – more times cold. He can't make up his mind if he wants me or not. When he does want me, it's something to write about – but when he doesn't, it's hell. Doesn't sound like me, does it? Never thought I was the kind that would jump when some damn man called. But here I am something like a member of a Sultan's harem. He has a harem, too, damn him. I am one of four. More damn fun for the kiddies. It's driving me crazy. Thank God my love affairs never last long. Gotta go now dear, so do write soon and think of me when you feel low and I guarantee you I'll laugh.

Love 'n stuff,
Lulu

Coast Guard Station
Alameda, Calif.
May 1, 1944

Dear Charlie,

I'm so sorry to hear that you broke your arm. What the hell is the matter with you? Did you forget my address or what? Well, anyway I finally got your address from home after about two months.

I'm now in sunny Calif. and that is a sad sack of shit. I've been here about a month and I can remember 2 sunny days.

I leave for Gunny school Friday so don't even answer this letter. We leave on the 19th for St. Augustine, Fla. for 4 months of school, then we get a leave. When I get out of school I'll be an E.M. 3/c. 50% of the class get rates and I think I'll make out o.k. I hope so anyway.

Well, what's new, Kid? How are all the southern belles? What do you do all day? Is it a school or do you work all day on the poor suckers that are sick? Are you going to get a rate out of it, or are you just going to be a pecker-checker for the rest of your life?

Drop me a line and don't forget. What the hell am I talking about? I just told you not to write. Well, I'll write as soon as I get there.

Love and kisses,
Freddy

17 Anise St.
New Britain, Conn.
May 1, 1944

Dear Chick,

Well, how are you anywho? We're all o.k. except mother, she still feels a little sick – she has a cold.

222

I'm over to Donnyjans now. This is my second home. Mrs. D. took Jean and me out for a ride in her convertible this afternoon. It was swell with the top down. It's been hot now for about three days and I hope it stays this way.

Guess what? I really had a swell time at the Junior Prom. We had about four tables joined together and the kids were swell. There was a nice crowd there, too (not all the ra-ras), Later about ten of us went out to Gabers. So I was really glad that I had gone after all.

We haven't heard from you in about four or five days. I hope you didn't break your arm or something.

There's no school all this week and that's just perfect. Although I have more work in English than I ever did.

Morry's station wagon just flew by. I saw the blue streak. One of these days he's going to go a little too fast for his own good.

Our May Crowning is next Sunday so I hope it's a nice day. We're going to have a living rosary this year. It should be very beautiful. Each girl represents a bead of the rosary. That's all for now.

Love,

Betty

Torpedo Squadron 29
FPO New York, N.Y.
May 2, 1944

Dear Charles,

I guess it is about time I wrote but I was on leave from the 15ᵗʰ to the 20ᵗʰ and right now I am trying to catch up on my writing and having a hell of a time of it.

I had a swell time but the time went by too damn fast to please me. I wish I could figure out where it went to.

I just remembered that little note you put on the back of the envelope and I don't feel a hell of a lot different and I damn sure don't feel ready for the grave as yet. I am having too much fun now.

I heard that Memphis was one of the best liberty towns around but that is only because the people haven't caught on to the sailors yet. It will change one of these days, they always do.

We have been doing quite a bit of work lately but I am not doing a hell of a lot now. The Squadron went up to Cape Cod while I was home but they didn't get in enough flying time so they stayed up there for ten more days and the rest of us that are left here aren't doing much except odd jobs around and going out nights. Tonight I am duty officer so I am trying to get caught up on some of these letters and also practice up on my typing.

Congratulations on making H.A. 1/c you ought to be able to get your rate pretty soon, but I hear that that is quite a job.

You were a dope not to have studied when you were in V12. Bray is doing o.k. now. I guess he is supposed to get out of there sometime in June but I don't know where he will go from there.

Swede Peterson is home for ten days. He is going to Pensacola now and then I guess he will get his wings.

I have been wanting to go up and say hello to Launa but I haven't had the time. I would like to see her though before I go out. I haven't seen her in quite a while.

Well, I guess this is all for tonight, I think I will hit the sack and get some sleep.

Don't work too hard and write when you get a chance. So long,

Mick

R. I. School of Design
May 8, 1944

Dear Charlie,

Received your letter today and read parts to the dorm. Some were shocked, others amused. Your friends were amused — you might know.

Darling, please be careful of that mad Russian. Remember it is Leap Year and she might leap on you some dark night. We girls are getting desperate these days. As for my hobnobbing with the elite of the Navy — Relax. He's gone now — and I have another. He's in the Air Corps, stationed at Brown. He's from Atlanta, Georgia, and is he smooth, tall, big brown eyes and sort of reddish hair. I guess I just go for redheads. No cracks. Met him last Saturday night at our big dance and from the minute he walked in there was nobody else in the place as far as I was concerned. He seemed to feel the same, thank God. Saw him again last night and will see him tonight. Right now I'm waiting for him to call — this time I think it will work. He isn't like John (the Ensign). Larry's pretty damn decent — oh, he has all the necessary vices including me. But he doesn't play dirty — and so far this letter is all about him. Guess it's pretty evident how I feel.

As far as 90% percent of the female population no longer being virgins, I'll have you know that the girls in this place are still virgins. (They don't date much.) And if you have your doubts about me, you can go to hell and we are no longer friends. Do you?

Spring is here and school is almost over. I'll hate to spend the summer in N.B. I think I'll work in Hartford at the Aetna Insurance Company. My father can get me a job there. And after work I'll spend my time at the Bond Hotel, entertaining in the officers' club. I can also get a job there. I don't plan to have a dull summer if I can help it. I wish Larry was stationed in Conn. There I go again.

Do you think you'll be coming home again? Soon, I mean. If so look me up. Dick should be leaving for the Navy soon, shouldn't he? This week sometime.

Tell me, where is Mr. Beach stationed? Give him my love when you write to him again. He was one of the grandest teachers I ever had. I can't imagine him in uniform – wonder how he looks – good, maybe.

Larry is coming down the hill now. Slow as molasses. He's just about the laziest Rebel I ever met. He probably won't get to the door for another hour. Well, I'll close now and please write again soon. Be good and keep away from those sex-mad WAVEs.

Love,
Lulu

91 West Street
New Britain, Conn.
May 9, 1944

Hi, Honeybunch,

I just got back from playing tennis in the park. I played with the "Spook." We ended the game at 5 -5. Meg was playing with Lorraine.

I guess that I didn't tell you that Mary Jane Ryan and I went down to New York last Wednesday. Boy, did we have a swell time. We went down on the 7 o'clock train. Then went straight out to Edgewood Park. I was never so surprised at any place. It's simply gorgeous. My roommate is Margaret Granbeck from New Rochelle. Ryan and I stayed there for lunch then went back to the "Great White Way." Went to the Paramount theater (not hotel) and saw Charlie Spivak and the world premier of "Going My Way" with Bing Crosby. The show was perfect. From there we went to Stouffer's for dinner. Had an extra special good time there. About 8 o'clock we went home just fagged out.

It was terrible having to start school again. I'm waiting for you to come home for my graduation. Would I ever be surprised. Just think we could have a smooth time at Beckley's and then maybe go to the shore – maybe? Well, hon, must get back to my homework.

Love 'n stuff,
Peaches

17 Anise Street
New Britain, Conn.
May 12, 1944

Dear Son,

Received your letter yesterday and you said you don't hear from us. It seems as tho Betty writes every few days. But you know how the weeks go by.

Betty keeps pretty busy with her homework and baton swinging.

It rained almost all week here, it seems like it will never clear up.

There's nothing much to write about. Nothing exciting happens. Lala, myself, Tessie and Mary Rosensweig played bridge last night. Our church gave it and what a crowd they had. They had a party on old man Andrews last Sun. in Ziegler's yard and quite a few neighbors went. Fannie is still moaning how hard it is to get by. Charlie was home sick for a couple of days but he is back working now. Little Donald is making his First Communion tomorrow. He is a good kid. But the other one is so fresh. He was swearing like the devil the other day and I chased him in the house. Fan got kind of mad but she got over it.

Willey Westerman is home for the first time. So are the two Pepe brothers. Kenneth was out until 4 this A.M. They had a party for the Pepes. He never works when any of the boys come home. Lala is wild. Tag is supposed to come home soon. I wonder if he will get married when he does. Aunt Anna has to give up working right away. She hasn't been feeling well and she went to the Dr. and he said she had a very bad heart. She is taking digitalis. I only hope they can do something for her. I will try to write more often.

Love,
Mother

U.S. Naval Base
Sampson, New York
May 15, 1944

Dear Charlsie,

Thanks for your birthday wishes. Let's hope that you and I will be together on my 20th year and that we have had or will be looking forward to D-Day. Wheeeee!!

Things are about the same here at Sampson. Last night I heard Gil Dodds speak and I was fortunate enough to shake hands with him after.

Two weeks from tomorrow and I'll be home. I don't know what's the matter with me – I'm not moved at all. I know that I'm the sort of a guy that agrees with most things, and no matter how bad things are I am usually less disgusted than most people. Maybe I'm not human! I feel just about the way I felt before leaving school. I do, of course, miss Mom and Dad. That goes without saying, but as for most of the other things in the "blood-pit," they're practically nil. What cha think??

Francine still writes. I received 4 birthday cards from her today. She met Mom Sat. and Mom told her it was my 20ᵗʰ year of material misery. So she bought four "late" birthday cards. Should I really take advantage of this stuff? Oh fuck it!! This is war!!

I've got an 8- 12 watch in 10 minutes so I'll stop this epistle (how the hell do you spell it) of St. Richard. Write!!

Oversexually yours,
Dick

The pisser should write soon! She's off schedule, isn't she??

VT 29 F.P.P
FPO New York.
May 16, 1944

Dear Charles,

I am duty officer tonight so I am using the typewriter again. It gives me a little practice and it is also something different. I don't know what the hell I will ever need the practice for but it may come in handy some day. I was home over the weekend but as usual there wasn't a hell of a lot to do but I always manage to have a good time. I have been going out with Esther Mathewson. Well, anyway I think you know who I mean. I went out with her first to get Morry's ass out but then I came to find out that she is damn nice(before you ask I haven't lost that little beat for Handcock yet, in fact far from it.)

We have been doing quite a bit of horseback riding. In fact, that is where I first started taking her and of course over to the lake. I let Morry take her to the dances at least most of the them but I took her over to a lake to a couple of them. It is a hot battle but a hell of a lot of fun. Why the hell do I always go after a girl that someone else wants, first Patty Lou etc.

I will finish this later, planes are landing now.

Well, the planes are in but some bastard has the typewriter now so I will have to finish it in ink. Please don't tell me about plane crashes. I have seen too damn many of them. I have begun to wonder if flying is safe.

I haven't seen Launa. I don't know how to get in touch with her. I don't suppose I will get the chance now. We won't be here too many more weeks. In fact, not half long enough, damn it.

Well, I guess it is about time to turn in now. I only have five hours to get some sleep before my early hop tomorrow. Write when you get a chance and don't work too hard. If you see Benny again say hello for me.

So long,
Mick

R.I. School of Design
May 17, 1944

Dear Charlie,

Seems to me, sweet, that you have a real case against love. What's your problem? Don't tell me you've been in love and she didn't feel the same way? I thought that the "Great Young" never fell. But since you know so much about it – me thinks you've been burnt – but badly. Have you? As for my not falling in love, relax it's too late. I'm in love with three men at the same time and it's getting pretty hectic. If I ever had to decide on one of them, it would be hell. Like betting on the horses, you never know which one is the winner. Oh, such is life.

Last night I met Red Gingrase in the Canteen here at school. Seemed good to see a familiar face, even if it was Red (the wrong Red). I'm only kidding. Gingrase told me Dick has gone into the Navy and is probably at Sampson. Can you see that bat in a sailor's suit? I can't. Haven't heard anything new from home lately. Except that the place is deader than a morgue. But then I knew that. I'll be home in about five weeks. Hell, but this year has just flown. If all my years are as fast as that, I'll be out of College before I know it.

My hay-fever has arrived and is making quite the showing. My nose looks like I've been imbibing a little too freely, and I can't see out of my eyes, every time I open my mouth I sneeze – other than that I'm perfectly all right. There's only one thing my heart desires and that is some roses– Four Roses. Maybe this weekend will take care of that. Emily's man is coming up and he always takes us both out. He's big enough to handle three women and capable, too. He likes to drink and especially with me.

228

Gotta wash my hair now. I'm going to the U.S.O. tonight to do my part to make or break the morale of the poor, unsuspecting service man.

Love,

Lucy

P.S. You know, dear, I love you best.
P.S.S. Relax, it's Leap Year.

17 Anise Street
New Britain, Conn.
May 17, 1944

Dear Son,

Just a few lines letting you know everything is o.k.

Thanks for the pretty card and the candy. It's too bad you got stuck on the candy. They must have had it left over from the last war. If you ever go in that place tell them about it. Betty gave me a nice pair of gloves and Donny gave me a bouquet of wild flowers and a card so that was o.k.

We had the garden plowed and we planted some seeds already. I am going downtown this afternoon to buy some corn and other seeds.

Your rhododendrons all dried up on the hill, even the laurel. So Donny said he was going to take care of your garden for you. It's so dry around here, we need rain bad.

Dad cut the grass twice already. It's supposed to be Donny's job. All he does is play ball and fight with Charles Farmer.

Pa is kept busy, he is working in Hartford this week. John didn't show up Monday or Tuesday.

I found your shorts but I can't find your trunks. Just as soon as I do, I will send them to you. Did you hear from Freddy? He was going to write to you. He is in the regular Navy. Anna sent him some money for he plans on coming home on a furlough. I guess that's all for now.

Love,

Mother

Hugh Reynolds died.

65 Arthur Street
New Britain, Conn.
May 18, 1944

'Lo, Lovie –

Received your letter this morning, and I am answering you immediately in that I'll probably be very occupied during my last few days in this "passion pit."

229

In continuing this "issue of passion," I'll once more remind you that I am protecting my virginity right down to my last ounce of strength. What damn fools we are!! Ah, but my sweet, it will pay off on D-Day!! Wheeeee!! What an offensive we'll launch!

At present my undies are out on the line drying in the sun. I literally urinated in my pants while reading your episode with that "fruit." He must have been quite the boy. I wonder if there are any of those boys running around loose in this part of the country. If there are any extras down there, send them up here for I think that the "toothless wonder" is getting sick of the "Community Chest."

I received my yearbook from Duke a couple of days ago. Charlie, it is really wonderful. It surely is great to thumb the pages and reminisce. But, you know, I feel as tho' I had never been at school, and that all of that is just a dream!! I suppose that you feel the same way about Harvard – no??

Saw your sister yesterday. She's having a hard time getting a ride to and from the school for the Girl's League Dance. I think that I'll let myself go and go to this great event. After all, it won't cost me a cent. I've been invited by an eleventh grader – guess I told you that before.

Saw Mary Jo Tuesday. She's working for a Doctor now – as a nurse she says. Poor Mary! She has no one with whom to go to Class Nite, Graduation or the Prom. Poor kid! I feel sorry for her! She said that she would give anything to have graduated with us so that she could have all of our remembrances – especially graduation nite. I told her that she should be going steady like "Hot Pants" and then she would be sure of dates for these important events. Then she said, "With a Spook?" She also continued by quoting you: "Some people rob the cradle, but Meg is robbing the graveyard." Oh my fuckin' dear!

Francine and I went out last Sat. nite and had a wonderful time. I was also at her house Monday and Wednesday nite. Tonight we're going to Lake Compounce – alone. Wheeeee!

Monday night I brought all of my old Archives up to the Valin house. Jean and Marie were in stitches laughing at the dirty jokes. They aren't so dumb. Fifi keeps telling me that she's madly in love with me. I let her kiss me on the cheek once in awhile. That seems to satisfy her. I hope Francine wears her glasses tonite. Then I can breathe on them and she won't be able to see what I'm doing. Wheeeee! Ya' ol' turd!

Well, Charlie, this is my last letter to you from the "Garden City." I'll drop you a line as soon as I get to Sampson. Take care and don't take any wooden nickels. If you do – you can split them with me. Screeeeeeeew!

Virginally yours,

Dick

US Naval Training Station

Sampson, New York

May 28, 1944

Hello, my lil' darlin',

Received your letter yesterday and was surprised and happy to hear from you. The Navy has changed you in no way, Charlie. I hope that it doesn't change me.

"Ya ole monkey piss," I can hardly remember what happened since the last time I wrote to you, for things have happened so fast and so furiously! I left New Britski Monday at 8 A.M. I spent the rest of the day in New Haven, taking in a movie in the afternoon. I left New Haven at 7 that night. Our group was quite fortunate, for we had troop sleepers from New Haven to Sampson. We arrived at Sampson at 8 A.M. Tuesday. Physical, needles, issue of clothing followed. We were assigned to our barracks and I began settling down. You've been through "boot" camp once, so that I guess you realize how strange and busy the first few days are – stenciling, checking clothes, squaring lockers etc. Did you have to square your "gear" when you were in boots? What one hell of a headache that is!!

The only free time I have for myself is between 5:00 – 8:45 in the evening. Furthermore, between this time I must wash all clothes that I dirtied during the day, wash and take a shower for the evening, and do guard duty or some detailed duty. Sunday may be different. I'll discover exactly how free I'll be this afternoon.

I have been told that the unit that I am in – "G-Unit" – is the best at camp. It is noted for its discipline and cleanliness. When the "gold braids" make a visit "G-Unit" is always presented to them.

I am now in my second week of training even though I haven't been here for a week. As you know, the Navy week ends on a Thursday and we came in on a Tuesday, so Thursday ended our first week. I'm now in my third day of my second week. Not bad!!

I still have my civilian hair. We get our haircuts tomorrow. Until then I'll be known as "barber bait." At first all of us recruits were labeled

231

"mothballs" because of our clothes smelling of camphor. After my hair is cut off I'll be known as "flat-top" or "skin head." When I leave for my "Boot" furlough, I'll be whore bait and when I return I'll be shark bait. The Navy has a name for everything.

There are a few fellas from the V12 unit at Brown University in "boots" with us. They felt pretty bad about coming here. I can now imagine how you felt.

Before I left I had a very good time. I spent most of my evenings with Francine Valin. Did we have fun!! Wheeeee! I'm not in love with the woman, but "ye gods" I think of her a lot and I promised her that I would spend most of my boot leave with her.

The night before I left home I made the rounds. I went to see Mary Jo and asked if she would like to go out to dinner. That we did!! Later I took Mary home, and on my way back I met Francine. What a session we had before we said good-nite and good-bye. Wheeeee! Bogart has nothing on me.

My uniform fits me like a boxing glove. Our whites and blues are being tailored now. We are wearing dungarees now.

Yesterday we were to have inspection. We were cleaned up to the nth degree. We waited in ranks from 10 to 4:30 in the afternoon, and the Captain didn't show up. Great!!

How about your shipment to California? Is there any chance of your getting home soon?

S'all for now, Mate. This note isn't up to my usual clowning standards. However, as time progresses I hope to improve.

Sexily yours,
Dick

Pvt. Joseph Rizzo
APO -26
Ft. Jackson, S.C.
May 29, 1944

Dear Sonny,

How in the hell are you, and your nurses and Waves? Have you gotten it from either of them? If you're as bad off as I am, you would take anything and I mean anything. Things are really sad around here—a weekend pass every other week—if we are in camp. When the pass finally comes up and you get in town, it seems as if the whole army received passes that night. Now I ask you what chance has an innocent boy like me got against all those other soldiers? I hope things aren't as bad down your way.

232

By the way, have you received a furlough lately? If not, you're slipping.

By the way again, have you seen our dear friend Benny? How is the dear boy? If you see him, tell him to write and send his address.

When and if you write, let me know the pieces you are working on (I mean at).

All we do in this damn infantry is march. Nite after nite. One night we did 28 miles in 7 1/4 hours. I wish to hell I had joined the Navy. Tell me what you are doing in Tenn. Aren't you a long ways from the water? I guess you are a fresh water Seaman. Well, write and give me some dope on N.B. if you have any. I don't have time to write anyone there but my Aunt and Uncle.

Hoping you get in,
Joe

17 Anise Street
New Britain, Conn.
May 29, 1944

Dear Chick,

You should have your shorts by now. We looked all over for your sun glasses but couldn't find them. If I do come across them, I'll send them, o.k? Perhaps Donny sold them to Waltie Rodin for a nickel.

We received the post card from you the other day. Hot Springs certainly must be a "snazzy" place.

Audry G, Virginia Green and I went over to Stanley Quarter yesterday. The pool hasn't any water in it but the refreshment stand was open. We just lay down on the sand all day and tried to get a tan. We didn't go home until about 8:30 p.m.

We have a two day vacation. We have Monday and Tuesday off because of Decoration Day coming on a Tuesday.

Mother is telling Donny to put some kind of wiring in the yard for the ducks. He always keeps them in a box all cooped up.

Your birthday isn't but a few days off. Is there anything you want Mother or I to get you? (don't answer that), If there is let us know.

I'm going to send this letter Air Mail because I haven't written to you this week and I don't want anymore arguments about not writing. That's all for now.

Love,
Betty

P.S. Don't forget to tell us about your birthday. Perhaps you want a nice flashy neck tie? Okay?

We just received a couple of letters from you so I tore off the old envelope and put on your new address. I hope it's right.

Please explain "Amphibious Training." Hope you enjoy your new station.

Love again,

Betty

17 Anise Street

New Britain, Conn

May 31, 1944

Dear Brother,

Well, kid how are you? I hope you like it at New River.

Isn't Camp LeJeune a Marine base? Did they put you in the Marines like Taggy? I hope not because Tag didn't like the Marines at all. (He was in the Navy though).

Daddy, Mother, Donny and I and the Narcums went to the Carnival in Berlin last night. It was stinky. The prices of everything are so high this year. (Donny sneaked into a Burlesque show when we weren't looking.)

I bet you had a swell ride on the train. Send me some of that perfume, o.k? You know, "Three Nights on a Troop Train." (Ha, ha!)

Gee, it's hot here. The summer's just beginning, too. Is it very warm at New River?

Mother got excited the other day when she found out New River, 'cause you usually get shipped out from there. Isn't that right? I guess that's all for now.

Love,

Sis

P.S. Have you heard from Dickey? How does he like the Navy?

Naval Radio School

Bedford, Pa.

June 2, 1944

Dear Charlie,

Here's hoping this letter reaches you. By the sound of things you must have been moving around or else they must be working the balls off you so you have no time to write.

How is the pecker checker coming along? This hole is just about getting me down and I do mean down. They work the ass off us from morning till night. Plus what they call the happy hour, which is misnamed. (A few times around the grinder.) I got a letter from Benny today and I see he is moving again. He already has a crow. Not bad. If I graduate within the top ten percent of my class, I will also get one. But the competition is a little stiff, although I haven't altogether given up hopes.

In about 3 hours I am leaving for good old N.B. It will then be about 4:00 p.m. I should get there Saturday morning about 3:30 a.m. This is if connections are good. It's only a short leave but better than none. I will have to leave Berlin about 11:00 Sunday morning. Because the skipper insists on tucking us in bed at 9:45 sharp. (Damn him),

Well, here comes that 4-F bastard that teaches us typing so I'll have to stop.

Don't forget to drop me a card.

As ever,

Tony

P.S. You must be pretty close to a crow yourself.

232 Mountain Drive
West Hartford, Conn.
June 2, 1944

Dear Charlie,

I am slowly going mad – I haven't heard from you or Ben in ages and I can't figure out what's the matter. Have you all gone on strike? Or is Memphis so interesting to you that you have forgotten all about poor little me.

It's so darned hot here that I wish I could forget about myself to the extent of going out and drowning myself in some ice water. There I go – griping again.

Tomorrow I have to go to a tea and how I love those things! It's our annual Alumnae tea at the Mount where everyone exclaims over everyone else and wants to know what you are doing and how is your love life. Then no matter what you're doing everyone says it must agree with you because haven't you put on a little weight. With me it's a little different – they'll all say how thin you are, but invariably they remark on your physical appearance in connection with what you are doing. I really enjoy them though and I gorge myself on the little tea cakes and cookies they have.

Last week we had a banquet at the Bond. Honestly, I never saw so many men all together since the war began. Of course, they were all over 35, but I'm developing a taste for older men and trying to develop a maternal

235

attitude toward 4–F's. After the banquet the staff went down to one of the
men's room in the Bond and had a little gathering. We had some wine and
stuff, but it broke up early. Boy! If I don't feel like an old hag at all these
business meetings and their intellectual speakers.

We were given Monday off with Memorial Day so that made us a
nice long weekend, but Marion and the baby came down and I couldn't go
anywhere. It was fun though, 'cause Marion let me take care of the baby
practically all the time and I was very dexterous in changing diapers and
the art of feeding.

Nancy and Morry are still in the throes of love. I wish I could find out
if Jane still mattered but I can't, and if I did, it wouldn't do me any good.
She'll be coming home for the summer in two weeks and then maybe she'll
get sick of him, but that's not very logical because there's no one else around
to take her attention.

I just got back from lunch if you'd call it that. On these hot days I seldom
bother to eat and today I had to buy shoes and a hat. Really, I think they
should extend our lunch hour to 1 ½.

I've got to get back to work now. I'll leave you with a hope and a prayer
that you will WRITE to me as soon as possible.

Affectionately,
Helen

P.S. I just received your letter from North Carolina so please just
disregard my anxiety at not getting a letter from you.

I was very surprised to learn that the Marines have been blessed with your
presence. I just love Marines! In fact, I went out with one for a month or so
(he was killed recently in the South Pacific) and what strength! What sinew!!

I think you may hear from Cheryl in the near future. I was talking to
her tonight and she has your address (I didn't give it to her.) From what
she says though, you are anxious to hear from her. Why didn't you tell
me? I could have conveyed your messages to her. I'd just adore being love's
messenger. Anyway, you might tell me what the story is.

Write again soon,
Helen

Remember, my pet, everything is strictly confidential.

U.S. Naval Training Station
Sampson, New York
June 3, 1944

Dear Charlie,

I received two letters from you via New Britain today. You bawled me out and I certainly deserve it. Can't do much about it except write more often. The best I can do is drop short notes (similar to this one) more often. The only real time I can sit down and write a real letter is on Sunday. I enjoy writing to you a lot, you know that, and I surely would write or would have written if it would have been at all possible.

Not to much comes off in "boot" camp as you already know. You take a lot of "crap" but besides that you do keep busy doing nothing. Today we had rifle practice and boat drill.

I roared my darn ovaries off when I read your lines about Meg being a pisser. You know, I wonder how she is getting along! Guess that after the Prom and Graduation she'll be on the loose again. Hot Pants!!

Poor Mary. I think that she's going stag to all the graduation events.

I read in the Herald that Lorraine Minton got a full tuition scholarship to Purdue University as an engineer cadet. How d' ya like that?

I got a letter from my parents today and they said that Mrs. Farrell had called and said that Dick has landed back in the U.S.A. He called from California. Gosh, I felt so good after I read this. If there's anyone that deserves a rest, I guess that it's Dick!!

Did you hear from Launa?

I sent one letter to your old station in Tenn. a few days ago (a week, to be exact). Did you get this?

I'm really looking forward to my leave!! I'm hoping that we might be able to get together once more before either of us gets into this mess though.

You know, I was going to mention the same thing about the only D-Day that we are waiting for now, (or did I). Speaking of cherries, I'll bet that when Meg's breaks, lemon juice will come gushing down. (assuming that it is unbroken).

S'all for now, Lamb. Lights are going out!!! I'll write again soon and you do the same.

Urinatingly thine,
Dick

17 Anise Street
New Britain, Conn.
June 4, 1944

Dear Son,

Wishing you were home for your birthday, but no such luck. Now that you are doing kitchen duty you can bake yourself a birthday cake. Here's wishing you a Happy Birthday.

Ma and Pa

U.S. Naval Training Station
Sampson, New York
June 4, 1944

Dear Charlie,

Received all of your letters up to the one you sent from Greensboro. So, my lil' lemon is in the Marines. My, but you're a busy beaver.

I'm not sure whether or not this will get to you. I've lost your address in Carolina. However, as soon as I hear from you, I'll write you a lengthy letter. I have had exactly no time to myself, especially during the week. Can you imagine, I haven't even abused myself in two or three weeks. I made up for it though by having two wet dreams in the last three nights.

Ye gads, I'm getting in pelvis deep with Francine. You should see some of the letters she's writing to me. I'll have some fun with her anyways when I get home.

How long of a training will you get at Camp LeJeune? Are ya' goin' to swim across or go by water skis?

That episode with the fortune teller really tickled me!! I guess that I'll have to get my fortune told, then I could ask if my bologna would fit in Meg's canal. Wheeeee!

When you get this — if you ever do — please drop me a card with your address on it immediately.

I heard from Jim Donnelly. He's in Colorado now.

I'm running out of ink, so I'll close. Write me soon! Don't forget your address, and remember D-Day.

Sexier than ever,
Dick

P.S. Gee, am I hard up for a female.

Naval Research Lab.
Washington, D.C.
June 6, 1944

Dear Charlie,

I haven't got any excuse for not writing except my studies .I'm stationed at the naval research lab in the radio material school.

The town is a swell place and we have a swell bunch of instructors but as far as regulations go the place smells. We will get boot haircuts, can't roll up our dungaree sleeves, get 10 - 15 hours EPD for getting caught without a squared hat and all that sort of thing.

I met the cutest chick from Chester, Conn. I haven't been out with her yet but who knows?

This town is so full of Waves it's pitiful. Those poor girls.

How have you been doing with your Wave friends? Will you be getting a leave soon? I'll be able to get home weekends when I haven't got the watch.

I had all my exams and graduated as you can guess.

If you get the ambition or time I'd like to hear from you. I've got to write Mom now so I'll sign off.

Love,

Ben

232 Mountain Drive
West Hartford, Conn.
June 6, 1944

Dear Charlie,

I don't feel like working – I'd rather write letters. Sometimes I just can't bring myself to write and other times, I don't want to do anything else.

We had our tea and it was just as I described. Meg (I can't remember her last name but you know who I mean) came as Barbara Donahue's guest and she was telling me that Dickey (I wish you'd call him Dick) is in Sampson.

I had a letter from Ben yesterday and he was on his way to Washington, D.C. How far is it from here? Why don't I just dash down there someday and see you both? Pardon me, while I wake up from that beautiful dream.

It's so darn cold here today and you should see me. I've got a white dress on and I felt so asinine when I went out to lunch. Everybody dashing around with coats all buttoned up and I – looking like an outdoor fiend in white.

Look, my lambie pie, I have to run now, but don't you think I've compensated for the long delay? Now you write to me and tell me all about North Carolina. Too bad I can't write with a southern accent.

Affectionately,

Helena

17 Anise Street
New Britain, Conn.
Tuesday D–Day
June 6, 1944

Dear Charlie,

Happy Birthday!! You're a big boy now. Today is the invasion day and we'll always remember it because it came on your birthday.

We've had a little excitement around here lately. Remember that man (he's 21) that used to chase the girls home, well, the kids from the Campus and Drug Store ganged up on him the other nite and took him to the Police Station. The girls have been making complaints about him scaring them, so that's what led up to it. His trial was this morning and he was acquitted and is being sent back to New Hampshire tomorrow. In court the judge said that he was examined and found that he had the mind of an 8 ½ year old. I'm so mad, now he can't chase me home anymore.

Sunday we went down to Tryon's cottage at Clinton. Neubauers went too. It was a cold day so I didn't go swimming but I laid on the beach and got an awful sunburn. I suffered yesterday, but today I feel o.k.

I bet you just love being on Mess Duty. You certainly got sick of it soon enough. You have pretty good hours though (I think so).

I've got to do the dishes now and then go to Novena later. So long for now.

Love,
Betty

P.S. Write your address plainer. We can never dope it out. Thank you.

Naval Research Lab.
Washington, D.C.
June 7, 1944

Dear Charlie,

I wrote you a few days ago but it might not catch up with you so I'll try again.

I can hardly believe you are in the Marines. I hope you'll like it. But as I have a rate and like what I'm doing, I wouldn't have it for all the ties and buttoned shirts in the world.

I went on a cruise up the Potomac last weekend with a few women I met. I hear from a few of my roommates that Camp LeJeune is the sexiest town with (they think) all the Beautiful American Marines. But we know

240

better. There are hundreds down here but I haven't dated any yet that I can brag about.

I just got a letter from Helena so I'll have to sign off.

Our time is completely occupied now. We get off from 6-7 every night and that's all. No weekday liberty as in Clarksville. I envy your nine hour day. Write soon.

Love,
Ben

17 Anise Street
New Britain, Conn.
June 8, 1944

Hi, Kid,

Gee, we can't understand why you didn't get any mail. We sent you a couple of birthday cards with some money in them. Lala sent a card too. And I mailed you a few letters before that too. We sent them to that other address (Mess Barracks or something) but I still think you should get them. Gee, I hope you do. Perhaps you could inquire about it.

We've got two more weeks of school and then vacation. I wish I was sixteen so I could get a job.

Domijans moved over to Black Rock Avenue. Betty Lee is over here now and her mother is coming over in a little while to take us over to their new house.

My baton lessons are getting harder but I'll get by alright. I go for my lesson tonite. So long for now.

Love and kisses, XXXXXX
Betty

R.I. School of Design
Providence, R.I.
June 10, 1944

Charlie dear,

I've been on the go for the last twenty-four hours with no sleep and little food. It is slowly beginning to tell. I seem to have trouble keeping my eyes open and my brain functioning. I expect to collapse sometime today from sheer exhaustion. To put it mildly I have been raising hell for five days, no it's almost two weeks now, and if I don't slow down there's gonna be a show-down. I've done everything from having liquor in my room to sneaking out after hours. If we didn't have a new house mother, an unsuspecting soul, and if it wasn't the end of the year, I doubt if I could have gotten away with

241

the fast ones I've been pulling. Of course, I'm not too sure I've succeeded in fooling the faculty. Only time and Lady Luck will prove that. Maybe you'd better start praying for me – again!!! In my next letter when I have more time I'll tell you about my escapades – and they are a far cry from our kiddish high school tricks. Right now I'm in class so this can't be very long, but I thought I'd let you know I haven't forgotten you. There's only one thing I want to tell you and that is cut out the sex in your letters, dear boy –you're slipping right back into your old habits that I used to nag you for. I know you say you just talk a good line, that it doesn't mean anything, but I don't like it. So relax a little – will you? Gotta close now for a while. Try to behave for a little while, or at least till you hear from me again.

Love,

Lu

Continuing from last week – How the hell did you get into the Marines? And are you one for good? Did I ever tell you I hate Marines! Well, I do. Sooooooo.

Been having a gayer time lately. Back to my old Ensigns again. This one is pretty nice. No, I'm not in love anymore. Some day I'll tell you the narrow escape I had. No, not what you'll be thinking. Gotta go again, dear, so write soon. I leave here the 16th, next Friday. So write before then.

191 Bristol Street
New Britain, Conn.
June 11, 1944

Dear Charlie.

Geeeeeeeeeeeee! It was good to hear from you after all this time! You know I always have time to write to you, regardless of any interest in people or things.

I nearly died when Mary Jo told me you were in the Marines now. What's the story? Did you get sick of the Navy whites or something? There must be some boys from New Britain down there. Danny Kelly used to be down there but he's somewhere in the Pacific now.

Things have been pretty dull around the old town lately. Not much doing but I manage to find something. (Don't get fresh, I mean tennis or going down to the "Swedes" to swim). Did you ever go down there in Berlin? It's neat but it's one h–of a long ride. It nearly kills Mary and I. We got to the end of Willow Brook Park the other day and just dropped there. (That's where I'm writing you from.) Class Night is next Friday night.

242

They'll probably make some rotten remark about Mary and I or else not even bother. We're a great asset to that school, let me tell you. The Prom is Monday or Tuesday and Graduation Friday. The dance afterwards won't be anything like the party after your graduation last year. Remember, that night you took Mary and I home and went out and had "a good time"? What a wild night. I guess none of us will never forget it.

 Write back right away. It's wonderful to hear from you again!

Love,

Meg

P.S. We'd better wait to talk about "between flings." O.K?
P.S.S. Excuse the messy letter but if I copy it over you'll never get it. I haven't heard from Dick, ask Mary for his address. He's at Sampson, N.Y.

17 Anise Street
New Britain, Conn.
June 12, 1944

Dear Son,

 Betty just received your letter and told me to write. Well, there is not much doing at present. Tessie was down yesterday and took us for a ride to lake Congamond. Donny enjoyed watching the speed boats. Betty didn't go. The Sodality had a picnic out at the park so she had to go there.

 Fannie got your letter and was she tickled about it. You ought to write to her again when you find time.

 So you don't like setting tables. I should think that you'd like it. It's much easier than being across on some little island like Tag was. What made them switch you to the Marines? They did the same thing to Tag and he didn't like it at all. But now they transferred him back to the Navy and he likes it much better. I wonder how Tommy is making out. I hope this war will be over soon. We just got your bond this morning. They are having another bond drive here, the kids had to buy stamps twice last week.

 Oh yes, we still have Prince around. No matter where he goes he always comes back. He doesn't touch Donny's ducks. He lays on the grass and watches every move they make. Some day he will probably grab one.

 I will try and get your razor brush when I get downtown. How about marking your clothes with indelible ink? I don't know if I will be able to get a stamp but I will try.

 Our garden is coming along fine. Neubauers have some of our garden and so have Narcums. I am going to the Teachers Meeting with Chas.

243

Farmer tonite. I wonder if Donny is going to pass. I doubt it. School doesn't bother him. Well, I guess I'll close.

With love,
Mother

Marine Barracks
Camp LeJeune, N.C.
14 June 1944

Dear Cheryl,

 I can't begin to tell you how good it was to hear from you. I wanted to write but didn't know if you would answer. We'd better let bygones be bygones or we'll be at it again. What makes us fight so anyway? I'm really glad to start writing to you again, we always did have a lot of fun together. Remember all the dances, Riverside and the Meriden Tower? I still laugh at the things we've done. Here 'Tis!

 The heat here has been terrific. In fact, I'm lying on my bunk now with just my shorts on.

 There isn't much to do here except go to the movies and to the beach on Sundays. I haven't left the base once in eight weeks. The movies here, however, are very good. There are five theaters here. I saw "Mark Twain" last night and "White Cliffs of Dover," "Mask of Demetrius," "Two Girls and a Sailor," and lots of good movies are here now.

 I could stand a lot of your cooking right now. The food here is alright but that's as far as it goes. I'd like to watch you making dinner someday. I'll bet it would be more fun than a barrel of monkeys.

 Virginia C. seems to be the same as she always was. Gad! I can see your dad stepping over the sleeping men in your living room now. That's what they call, "The blow that killed father."

 You once were having a picture made for me. I'd still like it if you didn't send it to someone else.

 I may not be here much longer but if you answer this right away, I'll get it before I leave.

Love,
Charlie

P.S. I hope that your mother is feeling better.

17 Anise Street
New Britain, Conn.
June 14, 1944

Dear Brother,

Well, kid, how the heck are you? We're o.k, including Prince. (I hope you got his picture). He's still running after birds, but very seldom catches one.

I was just reading the letter you wrote to Dad. I think you got a little ahead of time for Father's Day isn't until June 18th. Oh, well, it doesn't make much difference.

We have a new priest at St. Francis now. He stays with Father Brophy. His name is Father Webb, and, boy oh boy, is he nice. Red hair, freckles and very young. He was just ordained recently. I guess I'll try to date him up. (It's so funny, all of a sudden all of the young girls go to church every day).

Tonight we go to drum corps for drill. We have drill on Wednesday and Friday in the churchyard. Gertie hasn't been coming the last few times, so I've been leading the Corps. (More darn fun).

I had my picture taken at Lorings and if they come out good (slight chance) I'll have some made up and send you one, o.k?

We're having Composition now in English and I positively hate it. I always get the commas mixed up.

Betty Lee comes here for dinner now because her mother wants her to finish school here. Donny and Betty Lee have a wonderful time together. That's all for now. Love and kisses, XXXXX

Your Sweet Little Sister

Betty

P.S. Your razor brush is enclosed. I hope it's o.k.

232 Mountain Drive

West Hartford, Conn.

June 17, 1944

Dear Charlie,

Poor baby, I've neglected your letter for three whole days – how thoughtless of me.

My mom is in bed with the measles and while I'm waiting for the doctor, I can dash off a good substitute for a letter.

I was so excited all week – I had the faintest feeling that Ben might trip home for the weekend, but I haven't heard a word from him so I guess my woman's intuition has failed me.

I know what you mean about it being difficult to write to Ben. I found it that way at first, but now I just prattle on and on. I think it might be because he doesn't respond the way you would expect.

He doesn't call me Helena. Nobody does but you, and that really is a privilege to you 'cause I much prefer Helen, although I must say I'm flattered that you bother about a special name.

I have a thorough dislike for the author of "War and Peace."

Look, my sweet, if you're old and good for nothing, then you're certainly not good for marriage. Marriage requires the passion and fire of youth, and believe me, it's no trifle. I don't think a man is a success in life if he doesn't marry, have three or four children and keep them happy. I agree that a lover should see his proposed mate as objectively as possible because everyone has faults and marriage certainly doesn't overcome them. Now you've got me going. Mon Dieu! Let's stop here!!

Bring on the passion – I won't get disgusted. You know I don't pay any attention to you, and you have to keep in practice.

I haven't got a picture to send to you. I'll take some snaps this summer and send some of those – all right? I do want one of yours, though, if you'll send one. And be sure to write something on it. Darlin', honest I'd send you one if I had it, but no can do.

I went to New London to see Nancy last week and oh, what a marvelous time. Sunday night we went dancing – Duke Ellington was there. I met the darlingest Coast Guard and must have shocked him with my chastity. We went for a stroll on the beach and were talking and then he tried to kiss me. Of course, I didn't let him and after that he kept telling me that surely I was headed for the life of an old maid. I told him that wouldn't be so bad 'cause I knew two fellows who were going to be bachelors and I could live with them.

Then if my dress happened to slip above my knees, he'd tell me to pull it down. I was shocking his modesty. More fun!!

My brother arrived here today for a 15 day furlough. He can't come near home though because of mother. You should see her – she's all broken out with measles.

I'm so exhausted, Charlie, dear. I hope Ben surprises me this weekend. I need the relaxation. When will you be coming home again? We must get together more often when you do. I miss both of you lots and lots, but your letters are wonderful. Well, here comes old saw-bones. '

Night,
Helena

17 Anise Street
New Britain, Conn.

June 17, 1944

Dear Brother,

This may only be a half of a letter, but you said that's better than none.

By the way "Kiddo," I don't have any "night life." I stay in all night and do my homework. So there!!

There's going to be a Fife & Drum Corp meet at St. Agnes' Hall today and a dance for the different corps tonight. I'm going with our Corp, but of course I won't go in for any competition in twirling for a while yet, There's going to be a parade for Flag Day tomorrow and I think that I might lead it.

We had a party at Sodality last night. It was our last meeting till September. Jean and I were on the entertainment committee so we did our "College Rhythm" act with little red skirts and hats. We had more fun. I did a Hawaiian dance with a real grass skirt . "Mary Moonlight" let me borrow it. I had some pictures taken in it, so I'll send you one later. Our audience thought we were wonderful, so that was all that counted. Well, I have to go and clean the house a little, so I'll write again soon.

Love and kisses, xxxxxx

Betty

P.S. How's the table setting business?

P.S.S. Prince ran away again yesterday. First a man called at the Besco Drug on Arch St. and then Mr. Hagearty on Park St. Mr. Hagearty lives out this way, so he brought him home. I think he went shopping for Father's Day. (Little Devil).

Did you get your razor brush?

91 West Street
New Britain, Conn.
June 18, 1944

Dearest Charlie Lamb –

I purposely didn't write sooner 'cause I thought I'd wait till after graduation and tell you all the dirt. Well, I finally went to the Prom and Graduation Dance. You'll never guess who I went with – Joe Kenney. The prom was really swell. We went with Morry, the toothless wonder. After the dance we rode down to Lake Pocatapaug. No, we didn't go swimming together. The boys went in alone. Graduation exercises were over about 9:30 so I went home and got dressed. There were 2 dances. T.S. and D.K. at the Three Cups and Beta Mu and Alpha at the Wethersfield. You might know we went to the D.K. brawl. I didn't have as much as a smell of firewater to celebrate graduation.

Cal Wade, Betty Logan, Lorry, Jim Lynch, Jeff Donahue and a whole bunch of kids were feeling no pain at all. After the dance Morry, Nancy, Joe and I went over to Morry's house – had a swell time. I'm so glad I was able to go to the dances 'cause it made the last week of school just perfect.

I'm still working my fingers right to the bone – ain't it a shame!

The fourth of July weekend Meg, Joan DeWitt and I are going down to Joan's cottage at South End shores in New Haven from Saturday till Wednesday- unchaperoned, too!!(Waterbury Herald).

Tell me, Punkin – how in the hell did you ever land up in the Marines? I was nearly floored when I read your letter!

Dick Walton doesn't expect to be home until the 4th of July. They must have prolonged their boot training. Do you hear from him often?

Well, keed - I guess this is all the dirt for now – I'll see if I can dig up some more –

Please write real soon.

Oodles of love 'n stuff,
Peaches

P.S. Conway is home – shall I throw a party! When ya comin' home?

17 Anise Street
New Britain, Conn.
June 20, 1944

Dear Son,

Recc'd your letter today. It took a little longer getting here, you forgot to put Conn. after New Britain. We subscribed for the Herald and that will start tomorrow. I hope they won't ship you out for a while yet. Willie Westerman was only in three months and he was shipped across. He is in the Medical Corps. Did all the fellows send their clothes home? I hope that doesn't mean anything. We tried to get a stamp for you but it will take about 10 days. We will order one anyway. Can't you use indelible ink for the time being? What do the other fellows use?

I hope your pictures turn out good. Betty had hers taken but they didn't turn out so hot. I don't know whether she will have any more made up or not.

Nellie had another girl, born yesterday. I wonder if Pop Nealon is disappointed.

It rained here every day for the past week. The garden is growing swell. We took a ride to Plainville Sun. over to Almas with Ed and Oneida and Freddy's mother. We haven't had a beer party yet. Can't think of any more news but will write again. I have to get supper now. Pop will be home any minute now. I've got a chicken in the oven with baked potatoes.

I saw Donny's teacher and she said he was going to pass. Mattie Graham resigned so he is going to have his same teacher next year. So that won't be so bad.

Lots of love,
Mother

U.S. Coast Guard
Clallam Bay, Wash.
June 21, 1944

Dear Charlie,

I received a letter from you yesterday but I can't know what it said because the kid who was bringing the mail out to the cape fell in the river and the ink ran on all over the mail and you should have heard us guys bitch at him. Well, I guess there wasn't anything important in it, just shooting the breeze as per usual.

Well, I was up in a P.B.Y. over Alaska last week and I almost froze my nuts off. The Navy has two of them up on the lake now and I took a ride with them over the coast and up to Alaska. It was my first and last time up. Boy, do them things move. We left here at 6 in the morning and were back at 8 at night. I don't mind telling you I almost shit in my pants.

I haven't much time because we are leaving for the base in a little while and I'm on liberty in the evening and I won't get another chance for a week. There isn't a damn thing here new anyway, so I'll close now and write again when I get an answer to this letter.

Love and kisses,
Freddy

108 Park Lane
New Britain, Conn.
June 18, 1944

Dear Charlie,

Have I been neglecting you, baby? If so I'm sorry – packing and things took up my time those last weeks of school. But now I've nothing to do but write to you (oh, yeah). Forget about the ensigns, dear, that's a thing of the past. They're in Providence and I am in N.B. so unless they are there in October and come to see me, I've seen the last of them. All of them, damn it.

It is very boring in N.B. and so I am going to work. Don't faint, I did say work. In the telephone company if possible. I'll call you up, dear, and give you a thrill. Yes, I have heard about the scandal in the high school. So what – don't think it's the first time in our crowd. Hell, its been going on quite a while but it just never got around before. If that's their conception of fun all right – mine is quite a bit different.

Darling, the reason I hate Marines – is a Marine. I met him in Providence last winter and the less I hear about it the better. It was the second of my four mistakes in Prov. No, not what you're thinking – I don't play that way – remember this is me. Known in Prov. As "Ice cold Lulu" and I'm going to stay that way. No more love for me. I've got burnt twice and so from now on, it's purely platonic. Laugh if you want – but I mean it.

So last week was your birthday. Happy Birthday, dear – How old are you? Of age, I hope. All right I'll send you a picture in my next letter. You'll have a lot of fun laughing at it – but you asked for it – so don't complain.

How is Dickey and what's his address? Yes, I want to write to him – I've got to do something to kill the time – only 123 days until I go back to school. Wish it were only three days – that I could stand.

There is nothing to tell you so I'll close. In my next letter I'll dig up all the family skeletons and let you have all the dirt. Till then be good and don't dream of me unless it's clean.

Love,

Lucy

108 Park Lane
New Britain, Conn.
June 21, 1944

Dear Charlie,

Glad to hear from you, old boy. It seems from what you say that I probably won't see my latest Marine for quite a while. Am I to add you to my list of dates after the war? If so, you'd be quite a ways down on the list. It seems that I'll be pretty busy for about six months after the armistice.

N.B. is pretty damn dead to put it mildly. They're either too young or too old and that's no lie. But what care I – frankly, I'm a little sick of people. I get this way every once in a while. It will pass.

I have a job – three cheers. In the N.B. Coal and Wood Co. in the office. I told everyone I was shoveling coal. I like the job and the hours are swell, 8 –5. And I don't work Saturdays – also the pay isn't bad. I'll never get a mink coat for working this summer but it will be more than enough to keep me in cigarettes and cokes.

Two and a half months approximately, and back to the R.I.S.D. Happy day – I can hardly wait for the new term to start. If this year was as much fun as the last was— oh, what a life. I can understand why you dislike so many things about N.B. Because I feel the same way. Here I can't be myself – I'm too shut in by a small town and narrow-minded people. In Providence I can act natural. There, there is no tension, there is a reasonable quality of living. Convention, small town convention, isn't stuffed down your throat at every turn. I love Providence in spite of the dirt and smell and servicemen. I think I'd like any place that wasn't New Britain. Do I make myself clear?

Why do you insist on having my picture? I'd think you'd be ashamed to admit you know a girl with a face like that. Anyway, you can see me anytime at all by merely imagining the most disagreeable person you ever met – there I'll be. But maybe if I get up enough nerve I'll have one taken and send it to you. Send me one of you anyway, dear. I'd like to see you as a Marine – without the hat.

There's nothing to tell you because I've done nothing. I may go to the shore soon and visit my roommates. Other than that a very dull summer looms before me. Write soon, honey, and make it amusing. I'm in very low spirits. Harriman says my morale needs boosting, but bad. So do your part to keep up the morale on the home front.

Love,

Lucy

U.S. Coast Guard Station
St. Augustine, Fla.
June 21, 1944

Dear Charlie,

I received your letter the other day and this is the first chance I've had to answer it. I haven't got much time so this will be short and sweet.

First of all I haven't got the time and this school is driving me nuts. But I can stand anything for 8 weeks (and a leave).

Say how the hell did you get into the Marines? Did you ask for it or were you drafted? (That's what they call it.) Are you in the Marines or just working with them? I mean are you still in the Navy or what?

What did your mother think? Don't tell me, I know.

I've been writing to Joyce and telling her how you miss Cheryl and all that kind of stuff. So you can expect a letter with fish all over it. Cod. Why

251

don't you send her one with some pecker tracks on it? She'd go for that in a big way.

Let's stop kidding each other. Answer me just one thing, and no bullshit. Is there anything between you and Cheryl? I don't give a shit, I'd just like to know.

Well, I'll leave you with that thought.

Loads of luck,

Freddy

P.S. When I'm home on leave I'll take care of your dad's guns for him.

U.S. Naval Training Station

Sampson, New York

June 25, 1944

Dear Charlesie-Warlsie,

Oh, you really, really charge me! I don't think there are two people in the world that have as much fun reading and writing letters to each other as we do. I received both your Tuesday and Wednesday letters yesterday and was per-usually pleased, pronged and penisified at your remarks — whatever that means.

First, I'll answer all of your questions and make a few remarks about your lines. I'll jot them down just as they come to me.

I'm happy to hear that you finally received a few of my letters which I sent to Memphis. I thought that they had become lost. Well, I guess you know that my reputation has been saved a little at least by their arrival.

I was scheduled to leave here on July 18th, but now there is a question mark as to our breaking date. There have been a lot of rumors flying around about our leaving sooner. Also there is another rumor that O.G.U. is being stopped and that all "boots" upon graduation will go home and await orders. The leave is supposed to be guaranteed for 7 days plus all of the days after 7 that you await your orders. However, as things stand now, I'm scheduled to "break" on the 18th for a 7 day liberty. Speaking of leaves, will you be given a short leave after your training at LeJeune?

It doesn't seem possible that you've been in the Navy for a year. As you have said before the past year really seems like a dream. I could go on sentimentalizing but I don't think it's the right thing to do at present. 'Nuff said.

Jim Donnelly is in the Midwest someplace. I had his address at one time but I lost it. I believe that he's a buck private. You know, since I came

home I've induced (not seduced) about four fellas to read "Kings' Row".
You know, you and I should have a little commission coming for pushing
that book.

Today is Visitors' Day. It seems so odd to see civilians again. Women
especially!! I'm so hard up that I'd even look at Joan Jones. That's how bad off I am.

About Francine – as I said before I'm in pelvis deep with her. We went
out twice (pardon) three times when I was home. Also, I was writing her
at her little hole in the wall nightly for the last 10 days. The second date I
had with her, I started to buck like the cow's ass at fly time. Oh, my dear!
We French kissed each other so much that I felt turned inside out. After that
nite, I didn't see her once without kissing her before I left her. Does she eat it
up! I swear, darlin', that I'm afraid I really wanted to. I could have easily
broken our D-Day promise. That's how torrid it was. Since I arrived here
she's been writing very steadily – more than Meg ever thought of writing,
and her letters are really swell. You know these French anyway! The funny
part of it is that she keeps reminding me of the French that she has in her.
I don't know whether she's hinting or boasting. Before I left, I asked her
about Keith, and she said very calmly that she thought that that was all a
mistake. I'm sure that I don't really love her. However, she is something to
go home to and, brother, she suits me fine.

About the pisser. I feel sorry for her, too, Charlie. To this day, no matter
how many times I've given excuses and tried to explain my relationship
with her, I always wind up with nothing. Maybe, it's because I understand
her too much. I wonder how things stand with her and the Spook? According
to the schedule, he should be sucking air through his anus, and Meg should
be looking for something new. How is she responding to your line? Biting
as usual, no doubt!!! I've just got to say it again—What a pisser!!

I don't believe you should be sad when I get married (if I do). After
all, I'd let you screw my wife (as you've already suggested). Ya clown!! But
what would I be doing in the meantime – palming my poodle?

There's a fella up here that's really a character. He comes from N.B.
and is married and has one kid. That doesn't bother him tho for all he is
thinking of most of the time is getting "nooky". He can't get it up here tho
and the other fellas and I "kid" the hell out of him. He says that married
life is wonderful!

As for Launa, Charlie, I don't know. Your last letter to her must have
frightened her out of her pants. Truthfully, I don't believe that you could
change her feelings for you by telling her what you did. But then again I

don't know her as well as you do and you probably wouldn't have mentioned anything like that unless it were to bring results. Love seems so unfair at times. It doesn't seem possible that God could keep two people apart as he has in your case You must be beyond the point of disappointment by now. But I once read that people should not be disappointed by the works of God because it is only the material expectations of people that do not materialize that make them start doubting. You can take what I have just said for whatever it's worth. I keep thinking of it a lot when things don't go right for me.

By this time, I imagine that things in New Britain are all over as far as Graduation goes. I hope that Mary had a good time. I'll bet that she probably ended up going with her brother. Oh my dear!!

Things up here are pretty much the same. I haven't had a wet dream in a long time tho. I'm still leading the Barracks with four though – who am I kidding? I'm probably in last place.

That's all for now, my plunckin' plum. Hope to hear from you soon.

"Forever urine"

Dick

I repeat –" Hot Pants sure is a pisser." Oh! Monkey piss!

17 Anise Street
New Britain, Conn.
June 29, 1944

Hi, Brother,

How are you? I just got through scrubbing and washing the porch and my hands are numb. The porch looks clean now at least.

I'm sending a few pictures. Will you send the majorette picture and the one with the guitar back, and then I'll send you a smaller size that I'm having made up, o.k? They didn't come out too good but I guess that's the new film. We can't even get any more film now. If you can, try and get us some 616 film.

Jean and I are going swimming up at the pool this afternoon. My mistake, we're not going in the water, we're just going to lie down and get a tan. The water is too dirty to swim in. I prefer Shadsky's or B.A.B. Don't you??

That clipping about the dog was pretty good. Perhaps we should have a few of our Princey's experiences in the paper.

We just changed our minds. We're now going to the Reservoir. Five (5) of us are going. Good-bye for now.

Love,

Betty

232 Mountain Drive
West Hartford, Conn.
June 29, 1944

Dear Charlie,

I'm weak with exhaustion but I think I can get through a letter with a little rest between lines.

Mother feels slightly better now and I hope there is nothing to worry about anymore. She has been sick so seldom that it gets me to see her down. I'm on vacation now so that I can be with her and keep the house clean. Honestly, darlin', I think I'll be an old maid for sure. The house is so darned big that I no sooner get one part cleaned up when the other is all messy. This goes on indefinitely until I start banging my head against the wall! Today I scrubbed the kitchen floor and waxed it. My knees were giving in a little, though I managed to get some lunch, but E' Gad! What do you think happened? I went to put the milk in the refrigerator and stood right there and dropped it all on my nice clean floor!! Soooo – I spent the afternoon on my hands and knees again. I finally cleaned upstairs and got dinner and am now contemplating tonight's slumber.

You should have seen me doing the washing the other day. But I'll save you the details of that for another time.

Thanks for the morale-builder, sweet, but can a girl with practically buckteeth be exotic!! I have no illusions that Ben loves me – or ever will. But we have a lot of fun and we don't do each other any harm. Of course, I think he'd be willing to rent me out as long as it would be to you. How much do you think I'd be worth?

I'm going to scold you now. Why are you developing such a stubborn attitude toward not being married? That's the silliest idea I've ever heard and I don't want you to think about it any more. Why, with your sense of humor and romantic nature, you'll make a wonderful husband. And one other thing—I wish you wouldn't use the word "love" so loosely for your own good. Someday those three little words are going to mean something for you, and you shouldn't go passing them around.

You aren't annoyed with me now, are you, dear? I'm always pleased no end when I read your letters and I hope you won't freeze up on me now.

I went to Nancy's last night and sat around ' til 12 o'clock just talking and laughing. She's out with Morry tonight. She is just the kind of friend for me. Our natures are exactly opposite and it's a wonderful let down to be with her. In all the 10 years I've known her we never had the slightest argument.

255

Cheryl's mother came home from the hospital today. She still isn't well and I guess she'll have to go back for treatment in a couple of weeks. Well, my lamb, I think I'll toddle off, iron a dress, read a while and then stagger off to beddie-bye.

Affectionately,
Helena

St. Augustine, Fla.
June 30, 1944

Dear Charlie,

Well, Jack, what's cooking? Oh, Brother, take me back to Frisco. I didn't think there was any place in the world as bad as the west coast. But I know different now. I was never in such a hellhole in all my life. It's so hot you can't do anything. Our sea-bags haven't gotten here yet and I'm wearing dress-blues. And I don't mind telling you I don't wear them anymore than I have to. Well, I've bitched enough—now you tell me all about your place.

I got a letter from Joyce today and Cheryl wants me to send her your address. I wrote and gave her a line of shit like you told me to. I think that she came off in her pants because she seems to want your address in the worst way. So be all set for a big blow off.

Well, getting back to this dump (and it is a dump). We are staying at a hotel and the hotel itself is o.k. But we can't leave our rooms after class and we only get one liberty a week and that starts at 4:30 Sat. and ends at midnight. And that's all the liberty we get. No midweek or 48's. Well, I think I'll live 12 more weeks. (I hope). Well, I've got to run (to the head) so I'll sign off. Drop me a line and give me all the dope.

Love and kisses,
Freddy

17 Anise Street
New Britain, Conn.
June 30, 1944

Dear Brother,

I just got your letter this morning, but thought that I'd answer it now since I didn't go to school today. I was so tired from over the weekend, and then it was raining this morning so I stayed home. Saturday there was a drum meet at the Sacred Heart church. So our Corp was invited. There were about thirty different kinds of Corps there from all over. It lasted from 2 to 12 p.m. It was wonderful. The Junior Corps were judged in the afternoon, and the Senior Corps and baton twirlers at night. I never saw

256

such good twirling in all my days. It'll take me years to learn. Oh, our Corps got second prize for playing in the Junior Feminine Class.

I was majorette for the Corps yesterday. It was so hot I thought I'd faint at any moment. But I went through with it o.k. It is more fun to have people take your picture when you are marching by.

Gee, I wish I could get a nice tan. I got a sunburn that time down at the shore and the darn sunburn is still peeling. I'm a little tan though.

Fanny just came in and said she got a letter from you today. She's all excited.

Mother, Fanny and Lala are working out in the garden now. Those girls have so much fun. That's all, there ain't no more.

Love and "a smooch,"
Betty

P.S. I'm glad the brush was o.k.
P.S.S. Are the "chows" you get mongrels or thoroughbreds? Ha, ha!
P.S.S.S. Speaking of dogs, Baby Princey just knocked over a basket of clean clothes on the porch and then laid in them. Of course, he had to be all wet and stinky from the rain.

91 West Street
New Britain, Conn.
July 2, 1944

Dearest Charlie Warlie,

I'm so sorry I haven't answered your letter sooner – I really meant to – but just didn't get around to it.

When I came home from the shore two weekends ago, there was only 1 letter waiting for me and it was from you! I was so glad. Boy! Meg and I had a smooth time at the shore – it was just perfect. No chaperone – no mother.

Last Wednesday Miss Perry (the Dr's other nurse) and I went down to Beach Park with Dr. C. I came back literally "burnt to a crisp." My face is just about peeling off my head – at this point I'm rather repulsive looking (no cracks).

Meg is going to Parker's cottage for 2 weeks starting tomorrow –no, Jerry won't be there. While she's basking in the sun I'll be slaving – I tell you – there just ain't no justice!!

Salty Sea Scout Walton is coming home Tuesday. I hope to be able to see him for a few minutes at least.

Peaches! I'm sending you my graduation picture in hopes that you will send me your picture. Don't wait as long as I did. My picture is absolutely and positively stinkin' but I don't know when I'll get others taken so bear up with this one for a while O.K? Write real soon,

Loads of love 'n stuff
Mary Jo

17 Anise Street
New Britain, Conn.`
July 2, 1944

Dear Brother,

I'm just sitting around waiting for Audry to call. We're going up to the pool (not swimming) this afternoon. There was a tragedy there yesterday. A sixteen-year-old girl from Dwight Street drowned. You'll see it in Monday's paper.

There was a party under the old apple tree yesterday. Donny acted as bartender and he made $1.60. Irene and I went swimming up at the Res.

Daddy, Donny, Russell and Butch went to Indian Neck clamming today.

There's going to be another big Drum Meet Saturday. We're not sure of going because some of our drummers are on their vacations. If we do go and compete, I have to lead. I bet I'll faint right on the judges' stand.

I agree with you on the name Rhododendron for Nellie's baby. Nellie always liked rhododendrons. I wonder if she'll ask Fanny or Lala to be godmother??(Could be?)

There isn't any more news, so I'll say Goom Bye now.

Love and kisses,
Betty XXXXX

P.S. Donny certainly was glad to get that dollar from you. I think he bought some fishing stuff with it.

U.S. Naval Training Station
Sampson, New York
July 3, 1944

Dear Charlie,

I most certainly should have written you yesterday, for I had time enough to do so and wasted the greater part of the day. A bunch of fellas came in from N.B. and I went down to see how they were coming (not breathing hard) along. I really feel sorry for them! Look who's talking!!

I received your voluptuous volume of vigorous – can't think of anything that begins with "v" – remarks. You certainly must have a lot of time to write a letter of that length. It's perusually good to hear from you, Charlie. Don't stop now, Charlie, don't stop now.

You've been mentioning the book "War and Peace" so much that I'm making a promise to myself that I'll read the book someday. It'll have to be good to beat "King's Row."

I haven't heard from Mary in a hell of a long time. The last I heard from her was about 5 days before the prom. Since then nothing comes – including me. As for Mary, I've repeated many times how much I liked her, how I thought she was different from Meg, and that I didn't want to see her hurt. No, darlin', Mary's only half a pisser - in fact I don't think she even rates the title of a pisser. As for "Hot Pants" you know she should start putting out soon! No?

Speaking of nooky, you say that you believe Lucy is putting out. Is she still in Providence? Maybe I might see her when I go home in two weeks.

Dick Tarrell has finally arrived home for a 15-day leave. His side is badly chewed up, but otherwise he is fine. Mother said that she talked to him.

Launa should read that page that you wrote to me about her. Not that it would change things, but then you never know

Sweet dreams (wet ones),
Dick

17 Anise Street
New Britain, Conn.
July 7, 1944

Dear Brother,

Well, here I am again even though I haven't much to write. I'll find out tonite whether or not we're going to be in the meet tomorrow. Last night Mr. Walker showed me all the things to do if I do have to lead.

I guess you read about the Ringling Brothers Circus fire by now. It certainly was some fire. There were somewhere near 200 killed and I don't know how many injured. I guess that Barnum and Bailey won't have another circus for a while. I can bet they'll be sued for all sorts of things.

The radio is broke again. As soon as we get it fixed I'm going to buy some new marching records and try to twirl to the music. I've tried it by the marches on the radio and it's a lot of fun. Remember how you and I used to march around the living room with the candlesticks? More fun!!

I forgot to tell you before but your rose bush on the hill has beautiful roses on it this year. It's too bad that only the chickens can enjoy them. So long for now.

Love,

Betty

P.S. Sorry this letter isn't longer but there hasn't been anything doing lately.
P.S.S. Are you still out "on the range"?

U.S. Naval School
Bedford, Penn.
8 July 1944.

Dear Charlie,

I know it's been quite a while since I received your letter but we've been taking final tests and were busier than all hell.

It certainly must be a tough mess that you have gotten yourself into and my heart bleeds for you (Bull shit). All kidding aside, Charlie, how long do you expect to train and are there any hopes of getting back into the Navy? By the way, you may see me after all because most of the graduates of the school go out to join our dear friends, the Marines. So if ever you see a body laying around on the island be sure and see if it is me.

That is right, my brother took your sister to a dance but you need have no worries because he takes after his big brother and is a gentleman! Don't you say a damned word.

Benny must have stepped on a little more than shit. By the time he gets out of school he should be very close to a first class radio tech. You say your chances of getting a crow are slim, but don't get too discouraged because things turn out for the best.

By the way I graduate on the 25th of this month. And if I don't get my crow I shall have missed it by one man and no more. But I still have hopes. I am sure of 1st class anyway. So wish me luck.

When I was home last I went to a formal with Lucy Chanko – not bad. Dick Montville was there and also Bob Rock. Incidentally, those two boys are right here at this burgh. Between you and me, Rock looks like a goon in his uniform. We ended up in the same old place (the Boulevard).

You should see these little squirts around high school that think they are hot shit. It sort of makes me mad. Just a bunch of kids that are just starting to feel their "oats" and I do mean oats.

Well, I'll be seeing you on some island, I hope not. By the way, this weekend I am going home so I will stop and see your mother for a few minutes. If ever you get to New Britain, I wish you'd do the same. So long, Funky.

Your friend,

Tony

P.S. Excuse this half-ass typewriter. I'll blame the machine. Don't write until you hear from me again because it won't be long before I shove off.

U.S. Naval Station
Sampson, New York
July 9, 1944

Dear Charles,

How's my little sex-box today? Sexy as all hell, no?? Ya li'l darlin' ya! Are you still clinging to your virginity? You'd better be! What fools these mortals be!

Ye gads am I hard up for—I'll be damned if I know what for—I guess that it must be you.

Let's see! Today is the 9ᵗʰ. I have about 8 days left here. It'll be about 6 when you get this. I can hardly wait. I don't know why I can hardly wait. I guess it's because I want to get into N.B. to see Ginger. Ah happy day! Buck you fuddy!!

I still haven't heard from Mary, and what about Hot Pants? Has the Pisser answered you yet?

I haven't heard from Francine in over a week. I received a letter from her a week ago Saturday, and I also got four birthday cards from her on Monday. Since then, no word!! I doubt that anything is wrong , but if there is, there is no skin off my back.

I need a change of environment, I guess, for I almost feel that I have nothing more to say. Damn it! I'd really be getting bad if it ever got to that.

Have you heard about the Hartford circus fire? About 150 people (mostly children) were killed, and 200 plus were injured. I can't understand why things happen in this century of blood and misery.

I don't think that I'll ever find a woman that I'll really love. That's where you're one up on me. However, I don't feel that it's my right to even think of this with the indefinite future that's ahead of me. 'Nuff said .I'll write you just before I leave here and explain how things stand then. Take care Charlesie, and remember D-Day. Yours till mine grows an inch.

Gobs of love,

Umbriago

17 Anise Street
New Britain, Conn.
July 13, 1944

Dear Brother,

I received your excited letter today. I don't quite understand what you're going to do but that's o.k.

It's deader than heck around here. I wish I were down in New River with you. Then there would be some excitement!!

Did you see about those 616 films yet? Another thing, those two pictures I told you to send back. When I get them, I'll send some small ones like them.

Donny is at Billy Cabelus's for a few days and I have no one to argue with. The place is like a morgue.

Did you get those pictures you had taken?

Princey is still here and more stubborn than ever. He insists that the living room chairs are for him to sleep on. That's all for now. I'll write when there's more news.

Love and Kisses, xxxxxx
Betty

P.S. Where are they supposed to evacuate casualties? In California? (Explain.)

191 Bristol St.
New Britain, Conn.
July 13, 1944

Dear Dope,

How in Hell is everything? Excuse my English I'm in a smooth mood and so I thought I'd get relief from earthly cares and write to someone out of this world! Wasn't that darling? (Can't you feel those chills up and down your back? Close the window then.)

How's everyone down there treating you? Do they know who you are etc.? I wish you'd write me a crazy letter if you ever find the time.

I've been having quite a nice summer. Over the Fourth Mary Jo and I went to the shore, as she has probably already written you. I've been working at the Hospital. I have a new job there starting August 7ʰ. Boy, would you laugh if you saw me. Remember my dread of kids! Well, guess where?! Correct! Maternity!!! I'm kind of a receptionist or something and have to go up and down the floor filling out charts and making Birth Certificates. If all the kids are mixed up for the next few years, you can tell why. I hope I don't mix up any kids, it would be quite a joke. So that's my job—I'll tell you more about it in August.

I'm going down to Parkers with my sister for two weeks starting Monday. (Mrs. Parker is the only one there.) Dick is coming home Tuesday and I'm leaving Monday. It seems like I'm leaving town because he's coming in. Write me while I'm at the shore or when I get home. Be good, I'll try (just kidding)

Love,

Meg

P.S. No more cracks about who I'm going around with until I'm not — then you can go to town.

P.S.S. I'm going to LaSalle next Sept. 14. (Your favorite school!)

17 Anise Street
New Britain, Conn.
July 15, 1944

Dear Brother,

Well, kid, how are you today? Tessie is out on the porch with Mother and Daddy. She's talking a blue-streak as usual. Her "Dutchie" has been in Pennsylvania (working in the mines).

Jeanne Douglas called me yesterday and invited me to go to Sound View with them. We're going August 12.

Billy is down here with Donny for a few days. Now there's too much excitement around here. Charles Farmer and the kids had Donny tied to a tree a little while ago.

Irene gave me a "pin up" picture of herself to give you, so here it is.

Did you answer the letter that Jean Ziegler wrote you? I hope so.

I can't wait till the picture "Two Girls and a Sailor" comes. Van Johnson is swell.

Do you only have classes at night? What goes on during the day?

Well, Toots, I've got to go now.

Love and kisses,

Betty xxxxxx

P.S. I'll try to cure Donny of his writer's cramp.

17 Anise Street
New Britain, Conn.
July 19, 1944

Dear Son,

    Just a few lines to let you know we are all living. The weeks go by so fast. Do you want us to continue sending you the Herald? It will expire this week.

    Nothing much happens around here. Nellie had her Christening last Sunday.

    We are having a little party for Mrs. Schussler tomorrow, it's her 71ˢᵗ birthday.

    I went shopping today, I bought a couple of end tables and lamps. Pa might shoot me.

    Betty was all set to go to work on the tobacco farms for a couple of weeks. But it was called off. I'm against her working 8 hours a day stringing tobacco. She can't pick a few string beans without getting tired.

    We have a swell garden this year. I don't know why we planted so much. Your weeping willow is growing swell. But everything else is dried up. We need rain bad, our reservoir is very low.

    Jane Vidlak was asking for you. I don't know whether I told you, her husband divorced her and she married Heinie. She looked so hard, all she drinks is beer. I guess the Lake couldn't run without her. Well, I'll close for Betty is going over to drum corps and she will mail it.

                    Love from all,
                       Mother

                      17 Anise Street
                    New Britain, Conn.
                     July 20, 1944

Dear Brother,

    I'm sorry I didn't write for a few days. You see a bunch of girls and myself were going to work on a farm for two weeks. But our plans were changed yesterday when we learned you had to stay for a month. We were going to leave today.

    I'm going to Sound View with the Douglases on August 12ᵗʰ to the 26ᵗʰ. We're now going for two weeks instead of one.

    The ladies are giving a birthday party for Mrs. Schussler this afternoon at Fanny's house. "Old Lady's Reunion," you know?!

    Mother bought two nice mahogany tables and two white lamps for each side of the couch in the living room. They look swell. (Daddy hasn't seen them yet). He won't notice them anyway.

Donny made another swing up on the hill. You have to get on top of the old goat house to get on. I'm going to have him take it down today, that's if he will. Somebody's going to fall off before you know it .That's all for now.

Love and kisses, xxxxxx

Betty

P.S. Have there been anymore rumors about going to California or Siberia?

410 Carlton St.
New Britain, Conn.
July 22. 1944

Dear Charles,

Albert has misplaced your address so he wants me to send his letter to you. I imagine it was written quite some time ago. He called me this morning from Bedford, Pa. and he is graduating this coming Tuesday, July 24. He will then be home for five days and then be training with the amphibious forces in Virginia.

I'll have him write to you when he comes home as I imagine he must have a lot to tell you. I hope that everything with you is tops and that this mess will soon be over so you boys can get together and celebrate. The very best to you and regards from us all.

Sincerely,
Mrs. Victor DiAngelo

P.S. I got your address from your folks.

17 Anise Street
New Britain, Conn.
July 29, 1944

Dear Brother,

We received you letter today about going to California. I hope that you'll be able to stay there a while before being shipped out.

Monday we went down to Beach Park with the Narcums and Irene and I stayed overnight. Narcums have some friends there who have a beautiful cottage.

Thursday we went down to the lake and Donny stayed with Jane. Jane and Heinie are coming to New Britain some day next week.

Then yesterday we went clamming at Indian Neck and then to Beach Park again so today I'm all in. I have a beautiful sunburn, too.

Tomorrow we're having a party for Shirley Cabelus (Allen) under the old apple tree. It was her birthday Wednesday.

It's hot and sticky today. I can hardly hold this pen in my hand.

We didn't receive your picture yet, but I suppose we will shortly. I can't wait to see it.

When you get to California, send me some "Five Days on a Troop Train" perfume. O.K.?

Jean and I are going to Confession now, so I'll be going. Be sure to take care of yourself now.

Love and kisses, xxxxxxx
Your Sister,
Betty

91 West Street
New Britain, Conn.
August 2, 1944

Dearest Charlie honey —

I wouldn't for the world want you to call me sour-grapes, so I'm writing real soon!

Right now I'm in a visiting nurse car waiting for the old bag to finish giving her patient an enema — hope she comes out afore the results do. You see, I'm being a chaufferette today. She takes about an hour at each house, so I thought this would be a good time to catch up on my correspondence.

I came home yesterday from Bay View Beach in Milford. I was visiting the O'Connell's since Sunday. For a little excitement we went over to Saven Rock and I went on the Thunderbolt 5 times in the front seat, too. Last night Rob, Pater, Bob Marlin and I went down to Crescent Beach to see Meg. We left the shore about 12:30 and drove for about 10 minutes and we had a blow-out. Then we had to find an air pump. Then we lost our way so we got home about 3 a.m. Cripes, I thought Mother would hammer me but nary a word did she say.

There ain't much doin' around the old jernt — pretty darn dead as usual. Dr. C. gave me and the other nurse all this week off — not bad!!

That's a good one about Meg and me dragging you and Dick down to the garage and necking up a storm. That's one for the books!! Ya Clown ya! Here comes the old so and so, and so I must close.

With love and kisses,
Mary Jo

US Naval Training Station
Sampson, New York

August 2, 1944

Dear Charlie,

I hope that when you receive this that you're still at Camp LeJeune and not soon leaving for the West Coast. I've been in O.G.U. for 9 days now and my name has not appeared on draft. I haven't the slightest idea when I'll be leaving or where I'll be heading for.

I saw Lucy before I came back .She hasn't changed much, but I'm sure that she's had her tail bent a number of times since I last saw her. What a character! Have you heard any more from "Hot Pants"?? She should be home from the beach soon.

Yesterday I had my first liberty – a ten hour pass. I went into Canaandaigua, N.Y. and picked up a luscious hunk o' woman. Her name is Helen. We spent most of our time out at an Amusement Park similar to Lake Compounce. She was no character, so I can't think of anything comical to say about her. She's a damn nice "skirt" though.

Things seem to be going pretty good on the War Fronts. From the way many of the experts look at it the war should be over soon – they keep telling themselves.

I went over to see your parents before I left but they weren't at home.

How do you stand, Ducky? Do you know when and where you are going? ? Write soon and let me know. I've got to go on a work detail now, so please write and don't go looking for "nooky".

Love,

Dickey

51 Forest St.
Oakwood, Conn.
August 3, 1944

Dearest Charlie,

I received your card the other day and was so relieved to hear that you were fine. Remember you said in your last letter that I shouldn't write to you again until you wrote again because you were being moved? Well, I waited and waited until Helen told me that you had written her and said you were in California and about to be moved out. I felt better knowing you were alright, but rather hurt because you hadn't told me about what had happened. You know, it hurts to hear about you from her, but that's up to you, I guess, if you'd rather tell her these things.

There's not much I can tell you about your being where you are except I pray that you'll be safe and home soon, and I'm sure you will.

We certainly have had a complete change in the weather. It's been 95 and above all week, and today it dropped down to 75 – 80. We were all nearly frozen.

It's a good thing you can't see me tonight, Dear, you'd never like me what with my runny nose etc. from hay fever. I'm practically a wreck. Maybe you wouldn't care though. You've seen it before.

You know I was thinking about Meriden Tower tonight – guess because it's so breezy out. It was around this time last year that we were there, wasn't it? We really had some good times at dances and amusement parks etc. together. Didn't we? I'll be glad when we can do those things again. Can you imagine calling me and asking me if I'd like to go out? Those were wonderful days.

Mavis has been quite lucky. It seems that she met a soldier last spring and she's been having regular dates ever since. He'll no doubt be leaving soon, too.

I haven't heard from Helen lately, so I'm not too sure as to whether or not she and Ben are still writing. Have you heard from him? If so, where is he?

Mother and Dad got a letter from Fred Campbell the other day and we were quite surprised to hear that he is in France. He says he's fine and was even able to tell us about the weather there. It's hard to know what you can tell about without having it censored. You will probably have a lot you can tell me when you write, so how about getting busy on it? Seems like I've been writing for ages. Take care, and write soon because I miss you.

Yours,

Cheryl

P.S. I'm not sure the address makes sense or not because the post office put their stamp right in the middle of your writing, so if you do get it, will you remember to give me the address again in your next letter.

US Naval Training Station
Sampson, New York
August 4, 1944

Dear Charlie,

This is a short note to let you know that I am leaving Monday, August 7th for San Diego to attend Hospital Corps School. Of all the unforsaken places to go—I guess, I'll be o.k. though. For some reason or other, as I am writing this I feel that you are in San Diego right now. You mentioned something about going there in one of your letters.

I've got a work detail now, so I have to cut this short. I expect to arrive in California on Saturday, August 12th.

Urine,

Dick

-SIX-

THE SOLOMON
ISLANDS 1944-1945

IN EARLY AUGUST I boarded a troop train headed for California. Over the next four days our train meandered leisurely from North Carolina down through Louisiana and across Texas and New Mexico. Along the route we stopped for catered meals at the Fred Harvey restaurants. In California, without even a chance to look around, we boarded the APA *Sea Ray*, and headed out of San Francisco Bay into the wide Pacific. Scuttlebutt had it we were to lay over in Hawaii. Wishful thinking. Bypassing Hawaii, our unescorted, fully loaded troop ship proceeded south in the vast, empty Pacific. Strict blackout regulations were in effect. Day after day through the horse latitudes, we zigzagged to foil any Jap subs that might be lurking under the blue water. At the equator we forgot the enemy. A full day was given over to the hazing of us pollywog crossing the International Date Line for the first time. At the end of the day, now certified shellbacks, we moved ever deeper into enemy territory, the Southern Cross brightly overhead.

Some days later, on a dark and moonless night, the *Sea Ray* dropped anchor off the coast of Guadalcanal. The ominous, shadowy island had been secured earlier but was rumored to be rife with Jap holdouts. Small boats ferried us ashore. We made our way across the beach and stumbled in deep darkness through fields of knee-high grass. From the foliage of the tall trees came the unnerving shrieks of tropical birds. At an order from one of the sergeants, we spread ponchos, checked weapons, and hunkered down, fully expecting a Nip intruder.

Morning banished all fear. The island was a paradise of tropical breezes and sandy beaches. We set up camp in one of the vast coconut groves that ran along the long coast. The Canal, as the old salts referred to the island, had been selected as the home of a new outfit, the Sixth Marine Division. Because of the total news blackout and strict censorship of our correspondence, family and friends back home had no idea where I was until one of the guys managed to get word of our location to his mother through a prearranged code. She in turn phoned my folks, who were vastly relieved to learn I was far, far to the south of the firestorm that was about to descend upon Japan. Little did we know that the Sixth Marine Division would be in the vanguard of such action.

232 Mountain Drive
West Hartford, Conn.
August 9,1944

Dear Charlie,

I am supposed to be doing a memorandum – thus the stationary – and since I'm much too tired to work, I'll just take an hour off and write to you.

I received your luscious picture. My how you've changed! It's really very good. You look a little older because you look stern in the picture, but I like the more serious pose. And what the Marine uniform doesn't do for you isn't worth talking about! Definitely your type. I've had all the girls in the office drooling over it and Nancy thinks it's very good. I haven't told Cheryl about it and she won't ever see it 'cause she never comes to my house anyway. If I told her she'd say I was encouraging you and trying to steal her stuff although she has no claim legitimately. Thank you very much, my sweet, I'll cherish it all through life.

I went to Vermont this weekend and what a weekend! The train ride was terrific – filthy beyond imagination – and with no sleep all weekend I'm beyond recognition. Sunday I had a date, but they have the silliest law there - no dancing on Sunday – so we danced on the beach under a beautiful moon. Ben had planned on coming home, I think, but he said he might stay in Washington.

You sounded awfully mad in your last letter, darlin'. First you rattled on about Nancy and Morry and then about Ben, then about your work. I don't like to see you in a bad mood – you're usually so cheerful. You must be in California now and I'm going to worry every minute now about you. The war is going to be over soon, and then we'll be able to laugh without feeling guilty. There isn't anything to tell you so when I get all rested up I'll write you a nice long letter.

Affectionately,
Helena

VT 29 F.P.P
San Francisco, Cal.
August 14, 1944

Dear Charles,

I received your letter today. It took quite a while to get to me as you see I have moved. This one will probably take quite a while to get to you because you probably have moved, too.

No, I hadn't turned against you, a poor guy can't help it if he gets drafted into the Marines. But please don't start talking like you almost did in your letter. I know the Marines are winning the war, but what I can't understand is why the hell they don't send so many men home?

About the only people I heard from in N.B. are the family and relatives and once in awhile some one else gets ambitious and writes. Bray is out at Notre Dame, lucky guy. Well, that's all for now. Write soon and let me know where you are and what you are doing.

Your buddy,
Mick

232 Mountain Drive
West Hartford, Conn.
August 15, 1944

Charlie darling,

I received you card yesterday. I'll make a couple of good resolutions right now – first to write just as often as I can even if it would be just a note, and second to keep planning on that picnic to take place within the first month of your return.

Thursday

I've been so busy that I've had to abandon all letters that I started at work.

You should see me today, my pet. Tuesday night I took a flying leap off the bus and got a beautifully sprained ankle. It might have been a good idea to have stayed off it, but I'd rather be mean to myself. Don't tell anybody this, but I went dancing Tuesday night. My foot looked like a balloon and hurt like h----, but the fellow was such a good dancer I couldn't resist. He felt very guilty about the whole thing, but I was obstinate and made him take me. When I got home my foot was black, so I decided to take the next day off and rest. I went to my Doctor Wednesday and I think the poor man was baffled – my foot doesn't hurt very much and he couldn't understand why it had hemorrhaged so and didn't hurt – but we know, don't we?!! Now I'm all strapped up and have to wear my oxfords – curses! If Ben comes home, I'll die.

Our office force is going on a picnic Saturday – swimming, boating, everything you can think of and I have to go and sit. Oh, darn, I'm sick of living. This is fun though – everybody runs around and says "You poor little thing" and I just bask in the sympathy.

I'm going to miss you terribly, sweet. It used to be so nice to know that I'd get an answer to my letters to you just as soon as possible. I really looked forward to your cheery notes – I liked the pensive and serious ones too, of course. I won't give up though – I'll keep writing and hoping that you get them, and I know you will answer when you can. Make me first after your parents though, won't you?

I sent your address to Ben. It's two months since I saw him. I guess he's waiting for a formal to come home again but there certainly can't be one until October anyway. When there is one, we'll be sure to dance a couple for you. I'll tell Ben that I'm making believe we've exchanged dances so I'm dancing with you. Make sure you have a pretty girl for a date—Ben will be more willing to exchange then.

Must close now. My letters will probably be just notes, but you'll know that I'm thinking about you anyway.

Affectionately,
Helena

91 West St
New Britain, Conn.
August 16, 1944

Dearest Charley Honey,

Gee whiz – who do they think they are sending my lambie pie way off to "Jabroo?" At the rate you're going we'll never get a chance to get to Beckley's. It just ain't fair.

Yes, I did receive your picture and honestly it's absolutely handsome. I showed it to Meg, Mary Jane and Martha and they thought it was swell. I'm glad you sent the picture to me instead of H.S. Conway. Thanks loads!!!

Well, I'm no longer a working gal – as free as the birds in the trees. Tuesday I started to do volunteer work at the hospital. I've watched Basal Metabolism tests and lots of experiments in the laboratory. It's really very exciting.

Last Saturday nite I went out with Eddie O'Malley. Cripes! What a nite. First we went horseback riding in Farmington. Then we really did up Hartford. The Mark Twain – Josephine's Palace of Joy – Belvedere Inn and Palmetto all in one nite. I'm still sore all over from riding!!

I heard from Dick and the old so and so is out in Jabroo, too. I don't know – but something will have to be done about the home front morale pretty soon.

Last nite Meg and the Spook and Jess Munson and I went swimming at Churchill Park. It is really a nice place. Make it a "must" on your list when you get home.

Oh, yes, Kyttle, the boozer, is home on furlough. Boy! Has he gotten cocky – Judas – there's no talking to him. He still eats, sleeps and talks liquor. How you making out with yours?

If by any chance you are able to get hold of a hula–hula skirt or a sarong (with the top part) how about forwarding one to your "best gal?" Of course, I'd reimburse you for it. I'm serious – 'cause I'd really love one!!!

Well, punkin, this is all for now – you'll be hearing from me again soon – you lucky kid!!!

Take it easy with the native girls – and don't do anything I wouldn't.

Lots of love,
Mary Jo

Connecticut College
New London, Conn.
August 21, 1944

Hello, Darling –

There's a full moon and I got a letter from you today – so everything's rosy in spite of the test I fouled up. What is it about moons anyway? As the guy says – they do things to me.

So now you're going to study law – what next? You're as bad as I am about making up your mind. I don't approve of course – but that's neither here nor there. It takes so darn long – that's about as bad as being a doctor. It seems to me you ought to get through college as soon as possible (it can be done in 3 years, you know) and get started in business somewhere. Finally, I don't know how long you could stand being cooped up in that intellectual atmosphere for so long. But that's only my humble opinion – it's your life and they tell me you have only one chance to make a go of it. So I guess it's up to you.

I keep thinking about your coming home. Do you realize it will be about 2 years since I've seen you? And what's more – I don't think it's safe for civilians to keep men cooped up on an island for a couple of years – you're beginning to get me worried. I went out with a sailor last winter who had been restricted to the sub base for two weeks – needless to say I didn't go out with him again. But if that was a sample!! I'm going to meet you in a suit of armor – how about that?

274

By the way, Pris Jones is back at Conn. for summer school, so I guess that was a lot of bunk about her being kicked out for stealing. She just didn't seem like the type. I asked her if she was coming back next year – she said she didn't know yet, and they certainly wouldn't let her back if they'd once kicked her out.

Did you ever get a letter from Meg, Charlie? She wrote you one after the one you wrote to her and you never mentioned it. Maybe some of my letters don't get there either. That would be good for an excuse when you get so mad about not hearing from me. But we can cut out this horrible letter writing soon, I hope. You're right when you say we're not cut out for it.

I guess I'd better break down and do some Economics. I'm still about 6 chapters behind, and then I wonder why the tests are so putrid! I just ain't the intellectual type. Write soon, huh? Goodnight, Macushla.

      Launa

                  232 Mountain Drive
                  West Hartford, Conn.
                  August 24, 1944

My dear Charlie,

I hope you don't mind my typing your letter. Personally, I hate it and I very rarely do things that I dislike myself, but at least I look like I'm working when I bang away, and it makes a good impression. Maybe you'd rather have me use V-Mail. If you like it, just let me know. Some of the fellows don't.

How're things going, m' love? Don't let that pensive brain of yours do any overtime, will you, 'cause that's what starts a leakage in your morale. Remember that we are all missing you like everything. Ben was home last weekend and was down on Sunday. I went to a picnic Saturday and not having received his letter, I wasn't home early enough to go out Saturday night. I showed him your picture and he said you didn't give him any, but it was all right – I told him he could look at mine when he comes home. I also told him about our picnic and said that nobody could go but we two – oh, he was thrilled about that. He thinks the mutual relationship between the three of us is getting one-sided or should I say two-sided. I love to tease him.

I haven't anything to write you today. I haven't seen any movies lately, no songs to sing you, no poetry to quote you, not even a joke to tell you. I'm turning Puritan. I've been reading a lot and have just finished "Strange Fruit." It's rather raw, completely lacking in morals, for it's about a white fellow and a honey-colored negro girl, and was written mostly to

275

picture the negro situation in the South. The author really knows what she is talking about, but her style is funny. She keeps shifting back to the past, and I couldn't tell whether it was now, yesterday or tomorrow.

Did anyone tell you Freddy was supposed to come home? I was talking to Joyce and she said he was coming last Friday, but I haven't talked to her since and don't know whether he is home or not. I suppose your family enlightens you on these things. It's so rare that I hear about anyone from New Britain that I make it a point to tell both you and Ben. Benny said he was going to stop in and see your Mom and Dad Sunday.

Well, darlin', that's all of what I know today. This is one of those notes I said you'll probably get from me. I'm so anxious to hear from you. Don't forget, I'm next on the list after your parents

Affectionately,
Helena

Ozette Patrol Base
Clallam Bay, Wash.
August 25,1944

Dear Charlie,

I got your letter about 3 days ago, but I was leaving to go on liberty (a 72 at that) and I didn't get a chance to answer it until now.

Oh, Brother, what a time I had. I shacked up with this girl for three nights and did I have fun – we stayed at her place. (that helps save on the hotel bill) and went out during the day. I was in Canada and I had this girl and my buddy had her good friend and he stayed up to her place. He can just about walk. I can't. You should see them, nice, hot and French. I only have to put the last word down – that explains itself. It's a long story, so I won't even begin to tell you about it. There isn't much new, in fact there isn't anything new. I don't feel a hell of a lot like writing. I'm just writing to let you know that I'm still alive. (Not that you give a good damn but I thought you would like to know.)

Joke – This guy went into a drug store, limped up to the counter and sat down and ordered a sundae. The guy behind the counter looked at him and said, "Crushed nuts?" The other guy looked back at him and said, "No, infantile paralyses"

That's all,
Freddy

17 Anise Street
New Britain, Conn.

Sept. 5, 1944

Dear Brother,

We were so glad to receive that letter from you today! It's just about a month since we heard from you. We were all quite worried (especially Mother).

I came back from the shore the 26th of August. We had a perfect time. There were very few servicemen there because of the murder last month. One sailor had to ruin it for everyone else. There was an orchestra at O'Connor's this year and they were all kids, 16, 17 and 18 years old. We met all of them and had a lot of fun.

Two days ago, that was Sunday, we went to the shore again. We went dancing at night and went home about 12:30. The next day (Labor Day) we went to Soundview again. It was quite dead 'cause everybody was going home.

Today the Neubauers and our folks went down to Bob Tryon's cottage. They were going to go clamming. I stayed home for I had enough salt water for a while and besides I have to get ready for school tomorrow. I don't mind going back though. For my subjects I have Latin II, Biology, History and English. I guess I'll have to work sort of hard. I don't care. Jean Ziegler is going to the Mount for her Senior Year (no remarks??)

I bet you had a swell trip across the country. Thanks for all the pretty cards and the Indian pin. It was very cute.

I just love your picture in the Marine uniform. (Sure is snazzy.) You look as if you ran the Marine Corps! Bu still when I look at the expression on your face, you look as though you are laughing. I really do get a kick out of it.

Junie Ziegler, Ernie Glabau and a whole lot of other fellows are leaving for the Army the 31st of August. There really isn't anyone around anymore. I was glad to hear that somebody from New Britain was on the boat with you.

I hope you're feeling fine and aren't seasick.

Donny said he would write as soon as he got back from the shore. He has a lot to tell you. Donny and I fight more than you and I ever did, and we actually had some "pips." So long for a while.

Love from Everyone,
Betty xxxxxx

P.S. Take care now and don't try jumping off the boat.

277

New Britain High School
New Britain, Conn.
September 7, 1944

Dear Brother,

Well, how are you now? Have you reached your destination yet? I'm now in school for the second day. Everything is o.k. Here are the teachers that I have—Miss O'Sheen for English, Mr. Nordstrom, Biology, Mr. Catland, American History and Miss Benjamin for Latin II. How do they sound? Give me your opinion.

Donny is in sixth grade now. It's quite hard to believe. He'll be down at Nathan Hale next September.

Roger, Morty and all the rest of the kids are here at High School now. They go around with their mouths open as if catching flies.

Taggy called his mother from California yesterday and he's coming home in a week. I bet Auntie Anna is tickled pink.

I saw the picture "Show Business" yesterday with Eddy Cantor, George Murphy and Joan Davis. (She's a pip). It was a swell picture .I'll finish this letter when I get home.

Love, xxxxxx
Betty

P.S. I'm using a school pen.

At home
2:45 p.m.

Hi, Kid,

I just got home and noticed two V-Mail letters from you. I'm sending a few airmail stamps now, and then later I'll send some more, o.k. Gizmo?

I have some Latin and History homework tonight. I almost died when I went into Latin. I couldn't translate a word of it and I have two pages for tonite. So long for now.

Love and kisses,
Betty

17 Anise Street
New Britain ,Conn.
September 7, 1944

Dear Charlie,

How are you? We received two letters from you this noon. Last night Tag called his girlfriend Jean and Aunt Anna. He's in California and he'll be home in about a week. While you're across PLEASE sent me some *souvenirs. Tonight after school I'm going to the movies to see Pilot # 5, and 5 Graves from Cairo. The cub scouts bought a rabbit and were keeping it over here. So Sunday we had a beer party here and I made tickets and raffled off the first rabbit. Eddie next door won but he took a dollar instead but I made $3.50 and I still got the rabbit. Ha, ha! It's about 1:00 o'clock and I have to go to school now.*

Love,
Wart

P.S. I'll write soon.

232 Mountain Drive
West Hartford, Conn.
September 12,1944

Hello, my sweet!

I got both your letters today and it was wonderful to hear from you finally.

You're perfectly right not to rate people or write to them 'cause you feel you have to. I don't do it myself and I can't imagine why I mentioned your writing to me after your parents. I write because I want to and when I want to and I'm glad you feel the same. Maybe I'm getting ornery, but don't try to understand me either – I change my mind every other day – it's more fun that way!

I didn't tell Ben about our date for any special reason but I'm sorry, although by the time it comes into reality it won't make much difference to him one way or another.

He came home this weekend and we went to a new night club in West Hartford. You remember the "Puritan Maid" that was in Farmington, don't you? It's been made into a swanky sharp place called the "Algiers." It's very nice there, but nothing like the foreign atmosphere place you've planned for "our date." Let's make it a Russian or German place where an artistic individual plays a violin at the tables. Do you have a favorite song or anything to request? How do you like "Where or When"? That's been my special song for ages, and I think "Always" is fast becoming one of my stand-by's.

I went to a sort of family reunion last week. All my father's relatives – a couple whom I haven't seen for a good while. Those things are always gay – it starts, "My, hon, you've grown! and then you take out the package of cigarettes and they all fall over in a faint. Next time we see them, they'll look at my third finger, left hand, and if they find what they're looking

279

for they say, "Aren't you a bit young?" But if they don't, they say, "What happened to all the boy-friends?" There's just no pleasing them.

Your environment doesn't sound too bad. I hope I'm not the first woman you see when you come home – Mon Dieu! I'm afraid you'd be a little too bashful for me!!

I saw a wonderful picture Sunday and you mustn't miss it. It's "Janie" and all about 16 year olds and the fun they have. I'm hardly old enough to be saying this but when you're kissing the teens good–bye, I think most everyone agrees that 16 is a wonderful age.

Evidently, you didn't get my letter thanking you for the picture. It was sent to North Carolina, I think. Anyway, I said you're definitely the Marine or Jyrene type. It's awfully good and everyone in the office was drooling over it. You must come down to the office sometime – everybody is wonderful there. Some day you can take me to lunch!

I have enclosed "Prospice" for you. Just ask for anything you want, and I'll do my best to get it for you. Nancy said that we studied "A Psalm of Life" but I don't remember it. I haven't read anything lately. I'm such a bridge fiend, but now that winter is coming and Nan will be back at school, I'll have more time for books.

Incidentally, Nancy said to say hello to you for her.

Well, darling, that just about empties my head for now. My mother has been doing lots of canning and I have to run down the cellar and admire her rows of preserves. Mothers are wonderful, aren't they? Of all the people who can keep things going without a hitch, they do it best.

Ben dropped in to see your Mother and Dad Saturday. He says your family is well and that they had heard from you. Write soon, darling.

Affectionately,
Helena

17 Anise Street
New Britain, Conn.
September 10, 1944

Dear Brother,

Well, how's my Marine today? Cheryl from Oakwood just called and said she was worried about you 'cause you hadn't written to her lately. So we told her you were across. You'd better write to her before she breaks out in a barrel of monkeys etc. I wish you would tell me all about what is going on over there, but Mr. Censor would perhaps stop that.

It seems a little early to be talking about Christmas, but please tell us what you like, o.k?? And don't forget!!!

I have some homework over the weekend but not too much. We're having a Latin test Monday. I have more fun in that Latin room guessing at the sentences.

Gert Donnelly is going to be the Dress Major and I am going to be the Twirler for our Corps. Of course, I have the hardest job. Mr. Walker says I'll have to enter into contests next summer. I'll die of fright for sure!!

We haven't had any rain for a long time and everything is so dry. We water your weeping willow every day though. Well, so long for a while and I'll write again soon.

Love and smooches,

Betty xxxxxx

P.S. Send me home a Gizmo Native, o.k. (I think a Gizmo is a native.)

17 Anise Street

New Britain, Conn.

September 11, 1944

My dear Son,

Rec'd 3 of your letters today and so glad to hear from you. So you are on some island, I wish we knew just where, can't you kind of hint some way? Do you think you will be sent to some hospital? I'd hate to see you living in a tent and wading through mud. It's a good thing you were used to camping.

How is the food? I suppose it's all canned stuff. Is there anything you want us to send you? Write and tell us a little more about the island and yourself.

Cheryl from Oakwood called the other day and wanted to know if we heard from you. So I'm not the only one that worries over you. Benjamin was over for a little while on Saturday. He looks good. He was going over to see Helen. Freddy was home for 10 days but he said he was glad to go back. His mother almost went whacky when he was home. He stayed out until 4 or 5 in the morning. Lucky she had the car for him so he could get home at all. Tag got back and is in California. He expected to get a furlough and Jean has plans made for the wedding. But he called Sunday and said he didn't know if he could get home.

Pa is working steady. I guess he's planning on going hunting again.

281

I've been so busy canning and I'm not thru yet. I put up more apple sauce today and more peppers. Tomorrow I have to go to the dentist

Donny and Betty are back in school. Donny is getting so big. We had his tonsils out in August. He was pretty sick the first few days. But after a week he was running around again. He has quite a cold now. The mornings and nights are so cold.

Spuddy was home and his mother had a party on him. He is stationed in Florida now.

Freddy is going to S. Carolina. Donny is in the kitchen making molds and painting them. Betty just got back from Religious Instruction. Betty had a nice vacation this summer, two weeks at the shore.

Be sure you hide your money so nobody can take it. Freddy had money and other valuables taken on him. Have you seen any Natives? I hope you're a million miles away from the Japs. Were you seasick when you went over? I know a lot of fellows get seasick and I kept thinking of you. Because you use to get sick riding in the car. Well, I hope this war will soon be over so all you boys can come home.

Well, I guess I told you all the news and we will write every other day so you will get mail every week, and you keep on writing every day if you can and have time for it.

Lux Theater is going on so I will close with love from all.

We still have chickens and Donny's ducks and Prince is still around. He sleeps on the front porch hammock and barks all night long. It's a wonder the neighbors don't complain. That's all.

Goodnight and kisses,
Mother

51 Forest St.
Oakwood, Conn.
September 13, 1944

My dearest Charles,

You'll never know how relieved I was when I called home today and Mother said "yes" when I asked her, as usual, if your letter came. Seems as if I miss you more every day, especially when I'm in New Britain every day. I can almost picture you walking across Main Street. You will be soon though, I'm sure.

Because I was so anxious to know if you had gotten there safely, I just had to call your Mother and ask her if you had written home yet. She said she had been worried sick too until the day before I called the mailman had a letter for her from you. I think she's lovely, Charlie. I have talked to her several times before when you were home, but this time she seemed even nicer to me. I'd love to meet her when you get home again. Would you like that? You were worried about home because you told me you hadn't heard from them as yet, but it must have been the Post Office there, Dear, because she said Betty, your sister, had written that day, so you no doubt have the letter by now and feel better, I hope.

While reading your letter I found myself almost wishing I were on that island with you. The idea of having coconut trees and swimming in the jungle seemed like a dream, but then when you mentioned the monsoon it got a little too damp for me so I found myself under the weather again. It's really wonderful in a way when you think of all you are learning(Just imagine all the things you can tell you're children.)Seriously though, Charlie, from the news reports things are popping in the Pacific since our boys sank 89 Jap ships. You can't say just where you are but I hope it will never be too near those seas. Is there anything like that near where you are? Maybe I shouldn't ask things because you can't tell me anyway but write all you can.

Oh yes, so you believe in the superstition attached to catching the brides' bouquet? Well, Dear, I went to Doris Clapp's wedding (in New Britain), and I caught the flowers. Who do you suppose the lucky man will be? I'll have to wait until after the war to do much about it.

Speaking of weddings, a funny thing happened in our office. One of the girls in the office (Merlyn Wenger, do you know her?) came to work with a beautiful engagement ring. It seems that her boyfriend ordered it for her and although he couldn't get a furlough he sent it to his home instead and she went there to get it from his brother. I think she's lucky to have it, but if it were me I'd rather wait until he could give it to me himself because the sentiment attached to such a thing must be worth more than the ring alone. Don't you agree?

Helen and Benjamin went out again this weekend and had a swell time. I think that they'll still be going together after the war and it is wonderful to know that you will still want to go out with me then, or that is what I thought you implied when you said you would like to see me alone, and that we'd all have fun together. I can't help wondering if you feel the way you did the last time we were back together, or if you have changed. I wonder?

It's gotten awfully cold here in the past week and it's pouring out and I'm alone tonight and there's a mystery play on the radio, spooky, isn't it!

Did you know that it only takes a week to get your letters? That's good but it still seems like a long time between them. How would it be if we just wrote a few lines 2 or 3 times a week? Think you'd have time? I know I'd have it. Just like you did when you were at Harvard and I was at the Hospital.

Well, Dear, it look like I'll have to close for now, but remember I'll be so very anxious 'till I get your next letter – make it soon, won't you, and tell me a lot.

Mother and Dad both send their regards and say to take care. Until next time

Always yours,
Cheryl

P.S. Will you ever remember that we don't live in New Britain anymore? I noticed that you put it on the envelope but then crossed it out.

17 Anise Street
New Britain, Conn.
September 14, 1944

Dear Charlie,

Well, Darlin', how are you? I hope it hasn't been raining where you are like it is here. It's been pouring all day long and seems like it will never stop.

I can't understand why you haven't been getting my mail. We've been writing to you regularly. You should have some by now. (My arm isn't broken either.)

I just completed my Biology questions and will start on my Latin when I finish this letter. Ah! Homework. I was changed to Miss Carson's English class because ours was too large and oh, what a teacher. I hold my breath while I'm in there.

I can just imagine you running like heck when you heard that tank. I bet you were scared "shiftless." I bet that you were one of those fellows crawling along the ground. Huh, weren't you?

Donny just put the "Lone Ranger" on. He'll listen to that till he's 60 years old. Remember when we used to lie up on your bed in the cold room and listen to "Johnny Corntassel" and "Little Orphan Annie"? More fun. Wouldn't miss it for anything.

Cheryl French called again today. She said she had heard from you. She works for the telephone company, where you pay your bills. I never noticed her when I went in there. The next time I go in there I'm going to speak to her. I'll tell her how much you like her and everything, o.k.??! Well, I guess that's all for now.

Love and kisses, xxxxxx
Betty

P.S. I just, love the motto of your tent. It sounds so nice. I also like your N. Carolina friend's name, Elon.

U.S. Naval Hospital
San Diego, Cal.
September 14, 1944

Hello, ya' ole turd,

So ya ran off to sea on me!! Ya lil' devil ya!! You'd do anything for a laugh, wouldn't you? Don't answer that question!!

To begin with, "Breathless" I received your note from sea last weekend. Gosh, was I glad to hear from you. Before that letter, I was going crazy trying to think of a way to get in touch with you. I don't know exactly when you tried to look me up in San Diego, but I arrived here on August 11th. Parts of your letter were censored so I don't know when or from where you left the U.S.A. I suppose that we'll never know until after the war.

First, I'll talk about me, then I'll start asking you all the questions I have on my mind. I left Sampson August 7th and arrived in San Diego August 11th. I've been here for almost five weeks now. As far as I know, I'll be here for seven more weeks and then I'll be sent to a hospital – in the East, I hope. I have no bitching to do – not that there isn't anything to bitch about – am I kidding???

I've had four liberties so far. The last two weeks were spent in Los Angeles, Beverly Hills and Hollywood. Did you have a chance to get up that way? It's really quite the place for the servicemen. I have a connection that is strictly solid. I met a girl at the Beverly Hills U.S.O, and she invited me to spend the following day at her home. She has a beautiful mansion, swimming pool and all. I accepted the invitation and as a result have had two bang-up weekends. Last week, I spent Sat. nite at the famous Coconut Grove. Freddy Martin was playing. It was great. We had a picture taken of our party at our table. On the back of the "pic" I got Freddy Martin's autograph. The thrill of last weekend came when I was picked up by Al Jolson while I was hitch-hiking in Beverly Hills. He really was a swell guy. This weekend, I'm supposed to have a blind date with a redhead. What the hell! I'll try anything once.

285

You don't know how true I am to you, darlin'. I am clinging very fervently to my virginity. On the way out here, I had it offered to me on a silver platter in a couple of big city layovers. You see, lamb, I am still counting on our inevitable D–Day. I don't believe I have anything to worry about as far as you go! The only thing you can use now is a king-size porthole. Wheeeee! What fun you could have if you only had Meg and her braces with you.

I've been hearing from home quite regularly. I heard from Mary twice. The old girl worked most of the summer, went to the beach for two weeks, and is going to school Sept. 20ᵗʰ. Dick Farrell is home on a medical discharge. Lucy wrote me and I answered her letter last week. Most of the fellas have gone from the old "blood pit." Even the younger fellas from High School have gone – "Doc," Cal Wade, Dillon. Of course, Morry was and is still around – "Who'd 'ave thunk it?"

Guess who I met yesterday - none other than Jim Beach. He's in the Medical Corps and is stationed at the Hospital as a PhM3/c. He's anxiously awaiting orders that will send him out to sea. I told him about all the fellas and where they are now. He mentioned to me that Eddy O'Malley is stationed in San Diego, too. Do you know him?

You asked me about the book "The Light That Failed." Yes, that happened to be one of the few books that I've read. Gosh, you surely must have enough time for yourself. You've read enough books.

You know, Charlie, it seems so very odd writing to you this way – that is with you where you are or where you're heading. It seems that absolutely everything that has happened in the past is nil. I'd better knock it off or I'll be getting too damned sentimental and philosophical.

You mentioned that you were going to write to Launa. I see no reason why you shouldn't. I'm sure that she would receive it and furthermore answer it. She wouldn't be a woman if she didn't.

As far as women go with me, I think I'm getting like "Hot Pants." I'm taking pride in making a collection of women. I'm getting too damned fickle for my own good. No – I think that it's more that I haven't found the right one yet. Aw "nuff of dis luffink, leds stard fockink."

Now, listen here, "lamb." Take it easy and don't rape any snipers. Write whenever you can. Take it easy and don't urinate in the wrong foxhole.

Your best pal,
Dick

17 Anise Street
New Britain, Conn.
September 18, 1944

Dear Brother,

We received your letter today with your new address. Your medical job seems o.k. Why don't you just try operating on someone when the Doctor isn't looking??

Thursday we had a hurricane here. It was all over New England also. It wasn't as bad as the one in 1938 but it was bad enough. The apple tree (beer party one) was knocked over but with some ropes and pulleys Daddy got it back up. Darn it!! The apple tree in the back yard (left side coming from the house)was also blown down but that was old and about to kick anywho. There were loads of trees and roofs etc damaged in New Britain. The hurricane started about 9 at night and lasted until 2 in the morning. I was awake most of the night. We just got our electricity back today (Monday).

Guess what? I'm a cheerleader (I think) for the High School. Now calm down, I'm not turning into a "Rah-Rah." About three hundred girls tried out and 20 were chosen. (You ought to be proud of me.) We have two groups. The best Cheerers are going to be the group for the games, "Doc" is coming down tomorrow for inspection. It's altogether a new bunch of girls. Barbara F. and Audry Kraus also got in. We had more fun practicing. (Sore as hell.)

I got a bid from the Phi Sigma today, but I'm just forgetting about sororities. (I'm already in one. Ha, Ha, just kidding,)

School is o.k. We're having our first History test tomorrow.

Didn't you receive any of our other mail or letters yet? Will they forward it to you? (I hope so.) Well, so long for now, Doctor. Ma just hollered at me.

Love and kisses, xxxxxx
Betty

P.S. Tag is on his way from California. He's getting married on the 30th.

P.S.S. Don't you dare let any Japs sneak up on you. Walk backwards. (Ha, ha!)

17 Anise Street
New Britain, Conn.
September 20, 1944

287

Dear Son,

Rec'd your letter dated September 6ᵗʰ. So you have moved again. I hope you like it. That's the way Tag did, moved from one island to another.

Anna expects Tag home tomorrow. She's so excited about him coming home and so is Jean. I don't blame them.

They are having a little time finding a hall to have the wedding in. It's going to be on a Saturday, the 30ᵗʰ of September.

We had a hurricane here, it knocked down our trees but Pa put them up again. All except the early apple but we didn't care much about that one. But it knocked all the apples on the ground, but Pa made cider out of them so they didn't go to waste. We didn't have any lights for 4 days. But did it seem good to get them on again.

We got another bond Monday. How many men are on the island with you? Did you take care of any wounded men yet?

I hope you don't run into any Japs. We did receive your picture but you looked too sober in it. But it isn't bad. We can't buy any films around here so we can't take pictures to send you.

Well, I guess that's all for now. I hope you rec'd some of our mail by now. Poop Neubauer is loafing—he didn't like his job so he popped his boss and got fired. He has a car now. He bought Joe Neubauer's Buick but now he can't get gas to run around with.

Love and kisses,
Mother

232 Mountain Drive
West Hartford, Conn.
September 20, 1944

Dear Charlie,

Oh my goodness! I thought I mailed this ages ago. I've been in a state of oblivion for the past month.

I'd better put the poetry in the next letter. I haven't had time to type it, or even write it.

Every night I've been busy with a little chore the alumnae association chose me to do. I'm probably the only fool they can find to sell tickets. We are sponsoring a series of book reviews to be given by Father Kennedy. He is an outstanding reviewer and I'm very anxious to hear him.

Saturday night I'm having a bridge party. I'm really getting in a social whirl what with bridge, and plays at the Bushnell and intellectual book reviews.

I have planned to see one opera this year – that's all I can afford. I've already been to a couple of plays and I hope to see the Ballet Russe next spring.

Look, my pet, I've prattled on long enough.

Write soon and can you tell me more about your habitat? I'm curious about what you do all day, and about your environment and the natives, if that's what you call them.

Affectionately,
Helena

17 Anise Street
New Britain, Conn.
September 23, 1944

Dear Brother

How are you? Everything has been all right around the house, even Prince.

I still remember all those souvenirs you were going to send home, and so far I only got a few of them. As you know by now I got a paper route with forty-seven customers, It takes me about twenty-five minutes to finish every night and I get about 3.50 a week. That sister of ours all she does all day is holler and holler. Sometimes I feel like taking that club you sent home and hit her on the head with it, do you think I should? G'wan, big joke, tickle me I want to laff.

I got a good joke to tell you but I'll tell it to you after a few words. Right now it's windy to beat heck and cold. This too is one of the short letters so I'll sign off here.

Love,
Donnie

P.S. An Indian went into a hotel and asked for a room. The manager told him there were no rooms but if he wanted to he could sleep with a white man. The Indian said yes and went to bed. That night the white man got up to go to the bathroom and the Indian followed him in. Then the white man sat down and the Indian stabbed him. The manager came running in and asked why he stabbed him. The Indian said, White man shitum in Indian spring.

U.S. Naval Hospital
San Diego, Cal.
September 23, 1944

'Lo, Love,

289

I'm bitchin' like hell right now. I wrote you an almost complete letter yesterday, and for some reason I can't find it to send to you. Oh, my bleeding hemorrhoids'!!! What the hell, I don't mind as long as I'm writing to you. I can now make this one twice as long. The only thing I'm worried about is that some vagabond will pick up the manuscript and take it too seriously. I don't think that there are any two people in the universe besides us that can understand our letters. Wheeeee – but aren't we the unique characters!!!

I received your letter of September 10th yesterday, and oh my aching A-hole was I ever passionately happy to hear from you. Ya ole turd! You turn up in the queerest places. It really was great hearing from you, Charlie. It seemed so odd hearing from you and at the same time trying to visualize where you were when you wrote the letter. You know I believe it's because you and I have been living for almost 17 years in one set of surroundings, with one set of people, and one set of customs, and now that we're actually doing things it's difficult to adjust ourselves. Enuff af dis luffink, let's start makin' with the news.

Last weekend I went to Hollywood and Beverly Hills on liberty and what do you know – I met up with a "fairy" nice fella for the first time in my life. Wheeeee –Having a wonderful time, wish you were here to enjoy "it". It all happened about 12:30 A.M. last Sun. Another fella and I were hitch-hiking into Hollywood when a big Buick pulled up. I hopped into the back seat and discovered that I was surrounded by four inebriated "dogface" individuals. Before I knew it one of them had calmly pulled me onto his lap and was meeting with his "meat hook" toward my grocery department. Now you know how much I value my "family jewels"!!! At first, I was going to call for the chaplain, but then I was overcome with a fit of anger that sent the bend of my elbow into his mid-section. He seemed rather surprised at my sudden action and said that he usually didn't do that for every sailor. I soon made a quick exit by telling him to play with his own. More damned fun!!!

You know, Charlie, I've been thinking to myself—I really envy the censor who will be reading our letters. Never a dull moment.

Your description of the jeep etc. are really tickling affairs. You know, the only thing that I could think of when you were mentioning turning corners in the jeep with Mary and Meg as passengers was Mary's famous words, "Go like hell, Dick. Go like hell!" Just imagine what would happen if you, Mary, Meg and I were ever stranded on an island like that. No telling what would happen!! Course I could but I might reveal a corporation secret.

Your letter, as well as all of them, proved to be interesting as well as morale building. Ya ole turd, you'd even find something to remark about if your tongue was caught in Meg's braces.

I saw a great picture last night. It was "Waterloo Bridge." Rather old, but very inspiring. Sexy as all hell. Vivian Leigh took the part of a ballet dancer turned prostitute. It was a rather tragic "pic" but something out of the ordinary for a change.

Today I am on duty. Tomorrow I'll also be on the base. We rate liberty about 3 times a month. This gives me a good chance to get caught up with my letter writing, money, washing, and rest.

I really can't express how much I want to see you again. I swear – when we do meet Charlie, we'll have to stay up about one straight week to tell each other everything.

Mary and Meg have left for school. I'll probably hear from "Dynamite" Hennessey very soon. She owes me a letter. I wonder how the "Spook" and "Hot Pants" are "coming"? They most likely are, right in each other's drawers.

I'm in a reminiscing mood tonight. Will you ever forget Graduation nite, or my episode with Ginger, or our long talks about life and "Hot Pants," "Blackie" (McGuire), or the Spook? Those days have just got to come again, Charlie. They just can't be taken away from us.

Listen, Casanova Young, shake it easy with the natives. Remember you still have mine!!

Please take care, Chas. I'm prayin' for ya!!!

Your ever lasting friend,
Dick

51 Forest St.
Oakwood, Conn.
September 24, 1944

My Dearest Charlie,

Here I am again even before I got an answer for my last letter, but I expect one from you any day now, so then we'll be almost even. Seems as though I wanted awfully to talk to you tonight, I guess it's 'cause I have so much to tell you.

You have no doubt heard about the hurricane we had here. We were much more prepared for this one than the last one. The radio broadcasted warnings of the storm all that day so that all those along the shoreline would have a chance to leave. Property damage was quite heavy in some areas and it all but put an end to telephone service. Honestly, Charlie, those poor men worked day and night trying to restore service. My Father went in at 6:30 the night of the hurricane and didn't even leave his office until 12:00 p.m. the next night. They even asked me to work from 7 to 7 last Sunday, boy, what a day, the week seemed long too, having to work from Sun, to Sun, but it had to be done. They've got everything pretty well cleaned up by now, just hoping we don't have another bad storm before winter.

Speaking of winter, it feels as though it's here now. The leaves are all beginning to turn, and it's practically freezing out at night. No more sitting out after supper. Because it gets dark about 6:30 or so all there is to do at night is read. I went to the library last night and got three good books – those will keep me satisfied for a while.

You're probably wondering what else I wanted to tell you about. I was quite stunned when I heard it, because I never really realized it was as serious as it must have been, but it seems that Helen and Ben have broken up. She called me today and said it's been coming on for a long time, because every time they've been together they always wind up having an argument. She didn't say what they argued about, but I can imagine. Well, anyway, she told him if that continued he hadn't ought to see her, and he picked her right up and said he wouldn't, so I guess that means no more dates or anything. Then she called and said she had some news to tell me about she and Ben. I thought sure she was going to tell me they were engaged. It really wouldn't have surprised me, because last week it sounded as though they were so serious, but it looks like it's all over now, unless they change their minds again.

I was wondering who she'll go with now. From all the letters she says she sends you, she might be trying to have you. Is she having any luck? That's silly to think, but she tries to give me that impression.

Oh, by the way, Sophie Lincoln was in the office the other day and she, of all people, is engaged. Did you know that?

You know, Chas. my little "Black Boy," seems like I owe you a nice picture. Would you still like one? Just say the word and I'll have one taken for you.

I've still got yours on my dresser and I've put my little white elephant you gave me right next to it. Do you remember you had one, too? Getting back to pictures though, you have an altogether different uniform now. Tell me about it and what you are doing in your next letter.

Hit Parade's just going off the air and "I'll Walk Alone" was first. Have you heard it? It's pretty.

One more thing I want to tell you is that we have a new dog. Her name is Debbie. She's half Cocker-Spaniel and half Irish Setter – sort of honey color. You'll love her when you see her, that is if you like big dogs, she's about the size of a Great Dane! But I'll tell you more about her next time. Write a nice long letter soon because I miss you so.

All my love,

Cheryl

P.S. Mother and Dad send a big kiss.

P.S.S. Always be careful.

P.S.S.S. Have you heard from Fred yet? I don't think he came home, at least, I didn't hear anything about him.

17 Anise Street

New Britain, Conn.

September 25, 1944

Dear Brother,

I received a letter from you today and so did Donny. So you're back in your former place again. Are you glad to be back or would you rather be on the other end of the island again?

Tag is home and has been down here twice, but both times I've been out. He's getting married Saturday, the 30ᵗʰ. Ma said he looks about the same.

Well, N.B. High played Bristol Saturday and they smeared them as usual. 40 - 0 was the score. I got in as a cheerleader. So did Audry Kraus. We had more fun at the game. I was never so scared when we marched out on the field. We had to counter march etc, We wore maroon skirts with yellow sweaters and socks with maroon letters. I was letter W. "Doc" said we were swell.

I have an awful toothache. I'm going to the dentist tomorrow, but how I'll stand it till then I don't know.

I saw Benny at the football game, he stopped to talk but we're not allowed to talk to anyone while cheering, so I met him under the grandstand later (Ha, ha!).

I've Miss Curran now for English (the other class was too big). She certainly is an old pill. I positively can't stand her. Oh, well! Everything's tough now a days. I'm reading the biography of Mark Twain for English.

293

It's o.k. for a person who hates reading. It's nice big print, too. Well, that's all for now.

Love and kisses, xxxxxx
Sister Betty

P.S. I know you're a strong Marine, but take care of yourself anyway, o.k?

51 Forest Street
Oakwood, Conn.
September 28, 1944

Dear Charlie,

It's rather dreary and quiet here today so I thought I might be able to squeeze in a few lines between customers.

Everybody around here looks like they've lost their best friend, so before I acquire that look I thought I'd better busy myself by writing to you.

Football season started in New Britain last Saturday, and from the score it looks as though the N.B. team is fully as powerful as it has been in the past. They beat Bristol 40 to 0. It seemed good to see the kids all running around Main Street. The Bristol boys had a big dummy all dressed up in a uniform, sitting in a baby carriage. Looked as though they were having the time of their lives.

Mrs. Whipple was in the office yesterday and she was telling me that Roger said he had seen Jack Neuman and Jim Kilbourne. It seems like they are all on different ships, but they are all sort of anchored near one another at sea. It must have made him feel good to see a familiar face again. You haven't ever mentioned meeting any boys you knew before. Have you, or have you met a lot of new boys? How about a special "buddy"? Most of the kids have those, too, don't they?

I don't think I told you that Mother and I went to New York for a couple of days on my vacation. We had a nice time looking around and buying a few things for the day time. Then at night we went to see "The Searching Winds" by Cornelius Otis Skinner that was very good. The second night we went to the Paramount to see the Andrews Sisters in person. It would have been wonderful to see "Oklahoma" too but the tickets were sold out so far in advance that we didn't even try to get in.

Daddy and I decided to take the screens down last Sun. so we did that and washed the windows on the outside with the hose. I practically squirted the thing right on me so that when we finished I was just as wet as the windows. Shortly after that episode Helen came over to be cheered

294

up. She said something about wanting to go to Florida to see Larry and Sharon, if he's still stationed there next summer. I said it would be fun to go together, but it would hardly be worth it for two weeks, and anyway I think it would cost too much. Now that I'm working I don't like to spend my money quite so freely, and especially when I have so little to show for it!

Have you heard from Ben lately? If so, did he mention anything about he and Helen?

I realize it must be hard for you to write often, but goodness it can't be as bad as it seems now. All the kids in the office get at least two letters a week, and I've gotten exactly one from you in about two months. Maybe it's 'cause it's hard for you to get stamps. If you'd like me to send you some, just say so in your next letter, and by the way if there's any thing else like candy, books etc. that you'd like, please ask, won't you? I'd love to be able to do something for you. Well, my little Black Boy, business is picking up so I'd better close for now. Be careful.

Always yours,
Chery.

Connecticut College
New London, Conn.
September 29, 1944

Hello, Charles,

I guess you knew I'd write, didn't you? I don't know why I am – maybe you can answer that one. This whole thing is too complicated for me.

I've been back at college since the 21ˢᵗ and it seems as though I've never left. I've got a roommate this year so at least I don't have to talk to myself. She's simply fascinated by your picture (yep, it's on my dresser). She even went so far as to say you were darn good looking. Could be you have some shining qualities I haven't discovered?!!

I've only been back a week and they've piled so much work on me that I'm beginning to get those glamorous circles under my eyes. I must have been insane when I was making out my schedule last spring. I seem to be taking everything that I don't know how to do – math, chem, and all that stuff. Did I tell you that I intend to major in zoology? Now don't ask me where the devil I hope to get – I don't know. I originally had the idea I'd take a pre-med. But after a few weeks of labs, math, and chem. I'm beginning to have my doubts. I'll probably end up by chasing June bugs down in South Carolina or something – sounds great, hmmmm?

'Member Pricilla Jones? Well, she isn't back this year. I heard that she was invited not to return – she was supposed to have stolen money or something. But I probably don't believe it – I liked her.

I haven't heard from you since you were on the boat. I suppose you must have reached wherever you are going by now – but why the devil don't you let me know? What are you doing – and what is H.A? Hospital something, huh?

I'm certainly glad you want to go to college after the war. You've got the right idea. You're so young now that this set-back won't make too much difference.

It's quite a while since I've written to you –about last January, I guess. By the way, was it you who sent me that camellia? I've always thought so – and I'll be awfully surprised if I'm wrong. But I can't say thank you till I'm sure.

I went home to New Britain just before I came back. I saw Joan Rollins – she's going into training in New London this year. So maybe we can get together.

I didn't see Patty Lou. The last time I saw her it sort of struck me that we didn't have much in common any more. I seem to have grown away from all those kids. It's been quite a while since I've been home in N.B. I guess that's it.

No, I haven't heard anything about Mick since last Christmas. He must be overseas by now I should think.

Well, it's kind of late and I have an 8 o'clock French class tomorrow so I think I'll go to bed. Please write when you get a chance and let me know how you are. Goodnight –

Love always,
Launa

17 Anise Street
New Britain, Conn.
October 1, 1944

Dear Charlie,

How are you? Yesterday morning Tag got married—there were a few hundred at the wedding. They were still celebrating today and we just got home a few minutes ago. We took some pictures today of Farmer's dog and Prince and us and we will send them to you if they come out any good.

The 28th of October Lala is going to celebrate her 25th anniversary and I am going to be bartender. Fanny Brice was on the radio tonight at

6:30. Betty went to New London with Bobby Cabelus and the Arutes to see Jimmy. I asked daddy how old you have to be to be best man, and daddy said about 14 or 15, then he wanted to know why I asked and I said because I want to be best man for you so don't get married unless we know about it. Please.

I forgot to tell you that mother got me a suit with reinforced rubber shit droppers.

I'm studying harder than ever because I want to get that load of souvenirs.

There is some man on the radio playing music on a typewriter. Well, I have to go to bed now. I'll write soon again.

Love,

Donny

P.S. Sam Cabelus gives you his love. So does Dotty.

232 Mountain Drive
West Hartford, Conn.
October 3,1944

Dear Charlie,

I'm so tired tonight and I don't feel like writing, but for you I'll make the supreme sacrifice.

I'm so disgusted with life, darling—it was I feel as if everything happens to me. Maybe it's just the mental exhaustion. For the last two weeks I've worked to the point of desperation. My boss is an actual shrew and when she is off the warpath, then her husband is on. If education makes people like that, then I want no part of it.

The first spring day we have, I'll start looking for an inn with a strolling violinist. The song "Where Or When" isn't classical but it was popular about 10 years ago and isn't jazzy. Maybe you'd call it a popular classic, something like "Smoke Gets In Your Eyes." "Intermezzo" is very beautiful and I always fall into a spell when I hear Strauss.

I didn't get your telepathy message, but now that I know you're trying I'll concentrate real hard.

I don't know why I do everything you say, but here I am making up my mind to get the book of poetry. When I get through writing to you, I'll be cultured as a pearl. Know what I'm going to do? I'm going to type all of the poems I have liked and the ones I like in the future and keep them in a book. It's something I've wanted to do ever since I graduated.

I'm afraid, my sweet, that sarcasm is one of my evil traits. Probably Cheryl has written and told you that Ben and I have broken up. It was pretty definite when I talked to her, but now I'm not sure what our status is. I can't explain it to you, because everything is all mixed up and maybe it will be all right again.

Last Sunday we went for a walk in the woods. It was a tingly day and we ate apples and had fun.

Nancy is back at college. She and Morry are getting more serious every day and I've stopped thinking about it. He might grow into a wonderful man you know, and I'm beginning to think that when he settles down he'll really settle. Maybe he's wiser than any of us realize, getting the wild blood out of his veins.

Somebody told me once the fellows in service saw most of the present day movies. That was really a faux pas (French for mistake) on their part. I don't really believe I'd like to be sixteen again either, but there's another philosophy about 16 other than yours. You're old enough to make your own decisions at 16, but you're too young to be responsible for the results. There's always a way out. Well, my sweet, I'll be off to bed.

Don't ask me anything about Ben and me, please. I'll let you know what develops.

I'll send you the poems after I get the book, darling, and write soon.

Affectionately,
Helena

51 Forest Street
Oakwood, Conn.
October 4, 1944

Dearest Charles,

Another fairly quiet day and another letter to you. Towards the latter part of the month when nearly everyone has paid their telephone bill things become quite dull, and I can usually find time to write every day.

It's been all of a month since I heard anything at all from you, and as usual I'm beginning to wonder what the trouble is. I think when I do get something there'll probably be two letters together. I do hope I get one before the 5th of October because Mother and I have a little surprise for you but I don't want to mail it before I make sure your address has not been changed.

Well, Charlie, what's new? Are there many things happening to you or are things still the same? You are feeling well, I hope. You must have to be careful of colds if you are still having as much rain as you mentioned in your last letter. How about swimming? Are you still able to do that? It's getting so cold here that just the thought of water gives me goose bubbles. We had such a heavy frost last night that the ground looked as though it was covered with snow.

Oh, Charlie, how I wish you were here again. I suppose that's a rather silly thing to say because you must wish it twice as much as I do, but I like to have you know that I'm so anxious to see you again. I think that when I do see you I'll be so excited I won't know how to act. Let's hope I remember to act like a lady, at least.

I heard that Jacqueline Kincaid was in the hospital. She had her appendix out and is feeling much better now. Daddy said he saw her brother Calvin and he's in the Marines, too. Seems as though he isn't old enough to be in the service, but he must be because he is in.

I'm beginning to think I was wise when I took out hospitalization insurance. If I'm not in there before the week is over, I'll really be surprised. I didn't go to work Monday because I had a tummy ache. Tuesday I slammed my thumb between the adding-machine and my chair and had to hold it in water for an hour. Finally, when I was just beginning to be able to use that hand a fly came along and bit me on the arm. It's all red and swollen now — I don't know what that will turn into, and I'm afraid of what will happen to me next! If you notice that my writing is different in my letter for tomorrow, don't be alarmed because I'll probably have to learn to write with my left hand.

It looks as though everyone around here has joined some Indian tribe because they're all going around with red feathers sticking out f their hair. O.K, now I know it's not an Indian tribe, it's for the Community Chest and I've just been invited to join. The invitations are quite pressing. They say you are going to give to the Community Chest, aren't you? I pity the individual who refuses. I think the feathers are cute and just so you can see one I'm sending you mine. Now you can make like an Indian, too. If you don't have your little elephant with you, you can keep this instead.

The World Series are starting today, and even though I don't know too much about it I put a quarter in a little pool we started in the office. The inning that has the most runs will be the one that wins. I drew the 7th inning. It sounds as though it should be lucky. There are nine of us and 9 x .25 = $2.25 I get if I win. I'll tell you how lucky I was in my next letter.

Have you heard from Helen and Ben lately? I should call Helen tonight because she called the other afternoon and I was downtown. Maybe she heard from you – she usually mentions it when she gets a letter because she knows how anxious I am to know you're alright.

Guess I've done enough chattering for this time, so until tomorrow.

Love,

Cheryl

P.S. Mother and Dad send their love, and Debbie does, too.

P.S.S. Please write soon and as often as you can, and remember to take care of yourself.

17 Anise Street
New Britain, Conn.
October 4, 1944

Dear Brother,

We received your letter yesterday with another new address. That same day we had mailed two letters to you at the old one so I suppose it will take a few months for the mail to catch up with you.

There hasn't been anything doing except schoolwork. (And that I can't stand.)

Tag got married Saturday and it was a real nice wedding. The reception was at Jean's house and then later they went over to the Cabelus's. Dot, May and Sam and everybody was there. They all send their love.

After the wedding, Audry Kraus and I went to a Victory Dance at the Grange. It was o.k. We met two nice kids from Holyoke, Mass. there. They had come down to N.B. to see the game. I didn't see the game or cheer Saturday but New Britain won 36 - 16. It was an exciting game. (So I hear.)

Sunday I went to New London with Mr. and Mrs. Arute and Bob. Jimmy is at Admiral Ballard Academy and Mrs. Arute thought I might like to go up with them. We went through all the houses that make up the academy and etc. I also met lots of nice cadets. So that was that.

We had a Sodality party at Ziegler's house last nite for our president, Peg Heath, who is getting married. About 40 girls came and we had a perfect time. Father Brophy also came for a while.

Charles Farmer just came tramping in looking for Donny. Now he's shooting peas around the room. He's still a fresh kid.

Mother's got quite a cold but besides that everything is o.k. I hope you're o.k. too.

It seemed funny to hear that where you are summer is coming. Winter is coming here.

I guess that's all for now. Good-bye for a while and God bless you.
Love and kisses,
Betty

P.S. We sent a package with some cookies and stuff out today. We're going to send the cake next week.

P.S.S. I hope you'll be getting some mail pretty quick. Donny's even been writing quite a bit.

51 Forest Street
Oakwood, Conn.
October 6, 1944

Dearest Charlie,

At last I think I know why I haven't heard from you. I was talking to your Mother today, and she told me that your address has been changed. Now, this may become very involved but I'll try to explain. You see, I've been writing to you nearly every day but since I didn't know you had been moved, I've been sending them to the old place, and if you haven't been getting any of my letters you no doubt thought I haven't been writing, and you are probably awfully disappointed by this time. I feel badly too, because I wanted you to get those letters, some of them were nice and there was one especially nice for you. I imagine you'll get them all in a bunch now, but that's alright as long as you know I haven't forgotten you for one minute.

Your Mom said you had asked for a flashlight and your field glasses in her letter. Your Dad got you a new flashlight last night and if he mailed it today you should have them very soon. She was telling me that you and a Pal went beach combing and came back with fruit juice and apricots! Do you think they were on a ship that was hit?

From your new address I gather that you are right in the branch of the Marines that you wanted to be in, the Medical Corps. I'm glad you're still interested in that field. It's a wonderful one, I think. Just what type of work do you do? It's such a wide-spread field that it's hard for me to imagine just exactly what you are doing. I'm awfully interested.

Your Mom said that your cousin was married Sat. and that it was a lovely wedding. He said that he didn't get his mail regularly at all when he was across. And when it did come, he got several at a time. So cheer up, Dear, we are all writing and I think of you always.

Last night I wanted to read one of your letters so badly that I got all the old ones out and read those. Some of them made me feel awfully good, they were so funny. Then when I came to the one when you had Scarlet

301

Fever, I immediately wondered if you could have gotten it from eating cream puffs. Remember, I always thought that I got mine from those that you bought. I wonder?

Tell me in your letter if you have gotten any of mine as yet because I'm now through, I guess.

Well, my little Black Boy, I should close now because it's nearly time for me to go to lunch. Until I write again take care of yourself and don't forget to answer all my questions.

All my love,
Cheryl.

P.S. Do I have the address right? Tell me if it's not exactly right 'cause I have a little surprise for you, and I want to make sure you get it.

232 Mountain Drive
West Hartford, Conn.
October 9, 1944

Charlie, darling,

You write your best letters when you're tired. I've had two letters from you right in a row and it almost seems like when you were in the States and we used to write so often. I'm going to keep right up now and then I can vote myself the one girl in the world who doesn't owe her favorite Marine a letter.

I'm discouraged about that book of poems I was going to gather together. There's so many of them.

Your cider mill sounds fascinating. We must go there and drink the old Italian's cider right there. There was a song in the gay nineties whose first line was, "By the mill where they made sweet cider, I made sweet love to you." I won't hold you to that though, but I think it deserves mentioning.

I know Cheryl writes often. From what she says, she's so very happy about the whole thing. Tell the truth now, don't you encourage her a bit, just a teeny bit? What you can't tell her, you can always tell me. I'm very understanding, I've been told, and we seem to agree on every point beautifully.

Your theory on exhaustion is ideal. Of course, I don't ski but the rest of it is very appealing. Maybe you can teach me to ski and then I can absorb the complete comfort. We can have a blanket party. More fun!

I can just see myself in about ten years, reading over all your letters. I'm glad I don't have to read my own again. We write some really brazen letters, but if we enjoy it that's all that counts. I'm going to take a nice hot bath now, my sweet, and go to bed.

Affectionately,
Helena

P.S. *Please excuse cross outs etc – I haven't my own pen and this thing is temperamental.*

Oh, by the way, if you write me a request for a book of poems or anything else, I'll send it to you. The Xmas overseas mailing season has gone by and I think the post office has to have a request now. I'll make it your Christmas present.

17 Anise Street
New Britain, Conn.
October 9, 1944

Dear Son,

Today is Monday and no letter from you. I was going to write yesterday but was so sure of hearing from you that I waited until today and no letter today.

I didn't write last week for I was sick in bed with the grip. I got up Sunday for the first time and still don't feel so hot. I just can't get rid of this cold.

Old Lady Andrews died last week and so did Frank Malczynsky, the garage man, and now Willkie so I better watch my step.

Are you getting your mail regular yet?

Cheryl from Oakwood called the other day and is so worried, she hasn't heard from you in a month but she said she keeps writing to you. Why don't you write to her, she seems to be such a sweet girl. She's going to send you an Xmas package. I thought that was nice of her. I made a fruit cake for you today. We will get it out next week. I hope we can get a box big enough, it can only be so many inches around.

Betty sent out your binoculars and Dad bought a flashlight for you so I hope you get them all right.

I believe Nellie is sending you a box so you won't go hungry.

Tag was here today, he's going back the 21st. He said to send you a line and some fish hooks. Do you want them? I don't think you care about fishing.

Pa, Donny, and Buck Miller went over to the rifle range to do some practicing. Pa's going hunting in three weeks.

Donny's been such a good kid. All week he took care of me and the chickens and brings up the coal. He couldn't do enough. He said I took care of him when he had his tonsils out and now he will take care of me. He's some kid. He has charge of the chickens and Dad said he could have the egg money. That's what interests him the most.

Did Betty tell you about the wedding? Nothing exciting, no one got in the bag.

Sam, May and Dot were there. Sam sends his best regards and so does Dot. Her husband is in the Pacific somewhere, she hears from him 3 times a week. Do you only write once a week? Tell us more about the island and the food and natives there, do you have any shows there or do they have church services on the island? How many fellows are in you Co. etc?

Jane Rawlings is coming home this week. She's been down in Florida until now.

Babe Bristol is back, her husband was discharged from the Army. So I guess he will go back on the Fire Dept. Poop Neubauer is still loafing. He doesn't want to go back to the shop. He wants a job driving a bus.

Well, I guess I told you everything and try to write more often. And don't forget to write to Cheryl even if it's just a few lines. You should be proud to have a nice girl like her. Well, I think I'll close and hit the hay. I've been up all day and am so tired. Write more often.

Love and kisses,
Mother

17 Anise Street
New Britain, Conn.
October 11, 1944

Dear Son,

Today is Wednesday and no letter from you. I wish you would write more often. We heard from you just a week ago.

I am feeling much better today. Although my cold still hangs on.

Pa is cutting the grass and Donny is writing some Halloween play. Betty is going to drum corps tonight and I am going to bed early.

Pa shot a nice male pheasant yesterday morning. Donny looked out the window and saw him in the garden, was he pretty. So tomorrow we'll have pheasant for supper. Betty mailed the fruit cake out yesterday so I hope you get it alright.

Pa is working alone this week. John didn't show up.

304

Betty is having so much trouble with her English. She doesn't like her teacher. Did she tell you she is a cheerleader?

Fan was over this afternoon. Charlie is still trucking. Willie Westerman is over in England.

Well, I can't think of anything else to tell you so I will close hoping to hear from you soon. Freddy was shipped out but Anna doesn't know where to. Probably North or South Carolina.

Will close with love,
Mother

I'm sending you a picture of Pa and Don just taken recently. Too bad it wouldn't fit in the envelope. Will send it in next letter.

475 Glen Street
New Britain, Conn.
October 12, 1944

Dear Sonny,

I'm trying to write on your old man's machine but am not having much luck as this is a real relic if you know what I mean.

So you are with the old Sixth Marines now, what a life. I once told you not to become a chancre mechanic or you would be a leather head like me.

Did you ever get the letter I sent you from out there in care of New River?

I don't suppose you ever see any dogfaces out there now, do you? I never saw them except in the rear bases and they were a bunch of fidos if I ever saw any.

How do you like the gooks out there, or don't you have any? I'll tell your mother to send you some dime perfume to trade with the gooks.

October 15, 1944

Well, kid, it was quite a pause between the last of this and now, but you know how it is.

This morning your Pop and my father went for mushrooms. Donny went along and took your .22 with him.

Your kid brother popped off a cock-bird in the lot next to your house, some brother.

Your folks miss you an awful lot and you sure have got a couple of sweet parents. My leave is up the end of this week and it sure seems funny going back after all of this leisure.

Where are you now? All I can figure is that you may be on Saipan or somewhere at a base in the Solomons with a combat outfit but I wouldn't

305

say anything to your folks because they'd worry and I'm not going to be the cause of that.

Well, kid, I'm a poor writer and I can't think of much else to write about so I'll knock this off for now. Keep the spirits up and you'll never get down in the dumps so until next time loads of luck and keep your fanny down when you get in there and try and always keep a hole close by to duck into.

Cousin Tag

P.S. Wouldn't it be something if we could get into the same outfit somewhere? Tofo or Malolo, Sonny.

Naval Research Lab.
Washington, D.C.
October 13, 1944

Dear Charlie,

Here it is Friday and another week has gone to the dogs.

By now you must be in the thick of it. I hope you're getting along o.k. Have you got your rate yet? But you probably don't have time for that sort of thing, or to even think about it.

I've finally finished studying simple things like transmitters, receivers and normal gear. Radar is more interesting than the whole lot put together. I graduate Dec. 16 (if I don't flunk). I'm going to ask for a light cruiser or a destroyer. I shouldn't have to wait long for a ship the way they're being put out now.

I went home last weekend and had the most interesting weekend I've had in quite a while.

New Britain beat Hamden 13 -7, but your sister, a cheerleader you know, must have told you all about it.

I went out with Nell Talbot (lemon). Instead of being a lemon, I'd say she's all a fellow could ask for in a date. I've got to go to class now. Even if my letters bore you, drop me a line to let me know you're getting them.

Sincerely,
Ben

U.S. Navy Base
San Diego, Cal.
October 14, 1944

Dear Charlie,

I received your V-Mail letter and was ever passionately happy to hear from you. The last time I wrote you was about two weeks ago. I've written you two letters since I arrived here in Calif. This is my third. I can't understand why you shouldn't have received any of them. I sent them airmail. Also, you've said that you already received a letter from Mary, so you should soon get my other two letters.

I'll be leaving Corps School in November but where I'll be going I don't know. I'll probably know in about ten days. I'll write you my new address as soon as I know of it myself.

I haven't heard from many of the people back home! I hear from my father every day. I haven't heard from Mary since I've been here. She did, however, send me a card when she first arrived at school. My correspondence with most of the fellas, who we knew, is practically nil. I have no idea if they're in this country or abroad, or dead or alive. I imagine that Morry is still the same old "Rah-Rah." My weekends have all been great in Hollywood and Los Angeles. I'm really the original "Joe Gob" when I'm out the prowl. You know me – the original eager beaver. I am still looking forward to our inevitable D-Day. We'll have that day yet even if it's by remote control.

I am carrying on an indirect relationship with one of the most beautiful girls I have ever had the pleasure of coming in contact with. I've never met her. I received her address from a fella in boot camp, and I wrote to her before I left Sampson. I received an answer from her, and ever since then we have been writing quite regularly. She lives in Staten Island and her name is Olive Olson. Our letters are really something. I'm just dyin' to cast an eye on her. That's one reason I want to be sent east. I've just got to see that woman before I'm shipped out of the country. I sound desperate, don't I?? I'll tell you more about this "skirt" if things develop per schedule.

I received a letter from Lucy last week. What a "pisser" she is. Of course, she's always been that way. She says that there is nothing wrong with New Britain that a manly Navy Base wouldn't cure. When I was home on boot leave, she really had some rare tales to tell me about. She seems to love her "nooky." She must be making a lot of money now or doing it for love.

Remember the time that we told Betty S. that her stomach was sticking out? What characters we were. Remember how we used to tell about two prostitutes who ate raw vegetables while in the act? We used to imagine "Hot Pants" doing something like that. "Take it out deeper!" Wheeeee! I wonder who her latest is now. She's probably got a "squid" from Scully Square.

Glad to hear that things aren't too tough with you. You were never the one to complain very much. All I can say is don't go bringing back any "Ubangis."

Last weekend I did a novel thing. I flew back 130 miles to Lost Angeles by Western Airlines. It was really a thrilling experience which I'll not soon forget. All I could think of was wouldn't it be fun if you and I were at the controls. What top off would be to have Mary in the back saying, "Go like hell, Charlie, go like hell, Dick."

Two weeks ago I saw Jack Benny's first program of the season since he came back from overseas. Fred Allen was a guest and talk about urination in our pants – gads, I should really be called a pisser.

During my liberties I've also seen a number of movie stars. At least , it'll be something to talk about when and if I ever get back home. You really, really stimulate me!! I got your letter yesterday and what did I do but have a mighty naughty dream. "But, darlin', it's so nice to be bad."

Have you heard anything from home lately? It must really be great to get mail where you are. If you have yet to receive any, you should have enough to keep you busy for the duration when it does arrive.

I was just trying to think of something silly to say. You know, after this thing is over I'd like to get together with you for a couple of days and reread all of our letters. I've saved all of yours. We'd probably split our testicles laughing at them. We used to talk about the craziest damn things.

One thing I miss is those walks we used to take. The last time I think I fell in that small brook and really froze my right limb. Just so long as it wasn't my middle limb.

"Tings" in the good old USA is o.k, hope they're the same with you. I'll close, Charlie, and write when you get a chance. I'll be sure to write you once more before I leave here.

> *You pal and friend as ever,*
> *Dick*

> *9 Arthur Court*
> *New Britain, Conn.*
> *October 15, 1944*

Hello, Funnyface –

This is getting to be a bad habit. I haven't heard from you, of course – would sort of serve me right if I didn't, wouldn't it?

I came home to New Britain for the weekend – this town always gives me the creeps. I've been listening to records all morning – sort of depressing.

No one ever buys new records when I'm not here – so all we have are the old ones. And they remind me of so darned many things. I think I had more fun way back when I was in Nathan Hale than I've had since. Or maybe that's just because it's all in the past. Things always seem better when you remember them than they really were, I guess.

This letter is kind of a mess. I can't find any decent paper and I'm stretched out on the floor trying to write, so my writing is even worse than usual.

I saw your sister this morning on the way to church. She was arguing with another girl right in the middle of Arthur Street. We nearly knocked them down. She looks so much older than I remembered her. And cute, too!

Guess who came to see me at college last Friday – Joan Prentiss. She joined the Cadet Nurse Corps and she's going to be stationed in New London for the next three years. I guess that's a pretty stiff course – I hope she makes the grade. We had a nice long talk about all the kids and everything. Joe is overseas – she writes to him, I guess. She said he was terribly homesick and missed all the kids a lot. Why don't you write to him? I don't know what his address is but you could send it to New Britain and his family would forward it.

I thought Joan would choke when she saw that huge picture of you that's on my dresser. That started us off and we talked about you for about half an hour. After seeing the picture and listening to me, she decided you had changed – much for the better. That'll cost you at least a quarter for building up such a wonderful reputation for you!

They announced in church this morning that the youngest Gingrass fellow and some Harry Billings had both been killed in action. Any relation to Warren Billings?

New Britain took a good beating from Stamford yesterday. I guess there was nearly a free for all after the game. The paper said that all the kids were armed with rotten tomatoes to throw at the other team. The police were there and everything – good old New Britain! There's no place like it – yeh!

Joan told me that Prissy Jones has transferred to Syracuse but she didn't know any of the details.

I heard that Sally Lasher has broken her engagement. The week before the wedding she decided she didn't love the man. She certainly is a gay blade.

College isn't so bad now that things have started again. But education is still rather painful in spots – math for instance. I must be really thick for I just don't get it. Why should B + 2 over A something squared equal anything in particular? Well, it does but I'll be darned if I know what. I went to Harvard last weekend on a blind date – never had such a bad time in my life. He was tall enough but that's about all I can say for him. What a specimen – a violinist – imagine! I nearly had hysterics. Looks like I'm doomed to be an old maid. I bet I'll even hit 19 without being married – sad.

Sharon seems to think I should do the dishes – just so I won't get out of the habit. Hey, have you got off that boat yet? I wouldn't know. That's a hint.

As ever,
Launa

51 Forest Street
Oakwood, Conn.
October 15, 1944

My dearest Charlie,

I suppose I shouldn't be writing to you again tonight because I wrote such a long letter Thurs. night that I don't have much to tell you. But you've popped in and out of my mind so many times today that I won't be satisfied until I write just a little. I went to eleven o'clock Mass today and the priest gave such a nice sermon, and the music was so pretty that I found myself wishing that you could be there, too. Ever since you mentioned that you so seldom hear Mass where you are I often wondered why. Isn't there an Army Chaplain or would he be called a Marine Chaplain, there? Since I know so little about where you are it's hard to imagine what you have or don't have. I hope you have nearly everything you want, however. You know, I was in the Beacon Gift Store the other day and they have a lot of different pocket size games like checkers, cards etc. I was going to buy something for you but in order to send it overseas I would need a written request from you to show to the Post Office so how about asking for something that you'd like so I can send it to you? The man in the P.O. said I'd even have to do that with my picture, but I won't have any trouble because you did write that you would like one, so as soon as it's ready you'll have it.

Helena called late this afternoon and wanted me to go to the movies with her, but I had a couple of blouses to iron, and I wanted to wash my hair and write to you, and so I told her I was too busy. She hasn't heard any more from Ben since they made up but he'll no doubt be over to see her as soon as he's home again. You'll never know, Darling, how many times I've wished you were coming to see me. It's been about 9 or 10 months

310

*since we've seen each other, hasn't it? I could cry every time I think we had
another one of our usual scraps the last time you were home. You might have
come over were it not for that, but I guess your time was pretty much taken
up with someone else. You know, you never did tell me who you were with
besides Dickey W. that afternoon – I wonder if you still like her? There I
go being mean again.*

*It's getting so cold here that I wouldn't be surprised if there was snow
on the ground some morning. You'll laugh when I tell you, but I was so cold
last night that I decided to wear my little pink pajamas with the feet in
them to bed tonight. Remember how funny they were under the Christmas
tree last year? You really embarrassed me the way you laughed at them, but
anyway they're nice and warm.*

*Dad stayed in bed nearly all day with a cold. It's a bad one too, because
he's been coughing quite a lot, but next week is his vacation so he'll be able
to take care of it. Mother has been feeling quite well since she came home
from the hospital but she still has to be careful of her diet. Speaking of
Mothers, it's been quite a while since I called your Mother. She asked me to
call whenever I hear from you. We've become quite friendly over the phone,
Dear, and I think she is lovely. I haven't met her yet but she said she'd be
down to the office some day, and I'm looking forward to seeing her because
she sounds so sweet. Hope she likes me a little, too.*

*Well, here it is 11 o'clock and I'm still up! I'll be half asleep at work
tomorrow, and I really shouldn't be because it's very busy. All the bills are
coming in. I had something like 402 customers Fri. in one hour, that's what
I call busy. It was so crowded in there that they were all but hanging on the
light fixtures! Oh, before I forget, have you been getting any of my letters?
I do write often, Darling, because I get so lonesome and I know you do too.
I expect another letter from you soon 'cause you said you'd like to write
more often so don't disappoint me. Goodnight, darling, and as I say in my
prayers every night, God bless and watch over you.*

Love,

Cheryl

17 Anise Street
New Britain, Conn.
October 16, 1944

Dear Charlie,

*Well, Kid, how are you? I received your letter written the 6ᵗʰ today.
By the sound of your letter, you're in pretty high spirits.*

311

We're all at home. Mother's cold is practically gone. Oh, I forgot Donny's got poison ivy. He's always got something! Dad and Uncle Pete went for mushrooms a couple of times last week. Ma canned some and we've also been eating them up.

I was talking to Seymour Cohen Saturday. He said to say Hello to you. He was telling me what a tattle-tale I was when I was small. I don't remember, of course.

New Britain played Stamford Saturday and got beat 27- 7. They won the first three games though. We gave two Football Rallies in the auditorium last week. More fun jumping around doing the cheers. We're going to New London next Saturday to play N.L. Buckley.

I heard that Mick is at Pearl Harbor.

Say, is your friend Elon nice? Fix me up, o.k.?

I bet you had fun with those boars (pigs?). But why didn't you ride them? You told me that when you were small you rode them down at DiPintos.

Our drum corps is giving a Harvest Supper the 25th. The corps is going to play a few tunes and I think I'll try to do a little twirling for my first time in public. Oh Boy, this should be good.

Would it take much longer for mail if you just used regular mail instead of airmail? Why don't you try it and I'll tell you how long it takes, o.k.?

School is awful. I hate it. I can't stand History. English with Miss Curran kills me. Mr. Nordstrom slays me. I guess you now know how I like school. That's all for a while.

Love and kisses, xxxxxx
Betty

P.S. *Who do you think you are using Cashmere Bouquet soap, Heddy Lamar?*
P.S.S. *If you marry a native I'll kill you.*

17 Anise Street
New Britain, Conn.
October 16, 1944

Dear Charlie,

How are you? Good I hope. I was wondering if Betty told you that I sent away for some Lone Ranger tattoos and when I got them the address was Brother Hugo.

Mother is cleaning up for Betty's Halloween party and she said that I got a book that I subscribed for, I got it about two weeks ago. I just asked Mother a question and she got so mad she almost crapped in her pants.

Daddy was wondering if you were among the first to hit the Philippine islands because he heard on the radio that the 6th Army was the first to land. Now tell the truth, were you?

Mother wants to know if you see any nice natives where you are? If you do take the skirts off them and send them home for me. It's about bed time now 8:45 and I have to go to bed. I'll write soon.

Love and kisses

Donny or

Little Brother Hugo

P.S. My birthday is about 41 days away.

P.S. Can I have your 22 pump rifle?

51 Forest Street

Oakwood, Conn.

October 17, 194

Hello, darling,

Guess what? I got another letter from you, that makes three within five days. The only thing wrong with that is that it makes me want to hear from you every day, the more I have the more I want, but even though I don't get one every day, I know you're still thinking of me – as I always do of you.

You know, Dear, I've been awfully puzzled since your last letter. According to that you are just getting letters that I wrote weeks ago. If the last one you got was the one in which I told you about the hurricane, you must have loads more coming 'cause I've written nearly every day since then and that was about a month ago. But still these were probably the ones with your old address and if they had to be forwarded to you, that would explain the delay. You probably know all about it while I'm going around here wondering me little head off.

I bought a season ticket for the Mark Twain Masquers in the Avery Memorial. Have you ever heard of them? They're a group of actors who put on several plays. Last year I went with the kids in the office to a few of them, and they were very good, so I decided to get a season ticket this year. They put on "Life With Father" "Separate Lives" and three other good ones last year. You've seen "Life With Father" at one time or another, haven't you? That was especially good.

313

Father Kennedy is going to give three or four lectures on books and so Helena asked me to buy a ticket to that. Of course, I said I'd love to go although I probably won't read the type of book Father K. does. Do you think I'll hear about any good novels? They'll all no doubt be on religion. They'd better be good for I had to pay my hard earned money,

Tomorrow night St. Anne's church in N.B. is having a spaghetti supper and Ruth and Naomi asked me to go. I thought that since I love spaghetti so much, I guess I'll go. Do you like spaghetti too, darling? If you do let's go where they cook it the Italian way when you get home, and have some. Speaking of eating, 'member the time we bought the soda and sandwiches up at the tower, and how silly we got when we realized what everybody else up there was doing while we were having our picnic. That was the same night we had the blackout, wasn't it? It was wonderful up there so high with the wind blowing so hard, and still more wonderful being able to hold on to you so tight. Oh, and then remember the time we went to Compounce and on the way home Joyce had the measles? We had a flat tire and you had the jack to fix it in your hand while Freddy tried to hold the car up with his hands. Honestly, dear, I have to laugh every time I go over all the swell times we had together. They weren't always silly, we've been to a lot of nice places, too, like the dance at the Htfd. Country Club. 'Member how mad you pretended to be when I went off with that droopy kid from Kingspoint—were you really just a little bit jealous, darling? I like you more when you're that way. It's so cute to see you doing your darndest to completely ignore me.

You like to go back over things we did, too. I was surprised to know you remembered the walks we took when I lived on Commonwealth Ave. They date way back. You were right, I did have a brown suede jacket, but tell me what in the world made you remember that? That's another thing you always did. You'd never tell me or, I should say seldom tell me, you particularly liked things I wore, but you must have at least thought so to yourself if you remembered them that well. I hope you'll like the black dress I have on in my picture, and what about the shorts in the snap shot? Would it be possible for you to send me a picture or something of yours, it would make you seem a lot nearer.

Helena just called and she said she got a V-Mail letter from you today. Don't send me V-Mail, darling, it makes the letter too impersonal. I'd rather have your own handwriting. She also said you wanted to know all about she and Ben, so if you find out anything I didn't mention, tell me, too. Hon, I wonder if you call her pretty names like you do me. Tell me all about it in your next letter.

By the way, your face should be red. What's wrong with the name "Debbie" for my dog? Anyway I think it's cute and she sort of looks like a Debutante with her long wavy ears, reddish hair and droopy eyes. Of course, we have to overlook the tail, that doesn't exactly go with her feminine description. She's not small either, she's much bigger than your Butch.

Well, my darling, I could go on and on but I'd better stop so I can have something to tell you in my next letter. Answer awfully soon, won't you? Until next time.

Always yours,
Cheryl

P.S. Be careful, and by the way, do you still feel sick when you take those pills? Tell me if they still bother you.
P.S.S. Enclosed is a picture of what goes on in building across the street. I'm glad I work in the Commercial Business Office instead of the Traffic. Boy, would I be in a mess.

232 Mountain Drive
West Hartford, Conn.
October 17, 1944

Dear Charlie,

You poor dear – I didn't realize your morale was so dependent on my letters!! Mine has been so low lately though that I just couldn't convey any ill spirit to you.

I was sick in bed all last week. I must be getting frail or maybe it's just the femininity coming out of me at last. I don't mind being sick though – I crave attention and lately that's the only way I can get any. I stayed in bed and read all the poems in the book you suggested. It has a good selection and I'm enclosing the two you wanted.

I could get very dramatic about Ben and I breaking up, but remember, I am a realist and as a member of that school, I can't let my dramatic side run away with my usual contained self. It's the feminist situation – we still write and I imagine that I'll even see him when we can arrange it. I don't actually know if he feels as I do or not, but for me I don't think things will be the same again. We had wonderful times together and, of course, this is the first argument we ever had, so you never can tell. Everyone is changing so much, though, it scares me to think that none of us will ever be the same. E' Gad! There I go again. Well, you started it.

315

Mon Dieu! I'm having an awful time trying to decide what is and what isn't with Cheryl. She's been telling me that your mother called her and, of course, I'm thinking how wonderful everything is with you and the whole family when bang! comes your letter. I know that she hadn't had a letter from you in about a month until the other day when 3 arrived. She said that she wrote you very often and was quite worried about you – you lucky boy!! You two have been a puzzle since I've known you.

I think that you should be a bachelor and that I should be an old maid and we can sit back in our little café and laugh at the whole silly world. I have a little work to do tonight so I'll leave you now.

Affectionately,
Helen

17 Anise Street
New Britain, Conn.
October 18, 194

Dear Charlie Jr.

How are you? Daddy and I went to the movies today and saw Rainbow Island, he said it stunk. Prince is alright, right now—he is sleeping in the den on the chair. Yesterday afternoon daddy and I went fishing and got six perch and two pickerel. When we got home one of the pickerel almost bit Betty's finger off. Ha, ha!. Walter James and I set a few traps down near the hog sewer and someone took two of them. I got five new traps – two 1 ½ - one 1 – and two spring traps. (total $1.60).

Hambone Driscoll was drafted in the army. I can imagine him walking twenty miles to church or on a hike. I found one of the letters that I was going to send you in the drawer, and couldn't even read it myself. John, Daddy's old painter, was sent over to Pearl Harbor to paint ships. Well, I suppose you go swimming every day also. Well, I'll have to go to bed pretty soon.

Best of luck,
Donny

P.S. The Farmers were up to the State theater yesterday and some guy said, What's the difference if you go to heaven or hell? If you go to heaven you have a good time but if you go to hell you burn and meet all your friends.
P.S. You can take as long as you want to send those souvenirs.

91 West Street

New Britain, Conn.
October 18, 1944

Dear Peaches and Cream,

At last—I finally heard from you, The funny thing is that I was telling Ryan last nite that I hadn't heard from you in simply years.

Mary Jane and I are rooming together now and getting along swell. My first week here was terrific. I'd hate to live those days over again. My first roommate was a pip – she is taking the "Special Arts Class" which requires practically no homework so she'd be breezing all over the room while I was trying to study. She is married and if it were known she would be kicked out of school. Was I ever glad to get out of that room.

In the past ten weeks I've really got to love it here. Have met some real nice kids!

The studies are terrific! I'm taking Anatomy, Medical Practice, Chemistry, Hematology and Bacteriology. I don't have half enough time to study. It seems as though there is always something going on. Two weekends ago Ryan and I visited Barb Donahue at Marymount College – had a swell time. The second weekend I was here I came back from White Plains on a Saturday about 8:30 and who was in the lobby but Morry Blair and Elmer Fisher. I nearly died. It seemed so good to see someone from home. I went out with Morry and got Elmer a date that night and we went out dancing. Sunday they came back and took a bunch of us kids to see Sing-Sing Prison! Cripes, it's only about 6 miles from here. Hot Dawg! Maybe we'll be in for a little excitement.

Ryan and I are going home this weekend and guess who is home! Joe Donnelly! Barbara Donahue called me the other night and told me. Was I ever surprised. Hope I will see him for a while at least.

I haven't heard from Dick either in practically 2 months. I don't like it one bit (tough for me.)

Honey Chile – you know I'll always give up any date I might have (by some miracle-date, I mean) for you anytime you are home. Heaven knows when that will be!

The weekend of the 28th of Oct. Betty Logan, Barb Donahue, Meg, Ryan and I are going into New York and have one helluva time. I can hardly wait! We've been planning this trip before we all left for college.

Right now my suitemate is saying something to me – can't understand her – what a hick – she's from Orangeburg, Pa. Never heard of the joint!

I haven't heard from Bob in quite some time – can't figure it out – might be because I haven't written to him in over a week.

We sure do have a lot of southern belles up here. Ah sure do have to listen to them all talk. We have a Boston Deb here, too – she's very nice.

It took about a week to really get to know some of the kids, but once I did I liked it here so much more.

Last weekend we had a dance here. Terry Bolton (maybe you know her – she used to go around with Morry and went to T.C.C. She's very short, cute – from Waterbury) fixed me up. Cripes, he was a football coach from Peekskill Military Academy, He played football four years at Dartmouth. I expected a tackle any minute – what a brute. Had a fairly good time, though. The dance wasn't anything like the good ole shin-digs we had in New Britsky! Hallelujah when we can all go to one of those again and do the "farmer's shuffle." Well, box-time for lunch – so I'll close – and I want to hear from you again real soon.

Love 'n stuff,
Peaches

I have your picture up here and all the girls are crazy about it. I tell them you're the "killer" at home.(Don't forget my grass skirt,) Take care of the sweater-less sweater girls!!!

17 Anise Street
New Britain, Conn.
October 18, 1944

Dear Son,

Today is Wed. and what a beautiful day. It's Tag's birthday, I wonder if he will celebrate.

I must call Aunt Anna. I am going to give Betty a party next Tuesday. She only wants to have a few girls in. It doesn't seem like she is going to be 16, now she can go to work in the factory and earn her own living. Ha, ha!.

I am going downtown today for the first time in three weeks. I still have my cold but it isn't too bad.

Pa picked the apples last night. All we got was 3 bushel. The hurricane knocked the rest off. We are going to kill Donny's ducks but they are so big. We will have a nice meal. Pa and Donny killed the rabbit last week. The chickens come next. We haven't many left. We had quite a heavy frost here, almost everything is frozen.

Pa will have to take the screens down this week so I can wash the windows and he can put up the storm windows.

Tag said he was going to write to you. He said the natives like perfume.
He said to send you some and they will swap other things with you. I hope
you will be able to pick up something for Betty like a scarf for her head. But
I guess you will have to see them first.

How are the eats, do you get enough to eat? I suppose it's still canned
stuff. Betty tried to send you some Mary Olivers but they were all out of
them. If you send a request for anything we may still be able to send it to
you. Otherwise we can't.

I was talking to Aunt Anna. She said how Bob and Tag went hunting
today. Tag is leaving Sat. So long, will write again soon.

Love,

Mother

1173 Smalley Street
New Britain, Conn.
October 19, 1944

Dear Charlie,

It was surely a surprise to hear from you. I thought you were "pissed
off" with me for something or other. (I still think you are, but such is life.)

You must have some first class heels for censors if they send letters back.
I've never heard of such a thing.

I can't tell you very much about your sister because we don't have too much
to say to each other. I saw her at a game a month or so ago, she is certainly
growing up, she seemed a little "ill at ease" being a cheer leader for the first
game but she's on her own now and the crowd doesn't seem to bother her a bit.

As for Helena and I breaking up, you know how scuttlebutt goes. I don't
think we've actually broken up. We did have a little argument for which
I'm to blame but all matters have been cleared up and when the smoke lifts
I expect to see her again. Ungentlemanly? What sort of story did you hear?
I haven't heard a good story in a long time.

Will you send me Joe's address in your next letter?

There is really nothing new to talk about except a few unimportant
items. I've been getting home quite often, once or twice a month. Nell
invited me to her Sophomore Dance Nov. 4. Sam (my brother) got his mid-
shipman's uniform. He's in Chicago.

I've got a new hobby, I study calculus in my spare time. I've got to go
to lab now so I'll say bye for now.

Love,

Ben

P.S. Soon, OK?

U.S. Navy Base
San Diego, Cal.
October 20, 1944

Dear Charlie,

    This is just a note to let you know that I received your letter of October 9. I answered you – no, I didn't either, so I am going to write you an answer over this coming weekend. I sent you a letter Wed. October 18. In your last V–Mail letter you put down your address as being San Diego. At the time that I was writing you, I had the V–Mail letter with me and as a result I sent the letter addressed to San Diego. I don't know how long of a delay there will be before you receive this, but nevertheless you know that it is on its way. It will either come back to me first, or else the letter will be forwarded to Frisco.

    I'll write you again this weekend. Take care of "yours" till then and keep it out of dirty foxholes. Bye for now, my lil' hunk of imagination.

As ever,
Dick

U.S. Navy Base
San Diego, Cal.
October 21, 1944

Dear Charlesie,

    You lil' devil ya! I received another letter from you yesterday, and as I promised you in my short V–Mail yesterday, I am writing you today. Nothing more of interest has happened here, so I'll make comments on your letters of Oct. 9th and 15th. I feel in a crazy mood at present, so here goes.

    I'm glad that you enjoyed my little descriptions "avec la queer." I agree with you – we would have had a picnic if we were ever picked up together by a couple of "those boys." We probably would have had them "taking it in the ear for a beer," before we left the car. More damn fun!!!

    Yes, my lil' lamb, "Hot Pants" and Mary Jo are off to school. I'll bet that the girl with the "spontaneous combustive drawers" (Meg has a black market racket of importing males into the country.). I'll bet she'll be so under–sexed and hot when she has her first vacation from school that she'll be ready for anyone and thing. Those were really rare days that we had with Mary and the—oh, that reminds me of something. Can you imagine Meg saying this – "you've heard that Monty Wooley is the beard, Lana Turner is the cheat, Frank Sinatra the voice, and I am the jaw." But you should *see her sister, he says. As I was saying we surely did have some good times with those two skirts. We should have "plugged" them on our last night at Beckley's Beer Garden. Weren't we the little urchins tho, walking down the road while the women disrobed in the car. I'll bet that Mary's are like two watermelons with nuts. Meg's, if I remember correctly, were more like pancakes with prunes. Screeeeeeew.*

You know, Charlie, I still can't understand myself as far as my infatuation with Meg went. I've met a lot of girls since, and I've got to admit that Meg stacks up just as good, if not better, than any of them. Of course, if anyone were ever to marry the old "pot" I suggest to him to have her psychoanalyzed first. I imagine that she'd be a lot different if her family life were different. She's a "pisser" tho. I wonder if she squats when she urinates, or has she become a man?

"I'll Walk Alone" is still tops. This is the pay-off. Frankie Sinatra was singing this song at the Paramount Theater last week and he was hit with two eggs right between the seventh and eighth words by a civilian 4-F in the audience. One egg caught him between the eyes and the other hit his chest. Oh, my corroded cruller," that really "bulges my balls." As for my song, "Don't get around much etc" I've got a new motto, "Don't get it prone much anymore."

You asked if this school were as crowded as it was when I first came here. It is and even more so!!! In my barracks alone there are about 1,350 men. The Chaplain talks about one man to a bunk. Sometimes I wake up teething on my bunkmates toes – or I will be soon. I think the closeness of everything was too much for one old boy who sleeps across from me. He was surveyed out – for "ploughing somebody up the old dirt road." I thought that my "A-Hole" was mightily irritated some mornings.

I am on Mess Hall duty at present. I'll be leaving the old "den" Monday. Sometimes I complain about my plight but what with you doing 14 hrs. per day, I should think twice before I speak the next time.

Launa's writing to you didn't surprise me a great deal. If she were at all human, I knew that she would drop you a line to let you know she was thinking of you. I can't tell whether your being overseas and separated from her will help matters but it certainly couldn't make them any worse. To tell the truth, Chas, I don't know Launa well enough to tell you what to do. I don't see why you should or shouldn't have written to her as soon as you received her letter. You love her, and no matter how many times you've told her that, tell her again, again, and even again. Don't play hard to get whatever you do. It seems that no matter what you say to her it can do nothing but draw her closer to you than she is now. I've "done sed" my piece. Oh, another thing – she says that everything is all too "complicated." I know that if I were ever to tell a person that "the affair" has become "complicated", I'd know that back in my mind I wasn't sure of certain things, and that I wouldn't want to break off unnecessarily and regret it later. She's already told you that "it" could never work – that was the lowest or the furthest she could go. Now it's all too "complicated" for her – get what I mean? Maybe I'm just beatin' my chops in vain, but it's a thought anyway, and maybe it will give you ideas.

My mother got a big kick out of you signing your V-Mail letter to her, "With "love." Of course, you know Dad didn't like that, ya lil' wife lover. Only kidding, of course, but the folks did get a chuckle out of it.

I still want someone to love – no, I don't either. I think that I'll wait a couple of years before I do anything as drastic as that!! I'm talking about a woman, of course.

We have a "mighteous" First Aid teacher. He's a rather young fellow who has traveled all over the world. He's really a brilliant man. This morning he delivered an oration about the value of clinging to your virginity before marriage. He actually made me proud and glad that I hadn't lost my cherry. Now you see what Corps School does to you – I'm talkin' in riddles. But really there was something in what he says. We've still got a lot of time to dip it. I've got to report to the Mess Hall now, darlin', so take care and write when you can. Good-luck, "beautiful."

As ever urine,
Dick

17 Anise Street
New Britain, Conn.
October 22, 1944

Dear Son,

Rec'd your letter Thurs. with money order for $60.00. I also rec'd two bonds—we didn't get one last month. I will put the money in the bank for you if I can find your bank book. I looked around downstairs but tomorrow I will look upstairs. I know it's around somewhere. Try and send some home every month so when you get back you will have a little money.

Tag left Friday but we don't know where he's going to go.

You asked me if Lena was at Tag's wedding. Yes, she was but she had an awful cold. She is still working in Saybrook.

Today was a lonesome Sunday. Pa and Donny went to the rifle range with Buck Miller and Donnelly and Betty went to the show. I just hung around, I still have my cold. Pa and Donny got home a little while ago and Pa said how Donny shot the Enfield. Pa said he's pretty good. Anna dropped in for a minute, she said Freddy is headed for S. Carolina but she hasn't his address yet. Spuddy is in Texas going to school. Tess said how he has an awful lot of studying to do.

We are getting ready for Oneida and Eddies Silver Wedding next Sat. I suppose everyone will get in the bag. All the neighbors are invited. She has 120 invited. Betty was suppose to go to New London yesterday but it rained so just the players went down. So Doc Merliani took 18 of them to see the Holy Cross game in Worcester. Betty said they had a nice time although it rained. She saw Ned Ziegler there. Well, I guess that's all the news. I will be busy tomorrow and Tuesday baking for Betty's party.

Love from all,
Mother

51 Forest Street
Oakwood, Conn.
October 23, 1944

Hello, Darling,

How's my little black boy today? Hope you are feeling better than the last time you wrote and besides being upset from taking Malaria pills. Helena tells me you have a cold. It's a good thing I'm broad minded, or I would be very hurt. Do you know that you're neglecting me? You've written her two letters to my one. Oh, well, maybe her post office is more efficient than our little one in Oakwood. (I keep telling myself.)

Guess what I'm doing, Charlie?. I'm knitting a sweater! Lord only knows why I'm doing that 'cause I'm already up to my neck in things but now that I've started it I have to finish it or my mother will crown me. Well, anyway I knitted all Sat. night and Sun. and all I've got done is 4 inches. Boy, I never worked so hard for 4 inches of anything in my life but it's going a little faster now since I started it with larger needles. How would you like me to make you a pair of yellow or argyle socks when I finish? Would you wear them, darling, when you get home? If you would I'll make 'em for you.

I haven't been to a movie in ages, in fact the last one I saw was "Christmas Holiday." D. Durban sang, "I'll Be Loving, You, Always" in it, and it was beautiful. I bought it for the piano and between that

323

and "Together" my neighbors are really mad. I play them both so often. "Together" was in "Since You Went Away." By the way, do you see any movies, and how about the radio, can you get any programs, or do you have any there? Would it be possible for you to tell just a little about what you do and what things are like around you? My letters to you aren't censored are they?

We heard General MacArthur's broadcast after he had taken the Philippines. And it was so hard to hear him. He said the rain hindered them somewhat, and that makes me wonder if it could be the same rain you spoke of. Somehow hearing him speak seemed to bring you so much closer for the time. I wonder how near you are to him.

Have you heard from home recently? I hope you write often, Dear, because your Mom and Dad would worry terribly if you didn't. You'll never know how many things come into our minds when you don't write as often as you should. At least if you don't get our letters right away you don't have to worry about us. You can be sure they've been delayed at the post office or something like that.

Your little church in Belvedere is putting on a Harvest Supper Wed. night and since Ruth got two tickets free looks like we might go. Incidentally, the one at St. Anne's was wonderful. It's surprising to see the number of people who go to these things.

Dad just came into the room here and said, "Are you still writing! What in the world do you write about?" Guess I tell you most everything I do every day. Do you ever tire of my letters, Darling? You must have loads of them but I like to write often 'cause it's just like talking to you. Do you notice how I skip from one thing to another? Bet you wonder how so many things can jump in and out of my head.

Speaking of jumping, Joyce went horseback riding yesterday and her horse jumped and she landed on the ground. The poor kid nearly broke her back. She was lucky the horse didn't step on her. Guess I'll stick to my knitting, it's safer.

Well, it's getting late, Sweet, and I still have to return some books to the library. Member how you used to come to the library after me when you'd come over Saturday nights? Every time I go in there I imagine you standing in there with me. Be careful, Darling, and remember to write as often as you can.

All my love,
Cheryl

P.S. My picture won't be ready till Nov. 1, so don't think it's been lost. I had a wallet size one made. O.K? It's colored, too!

232 Mountain Drive
West Hartford, Conn.
October 24, 1944

Dear Charlie,

Enclosed is the poetry I have been trying to get off to you.

Nothing very exciting has happened. I have been gallivanting around quite a bit and am getting weary of it. Guess I'm just a home body at heart.

I'm going to another party Saturday and next Saturday. I have my choice of the Yale-Dartmouth game or a pajama party. The pajama party sounds intriguing and I could go to both, but I'm not very fond of sitting up all night in pajamas and smoking my heart out. E Gad, I sound corrupt, don't I? So that you won't be disillusioned with me, I'll let you in on a secret – just the members of the female sex are invited to the pajama affair – don't tell anyone. I like other people to think I'm risqué, Night for now.

Affectionately,
Helena

Monday. It might be nice if I mailed a letter when I wrote it. Ben was home this weekend. He called me and we had a gay little chat – silly isn't it?

17 Anise Street
New Britain, Conn.
October 25, 1944

Dear Brother,

We haven't heard from you in a few days but we hope to soon.

Everything's o.k. here at home and hoping you're the same.

I was "sweet 16" yesterday. I had an "all girl" party last nite. There were about ten here and we had a swell time. We played all crazy games and etc.

I didn't go to school today for I was dead tired and slept till 10:45 – I'm getting like you use to be.

Our harvest supper is tonite. I was supposed to twirl, but I'm not sure now. We're having another mix-up in the Corps. This time it's Jean Ziegler. She's trying to run everything. I'll tell you how it turns out.

Mother went shopping today with Fanny.

Donny is some character and does the craziest things. The other nite he and "Walty" went over to Burns Hill and were throwing tin cans at the

Greek lady's chicken coop. He said you told him about it so he though he'd try it. Hot sketch, he is!!

Lala is having a 25th anniversary celebration party Saturday. She's expecting quite a crowd. It's going to be at the Junior Mechanics Hall.

Last Saturday we were supposed to go to New London, but it was raining and was too damp. The team went up and played though and also lost , 6 – 18. They played a wonderful game though.

Doc took about 13 of us from the band and cheerleaders to Mass. to see the Holy Cross – Brown game. You see, we were disappointed about not going to New London. The game was neat and ended in a tie score 26 – 26.

After the game Doc took us through the college and chapel etc. Holy Cross is really a beautiful place. We got drenched from the rain but we didn't care. Doc wanted me to twirl for the band but I can't very well be in the band and corps both. Drum meets usually come on a Saturday. (Capish?)So long for now and take care of yourself.

Love and kisses, xxxxxx

Betty

Connecticut College

New London, Conn.

October 27, 1944

Dear Charlie,

This is going to be kind of short 'cause I'm so tired I can hardly keep my eyes open. I've been having tests and papers due for the past two weeks – and I haven't had one night of eight hours sleep since they started. All this education is kind of rough at times. But that's enough of griping for one letter I guess.

I got your letter yesterday – that was pretty quick considering where you are, wasn't it? And please notice the prompt answer. I've turned over a leaf – I'm an entirely new woman. I wonder how long this will last?

About that good advice I was supposed to give you – I don't know how good it is but anyway – I definitely wouldn't go out for pre-med. It sounds o.k. in the abstract but it's really one helluva job. It takes an awful lot of brains – no, I'm not insulting your intelligence. I've given up the idea of being a doctor myself. It takes more than I've got and it also takes money – and plenty of it. Not only to get through school but about $6,000 after that to set yourself up and you'd be about 35 before you'd be financially able to think of buying that little white shack you mentioned. It's up to you of course, but I wouldn't if I were you.

Why don't you try to get to college when you get home? You'll only be about 21, and that's a lot younger than most of the fellows who will be starting in. You know what college is like from going to Harvard – it's a lot more work than most people think, but I honestly believe it's worth it. You're in no hurry to get anywhere and you can spare the four years. And you'll be able to get a better job when you get out, don't you think? And to use the old expression – I think you're definitely college material, my friend. But people never listen to advice anyway, so why don't I shut up.

I haven't seen Joan since that time she came up to see me. I was supposed to call her, but I've been so busy I haven't had time.

Nancy Halloway is still up here. She went home to see dear Morry this weekend. They're still going as strong as ever I guess.

Joan said she thought Connecticut was simply beeoo-otiful – she was very much impressed. You've never been up here, have you? I'm afraid I'll still be here when you get back – you'll have to come up and see it. How about it? Seven hundred and fifty beautiful women – that should tempt any man.

You said you wouldn't be home until '46 – and you sounded pretty sure. That's quite a ways off – don't you think you'll get home at all before that? I'm afraid my Xmas vacation is going to be one big bore this year. Oh, well, "things are tough all over."

I'm practically falling asleep and I still have to translate ten pages of French so maybe I'd better stop. For a "kind of short letter" this sort of dragged on, didn't it? Write soon and take care of yourself, Charlie.

                              As ever,
                              Launa

                                        Naval Research Lab.
                                        Washington, D.C.
                                        October 28, 1944

Dear Charlie,

I'm sorry to hear you're pissed off but how do you think I feel after not getting an answer to my first three letters? If you wanted to hear from me you had a funny way of showing it. But I don't feel like arguing.

What is the idea of calling Nell a "cheap slut?" If you have any basis for your remarks please write them down with the rest, if not shut up!

I haven't seen Helen for about a month.

                                                      Monday

Good morning,

I went home Saturday. I pulled in about 2015. Johnny picked me up and drove me home. I had a little chow, chatted a while with the folks, then started out to complete my date with Lemon. About 2130 we went to the movies, she did nothing to classify her as a "cheap slut." We left the movies about 2315. I drove out into the country. It was a beautiful evening , the moon was full and the air was crisp. I parked the old buggy on a little rise so the moon would shine through the window. We spent the next half hour or so mushing it up. I still got no indications of "cheap slut." She is as straight as a die. About midnight a patrol car pulled up. I opened the window and he said, "What's the matter?" I was in a gay mood so I replied, "Not a thing." He said, "You shouldn't be parking on a hill." I told him it was such a beautiful night and the view was so perfect that I thought it was a swell place to park. I could see him getting a little pissed off so, as I didn't have a license, I consented to move. I found a nice spot down the road a piece and parked under a big oak. I got her home about 0130. The whole evening was innocent to the nth degree so you can get pissed off at me again because in my five months in Washington I'm still a virgin.

Sunday morning I went to 1100 mass. I returned home and had chow. I sat around and straightened out my notes from the last few months.

I won't be fool enough to say I'd rather go out to sea than be on a shore station near here, but I'm really looking forward to getting out there and doing a little of my share.

I phoned Helena Sunday. What caused our argument was really inevitable so we both agreed. After going out with her for so long, I didn't hesitate in getting a little chummy. Well, she felt for some reason it was o.k. as did I. Of course, when someone gets "chummy" (pleasant way of saying it) it begins to get one a little over anxious. We both decided it was getting a little too rough so we wrote 2 or 3 blazing letters to each other and we are feeling much the better for it. She's still the nicest girl I've ever dated so I expect, unless she has made other plans, to see her soon. Here's hoping this letter finds you a little less pissed off than the last one.

Love,
Ben

17 Anise Street
New Britain, Conn.
October 30, 1944

Dear Charlie,

Donny received your letter today. Glad you got his and Pa's.

I suppose you will have to wait a week for him to answer it. He is out with the Farmer kids blowing horns and ringing doorbells. I suppose tomorrow they will get dressed up.

Well, the party was a success. There were about 95 there. No one got too drunk. Pa got feeling good. When he kissed Mrs. Ziegler you know he had a good time. He even danced. Lala got some nice gifts and quite a lot of money

Donny helped for a while but he had a toothache, he went home but came back again.

Betty's looking for some pictures to send you.

Billy Ziegler got married, he had the girl home this summer. I think she's from Wisconsin. Bert Teske joined the Navy, he is waiting to go.

I see in tonight's paper where Danny Bray graduated from Notre Dame and now he is an Ensign.

Pa's getting ready to go hunting, he is leaving Friday. I hope they have good luck this year. We could stand a little deer steak.

Did you get any packages yet? I heard they weren't going to keep them here, supposed to send them right along.

Tag was home Sunday. I guess he will get home every weekend.

Benny was home again but I didn't see him. Betty says he is the sloppiest sailor she ever saw. Meow! He still says, Hiiiii.

I'm glad that you don't like beer and don't shoot crap either.

We got a film today so we will be able to take some pictures . Donny got it over at the Drug Store. Well, I'll close. Betty will write and give you more dope about her friends.

Love,

Ma

Connecticut College
New London, Conn.
October 30, 1944

Dear Charlie,

So you've finally broken down – I'm glad. That farce we were carrying on was beginning to get on my nerves. All the formal letters – well, it just wasn't us. It was too much of a struggle.

I got your letter this morning and I've been trying to decide all day what to say to you. I've never lied to you - you know that – so I guess I'd

329

better not start now. Maybe you were right when you said I was waiting for a knight on a white horse. But I still seem to be waiting for something I can't seem to find. Can't I look a little longer though? You seem to be trying to back me up in a corner – can't you see that I can't answer you now. I don't know the answer. I guess I'm really being truthful for a change – there have been times when I thought I loved you – many times. Last Xmas it nearly killed me to keep laughing at you – but I guess you know that. The day I got back to college I nearly sent you a telegram – I even had it all written down. But then I got scared and went to the other extreme. I've never been able and I still can't tell you I love you. I know how much you mean what you've said to me – but until I can match your sincerity I can't answer you. I've always told you no before - but this time you asked me to be honest – and I'm afraid it's turning out to be quite a mess.

As I've told you before, we're too much alike. I guess maybe that isn't good. I want someone I can look up to – not just straight across at (no, I'm not talking about height, you dope!). But still I can't seem to forget you. Even when I don't hear from you and don't write to you I keep thinking of you – and I know you're thinking of me. It's such a damn mess! I made such wonderful resolutions the last time. First, I sent all the letters back – then I kept them but didn't answer – and now look where I am. The whole thing is probably that no fellow has loved me the way you do. I'm afraid I told you all about my love life last Xmas after the zombie. But they were all different. They came and I knew they'd all go eventually – no great loss to anybody. I've covered four pages and haven't said a damn thing yet. This letter is taking 10 years out of my life, you rat! How do I get into these situations anyway?

Well, I guess I can always get behind that old safe wall – we're too young anyway. The war has to be over and we both have to struggle through college – and that's quite a long time. I'll still be here when you get back – can't we let things ride till then? But for heaven's sake, don't let anything happen to you. You're about the only thing in my life that I can count on. Remind me to tell you about my life sometime – it's quite a hellish mess. You really know very little about me when it comes right down to it, m' love.

I'm beginning to sound like a sob sister – you've got a hell of a nerve trying to break me down like this. Pardon me while I rave and rant for a while – have to get back to normal.

I wrote you yesterday so you really can't expect me to write anymore, huh? It's 12:30 and I have to be in a French class at 8 tomorrow. Goodnight Funnyface.

Love always,
Launa

P.S. It's Tuesday morning now and I slept through my French class – your fault, of course. I told you that this letter completely wore me out. I just read the letter over, Charlie, and I seem to have hedged around the whole subject. The answer in a nut shell is that you don't measure up to what I want – and yet I can't let you alone. If you could break things off yourself, things would be much better. The whole thing is up to you – think it over and go ahead.

P.S. My roommate sends her love, but she seems to think I take care of myself pretty well.

U.S. Navy Base
San Diego, Cal.
November 1, 1944

Dear Charlie –

How's my little "dove" today? I haven't received any mail from you in over a week, but I'm getting ready to leave here, so I'll write you a farewell letter from sunny California. I'm being sent to Charleston, S.C. for my ward training. I had a choice of hospitals in S.C, Fla, Tenn. (Memphis), Okla, and Cal... I could have gone to any one of them but I took S.C. with the hopes of making a quick dash home or spending a few weekends at Duke. That's the only reason I took S.C, otherwise I would have gone to Memphis to look up your woman who has been writing to you etc. I'm sorry to leave Cal. for one reason. I finally met my "meat." I may be denying this in a few weeks, but at present I feel definitely certain that this woman is that something which I've always been looking for. (Sounds like the D.W. of a few years ago, doesn't it?) I'll tell you about our "fleeting meeting." I met her, that is "Peggy"(that's' a miserable name, isn't it? Makes me think of a prostitute every time I repeat it.)Anywho, we met last Sat. at a dance in Beverly Hills. She was reclining on a soft chair in the lobby sipping a "Mickey." I walked up to her, rather uninterested at first and told her that she'd catch cold if she kept her nose too long in the glass. What a "pisser." No she is not either. She just drinks too much – like a sponge. The little things that she does and the way that she handled me, fascinated me!! We discovered that we have a great deal in common, and

331

we had quite a fling until 2:00 A,M. (No, not that kind of a fling.) I met her Sunday and spent the afternoon with her, too. It was like pulling the roots from under me when I left her. Funny thing about it was that she reminded me of Meg quite a bit. She's blonde, blue eyed and 5 ft. 6. No jaw though, lovable as all hell!!! Oh, my fuckin' dear – "For the first time" – La-de-da – Aw screeeeeeeew. I have on eternal hope and that is that I will get a few hours in LA so that I can spend the last few hours with her. I sound desperate as all hell!!!

I received a letter from Mary yesterday. What a "pisser." She claims that she was home a short time ago and she went out with Joltin' Joe Donnelly. Wheeeee! But she says that she still loves us!!! Cute ole pot – hasn't she? She mentioned that she was just recovering from a urinating spasm which she acquired from reading your latest letter. Ya old turd!!!

It's been so long since I last heard from you that I have no idea what you are doing or where you might be. Take care, Charlie. I'm praying for your safe return.

I haven't received much mail from persons other than Mom and Dad lately so I haven't got much "scuttlebutt" from the home front. The old "blood pit" is probably the same.

Hope to hear in your next letter that you have discovered a solution for Blair and Fisher, Inc. You should be quite content in hearing from her.

I haven't been doing any reading lately. I've decided to join the Book Guild or Literary Guild. The first book which I'll get is "The Razor's Edge" by Somerset Maugham,

I leave here Nov. 3rd Friday. It will take almost 5 days to get to S.C. You can send your letters to U.S.N.H. in Charleston. I imagine that you'll have to include the word "staff" in the address. I'm not sure of my exact address. I'll send you a V-Mail letter as soon as I arrive there.

S' bout all, Charlie. Good luck in whatever you do and God Bless You!!!

Sexfully urine,
Dick

P.S. Darlin', I'm hooked.

Connecticut College
New London, Conn.
November 1, 1944

Hello, Stinky,

Happy Halloween!!! Of course, I'm a day late but at least I've got the right spirit.

Aren't you simply overwhelmed with all this mail? Reason? Why a full moon, of course. Or maybe you don't notice moons anymore.

I'm feeling kind of punchy tonight. I've spent all afternoon and all night on an English theme about Fate and Fatalism. I'm afraid it's going to my head. I don't believe a damn thing I'm saying but it certainly makes a nice theme. You're a fatalist, aren't you? So is Sharon – you two ought to get together. She and I argue about it all the time – but I'm still not convinced. But what's all that got to do with the price of beans anyway?

My poor roommate just dropped a whole jar of jam all over the floor. There are about ten females in the room – and they're all talking at once. Women – I'm so sick of them. How would you like to live with 750 of 'em – I know, you'd love it.

Your last letter got here in less than a week – pretty sharp, huh? I decided it probably got here on its own steam.

I'm afraid I'm not concentrating very well. I didn't have much to say to begin with.

I've decided how I'm going to spend Xmas vacation. There's a new book out "Forever Amber" I think. It's a couple of thousand pages and better than "Gone With the Wind." That should last me a couple of weeks. Sounds exciting, no? No! Damned inconsiderate of you not to be home, m' love.

There seems to be a conspiracy to keep me from getting any sleep around here. The women are just beginning to warm up to their subject – men, of course. Pardon me while I kick them all out – or I'll probably sleep through my French class again. I still blame you and that damn letter for the last time. Good-night, darling – write soon.

Love,

Launa

51 Forest St.
Oakwood, Conn.
November 3, 1944

Hello, my darling,

How are you? I'm quite lonesome for you tonight and the only way that I can feel a little nearer to you is to write, so get ready for a lot of reading.

Before I write one more word I must tell you that I get two letters from you every week, and it's wonderful. I can't understand whatever happened at first but I get them and am always looking forward to them every week now. You seemed so upset in every letter you wrote because I wasn't getting them that I was almost afraid, but it's swell now, Dear, so

333

don't worry anymore, just keep writing letters. You said that you write to me oftener than anyone else, and I believe you too since I've been getting them. I'm beginning to think that you think of me as often as I think of you. It's funny, Dear, when you were home I thought of you, but never like I do now. It's so different. Guess we took one another for granted 'cause we knew we'd see each other on Sat. or Sun. , but now I think of you and wonder what you might be doing while I'm working, or getting ready for bed or even walking down Main Street. How often I wish we could be dancing together when a pretty song, or one that we used to like, comes on the radio. Do any of these things enter your mind, Charlie, or does it all sound confused to you?

Mother and Dad went out last night and rather than stay alone I invited Marilyn Wenger, one of the kids at work, over to sleep with me. Also you remember I told you quite a while ago about her engagement. Her boyfriend is in Miss. and she hasn't seen him in almost a year either. She feels exactly the way I do, wondering how different he'll be when he comes home, and she worries as much as I do about you. I don't think you will have changed that much when you come home. From your letters you, of course, seem older, but that's to be expected – you're more serious too, but we can't be nutty all of our lives. I guess, just once in a while (maybe on that date we have to play weegie board, we can, O.K?)

Getting back to your letter, you're a fine one, laughing at me when I ask you if it gets a little cold there. Sweet, how in the world do you expect me to know what it's like! I know now though and from now all I'll mention is the heat – then you won't laugh. Talk about laughing, do you realize you're still writing New Britain on my letters and then crossing it out. I see it so don't think you're fooling me – will you ever remember that it is Oakwood? Thank goodness we're not moving back to N.B. till after the war, or you'd be in an awful mess and I'd never get my letters.

Say, weren't you in a bad mood, my little Black Boy, when you started that last letter? I'm glad you waited and started again when you felt better or we might be up to our old tricks (arguing) again. I don't think it's as much fun to argue in writing. 'Cause then I can't see your eyes, and that's what I love when you're mad. They're nice when you're in a dreamy mood, too.

What's this about your brother begging you not to get married until he's old enough to be your best man? Have you led him to believe you intend to? If so, who's the girl friend? Really, Chas, the least you could do would be to tell me about it. I had no idea you liked anyone. Seriously though, *that was cute, wasn't it? He probably heard (hang on) Merton Savage is engaged!! And if he had enough courage to tell a girl he likes her that much anything could happen! I don't know whether it's from the war or not but there are hardly any girls around who aren't at least engaged. Incidentally, I hope you will wait till your brother is old enough – don't go marrying any old body!*

You never mentioned writing to people you met while you were stationed at different places before – tell me about them, were there a lot of pretty girls? Not that I mind, but was just curious. And maybe, Darling, I would be, as you say, just a wee bit jealous, would you mind if I were or wouldn't you care either way? Hope you write the right thing.

I was so sorry that your buddy left and that he had such a difficult assignment. There's not much anyone can say to make you realize that. I can appreciate how you must feel, but just believe that he'll be alright. All I can do is pray that you will be safe and I do so often, Dear. I'm keeping my fingers crossed (for you, too) so that you will get with the tanks or the artillery just as you'd like to. You may, so just keep hoping – with your chin up high.

I got a letter from Roger R. the other day and he said I could probably gather where he was from the newspapers. He said he'd like your address because he thinks he's somewhere near you. Wouldn't it be swell for you both if you met? Seems that any familiar face would look good.

Tuesday was Halloween and it was so cute to see the little kids costumes with their great big bags for candy. I didn't go out but I felt like it. 'Member the party we went to at Ben's house one year – we had so much fun, didn't we? Remember the sandwiches etc. all over the floor? What a mess!

Helena called the other night and she's been in a terrific mood with me lately. She seems to resent the fact that you and I write so often, and that we keep it up. I don't see why she should, she and her friend Ben are together again. I should think she'd be glad, the way we are about them when they're happy, but she doesn't seem to be. Oh, well, maybe she just wasn't in a good mood. Anyway, I'm not going to bother.

I made an appointment to have my eyes examined Tues. I've been having awful headaches and maybe it's because I need glasses—reading ones only, I hope. If I get them we'll both look important.

Did you get any of the boxes or snapshots I sent you yet Darling? I'm getting my good picture tomorrow and I'll mail it to you. I hope you get it – do you think it would be taking too much of a chance? It's wallet size, and tinted. It won't get in your way.

Well, Sweetheart, I should close now so I can knit a few more rows on my sweater. I've written so much as it is that you'll probably have to pay for postage due when you get this one.

Write often because I look forward to your letters more than anything else. Goodnight, and be careful and mind the guard when he tells you to keep your clothes on, after six like a good boy.

All my love,
Cheryl

P.S. I'll get you some stationery tomorrow, Dear, and we'll play my games when you come home.

LST 925
San Diego, Cal.
November 4, 1944

Dear Charlie,

I finally heard from you, you old "pecker checker." But I don't blame you as it had to go home and then come all the way back to this mud hole. The letter I mean.

Charlie, I am on L.S.T. 925. I may be very close to you right now, so keep your eyes open.

I get liberty Sunday, so I guess I'll spend it in the native village trading. Don't worry, there are no native women on the island. Even though I must admit they get lighter and lighter every time I see them.

I haven't heard from Lu, Charlie, in a heck of a long time so I guess she will have to wait till I get home. I think I can really talk "turkey" with her. It's about time you heard from, or I should say, are you getting some place with Cheryl and Helen. Two cousins battling over one man. I can hardly wait to see the finish. Write soon, Chas. or telegram.

Me,
Tony

Naval Research Lab.
Washington, D.C.
November 5, 1944

Dear Chxarlie,

You can see it's morning. I can't even spell your name.

Informed sources have it you expect to go into action soon. Good luck.

Saturday I went to N.B. I got on the train in Washington only to find that I had lost my ticket. I had to pay full fare on part of my trip home and back.

I pulled in an hour late at N.B. It took me about an hour to phone, wash and eat so it was about 2200 before I called for Nell. We drove to West Hartford through the worst fog I have ever seen. It was 2300 before we found St. Joseph's. The nuns in the reception line must have had their own ideas as to how the earlier part of the evening was spent, because they commented on our timely arrival. We danced around for about one hour and had a little punch in between. There were a few people we knew. Dick Pike (used to go with Ericson) now with Ann Stevens. Red Fremont with some unknown Mary Jane. Barbara Bell with some unknown. Ann Collins was there for a while, too.

We looked all over afterwards for a place to eat but had no luck at all so we stopped someplace and had a cup of coffee and doughnuts. The rest of the evening was spent the way the latter part of any evening is spent.

All in all I had a swell time and I think the rest of the gang had the same.

Red Fremont, Mary Jane and another couple shared the bar with us.

I couldn't get out of the sack in time for 1100 mass. It was my little brother Rickey's birthday so I stopped and got him something. I had a home cooked meal which I really appreciated.

I dropped in to see your family Sunday afternoon. Your mother is looking fine and Donny is growing into quite a little man. Donny will probably tell you about what he caught when he went hunting so I won't spoil it for him.

After talking to your mother for a while, I stopped in to see Helena, only to find her in bed. We talked for a while and I kidded her about the tough night she must have had, because she was in bed when I got there. It was quite late in the afternoon.

Cheryl is looking swell. Mr. and Mrs. French are also looking good. What gives between you and Cheryl? I think she has it pretty bad. She looks just like the picture she is going to send you.

I'll have to sign off now because class is about to start. Write soon, and let me know if there is anything you would like from the States. Just say the word.

Love,

Ben

337

Hdq. Bn. 6*th* Marine Div.
San Francisco, Cal.
November 5, 1944

Dear Sis,

I'm too tired to write tonight but I know you want to hear from me as I haven't written for two days. I haven't heard from anyone for the last three days. Not even Cheryl. I got one letter from Launa and in a P.S. she wrote, "It's so nice that dear Cheryl and I have such a nice picture of you." I damn near choked when I read it. I wonder if those two met on the street or something. Let's hope not for my sake.

Cheryl said she was going to the Harvest Supper given by the church. Did you see the beast there? "Beast" is the favorite gyrene term out here now. Everyone is a beast (a gyrene is a Marine).

It's been raining for two days now and I'm beginning to feel the ground under me starting to get slimy. I always hated mud.

I may be transferred soon to the same outfit Elon is in. I hope so 'cause I'd like to do a little medical work for a change. It's late now, little darlin', and I have to hit the hay. I'll write again tomorrow.

Love always,
Charlie

17 Anise Street
New Britain, Conn.
November 6, 1944

Dear Son,

Today we rec'd two letters from you, one for Betty and the other was mine.

So glad to hear you are getting good food. When Tag was over there he said the food was lousy.

Aunt Anna said how Tag received you letter. He was home again Sunday. I don't think he cares much about the place he's at.

Benjamin paid me a visit yesterday, he looks real good. He said he may take a ride to Oakwood to see the girls. He said he had a little squabble with his girl a couple weeks ago. I told him to go over to see Cheryl.

Well, Pa left Friday for Maine. I haven't heard from him yet.

Donny went hunting Sat. afternoon and came home with a rabbit and a squirrel. I guess he is going to be another hunter. I hope Pa brings something home.

Betty got your letter where you told her to study hard and get good marks. She took a ride to New London with the Arutes and Bobby yesterday. Bobby got awful tall. Aunt Anna's boyfriend Charlie Niemas is at Cedar Crest. I don't know whether you know him or not. I took a ride with her to see him. Freddy is in Georgetown, N.C. but Anna said he wasn't going to stay.

Danny was home and is he proud with his Ensign outfit.

We had a few snow flurries today and it's so cold and windy. I guess the old winter will be here soon. The place is so quiet around here. I suppose Pa will make up for it when he gets back home.

Well, tomorrow we vote. I really think Roosevelt will get in again.

Betty's out in the kitchen giving herself a permanent wave and Donny isn't home from school yet.

Oh, yes Tommy is in the hospital over in England, his leg bothers him again. He probably will be discharged if it doesn't get any better.

Oh, I must tell you about the dog. I washed and ironed three pair of ruffled curtains and put them on the living room chair and the dog went in at night and slept on them. What a mess they were. If I wasn't afraid to use the gun I would have shot him. I'm still mad at him. More trouble when we keep him down the cellar. I wonder if you could use him over there. Well, I guess I told you all the news. Will write again this week.

Love,
Mother

51 Forest St.
Oakwood, Conn.
November 7, 1944

Dearest Chas,

Did you ever try to write in bed? Awful isn't it – well, I'm going to try anyway since I've got a lot to tell you. I'm not too sick now but I went to work at eight this morning and finally I had to have Dad bring me home at nine. I felt like I had an army of gremlins in my stomach. Oh, what pain – my mother put me to bed with the heating pad and it feels better now. Hope I can go to work in the morning 'cause three other girls are also out and we're very busy.

You know what I got in the mail this morning? A little turtle. One of the girls is in St. Petersburg, Fla. on her vacation (Helen Fagan, you know her, don't you?) well, anyway my poor mother nearly developed heart trouble when she opened the box for me and saw a little turtle crawl out.

I was up here in bed and when I heard her scream, I nearly died myself. Oh, I hate the thing and my mother won't even touch it. She's so afraid, it's really funny – she stands a foot away from it and talks to it. You'd think it was like a dog. I'm going to give it to the boy next door, maybe he'll like it.

I had company yesterday Sunday afternoon. I was upstairs taking a nap, since I didn't feel too good then either, well, anyway, the door bell rang and who was it but Benjamin. I nearly broke my neck trying to get dressed because he only had one hour until train time. Daddy entertained him till I got downstairs. He looks very good and he's getting awfully tall. The navy has certainly done a lot for him. Of course, you were our main topic of conversation. I had to laugh at Dad – because when Ben asked me what I do every night Daddy said "she has to write to Charlie every night." Coming from him, it sounded so funny because you know how he usually is about things like that. I never thought that he particularly noticed that I was writing. I guess Ben had been over to see Helen for a few minutes. He said he had gone to a Sophomore hop with Nell Talbot at St. Jos. the night before. But then he said Helen went to a pajama party somewhere, so they were even. I think they'll be together again especially since he's coming home Christmas. Don't worry, she won't pass that up.

Well – tomorrow is election day and it's been quite an exciting campaign. The speeches on both sides have been quite nasty but I suppose that kind of talk always accompanies election speeches. By the time you answer, our new president will have been elected – but from the looks of things now, Roosevelt seems to be the one most highly spoken of. I don't know too much about Dewey's policies, but they certainly haven't been put across the air too well. I wish I could vote, it would be one more for Pres. Roosevelt. What's your opinion, Chas? You ought to hear Ben talk, he's a strong democrat. He said most of the boys where he is are, too. How about in the Pacific? Well, tomorrow will tell. Guess it's right to hope the best man wins now.

It snowed here all day and it's sooooo cold – your lucky it's warm where you are – winter is fun but not during these times. Remember how we used to slide on Commonwealth Ave. and how you would never pull me up the hill? Oh, yes, fine thing you accusing me of going off on that Halloween party. How about your little skiing sessions with Virginia Campbell? Now who's the little devil? You're still up to it too, not giving me your picture, but giving it to Helen if you please. How nice. I have to laugh 'cause if I ever wrote to her Ben, she'd burn. Oh, well, I always was broadminded, my "Honey Chile."

340

You know I ran across that snapshot of you, Joe, Fred and Dickey taken together. You look nicest (I think) but it's good of all of you.

Have you heard any more about new orders? Can you let me know when you do, Dear? Ben said that he saw your Mother and family, and they are all well. Did she tell you we met in the office last week? It was funny – I took her bill and said as usual – good-morning – then when I saw the name I said, "Oh! Morning, Mrs. Young!" I must have looked surprised 'cause she laughed. We didn't have much time to talk, but she seemed awfully nice. Now don't go thinking what you wrote in one of your other letters.

Well, Dear, I'd better close before I make a complete mess of this. There's not much sentence constructure etc, but all I care about is that you can read it and that you get them often. You will forgive me this time, won't you? Goodnight Sweetheart and be careful.

Always yours,
Cheryl

Keep writing often, I never tire of your letters. I'm mailing my picture tomorrow, so tell me when you get it.

Connecticut College
New London, Conn.
November 8, 1944

Hello, Darling –

How's the light of my life? I got two letters from you today – did wonders for my morale. I was beginning to think this was "Down With Launa Week" – only one letter from Mon. to Wed. It's amazing – your letters get here in less than a week. But I am furious – you don't seem to have gotten any of mine. I have been writing – honest. You'll probably get them all at once – which will be very boring.

I've finally settled down to studying this week. My marks have been just awful. I don't know what was the matter with me. I just wasn't interested in anything. But things have taken a turn for the better so I guess they won't bounce me this year.

I've spent the day mourning about elections. Not that I didn't expect it – but hell – you'd think people would wake up after 12 years. Oh, I know you're a damn Democrat – but at least that gives us something to argue about. Why do I love to fight with you? But to get back to elections - I swear I'll never take an interest in politics again. I've made more enemies in the last two weeks than I've made in two years. I'm convinced that the

341

majority of the people are too stupid to know a good man when they see one. I suppose you wanted the old fool in again for four more years – well, you've got him. And I'll bet five dollars you'll be sorry. But there's no sense in blowing my top about it now, is there?

You get me so confused – what was the nightmare you had about me in Norfolk? And what's the connection between that and you're going to the hospital? I'm in a fog – as usual.

Your letter was dated Halloween and I just remembered – that's when Benjamin Navikas (how do you spell it?) had his party. I went home last weekend and found an old diary of mine in the closet. What a riot! I was quite a gay blade back in '38, you know it?

My roommate is about to write you a note – you lucky boy. She's been hearing about you for two years – you've become sort of a family tradition or something. She's cute – want to get fixed up? She's already got a man – but you're such a determined guy I'm sure that wouldn't bother you. She's decided not to let me read it so don't hold me responsible for anything – I imagine it's quite gay.

It's 12:30 and I'm going to part with a pint of blood tomorrow so I guess I'll go to bed. Goodnight Stinky-Love always,

Launa

Dear Charlie –

This is Beth – Launa's roommate – speaking. I've heard so much about you and have been gazing longingly at your picture since last September – so when I heard you sent your regards to me, "I sez to myself sez I" I should write dear old Charlie a line.

Launa and I have been having a gay old time – you know, Charlie, just in case you're interested, and I know you are – she is really very easy to live with – and lots of fun. But I guess I don't have to tell you that. We've decoded that Con College would be a wonderful place if they would cut out all the classes!! Well, it sounds good, doesn't it?

I started this merely to say "Hello!" and now I've said it – to be serious for just a moment – Good luck, Charlie – and have fun!

Beth (alias Launa's roommate)

If this sounds slightly confused it's because we've been drinking "hard cider" all night.

17 Anise Street
New Britain, Conn.
November 8, 1944

342

Dear Son,

Today is Wednesday and we just rec'd 3 letters from you, that makes 5 we rec'd this weeks, seems good to hear from you steady. The mail is coming through fine.

No much news. We voted yesterday and I see where Roosevelt got in. Just as well, probably the war will end sooner I hope.

Pa is still away, I haven't heard from him yet. He will probably call tonight or tomorrow. He is always hunting when it's our Anniversary, not that it matters much. I guess that we will celebrate our 25th, that's if the war is over. So you and Cheryl can come. Ha, ha!. I saw her the other day. But I didn't get much of a chance to get a good look at her. But I will the next time.

Do you remember Billy McClellan? His mother called me and she wanted Mick O'Leary's address. She said how a new crew of men were transferred to an aircraft carrier Billy was on and it happened Mick was one of them. Was he tickled to meet someone from home.

Merton is somewhere in France. I saw his mother yesterday, she thinks he is headed for Germany.

Well, I am going downtown with Lala in a little while. I went to the show last night with Anna and saw "Since He Went Away." It was very good but awfully sad. I should have brought a Turkish towel with me.

Nellie was over to Lala's the other day and wanted to know where you were. If you have time you should drop Nellie a few lines and make her feel good. Ask her about her new baby. Well, I guess I'll close and get dressed. Oh, yes, Donny got your letter today where you lectured him about using vulgar language. I wonder if he will write again. Do they censor your letters?

Love,
Mom

17 Anise Street
New Britain, Conn.
November 8, 1944

Dear Charlie,

We received three letters from you today and two yesterday. We are getting mail regularly now.

That was a nice lecture you gave me. Thanks a lot. But Cheerleading, Drum Corps etc. don't interfere with my schoolwork at all. I stay in every night except Wednesday (religious school) and Thursday (B. lesson). My *schoolwork is o.k. but I just can't stand my English teacher Miss Curran. She's very unfair and doesn't explain anything. So there — you said you received an A in Biology. If I had Mr. Beach I'd receive an A+ Clarence is o.k. but bores the life out of us. You were mistaken when you said he was a fair marker. He flunked half of his class last year.*

I'm having a Biology final tomorrow and I took a History test today. Mr. Catlin is my history teacher and I just adore him. He's hard as heck but he talks my language, you know what I mean.

I hope you're o.k. Everyone is okay at home (We still have Prince.)

Freddy was shipped out yesterday. From New York though, so you can't meet him. Ha.

Dad is coming home Sunday. Aunt Anna comes here practically every night. Ma and she went to the movies last night and they're going again tonight. Ma's getting to be a "Movie Rat."

Don't die, but Donny's going to be an altar boy. So he says. I told him he has to be especially good and he said he'd go on a diet. I guess he must be going to reform.

By the way, where is Dick Walton now?

That was a hot one about Cheryl sending the chocolate cake.

When Benny came home, I saw him at the football game with "lemon." She's a hot sketch.

I went to New London with the Arutes Sunday to see Jimmie. He's a neat kid but that's all I'm going to tell you. He gave me two gold midshipman's anchors from his uniform (he's a cadet). He is coming home Thanksgiving .That's all for now.

Love and kisses, xxxxxx
"Sister"

51 Forest St.
Oakwood, Conn.
November 8, 1944

Dearest Chas,

How is my "bachelor" friend today, and when did you predict such an interesting future for yourself? Surely it must have been in one of your serious moments, but if I know you, that won't last long.

This wasn't intended to be a letter, but just a little note to send along with my picture. The folder isn't a particularly good one, but I was sort of afraid of sending a better one since I'm not really sure of your getting it. I am planning on having one sent in a little gold miniature frame for you as soon as you get home—if you still want one, but after reading your letter for today I might have to change my plans. What would a bachelor want with a girl's picture?

Write and tell me whether or not you get it – I'm keeping my fingers crossed until I hear.

All my love,
Cheryl

P.S. Don't be critical, you remember how much you disliked my graduation picture? I'm almost afraid you'll think this one is as bad. I look as thoughtful in it as you do in the one I have of you in your Navy uniform.

Naval Research Lab.
Washington, D.C.
November 9, 1944

Dear Charlie,

There isn't anything new in Washington to write about but I'll just shoot the bull.

Your imagination is better than any wet dream I've ever had or hope to have. Maybe it'll develop when I ship out.

I think you're right about lemon in comparison with Helen. If I have the right to compare, it's still Helen for my money. I think that fight we had was the best thing that could have happened. She doesn't know how I feel, and I don't know how she feels. We'll just have to feel each other "out". (and I don't mean "up"),

I've been wondering if you've run across any queers yet. Being way out where there are no women, they should be doing a pretty good business.

You've never told me what you plan to do when this mess is over. Do we go to college for a few years? Go to work? Get married? If all goes well, I expect to spend a few years at school in upper New England, I hope.

I suppose you heard about the snow storm they had in Conn. I've been hoping a little of the snow will stay until I get home this weekend. Come on winter, my skis are getting rusty.

Have you run across any nice natives yet? I've been hoping to hear some weird tales of shapely native maidens. But knowing you as well as I do, I wonder.

What do they let you write? Can you tell me what sort of work you do? You know a typical day's routine. I don't know if you're at a field hosp, a naval base, a couple of tents or some god forsaken shit hole or where you reside. Do you wield a mighty needle? I just remembered I'm due for boosters this month. I hate those damn needles.

Tuesday night I had liberty. I went to the K. of C. There were more pretty women. I danced with a blond from Miami who really left me standing on end. Not what you're thinking either. My liberty expired at midnight so I had to confine my activities to dancing. I also met a girl who lived in Hartford for 8 years. She just liked to cuddle close when she danced. You could really toss her around with no strain. I'm still drooling. When we would dip, she would make things so nice, I don't know how I lived through it. Now I'm down on all fours – Ah oooooo!

By the time you get this letter I'll have four weeks of school left. I'll be home for a while before Christmas. Do you want me to do some shopping for you?

Ben

17 Anise Street
New Britain, Conn.
November 10, 19444

Dear Son,

Today is Friday and it's such a gloomy day. It's raining and so dark, so I thought I would scribble a few lines.

Cheryl called yesterday and we had quite a talk. She is so happy because she hears from you. She told me how she sent you a picture of herself. Benny did go over to see her Sunday. Did I tell you how Freddy was sent out? He has an APO number New York.

Pa called the other night but I was out, that was Wednesday. They didn't have any game yet. He told Donny and Betty how they had 18 inches of snow up there.

I cooked Donny's rabbit for supper last night. He asked Walter Roden over because he was with him when he went hunting, and Freddy's mother was over. The rabbit was swell, it must have been a young one.

Betty said she was going to march in the parade tomorrow, Armistice Day. I wish you could tell us what island you are on. Irene Manning's boyfriend told her by starting every paragraph with the letters. If you do that put a line under your name Charles.

Well, there's not much happening around here. Mr. Westerman is sick with arthritis. Kenneth Neubauer isn't working yet. He wants to drive a truck. Oneida said how the Ferndale Dairy called him and he is supposed to start tomorrow. I wonder if he will. Tommy is still in the hospital with *his leg. Tag thinks he should be discharged. Tag thinks that he may have to go across again because they are so short of medical men. I am sending you a picture of Don and myself, it isn't so hot but you can see how tall Don is. He looks so tall in long pants.*

Love,

Mom

U.S. Naval Hospital
Charleston, S.C.
November 10, 1944

Dear Charlie,

How is my "voluptuous vulture" tonite? From the tone of your latest letter, you sound like you're in rare form. I am writing you from Charleston, S.C. Damn it, I'd give my "unfiltrable" chastity to be back in California. Charlie – don't laugh at me now – but I've finally found my match. It's that girl I wrote you about in my last letter. Don't call me a second "Hot Pants," as I know I'm not that bad! Before I left Cal. I met Peggy at the LA. station and spent two hours together with her. I've never missed or yearned for anyone as I have for this "flame" I don't believe in love at first sight, but, darlin', for the first time in my life I am certain of a woman. Sound odd? It seems odd to me but that's the way it is" We made no promises to each other except that we'd write regularly etc. She's really tops. What da ya tink? Should I marry her?? Eek!! What a thought!!! Aw screeeew!! I'll write more about her later!! I look upon her as being a necessary evil right now. "Evilize" me, honey.

What an island you must be on. I bet that we could "rip" the hell out of the place if we were together – gooks and all!!!

I agree with you. We should have definitely leaped into the car and "nookified" the two "pissers" when we were at Beckley's. I bet they they've never even seen the nozzle on a king-size one like yours or mine. But then again, remember that afternoon at Beckley's?? Those rude boys jumping into the water with their "emotional antennas" in the air! Don't let me look, Meg would say, straining her eyes.

Speaking of Meg – how do you like the enclosed sketch? "Scintillating Meg" – oh my fuckin' dear, when I saw that, I roared till my testicles started to hurt. If that doesn't fit her to a "T" I'll evacuate my bowels. At first I was going to send the sketch to her, but I decided that you would appreciate it more. It came out of a hot spicy book I was reading while en route to Charleston.

347

I am temporarily unassigned to a ward. I'll start my duty on Monday, I imagine. I'll probably draw the maternity ward. Won't I be the eager beaver if I do??

I figured that when I got to Charleston I'd be able to get home on weekends, but as of two weeks ago all 72 hour passes have been done away with. That leaves yours truly loaded with nowhere to drop his load. However, Mother and Dad are proposing a trip south to see me. That'll satisfy me. You know, Charlie, of all the things I do, I never forget my parents. They're always foremost in my mind.

From what has happened here at the hospital, I judge that I won't be here very long. It's either F.M.F. or amphibs from here. It doesn't make much difference – Fuck the Navy anyway!! I do want to get to Conn. and Cal. once again tho before I leave this damn country.

It's late, darlin,' so I'll close. I'll have more news for you next time. Take care and write.

> *Fairily yours,*
> *Dick*

> *Connecticut College*
> *New London, Conn.*
> *November 10, 1944*

Hello, Stinky,

I hate to mention it but this seems to be turning into a one sided correspondence. I guess I'd better start waiting for some answers before I completely collapse from a case of writer's cramp.

I haven't said anything about that frighteningly serious letter I sent you. It was quite out of character and I'm trying to forget the whole thing. But if you want to do the intelligent thing, you'll tell me to go to hell and stop writing. Needless to say, if I don't get any letters from you, I won't write any. It's up to you, m'love. 'Nuf of this stuff.

I just finished a French theme about the Blood Bank. Did I tell you about the gay time I had down there? They ask you fifty million questions about do you have swollen feet, scarlet fever and all that stuff. I'm so blooming healthy that it's disgusting. Then they led me into this room where everybody is stretched out on beds – gruesome. Well, to begin with they couldn't find any of my veins – I began to wonder if I was bloodless. Anywho – they finally stuck the damn thing almost through to my elbow (no, it didn't hurt). I felt quite unusual with such queer veins – a very unique case no doubt (and I don't mean mentally). They play an organ through the whole procedure. I felt as though I were at my own funeral. Have you ever heard "Mairze Doats" on an organ? You're missing something. Then, of course, they had to play "Night and Day" – ironic????? Anyway, I didn't faint and I got a big kick out of it.

I've been writing to kill time while my hair dried. And it's dry so I guess I'll go to bed. It's pouring rain, I have to study all day tomorrow for a math test and this hell hole is beginning to get on my nerves. Why the hell can't you come home and stir up some excitement? Guess I'll have to wait. Take care of yourself, Charlie, and write soon, huh?

Love always,
Launa

Naval Research Lab.
Washington, D.C.
November 11, 1944

Dear Charlie,

Well, here it is liberty call and I'm calmly writing. I'm so tired I'm staying in today and taking a nap.

I wasn't trying to belittle the U.S.M.C. I'll agree they're a rugged bunch and take more risk than the average Navy man, but they're not running the whole war by themselves.

I passed again. We had a neat lecture on the side, about life in the Fiji Islands. The officer was telling us about the native women. He said if you go on shore for liberty and want to have fun don't stay near the coastal towns, go inland to some small village. The natives bathe 4 or five times a day. The women are a tan color and very light considering the climate. All you do is make friends with the Chief, he marries you, not legal in States, and you are all set.

I think the need for R.T.'s is a little less so if all goes well our school day will end at 2:00 instead of 2:30.

I can see you with a tan and moustache. Hmmmm....I've got to write to Helen now.

Love,
Ben

17 Anise Street
New Britain, Conn.
November 11, 1944

Dear Brother,

Well, Kid, how are you?? We received a V-Mail letter from you yesterday. I'm sorry I haven't written for a while, but the time goes by so quick I never have time to do anything.

Dad left for Maine last night. I'm certainly glad he did. I'll tell you why. Yesterday Mother ironed all her nice ruffled curtains and laid them over a living room chair. Last night Princey pushed them all off and laid on them. You can imagine what they looked like. Boy, oh, boy, was she hot (and I ain't kidding), She almost killed the dog and would have shot him if the gun was loaded. So she claims we're getting rid of him. So that was that (good, huh??)

Halloween our religious class gave a party. Most of the kids that came never went to religious school in their life. We had a swell time dancing and amateurs etc. I also did a little twirling routine. I have about 35 moves in twirling now and I love it.

I never met Cheryl but the voice on her slays me. She talks like she's talking to a dog or something. Oh, she's just cute, that's all. You know you love her. G' Wan!!

School is o.k. And I don't skip either.

New Britain High plays Old Lyme today. The band and cheerleaders aren't going though. I guess it's too far.

The cheerleaders have new uniforms. We have white flared skirts, heavy maroon sweaters with gold letters and we ordered the neatest hats but they didn't arrive yet. They're English (white) sailor hats with a maroon tassel. Pretty snappy, eh' what??

That's all for now. I'll write again soon.

Love and kisses,

Betty

P.S. Be a good boy and don't do anything I wouldn't do!! I hope that you'll wish Ma a happy Anniversary (It's on Nov. 9th) even if it's late.

51 Forest St.
Oakwood, Conn.
November 12, 1944

Dearest Charlie,

I wish I could find just the words I want to tell you how happy I was when I called home this morning and heard Mother say I had two letters from you. Honestly, Darling, the whole world seemed to brighten. I guess

350

it's because I was beginning to think you had lost all interest in me because you had stopped writing. Does that sound silly to you? No, I don't think it does, because I can tell from all the wonderful things you said, that you care, too. The kids at work all wanted to know what happened to make me so awfully happy all of a sudden. – Promise you'll never go that long without writing again, even if it's only a half a page. I'll know you are well and all right.

Do you really like me better when I'm mad and about ready to explode? I'm afraid if that is the way you remember me, it's not a very pleasant memory. You know, Dear, I wasn't half as mad as I pretended to be. I just did it to see that sort of timid look in your eyes. I loved it even though I knew darn well you weren't paying a bit of attention to me. Your flowers were always dearer to me than any others I got from anyone else, too.

When you get home can we go to a lot of places together? And will you send me more flowers like you used to? It is a wonderful feeling, as you say, to know that someone is so anxious to see you again. Yes, we will be older when you come home, but that has its advantages, too. I can hardly wait either, Darling.

It was quite a coincidence that the man who took your Xmas box for me in the Post Office should have just mailed one to you himself. I don't remember his name but he lives on your St. He said that Betty, your sister, had just mailed one, too. So, if you get them all, and the cake is at least soft, you will have fun eating. Mom made you a chocolate cake (the kind you liked here once before) and I'm just praying that it won't be all squashed or like a brick. Incidentally, Dear, your Mother said you wanted candy so I sent some Mary Olivers. Did you get that package yet? I do hope they'll keep on the way, but it is just a journey for chocolate. Oh, well, if you do get them it will be worth the chance of sending them.

I know how badly you want a picture of me, so I had one taken yesterday, and I'm waiting for them to be developed. It might take quite a while, but as soon as they are ready you will have one, but I've enclosed this snapshot for now, because a picture does mean so much. I don't know what I'd do without yours. It really brings you so much closer. This was taken 2 years ago, and I don't look too much like that now, but at least it's something for the time being.

I was talking to Helena tonight, and she said Ben wrote again and it's beginning to look as though they'll be going together again, guess they're planning on forgetting the past and starting all over. For a while I began to think you had decided to change cousins – she said she sends you poetry etc.! Let me get some for you, Dear, pardon me while I get mean. I have a lot of good poetry books, too.

Oh goodness, I don't know what Benjamin means when he says he's been over to see me.

Why, I haven't seen him in over a year. In fact, I think you were with him when I saw him last, and as far as my ever liking him goes – well, don't ever give that another thought. I think too much of you for that.

Nothing has happened in N.B. except that the N.B. football team is still winning every game, that's what the paper says anyway.

Fred hasn't been home, or if he has he didn't come over to see Joyce. Guess that's practically over by now. Jimmer Walsh came in the office yesterday to say goodbye. He was leaving for Camp Shelby in Miss. at one o'clock that morning. I didn't see him at all while he was home either – see how much I think of you. Bet you go out dancing with all the cute little black girls where you are. Can you do any of their tricky dances? Bet none of them can dance as good as we do together, can they? Oh well, enough silly chatter. If I don't get to sleep I'll never be able to go to work in the morning, so I guess I must close. Goodnight for now.

Love – kisses,

Cheryl

P.S. I always remember you in my prayers, but it is a good idea to say your new rosaries, too.

P.S.S. Do those pills still bother you? Well, that's still better than malaria, so take lots of them.

Love from Mom & Dad and Debbie, too. I'll write tomorrow and you do the same. Do you have enough paper, envelopes etc? If not, say so and I'll send you some.

17 Anise Street

New Britain, Conn.

November 12, 1944

Dear Brother,

Daddy is supposed to come home today, but as yet he hasn't.

Aunt Anna is here today and she has been here practically all this week.

Last night I slept over at her house and then we came back here this morning for church.

Freddy hasn't been shipped yet (we thought he was). But he is assigned to a ship and waiting for his orders to leave.

Yesterday was Armistice Day. I marched with the cheerleaders in the band. We almost froze to death. It was damp and cold.

New Britain played Hillhouse yesterday and got beat 40 – 0. That bugger Jackson was on the Hillhouse team and, boy, can he run. He made all the touchdowns. When he runs he looks like an animal and none of the N.B. players dared to tackle or block him. An American-born Jap played center on the opponents team. He was also good.

Aunt Anna has a Polish program on. You know that kind of music that Mother and Julius used to dance to (laugh). Julius would put his foot through the floor any minute.

Donny is the funniest thing. He's getting so fat. We're always kidding him about it and he gets so mad.

The funniest thing happened the other night. Donny took a glass and put some soda in it, but he didn't know the glass had some egg whites in it. He drank the soda with the funniest expression on his face. The egg whites were all over his chin and hanging off. He was so mad and Ma and Aunt Anna almost died laughing.

Marks closed Friday and I had four tests. I don't know how I made out yet. (I know I passed though).

Last week I had a big test on the Revolution in History. It was so hard and I knew I didn't pass it. The next day Mr. Catlin called me over to his desk and said I got 54 but he was going to make it a 70. I was the only girl that passed. (about 3 boys passed), You see, Mr. Catlin and I get along swell. I was about the only one that passed the Biology test also. I got 82%. You see I'm not smart and I'm also not dumb. (Get it?)

Love,
Betty

P.S. Be a good boy now!!!

51 Forest St.
Oakwood, Conn.
November 12, 1944

My dearest Charlie,

It's been a few days since my last letter to you, but so little has happened that I'm afraid my usual conversation might become tiresome, so rather than have you bored with my letter I thought I'd wait, but monotonous or not I couldn't wait any longer, 'cause I'm getting lonesome for you again, so I'll take the best way out by telling you about neighborhood gossip if I have to.

Last time I wrote I was out of work for a couple of days with a cold, sore throat etc. but staying in bed seemed to take care of it because I'm back to the old grind, all better now.

About the only exciting thing that happened around here last week was the president's reelection and even that isn't considered exciting any more after three previous terms, but anyway the majority of us are quite satisfied with the outcome – did it meet with your approval? You know the Marines have established quite a reputation for themselves and since you've become one, you sound like you're becoming a hard man, Chas! See, even the papers agree with me. Just look at what you're going to be like if you're not gentle, so from now on I expect you to be more (shall we say affectionate?)

Oh, Charlie, I had my eyes examined last week and as much as I dread it I'll have to wear glasses. Dr. Fissure or is it Fisher? Anyway, he said I'd just have to wear them for knitting or reading so I'm not too bad yet. I got the kind of frames that slant a little, They really don't look bad, just terribly business like,

I was just talking to Helena and she said she and Ben went out to a movie etc. last night, and they had an awfully nice time. She said he was particularly nice to her. It pleased her so when he commented on her new dress and her hair etc. Guess you are quite an impressive lecturer since you gave Ben heck – he seems to respect her much more. She's lucky to know that someone likes her just a little, I'm happy for her too because she felt rather low when they were arguing, but then who wouldn't? You know Chas, I don't think there's anything worse than scrapping with your honey chile, do you? But I'd never do it, would I?

You remember Nancy Halloway, don't you Chas? Well, you knew she and Morry Blair were going together quite a while now, and though it's sort of on the quiet side it's beginning to look like they may be serious. As you know, I never gave two cents for Morry, but Nancy is a swell kid. Maybe she can change some of his loud and bold habits. I hope so anyway for her sake. If I remember correctly one of our many arguments was over him. Didn't you like him, or am I thinking of someone else? Helena and I agree 100% on this matter. Guess he wasn't too nice to her either.

Did Ben mention seeing my picture on the piano when he was here? He seemed to like it a lot because he even told Helena about it. There's not any glamour or any of that junk attached to it but I don't think the lack of that will disappoint you. I hope not anyway

I'll bet I'm a thousand miles off, and you'll never be able to tell me if I am or not, but I think from some of the things you've told me that you're near the Hawaiian Islands. Now if I'm way off, don't laugh. I can almost hear you now, just like you did when I wanted to know if you were warm enough, but if it was a good guess you can tell me when you come home. I know it's hot on the Hawaiian Islands and they have coconuts and little black girls who like blonde hair, but I suppose there are loads off places that could be adapted to these things. This is one time when you really have the upper hand – all I can do is make some awfully rough guesses and you know just how wrong I am, but you still have to let me keep wondering. Go ahead and laugh, you little devil. I know you will anyway so I'd better stop being so imaginative.

Did you ever play cribbage, Charlie? It seems to be quite the game here. Mr. and Mrs. Fox come over every Sunday night and he and Dad play for hours at a time. All I hear is 15 two, 15 four and four are eight, or some such noise like that. If you ever want to stand in with Dad, instead of offering to build a fire in the fireplace (with coal) ask him to play a game of cribbage then you'll be tops. Will you ever forget the fireplace episode? I never will forget the expression on your face. Honestly Dear, you turned as white as this paper. Gee, you were funny.

Did you know Danny Bray is an Ensign now. Ben says you can't get near him with a ten foot pole, he's so proud. Gosh, I don't even think that I'd recognize him it's been so long since I saw him. Seems as though all I can connect him with are steam boats, clams and saddle shoes for a formal. Will you ever forget how he enjoyed eating after a dance? Helena won't, or the saddle-shoes either!

I asked Dad to try and get a film so I can send you some pictures of Debbie before it snows. I'd love to have you see her. You'll like her a lot. She's been so jealous of our new turtle—the size of her, it's really funny. I told you I named the turtle "Bill" on account of its "greenback," didn't I? I'd better stop this – right now.

Did you know Freddy is across? They think he is in England or France. Have you heard from him lately?

Shirley Lucas was over the other night. She's taking piano lessons and she wanted a little help. She plays beautifully by ear, but she wants to take classical so, she's doing it. I think she's foolish myself, spending money on lessons when she can play anything by ear, but she has a one track mind, if you remember. I suppose it's as good a pastime as any.

Well, Dear, I'll have to put two stamps on if I write anymore, so I'd better close now.

Just one more thing. I was quite surprised to hear that you have such a wonderfully established hospital, with so much of the necessary equipment. You said you all had just completed it – did you mean the actual building of it? Do you give transfusions and hypos and, although it does lower your dignity, carry a few bed pans? I often wonder if you'll be interested in the medical profession after the war, since you have had so much experience lately. Have you given it any thought? I really must close – so Goodnight, sweetheart, and be careful.

Always yours,
Cheryl.

P.S. Would you like some of the crossword puzzles from the paper, or don't you like to do them? I'll cut them out and send them to you if you like.

Naval Research Lab.
Washington, D.C.
November 13, 1944

Dear Charlie,

It's about 80 – 90 degrees outside and this sewage disposal plant smells like it.

I've been going through the same old life, eating, sleeping, studying etc. I haven't met any enchanting women yet. I've got the duty this Saturday so I don't expect to. But I have a little consolation. We're having a beer party Saturday and if I haven't got the watch while it's progressing I'll sure be feeling pretty good.

Sam had 15 days leave and he's now going to pre-midshipman's school in N.J. We were at the lake (Poc.) last weekend , I went canoeing in the moonlight but I won't tell you about it because your stories will make mine look tame. Sunday I went sailing with Tommie (Evelyn Thompson) I think her first name is Evelyn. She bailed while I sailed. She's been going down every weekend about 0100 Sunday morning to a party of some sort. If I head for the lake in a few weeks I'll sure as shooting look her up.

I don't know whether you've seen the photos enclosed but I think they're pretty good.

What are you going to study at school?

LETTERS FROM THE ATTIC

Wednesday

When will you get another leave? Try to get one around Christmas if you can manage it.

Love,
Ben

232 Mountain Drive
West Hartford, Conn.
November 14, 1944

Dear Charlie,

I just succeeded in extricating myself from the depths of your letter. I can't imagine you thinking it was short — it was long enough for me and nice and gossipy just the way I like it.

I haven't much gossip for you 'cause I'm turning over a new leaf, my pet. Can you imagine it — no more letters with ironic sentences or ambiguous notes sprinkled here and there as is the custom, but my own honest opinions, good or otherwise, but honest and above board.

Saturday night I went out with Ben. We had a quiet date but I like them like that and we talked about many things. He really has a lot behind him and plenty ahead of him — he is so perfectly honest with himself and everyone else and anyone who doesn't give false impressions should do all right. It means a lot to me to have him shipped out, but as you said, I think he'll find himself then and be a better man for it.

I haven't done many other things lately. Three colds have kept me in bed quite steadily and I'm disgusted. Mother has dragged in all the vitamin pills that she could buy and at every meal I get a combination of A, B, D, C,G, etc. plus some solid food which I hardly need after such a hearty conglomeration. I just sit and look at it (the pill I mean) and after something like "All that meat and no potatoes", which is usually interpreted as "Shoot the taters to me mater."

I just switched typewriters so don't be alarmed by the mammoth letters.

I should discuss your paragraph on love, but I'll spare you that. I think maybe you have had your love but I think you will find another or even the same. It's hard to renew relationships by mail, but have you tried? You have many people's respect and friendship and I know you are fortunate in loving so many people. I have loved many of my girl friends and a few men with the kind of love you mentioned and it's really much better than a simple friendship.

Nancy and I and she and her college friends have been discussing religion quite avidly lately. She has a problem on that score, you know, because she hardly ever goes with Catholic boys. It's funny how some Protestants are bigoted about our religion so much so that discussion till doomsday couldn't clarify matters for them. Anyway her roommate doesn't go to services but they were talking one night and she said someday she would go to church but that she just didn't now. Eventually she decided to read a little of the Bible while Nancy said her night prayers and she opened to a quotation (I don't remember the exact words) something like "Outwardly ye are filled with charity and goodness, but inwardly ye are filled with hypocrisy." The poor girl was amazed and decided to go to church Sunday. It might be coincidence but it's interesting anyway.

Your dictionary is forthcoming. I never thought of anything like that and am glad you mentioned it.

How do you like Cheryl's picture? Ben said it was very good though I didn't see it myself. I haven't seen her in quite a few weeks but we talk on the phone very often – she's a heck of a lot of fun when I'm in the mood for it.

By the way, where is Dick Walton now? The couple of times I met him gave me a very good impression and I would like to know him better. I think he'll be a happy successful individual, too. Does he have a girl at home? Did you think Meg Bolan and he were suited for each other? I never knew her well and I used to wonder what they had in common.

Saturday morning Nancy popped in the office, bag and baggage, with, "Hello, I'm home." We started gabbing and set the whole office astir. I spent the afternoon with her just lying around and talking.

I'll be busy this week – there's a lecture tonight, movies tomorrow night and a turkey bingo Thursday. Mom says if I don't win a turkey I'd better plan to camp out for the holidays.

I think I'll write a note to my brother. I need his advice. Maybe you can help, too. I must have told you that I was practically broken-hearted 'cause I couldn't go away to college – so much so, in fact, that I wouldn't consider living home and going to St. Joseph's or New Britain Teacher's. I still want college and I'm afraid I'm going to lose my desire now that I'm earning my own money, etc, so I was thinking of taking extension courses at Trinity so that I could be earning money too and still not forget what it is to study. Then if I went to college I'd have credits ahead of me and could probably work while in college. Of course, if I decide not to go to college in the future I'd have no certificate or anything much to show for my effort at Trinity and I can't decide whether that would do much good. You can tell me another thing, too — if a fellow goes to college, how does he feel toward a girl who hasn't the education he has? If you go to college when you come home, are you going to insist your wife be a college grad? You don't have to answer any of this, darling. I can't expect you to read into your future and know what you want, but it helps to put these things on paper.

Be good and write soon and tell all the natives I'm asking about them.

Affectionately,

Helena

51 Forest St.
Oakwood, Conn.
November 14, 1944

Dearest Chas,

It's 9:30 p.m. and just about time for me to get ready to go to bed but before I do I'd kind of like to say my usual goodnight to you. If I keep this up you'll be getting a letter from me every day next week, my last night's letter was so long that it should last you nearly two days so you really will be busy

Today is Monday and although I didn't get any letter from you I haven't begun to wonder, because I did get one on Thursday of last week so I really don't expect one until maybe Wednesday. Of course, if I get one before this, you can be sure I won't be disappointed. You know you've sort of spoiled me, Darling. I've been getting at least two letters a week from you for the longest time, and I'm afraid that if you stopped now I'd be very lonesome — You won't stop ever, will you?

We've been so very busy in the office since Saturday that I'm ready for bed at seven every night. I never get there till at least ten, however, by the time I do all my little jobs at home (feeding my turtle and trying to keep Debbie from being jealous) then there are always supper dishes to dry — speaking of dishes, you never have to do them, do you? Guess that only happens when any of you are on K.P. — and you'll never have to do anything like that — you'll always be a good boy, I'm sure

Tomorrow night Father Kennedy is giving his last lecture. I believe this subject is about war, politics and peace. I hope his last one is as interesting as his others, he was really good — and he has a wonderful sense of humor.

Have you gotten any of your packages yet, dear? Bet you're awfully anxious for a nice bit piece of fruit cake etc. But say, I hear you've been having steak! You must really rate. Are you sure it's steak? Gosh, we don't even have that. Next thing you know I'll be asking you to send me some of those delicacies.

The telephone has been ringing constantly since the air workers and bond salesmen started their work on the latest bond drive. Dad is chairman again and he's so anxious to make it as successful as the last. It takes a lot of planning and organizing but he gets so much satisfaction out of it when it's over, and West Hartford and Oakwood have exceeded their quota.

Can you guess what my favorite color is, Charlie? Yes, it's blue. I hope you like it just a little, too 'cause it seems every time I buy paper it turns out blue, either light or dark. If you didn't like it you'll learn to after all my letters. Do you like any particular color? Goodness, how did I ever get on such an out of the way subject?

Oh, it's 10:30 and I should press my skirt and blouse for work tomorrow. I feel like it now that I've written even though I didn't say much. It's funny how much better I feel when I know you'll be getting a lot of letters during the week. You know, you've never even told me whether or not you'd miss them if I didn't write so often. Will you, just a little? Be good and take care of yourself. Goodnight, darling –

Yours,
Cheryl

232 Mountain Drive
West Hartford, Conn.
November 14, 1944

Hello, darlin',

Of course, I haven't forgotten you. By now you've probably got loads of mail from all of us. Five days is an awfully long time to be without mail. I'm usually frantic if I don't get any in such a long time.

You poor boy – if Cheryl met Launa on the street then I'm afraid you're a dead duck. Cheryl never knew that I was aware of your feelings for Launa and she used to tell me that you took Launa out after having fought with her. And if both of them knew that I have your best picture of all, I think my goose would be cooked, too!!! I said in my last letter that I wasn't going to gossip so I won't go any further but I get quite a bang out of the whole situation.

When you describe yourself as having a beard and a mane of hair, I have to run and look at your picture just to assure myself. Don't get too rugged, my pet – remember most of us like our men gentle and just masterful enough to produce meekness in us but not fear.

I didn't see the movie "Gung Ho" and I'm glad now. "Guadalcanal Diary" was quite enough for me, and knowing you're transferring to something like that, I'll probably chew my fingers off with anxiety.

I'm going out with Ben again tomorrow night. He's been home every weekend for quite a while, but I've been out with him only twice.

Yesterday was Thanksgiving, but it was a very quiet one for us. When my Dad was living, the holidays were always very festive and now they seem to get more solemn every year. Mother, my Aunt and I had dinner at home and then we visited relatives in Massachusetts in the afternoon.

I liked your quotation from "Spring Sadness." If you write some free verse, will you send it to me? I can't say that I'm fond of poetry on death, though most work on that subject is especially beautiful.

I'll send you the Shakespeare sonnet next time.

I haven't had a film, my sweet, in simply ages, but as soon as I get one I'll pose pretty for you.

I love to have you quote things. Here is something I like – it's rather light but it was very appropriate for me about a month ago. Oh, I can't put it here – I'll type it on reverse.

I know this is easier said than done, but try not to be too lonely. Just think of your homecoming and of all the people who will be so happy that you're back with us again.

Affectionately,

Helena

Oh, darn, I changed purses today and left the poetry I carry with me home in my other purse.

I don't want to delay this another day and so will wait till next time. You'll certainly learn the patience of virtue, won't you? Every time I write, the enclosures wait for the next time. Oh, well, you like me that way, don't you?

Connecticut College

New London, Conn.

November 14, 1944

Hello, Stinky Darling,

Isn't this romantic? Someone just looked over my shoulder and saw that rare salutation. Can I help it if I'm so tired that I'm punchy? I didn't answer the letter I got from you yesterday— I was rather undecided how

361

to go about it. Exactly what did you expect I'd say after reading about your love life for six whole pages? Should I be gay? If I got mad, it would give you too much satisfaction. Funny how I know you so well. So I guess the best thing to do is say nothing. But you did sort of overdo the Cheryl angle, don't you think? The whole thing was simply too sweet for words. 'Nuf said.

I got two letters from you today – that makes it a good day in spite of everything. Tuesday is my worst day—I have classes from 8 a.m. straight thru to 3:30 with no time off for lunch. I gape into a microscope in Zoology lab for three hours (by that time I'm nearly cross-eyed) and then go into chem lab and stand up doing some stupid little old experiment for three more hours. Sounds great, huh? And on top of all that they popped a math test on me at 4 o'clock . And seeing as how I didn't get to bed till 1:30 last night I'm simply dead. You always seem to write to me when you're exhausted, too – no wonder our letters are so punchy.

That place sounds horrible – and your little Jewish friends even worse. But now that you've got your orders I suppose you'll be moved. And as for your being with Carlson's Raiders – I guess maybe you know how I feel though, don't you? I'll let Cheryl give you the long sentimental line, but, Charlie, please take care of yourself. I'm afraid you've become a very important item in my life – much against all my common sense, of course. How do I get off on these tangents anyway?

Time off – I just had to comb my roommate's wig. No, she doesn't wear it all the time – only for special occasions. She's in a Greek play and has to wear a hideous black wig. We've all been trying it on – and I've decided I won't get my hair cut after all. I had intended to, but after seeing myself in a short black wig, I changed my mind. I looked sort of moth eaten.

It's really fall now – and just beautiful up here. The college is up on a hill and we have a beautiful view of the ocean. I love the fall – but I guess you do, too. The leaves are all off the trees now – and we even had a couple of flakes of snow last week.

Speaking of snow, I'm working on the idea of going up to North Conway this Xmas to go skiing. I don't know if I'll be able to wrangle it. But I'll go crazy sitting in New Britain doing nothing for three whole weeks. That town depresses me anyway and you aren't going to be there. Hell, what a Xmas. But I should gripe when you're way out there. Spoiled brat, I guess.

I'm about to collapse – I don't think I've ever been so tired in my life. Pardon me while I see if I can make it from the desk to the bed. Goodnight, Charlie

As ever,

Launa

P.S. You keep saying that I don't write to you. I'm writing but you just aren't getting them. I'm afraid I've got the habit now – so don't worry about my stopping.

17 Anise Street
New Britain, Conn.
November 16, 1944

Dear Son,

Today is Thursday and it's raining cats and dogs. I waited for the mail man thinking we may hear from you. But Betty rec'd a letter Tuesday, first one since last Wednesday.

Today Marion Douglas is getting married. What a day. I want to go to church and see her but I may get soaked. She's getting married in the church on East Street. Betty's going over to the house afterwards. They are having the reception at the house.

I went to the Parents and Teachers meeting the other afternoon. I saw Donny's teacher. She said he is doing much better. He was in a play and it was good. I didn't go down to see Betty's teachers but I guess she will do alright. (I hope).

Kenneth is working for the Ferndale. I wonder how long he will last. Well, Pa got home Sunday. They didn't have any luck. There was an awful lot of snow although they saw quite a few. Well, they had a vacation anyway.

I think they're going to let Tommy come back to the States and put him in some hospital. They may operate on his leg.

Well, I guess that's all the news. Well, next week is Thanksgiving. I guess we will have one of Donny's ducks. I think turkeys will be kind of scarce. I hope you will have a good dinner. Did you get any of your packages yet? I imagine they will hold them up until Xmas. Well, I must get dressed. I have an appointment with the dentist and then I will go to the wedding.

Love,

Mom

Connecticut College
New London, Conn.

CHARLES YOUNG

November 16, 1944

Hello, Angelpuss,

    Here I go again – this is getting to be a habit. I can't understand why you're always griping about not getting any letters from me. It must be the mail m'love – 'cause I'm wearing myself out writing to you. Do you appreciate me, you Goat? "Greater love hath no woman" – or something.

    It's so nice to hear all the news about my friend(?) Cheryl. Bless her little heart! Tell me, darling, when's the wedding? Don't you think you're a little young to get married? And don't give me any of that stuff about "How does it feel to be loved?" It must be wonderful to be a Casanova like you and have so many adoring females drooling over you. Do you get my point or shall I continue? I'm learning to control my temper though, aren't I? Seriously, you and she would probably make a good pair. It's something to think about, anyway. How can you stand me when I'm so sweet?!

    We practically had a blizzard tonight. I had to go to chem. class at 7 and when I came out it was snowing so hard I couldn't even see the dorm. (By the way, imagine having a class at night – what hell!) Remember the storm we had a couple years ago when the trees were all covered with ice and everything looked like a fairyland? Well, it was just like that. It looked so beautiful and everything that I got upstairs and couldn't study. 'Member the walks we used to take in the snow? We'd get home and decide to go one more time around the block. But I guess we shouldn't rake all that up.

    It's only 1 a.m. – that's a nice hour. But we've been drinking cider all night and I'm afraid it's a little hard – so I feel pretty good. I still have about three hours work to do, but the cider hasn't boosted me up that much. If I can get enough done before tomorrow night, I'm going home for the weekend. There's nothing doing here and this place drives me crazy when I have to stay cooped up like a nun. I'm just not the type. So you'll probably get the big thrill of a letter from New Britain. What a life – as the little man says – "I'm leading a vegetable existence." My roommate has gone to bed and the light will probably keep her awake, so I'd better go, too. Goodnight, Stinky.

        Love always,
        Launa

          17 Anise Street
          New Britain, Conn.
          November 18, 1944

Dear Brother,

 How are you today? I'm o.k. but right now I'm very tired. Today New Britain High played Hartford High. The band and cheerleaders went up, too. We had a swell time. It was freezing cold but the cheering warmed us up. The score was 26 – 12 in favor of New Britain. The Municipal stadium was o.k, but I think New Britain has the best football field of all the schools.

 I went to Confession after I got home from Hartford. The Sodality is giving a Communion breakfast tomorrow at the Burritt. I never went to one, but I guess it will be interesting.

 Kitty and Frank (your friend) and Aunt Anna are here tonight. Mother and Dad and the rest of them are always singing "Down In The Valley" and "Have I Stayed Away Too Long." They love those two songs. (There they go again.)

 That was funny about the crabs. I think I'd die of heart failure if I ever found a crab in my bed. It's a good thing they're not about ten feet long with big claws.

 We get out of school Wednesday noon for our Thanksgiving vacation. School is o.k. We receive our report cards Monday. I'll let you know how I make out!!

 In English we're reading "A Tale of Two Cities." It's a very interesting book.

 I'm glad to hear that you thought you'd be in your present situation for a while.

 Marion Douglas got married Thursday. She married a Polish fellow from Middletown. She had a very nice wedding. I guess that's all for tonight. Goodnight.

Love and kisses, xxxxxx
Betty

P.S. Aunt Anna is going to stay here tonight. Her landlady died this week and I guess the house is kind of spooky.
P.S. Princey is still kickin' around the house and he sends his love.

Naval Research Lab.
Washington, D.C.
November 18, 1944

Dear Charlie,

 You, too, should be flattered, if that's possible. This is the first letter I'm mailing all week. I started one to Helen yesterday but never mailed it.

365

I went out with Helen last weekend. We went to a movie about 21:30 and then went out to eat and etc. We talked quite a bit about you (?) and not the kind you expect. I think we really did very well. Your suggestion about putting all my eggs in one basket was a good one. You can't imagine how many times I thought about marrying Helen or at least getting engaged. But something (usually with skirts) usually detracts me every time.

I wasn't bitching because you hadn't written, but because you're in one of your lonely moods, no doubt, and asked me why I hadn't written more often. The way I see it you don't write to anyone unless you feel they would like to hear from you. Do I make myself clear?

I enjoy writing to you not just because you say mail means so much, but because I consider you a friend. You can get pissed off all you like. I enjoy reading your letters when they're hot and heavy.

I have a few lousy shots of me, I think I might find one. Speaking of pictures, I don't have one of you and Helen has, which only adds to my sorrow. I'd expected one, small as it may be.

Tuesday Nov. 21

I never did get to finish this letter last week. I've been studying for a GI test for RM 2/c. I've still got my hopes.

I hate to admit it, but I see what you mean about Lemon and her trying to get her claws into someone.

I've got a date with Helen next weekend. I've heard rumors about there being a Thanksgiving Formal. I hope so because it's been quite a while since I've been to one of them with her.

I think you've gained a world of wisdom in the last six months. How did you do it?

Are there any books that you'd like to read that you can't get your hands on? I'm sure I can get them for you if I'm allowed to ship them.

We had about four inches of snow in New Britain, my brother tells me, last week. By the time I got there it was all melted again. I'm going to get a few days of skiing in during my leave or bust.

I went home last weekend and took a few snapshots. You should get one less than a week after you receive this letter.

What sort of talk is, "Write to Al, you don't mind, do you?" Are you trying to get me pissed off or did you just want to say something cute?

I'm sorry I can't tell you about election night in Washington because we only get liberty on weekends when we don't have the duty and once a week until 2400. At last I'm in the 7ʰ division (the last, thank God). I have an "arm band" which allows me to drag the chow line and to supervise instead of work at Cleaning Stations. I'll get my orders three weeks from today.

I'm enclosing a clipping, I hope you haven't read it before.

With all the trouble I've had with skiing, I'd still rather ski than do anything else whatsoever.

Did you receive your picture from Cheryl? How do you feel about her? I think that she has the idea that you are the only one etc. And you feel the same. But your letters don't seem to confirm my suspicions. If it isn't any of my business, say so. I don't mind.

After chow

I just went over to the Base post office for some airmail stamps. It's just about freezing out and the wind is blowing to beat all hell. It looks like snow, I hope.

If you see Al, say hello to him for me.

Our Glee Club sang last night and we had a movie "And Now Tomorrow" so they started the show with us, then the movie to kill the stale taste we left. We're going to sing on Thanksgiving at one of the best USO's down town. It'll be a break because I think we'll have the official liberty until 2400.

I guess you can tell I am running out of words with any importance to you so I won't ramble on any more.

One of many,
Ben

P.S. You still haven't told me about the hula girls.

9 Arthur Court
New Britain, Conn.
November 19, 1944

Charlie, darling,

Hello – talk to me. I'm sitting in the living room in the chair near the Vic and Sinatra is singing "Night and Day". Now I ask you – is that fair to my morale? It's funny what music can do. And ever since last Xmas, you've haunted this room. You're even beginning to haunt me. I hear from you so much that I couldn't forget you if I wanted to.

Sharon just walked by and casually mentioned that I should be careful what I put down in black and white. I hope you don't intend to hold me to all I say in letters – I'd be a ruined woman! But I guess you know me better than that. So I can go ahead and ignore all the good advice. I'm likely to say most anything on a Saturday night when I have to sit and talk to the

367

dog. Even Sharon has deserted me – she's gone to bed. I guess I'll have to take up talking to myself.

You asked me for a picture in your Xmas card. M' love, I just don't got none. No kidding, I've got a camera but it's impossible to get any film. So I'm afraid you'll have to wait – you do know what I look like though, don't you? Or are you writing to some Scarlet O'Hara in your imagination? Sometimes I think you are. You're the most idealistic creature I've ever seen – I wish I could bring you down to earth. Are you going to live in a two room flat for the rest of your life dreaming beautiful dreams? Hell – why don't I give up?

'Member Ed Winthrop – the one I was going to marry a couple of years ago? Well, I got a letter from him Friday and he expects to be home for Xmas and he's going to announce his engagement to the girl I took him away from originally. Now sing me a couple of bars of 'Time Waits For No One" – and it sure is passing me by. Oh, well – he was going to stick his wife on a boat and take her for some kind of cruise for a honeymoon – I probably would have gotten seasick anyway.

My writing to you is getting kind of difficult 'cause I never have much to say, And if you get my letters all in a bunch – and I'm afraid you are – it'll be even more boring. Oh, well – maybe you'll get sick of me and that will settle the whole problem. I wish something would settle it.

By the way, Sharon said to say hello to you for her. She always liked you – some people have funny tastes in men, huh?

We went to the movies tonight and they showed a short about the taking of Saipan. I guess we don't know what the war is all about here. It's so damn stupid to feel so absolutely useless. And we gripe because the food is so lousy up at school. What a farce. It seems as if the whole world is filled with unhappy people right now. I pray with all my heart that it will be over soon. For a girl who didn't have much to say, I certainly covered enough space. Guess I'll go to bed. Take care of yourself, Charlie.

> Goodnight, darling,
> Launa

> U.S. Naval Hospital
> Charleston, S.C.
> November 19, 1944

Dear Charlesie,

You really "pickle my piss!" Received your letter of November 10ᵗʰ today. "Ya ole turd." Was more than happy to hear from you. I was just in the mood for one of thy masterpieces. Now I'm all stimulated – Screeeew!

It seems that slowly but surely I'm getting to know Launa - thru you. I can see what she's driving at – no, not your cherry! I guess most women are like her – that is waiting for their "Knight on a White Horse." You know whom she reminded me of when she said, "Can't I wait a little longer??" Yes, you guessed it – Meg. Only not quite in the same sense of the word – Launa knows what she wants and "can't seem to find it" as she says. Where as Meg doesn't know what she wants and is always looking for it. I know that if you ever married Launa, Charlie, you'd be happy and everything would turn out perfectly. You know, she's the one and only woman you've ever thought anything of or ever will think anything of, for that matter. She's already told you that she can't forget you. Now I know definitely that if I had someone on my mind who kept repeatedly coming back to me in my thoughts, I'd surely know that there some degrees of love connected with it. There just couldn't be any other answer for it. To tell you the truth, I get the impression that she is slowly weakening and beginning to see that you are the only one that she has cared anything about and that she has to make up her mind soon. She even explained to you that she was ready to send you a "telegram" last Christmas and got "scared." What I'm trying to say, Charlie, is that this frightened feeling which almost every human has, is starting to wear off. It has to wear off sometime. If it doesn't or if it never had before, I don't see how anyone could have ever made up his mind to finally get married. It seems to me that you've gone too far with the deal already to start asking yourself if everything would work out if you finally did get her. There is a future in it and deep down inside you know it. "Enuff of dis luffink – you should see her sister."

Charleston really gives me a "jubilant jagged jab in my jolly Joe-hole." I'll be here through December 11ᵗʰ then I'll be eligible for transfer. Where in the hell I'll go from here I don't know!

Your Mother's P.S. about Cheryl really "tickled the tender tissues of my timid testicles." She'll never know if she doesn't know now. I'm thinking now of the experiences which you had with her. Oh my stinkin' dear!

I've already told you about Peggy. I'm afraid you got the wrong impression of the little darlin'. Seriously now, Charlie, before I go any further, I'm going to say that I'm not sure whether or not this is another infatuation or the real thing, One thing I do know is that I've been hit hard and the separation hurts. You must get tired of hearing about my "flickers". One of these times I'm bound to be right. Who knows?? Maybe this is "T-Time". I'll have to ask her about that extra storage tank business.

Perhaps I exaggerated her fondness to indulge, but I know she wasn't brought up on a breast. Cripes! What am I saying? The woman claims she is madly in love with me – a fact which I hope to learn more about. If I ever hit California again – and I probably will – I'm liable to take drastic steps!! What the hell am I talking about – I'm a bachelor at heart. Screeeeeeew. Damn it!! I don't know what I want, when I want it, or how I want it!

Incidentally, I have yet to meet that "Southern Iceland" chicken. I'll probably hand you the same story about her. No, I won't either!!!

Mother and Dad are intending to come down here to see me for Thanksgiving or Christmas if I'm still here. It'll really be great to see them again. I know that I really love my parents!! That's one thing I'm certain of.

This is a crazy letter in spots, but I don't give a damn, do you?? I guess that we were just made to be crazy. Adieu, my pet. I've got a special watch coming up in 15 minutes. Write when you can.

As ever,

Rich-Hard

17 Anise Street
New Britain, Conn.
November19, 1944

Dear Brother,

Well, Kid how are you today? It's been snowing here all day today and I think it's hailing now. It seems that every time we have skating it snows.

We went skating Friday and Saturday nite but it seems that kids our age are getting too old for skating. There seems to be all little kids about 9 and 10 years old. I guess I'm getting old, that's all.

The girls went to the movies this afternoon but I stayed home. I just finished an outline for English. The book we're having is "Sir Roger De Coverly Papers." We just started it so I don't know how it is yet.

I darn near split a gut when I heard about those two gooks. I bet they really were a scream. What do they make "Gizmo Juice" out of? It sounds good. You should have taught them a new song like "Marzie Doats".

Dad was glad to hear from you. He received both your letters at the same time, even though they were dated quite far apart. Donny also received your letter. He goes quite big for trapping now. He sent away for five new traps and he has them set down in back of Farmers.

Tessie has been here all day long. We were talking about the time we lost the gun in the coal bin and she had to scrub us with cleanser and a scrubbing brush to get us clean. (More fun.)

370

I'm sending two more of those service men's clippings. Sorry, but I forgot to send last week's. I think they're quite interesting.

Freddy went back Friday, then thought he was a day late.

Francine Valin is engaged to Lennie Hopkins.

Junie Ziegler is home on a thirteen day furlough. He's stationed in Kentucky. He's with Ernie Glabau so that's nice.

I got a letter from Jim Friday. He got his application from the Merchant Marine Academy. If it's accepted, he starts training for an Ensign's commission. (Goody) I love Ensigns!! It's time to close now.

Love and kisses, xxxxxx
Betty

P.S. We mutilated worms in Biology Friday. It was lots of fun. Our new saying is "Hot Spit and Monkey vomit," (Cute, eh?)
P.S.S. Watch out for the "Gooks.

17 Anise Street
New Britain, Conn.
November 19, 1944

Dear Son,

Betty just wrote so there is not much to write. Tommy went back yesterday. They are supposed to operate on him. Pa took Tom, Shirley, Tag and Jean ice fishing down to Lake Pocatapaug Sunday but they didn't get anything. Tag gets home every weekend. We haven't heard from Bert since he went away.

Nellie Nealon is at the N.B. hospital. She was operated on yesterday for a tumor and she had her appendix out at the same time. Joe said she was very sick and will be for the first few days.

Fan and Lala were over yesterday. Fan feels much better now. She gained a couple of lbs. The boys have trouble getting cigarettes. They are scarce and they have to roll them. Donny keeps going in the drug store and buys tobacco and he rolls them for Pa. I wish he would give up smoking. They only make him nervous. I hope you don't start in again.

What kind of training are you getting now? I suppose you sleep right out in the open. You will be a regular gypsy used to all kinds of living. Well, Pa is going to take me shopping now so will close.

With love,
Mother

17 Anise Street
New Britain, Conn.

November 20, 1944

Dear brother Charlie,

    How are you? This afternoon I went to the movies and when I came home Betty was writing a letter to you so I thought I'd write one to you also. Betty is turning the quiz kids on now and Jack Benny is going off, the goon. As you know I roll daddy's cigarettes and in another six months you won't be able to buy a pack of tobacco so we got twelve packs. Daddy said it should be good for trapping in back of the Blue Danube but that's what I want you to answer. It snowed so hard Thursday that there wasn't any school Friday. I wish I knew what to write but I can't think of anything to write. By the way, has the Red Cross sent you or the other fellows any cigarettes? We can't even get a pack of kool cigarettes. I can't think of anything else to write, so I'll sign off.

Love

Donny

P.S. I enclose 1 stick of gum. It's not poisoned.

Connecticut College
New London, Conn.
November 20, 1944

Hello, Eager Beaver –

    Good name for you, no? There were two letters waiting for me Sun. night and I got three today – that's five letters I owe you. You better be careful – I'll be spoiled.

    I'm completely exhausted. This lack of sleep is beginning to get me down. But I'm happy – you couldn't have said anything in your letter that would have made things better. I've waited so darn long for an answer to that horrible letter I wrote you – I shudder every time I think of it. Don't ever try to tell me that honesty is the best policy – I got myself so mixed up I didn't know whether I was coming or going. But you seem to have cleared everything up. How the hell do you understand me so well? At least now I can go ahead and say what I feel like saying without worrying how it sounds or what you'll think. You're wonderful, darling –and by the way I mean that. I haven't felt so good in ages.

    As you said, by the time we see each other again, we'll both be different. I'm sure you won't be the same when all this is over – and I probably won't either. Cheer up – maybe you'll learn to hate me. At least we'll be older and maybe I won't be quite such a crack pot.

372

I'm afraid that it's only two thousand bucks altogether that you'll get from the government – but that'll take you quite a ways through college if you go to some university. Although I don't know if I'll approve of those co-eds!

What do you want to do when you graduate – or am I looking too far ahead? I seem to be the only ambition in life that you ever tell me about. Love isn't all there is to it, my friend. Since you don't have to worry about me anymore, you can put something else in that one track mind.

I started with a big piece of paper just so I'd only have to write one page—but it didn't work. How did I ever meet you anyway? I'm so blooming tired I can't even write. Beth just suggested that we both commit suicide – best idea I've heard yet. Gee, I'm getting tired of going to school – as I said before, a vegetable existence. That phrase describes it perfectly - I'm beginning to feel like a dried up old carrot. I hate carrots – I suppose you like 'em. We really don't agree on much.

As I told you in my last letter I haven't got a picture to send you. But you'll get one as soon as I can get hold of some film.

Nancy's roommate was up here today when I was out. She left a note for me on your picture which is perched on my desk to keep me from concentrating. She'll no doubt tell Nancy, and Nancy will tell Morry – and here we go again. Freddie (that's her roommate) says she thinks Nancy and Morry the Goon are going to end up by getting married. Can you think of anything worse? So then we had a long discussion on being married to a man with no teeth. Fascinating –

I'm glad you finally went to communion. I went last month too for the first time in about a year. As a matter of fact, I was even excommunicated (what a word) from the church – I didn't go around Easter time. I didn't think it made a darn bit of difference one way or the other. But it does – a hell of a lot. But I guess you know that as well as I do. You miss your religion when you haven't got it – it helps a lot.

I can't keep my eyes open and tomorrow is the day I go from 8 till 3:30 with no let up. Honestly, I could sleep for a week.

Thanks, Charlie, for making things so easy – not many people would have done it. Goodnight, darling.

Love always,
Launa

VT 29 FPO
New York, N.Y.
November 21, 1944

Dear Charles,

I guess it is about time that I wrote to you. I hope this letter gets to you. I hear you are or at least you were in Sick Bay again. What's the matter, was the leave too much for you? Well, maybe you will be able to get another sick leave out of it.

No, I haven't made second class yet but I hope to soon, you notice I said hope to, it is kind of hard to get one in this squadron because we have a shit house full of second class men but as soon as a few of them make first class maybe I will have a chance.

My address is Fleet Post Office because people aren't supposed to know where the squadron is after we ship out and it is a lot easier to use that now instead of changing it afterwards, but I guess it will change from San Francisco to New York sometime in July because I think we are going down to the South Pacific sometime around then.

Hotch is in Norfolk and as for Neuman and Whipple, I don't know where the hell they are. Now, most of the rest of the boys are still in the same places they have been.

Don't mind the dirty paper. I just finished kindling fires and there's no place to wash my hands in our cruddy room.

I went to New York over the weekend to see my cousin and really had a swell time.

Well, I guess that's all for now. So long, be a good boy and write soon.
Mick
Hope this gets to you.

17 Anise Street
New Britain, Conn.
November 21, 1944

Dear Brother,

I received a letter from you today and so did Mother. Be sure to tell her how you like your new situation.

Mrs. Reynolds just called to tell me there was a pheasant out in the lot. Ma and I just went out and we saw it, but it flew away. It was a big one. Mr. Westerman said there's a lot of them in back of his house.

Tomorrow is Thanksgiving but we're not going to have a turkey. I bet you'll have a nice dinner.

We got out of school today until Monday and we didn't get any homework. Our report cards came out Monday. I got a B (88%) in Latin and C in English, History and Biology and an A in gym. You said Mr.

Nordstrom was an easy marker. He gave C's and D's only in the class. I deserved at least a B. I passed all my tests and got good marks on my written work. Oh, well, we all can't be as smart as you.

I think that Benny has a case on anybody with a skirt. Don't you think so??

I saw the picture "Show Business" and I liked it very much. George Murphy was good and I love the song "It Had To Be You."

New Britain High plays Buckley tomorrow and Buckley claims they're going to win, but they'll find out. It's been raining now for four days so I hope it stops for the game tomorrow.

Daddy isn't working today so he went to the movies. Donny and Walty also went to the movies.

You really kill me with some of those corny sayings etc. you write in your letters. They make me laugh though. So long for now.

Love & Kisses,
Sister

Conn. College
New London, Conn.
November 21, 1944

Dear Charlie,

It's pouring rain out and it's been a terrible day all around so I'm in a stinking mood. I finally got two letters from you today. And if you don't stop griping about my not writing to you I'm going to give up entirely. I have no intentions of stopping and I'm writing as often as I can manage. If you aren't getting the letters it's because of the mail and not me. I also received your sweet little V-Mail letter Sat. morning — thanks. Just what the devil do you expect? I do write to other people occasionally — I'm not afflicted with the one track mind you seem to have.

And by the way — you'd better slow down on these letters. I'm afraid they're getting here on their own steam — if you know what I mean, and I think you do. As I've said before, there are a heck of a lot of things in the world besides love — believe it or not. Do you ever think of anything else? If so, I never hear about it. And to use the old phrase — you're too young.

I gave Beth your note. She was rather shocked — hope you're happy.

Xmas vacation starts Dec. 14th — so I'll be in N.B. anytime after that. Your last two letters took about 10 days — so you can plan from that.

You're just rubbing it in by telling me about all the books you read. I haven't read any fiction since last summer — which seems at least a year

375

ago. But I'm afraid I'll have a chance to catch up on all my reading during Xmas. Sounds gay, no? NO!

And I told you I'd send you a picture as soon as I could get some film. I may be able to buy some next week. So you see I'm not just "having another tantrum" over that either. Just who do you think you're writing to – your kid sister?

I'm dead tired and it's only 5:30. And I have a paper due tomorrow at 8 which I haven't even begun. I guess this isn't a very cheerful letter. – but I "must write".

Take care of yourself, Charlie – and I'll write when I'm in a little better mood.

As ever,
Launa

17 Anise Street
New Britain, Conn.
November 22, 1944

Dear Charlie,

How are you? A few days before Thanksgiving we killed my ducks and found gold in their crops, they were very small. Mother just let Prince up from the cellar and he's lying here snoring.

I am doing pretty good in my school work now. I got a 75, 82, 94, and 93 in my work last week.

Do you remember in the last letter I asked you to send me home a native, all I got was a four legged cannibal. Maybe Betty will beat me up but the other night when Betty went out with the boys they came home with lipstick all over their faces. You know what that means. Love at first sight. Betty is lying down on the couch otherwise I wouldn't be writing these things.

We're going to have corn and mushrooms for supper. I was just wondering what you had for Thanksgiving. We could not get any turkeys in New Britain because they said they were all going overseas. I'll bet they were not. Just got the paper and Mother is sitting down reading it. Mr. Nixon's picture is in the paper for being the head of the board, the same as the old job. Well, there's not much to say so I will sign off here. Love and kisses,

Donny

P.S. I wish you could be here for my birthday.

9 Arthur Court
New Britain, Conn.
November 23, 1944

Hello, Darling,

Things would be a lot easier if I could read your writing, Stinky. The letters are o.k. but when it comes to writing the address you must think I'm psychic. I hope you get this – I just took a good guess at what it said. Why the new address? Are you being moved? I suppose that's it.

I got two letters yesterday. I love the way you have no inhibitions about what you write. I guess you know the letter I'm referring to. There's nothing unusual about the whole thing. It's just the war – we all seem to think we have to have everything right now – just so we'll be sure to get it. Hell – sometimes I'm so sensible I make myself sick. I'm afraid I can't discuss the whole thing – I'm not quite as uninhibited as you are. You know me – like a clam in a shell. And I never seem to come out of it.

It seems so funny to hear about your going swimming all the time. It's really quite cold here now – and I'm not looking forward to winter this year. Please don't let me get old and stodgy – but they don't seem to be half as much fun as they used to. I haven't been skiing in at least two years. I wish I could go up north during Xmas vacation to some ski lodge or something. 'Cause I'll go nuts if I have to sit in this town for three whole weeks. I suppose I can call up Patty Lou and we can go to the movies or something exciting like that – gay! And then sit and think about last Xmas. See what I mean? I'll begin tearing my hair out – will you love me when I'm baldheaded? Don't say yes or I'll know you're lying.

I just finished stuffing myself with turkey. They were almost impossible to get this year but Sharon got one on her good looks I guess. Did you have any kind of a Thanksgiving? You were the ones who were supposed to be getting all the turkey so I hope you got some. You even barged in on my Thanksgiving though. Phoebe was in the middle of grace (once a year we have grace) and the damn Vic started in on "Night and Day". So grace wasn't too successful as far as I was concerned.

You haven't mentioned Cheryl lately – deah. I don't mind as long as I hear about it (it says here). Don't tell me she isn't being faithful! Or are you just keeping me in the dark? Too bad all your women aren't as faithful as I am – ouch – I'd better duck for that one. One good thing about letters – you can say most anything without getting hit. You always did abuse me anyway.

I've been writing this letter on and off all day. Every time I get started somebody comes along. Now I have to dash and get dressed. I have to catch the bus back to that nunnery in half an hour. I'll write you tomorrow, Stinky. You said something in your letter about the fact that we're both so mixed up that we ought to stick together – I'm afraid that you hit the nail on the head. Take it easy, m' love.

Always,
Launa

U.S, Naval Lab.
Washington, D.C.
November 24, 1944

Dear Charlie,

I'm afraid this is going to be another morning letter. I've got a tough inspection tomorrow, which if I don't pass will cause me to lose my weekend liberty.

Last night our glee club sang. The turnout was better than we had expected. (They didn't know what they were in for.) All the numbers were done very well except one. It seems we had sung the introduction one way for recordings and the other for performances. Well, about 5 fellows started two measures before we were supposed to. It worked out swell, the conductor just very slowly built us up in a beautiful crescendo and the audience never knew the difference. After we had finished singing, the band from the "Navy School of Music" came in and played for dancing. I found a very nice partner, who although we had met each other was just as much at a loss as to where, as I was. The music was good and the gal very nice so I danced till about 2300 when I had to start back to the base.

You said something about spending a few years in Europe. I can't see any attraction in any European country except Norway or Sweden for its skiing. I've thought of traveling over the globe after I graduate from college but I've got a long way to go.

I won't tease you about Cheryl anymore. I can see it's Launa 100%. I don't blame you a bit, she's quite the girl.

Roger Arcand is still in Italy and I guess he plans to stay for a while. He and a few buddies just finished a house, it even has a large open fireplace. Italy, he says, is a filthy place.

Saturday, Nov. 25—0655.

I don't blame you too much for worrying about the speed at which this younger generation is growing up. I suggested to my little sister that she attend a girls school. She said she didn't want one where there were no boys. I suppose our parents were quite worried about us though.

Monday ,Nov. 27—0640.

I spent the weekend at home. The train pulled in on time and I got home about 2000. It took over an hour to eat, wash and say hello to the family. About 2130 I was knocking on Helen's front door. She had on a black evening dress with white shoulders covered with tiny white ruffles, it was very becoming. We ended up at the "Lobster." The rest of the evening was spent as could be expected. Sunday morning after church I fooled around with the kids till it was time for chow. We had our turkey dinner then. The whole family was present with the exception of Sam who won't get his commission till the middle of January. Sunday afternoon Johnny built a fire in the fireplace and I sat around for a while. My cousin Rita dropped in and we took a few more snap shots.

I'm going to a formal next weekend. I don't know where it is but I think Helen will find out in plenty of time.

I saw Sara Preston at the Berlin station but she was busy gabbing with a bunch of girls so I didn't interrupt her. Write soon.

Your friend,
Ben.

Connecticut College
New London, Conn.
November 24, 1944

Hello, Stinky,

My roommate is standing in the middle of the room spouting her part in a play – the radio is blaring and a couple of kids are sitting on the floor playing bridge—so I'm finding it kind of hard to concentrate. More women! And on top of it all I can't talk. It's about 10 below 0 out (well, almost) and we had to play tennis for gym. And like a moron I got hot so I took my jacket off –so-o-now I've got a beautiful cold and every time I start to say anything all that comes out is a squeak – more fun. And to top it off all of these jerks started talking about Roosevelt and I couldn't even put in my two cents. I just have to sit here and fume. Life is so difficult.

No letter today. I expected one somehow and when it didn't come I was furious. I told you that you were spoiling me. I was raving and ranting about it and Beth piped up, "I thought you didn't love the guy" – so I tried to explain and got all screwed up. Is life so complicated or do I just make it that way?

379

The latest news about the Darcy family is that Marvin is thinking of leasing an apartment by the year somewhere in West Hartford. That entails selling the house in New Britain which I suppose is a good practical idea – only that's about the only home I ever had. I'm afraid we Darcy's have gypsy blood in us somewhere—it seems to be against our principles to stay any place more than a couple of years. Damn monotonous, too. When I finally do get a home, "I ain't ever gonna roam law'd". By the way, don't misunderstand all this. All I mean is a definite home is a pretty nice thing to have, but what the hell, I'd probably die of boredom anyway.

I think about you often, Charlie – too much I'm afraid. Maybe it's because all the males I've seen lately haven't hit the right note – I don't know. Anyway things are getting worse instead of better – and all by mail too! I must be crazy, huh?

It's late so I guess I'll go to bed. If I don't get a letter tomorrow I think I'll explode – 'cause that means I'll have to wait till Monday. I know –T.S.—'m really abused. Goodnight, darling –.

Love always,
Launa

17 Anise Street
New Britain, Conn.
November 25, 1944

Dear Son,

Well, at last I have got up the ambition to write you a few lines. It seems there is nothing to say as Betty and Mother write quite a few times each week.

I went on the annual hunting trip and as usual got nothing. Harold, Russell, Walter Miller and Buck Miller went along as usual. None of us got a deer although we had glimpses of them for a few seconds. I got one shot in but it was lousy, saw the deer for only a few seconds. We had snow up there the first day in camp, it snowed for 24 hours or more, about 15 inches on the level, then there was crust the rest of the week with the exception of the last day. We made a drive and put three out but the ones on the stands missed. All we did was eat a lot of meat that we brought with us and consumed a lot of booze every night and morning as the camp was on Silver Lake (one of the Rangely Lakes in Maine), Deer can be bought up there at 25 dollars apiece and there are plenty of them. The natives jack them at night and sell them to city-slickers. I couldn't buy one and tell Donny that I shot the deer. That's like hitting below the belt and unfair. We had a good trip all the way coming and going, it was hard work hunting but every morning you want to do the same thing over again.

We got a letter from one of your pal's mother, named Wheatly from Ridgewood, N.Y. Mother is greatly relieved in knowing the whereabouts of Kid Klutz.

Thanksgiving Day we stayed at home, the Cabelus's were here for dinner, I no more than got started eating when I bit into an olive with a seed in it and first thing I knew one of my front teeth was where it shouldn't have been, in with the duck, we had no turkey, they were scarce this year. In the morning I went hunting with Walter Miller up to Pleasant Valley, there were plenty signs of game but I couldn't catch up with anything worth shooting at. I was supposed to go again today but I had to finish up a job which is the last one I am going to work on the outside this season. It was so cold that I most froze. It is now 7 P.M. Mother and my sister Anna went shopping for a present for Kitty Narcum, they are celebrating an anniversary tomorrow.

We also received two V-Mail letters today, one was typewritten and says that you moved and that you do not do latrine detail anymore. You must be a pip for getting this sort of work. What do you do — duck work detail all the time and the latrine detail is punishment? Well, so long as you like the present job that's all that matters.

Two more bonds came from the Navy Dep't this week and I believe you have around $350.00 worth already. When you get a grand, maybe you'll lend it to me. Oh yeh! Keep it up and save your dough, you'll need it when you get back. Am enclosing the finn you asked for. What do you spend your money on in the jungle? Are the natives wise and take it away from you or have you got a native belle that you're playing around with? Well, you know that familiar Navy saying, Any old port in a storm! Be careful though, keep away from the Gooks or that dame up in Oakwood is apt to be jealous.

I think that Betty is taking a shine to Jimmy Arute, he was down Thanksgiving. He's a cadet in the Coast Guard at the Coast Guard Academy in New London. When he came into the house I asked him if he plays in a band. What a uniform, he looked like an admiral in the long blue overcoat and the blue uniform he looked dippy. Bobby Cabelus was with him, also another kid called Porky, he's in the navy and just got back from Europe, he's on a destroyer and has already been in three major engagements.

This is all I can think of right now and I will do my best to try and write more often. This damn typewriter print is lousy and I make more mistakes than usual.

I told Donny tonight that each of us has to write a letter every other day and it's his turn tonight but he persuaded me to write tonight – it's his turn tomorrow.

It seems to me although I do not know for sure Betty or Mother write at least three times every week, some of these must be lost or sunk on the way.

Hope this will find you in the best of spirits and good health, everybody at home is feeling fine, also Prince, he stays home now and does not wander away. We would have got rid of him long ago if he wasn't your dog. I think if he did go away we all would miss him, he's part of the family now, we had him too long. Well, so long for now, and I hope again this finds you o.k.
Your Pop

51 Forest St.
Oakwood, Conn.
November 25, 1944

Dear Charlie,

I just finished reading your letter and I must say it did more than upset me. I never realized it, but it seems as though I've created some sort of an impression on your mind, quite unknowingly, that can't continue to go on without being straightened out. I'm almost afraid to think of what you believed I've been hinting at. True, I have asked you about things we have done in the past, but only because I thought it might be sort of relaxing for you to think back over the fun we had with all the kids. You see, I too realize it's been a long time since we've seen each other and that we're getting older and our ideas and our ambitions have thoroughly changed. I didn't think, however, that this meant we couldn't continue to be good friends. I've been thinking that anything I could write or do for you might make you just a little bit happier since you are away from home, and you must realize that I've felt under no obligation to you at all – it's no more than I would do for any good friend under such circumstances.

I'm not writing this to be mean at all, but only because I feel you've taken my letters much too seriously as far as connecting all the foolish engagements and marriages at home with you and I. I assure you that I haven't even begun to think along those lines, particularly with such an unsettled future to look forward to.

Incidentally, don't you think it a better idea to keep what goes on in our letters just between us? I think it's only fair to me since I am the one who is being played upon.

Let's hope that this will put an end to all the doubts you might have had about me. Please believe that you won't hurt me at all by having all the friends you like, because that's the way it should be for both of us.

Sincerely,
Cheryl

17 Anise Street
New Britain, Conn.
November 26, 1944

Dear Brother,

We received two V-Mail letters from you today. I think that in one of them you were a little angry. But I bet you're o.k. now. (Aren't you, you little devil?)

We received a letter from Mrs. Wheatly a few days ago and we were very glad to hear from her.

Aunt Anna, Uncle Pete and the other Aunt Anna were here for dinner Thanksgiving. I hope that you had a nice dinner. New Britain lost the game to Buckley for the first time in about 15 years. Buckley really had a neat team. The score was 13 – 0. The game was awful though.

Jim Arute came home from Admiral Ballard for a Thanksgiving vacation. Thursday nite Jim and I and Barbara Larson and Salin (George)) and Vera Dillon and Bob Cabelus went out together. We had a neat time. Barbara Larson is quite the girl now. Remember you used to think she was so small etc, but she's changed quite a bit.

Father Webb is taking about five kids to the Yale-Virginia game at the Yale Bowl today. I've been trying to go, but I'm not sure. Barbara is going and she doesn't want to go unless I go too. Get it? She's going to talk to Father and then call me. I'd love to go and see what the Yale Bowl looks like.

You said you go to your old place to take a shower. I bet by the time you come back you need another one. I'm glad to hear you like your new situation.

Oh, Father just called Barb and said I could go. I think I will but I don't know what to do. I'll write to you tomorrow.

Love and kisses,
Sister

P.S. I hope I have a good time. Gotta go in 15 minutes.

17 Anise Street
New Britain, Conn.
November 28, 1944

Dear Brother,

Well, I went to the Yale-Virginia game Saturday with Father Webb and the kids. We had a swell time. The score was 6 -6 and it was a wonderful and exciting game. The Yale bowl is really nice. We had seats in the second row on the 45 yard line. I had three sweaters on under my coat and we had a big blanket. It was actually freezing cold. We ate at the Village Inn on the way home. It's a ritzy place.

We got home about 8 o'clock. Jimmie, George and Bobby C. were here when I got home. Barbara, Vera and I were suppose to go out with them that night. We had quite a mix-up. Mrs. Larson didn't want Barbara to go at the last minute but we got straightened out finally. We went out about 9 o'clock.

We had a turkey dinner at Narcum's yesterday. It was their 21st anniversary and they had a few people over to help them celebrate. So long for now.

Love & Kisses, xxxxx
Betty

P.S. Donny and Irene went to the Newington theater yesterday. I think he likes her.

51 Forest St.
Oakwood, Conn
November 28, 1944

Dearest Charlie,

Your letter for today was a particularly nice one. Sounded like your old self again.

So you finally got my picture. If you're sincere about it you must really have been pleased. But what in the world does Gloria DeHaven look like? Probably like Joan Davis, well, anyway I won't rest until I see a picture of her then I'll know whether the fellows in the tent were paying me a compliment or otherwise.

Seriously though, I'm glad you got it, since you did ask for one. Now you have some idea of how I've changed in the past year. Do you notice much difference – good or bad?

Sure I remember Billy McClellan. How could I forget? I can't picture him in a sailor suit, he was so little. All I can do is picture him and Benjamin standing outside in my driveway on Commonwealth Ave. yelling at me when I had Scarlet Fever. They were devils. Weren't we all then?

So you're so hot it's hard to write. That to me seems almost impossible since it's so cold here, but this enclosed picture might help to cool you off. Remember when you went on that skiing trip you sent me a folder full of pictures of the Lodge etc. in VT ? Was this one of the paths you took? No wonder Ben broke his leg. It's a wonder he didn't do more than that. You can show this to some of the fellows, bet they never thought you had it in you!

I see you've mentioned Ben and Helen again. Whatever are you trying to do? First you write to him and lecture on all of Helen's good points, then you write to her and tell her he's not worth having, then you wind up saying "Maybe she doesn't love me anymore, huh?" Personally, I can't figure out what you're driving at. Could it be that you'd like her for yourself? No, couldn't be that 'cause in the next line you say it would be fun if we could stand up for them when they get married. I don't know, looks like you've got me wondering more than either of them. What this thing calls for is a party for the 4 of us to see who's in love with who, you and Helena, or Ben and she.

You make me laugh with all your changes of girl friends anyway. It really looks bad for the one you choose. Never mind, Sweetheart, just pour you little heart out to me. I'll be tolerant with all your troubles.

Oh, before I forget I must tell you about Charlie Cantrell. He's been home on a ten day leave and he's leaving tomorrow to go back to camp then he says he'll be going into the Pacific somewhere, too. He's a 1ˢᵗ lieut. in the Marines and I believe he's also in some medical branch. Wonder if you'll ever meet him? He's a swell fellow, I'm sure he makes an excellent officer, too.

It was wonderful to hear that you're finally settled as far as work and moving around is concerned. It's quite a relief to know that your work is easier and that you'll have more time for yourself for writing (as you said.) At least it sounds as if you're going to be safer than you'd be if you were in the infantry. I guess my prayers weren't overlooked after all.

Thanksgiving Day was the nosiest one I've ever spent. You see my Uncle was here with the three children and I was nearly batty by the time they left. Oh yes, they even wanted me to play football in the mud!

It's less than a month till Christmas and I haven't bought a card yet. I suppose I'll do what I did last year. Wait until the last week, then get a cold and have to stay in bed, shopping or no shopping. Well, we managed to exchange gifs anyway, didn't we? I still have the pretty slip you bought me. It's still like new (I use nothing but Lux flakes on it.) One would think I was working for C.B. DeMille.

Ann Rollins was over yesterday and she was asking for you. She taking her mid-year exams at St. Jos. and they're terrific.

One more thing, you remember Art Collins, don't you? He went to one of the teas with Mary LaPorte. Well, he's an ensign, you know, and he's been taking Agnes Knapp to dances etc. and, boy, the sparks must be flying around Mary LaPorte's house! I'll tell you more next time.

Write soon 'cause I'll be waiting.

Love,

Cheryl

R.I School of Design
Providence, Rhode Island
November 30, 1944

Charlie, my pet,

How's my favorite Marine? From the sound of your letter, dear, you're not too happy. What's the trouble – silly question, isn't it? There you are thousands of miles from me and good liquor – so your low spirits are understandable. No conceit in me –classing myself with Vat 69 or Schenley's Black Label. Miss me? That's what I thought – oh, well, it is still Leap Year.

Darling, I wasn't insulting your mouth – after all, dear, it serves the purpose – and if I remember rightly it served rather well. About French kissing – yes, I've tried it – I don't like it – sorry. I could say I did and then have to prove it when you return. So I'll tell you the truth for a change. The trouble with this world is that the men have all of the fun at the expense of women. I wish I were a man sometimes. How would you like me as a man? I think I'd be rather nice.

Just looked at your picture and wished I hadn't. Every time I do I think of all the fun I had with you – and now there you are and here I is and I'm bored stiff. (This is no line, dear, in case you're reading it skeptically) Right now I'd give five years of my life for a date with you. I haven't laughed till I was sore for ages. Come home, baby, and amuse me – Now tell me you'd rather stay in the South Pacific – Even Red said he liked to see me as long as it was home.

Charles, my pet, I have come to the conclusion that you're a big boy now. You seem to have grown up – Not flattering – I should have said you've changed. Did I detect a little sarcasm and a sly dig in your last letter? It didn't seem like you at all – maybe it's my imagination, I hope so. Please don't get the way I used to be – it's a horrible life.

We've had an epidemic of sex fiends lately and it's getting damn annoying. There are more naked men floating around and I'm about sick of it. I met one tonight so we called the police. Then there is the guy across the street who puts on a burlesque every night for our benefit. I told the police about that also. There have been four rapings in two days – and right around school. The police asked if I'd testify in court if necessary so if you see me in the papers in connection with a raping – think nothing of it. They think the guy I met tonight is the one they're looking for. You might know I'd be the one to see him – I walk up to trouble and take it by the hand. Hell it just got me mad – I'm no prude and I have Life Class every day but I'm getting tired of so damn many nudes. I prefer my men clothed.

We're having a dance next week and so I bought a new gown. Sexy as hell. I've been on a diet you know so I'm quite a bit thinner than I was a year ago—but living on black coffee is a tough life. Come home for the dance, will you? I feel like doing the polka—how about it?

I've got homework to do now so I'll close – but since you insist I owe you two letters I'll write tomorrow again – but be an angel and write to me soon.

Betty Harriman is coming up for the week-end and Frannie Murphy is in the country and is stationed in Boston for a few weeks so he's coming up also. We should have a gay weekend. Be good, dear, and write!

Love,

Lulu

P.S. You b-d – here we are without cigarettes and you have cartons. That's the only reason you can out smoke me. Say, do you know a good marijuana market? I'm desperate.

'Night, Lu

17 Anise Street
New Britain, Conn.
December 3, 1944

Dear Brother,

How are you today? It's colder than a bluebird's wing out here. The temperature this morning was 8 above 0. Donny is down at Moon's pond skating now. Today is Donny's birthday. He's getting so he doesn't want toys anymore. Remember for Xmas how he always wanted toys and I gave him the gloves and he almost kicked off. I shouldn't talk. I'll never forget that black briefcase you gave me. Boy, did I cry. I just sat there bawling and making faces at you. I certainly was a pip.

We received five letters from you all at once Friday. Three were V–Mails and two airmail. The typing was very easy to read, too.

We were happy to hear about Irene Manning. It was a job well done

If you must know about Jim, I'll tell you. He's a cadet at Admiral Ballard Naval Academy. He's seventeen and very nice. Isn't it funny how I go big for fellows whose fathers are in the construction business? I'm only kidding. George DiAngelo, that big handsome brute. He's a case for the birds, if they can find him. This Jim Arute did not go with Lorraine Henry. That was his cousin Jack. Got it?

Dad went hunting up to Cornwall yesterday afternoon. He came in about 12:30 last night. They couldn't find the place to go hunting so they sat over to Buck Miller's house and chewed the rag. Some rag.

You certainly have a hot time with all your girls. But you love it, don't you??

I'm sending this picture of Ma and Pa. You said a while ago you wanted one.

I guess that's all for now.

Love and kisses, xxxxxx
Betty

P.S. If you kid me or say anything about Jim, I'll fix your wagon good. I wouldn't mind but everybody reads my letters. Get it, Kid!!
P.S. Ma went to a bazaar last night. Some sailor (his name is Tommy) was there. He's going to come to see me this afternoon. I only saw him once but I'll take care of him. But good!

Connecticut College
New London, Conn.
December 4, 1944

Hello, Darling,

I deserve a good swift kick and I know it. I just finished promising you I won't stop writing and then I don't write for a solid week. Honestly,

Charlie, I'm terribly sorry. Xmas is coming on and they seem to think they have to send us home in a state of total collapse from over-work. I had a huge chem. test last Friday and I spent most of last week cramming for it. I'm pulling off a snazzy D in chem. so far so I had to really shine on that exam. I don't know how it turned out but it better be good after all that effort. Anyway, to get back to where I started – I'm awfully sorry –and I hope I'm forgiven. It wouldn't be so bad only that last letter I wrote was such a stinker. This place gets on my nerves about this time every year and I get mad at everybody. Someday you're going to tell me to go to hell – and I guess I deserve it.

I rode home on the bus to Hartford yesterday with Nancy – she isn't coming back next year. Little old Conn. is too tough – she doesn't think it's worth it. Maybe she's right. She's going to some school in New York, I think.

Speaking of New York, I'm going to take an apartment there after I graduate. Minch (she's the one I roomed with at Briarly) will graduate from Smith the same time I'll get out of here - so-o we're going to get an apartment and work in New York. Sounds quite gay, don't you think? But two years is a heck of a long way off.

I've got some great news to tell you. It isn't supposed to be announced but I guess you can't tell anyone (by the way, please don't) – Min is going to have a baby. I can hear you blowing your top now. Who ever would have thought that of Miss O'Hare! But I think it's wonderful – and I hope it's a boy. But it won't be till spring – so don't broadcast it, huh? I suppose you'll write and tell everyone – that's what I love about you, dear – you're so trustworthy.

Ten more days and I'll be out. Three whole weeks of being a lady of leisure! But kind of a bored lady of leisure I'm afraid.

By the way – I haven't heard from you since last Monday. Maybe that had a little something to do with my not writing. Has Cheryl taken my place? Or have you found Dorothy Lamour on the island?

I have to copy an Eng. paper before I can go to bed – and it's twelve so I'd better get started. Take care of yourself, Jasper, and write soon.

Love 'n kisses,

Launa

Naval Research Lab.
Washington, D.C.
December 4, 1944

Dear Charlie,

Your mood certainly has changed for the better. Your letter certainly put me in a good mood. I'll be looking forward to hearing some of those stories as disgusting as they may be.

I'll probably be sorry as you say, but I don't feel ready for marriage yet. I've got so many things I have to do before I take that beloved step. I'm entertaining and thinking about the engagement but haven't taken any steps yet. You certainly have got it bad, I guess, you've always loved her but let other things get in the way. If I were as madly in love as you are I'd get married tomorrow.

Saturday night Helen and I went to a dance at the Teacher's College. We had no tickets or pass of any kind. The door was open so we walked in. It was the Junior Prom. Morry was there with Nancy Halloway. I think they're both wrapped up for good. I ran across that old girl Patty Lou who is just as cute as ever. Peggy Glacin, Irene Stagaria, Gloria Brody (chubby) and quite a few others were there. We had a good time but things weren't like they used to be. All the old crowd has shipped.

After the dance we went over to Helen's and she made coffee and we had a little party.

I came so close to asking her the question, I shudder to think.

Sunday was spent in a quiet way. Church, dinner, lounging around the house and I dropped in to see Ginnie Campbell. She told me all the local scandal and we gossiped about everyone and everything that happened and is going to happen. I'm planning on a ski trip with Ginnie, her boyfriend, Soupy and myself. You will probably frown upon it but such is life.

So you can't wait till I ship out, you old turd you. I hope I draw some FO job. Then will you be pissed off.

Monday Afternoon

I just got a letter from Al, he sounds in swell spirits. Every time I get a letter from you or Al, I feel like an FO.

Army beat Navy 23 – 7. Do you get all the news by radio?

Tuesday Dec. 5 -0650.

I had exams Friday. C+ and A were the grades. Just one more exam and I'm through. You should get this letter about next Wednesday. Well, I'll be taking the exams then and right after the exams we'll get our orders. I've been looking forward to that date so long it seems hard to believe it's here. I still got my eye on a cruiser.

*Write and tell me about the beautiful natives. You must think they're
white by now.*

Your friend,
Ben

17 Anise Street
New Britain, Conn.
December 5, 1944

Dear Brother,

*How are you? We received your letter Friday noon. Thanks for the two
bucks. I was just thinking what I should get you for Christmas.*

*A few days ago Mother went down the cellar and looked in the cabinet
and the covers were off some of the jars so daddy took a few traps and set
them in a box yesterday. We caught one rat that was about 9 inches long,
today we caught one that was about 4 inches long. So we set them again
but to get off the subject about rats for a while.*

*Daddy is a tight wad so I don't think we are going to get a Christmas
tree this year.*

*Daddy and I just got finished cleaning the guns out. Well, I got to get
ready for bed now.*

Love,
Donny

*P.S. What kind of pictures are they, pin-up girls? If they are you should
get 100.*
P.S. Forget the tight wad stuff – it was just a joke.
*P.S. Guess what daddy got me for my birthday. 4 POUNDS of peanuts
and they are all gone.*

Edgewood Park
Briarcliff Manor, N.Y.
December 6, 1944

My dearest Snookums,

*I was so surprised to receive a V-Mail letter from you, personally I like
your personal letters better. But gosh darn – it was swell to hear from you
again. Honestly, I wrote you a nice big fat letter about a month ago and I
have been waiting to hear from you. I kept telling Dick to tell you that you
owe me a letter. Now were even, o.k?*

*Only two more weeks and I'll be home for Christmas. I know it won't
be too much fun after all – you and Dick won't be there. Just imagine New
Year's Eve without you (and Green) to give me a kiss! Heck I hope someone*

391

will be home to have some fun with. Darn you, you didn't know when you were well off at Harvard – home whenever you cared to come practically.

I think I'll be working at Parker's this vacation and just think – you won't be able to steal any hankies or perfume for your Aunt for a present. I hope you don't think I'm trying to gloat or make you feel badly (as if you could) honestly I'm just kidding around.

These last two weeks before vacation are full of exams. Cripes—I feel I'll be too learned when I leave this den of iniquity. I just spent practically the whole afternoon studying for a Medical Practice exam. What a course this is but the good part is that I really feel as though I have learned something.

Last Saturday Ryan, Martin and I spent the day in New York and had a rip roarin' time. We went to the Paramount Theater and saw "And Now Tomorrow" and heard Andy Russell. I swear he is the second Frankie. Then we had dinner at Stouffer's and had time to window shop. The stores in New York are so crowded they have to have traffic directors inside them, imagine! We still had time to spare so we went to see Abe Lyman and "The Very Thought Of You." If you happen to get the chance to see that picture, don't miss it. I haven't sat through such a good picture in years. Abe Lyman literally stunk!!!!!!!!!

The night before we go home for vacation is supposed to be Hell night. All the seniors come around about 5a.m. and throw water at all the juniors and pull us out of bed. If anyone disturbs my sleep they can start bucking for the Purple Heart. What a dead head, huh?

I don't know if I told you in my last letter that I am on the tennis team and, boy, am I getting to be good. We have practice every Monday plus two other periods every week. All I want out of all this is a E.P. tennis jacket.

Mother wrote to me today and said that Jean Holcomb's father died of a heart attack over in Holland November 16. Tings is rough all over.

Meg and I are planning some big times when we get home – boy! oh boy! I'll be able to smoke when I want, eat and sleep when I want. I can hardly wait.

They laughed as I came out in my shorts, but when I bent over, they split.

They laughed when I sat down to read the evening paper. How was I to know the john door was open?

I nearly died the other day. I got a V-Mail Christmas card from Louie Carlo. I brought my class book up to school – the kids howl when they read some of the names.

I told you before that all the girls want to know who the picture of the Marine is on my dresser. They all want to meet you some time! I keep telling them that you are the Moron, Wolf and Clown of New Britain – but that doesn't seem to make any difference to them. What can I do??

This Saturday the Med students are having a dance. We're supposed to get fellas from Cornell, Yale, Columbia and a few other places. No doubt I'll get some four-eyed civilian. Just my luck. Well, cuddle bunny, this is all for now. Have as Merry a Christmas as you possibly can. It won't be too long before you will be home again.

> *Love 'n poiple passion,*
> *Mary Jo*

How are you coming on my hula skirt?

> *Sixth Marine Division*
> *FPO San Francisco, Cal.*
> *December 8, 1944*

Dear Sis,

I just received the letter you wrote when you were sitting by the telephone waiting for an invitation to the Yale – Virginia game. I saw the Yale – Dartmouth game last year with Sara P. I hope that Yale gets beat royal. The Yale Bowl isn't so hot. When you're in training up in Boston, I'll come up often and I'll show you the Harvard stadium. Now that's something. So start studying so we can do it, huh? Maybe I'll go back to school in Boston after the war but I sorta think I'll go to New Hampshire or Vt.

You must know what Mrs. Wheatley told you is strictly on the q.t. Her son and I were pretty good friends. He's with an outfit about sixty miles from here.

I still remember Barbara Larson as a freckle-faced anemic looking kid. I guess Rhododendron Nealon will be driving a car when I get home.

Have you been up to see Helma lately? I'm going to send her an Xmas card. If she's still at the Memorial Hospital, she'll get it.

I'm sending everyone I know cards. Give them all a break. Even Father Brophy. I've got seven or eight made up. Only about fifteen to go.

Does Bobbie Cabelus dance now? You and his friend (the dogface boy) and Jean used to cut up the cement in the cellar. Do you see Jean very often?

I tried out my flashlight last night and it works pretty good. Darn good, in fact.

A joke (you know, what you laugh at.)

A Rabbi went to an east-side tenement and knocked on the door and said, Rabbi – "Madam, I've brought you the gospel."

Mrs. Goliding – (calling her husband). "Jakey, you forgot to pay the gas bill." (Laugh anyway).

Gotta write to Launa Darcy now. Bye –

Love,

Charlie

P.S. I hope that five spot is on it's way.

232 Mountain Drive
West Hartford, Conn.
December 8, 1944

Dear Charlie,

I don't wait weeks before answering your letters. I always sit right down and answer immediately – so there, too! Pretty soon Ben will be overseas and then I'll have the two of you hounding me – I might just as well give up my job and sit and write to you both all day.

And shame on you for inveigling me into gossip by saying it's just news and by calling it "scuttlebutt." I don't care what you say, gossiping is a lowdown trick, but I love it – don't you?

There's one person I won't talk about though, and that's Ben. You two are much too friendly and if I have anything to complain about it I'll do it to him. I will say, though, that we are getting along pretty well (oh joy!) and I feel very good about the whole thing.

I think your problem about Cheryl is solved. Keep writing to her. So far as I know she received a letter from you in which you set forth all the things you wanted to get straight, like the fact that you do write to other girls etc. I think that you should write and be friendly enough. Sometimes we girls take things too seriously and we need to be straightened out. She's a nice girl, once you learn to ignore her possessiveness.

I've been running around like mad to get my Christmas shopping done. Everything is very expensive this year and most of the time the stores have just sold the last thing you wanted in the size you want.

By the way, the dictionary I bought you and haven't as yet sent is quite small and doesn't have many meanings for the words, but it's a Webster and I wouldn't take anything else.

Thanks for the advice on the desirability of an educated wife. I've also seen some highly educated people who are as repulsive as sin – in fact, I work with a couple of individuals who think they are Mr. & Mrs. God Almighty, and we have some gay times because I refuse to acknowledge the supposition. Anyway I don't think a few courses would hurt me and I would rather enjoy a little studying again. Thanks also for you compliment on my personality, or whatever it is you think I have. Some day we'll really have to get to know each other, except by mail, and then you'll find out about the things I haven't.

Don't you think that whatever clicks stays clicked longer if people have things in common? I can't think how awful it would be if I married somebody and, though we were madly in love, just couldn't get along. Of course, I don't believe in love at first sight, so I imagine that people who do fall in love spontaneously have to find out about each other after they know they're in love. But I believe you can't love anyone without knowing him or her and finding out what there is to fall in love with. To me, love at first sight, or the click that is necessary to you, can only be physical attraction. 'Nuf said on that – I'll be getting way off the track.

(Did you think your typing was bad? Look at mine, and I work at it all day.)

I should say that your old flame is all aglow. Six letters should have sent you reeling, depending, of course, on the type of letter. Are you writing back and forth again? Don't make things too easy for her. I wish I knew her – I'm sure she's very nice. But like all other women she wants to keep a man guessing.

I just wrote a short letter to Ben. If scolding him produces longer letters, I'll have to start being a shrew. I'm afraid I could easily slip into the habit of nagging, and that's why I hate to start scolding. Besides you need the long letters ,more than I do, so I'll grin and bear it.

There isn't much news in this letter, just a lot of trifles, but it's long. I double-spaced so you could read between the lines – then you'll have twice as much as I've written.

Your poem next time, my pet, 'cause I'll have to go to the library and I won't have the time for a couple of weeks anyway.

> *Affectionately,*
> *Helena*

4th Battalion 15th Marine
Sixth Marine Division
FPO San Francisco, Cal.
December 10, 1944

Dear Mom –

This is just a letter to let you know I haven't heard from you in ages. I guess it's the post office's fault. I got a letter from Launa today and it took nineteen days to get here. She said she's been writing every day. I hope to get a whole pile of letters soon.

Will you take about twenty dollars out of my bank and buy a present for Sis, Donny, Dad and yourself. I thought that I was going to get paid this month but we have to wait now until the fifth of January. I should be able to send home quite a bit then.

Nothing of any interest has been happening around here. We have classes for a few hours every afternoon. They are rather interesting and make the day seem much shorter.

I sent out about twenty-five V-Mail Xmas cards. I even sent one to Father Brophy. All the old girls in the neighborhood will get one, too. I guess I told you that I sent one to Helma.

Benjamin should be home for Xmas. I guess he will stop in and see you. Dick's folks may go down to S.C. to see him. Most everyone will be away this year. Launa said things are so dead she is afraid that she will get stodgy (she reminds me of Barbara Jason).

I'm still waiting to hear from Dad. Did he break his arm or something?

Well, Mom, I'm going to see Sophie Tucker in "Follow the Boys" tonight. I get a kick out of her. So I'd better sign off.

They gave me six cokes yesterday. Big deal! They sure hit the spot.

Love,

Charlie

51 Forest St.
Oakwood, Conn.
December 11, 1944

Hi, "Black Boy"—

How are you today? Seems as though you're in the best of spirits from all the super letters you've been writing me. May I ask what your source of inspiration might be? If it's my picture, I should have sent one ages ago – believe me I would have, too, had I known what its effects would bring. Then, too, it might have been the candy. I was so glad to hear that *they hadn't spoiled and that you enjoyed it so much. I'll get another box tomorrow and mail it to you since your Xmas box wasn't so good. That'll make up for it. O.K?*

I haven't gotten an answer to that shall I say "cool" letter I wrote you. You know, Chas, I practically sizzled when I heard you were in love and felt that you would have to tangle with me over it. Now that I've cooled off, however, I want you to know how I feel about things like that. You know we'll always be the same to one another no matter what, so why worry about all your weaker moments? In the meantime, just pore your little cupid heart out to me about your affairs. I'd just love to console you, Honey Chile.

This V.F.W. sounds quite interesting and it certainly offers a good opportunity for you since you'd like to go to college after the war. Have you written your Dad about it yet? Wonder what he'll think about it! And by the way – what's up between you and Ben? For you to say "I vant to be alone" makes me wonder. Truthfully though, if you want my opinion, you two aren't much the same. He's still rather flighty, if you know what I mean.

What's all this about your being entertained by the Campbell twins? Lucy Conway and Marie Fagan? You never mentioned this before – what's the story? Sounds like you took a special liking to ginger ale that night. Boy, it's a good thing your sister caught on when you got home, or your family might not have appreciated it.

Wasn't it nice of the Stanley Works to send you a lighter. Makes you feel as though you're finally thought about, I bet. What else have you gotten? Helena told me you asked her for a dictionary. Did you get it yet?

How's the food lately? Any better than it was the last time you wrote? Is there anything else that I could send you that might taste good to you? Anything – if so, do tell me.

Everyone here has been busy shopping for Christmas. It's so crowded in the stores that you nearly get knocked over. I waited in Davidson & Leventhal Sat. for my mother, and by the time she came I was a wreck. I still have a lot more things to get. Helena asked me for earrings so that's one present I won't have to worry about. I've got my mother's and father's to get and that is a problem.

Oh, Charlie, we had to give Debbie away last week because so many neighbors complained that she was scratching their storm doors etc. I miss her terribly, but she'll be happier where she is now, on sort of a farm where she can run as much as she pleases. I'd like to get another little one like Fluffy, but I'd no doubt get shot if I suggested it now.

I wish you could see the pretty new gabardine suit I got Sat. It's a tailored, ice blue. It looks nice on, too. Think you'd like it?

You wanted to know who Ruth, Norma, and Marilyn were. Well, they're all kids I work with, and don't worry about you're slipping because you didn't ever meet them, you see. Norma's from Plainville, Marilyn's engaged and Ruth went to St. Jos. — she's 21 — feel better now? You see, you haven't lost your Sinatra appeal at all — in fact, you'll be horizontal if what you say about your looking like him is true.

Did I tell you Jack Neuman is home? I saw him yesterday, and he looks good, but just a little drawn.

I got a V-Mail Christmas card from Billy Bean today. Remember he's the one I met three or four years ago on our vacation. He's in New Guinea now. I thought it was nice of him to remember me after all these years, but then he's not the only one — you haven't forgotten after all this time that's gone by since we last saw each other either, have you, you little devil you.

Well, Honey Chile, I'd better close so I'll have something to write about tomorrow. Be good —

Always,

Cheryl

P.S. I said Marie R. and Roger were engaged.
P.S.S. Note the green ink, also the grey envelope. Like the color combination?

Connecticut College
New London, Conn.
December 12, 1944

Hello, Darling —

No, I'm not mad or anything — just slightly burned around the edges. Just 'cause I used to get a letter every day and then didn't hear from you at all for almost two weeks — why should I be mad? I thought some Jap had hit you with his pea shooter, you jerk! At least when you don't hear from me you know it's nothing worse than an English paper or a math. test. I got three letters today — that helps some — but you're still not forgiven. And I don't know what you're talking about — only eight letters from me. For a while I wrote you every night — and I write at least twice a week. I don't think you're getting them. I'm not kidding you — that's the truth.

I can't imagine you any taller. Do boys still grow at 19? Or maybe you're only 18 – I can't remember. But I guess you were older than I am, huh? Anyway – shall I wear spike heels the next time I see you? Now tell me you've grown to look like Jimmie Stewart and I'll say yes in a minute.

It amuses me no end to hear how positive you are that we'll get married. To tell you the truth, my friend, I don't want to get married for a long time. So many of the girls up here are getting engaged or married – and we all feel kind of jealous now and then. But why should anyone want to tie themselves down at 18? I can't see it. "I'm too young and fair for all that." But wouldn't you choke if I said, yes? Just think, you'd be saddled with some female that can't cook or sew and hates to clean and wash. And don't tell me kissing is more important than cooking – you wouldn't think so if you were hungry, m' love. And to top it off, I intend to work for two years after I'm married – I know that would make you happy – yeh. And I'd probably never do anything you told me to. So – you'd better think it over before you go around proposing to strange women.

I started this up at school and never had a chance to finish it. Now I'm home and slowly going insane. I have to go and help Phoebe – so I'll mail this darn thing and write you again tonight. Damn, you have no idea what a hell-hole this town is without you, darling.

Love always,
Launa

4th Battalion 15th Marines
Sixth Marine Division
FPO San Francisco, Cal.
December 13, 1944

Dear Donny,

It sure was nice to hear from you. It seems like ages between your letters.

So you found gold in your ducks, huh? If you weren't a Cub Scout, I'd think you were telling a fib. Are you sure it was silver and not gold?

I'm glad that you're doing so well in your school work. You should get much better marks than Betty this time.

That four legged "gook" that I sent was all I could find. I asked the Chief of the village for a little fuzzy wuzzy girl, but he said they didn't have one your age. The cannibal was all he could spare for now. Does Princie get along alright with him?

399

So Betty paints the boys with lipstick? You'd better keep an eye on that sister of ours.

You aren't doing so bad yourself, old man, from what I hear about you and Irene. That Newington theater is quite a smooching place. Don't ask me how I know, 'cause I won't tell you.

There isn't much going on around here. That is, nothing exciting. I guess you are still anxious about souvenirs. Just hang on to your britches for a few months and I'll be able to fix you up fine. Is that okay with you?

Well, Don, I've got to hit the hay now. I'm in bed every night at nine. Taps are sounded at ten o'clock. I'll bet that you are a night hawk just like your sister.

Goodnight, sleep tight and don't let the bed bugs bite.

Your brother,
Charlie

Sixth Marine Division
FPO San Francisco, Cal.
December 13, 1944

Dear Dad—

I received your letter of Nov. 25 today and was really glad to hear from you. I wish you'd write to me more often.

We've been awfully busy here for the past few days. We moved our camp. We are now on higher ground and much nearer the ocean. This new tent of ours is super. We have four men in the tent and this one has a wooden deck. We had gravel before. Our tent is about fifteen x fifteen and is the pyramid type.

If you've noticed the envelope, you'll see that I'm a PhM 3/c now. Yep, you just can't keep a good man down. My rank on the test was 4.0 (that's 100% to you civilians.) Now I rate with a buck sergeant and get seventy-eight dollars a month plus the twenty-five percent overseas pay. That's not bad. I'll be able to send home about fifty dollars every month now. I guess it will go into effect the first of January.

When I told you we had latrines that wasn't punishment or E.P.D. (extra police duty). You see, all the fellows were corpsmen. It was sort of a transfer center. We had to dig and everything else. Now that I'm with this artillery outfit, my work is strictly medical. You know, I've never had a black mark on my record or been called up for anything, yet. That is, I've never been caught. My friend from N.C. never worked when we first hit this island. Things were so screwed up that no one knew where anyone was.

We used to swim, beach comb and explore the jungle all day, every day. I'll never forget those times. Boy, we had fun. After a person gets used to the service, he knows where and when not to dope off. I'm an old salt. I like this new work, however, and it's a pleasure doing it.

I received quite a stack of mail today. A letter from Donny and Betty, one from you, two from Cheryl, one from Helena (West Hartford), one from Ben and one from Lucy (Providence.). You see, your son is international. With all those war bonds of mine I'd better be careful or I'll wind up behind the eight ball as those poor Cabelus boys did.

I found a Jap canteen in the boondocks today. It has a bullet hole in it. Don't tell Donny but I'm going to send it to him if I ever get down to the post office. It's a nice souvenir. It has Jap writing on the bottom. I'd like to be able to send him more, but there isn't any around here anymore. The gooks sell them at outrageous prices. In about two or three months I'll be able to send him all he can use.

You asked me what we spent money on here. Well, I spent four dollars the other day. I bought two pair of shorts for $1.50 each and toilet articles. I spend about ten dollars a month.

Benjamin is always asking me about the hula girls here. I've seen about five of them and they had boobs on them that looked like shriveled pancakes with dried prunes on them. The natives also have every disease imaginable.

Do you know the difference between Mrs. Roosevelt and the Panama Canal? Well, one is a busy ditch and the other is a dizzy bitch. Well, I've got to answer some of my fan mail now so I'll close. Write soon.

With love,

Charlie.

17 Anise Street
New Britain, Conn.
December 14, 1944

Dear son,

Just received three of your V-Mail letters. I think if you wrote a little larger we could read them better. You asked for film — we can't get any around here. I've been trying to get some every time I go downtown. The next time I go I will get your shoes but I guess it will take a while to get them. I can't understand why you don't get our packages. I went to the Xmas Guild party and they had a few letters from the boys overseas, thanking them for their Xmas packages so I hope you get one and don't forget to write and thank them also at Stanley Tool.

401

Pa is 45. I invited a few couples in tonight, he doesn't know about it and Violet is coming over to play piano. So we will have quite a session. They can all get drunk on cider and then they can sing like the birdie do. Ha, ha!

Well, I've been trying to do a little Xmas shopping but everything is so expensive.

We got a bond today.

Donny doesn't want much this year. I bought him an airplane model and a knife to cut them out with. I don't know what I will get for Betty – almost anything I guess. Pa is still working alone. John left already. I wonder how long he will stay. We were down at Cabeluses Sunday and Tag was home. Betty thinks he got awfully fat. He likes Brooklyn much better. I guess it's because he can come home every weekend. He said he likes the Marines better. He had his Navy suit on and it was so tight on him. He had it made that way – if he ever let one flicker it would split it. Ha,ha!

Well, I guess Betty and Jimmy are really getting serious. He took her to the show Sat. and she had a letter from him yesterday.

Donny is in the kitchen wrapping Dad's present. He bought a cigarette lighter and three brushes. You know Dad never uses brushes but he'll say they are all right. He's been rolling cigarettes for Dad. They're hard to get and Pa pays him for them. He gets about 20 out of a 5 cent pack of tobacco. I hope he doesn't start smoking them. Do you smoke yet? I hope not. Well, I will close now for Don will mail this for me. Merry Xmas to you. I hope you will be home for the next one.

Love,
Mother

17 Anise Street
New Britain, Conn.
December 14, 1944

Dear Brother,

We received two V-Mails from you today. You acted a little mad, but I knew that you really weren't. Mother and Dad wrote a letter to you today. So I hope you get some mail now.

Guess what? Jane Rawlings had a baby boy. She's going to name him John Howard.

Last night we had an earthquake here in New Britain. It lasted only about 6 seconds. It was about 11:15 and the whole house shook. It was nothing serious though, but it scared the heck out of me.

Princey came home today with a big long rope on him. I guess someone tried to steal him.

Tomorrow is our last day of school. We have 19 days off. We had our "Tale Of Two Cities" final today. I hope I passed it.

Today is Pa's birthday. He's 45. We're having a party for him tonight. Violet's going to be here. I suppose Donny will ask her to make that monkey face.

Jimmy Arute and I went to the movies last Saturday and then to Gabers. He's really a character. He hates high school and all its Rah Rah's and calls them "Precise tools." He's coming home again the 22ⁿᵈ until New Years.

Gee, I certainly wish you were going to be home. I hope by next Xmas the whole darn war will be over. I guess that's all for now and have a nice Christmas (if you can).

> *Lots of love and kisses, xxxxxx*
> *Betty*

> *17 Anise Street*
> *New Britain, Conn.*
> *December 14, 1944*
> *My Birthday – 45*

Dear Son,

I got your letter where you say you are in a light artillery outfit, and you wanted some information about joining the V.F.W. Well, you can do as you please, I don't think it will hurt you one way or the other, you could also join the American Legion at the same time. All these Vet. Organizations will do all they can when the men come home.

Also received you letter yesterday about wanting a pair of loafers. These I will get for you sometime this week, also the film you asked for, if I can get it. This letter was received today.

No doubt mail not reaching you, Sonny. I don't know what to think. Betty writes at least three times a week or more, Donny throws in a letter about an average once a week and Mother writes either once or more every week. Well, myself, I wrote you once since I came home from the hunting trip about three weeks ago, the last time I wrote and you have undoubtedly got that letter by now.

Today is my birthday. Got thru work about 3:00 and came home to find mother putting a candle on a cake for me. Imagine! Lala and Fanny were also over and we all had a highball. They just left. I thought I ought to get this off to you so that you may get it for Christmas. It seems so long for a letter to get there and a reply usually takes the better part of the month. I hope this finds you in the best of health and that you have as happy a Xmas as possible. It seems you are over for a couple of years.

We've all been busy at home, myself working every day and Donny, Betty and Mother doing a little Xmas shopping now and then, buying the usual presents for all the relations etc. Donny just got home from school this very minute, 3:45, and he brought in an ash tray made of pewter that he made in school. This I suppose is one of his presents from him to me. Mother got me a tie and shirt. Lala was the only one who remembered me with a birthday card. What else could I expect, my old girls all seem to have forgotten me. Speaking of girls (Flash) Jane Rawlings had a boy yesterday, that's news. Drop her a card or something telling her how you are doing out there in the jungle, that ought to give her a laugh.

Buck Miller called about going hunting on Saturday. We're going up to Cornwall where you got that big buck.

This is about all for now, son. I'll try to prod them into writing more often, so good luck for the Xmas holidays, I hope this finds you feeling fine.
Your Pop

Brooklyn Navy Yard
Brooklyn, N.Y.
December 14, 1944

Dear Charlie,

I finally got my orders. I've got a destroyer the John A. Bole (DD775) detail in Brooklyn. And I got 9 days leave and 1 day traveling time. I'll have to report back December 27.

There were quite a few amphibs assignments so I consider myself lucky to get a destroyer, although I wanted a cruiser. From all I can pick up from the old salts, she's a new job being fitted out. I'm hoping she is for I want to see Sam in his Ensign uniform before he and I ship out. He's got about a month to go.

I take it you've been transferred or something of the sort because I haven't gotten any letters for over a week.

Last night I went bowling with a few buddies. It's sure going to be tough to leave all the fellows. I still don't know whether I'll make RT 2/c but I've got my fingers crossed.

You'll probably cuss me up and down for writing such a short letter but....

I am going to spend a few days at the Ranch Camp. They had 5 inches of snow a week ago and a recent snow storm .I'll write when I get a little time.

Your friend,
Ben

Sixth Marine Division
San Francisco, Cal.
December 17, 1944

Dear Sis,

It's been a few days since I wrote last. We've been awfully busy around here and the time goes by awfully fast.

I received two packages today. One was from Boston and I can't imagine who sent it. There were lots of good things to eat in it. The other package was from the church. I haven't opened it yet. I'll keep it till Xmas.

I went to church this morning and this afternoon we inventoried our medical supplies. Interesting!

The mail station stinks as per usual.

So you can tell by the letter I'm in a grouchy mood. I always am when I just wake up. I fell asleep for an hour after supper.

We are supposed to get paid tomorrow. I still can't believe it. I've received ninety dollars in the past four months. Starvation wages if I ever saw them.

I suppose that you'll be doing a lot of skating over Xmas and New Years. How is Donny coming along? Does he still run around on his ankles?

Well, I've got to close this letter. Be good and watch the construction gang

Love,
Charlie

17 Anise Street
New Britain, Conn.
December 18, 1944

Dear Brother,

I received two letters from you yesterday, so I thought I'd better answer today.

Aunt Anna is here now. She and Mother are going to the movies tonight. They both love Joseph Cotton. He isn't playing in the picture, but they'll perhaps find someone they like.

405

Yesterday I saw the picture "Laura." Gene Tierney took the part of Laura. It was an excellent mystery picture. I'll have to look up the book and read it.

Jim came home yesterday for the weekend. We're going out tonite to a movie or something. There's a neat show in the Roxy (only fooling, we're going to the State).

We only have one more week of school and then vacation. It doesn't seem much like the Christmas season now though. I hate the thoughts of Xmas shopping. I haven't any money anyways. Don't tell me to get a job either 'cause I don't want one.

I'm enclosing tonite's Home Front Digest. Ma sent one last week also.

Donny shot a big rat up by the chicken coop. He was on the coop when he shot it. He said it was flying through the air.

You asked about Myrt, Peg and Eunice, well, Myrt is going to N.B. High again – she's tagging a p.g. in Nursing. Peggy is working at the college and Eunice is working in some factory office. Myrt says she's going to school so she won't have to work.

That's all for now.

Love and kisses, xxxxx
Sister Betty

P.S. You know darn well you like Cheryl. G'wan (only fooling, honest).

9 Arthur Court
New Britain, Conn.
December 22, 1944

Charlie, darling (sounds good, mmmm) –

I'm sitting in the dining room drinking coffee to try to keep from freezing completely. It's down to 10 and I'm sure it's not more than 15 in this house. The old furnace is on its last legs. I guess maybe it's a good thing we're selling the house, although I hate to in a way. But let's don't go into that. And I suppose you're sitting down there on your island nice and warm. Good old New England! Don't let me kid you – I love it.

Today is a good day. I managed to get three whole packages of cigarettes! Don't laugh – that's like finding a gold mine. I stood in line in Liggets for 20 minutes to get one miserable pack of Phillip Morris – which I loathe. I tell you – we civilians have a tough time.

Sharon, Phoebe and I went to the movies tonight. Boy – all this night life is going to kill me. I don't think I have ever been so bored in all my life. There's just nothing to do. At least up at school I have something to keep me busy all the time. I've tried reading some hot books, but I must be slipping 'cause I never get interested enough in who is making love to whom to finish them.

I went into Parkers today and saw Mary (is that who I mean?). She's cute—looks full of the devil. She asked me if I ever heard from you – is she kidding? She said she looked forward to your letters because you were such a riot. So we decided you were a hot rock – and she told me she didn't have any stockings, and that was that.

Patty Lou and I went to Hartford last Sun. She looks quite glamorous lately. She's still working in Manning's. We went in and had a cocktail to celebrate the great reunion and went to see Cab Calloway at the State. We polished it off with a dish of Italian spaghetti. She's a great gal – I told her I was going to marry you just to see the reaction. It was just what I expected. But don't worry darling – I like you – very much. My, aren't I sweet lately?

You made some crack about my skiing, Goop. I did learn to ski but you never saw me. I used to go up to Black Panther almost every week with George Howe and those kids. Where were you? I guess that was one of the times we were off – we always were more off than on. And about that week up north after the war – I accept your invitation. I never did like people with their nasty ideas. Maybe we could take George along as chaperone. By the way, Fido sends you his love. He misses you to growl at this Xmas. I sort of miss you to growl at, too.

You say the dumbest things. I'm not afraid you'll get tired of me. It's just that I can't see how people can stay married to each other for years and years. I should think they'd get sick to death of each other. What happens when the moonlight and roses stage is over? I suppose they sit and talk about good books or something. How gay! I'd go nuts. Maybe I'm an advocate of free love and don't realize it. But I doubt it.

You keep telling me to make up my mind, Charlie. How can I when I haven't seen you in a year? I'm waiting to see how you turn out, m' love. Maybe we'll both be so changed by the time we see each other – well, anyway – you get the point. I honestly don't think you'd care to be married to me. As I told you before, you want a little yes-girl. Did I ever tell you I intend to work after I get married? I hate aprons and I won't be stuck in a grimy little kitchen for the rest of my life. You see, Stinky, the moonlight and roses isn't the only angle.

You asked me about what you should do — I'd say no definitely to journalism. Maybe I'm wrong — but that's awfully indefinite, And writers are a dime a dozen. That interstate commerce sounds good. And so does law if you want to spend that much time in school, I'm glad to hear you have some ambition — 'cause I've got gallons of it. I'm going places and I expect you at least to keep up with me. Nasty crack, huh?

I could rave on for hours but it's one o'clock and besides, this is too long already. Goodnight, Goop — I wish you were here. 'Nuf said.

Love always,
Launa

17 Anise Street
New Britain, Conn.
December 23, 1944

Dear Brother,

How are you today or should I say tonite? Mother and Dad went to a party for Joe Henry tonite. (He's home from the Pacific after about two years.) Donny's in bed so I thought it would be a good time to write to you.

I was just listening to "Jam Session." It's a program with all the best records in Jazz.

We got out of school yesterday for our Christmas vacation. I went shopping with the girls this afternoon and tonite with Aunt Anna. I'm worn out. Christmas shopping sure is a problem.

This was really sharp about the kid who had "the bug". I bet you just stood there and pretended to know what he was talking about. (Didn't you?)

I wish you would please tell me what type of medical work you're doing. O.K.? (If you're doing any.)

Dad bought three new records. They are "White Christmas" and "Adeste Fidelis" by Bing Crosby and "Meet me in St. Louis, Louis" by Judy Garland. Dad always was a pip at picking out records, but these weren't too bad.

I saw Launa downtown today. I didn't speak or anything. Perhaps she doesn't know me anyway. She looked very nice.

You know that Dad wouldn't let me drink hard cider, even if it helped me to do my work. Launa must certainly sleep "tight."

Dad's party was pretty hot the other night. Violet played practically all night without stopping and Dad got lots of ties for presents. He also got some shirts, socks and hankies.

I think I'd better go to bed. I'm getting sort of tired. I'll write again soon. Goodnight.

Love and kisses, xxxxxx
Betty

P.S. Merry Christmas and a Happy New Year.
P.S.S. Bill Ziegler got married quite some time ago. (Perhaps I told you). Junie will perhaps be next. Donny Ziegler is being shipped out. Freddy is on his way across.
P.S.S.S. We're glad you got the fruit cake. How do you like it?

Sixth Marine Division
FPO San Francisco, Cal.
December 24, 1944

Hello, little Darlin' –
   How's little Mono, today? I've been having fun all day.
   This morning after church I took the jeep and went way down the island to see Elon. I had to take a fellow down that way so that's how I happened to get the jeep. Anywho, on the way down we picked up three gooks. They were all in the bag. They gave us a swig of gizmo juice and I can't talk yet. It's a wonder my teeth don't drop out. One had an old broken down mandolin and he began singing "You Are My Sunshine" and "Shoo-Shoo, Babe" in English. I damn near died laughing.
   When I picked up Elon we went down to the Service Center and had cokes and ice cream. I also bought two shirts for five dollars. They are beautiful. Don't ask me where I'm going, you clown! I need them for my morale. If I have a nice shirt, clean trousers and my low shoes to put on, I feel perfect.
   I'm going to midnight Mass tonight. Christmas carols and everything.
   I opened the package from the church today and guess what? Olives, yep a whole bottle. There was also a box of candy, crackers and a small fruit cake. I'll write a letter thanking them soon. Well, I've got to go now. Bye, and don't get crocked over New Years.

Love and kisses
Charlie

4ᵗʰ Bn. 15ᵗʰ Marines
Sixth Marine Division
San Francisco, Cal.
December 24. 1944

Dear Mother,

I just finished dinner. I'm so full I could sit under a coconut tree and stay there for a week. I guess they planned on one turkey for each person. And ice cream! Gallons of the stuff. They served from two o'clock until 3:30. I'll be getting fat if I'm not careful.

Last night I went to the midnight Mass down at Headquarters. There were lights strung up to two palm trees, one on either side of the road. The big palm branches were all lit up with different colors. Between the trees, stretching across the road was a big Merry Christmas sign. It was really very pretty. I guess I'll never forget it.

I went to Communion at the midnight Mass. The altar was decorated with dyed parachute silk. They even had a crib. There were an awfully lot of fellows there. I think I'll write and tell Father Brophy about it when I thank him for the package.

My mail hasn't been coming thru at all lately.

Last night the movie "Jane Eyre" was here. They are also having a double feature tonight. Well, I guess that's all for now. Write soon and Happy New Year.

Love,

Charlie

17 Anise Street
New Britain, Conn.
December 25, 1944
Christmas Day

Dear Son,

Well, this is the day that we have all been looking forward to and hope that today you will enjoy yourself the best possible. Such is life.

It is now about 9:45 A.M, Mother, Betty and Donny have just come home from church. Myself, I am the usual heathen, but don't forget I do as much praying as the whole family, mostly so the war will be over and you can come home and start a natural life again.

While the family was in church, I played your Victrola practically for the first time. Betty was playing your records with Bobby C. last night and I happened to look over some of them. I played By-yu one of your favorites and it made me think of the times you always played that number. Also played White Christmas and Donkey Serenade, some others, I forgot the names.

410

Donny got up at 5:30 this A.M. to look over the array of presents, he got a lot of toys. I don't know what the rest got but I got plenty of shirts and ties. Aunt Anna, Freddy's mother got me a pair of house shoes. Your loafers were sent out by J. Keavers a couple of days ago and I hope that you are still at the same place and they finally catch up to you. I tried them on and they fitted me perfect, we couldn't get any narrower size. If they are loose fit in a piece of corrugated paper for inner souls.

Tag was home last weekend and I went hunting with him and Bobby up to Cornwall. Tag showed me where you brought down that buck deer. I always thought you got it in another place I had in mind. No, we didn't have any luck. Bobby got a cotton-tail, we had the two dogs with us but they didn't scare anything up.

Tommy got home from England on Wednesday. Tag also came home and we all went down to Glen Street, and what a reunion the two boys had, they were like a couple of sweethearts.

Freddy also came home during the weekend, they had dinner at the house yesterday but Donny and I happened to go ice fishing. He pestered me all week and I just had to take him although Mother was in a dither about us going. We went to McCoy's, just Donny and me, and what luck we had. Altogether we caught about 25 fish, We did bring home four nice pickerel from 16 to 18 inches and 6 nice size perch, just the limit. We stayed only a couple of hours.

In one of your last letters to Mother you said that I might have broken an arm for not writing to you. This is the fourth letter I am writing since I got back from hunting, wrote the last one on my birthday the 14th and Betty noticed I had the wrong address or wrong number of Marines. I believe it should have been the 6th instead of the 5th, probably all of the letters were addressed that way, I couldn't say, am sorry if you haven't received any of them although you might get them eventually.

We have plenty of snow here today, it's sleeting right now and Donny just brought me in a present from Mr. Farmer (a pack of Camels) what a real luxury. Natey Koppel also came in with a present, Donny didn't have one for him so he is around now looking for a half a buck to give him, Betty is upstairs trying to find the dough.

Joe Henry came home last week from the S. Pacific and he said that he was on Guadalcanal for a long time and it is now a big base. They had a party on him at Van's and what a party it was. We didn't get home until 3:00 A.M.

As for myself I have been working right up to Saturday and have plenty more for this week, something unusual for this time of the year.

Well, son, I hope you enjoyed the day and are getting along fine, I will try and write you at least once a week, am just beginning to realize that you should get more mail.

With love from the whole family,
Your Pop

9 Arthur Court
New Britain, Conn.
December 26 , 1944

Dear Goop,

I got your Xmas card a couple of days before Xmas – very cute. And I got five letters today – so I'm not doing bad at all.

So I was nearly a divorced woman – what a panic. You should have mailed the letter and let me read it. And stop trying to make me jealous of whoever is writing to you – it can't be done. I don't give a damn one way or the other, m' love. I guess that settles you. Do I give you a detailed description of the men in my life?—there are a few besides you believe it or not. Let's not be childish.

I started this yesterday but had to stop 'cause I was in such a foul mood. This place is beginning to get on my nerves. But now I feel better. I dragged poor Sharon out for a walk with me after dinner. It's snowing and it's just beautiful. We walked over to the park –by the bridge— and needless to say I thought of you and missed you very much. What a life.

You're a very smart little bird. You leave a very flattering picture behind you and then you bombard me with all those beautiful letters. It's very possible that between now and 1946 I'll slip and decide that I'm in love with you. But won't I just be kidding myself – and you? I think so. You can't decide you love someone when he's so far away. We'll have to wait 'til you come home to do any deciding. That's the only fair way to do it – yes? Please be content to wait. I know I'm being disgustingly sensible but it will be much more fair to you in the end, Charlie. Hell – this mess has dragged on and on for so long. I don't see how it will ever be settled. Oh, well – let's don't worry about it.

Phoebe met Mrs. Whipple and she asked her if I was home. Phoebe said yes, and Mrs. Whipple said "Well, you tell her that Roger is home!"

Is that my cue to run up and pay little Roger a visit? Now there is a man you really have to worry about. Honestly, what a panic. Does he look like the answer to the $64 question to you – well, he doesn't to me!

I saw Donald Leary up at the drug store last night. He said Mick is in the Philippines and wanted to know why I didn't write to him. What a question to ask me!

We didn't even have a Christmas tree this year. Everything is so mixed up about selling the house and everything. It's the first time in my life – and the last I hope – that we haven't had a tree. I didn't realize I would miss it so much. It really didn't seem like Christmas without one.

Phoebe is trying to chase me to bed. I've had a cold ever since I've been home and she thinks I'm run down – can you imagine me run down? What a farce! It's just this monotonous life that is getting me down. I'll almost be glad to get back to New London where something is doing. Goodnight, Stinky – I miss you too much.

Love always,
Launa

P.S. Have you been promoted, Goop?

9 Arthur Court
New Britain, Conn.
December 26 , 1944

Hello, Stinky –

This is going to be short 'cause it's late and besides I haven't anything new to tell you anyway. But there's a full moon and it's shining on the snow – well, you get the general idea. My thoughts aren't where I wish they were. At least up at school I can grind my teeth and wrap myself in some Chemistry or something and forget all about you. But here it's different. Oh well, let's skip the subject.

Maybe you already know it but Patty Lou told me today that Francine Valin has a rock as big as her head – from Lennie. They're supposed to be madly in love – ah bliss! I tell you, everybody's doing it – it gets discouraging. I'm beginning to feel like an old maid at 18 – in spite of the fact that I wouldn't be tied down for the world. (It says here).

Marvin bought me a fur coat today – bless his little heart. It was a Christmas present slightly late 'cause we couldn't find what we liked. I'm quite thrilled

Dear little (?) Benjamin came over to see me yesterday. I met him down town a couple of days before – he certainly has changed. It must be

413

at least three years since I've seen him – quite an improvement. He told me where you are – he's just been over to see your mother. By the way, do you know that I wouldn't even recognize your mother if I fell over her? But to get back to Benny – he'd been up north skiing. It sounded wonderful – it made me determined to go up north with the kids in Feb. after mid-years. We talked over old times – even the time he had a crush on me. I don't remember that but he assured me he did. What a riot. I'm afraid he thinks I'm in love with you – and always have been. What have you been telling him? Anyway, he's going to come back in 10 years and see how things work out. I can't get over the change in him. But his fingernails were dirty – stop laughing! That's the standard joke up at school – everybody kids me because I can't stand boys with dirty fingernails. They think I'm crazy – but there is something about it that nauseates me. A boy either is or he ain't – and if he has dirty fingernails, he ain't. Go ahead and laugh – everybody else does – even my family.

I went to a New Year's party last night in Watertown. I'm telling you about it because I know you can't begrudge me one date in three weeks. I stayed overnight with J.D. (she's a girl, cool off!) – she's the one that gave the fool thing. You should be very proud of me – I was one of the three females who didn't completely collapse – it turned out to be quite a brawl. You should meet J.D. – you'd like her – quite the ra-ra girl.

Well, Charlie – it's exactly one year ago tonight that I saw you. A year is quite a while. I went over to church alone this year. I was so darn lonesome I wished I hadn't gone. Then I took a walk over by the bridge. It's cold – and the stars are out. The little brook was bubbling like mad and I could hear the ice cracking – you know that hollow sounds that seems to go all across the pond. Hell, I hate to be alone. I seem to have a horror of being by myself lately. I used to love it – but now I give myself the creeps, I guess.

I go back tomorrow – when I think of what I have to do before Feb. I could curl up and die. Mid-years come at the end of Jan. and I have a 20 page English paper and a 10 page chem. paper due before then. So if the letters are scarce you'll know why, but I'll try and write often – honest.

Ginnie Campbell is going steady with a 16 year old boy. Patty Lou has taken to going out with a boy 17, and I've picked up the fellow who works on the fruit counter in King Cole's. I tell you – war is an awful thing. My little grocery boy is a Wop and he has seven stitches on his stomach. Never mind how I found out either – well, if you must know, he only told me about 'em. O.K. so I've never been out with him either. But he has got pretty brown eyes. Poor Phoebe nearly died as he was getting her some grapefruit and told her he thought I was wonderful and he wished he'd been out with me New Year's Eve—can't you imagine the expression on Phoebe's face. She was horrified! So we picked up our grapefruit and left – eh! that love should be so short-lived. – oh nuts!

This letter is much too long. 10 pages! I suppose I should be glad that there's no one to corrupt me with zombies – but somehow I'm not glad at all. I miss you, Charlie, more than I've ever missed anyone. Damn you to hell!!

Launa

12:45

Here's that girl again! I seem to have a hard time finishing this. I got a letter from you this morning and as usual you made me feel like a heel for not writing. I refuse to write every day – in the first place there's nothing to fill up th letters with. And in the second place, even if you were my husband, I wouldn't write that often. I just ain't the type. In spite of this my conscience still doesn't feel any better – grrr- you annoy me. Naturally. Life does have it's little bright spots.

Marvin can't seem to find an apartment in West Hartford. He's going nuts. Sharon gets sworn in tomorrow and will be leaving the end of January. We'd like to have some place to go by then but I'm beginning to doubt it. After thinking it over I'm not too gay about the apartment idea. I'm afraid I'm a country gal at heart and the idea of being five flights up overlooking Farmington Ave. doesn't exactly appeal to me. But so what? You must "come up and see me sometime" –what crap.

U.S, Naval Lab.
Washington, D.C.
December 27, 1944

Dear Charlie,

My leave is all used up and I'll be getting back to the old grind soon.

I got home from Washington Sunday 17ᵗʰ· That day Helena and I went to a movie.

You will probably be very disappointed in me for the next part of my leave. I took a train Monday noon for Vermont. I got there about 2000. I stayed at "Strons." (Erling Stron is a great Norwegian flyer) for Monday night. It was a swell stop except for the lack of fellows and girls my age. Tuesday I went skiing at the toll house on the open slope. I was a little shaky but I caught on in a little while and was doing a reasonable stem christy. My technique was pretty poor so I took lessons on Wednesday afternoon. We had a swell class. It consisted of a graduate from Harvard med, one from Cornell, and a Yale fellow. There were also two swell gals from Vassar (both blonds). I moved to the lodge Tuesday night for a little more excitement. We had a "ping pong" table and a tavern with no liquor. We danced and fooled around a little but we were all quite tired. Wednesday afternoon I learned quite a bit. The instructor was very good. Thursday morning we had about six inches of fresh powder, so Art and I decided to try the "Nose Dive." The snow was wonderful. I took a couple of beautiful spills on the seven turns but suffered no broken bones. Art sat on his ass going down a steep part of the dive and ploughed into a stump which sent him sailing in the air. It knocked the wind out of him and we thought he was really hurt bad. He didn't do anymore skiing that afternoon anyway but felt much better later in the day. Friday I went up to the mountain again and took the toll road in the morning and the dive in the afternoon.

I left Friday night and had the pleasure of meeting another blond from Vassar. She was even prettier than the others and was twice as friendly. She invited me up if my ship doesn't sail too soon. We rode all the way from Montpelier Junction to Hartford. She lives in West Hartford. I'll probably be sorry for not spending all my time with Helen but I can't see it. Saturday night I had dinner at Helen's, then Mary LePorte, another sailor, Helen and myself went to the Bond for a few drinks and dancing. Mary is about the same as ever, although her hair has gotten a little darker. Sunday night I visited my Aunt Rose in Hartford. My cousin Irene was there for Christmas. Monday (Christmas) I spent at home and with my Aunt and Uncle in New Britain. Tuesday I slept soundly and dropped in at Alpha. Pris asked how and where you were. Jane and Martha Baldwin were there, Ryan was there, I guess most of the older girls were present.

As you can tell by the writing I'm slowly slipping off to sleep. I rode a train last night and am quite tired. I checked in at the base at 0700 this morning and got a few things settled. My ship isn't here so far as I know. I had a liberty card made out and have liberty till tomorrow morning. I haven't decided whether to go home or stay here tonight. I think I'll stay here and get some rest. My mail hasn't caught up with me yet but I've got hopes of a few letters.

Your friend,
Ben

4th Bn. 15th Marines
Sixth Marine Division
San Francisco, Cal.
December 27, 1944

Dear Mother,

There isn't much to write about tonight. I wrote to Betty just last night. I got a letter from Ben and the most beautiful card you ever saw from the Farmers. They wrote little notes all over it and I really got quite a thrill out of it. I wrote to Fanny last night. Betty said she wasn't feeling too well so I thought I'd cheer her up a little.

Tell me about this gook Betty is running around with. Don't let Betty read this or she'll have a fit!

Benjamin has been assigned to a destroyer. He thinks he'll get another rate. Cripes, they don't even have to work for their rates, they just get them handed to them. That's because they need so many radio men. I guess I'm just a little jealous.

That Launa is a pip, no kidding. I didn't hear from her today. I'm going to give her holy h– when I write to her tonight. She gets so mad when I give her heck. If you knew how we argue through the mail. She's not a dead head like Cheryl.

So Tag likes the Marines, huh? How does he get along with his wife? I'll bet he's sorry he didn't look before he leaped.

I was snowed under when I heard about Jane having a baby. I'll bet that Grandma Rawlings darn near took the gas pipe.

I haven't heard from Dick in over two weeks. He must have been transferred somewhere.

Well, mama dear, I guess that's all I have to say for tonight.

Love and kisses,
Charlie

U.S, Naval Lab.
Washington, D.C.
December 29, 1944

Dear Charlie,

Some of your mail finally caught up with me. It was sure swell to hear from you again. I thought you had gotten into one of your pissed-off moods again. I am expecting one of your special letters pretty soon.

I did see Launa over Christmas. She sure was looking swell. I guess you know I had a crush on her once. I was walking toward the bus stop

417

when we spotted each other in front of the Strand. She was very pleasant. We said the usual greetings and went on with our shopping.

I was assigned to a pretty good detail, they made me M.A.A. I'm on for two days and off for the next two. I'll get New Years weekend off.

When I get my liberty, I'll see if I can pick up the film for you. Although I have my doubts as to my success.

What did you mean didn't I guess it was Launa? I wrote in a few letters I guessed it was she. You can trust me not to say a word. I did tell Helen before I received your letter that I thought Launa was the one, but I won't elaborate on the subject now that I know how it is.

I noticed on your last letter that you are a PhM 3/c. Good work!

So far as I can figure out, my ship hasn't even been commissioned yet.

Helen and I aren't on the same status as Launa and you. I don't know whether she loves me or I her. I think she's very nice, but between you and me I don't feel that deep love I should. If I'm stationed here for a while, I'm not going to make the mistake you think you did and date a few different girls.

I'll let you know how poorly I do with Martha, the gal I met in Vermont.

I'm getting to be quite a FO. I slept on my last liberty. I didn't even have the ambition to get a date.

I've got to be going now. I'll write as soon as I get another chance.

Your friend,
Ben

17 Anise Street
New Britain, Conn.
December 29, 1944

Dear Brother,

I just came home from school and found a letter from you. I also received one yesterday. It was the letter with all that crazy stuff in it that you didn't think anyone should see. But when I got home my mail was all opened up already.

You certainly have a nerve asking mother about Jimmie. I don't know what you think but I'll fix your boat if you make any nasty remarks. (got it, kid?)

New Years night was Jimmie's last night home so he had a few couples over for a gathering. (You know and not a smooching party.) He said he's not coming home till June but he'll be home before then. He's only in New London.

You certainly seemed to have a nice Christmas. It would be a good idea to write to Father Brophy and tell him about your Xmas mass etc. He'd appreciate it a lot to hear from you.

I'm now at Aunt Anna's house. I came down here for supper with her. Fred was suppose to go back today at 4:30 but he didn't go. He said he's leaving tomorrow morning.

There was skating yesterday and this morning, but the sun came out this afternoon and now it's ruined again.

Gosh, it seems awful to be back in school. Our next vacation is in February. Oh, well, I'll live through it.

Aunt Millie was wondering if you received her package yet. Fanny was very glad to get the letter from you. She's o.k. now but still a little nervous as usual. That's all for now.

Love & Kisses, xxxxx
Sister

Sixth Marine Division
FPO San Francisco, Cal.
December 29, 1944

Dear Dad,

I'm glad that you answered my last letter so soon. I w hoping you would.

I have a slight head cold now. It's so damp here lately. It rained all afternoon and everything is floating around here.

To hell with the VFW and AL. I was just hyped up about them for a minute. You know how I am when I get a brainy idea.

Some of the fellows (about 4) are being sent back to the States. I wouldn't want to go back now. The firing hasn't even started yet. Some of the fellows say the Sixth Division is getting a bit of publicity in the States. Have you seen anything about us?

From what I hear you had a pretty good birthday party. I'm sorry that I forgot about it but here it's hard to keep track of the days.

I guess I told you before that Benjamin has his orders to go aboard a Destroyer. I don't envy him too much. I had enough of the water on the trip here.

I can't tell you how bored I am with this island. I've never been in one place so long since I've been in the service. When we do move, I suppose

I'll be moaning and bitching. Time goes by much faster when you move around. I could be ready in five minutes if they would only say "go." Well, Pop, I guess I've covered everything there is to cover. Take care of yourself and don't work too hard.

Love,

Charlie

4th Bn. 15th Marines
Sixth Marine Division
San Francisco, Cal.
January 1, 1945

Dear Sis,

I wrote to you last night but I lost the damn letter.

Jan. 3, 1945

Eeeeeeek! I still haven't finished this letter! I'll finish it now if it kills me. It's so darn hard for me to write when I don't hear from you.

Cheryl hasn't written in ages. I guess it's best but she was a good supplier of mail. I guess I sort of "took her for a sleigh ride in the good old summer time." Remember that record?

That Launa will be the death of me, yet. She doesn't write for a whole week and then she writes telling me how sorry she is and that she adores me (Ga 'wan) and she'll write more often. She even says "honest." I get so mad that I could spit. I haven't written to her for three days. Boy, does she gripe when I don't write. But then she writes like hell and vice versa. Silly isn't it? You'd better tell Ma and Pa to stop reading your letters. Tell them if they want to hear from me they should write more often. If they continue reading your letters, I'll have to start feeding you the bull.

You know what I think I did? I think I wrote a real hot letter and accidentally put it in with Pa's letter. Something will be sucking wind if I did and it won't be my mouth.

Ooooooooooo. Everything happens to me .We have to give shots today. Hundreds of them. We also have to get one in each arm. Oh, my aching arms.

I had some pictures taken the other day. A gook came in with his little son. The kid had a cut foot so we bandaged it. Then my friend took my picture with the gooks and I took his. We borrowed a camera and a fellow let us have four pictures on his film. I'll send them home if they come out good, and don't ask which is me!

420

The food here is pretty good now. We had plenty of turkey for New Years and Christmas.

I just finished reading "A Tree Grows In Brooklyn." It was worse than "Tobacco Road."

Now don't break you leg rushing to the library. You wouldn't like it.

One of the fellows said the "Sixth Marine Division" was getting quite a build-up back in the States. Have you heard anything about it? I guess you know your big brother is leading a rugged existence. Bow Wow, Grrr! I chew nails and spit rust just for the fun of it. G'wan!

You know something, I'm bored. All this sleep and no fun is getting me down. The sooner we shove off the better. Tell me something, did the President make a New Year's speech and did he say anything about the Marines in it? The way the scuttlebutt (rumors) flies around here would make your head spin. Every time someone goes to the head (toilet), he comes back with all the "straight dope" as to where we are going. I'm just waiting for someone to say Siberia. That will be the end.

Well, little Darlin', I've about written myself out. Write soon and give me all the news. I'll try to write more often, but I wish you all at home would, too.

Your loving brother,
Charlie

17 Anise Street
New Britain, Conn.
January 1, 1945

Dear Brother,

Well, today is New Year s Day and what a day! It's raining like heck out, we only have one more day of our vacation left and then we go back to the old grind again.

I noticed on your last letter you had PhM 3/c. I see you got your rating. Tell me more. Do you have a better job now and etc.?

Last night Ma and Pa went out to a New Years party. Irene stayed here with me and Jimmie came down and we had a few kids over. Then we went up to Hetzler's where Barbara L. was taking care of kids. It was a wonderful New Years Eve.

Irene is still here and now she's playing the piano. The girls are coming over this afternoon.

Donny got a game for Christmas from Tessie. It's a gambling game called "Snake Eyes." He's been playing it every day since he got it. It's lots

421

of fun, but I lose too much money. At the end of the game Donny has to have the same amount he started with or there's trouble. (some gambler)

Benny was home for a few weeks and he came down to see us yesterday. He brought Mother a nice Poinsettia plant. He's waiting for his orders to be shipped out. He still the same old Hiiiii boy.

Freddy brought down some new records. One is "Rum and Coca Cola." It's swell. He lets us take the records for a few days and then he brings them home.

The girls just came over, so I guess I'll close now.

Irene and I didn't get our dinner yet so I think we'd better cook us something. Bye now.

Love and kisses, xxxxx
Sister

VT 29 F.P.P
San Francisco, Cal.
January 2, 1945

Dear Charles,

How are you and all of the rest of the gyrenes, all o.k. I hope. I don't know why I keep writing letters to you when all I get back is a lousy V-Mail and the typing is double-spaced, boy you can think of more ways of shortening letters than anyone I know so if the next one I get isn't a letter, you'll see how short a letter can be.

Well, Charles, how is the love life, getting much or are you being true to Launa? Sometimes I get letters from the women and sometimes I don't – boy – I can't figure these out but I guess they have fooled a lot better men than me, so what the hell.

I see Dick quite a bit and we sit down and shoot the s---for a couple of hours. I hope he and I are able to get home together, he has some pictures of some nice stuff from Plainville and Bristol so I got plans. There are about ten or fifteen of us from Conn here. Boy, if we all got together, what a time.

Do you remember Shirley from Torrington? One of the fellows here went to school and then worked with her, so I am really getting the word, but from it and the letters I have been getting from her I think I will have to take a trip up to see her some day while I am home.

Did you get your rate yet? I had plans for one once, but now I'm beginning to wonder how all these guys back in the States are getting them, however, I hope to get second before I get home.

I don't hear from the boys much anymore either— guess the liberty is too much for them back there. How is Bob getting along with his girl, are they married yet? I heard how he got engaged. Boy, how that guy surprised me, and everyone else, too, I guess.

I got a letter from N.B. today and the way it sounded Len and Francine got engaged but I don't know for sure. Well, I guess that's all for now, Charles. Be a good boy and write soon and I mean a letter.

Mick

17 Anise Street
New Britain, Conn.
January 3, 1945

Dear Brother,

The picture of the chapel and cemetery you sent was nice. I'm going to show it to Father Webb.

The Sodality and St. Francis Boy Scouts are giving a party for Father Webb. He's going to be 26. All the kids chipped in and we're going to give him money.

Sunday the C.Y.O. is sponsoring a communion breakfast at the Hotel Burritt for the Catholic High School students. It should be really nice. There's going to be a guest speaker and the Acapella Chorus is going to sing.

Also the High School Band Concert is Friday night, but I'm not sure if I'm going. Gosh, I've got to get a job somewhere. I'm always broke. I've been having some new clothes made and they cost money. Oh, well, that's all for now.

Love & Kisses, xxxxx
Betty

Connecticut College
New London, Conn.
January 4, 1945

Hello, Darling –

I got three beautiful letters today. By the way, did I ever tell you that you write the best letters of any male I correspond with? Well, you do. I love every one of them – even when you're in a bad mood.

I'm glad you finally heard from me – I was beginning to feel like God's lowest creature. It's funny, you're letters are so different when you haven't heard from me in a while. Sort of distant or something – but I guess I can't blame anyone but me for that, can I?

Charlie, you probably don't want to hear this – and I'm not trying to lecture again – just a bit of common sense. Please don't think about getting married and all that stuff so darn much. Not that I care – only you've got me doing the same thing and there's no future in it. You won't be home for a hell of a long time – and when you do get home, you'll want to go to college and get a decent job before you'll want to marry anyone. Everyone is the same way – they feel as if there's so little time that they have to grab at everything. I feel the same way. You have never seen so many diamonds in your life as the females up here are carrying around. Can I help but be jealous? But as I said – there's no future in thinking about it. It just ain't bright. It just makes you more discontent than ever. Do you see my point, or am I talking to the wall? We'll just have to wait so we might just as well take things as they come. Why do I always get all mixed up when I try to philosophize? Better shut up, huh?

About the size ring I wear – do I have to tell you what I'm thinking? I'll tell you because I'd like a "ring from the orient," – a "friendship ring" – and because I trust you not to be a crazy school boy, that should do it. I take either a 6 or a 6 ½. I can always have it made smaller and I'm really not sure.

I'll look for your film the next time I go down to the big city. It must be nice to have so many females of whom you can make such a request. That's a dig, you jerk!

I have quite a merry tale to tell you – you'll get quite a charge out of this. Before Xmas I had been going out with a stinky little sailor – S1/c – "little Dickie-boy". Sounds like a canary, no? He's a perfect ass, but he used to bring me cartons of cigarettes and even gave me two beautiful sterling silver pins! But I managed to frighten him to death so he didn't dare to hold my hand. Maybe I should be a school teacher. Well, anywho, I met him in N.L. Wed, night and nearly died of shock – he was supposed to have left the first of Jan. Now he's going to be here till Feb. But I decided I'd rather roll my own (you think I'm kidding?) than go through that all over again. He called tonight and was all set to spend Sat. and Sun. with me. But I wasn't all set to make with same. I had tried before to palm him off on somebody else – even got him four different blind dates. But no go. His mother must have been frightened by a homing pigeon. So tonight I told him I was announcing my engagement next week – where do I get those brainstorms? He wanted to know what the poor fool's name was. So-o I popped out with Charles Young.(See, you're on my mind?) He had to know all about you and he expects to meet you when he goes overseas – that should be pleasant. He wishes us all the luck in the world, darling, and knows you must be a swell guy to get me. Are you deeply touched? We've been having hysterics ever since I told him. Honestly, what women won't do for cigarettes! I wish you could see him just for the laughs.

What a stupid letter. I've had a splitting headache all day – a brain tumor, no doubt. So-o I've been acting like a fool and haven't done a bit of work. This letter is just about as whacky as I feel.

You asked me how tall I was 5 -7, no shoes. I won't discourage you by telling you how tall I am in spike heels.

You said one thing in your letter that sort of gave me the creeps. Quote: "I guess you know I'm not fooling around anymore". I sort of gulped at that. I haven't said I loved you (that I don't know) and I haven't said I'll marry you. I said I missed you and I do. And that's all I can truthfully say until I see you again. You know I'm not careful what I write, so blame it on the moon or something if I'm amorous. There's no sense in trying to explain any more – you know what I'm trying to say anyway, don't you?

Beth's grandmother died so she won't be back until Sun. (Beth, I mean). So Betty is going to sleep in here to keep me from getting lonesome. She's the type that likes to get to bed before 12 so-o I'd better start looking tired as it's 11:30. By the way, I'm doing pretty well on the mail, aren't I? I deserve congratulations, no?

My headache is gone for the first time since noon. See what you do for me? Goodnight, darling –

My love always,
Launa

51 Forest St.
Oakwood, Conn.
January 5, 1945

Hi, Honey Chile –

How's everything today? This is only going to be a quickie 'cause I'm writing it between customers, but as long as you know I'm still thinking of you is all that counts.

I called your Mother this morning and we had so many things to tell each other. It's funny, the first time I called her our conversation consisted mainly about you with a little bit about the weather. But now we cover most everything, including "the bottle of holy water" you expected from the church at Christmas. She told me about the Mass and the altar they fixed *for you boys. That was really swell, wasn't it? Must have seemed a little more like home.*

Did you know that Freddy was home over the holidays? Your Mother asked me whatever happened to him and Joyce? I don't really know either, do you? She has a lovely picture of him that she showed me just the other day and she appeared quite pleased with it, but something must have come up since then.

I got some sad news the other night. Roger told me that Billy Gingras had been killed. It must have been in the paper, but I didn't see it. Had you known about it? Gee, it's such a shock when you hear about these things happening to kids we went to school with. It's an awful thing.

You know I think I forgot to congratulate you on your new rating P.M. 3/c. If you don't slow down, you'll be a licensed physician soon with a little business of your own.(You know— like the master minds.)It's just about time for me to leave for lunch, so I'd better close. I'll write a nice long letter when I get home. Until then –

Always,
Cheryl

P.S. Has anything happened to your arm or pen? I'm not exactly swamped with letters from you.

Connecticut College
New London, Conn.
January 5, 1945

Hello, Stinky,

How do you like the stationery? I don't got none so I guess you'll just have to create a taste for lines.

This letter writing is getting to be a habit, aren't I wonderful? I didn't hear from you today – but I keep right on writing. What faithfulness! What dependability! What crap!

I'm sitting here like a bump on a log waiting for some horror who's going to be a Methodist minister – can you imagine! It's a blind date (again!) and he'll probably be worse than the average. I don't feel lucky tonight. I'm sure no other female gets stuck with more jerks than I do – it's pathetic. "Papa, won't you please come home." Don't worry, darling—my heart still belongs to Daddy and my taste doesn't run along ministers. Either he'll convert me or I'll convert him. I'll finish this tonight when I get home and tell you the story. My motive is purely to get out of the horrible Friday night supper – honest.

I spent three hours this morning cutting up worms. How gay. Have you ever peered at the intestines of a worm for 3 hours on an empty stomach (mine I mean, not his). Well, if you're ever invited, don't accept.

I'm going downtown tomorrow (big day) so I'll look for your film. Sweet, aren't I?

I don't like to be kept waiting by a darn minister! He's now a half hour late. I don't think I'm going to like him.

You asked me what I was going to do when I graduated – if ever. I want to take an apartment in New York with Minch – she's the one I roomed with up at Briarly. She'll graduate from Smith the same time I finish my sentence here. And get a job of course. N.Y. would be fun for a while – but not permanently. I'll probably end up in a stuffy old lab somewhere although I'd really rather go into business. – advertising is something. The buzzer just rang –

12:30

Not too tough – but still not my type. His father is a minister, too – how charming! He's a very nice guy but much too passive. Not even slightly crazy. In other words, he isn't the Knight on the White Horse – so I guess I'll stick with you, darling. Do you think I'll ever meet anybody as crazy as you are? I'm afraid not.

I'm dead tired and I can't decide whether to do my French now or tomorrow morning at 5:30. Guess it'll be tomorrow. That gives me about four hours sleep – great! Why don't I go to bed and stop boring you with all this stuff and nonsense, hmmmm?

Guess, I will. I'd rather write to you but I haven't got a darn thing to say. Wish you were here – we never seem to run out of things to say when we're together. I'm falling asleep. Goodnight, my darling.

Love always,
Launa

32 Sigourney St.
Oakwood, Conn.
January 5, 1945

Hello, darling –

Here I am again, see how much I think of you. This is my fourth letter this week and today is only Wednesday.

I'll bet from the above address you'll be thinking we moved and I don't know the number of the house, but we really haven't. You see Marilyn Winger stayed over at our house one night last week when Mother and

427

Dad went out and nothing would do, but that I come over for dinner and stay with her tonight —so that explains the change of address. Marilyn is the girl I told you about in one of my other letters – 'member my telling you about her engagement? We've been having a lot of fun together. Did you ever hear of her before? Well, anyway, she's writing to her John, and so I just had to write to you. You ought to see how we're in our pajamas with our hair up. She's lying across the bed and I'm sort of sitting in a chair with a box on my lap for a desk, and oh, how could forget to mention that Frank Sinatra is causing all his listeners to swoon – all but us, darlin', and we were just saying that he's kind of a poor excuse for a man.

Saturday night five of the girls from the office are coming over here for a spaghetti supper. Norma's mother can make the real sauce so she's bringing that and I'm just going to cook the plain spaghetti – that ought to be easy. Of course, the setting won't be quite like it was at St. Ann's Church since all these kids are as Irish as Patty's pig, but we'll get Italian bread, cheese etc. and it will be just as good   .

You know Ruth and I didn't go to the lecture after all last night. After supper we sat around talking with Mother and it was so warm in and so cold out that we decided to skip the lecture. We knitted instead and, Charlie, my sweater is 10 inches long now – isn't that wonderful? I'll have it finished before 1960 just to show you.

Tomorrow should be a good day for you, if the mail isn't being held up, you'll be getting my picture – it will be just eight days since I mailed it. I do hope you'll like it just a little.

I'm in sort of a dreamy mood tonight – you used to talk about all the little funny things we did together, too, but you haven't mentioned anything like that in so long – you're not beginning to forget me, are you, Charlie? You'll no doubt be laughing at me again but I was just wondering – I know you'll ignore all this because even when we were together, I always said it was like pulling teeth to get you to tell me things. The last time we went to the tower you were like I've always wanted you to be – remember I asked you why you ever came to be with me on your last night home – of course, you said a lot of things that night, but it's been so long since then, that I wonder if you are changed.

Something tells me we'll have wonderful times together and with the kids we know when you come home. I'm looking forward to these days more than you'll ever realize. You said once you could hardly wait. Don't change, darling.

I'd better stop, it looks like Marilyn is nearly through, too. I'd forgotten she was here. Funny how I forget everything around me when I write to you. Guess I concentrate too deeply.

Aren't you going to write to me this week at all? If when I call tomorrow Mother says no mail again my whole day will be ruined. I won't really give up and feel awful until Sat. (Cause I just know I'll have one letter tomorrow or Fri.). I told you that you have spoiled me writing twice a week. Now I expect that all the time. Marilyn gets a letter every day but John is only in Texas. I'm quite pleased with two a week, especially when you consider the distance. Oh, Guy Lombardo is on the radio and he's playing "Frankie and Johnny." Remember the night we saw him at the State?

Can you tell me anymore about the hospital? You've no doubt got more than three patients by now. Tell me all you can when you write.

Hope you're being a good boy and are still keeping your clothes on after six like you should. You know that sounds bad to anyone who didn't know what I mean. But no one else sees this but you, and I'm sure you understand. Night, my dear – write soon.

Yours,

Cheryl

P.S. Did you know Marie Keegan and Roger Cowles were engaged? Well, he's home on furlough and they seemed so happy together today. I met them in the bank. I'm sure you know Marie anyway. She seems to be a nice kid.

P.S.S. You'll overlook all the cold cream smudges, won't you?

Love again,

Cheryl

4th Bn. 15th Marines
Sixth Marine Division
San Francisco, Cal.
January 6, 1945

Dear Sis,

That letter I got from you was a pip. One sheet of stationery and torn in half at that. You really, really charge me at times.

I read the clipping about Tag. I always had an idea he was in action instead of a defense battalion. That's why he was over here so long. Don't say anything tho 'cause he probably gave Tommy a big story of all the battles he was in. I'd rather be with an attack outfit than a defense battalion.

429

Whew, what a letter I wrote to Launa tonight. Did I ever crawl! You see, the mail is all mixed up again and I hadn't heard from her in ages. Sooooo last night I wrote and told her to take a flying leap in the lake and that if she didn't write more often she had better not write at all. That was last night. Tonight I got a load of letters from her so I had to crawl and apologize. Every time I open my mouth, I stick my foot into it.

I lost Kitty's address and Tessie's, too. You can thank Kitty and Irene for the cards.

I think I'll write to Tony DiAngelo tonight. I haven't written to him in ages and I owe him a letter.

There isn't much to write about tonight. As I told Pa, it's hard to write letters if I don't get one to answer. You didn't say a thing in your last letter. What's the matter, are you getting "jungle jolly" or going "oriental" on me? These gooks out here could probably write and tell me as much as you did. Well, lil' Darlin', take care of the construction gang (Georgie, too).

Love,

Charlie

17 Anise Street
New Britain, Conn.
January 6, 1945

Dear Son,

Your letters of the 13ᵗʰ and 29ᵗʰ of Dec. were delivered today so I thought I must just as well answer them as soon as possible for you know how I am when it comes to letter writing, always tomorrow.

Am glad to hear that you have got a better rating, about six months from now you no doubt will get the second class and then later a first, that's the rating Tag has. It all takes time.

Well, the New Year has started again. We at home had a hectic one if you may call it that. Mother and I started on a round of parties on Saturday and didn't wind up until New Years day around 3 in the morning at our house. Saturday we went to a banquet with the Narcums and Tessie to Waterbury, Sunday we went over to a place on Greenwood St. for a New Years Eve party, what a time, and Monday we landed at a guy's house in West Hartford that was the cats, he had liquor down the cellar stacked to the ceiling, just right for me.

Went to work again Tuesday. Harold DiPinto worked with me this week and finished up last night. Today I'm loafing, just running around getting a few bills collected and this afternoon I'm going to get a new tire for the truck. Got a tire certificate from the ration board this morning.

I note in your latest letter that some of the men are being shipped back to the States and, (you don't care about coming back as the fun hasn't started yet.) there must be fighting blood in your veins and I'm sure you don't get it from me. If it was me I'd swim across to get home and then crawl across the country. Maybe I'm what they call a home guy. Well, anyway that helps home morale if you don't start griping and am sure that all the boys would rather be home than out in the jungles fighting the Japs. Regarding the 6th Marines, can't say offhand any particular instance of publicity they have had but I do remember a few months ago about this outfit being mentioned as doing a lot of battling on the islands. I hope you stay at the same place because after all if you move to a new place it happens always that it was worse than the other. I was the same in the last war, always wanted to get out of the place where I was, just to keep moving.

We got quite a few letters from you this week, some were mailed the middle of Dec. and the last was dated the 21st, no the 24th or Xmas Eve, I got a kick out of the time you picked up the gooks and they played the mandolin. They may be called head-hunters in the jungles but I think we have the same here only they are called tail-hunters or wolves. When they play, "You Are My Sunshine," they can't be very wild.

You seem to have quite a time writing to the Gals as I read all the stuff you send Betty. A chip off the old block, I guess. Done my share of it when I was in the Army but when I got home they all stunk for a couple of years. When the time comes, we all fall like a ton of bricks.

Well, this will be all for now, lots f love from everyone.

Your Pop

232 Mountain Drive
West Hartford, Conn.
January 7, 1945

Hello, love,

I feel so ashamed of myself – your letters are always so cheerful and they do such wonderful things for my morale and I do practically nothing for you. I should write you a million more times than I do – forgive me – mon cher. I've made some New Year's resolutions that I intend to keep.

Did I say I didn't like gossip? What a thing to say. Charlie, my pet, you just can't make a statement that you're through with love without telling me about it. How can I be your confidante unless you tell all? I can't believe

431

anything I hear around here and you wouldn't want me to get things misinterpreted. Come now, tell Helena all about it.

Ben is stationed in Brooklyn now waiting to be shipped out. We've been having some wonderful times and I know it's going to be very difficult when he leaves. He gave me a lovely silver pin for Christmas which means more to me than anything else I got. I got lots of presents this year, too – a gown, a negligee, gloves, perfume, a sweater, a bond and all the other doo-jiggies women get. Nancy gave me a cigarette case but I gave up cigarettes for the New Year. Oh, you'd die if you could see me smoking Ben's pipe. I like the taste of them, so now when he lights up it's for both of us.

New Year's Eve we went to a party at Nancy's, and what a party! We made a wreck of the house and I guess Ben and I were the only sober ones there.

I loved your paragraph on Christmas, darling. I thought of you so often during the holidays, but I can't be sad – it's a new year and there must be better things coming.

I'm not in a writing mood, dear, I want to talk to you, but I can't seem to write.

I wish I had something to quote for you, but I haven't read anything lately. I've enclosed that light bit of poetry I mentioned a while ago. Read it slowly – it's very realistic and there's something about it that makes you want to cry even though it is light.

I promise to write more often now – just like we used to.

Affectionately,

Helena

Charlie, you've been promoted! Why didn't you tell me? Congratulations!!

> *4ᵗʰ Bn. 15ᵗʰ Marines*
> *Sixth Marine Division*
> *San Francisco, Cal.*
> *January 8, 1945*

Dear Mom,

You really don't deserve this letter 'cause I haven't heard from you or the rest of the family in over a week. But I'm going out on maneuvers in the jungle for a few days and won't be able to write. I know how you worry when you don't hear from me. I don't know whether we will be gone two days or four. By the time you get this letter, I'll be back so it doesn't matter anyway.

I got a little sunburn today. I didn't have my hat on when I washed clothes this morning. I never washed so many clothes in all my born days. I traded a fellow a mattress cover (I had three of them) for a sheet and now I have a super duper stateside cot.

I managed to get a pair of moccasins, too. The p.x. got two hundred pair in. They were only two dollars a pair. They aren't half as good as loafers 'cause there is no arch in them. I hope I'll get my loafers soon.

The fellow that took my picture is going to get the prints next Sunday. I'll send the picture right home.

Ray Wheatley told me that you sent his mother an Xmas card. She thought that was very nice. Did you get the card I sent, and what did you think of it?

Did I have a treat today! The p.x. got in some Kraft pimento cheese spread. We could buy two jars and a box of saltines. They really went over big.

Well, Mom, I guess that's all for now. Write soon 'cause I'll be waiting to hear from you.

Love,
Charlie

Connecticut College
New London, Conn.
January 9, 1945

Dear Charlie,

I've been blowing my top all day over the letter I got this morning. But I'm so blooming tired right now that it's kind of hard to work up a good healthy rage. I don't know what happened to the letter- it was written Dec. 11 and it only just arrived. I'm not sorry for anything I said – I can't even remember what it was. It was long before Xmas when I was in a bad mood – T.S. I do hope I didn't hurt your feelings, deah!

Also, my favorite idiot child, there are lots of things more important than love – self-respect, material success (Yes, I mean it). You asked me what kind of a woman I was – I got a kick out of that. You should know by now – guess I'd better shut up.

All right –so I'm a spoiled, self-centered adolescent – so what! Naturally I don't know what war is like – is that my fault? Are you blaming me? What do you expect me to do – go out and join the WAC? I can't even do that – too young again. Damn it – don't you think I know I'm useless

433

sitting up here on a hill studying chemistry? But what would you suggest? You sure like to rub it in, don't you, Charlie. Thanks –

And I'll believe you've caught up with me when I see it. Have you suddenly blossomed into a great big handsome man? My, my – Dry up, will you?

This letter should fix things just fine. How the devil can I blow my top by mail? By the time I get an answer, I'll have forgotten what I said.

I finally found out about your promotion – congratulations. As you said, you'd better look out or all of your women will be after you for your money. By the way – say hello to Cheryl for me when you write.

I'm tired – and I'm mad so there's no sense in writing anymore. Goodnight.

Launa

Just read it over. Pleasant thing, aren't I? Here come those divorce papers again!

17 Anise Street
New Britain, Conn.
January 9, 1945

Dear Brother,

Well, it's been snowing here all day long and it's just stopping now. I certainly am getting sick of snow. There hasn't been any skating, of course.

Today we Cheerleaders had our pictures taken at Johnson & Petersons. I hope they come out o.k. They're going to be in the Beehive.

School is running along o.k. Next week I'm going to be having a big test in all four subjects. Latin is about the easiest subject I have.

Say, do you know if Mr. Nordstrom has a wig or not? All the kids are trying to convince me he wears one. I doubt it very much though.

We can get WHN on our radio and all afternoon there is swell music with little advertisement. They play both old and new songs but as you say the old ones are always the best. "Blues In The Night" is playing right now.

Princey always lies on mother's living room chair so she made Donny get a long board and hammer about 20 nails into it. She puts it on the chair and when Princey lies down he jumps right off the chair again. (Pretty good, huh?)

Sunday I stayed in and read poetry all day from your blue poem book. I love to read them. I like the poems "Rags" and "Vagabond House" and "The Mistletoe Bough" about the best.

I'm going to have my eyes tested because I think I need glasses. I always get headaches when I read. I don't think I would mind wearing glasses if they were just for reading.

I'm sorry this letter is so short but I haven't any news to report. Bye now.

Hugs and kisses,
Betty

P.S. Tell me what you did in the jungle.

17 Anise Street
New Britain, Conn.
January 10, 1945

Dear Son,

I suppose you are wondering what happened to me. But you know with all the holidays I just neglected you. But now with the holidays over I will write every week. Betty just wrote to you today but I will mail mine tomorrow. Well, I am glad you are still where you are. I know you are safe. Tag said not to complain. He said he was on one island for 16 ½ months. No wonder he got married so soon when he came home. Jean is a nice girl – they get along very well. He even takes her hunting with him. He gets home every weekend. Tommy is supposed to come home today. He is at the Memphis hospital. He is having his furlough and when he gets back they are going to operate on him.

Your girl Cheryl called the other day. She wanted to know if I heard from you. She said how Lennie Hopkins was engaged to the Valin girl, Francine. Lala saw Cheryl in the Conn. Furriers about Xmas time, she probably bought a new fur coat.

Benny was here for Xmas and be brought me a beautiful poinsettia. Freddy was sent back to Norfolk, VA. He must have been in the brig because he went back a day late. Something seemed to bother him, he just didn't care to get back.

Pa just left for the Royal Arcanum and Betty went for baton lessons and Donny is over to the drug store. I am home alone and it's so quiet. The dog is still around. I don't know what we are going to do with him. We leave him up here and he sleeps on the best chairs. We put him down the cellar and he wets on Dad's wallpaper. What a dog. I wish the Army would take him.

Mrs. Leary called when she got your Xmas card and she was so happy.

435

She said how Mick sent her a beautiful plant. Not much new in the neighborhood. Oh, yes, Chas. Farmer went to the Firemen's ball and got all in the bag. He drove his car as far as Hartford Ave. into a snow bank and the cruiser brought him home. Good thing he knew the cop or he would have gotten arrested. When Fan saw him she screamed so loud she said she thought all the neighbors heard her. She was up all night with him. She said she wasn't over it yet. She will have them kids nuts.

Did you get the Xmas box Millie sent you and she said she sent you five dollars. Let her know if you did and don't forget to thank her.

Anna was laid off in Htf'd. She is working in Landers.

Lala and I went downtown today. We were going to the show but we changed our minds. We saw Fibber McGee and Molly Monday and it was lousy. Pa and I saw Pin Up Girl last night and it was good.

The lot of Sonnenberg's next door was sold to someone by the name of Wentland. We saw it in the paper.

Did you get the shoes yet? I'm afraid they're going to be too big. Did you get the five dollars Betty or Pa sent you? You didn't mention it in your letter. Well, I guess I told you everything. Oh, yes, I met Mrs. Bordiere and Richard is in the Navy and Josephine is a Cadet Nurse. Dickey Nickson is in the Navy. He is at Sampson.

Love,
Mother

17 Anise Street
New Britain, Conn.
January 11, 1945

Dear Son,

I got your letter of the 3rd of Jan. today so thought I would answer right away before I get lazy again.

Tommy Cabelus came home for a couple of weeks, believe he came home yesterday, he's coming over with Shirley for a visit tonight and I'm banging this letter off while waiting for him.

You say that you were issued a carbine, this sounds as though you're on the move pretty soon. There is nothing I can do about it but I wish you would stay away from the fireworks if at all possible. Still you will see more of the country and the experience will be worth a lot in later years. Latest news about the war is we invaded Luzon, you probably get all this first hand, it doesn't sound so bad so far but I think there is going to be plenty of fighting before the thing is over with.

I wrote you a letter this past Sunday and told you the news to date. Have been working in Plainville all this week and boy is it cold, I almost froze working inside a house with the heat on full blast all day. It was around 10 below and that's plenty cold.

Donny bought a few muskrat traps last week but so far hasn't caught anything. We're trying to trap some rats up in the chicken coop but no luck so far, guess they're too smart for us.

Prince is in and out of the house all day. He doesn't seem to get used to the cold, always in front of the stove, just where we go into the dining room. Some times I feel like calling up Rouski, the dogcatcher. Mother, I think, is superstious(maybe it's spelled wrong, the hell with it). She thinks a lot of Prince because he belongs to you, otherwise she'd throw him out.

Last night I went to the Arcanum meeting and got home around midnight, was supposed to go to the movies tonight with Donny but can't go, Tommy is coming over. Uncle Pete has been sick the last few days and is not working. He gets some kind of cold every winter.

Mother wrote you a letter yesterday, also Betty. I told Donny to write you one tonight but he's got a blood blister on his thumb, his excuse for not writing tonight. Says he'll get one off tomorrow maybe.

I've been telling Donny the past few weeks that in about July we're going to Maine for a couple of months hunting and fishing. It's a lot of boloney, I know, but I really would like to spend a couple of months up there and away from all the work. I make enough to loaf half the time if I want to.

I don't know if Mother told you in one of her letters or not, we paid off the mortgage on the house and now it's all ours, even paid Barney a Grand that we owed him on a second mortgage. Some day in the near future we may throw a party (They throw parties now whenever a mortgage is paid off). The lot next door to us, Sonnenberg's, was sold last week so that lets us out of buying it. I never did want that lot anyway, too much to take care of.

Well, this is all for now, Sonny. Tom is here with Shirley so I'll sign off and write again in a few days, and hope this finds you feeling fine. With love from all,

Your Pop

17 Anise Street
New Britain, Conn.
January 11, 1945

Dear Brother,

Well, how is my little "Gook" today? I certainly hope those pictures come out and you can send them home.

I bet you're glad Cheryl hasn't written to you. But she called up last week and said she hasn't heard from you, but she wrote to you. I guess you'll have to take a more drastic step.

I haven't heard or read anything in the papers concerning the Sixth Marine Division. I guess it's because I don't read the front page thoroughly enough. I guess I'm just a "proverbial ass." That's what Mr. Catlin (my history teacher) calls the kids when they don't know the answer.

There is skating today but I'm staying home. I have to go to Religious School and then take my baton lesson. Father Webb comes after us if we don't go to religious instructions, but I like to go. For next week we have to have an essay on "Evolution." I can't imagine how I'll ever write it.

I'm starting to read "My Antonia" for English. It's a historical novel. I chose that novel because the print is about an inch high.

Dougie Driscoll quit school yesterday. I guess he figured he won't pass all his subjects and he won't graduate in June. He was in my homeroom and that's only 11th grade. But I think he was crazy to quit anyway.

The Press Club is giving a dance Friday. I'm a representative so I have to sell tickets, but I'm not going. Those dances in the gym are usually pretty crumby. In fact, anything the High School gives stinks. I wish I was going to a different school. I think I'll join the "Plops." That's the Parachute Landing Organization Patrol. That's all for a while.

Love and kisses, xxxxx

Betty

P.S. What is Launa studying at college or is she just going there for the sake of going?

Bye now and don't get disgusted. You could be a lot worse off.

4th Bn. 15th Marines

Sixth Marine Division

San Francisco, Cal.

January 12, 1945

Dear Sis,

I'm out in the jungle now with all the bugs and lizards. We've been out here for three days and are going back to our camp tomorrow morning. If we go out all next week I'll be able to write but there won't be any place

438

to mail the letters. So don't worry if you don't hear from me for a week. You'll get a stack of letters to make up for it.

I'm not going to write to Launa anymore, and this time I mean it. I don't care if she writes two times a day, I still won't answer. (Yea, it says here in fine print.) Ga' wan!

There is no ink here so I'm using merthiolate (something like iodine). I bet you thought it was blood. Eeeeeeek

I got a Christmas card from Aunt Mildred and Aunt Stella the other day. It had ten dollars in it. I haven't had time to write to them yet but I will soon.

No one sent me a pen for Christmas. Just what I needed. I should think by the blurs and smudges that people would catch on. I'm using another fellow's now. Don't send one though 'cause they're expecting some in the p.x. I'll tell you if I want one later.

Freddie seems to get home quite often now. I wonder why he never writes??? He must have forgotten how. All Coast Guard men are dunder heads. By the way, what happened to your ditch digger? You haven't mentioned him lately.

I finished reading "Frenchman's Creek" last week. It wasn't very good. Not much to it. Well, I'll leave you now to decipher this. Don't let your foot go through the ice when skating!

Love,
Charlie

R.I. School of Design
Providence, RI.
January 15, 1945

Hello, darling,

I think I'm going crazy. Or rather what I really think is that the rest of the school is going crazy. God, this has been the weirdest day – the boys all act like fairies – the women are all so damn frustrated it's pitiful. Oh, hell, I feel like swinging from a chandelier. Now do you get my mood, old boy? Maybe I can sleep it off.

Say, I don't like that friend of yours, the one who said that some women are easily raped – he sounds like a connoisseur of the subject. Keep away from him, do you hear? For your information the sex angle in Providence is now dormant and I'm still in possession of what you call my little white flower. Just finished reading "Shore Leave" and as a result my mind is probably the vilest on the Atlantic Coast. I suppose you're still taking care of the Pacific?

In regards to your letter of Nov. 21, 1944, in which you stated that Rita (my roommate) reminded you of that poem called the "Bloodless Love of Virgins." She'd have you know that it isn't blood in the veins but tomato juice. Do you follow me?

You know, sugar, I've been working up my old burlesque routine just in case I don't graduate from this joint. In fact, I've been practicing so regularly that Rita said at some future date I'd be a burlesque queen. She'll probably be a scrub woman and Emy would be the only one to succeed in her chosen field. Hell—Gypsy is making good money. My first roommates decided I had a tendency to be an iceberg so in order to thaw me out – warm me up – get me hot—they put my bed next to the radiator. Now Emy is complaining I'm thawing too fast. Could it be because I went out with her man last night?

Going to the symphony tomorrow night and try to improve my mind – if possible. Ever heard the Boston Symphony? Didn't think so. You go in for sexier music, me thinks.

So far I haven't told you a thing that's important or sensible. But frankly, I'm not in the mood nor can I think of anything. So, baby, you'll have to be satisfied with this tripe.

By the way, how are you – still controlling your emotions I hope, or aren't there any women where you are – wherever you are – and, boy, would I love to know. I'm learning to be a Mata Hari – progress is slow.

Well, honey, I'm going to bed now and tomorrow if I feel like a human being again I'll try to write a sensible letter – take care and be good –

Love,
Lucy

17 Anise Street
New Britain, Conn.
January 15, 1945

Dear Son,

Today is Sunday and what a day. We went to church this a.m. Pa took us and we ploughed home through all the snow and it's still snowing. Donny hopes it keeps up so there will be no school tomorrow.

Pa took Donny to the show this afternoon and Betty and I stayed home. Pa is on the couch sleeping, Betty is in the big chair studying, Donny is in the kitchen making cigarettes for Pa. Prince is in the big chair in the den sleeping and here I am writing.

I rec'd your letter yesterday saying you were going into the jungle for a few days. But I hope you're out of there by now. I can't wait until we get those pictures of you. I didn't think you would see Ray Wheatley anymore. I thought he was transferred. I was glad his mother got my card. Your card was very nice. I guess all the service men sent that kind. Anna is working in Landers and she likes it. She heard from Freddy and he said he was in the brig with 14 other fellows but he said he doesn't mind it. He has kitchen duty and he can only write home twice a week. Mrs. Savage said how Merton was slightly wounded in action but they haven't heard how bad. I hope you don't have to go in any action for a long time.

Tommy was down the other night. He looks swell. Is he glad to be home again.

Donny decided to write to you now. He is going to tell you all about him and Daddy fishing yesterday.

I heard how Nellie Nealon is going to the Boston hosp. the 17th. She's supposed to have a large tumor. I still don't see anything of her. Mr. Westerman has Arthritis very bad, he limps as he goes to work. Pa hasn't heard anything from John. We don't know where he is.

I went to see "15 Min. Over Tokyo" with Oneida the other day and it wasn't bad. Kenneth is still working for the Ferndale Dairy. He has a route of his own. Oh yes, he has a girl friend by the name of Thelma. He goes to see her twice a week. But he had an argument with her last week, she heard how he came home all in the bag and he was supposed to see her that night. So she gave him a bawling out so he picked up his hat and coat and went home. Well, I guess I told you everything. Oh yes, we are going to give Mrs. Lincoln a house warming. Mrs. Savage called and wants some of us neighbors to get together and go up to her new house. Do you know they made a beautiful house out of their garage? Did Betty tell you how Sophie Lincoln is engaged? Well, I'll close with all my love. Betty will write tomorrow.

Mother

51 Forest St.
Oakwood, Conn.
January 16, 1945

Dear Charles –

Here it is Monday morning and the beginning of another week. It should be a very quiet one here at the office because since all the bills have been paid, and the new ones are still being made up in the New Haven office, I look forward to this time of the month because it's the only time I can ever write personal letters in the office.

I found your letter waiting for me when I got home from work on Saturday. It was your Christmas card to me, and it was so much nicer than those that you bought. You know, Charlie, we almost had an awful misunderstanding over something neither of us meant to happen, but now that it's settled we should be able to be as good, if not better friends. I still can't help thinking that you were led to believe that something existed between us that really didn't. Couldn't you have been influenced by Helena and Ben? You see, it's kind of hard for me to put you back on the right track, when you are always hearing these other remarks as to the way I feel from outsiders. Oh well, it's over now, thank heavens, and I hope everyone else is as happy over its outcome as we are.

I've just got to tell you about the funny thing that flashed through my mind when I mailed your letter on the way home from church yesterday morning. We were having quite a blizzard, so bad that the mailbox was all covered with snow, and as I put it in I thought of all the changes of weather it would go through, and then finally land in your hands, where it must be so very hot. Have you ever thought of anything like that when you've gotten mail that has been so far away? Gosh, how'd I ever get so involved? I'm practically racking my brain here trying to get one little idea across – boy, after all that work, I hope you appreciate it as well as get it.

Did I tell you that Lennie Hopkins and Francine are engaged? I was quite surprised. I thought that she liked Brian. She was supposed to have been engaged to him, too, at one time. Personally, I don't care for her anyway and the way she's been acting doesn't alter things much.

How is your work coming along? Are you performing any operations yet, or wouldn't they trust you with a knife in your hands? Can't tell – you're liable to be "a cut up."

Roger called last night again. It's hard to get used to having boys call me. It's been so long since the usual Sat. nite dates. He's coming over Wednesday. We'll probably go to the movies to see "Meet Me In St. Louis" with Judy Garland and that cute little girl, is it Margaret O'Brien? It's supposed to be good, so if it ever gets to where you are, don't miss it.

I was talking to Ann Collins yesterday and she told me all about the New Years Eve party at Nancy's house. She was on a blind date with Buddy Killbourne. From what she says, it was quite the brawl, what with having to sober them up with black coffee etc. I guess she was sort of disgusted. Can't say that I blame her too much. During these times those things don't seem quite right to me.

Helena said she got another letter from you. She claims you don't write as often as you could though. Come now, you're not slipping, are you? She looks forward to your letters so don't disappoint her. Well, pal, I'd better close now 'cause business is "pickin' up." Write awfully soon.

As ever,
Cheryl

P.S. Our front steps are as icy as ever. I practically go up and down them on my hands and knees.

Connecticut College
New London, Conn.
January 17, 1945

Charlie, darling –

It's so long since I've heard you, for the first time you seem very far away. So I dug up all your old letters—just to put me in the mood. That it did!

I've been out painting the town – we had a big celebration. This is our first night off campus – first date in a week. Guess I'm entitled to it, no? Not the Knight on the White Horse so don't worry.

I finally got the birthday present. You're wonderful! Or did you know that? I've named them Goop and Droop. Droopy is the one with his head down and Goopy's the other one. They sit on my desk right underneath your picture. The whole affair is quite distracting when I sit down to cramming some math. Did you really make them from shells you found on the beach? No one will believe me. I'm crazy about them – who else would ever send me anything like that? No wonder I keep writing to you even though you're through with me. Why is it that I can't resist making cracks? Seriously – thanks a lot Charlie – I'm afraid you spoil me.

We had a three-hour bull session last night. We discussed philosophies of life – and evidently mine is all wrong. The general conclusion is that I'm a "hard woman." Beth is threatening to write and tell you what you've let yourself in for. I'm getting the biggest charge out of it. Did you realize I was such a horrible creature? Or maybe you did. There I go again.

You won't believe it – but I'm sitting here calmly minding my own business and some crack pot on the radio starts singing, "Night and Day." It's a busy time, isn't it? This is just one of those nights – better just ignore me. As people keep telling me, "Distance lends glamour." – which probably works both ways in our case. But frankly, Stinky, men bore me to tears. As I figure it they're all basically the same. You put on a little act for all of 'em and they all go for the same kind of stuff. You're the only one that doesn't get the same old act out of me. And you're the only one who doesn't bore me. But then, I haven't seen you for any length of time for about four years. Oh well – there's no use pondering over it. There's no solution till you come home—one way or the other. It's quite late and I have an 8 o'clock class tomorrow. Goodnight, Stinky.

My love always,
Launa

4ᵗʰ Bn. 15ᵗʰ Marines
Sixth Marine Division
San Francisco, Cal.
January 17, 1945

Dear Mom,

I haven't heard from any of you in about a week now but I expect some mail tonight.

I've been out in the field training for the past three days and am going out tomorrow for five days. So you see my mail will be pretty irregular for a while.

I got four letters from Launa yesterday. A fellow brought them out to me when I was in the field. She says that she is going to move to West Hartford and that they are going to sell the house on Arthur Court. I'll have to get Pa on the ball so I'll have a decent car to go courting in when I get back.

I also heard from Cheryl after about a month. She says that she called you up. Mary Hennessey also wrote me quite a letter. I haven't heard from Dick in over a month. He must be getting shipped somewhere.

My pay account is finally up to date. I drew one hundred dollars and am enclosing a money order for ninety dollars. As I told Betty, I'll be able to send about fifty dollars a month home from now on.

The food here has been lousy lately. All we get is canned corned beef hash. We are going to eat K-rations all next week. Those are units of food all packaged up.

The weather has been pretty good lately. We haven't had much rain.

I got a letter from Mick the other day. He didn't say much. He said Roger Whipple had been over to see Cheryl. Launa said that Roger didn't *look like the answer to "the $64 dollar question" to her. She's a pip. Benjamin went over to see Launa. The wolf. I told her that it was a wonder he didn't make a play for her. Well, Mom, I guess that's all the news for now. Write soon. I made a birthday present for you and mailed it today. You should get a kick out of it.*

Love,
Charlie

17 Anise Street
New Britain, Conn.
January 17, 1945

Dear Brother,

Well, how are you today? I received a letter from you this week and I guess it took me quite long to answer it.

I just got home from down town. I bought a new black hat. Last week I got a dark green coat and black shoes. I'm going to be all decked out for Church tomorrow.

We've been having sub-zero weather practically every day but today it's pretty warm out.

Last night a bunch of us kids went skating but we only stayed a few hours because it was so cold we almost froze.

Jim was suppose to come home this weekend but I received a letter from him saying that he won't be able to get home till next weekend. That's rough.

I saw Launa go whizzing by when I was down town today. She had on a fur coat and she looked pretty slick. I thought you said you weren't going to write to her anymore. But she seems to be writing to you often enough when you get three letters at once? (Ga 'wan, you know you love her.)

Mother was certainly surprised when you said you made her a present. I can't imagine what it could be and neither can she. Donny got twelve more traps today. I don't know what he wants so many for, 'cause he never catches anything.

I can imagine you go pretty big for those K-rations. You certainly can't get filled up on those things.

I think I'm going to be in a fashion show next week at school. A group of 25 girls are going to model gowns and dresses for some store. More fun!! I'll perhaps trip on the gown and fall down on the stage.

Do you ever hear from Joe Rizzo anymore?

445

CHARLES YOUNG

Donny and Walty just got back from setting traps. They set muskrat traps. Walter is going to be at Senior High School next year. These little shavers are growing up fast. I have to close now but I'll write again soon.

Love & Kisses, xxxxx
Betty

P.S. Please take good care of your self so I won't have to worry.

4th Bn. 15th Marines
Sixth Marine Division
San Francisco, Cal.
January 19, 1945

Dear Dad—

I'm out in the field now and a fellow just brought me a load of mail. I haven't heard from Mother or Betty in ages. All the mail today was from different girls. I haven't heard from Dick W. in an awfully long time. I'll bet he's being shipped somewhere.

We are living on "K" rations now. "K" rations are small packages of concentrated food. There is a breakfast, dinner and supper unit. It's about the worst stuff I've ever eaten. We only have to eat it for four days, so I guess I won't starve.

You certainly rang the New Year in right from the sound of your letter. No wonder Mother hasn't written. You didn't ruin the garage doors again, did you?

I got a big kick out of your saying there was fighting blood in my veins. I have no desire to engage any Jap in a knife fight. It's just the excitement of the bombing and the artillery that I'm dying to see. I'll probably be scared stiff at the time, but anything is better than this rock. There is nothing to do here. You get tired of training all the time. The quicker we leave this place, the sooner we'll all get home. Amen.

I'm not with the 6th Marines (that's a regiment). I'm with the Fifteenth Regiment, Sixth Marine Division. Our Division is brand new. It's never been used so we are raring to go. There are a lot of veterans from previous operations so we really have a crack outfit.

That's about all the news for now. I have a slew of letters to answer.

Love,
Charlie

4th Bn. 15th Marines
Sixth Marine Division

446

San Francisco, Cal.
January 21, 1945

Dear Pop,

I still have a letter here that I haven't mailed to you yet. We aren't able to mail our letters out in the field but we get mail and have plenty of time to write. You'll probably get two letters at once, but remember you'll owe me two then.

I just finished a five page letter to Betty. I wish you'd have her decide what she's going to do after H.S. I wish you'd make her go to college. You don't know how much it means nowadays for kids to get all the education they can. When I was in H.S. I was all fouled up and didn't know what to do. But it's different with Betty and Donny. If they get started right is all that counts. It only costs about six hundred dollars a year. If Betty decides to be a nurse, it's only about five hundred. We can always cash in my war bonds if we have to. If she goes to work in a factory she'll be getting married when she's nineteen. I don't know about you, but I don't want to be an uncle to a bunch of wild kids. You'd be their Grandfather. That sounds funny as hell to me and you'd better not let Betty read this. Have her see Miss McCawley (girls' high school advisor) and she'll know what the straight dope is. I wish she'd train in Boston. If she gets an application in this year, they will send her a catalogue and she'll know what subjects to take next year. Get after her, will you, Pa? I don't want her to start working when she gets out of H.S. Cripes, she'll only be seventeen. I want to see my little sister have a lot of fun and college days are by far the best days. I'm going back to school if I have to start with Donny. I hope you won't think I'm being silly.

My heart sank when you told me Sonnenberg's lot was sold. Now we can never have a decent yard. I'll have a house right next to my bedroom windows. Gotta run. More later.

Love,

Charlie

4*th* Bn. 15*th* Marines
Sixth Marine Division
San Francisco, Cal.
January 22, 1945

Dear Mom,

I sure was glad to hear from you. It seems like ages since you last wrote.

447

I wrote Pa a letter that will probably make him suck on the gas pipe. I'm sorry I sent it now. I felt pretty bad about us losing the lot. I won't go into that again.

Cheryl has been writing pretty often again. I've been answering all of her letters. I'm thru with Launa. This time I mean it. What a battle we had thru the mail.

Cheryl said that her father bought her a fur coat for Xmas.

I got a big kick out of Charlie Farmer running into that snow bank. I'll bet Fannie is still hollering. It's a wonder he didn't take Nellie to the dance.

I didn't get the shoes yet and I didn't get a package from Aunt Mildred. I got a money order for ten dollars from Aunt Mildred and Aunt Stella. I wrote and thanked them for that.

At last we got some decent food in camp. We've been living on corned beef and canned hot-dogs with sauerkraut for the past three weeks. I guess we'll get fresh meat now for a while.

I haven't heard from Dick in ages. I'm sure he must have shipped out.

Well, my best girl, I guess that's all for today. I have to answer a letter that Sis wrote.

Love,
Charlie

17 Anise Street
New Britain, Conn.
January 24, 1945

Dear Son,

Rec'd your letter with the money order today. I will put it in the bank for you. That will make $214.38. Try and save all you can so you will have a roll when you get home. Mrs. Savage said how Merton has $900.00 saved. He sends home a $50.00 bond every month.

We didn't hear from you in about a week. I was kind of worried. I surely thought you were sent to some other isolated island.

Not much happens around here. Pa isn't working this afternoon. He bought a new grinding wheel and he's putting it on the bench down in the cellar.

It's been so cold here for the last three days, 5 and 6 below. Everybody's car was frozen. Pa couldn't get his started.

Donny sent for my traps. I guess he's going to be a trapper. He got up at 5 o'clock the other morning to look at his traps. Betty isn't home yet. She must have gone to the show. She keeps pretty busy with her homework.

She does quite a bit of reading now. That's something she would never do before. Well, I guess I told you all the news. I am waiting for Pa to take me shopping.

Love,

Mother

4ᵗʰ Bn. 15ᵗʰ Marines
Sixth Marine Division
San Francisco, Cal.
January 25, 1945

Dear Dad,

I forgot to mail this letter last week so I thought I'd just add on to it.

There is still nothing exciting happening around here. We've been drawing clothing, etc.

I went to clean my carbine this morning and found a wasps' nest in it. I just cleaned it three days ago. The wasps get into everything. The other day we found some in the Doctor's stethoscope (the apparatus for listening to the heart).

You mentioned going on a trip to Maine with Donny. Cripes, don't you know there's a war on? Besides, why don't you wait until after the war and take me with you?

I'll bet that you were glad to get the mortgage paid up. Now you don't have to pay the extra interest, and you have no excuse for not fixing up the old homestead. Put in a bathroom upstairs and fix up the kitchen for Mom. You know we ought to build a gable on each end of the store rooms upstairs. Then you could put a bathroom in one corner and extend my and Donny's room. After all, I have to have an apartment 'cause I've decided to become an old bachelor. Me and Swanee will be buddies. We also have to show our neighbors up. (the new ones).Well, I've got another letter to write so I'll close now.

Love,

Charlie

232 Mountain Drive
West Hartford, Conn.
January 26, 1945

Charlie dear,

I've written two letters to you – you must have them by now. It seems to take so long for my letters to reach you and I always feel so hurt when you

449

say you're not hearing from me. Nothing's happening to us , darling – it's the U.S. Post Office.

I think what you say about Ben is true and I'm willing to discuss it with you. After all, who could know him better than you and I? Don't think it's wrong for him to love the whole female race. I'm fickle myself. We're young and I've always felt the freedom of youth should be enjoyed, so much so that married life won't be like a harness. However, I think I'm more constant than Ben. I'm sure you know how I feel. There's just one thing I'm afraid of – I'm afraid I'm going to be understanding and tolerant too long and then some day I'll be hurt. I'm just the type that can take it though and come up fighting, and until something definite happens, I'll be here just as I have for the past three years. The skiing up north was a little bit of all right – and the portion of the female race that was up there wasn't bad either!! You see, I'm not completely a fool, darling – I'm just trying to play the game in the smartest way I know. Any suggestions will be greatly appreciated!

I have been working very hard lately. My little typewriter and I turn out more work than anybody else in the office. Enclosed is a cute cartoon – I'm going to write to Washington for one of those attachments.

I'm very excited right now because my brother is coming home the 30th of this month. My sister-in-law's brother is home from 2 ½ years in the South Pacific and naturally Marion wants to see him. So Larry asked for a furlough and got it and now he, Marion and baby will be trekking home for 15 days. I'll have to teach Sarah to say Aunt Helen while she's here. After all, I'll be 20 in February and have to have something to make me know it.

Again, congratulations on your promotion. Ben said you had it sometime before Christmas. If I'd known I would have written a special letter. I'm very proud of you.

I enjoyed "Frenchman's Creek" very much. The picture was half as good as the book. Right now I'm studying a textbook on "Municipal Government in the United States" to give me a good background for the kind of work I do.

Can't imagine from whom the anonymous Christmas card could be. I sent you one with my name printed – didn't you get that either?

I must wash out some stockings and things now.

Don't worry too much about Ben and me. I'm having fun too, you know, and this is all a part of growing up.

Affectionately,
Helena

Connecticut College
New London, Conn.
January 26, 1945

Hello, Darling –

By the time this arrives you will probably have divorced me for the sixth time. I can't even remember the last time I wrote. But then – I haven't been hearing from you either. And when I found out it wasn't because you'd been moved, the temperature rose 10 degrees. I expect another "Dear Launa – I'm through" letter any day now. We lead such a peaceful existence.

I've been working like a dog lately. For some reason I let everything slide for a couple of months – too much of a rah-rah girl, I guess. So – now that mid-years are about here, I'm beginning to regret it. It makes for twice as much work. Mid-years start next Wednesday, so if you don't hear from me, you know why.

I'm going home tomorrow 'cause Sharon goes in the WAC Monday. And seeing as how I kissed all the boys goodbye I guess I can afford to kiss her goodbye, too. Damn generous of me, no?

It amuses me no end how positive you are about us. I got two letters today and there seems to be no doubt in your mind – if any. If I may say so, you're getting a little conceited out there on your island, aren't you? I guess we've argued enough for a while, so I won't press the point. I'll admit it would be swell if things turned out as you expect them to. But I'm afraid I don't have the faith you do. Beth keeps asking me, "What are you going to do when he gets home?" Damned if I know. But there's no sense worrying about it now. Either it'll be there or it won't. Why do I keep talking about the same thing all the time – we go around in circles.

I must say your description of the native women left me gasping. As you said – a bit crude. But at least I don't have to worry about your running off with a voluptuous dark skinned native. And maybe it's a good thing you'll be hitting the west coast first. "I'm too young and fair for all that!" I've been slaving all day and this just ain't human!

The one bright spot in the day was when I got two letters from you. You had received my nasty little note, but I'm afraid there's another coming – which is even worse. Heaven help us. If you nearly blew your top at this one – I dread to think what you'll do at the other one. I'm just glad I'm not there. As much as I love to fight, I didn't care for this argument too much. It was kind of different. And anyway, there's no sense in fighting by mail – it takes too long to answer and by the time you get the answer you're not in the mood anymore – and vice versa. I told you off and you told me off, so let's skip it. But I'm afraid this isn't the end of it – you haven't received the other letter yet. And I'm afraid that is just about going to do it. T.S.

To go on to something more neutral – the K-rations sound horrible. I'm afraid you're going to make me learn how to cook before you marry me. I don't image a can of spam and some crackers is going to go over so well – O.K, go ahead – brow beat me – see if I care!

I'm in the middle of my second pack of cigarettes and I feel like a walking case of T.B. This has been one of the longest days of my life. I wish I could go out and raise hell. But all the men I know are so damn stodgy. I've come to the conclusion that men are asses – no doubt about it. For heaven's sake come home and unconvince me, will you? Such a damn fool bunch of morons I've never seen. I'm trying to decide if it's better to sit home and knit – no doubt you'd approve. Hell, I wish you were here. Beth keeps telling me I'm building you up in my mind – could be. How the heck would I know? But I miss you anyway. This is a heck of a letter. I'm beginning to see double at this point. Goodnight, darling – and I hope you don't completely explode over that letter.

Launa

4th Bn. 15th Marines
Sixth Marine Division
San Francisco, Cal.
January 27, 1945

Dear Bobo –

I just got your letter and Mother's. I was really glad to hear from you because I hadn't heard from anyone in over a week.

I was down on the beach this afternoon looking for shells and I found a souvenir for you. I'll mail it as soon as I can get something to wrap it in. It isn't much. I'm also sending you my binoculars. You can have them if you can use them. They aren't of much use out here. You probably won't get them for two months or more. The package will be too heavy to send airmail.

It's kind of early for trapping, isn't it? I should think that all of the brooks would be frozen.

I went swimming today. It was the first time since Christmas. Hardly anyone ever goes swimming here. If it were fresh water, I would go every day but I'm pretty sick of salt water.

The food here is terrible – we haven't had any fresh meat or vegetables for six weeks. I'll be glad when we get out of here. Boy, I'm sick and tired of this rock.

We were just given another issue of clothing. Tomorrow we are going out to the rifle range for a little practice. Well, Fuzzy, I guess it's your turn to write again. Don't wait so long next time to answer.

Your brother,
Charlie

232 Mountain Drive
West Hartford, Conn.
January 27, 1945

Dear Charlie,

Here is the picture of Ben and "your pride 'n joy" which I promised you. We had just had a glass of wine and can't be held responsible for facial expressions. The night started out to be beautifully – you know, dinner, exchange of Christmas gifts, all in a nice homey atmosphere—until one of my old flames popped in accidentally and put everyone on the alert. Ben was a good sport about it, I was deeply mortified and the other fellow was incredibly unaware of any discomfort.

I hear you want some films. I'm sure I can get some for you. I have two here but they're 616's and you want 120's, don't you? I'll probably have more snaps to send you soon.

Affectionately,
Helena

Oh, I almost forgot – a joke: One broom says to the other broom, "Let's have a whisk broom." The other broom says, "We can't have a whisk broom 'cause we never swept together."

9 Arthur Court
New Britain, Conn.
January 27, 1945

Hello, Eager Beaver –

I thought I'd better write now before all the desperate cramming starts tomorrow. I'm writing my 20 page paper all day tomorrow, so I don't imagine I'll have time. I wish I could just sort of crawl into a hole for the

453

next couple of weeks. Pardon all the messy writing, but someone is jumping up and down on the bed – this place is a mad house.

Sharon leaves tomorrow morning. It sounds wonderful – wish I were going. She's going to be in the air corps – more fun!

I went downtown yesterday and rode home with Donald Leary on the bus. He's grown up quite a lot. Reminds me of Mick. He's going in the Marines in June as soon as he graduates. He said they haven't heard from Mick in over a month – have you? He also gave me all the dope on Francine Valin. She is engaged to Lennie, but everybody seems quite het up 'cause Brian came home and she started going out with him again. Ah women! Wonderful animals.

Donald and I hashed over the times you, Mick and I used to go skating all the time. We talked about you naturally. He had the nerve to ask if I "was going" with you. I laughed and said no. Then he asked me about dear Cheryl – more fun! By the way, I think that she and dear Roger would make a lovely couple. Not as lovely as you and she, however. Aren't you even slightly jealous? Come on, confess! I don't know how she can tolerate Roger though. He repulses me – ugh

Talk about being repulsed – I sat next to some horrible Mississippi sailor on the bus from Hartford tonight. Now I know why the north and the south never got along. He finally decided I was a "damn Connecticut Yankee" and left me alone. God deliver me from all "southern gentlemen(?)"!

Hey, there's a full moon. I guess we'd better not go into that – I guess you know what, hmmmm? Hell, aren't I the coy little thing?

You made some remark about not coming back, darling. Let's not dwell on a gruesome subject. But whether or not I love you, I don't know. All I know is that I need you – very much. And God wouldn't do that when we have so much to settle. Funny – but lately I seem to believe much more in God than I ever have before. (not just because of exams, either). I may be a religious woman yet – perish forbid! How the heck did I get so serious?

A mob of screaming females just came in the room so I might just as well quit. Maybe I should begin telling you what you tell me – please write.

Goodnight, Stinky,
Launa

91 West Street
New Britain, Conn.
January 27, 1945

454

Dearest Peaches,

You're crazy. I wouldn't be so dumb as to write a letter in December and mail it in January! Unless I made a mistake in writing!

Cripes, right now I could spit! Meg came down from LaSalle Thursday nite to spend the weekend with me. She and Pater and Bob and I planned to spend the weekend in New York. Well, last nite Bob said he has to fly today and tomorrow. Meg went into the City this morning anyway — boy, war is hell! See Bob is stationed over at Stewart Field, New York. Right next to West Point! So near and yet so far. I went up to see him last weekend — had a swell time. Oh, well — I guess you can't possibly have two good consecutive weekends. Soooo — while Meg is in the big city probably getting blotto with Otto, I sit here. All the kids have gone away this weekend. I have a couple of exams this week that I suppose I should just give a little time — very little, I fear.

Oh, but, Honey, of course, I still love you — naturally!!!

As far as I know, your "little Dickey" is still in South Carolina. The last letter I got was from there anyway.

No, sweetness, I'll never forget those wild rides — especially the nite you and Dick and Meg and I stole your Aunt's car to go to Kay Casale's graduation party and you forced me on Joe Green's lap — "Just wanted to know where you were." I'll never forget that! And H.S. Conway didn't know I came with you and started wolfing you all over the house! You screaming, "Stop, stop, I love it." Then you went out and had a good time.

Thanks for the compliment about "Nancy" — you know, flattery will get you no where these days!

We have a new lab teacher. Boy, he embarrasses the shellac out of us. He says he can't wait until we have X-Ray classes next year because we can have a lot of fun in the dark room! I can hardly wait! Well, tweetie — I simply must start my work! Rah ! Write real soon.

Love ya,

Mary Jo

I'm still waiting for my grass skirt. I have a job at the Hawaiian room — simply have to furnish my own costume.

4ᵗʰ Bn. 15ᵗʰ Marines
Sixth Marine Division
San Francisco, Cal.
January 28, 1945

Dear Mom,

Today is Sunday and as usual there is nothing doing.

I went to church this morning. The chapel is only about a mile from here. Another fellow and I have been going to Communion every Sunday. We check up on each other.

I guess that I told you that the pictures we took didn't come out. All the cameras in our outfit had to be turned in last week.

I've been working on some shells again. This friend of mine's father is a jeweler and this fellow is going to make a shell necklace for me if I can get him the shells. I'd like to send Betty one if I can.

What is Freddy in the brig for? As Pa would say, "He's crazier than a bed bug." What's his rate now?

We are having steak for dinner today. It will be the first fresh meat we've had in six weeks.

You said that Sophie Lincoln was engaged. Now I've heard everything. Well, I'll close now. I want to write to Benjamin. I owe him a letter.

Love,
Charlie

17 Anise Street
New Britain, Conn.
January 30, 1945

Dear Brother,

I received two nice long letters from you yesterday. It's funny how you can have so much to tell me and I can't think of a darn thing to tell you. I guess, I'm just leading a boring life, that's all.

I have an awful cold so I stayed home from school today. I'm going to study for our Latin test. Miss Benjamin said if I got 80% or over she would give me an A on my report card. The last time I got a B with an 88% average. History is the subject I have my trouble with. I just can't understand it no matter how much I try. Oh, I'll get by alright, I guess.

Mother and Lala are going up to the hospital to see Nellie this afternoon. All the neighbors chipped in and they are going to buy her a gift. (That's nice)

What kind of a band do you have there? Johnny Elastic and his Rubber Band?

That's a date about our going skating. But don't you dare skate fast and let me drag behind as you always did.

Sunday afternoon a bunch of us kids went skating and we had a swell time. We played Ringalievio with Father Webb. He certainly is sharp on skates and no one can catch him. The way he runs around and etc. you would never take him for a priest. My muscles were so sore Monday morning I could hardly walk.

It was Monday, too, that I was in that Model Fashion show. There were abut 25 girls and we modeled spring and summer fashions. I wore a loafer suit, if you know what that is. Some people call them "Frank Sinatra Suits." They have a jacket with a solid color for the sleeves and back and plaid in the front, with a solid color skirt. It was really nice. Perhaps I should have run home with it on!!

Perhaps R. Whipple and Cheryl would make a good pair. I saw Roger the other day, and I don't think he looked like the answer to the $64 question either!!

Our gangster cousin Bert was home from the Navy and he was traipsing around N.B.H.S. like a B.T.O. I never even knew he went to High School at all. Perhaps he didn't. He's as handsome as ever!! Gosh, I hope he asks me to go out with him. (Are you kidding?)

Donny found a rabbit's foot in one of his traps and later he found the dead rabbit in the hole. He felt so bad that he cried and wouldn't eat his dinner. He said he was never going to set another rabbit trap again.

I was quite disappointed about the snapshots. I would have loved to have seen them. I hope you haven't changed much because when you come home, I at least want to recognize you. I bet you're big and fat already, huh? I guess tat's all for now.

Love and kisses,
Sister Betty

P.S. I was very glad to know that you're going to Communion often. I'm really proud of you.

An important P.S.S. I really don't know what to do about my post-graduation plans. Dad wants me to go out here to T.C.C. but I don't care for that. I would like to be a nurse but Dad doesn't go big for that. I'm quite confused and it's bothering me. Dad said he doesn't want me to go away when I can get an education right here. (Isn't he silly?)

4th Bn. 15th Marines
Sixth Marine Division
San Francisco, Cal.
January 31, 1945

Dear Sis,

How's the goon child today? I received your letter last night. It was the first mail in quite a few days. I also heard from Lucy. She's still going strong in Providence.

Mr. Sandberg doesn't wear a wig. Cripes, Elmer isn't that old. The only one with a wig is that French teacher, and I doubt that.

I haven't mailed yours or Donny's package yet but I will tomorrow. Yours is light enough to send airmail but the other package is quite heavy. I suppose Mom got hers by now.

I sent Launa two of those little turtles for her birthday. She was quite pleased with them. I'm not writing to her anymore. It's a long story.

Cheryl has been writing quite often. I'm looking for some new stock. Just call me Benjamin. I love them all.

I saw "Coney Island" last night. Mother would like it a lot. The night before that I saw "Conflict" with Bogey. It was swell.

Thanks for sending the Service Man's News. Well, I guess that's all for today. Write!

Love,

Charlie

17 Anise Street

New Britain, Conn.

February 1, 1945

Dear Son,

Got your letter of the 12th saying you just got back from a few days in the jungle and that you were going back for a couple more weeks. Also your letter to Mother how you are getting plenty of grub now. Glad to hear it, also that you are in the best of health.

Your letter says I'm supposed to "suck the gas for selling the lot." I haven't got the letter yet so I suppose there is plenty in it, you must have been letting off steam, say what you think and get it over with. I thought of buying the lot for years but what was the use of having it? More taxes and nobody to take care of what we have now properly. The fact is, Son, we might sell the place when you get back and get something better. We always talk about remodeling the joint, but it will take plenty moola for that and sometimes it doesn't pay, you still have an old house. Well, so much for that.

It's the 1st of February you will note above, and, boy, is it cold, close to zero and way below since last week and talk about snow, more than we've ever had, a little comes down every two or three days. The driveway is a *mess, I shoveled it the first time it snowed and gave up. I manage to get the truck up in front of the garage and keep the Auburn in the garage most of the time, "my Sunday Car" running better than ever.*

I worked over to Tessie's and got through last night. Dutch, her husband, is still in PA. She goes down every week or so to collect the old dough. You know Tess, the gal for the moola. Betty says this means "money", reminds me of some sort of cow. Speaking of cows reminds me of Mother and I trying to get some meat yesterday. The stores were all sold out and you couldn't buy a decent piece of any kind of meat for love or money. We finally compromised and bought a 20 cent soup bone. Had soup for dinner and supper also some pork sausage with Delmonico potatoes for supper. So you see we still eat.

We also got the package you sent Mother. The turtles are quite ducky. Do you polish up the shells to have them shine so? How about sending home a Jap rifle gun of some sort. I'd like to see what they look like.

Last week Tommy and Tag were home for the weekend. Tommy is now in Memphis hospital, he is going to be operated on for something or other that has to do with his leg. Tom, Tag, Shirley, Jean, Billy and Donny and I went fishing to Pocatapaug last Sunday but didn't get a fish, it was lousy. We did however have a fine time eating sandwiches and drinking cider on the lake. No, we didn't stop at Jane's, although Donny wanted to, we had too much of a crowd.

Mother is mending my coat right now, so I thought I would rattle this off and at the same time try to keep my word to keep writing you although there is nothing to gab about. Betty took some pictures about two weeks ago, but I don't know whether she had them developed or not. I'll ask her next time she's around.

Well, so this will be all for now, hope this finds you in the best of spirits, everything on the home front is o.k. So long.

Your Pop

232 Mountain Drive
West Hartford, Conn.
February 1, 1945

Dear Charlie,

You're right — marriage and its headaches aren't for us — what we want are picnics and dances!

I must, however, make one further comment about your paragraph on "clicks" etc. I agree that respect is the thing. I don't think it's necessary to be in love (blindly in love, I mean) to make a perfect marriage. So now we agree perfectly.

May I comment on you and Launa? You still write, don't you? Somehow, it seems to me that when love is over, all contact should be stopped. There are memories enough to haunt you without reading impersonal letters. I realize how hard this is to do because when Ben and I had our little argument this summer we went on writing trying to be nonchalant.

'Nuf said – now let's get out of this rut.

Of course, I haven't forgotten about our picnic. Your year and a half will go by quicker than you think. Maybe we ought to start planning the luncheon – I'll have to learn how to prepare deviled eggs and salads. And don't forget, you're supposed to take me to the rustic old Italian's farm to drink cider. Then we're supposed to go dancing. Sounds like fun, huh!

Ben went skiing last weekend again. He's really a fanatic about the sport, isn't he? You're quite fond of it too, aren't you? How about instructing me sometime?

I'd better buzz now. Write soon – it's fun to get letters often from you. I've had 3 in two weeks.

Affectionately,
Helena

FPO San Francisco, Cal.
February 2, 1945

Dear Charles,

How are you? I got your letter last night with the pictures so with the good will power I have I will send them back. I didn't recognize your sister until I read the letter. What a change, and no addresses given out, except to my buddies, about fifty of them. You don't mind that, do you?

Cheryl looks nice, especially the part you mentioned .What's the story, huh? That's all I need to say.

I see Benny is a big time operator, second class and just out of school. I will probably be third for the duration unless something comes up. While speaking of rates, congratulations. I saw you made third, when are you going up for second?

As long as you're still blowing your top, you're o.k. Say, I am giving small stores a great business out here.

What about all the women there? Any nice ones? If so, when you leave I could use some addresses as I expect to be going by there some day and maybe I will have a few days.

You had better watch that Whipple kid. You can never tell, between his mother and Launa's mother, you know.

I see my brother is getting around lately. I don't know where he gets the word on me but he has it.

You asked how long I was suppose to stay out here, well, when some one comes to relieve us we can go home. Of course, you can't tell when they will get here but we do a lot of sweating every day, hoping they will get here soon.

Do you remember Shirley from Torrington? I got a box from her and she is showing off her cooking. Ouch! I guess I will have to go up to see her, but I will have to keep my distance, well, most of the time anyway.

Well, Charles, I guess that's all for now. Don't forget to look up some women around there, take care of those gyrenes, be good, stay sober and watch that top of yours. Write soon.

Mick

17 Anise Street
New Britain, Conn.
February 2, 1945

Dear Brother,

Oh, what a beautiful morning – oh, what a beautiful day! I feel good this morning. There is thirteen inches of new snow and with the other 12 we have 25. The drifts are high as heck. I guess the plow won't be down until this afternoon. Gosh, I never saw so much snow in my whole life. Perhaps the mail-man will never come down and take this letter. Donny and Dad are making plans about shoveling out the driveway. The sun is out and the snow is sparkling. It reminds me of the first verse of "The First Snowfall."

Gosh, I hope I'm not making you drool or anything.

Well, I must get busy now before Mother starts yelling at me. Good-bye.

Love and Kisses, xxxxx
Betty

P.S. Yesterday I got a returned letter to me that I had written to you from Soundview the summer before last. It had all sorts of stamps and marking all over it. It didn't pass because there were some shells in the letter. They certainly took long enough to send it back.

17 Anise Street
New Britain, Conn.
February 5, 1945

Dear Brother,

    I received my report card today. I got an A in Latin and C in History and English. I went down to see that old crud Miss Curran about my mark and she started harping about the day I was absent on November 13! Cripes, what does she want anyway? I've been getting good marks in there lately so I thought I deserved at least a B. Oh, well, such is life.

    We haven't heard from you lately so I figure you are out in the field again.

    Yesterday Tag and Jean and Aunt Anna and Uncle Pete came down. Tag sure is lucky to be home every weekend. He has an idea about starting a book on all the places he's been and what he's seen etc. It sounds o.k. but I can't imagine how far he'll get.

    Jim came home for the weekend and Saturday night we went to the movies and saw "Something For The Boys". It was o.k. I also saw "Winged Victory." That was really good.

    Say, what the heck happened between you and Launa? I don't see how you could have such arguments just through writing! You know you like her so I don't understand why you should argue with her, or did she start it all? Or perhaps you will be better off as a bachelor. I guess I'll be an old maid, too, and bring my kids up the same way.

    Donny got a pretty good report today. But I swear that kid is going to be a devil in a few years, not saying that he isn't one now!

    The little clipping I'm enclosing was quite a coincidence so I thought you might like to read it. I'm also sending the news clipping from the Herald.

    Dr. Mellion, the school physician, is home from the army, and he gave a very interesting talk to the students today about the action he saw overseas. He was in France at the time of the invasion.

    We had four inches of snow last night. I don't know when the winter will end. I bet for you it's just the opposite. I guess warm weather does get quite sickening after a while.

    Dad received your encouraging letter but he still doesn't wish me to go away to school. He insists upon T.C.C.!!!

    I didn't receive my Biology mark because old Clarence has to be different and not mark our cards until tomorrow.

I guess that's all the talk for a while. As you notice this is the first typing I've done in years.

Love and kisses, xxxxxx
Betty

P.S. What picture of me did you show to the Gook?

P.S.S. Nov. 13 was just a day I was absent so don't think I skipped on that day. I never skip on the 13th 'cause that's unlucky!

P.S.S.S. Those little turtles are darn cute. Their shells are very pretty. At first I thought you were sending Ma a bar of Lifeboy for B.O.

51 Forest St.
Oakwood, Conn.
February 5, 1945

Hi, Chas,

I got another letter from you Sat. and was quite pleased. I had to laugh though at your opening paragraph. Whatever gave you the idea that I had forgotten you? Evidently my letters hadn't been getting to you, but if there is any delay I wish you'd blame it on the post office and not on me. O.K?

Do you save your letters? I do, and it's amazing to see all I have gotten from you. Let's see, I get nearly two a week and that's been going on for nearly a year now so you can imagine all there are. One night I decided to go through them all, and after finishing them I was worn to a frazzle. Gee, we did nothing but agree for a time, then we'd no sooner get straightened out but we'd get more involved. We were always mad when you were home, but who'd ever think we could argue via mail. The only thing wrong with this is that by the time I get your answer, I've had time to calm down, then it's hard to get back into that fighting spirit. Oh, well, we never give one another a chance to be bored anyway. At least we always end up happy. I think I used to magnify things a whole lot though – sometimes you were in such a daze when I pounced on you that I really felt sorry, but then again you put plenty over on me. Am I right? By the way, you never did tell me who your latest heart throb was, and don't think I didn't sense the fact that you were madly in love for a time there. It seems to have faded out a little now though. Come on, tell me about her. You're always pretty well informed as to who I've been seeing, so I just wondered who had been making you so moody. Whatever you do, please don't go into the gruesome details of your being a bachelor again. I assure you that you've thoroughly convinced me of that, but I still think that you could have liked someone without upsetting your plans for the future.

463

Who's been telling you about Roger? You said he gets home often but yet he doesn't. This was the first time in two years. That's a heck of a long time to be away I think. Do you think you're due for a leave, or is there a certain length of time that you have to be there? If so, you must have half of it over by now. I wonder if you'll come over to visit with me when you come home? I promise I won't get mad if you call me the last minute. I'm much more understanding than I was two years ago. Guess I was noted for that. Roger was telling me that Maurice Blair wanted to know how he could possibly get along with me. Roger told him he didn't have any trouble, Ugh. Morry's not one to talk.

Well, Honey Chile, there isn't really much to write this time, but it will hold you over till my next real letter. Be good and write soon.

Love,

Cheryl

P.S. Will you overlook any traces of a nasty mood? I came to blows with one of the girls in the office and I'm still on the moody side. These people that are so self-confident infuriate me.

P.S.S. I'm still looking for some film. If you happen to get some send me a picture of you. I'd love to see you in your Marine uniform. By the way, have you heard from Billy Mc. yet? I hope he's all right.

17 Anise Street
New Britain, Conn
February 5, 1945

Dear Brother,

Not much happening today but I thought I'd drop you a note anyway.

School is alright. I guess Mr. Sandberg went on a ski trip because he wasn't in school today and won't be until the end of the week. We have an old nutty substitute.

Ma's listening to Joan Davis now. She's a pip (Joan, not Mother.)

Mother said you should have sent those turtles to Cheryl instead of Launa. She would have appreciated them more. (G' wan, I can see you sending them to Cheryl.)

The Sodality is giving a party tomorrow. It's going to be a dance, too. Father Brophy is buying the soda and all the girls are going to bring something. Father Webb is helping the Sodality give it. I guess that's all for now.

Love & Kisses, xxxxx
Goodnight, too,
Sister Betty

P.S. I wish you would give Donny a lecture on behaving. He's as fresh as heck. I've tried everything.

> 65 Arthur St.
> New Britain, Conn.
> February 6, 1945

Dear Charles,

Received your letter this morning. I'll bet that you are sore that Dick doesn't answer your letters but I'll see to it when he comes home. Over the weekend, he will write to you.

He has been busy—he didn't write anybody. He is stationed at Brooklyn but for how long I don't know. I sure am glad he is close by and I can see him weekends. I haven't his address, as he hasn't given it to me.

I hope you're well and happy—it's a long time since I saw you last. I hope you can surprise me and drop in sometime.

I bet your mother is waiting and praying to see you soon. All the boys are all gone. Dillon just left a week ago for the Army Air Corps.

We sure are having an old fashioned winter. Sure will be glad when the good old summer comes along.

Dick is coming home this weekend. He said he would go and visit your mother. He will write you over the weekend and give you all the dope, so take care of yourself and God bless you. I remain as ever,

> Mrs. Richard Walton

> 17 Anise Street
> New Britain, Conn.
> February 7, 1945

Dear Son,

Having a few minutes to spare, I thought I would answer your letter. Today is a beautiful day, the sun is shinning but it's pretty cold out. The radio said it was zero this a.m. Not much happening around here. I suppose Betty told you how Tag and Jean and Pete and Anna were down Sunday. We played set back in the afternoon and they stayed for supper.

Tag smokes like a trooper now. He even takes a drink - he didn't refuse a drink Sunday. He is writing a book on all the experience he had being in the Navy and all about the islands and the people on them. I hope he makes some money on it. His six months will be up soon and I don't know what he will do then.

I am making bread this A.M. I made it the last few weeks now. Pa thinks I should make it every week.

Pa manages to keep busy, as a rule he loafs a few weeks but not so far. Maybe next week if nothing shows up.

Donny bought a few more traps. He set some in back of Willie's pond and he got a rabbit foot in it. He felt so bad he couldn't eat his dinner. He finally went down and got the rabbit out of his hole but it was dead. He said he wouldn't trap for any more rabbits. He's been sliding almost every night after school.

Did Betty tell you how she joined the ski club? I wonder how she will make out. I think she'd better practice on Swanson's hill.

Nellie is coming home from the hospital tomorrow. Fanny can't come over much in the winter time. She is always so cold.

Kenneth is still peddling milk. Lala has to help him with his books every nite. I guess he isn't too smart.

You said you were thru with Launa. What does she do, try to tell you what to do? Just tell her you don't have to take any of her crap. Tell her there's too many fish in the brook. She always reminded me of Kathryn Hepburn, a little spit fire. Just tell her where to get off. I still think Cheryl is the old faithful. But I know you don't think so. Well, Son, don't let any of them get you down. There's plenty of time to pick one when you're home again and going to school. There's the place you meet the Babes. Well, cheer up, you still have me.

Love and kisses,
Mother

17 Anise Street
New Britain, Conn.
February 8, 1945

Dear Brother,

I received a letter from you yesterday and so did Mother and Donny.

Boy, are we having a blizzard today. This morning it started snowing and it certainly turned into some storm. The drifts are about five feet high. I know there won't be any school tomorrow so I'm not planning on going.

Old Clarence broke down and gave me a "B" in Biology. I almost fell through the floor. He gave "D's" to half the class.

Eddy Wallace got a medical discharge from the Marines. I was talking to him the other night. He's trying to get a job at the Post Office. He asked about you and wanted to know if Uncle Bernie is still living with us That's all, kiddo. Write!

Love,

Betty

51 Forest St.
Oakwood, Conn.
February 8, 1945

Dear Charlie,

Here I am again, this must make the third letter this week, but I got another one from you last night and you said you weren't getting mine as regularly as you should so just to keep your spirits way up high I'll keep at it. I hate to have you feeling lonesome. It makes me feel so badly when you do, so come on, help me a little by talking about all the things we'll do when you come home. Oh, just the word dance seems like such a thing of the past. You want me to teach you over again, but just between us, something tells me it's going to be sort of a half and half proposition.

Where in the world do you think I could be getting all this practice? You know, I don't think you really realize how little there is left for girls to do, since all you boys have gone away. Honestly, there's absolutely nothing to do especially for weekends except go to the movies or knit or talk with the girls. Of course, I was kind of busy when Roger was here but you know how fast three weeks go by. They just flew, and the next thing I knew I was saying goodbye to him, so you see, Honey chile, one is forced to lead a calm, uninteresting life.

You'll die when you hear this, but they tell me Ben is quite the dancer. There must have been an awful lot of improvement made because if you remember how mad I'd get when we exchanged dances with him. Oh, it was worse than words can say. It's funny though we danced so much together, that it made it hard for me to follow anyone else, so maybe it wasn't Ben's fault after all. They couldn't all be as good as you are. (I can almost see your head swelling.) Anyway, so I should have understood or rather overlooked any mashing of toes that might have been done.

I'm thoroughly disgusted with the weather. We're in the middle of a blizzard and I just got the last batch off the walk! You'd have died if you heard my mother when I got home from work last night. You see, the boy who usually shovels our walk was sick and as a result ours and the Lucas's were the only ones on the street that were covered in solid ice. Well, anyway Mrs. Lucas was telling my mom that the police stat. called and said she'd

467

have to do the walk before the next day. Of course, my mother laughed hysterically at that. Imagine having the police call. Well, it wasn't so funny when the doorbell rang a while later. Who was it but a cop and he actually threatened to send her to jail if the ice remained on our walk. You know my mother – she was scared stiff – guess she believed him – well, anyway she won't have to go to jail – I shoveled and chopped for two hours and I'm so d– stiff today I can hardly move. Believe me I'll never complain of the heat again. As long as there's no shoveling to do. It's really tough because my father can't do anything like that either on account of his stomach. See how wonderful it is without you strong handsome fellows around.

I don't think I told you about going to New York, did I? Norma, Ruth, Marilyn and I are planning to go the first weekend in March. If we leave right after work Sat. noon we'll get there at 4 o'clock or so. Then we'll probably stay at the Biltmore. We'd like to see a play, preferably "Bloomer Girl" and then maybe shop some more, eat and go to bed. Sun. we can go to church, eat, see a movie and get the 6 something train back home. It should be fun for a change.

Did Helena tell you her brother and his family are here? He got a 10 day leave from Ft. Myers. The baby is darling. I think she resembles her cousin – Cheryl.

If you don't stop growing you'll tower over me. I'm about 5 ft.4 inches though so that's not short either. You must be as brown as a berry. Have you gained much weight? I'm awfully anxious to see you again. Hope it will be soon. Well, Sweet, I'd better close as business is picking up. Be good and write often.

Always,
Cheryl

P.S. Mother and Dad send their regards.
P.S.S. Leave it to Freddy – in the brig again!

17 Anise Street
New Britain, Conn.
February 8, 1945

Dear Brother,

We haven't heard from you in about a week now but I certainly hope we will soon. I guess I haven't been writing as often as I should either but where all the time goes I don't know. I have to study hard this week because we're having finals in English and History.

I started to read the novel "Red Badge of Courage" tonite. It's about the Civil War and pretty dry, too.

Frannie O'Day's mother died a few days ago. Mother and Lala went with the Guild to her house to say the rosary.

Russell and Butch are here now. As usual, Dad is giving them cider. I think Pa would die without his cider.

It snowed a couple inches again today. It seems like it'll never stop snowing.

Tag and Jean, Shirley and Tom and Dad and Donny went fishing Sunday. They didn't catch a thing though.

Today I got a stomach ache in school so I stayed in the nurse's room for the last two periods. I lay down and almost fell asleep. The nurse doesn't care how long you stay there as long as you don't want to go home.

There was skating yesterday, but since it snowed there won't be any for a while. I don't care though 'cause I don't care to go anymore. I guess I'd rather be a "home girl."

Jimmy is coming home next week and then I won't be a home girl??

Could you give me some advice on some good books to read? I'm getting so I like to read now. I guess you've read most of them here at home so you should know which ones are good.

I guess that's all for now.

Love and Kisses, xxxxx
Little Sister Betty

P.S. Do you still hear from Cheryl, kiddo?

475 Glen Street
New Britain, Conn.
February, 8, 1945

Dearest Nephew,

Your letter sure was a pleasant surprise. It came as a sort of birthday gift. I celebrated a half a hundred on the third of the month. Uncle Pete gave you a compliment saying you write nice letters.

Yes, it is swell to have Tom and Tag back in the States. Tag comes home every Saturday and goes back Sunday night. His six months in the States will be up the 20ᵗʰ of March and he expects to be shipped out again. He wants to go back with the Marines again. It's snowing very hard just now. We sure have had more than our share this winter, at least, Tag is seeing plenty. When he first got home, he was so disappointed because we had no snow, after not seeing it so long. He sure got a thrill. Tom is stationed at Memphis, Tenn. He was home from the 10th of Jan. till Jan. 23. He's having more x-rays taken and then he will be operated on for his back and leg. The cartilage has been torn from all the vertebrae and rest on the nerve in his leg which is very painful at times. I hope it all turns out successful. I let Tag read your letter. He said you're having the same experiences he had with the gooks because they steal anything they can lay their hands on.

You asked about Jimmy Arute. He's a very nice boy. He's a pal of Bobs. He goes to Admiral Ballard Academy at New London. He was home last weekend. I think he will go places as he's ambitious and he loves going fishing and hunting. Don't worry about Betty. She can take care of herself. I hope this clears things up for you. Any other information you want just write and let me know and I'll try to oblige. You don't want your hair to turn white worrying about my favorite niece. Ha, ha!. Love and best wishes from all.

Your loving aunt,
Anna

17 Anise Street
New Britain, Conn.
February 9, 1945

Dear Charlie,

How are you? I received your letter the other day. I was wondering what the souvenir could be, Maybe a Jap torpedo that floated up on the shore.

On my report card I didn't get such a hot report in arithmetic etc., but as soon as the teacher comes back I'll ask him why. Our teacher was sick so we had a teacher taking her place this week. Right now your dog Prince is laying down beside me while I write this in the living room. For this month I'm a traffic officer in school so I have to be a good boy in school. I can't throw snowballs either. Ha, ha!.

This afternoon Daddy and Mr. Neubauer had a snowball fight with Madeline, Donald, Walter and Kenny P. Boy did they throw. Speaking of trapping, about what time before March 15 would you suggest for trapping and also where, that's what I would like to know, and make sure you write and tell me whereabouts. Friday is Mrs. Farmer's birthday and Mother, Daddy and the Neubauers are going over there. Cigarettes are so scarce to get I have to roll them for Daddy. I think you should send a carton of cigarettes home instead of some souvenirs. I was supposed to help Kenny Neubauer deliver milk tomorrow but instead he got some other kid to help him.

Betty took some pictures of me and daddy shoveling the driveway, in some spots the snow is about six or seven feet high. Are there many snakes on the island that you are on? The snows must have been pretty bad around because the plows haven't been around yet. Betty asked Daddy to fix up one of the old pairs of skis you had so she could go skiing. My skis are in perfect condition to go skiing. Well, there's not much more I can think of so I'll sign off.

Love,

Donny

65 Arthur Street

New Britain, Conn.

February 11, 1945

Dear Charlie,

Dost thoueth remembrest me? I am the fella with the lame brain and broken arm. If I remember correctly, I haven't written you in months. I'm very much ashamed, Charlie, and I want to apologize. I do think it's gone beyond the stage of apologizing, so I'll not bother. I don't exactly know what type of punishment I deserve. Oh!! I am such a bad little boy!! I guess I'll go out and smash my cherry. Wheeeee! Seriously, though, Charlie, my not writing was inexcusable. I was, however, very busy in Charleston. I missed a lot of sleep and lost a lot of weight while I was there. – Lost weight from working too hard. Don't get any ideas.

I'm through with the most difficult part of this note, so I'll get down to the "bare" facts and news. To begin with I'll tell you how I stand. I left Charleston on January 31ˢᵗ. I am now stationed in Brooklyn, N.Y. on the hospital ship USS Mercy. Word has it we'll be shoving off on or about Feb. 28ᵗʰ. Whether or not we'll do S.P. duty is not known. I'll keep you posted as to what the sailing date will be.

I arrived in Brooklyn on Feb. 1st and am having a rare time for myself. This is my 3ʳᵈ time home. On the day that I arrived in Brooklyn I came home for a couple of hours. Mother and Dad never expected me. I had told them that I'd probably be sent to the F.M.F. and start heading West again. You can imagine their surprise when I walked in last week. I was home last weekend. I was A.W.O.L but didn't know it. I got away with it but had to do a lot of fancy talking. This weekend finds me out on a 72 hr. pass. I have to report back at 7:30 a.m. tomorrow.

The old place hasn't changed very much. It does look a little different tho' as Conn. is just recuperating from a blizzard. I've seen almost none of the

471

kids with whom we went to High School. New faces and adolescent kids maturing are about all you see. However, last week I saw Mary. She was home from school for the weekend. Nice as ever but gaining a little weight. Eeeeeek! No, not that. I saw Ginger Dillon yesterday morning. I nearly came in my pants after taking one look at her. Can you ever forget the case of the missing toilet paper? Met Benny on the train last weekend and also saw him in the chow hall. He's got a ship and will be leaving soon. Now and then you see familiar faces but they're almost meaningless.

Here's the pay-off, Charlie. When I got in last weekend, I called Mary's house and received no answer so I called Meg – Meg was away at school but her mother answered. I inquired about Mary, asked her how Meg was – you know all that "blaze blah." Her mother wrote to Meg telling her I had called to see if she were home. Well, this caused "Hot Pants" to write to my mother asking her for my address, when I'd next be home, and to call on her when and if I did get home. I called her yesterday and met her in Liggetts. Here is the story – I walked into the hangout and Meg gave me her "braceless" smile. We sat down and talked. As it happened there was a frat dance at the Edgewood last nite, so I said to myself, "What the hell, I'll ask her to the dance." But first I said, "How are you and the Spook doing?" She made a sign of disgust and made an unrepeatable remark about him. "Oh," I said to myself, "Poor Spooky." I kidded the hell out of her for a while and then asked her to the dance. Then the fun started. She said that she'd promised the Spook she'd go with him. For the next hour or so I kept casting remarks at her trying to make her break the date. I said, "You're not very good at keeping promises. Come on, Meg, I'm in the mood for you. We'll have the whole front and back seat. What about it?" She proceeded to explain that it was their last date together and Pater considered it a date "for old time's sake" I said, "Well, for now time's sake, come to the dance with me." It didn't make a damn bit of difference if she went to the dance with me or not. I didn't expect her to beak the date, but I figured that she'd be liable to do anything and that we'd have a good time together if she did break the date. I kept telling her that it made no difference to her or to him if they kept the date. Now get this – Meg said, "It doesn't make any difference to me, but I know that it would make a difference to him." You see that she's still a "pisser." That remark really tickled me. During the course of the afternoon we listened to some records at "Dirty Gertie's" and I kept saying, "Well, what time will I see you tonite etc. etc. " Every time I said it, she almost gave in. Wheeeee! Before I left her I asked her jokingly to kiss me. She didn't want to because she complained that there were too many people on Main Street at the time. I said that a handshake would have to do. She started shaking hands and she squeezed it (my hand) very tightly and looked very sincerely into my eyes with that "wantsome" look of hers. She asked me to promise her to write. I told her that I didn't want to promise because I knew that I wouldn't write. That slightly surprised her, but she couldn't say anything about it. She asked me to call her today. I may call and see if she still loves me and mine. Doesn't that really charge you, Charlie?? "Lassie Comes Home" from the pup family of the same name. She claims that she'll be home next week. I think I'll ask her out. I wish that you were here to guide me as to where I should drop my first load. "Enuf of dis luffink."

I don't quite understand you as far as Launa goes. We'll have to leave this as a topic of discussion when we meet. You haven't explained everything in full detail, and I don't know Launa very well.

I like "Dolores." Swinburne must have been quite the Errol Flynn. He makes it so realistic. Some day I'll write my sequel to it. Maybe next week, after I go out with Meg.

Have you heard from Lucy or Cheryl lately? Are they all still desirous of your "olive"? They are all probably turning green with envy.

Here I am, Charles, a man torn between two loves. But my motto is to take one love at a time, and that's exactly what I've been doing. I still write to Peggy, the Los Angeles girl. Our letters are not as frequent and passionate as they were at first. I do know that I have a warm feeling for her, but time and distance has changed things a little. If we ever meet again, I do believe that "things" will start all over again. At present I'm having the time of my life with that "South Iceland" girl Alice. We've had about three dates together and are planning to see each other as much as possible before I leave. She's blonde, blue-eyed and ever lovable. Maybe it's just another passing fancy. I guess time will tell, but I'm going to get as much enjoyment as possible.

Latest: Francine Valin is engaged to Lennie Hopkins. I haven't seen her since I've returned but intend to do so. You always said that she liked the guy.

I saw your sister yesterday and also this morning. She looks about the same. No weak ankles or anything.

I haven't seen Maurice or Elmer. I guess that they must feel pretty low with the government deciding to draft 4-F's. Wouldn't it be a howl to see Morry in uniform? I bet that if he ever got in he'd try to run the place with profits from Black Market gas. He'd probably get the Executive Officer to allow him to take his station wagon with him. I've been told that he's still the same "rah-rah."

I expect a leave from Friday Feb. 16th to the 23rd. I only wish that you were going to be here to spend it with me. I'll probably be back in July for awhile, so maybe things will be changed by then.

I hope that things are o.k. with you, Charlie. Take care of yourself. I want to be able to keep that D–Day date one of these days with you.

I'm going to see your parents before I leave, so I'll tell you in my next letter how "things" are at home.

I promise that my next letter to you will not be delayed as long as this one was.

I'll say goodbye only for awhile. I advise that you not write until you hear from me next. My mail situation is all screwed up. You'll have my permanent address on my next letter. Take care now.

Your pal,
Dick

P.S. Congrats on your new rate
P.S. Forgot to tell you. I was told this morning that the band didn't even show up at the dance last nite. That must have burned the Spook's sheet.

17 Anise Street
New Britain, Conn.
February 14, 1945

My dear Son,

Today is Valentine's Day and Donny brought home quite a few from school. Do you remember those days? He sent me one thru the mail, I got quite a kick out of it. He couldn't get one with Mother so he bought one with My Best Friend on it.

He is listening to the Lone Ranger and Betty is at Church taking her baton lessons.

Pa is in bed, he's been sick all day with a cold and sore throat. I told him shoveling so much snow and the snow ball fight he had didn't do him any good. He was out selling links and chains Mon. Tues, he got rid of all the chains we had. He must have sold over $200.00 dollars worth. All we have *left now is a few cases of Jiffy Links. Too bad we haven't any more stock on hand. We had so much snow this year and I guess we are due for more.*

I guess I told you how I got the turtles and they are pretty. Betty got her necklace and bracelet, now it's Donny's turn to get his souvenir.

You asked me why Freddy was in the brig. It was because he went back a day late.

Betty saw Dickey Walton and he said he was coming over Sunday to see us, but he didn't show up.

Dottie Cabelus and her girlfriend were over to Aunt Anna's for the weekend. Tag was saying how they are starting to send the fellows overseas again. Their six months are up. Tag's will be up next month. I suppose he will go over again. Bert Teske is down at Norfolk, Va. Do you remember his cousin Ray? He was only in the service four months and he is over in the Philippines now. Mrs. Savage hasn't heard from Merton in quite some time. She is so worried.

We went over to see Jane's baby the other day, Lala, Fan and I. She is so happy. The baby looks like her husband. All she does is pray for the war to be over so her John can come home.

We went over to see Nellie the other afternoon. Lala and I and then Pa and Eddie came over. They were half in the bag otherwise I don't think they would have gone over. We finally saw the baby. She's getting so big. I told her you said she should name her Rhododendron – she laughed.

Westermans are having their house covered with those white shingles. It looks good. Well, I guess I told you everything. (do the boys get any cigarettes over there?) They are so scarce around here. Donny keeps buying tobacco for Pa, he is going to make sure Pa doesn't run short of cigarettes. Even Lala rolls hers. Well, I guess I'll hit the hay. I feel lousy. I must have caught the cold from Daddy .Take care of yourself.

Love,

Mother

91 West Street
New Britain, Conn.
February 16, 1945

(How do you like the scent of my "Pink Passion"?)
Hi, Sweetie,

Was I ever glad to hear from you this morning. Your letter couldn't have come at a better time. – no kidding. We haven't laughed so hard in a long time! I nearly died when I read the envelope – you joker- what were

475

you thinking? "The House of the Good Shepherd?" You weren't far from wrong.!!

Darn it all – I hope you received my letter – AIR Mail! I'm not used to sending air mail letters – that's why I probably forgot.

This is the first weekend I've stayed in this berg since I got back from Christmas and it is hell! Cripes, there isn't a darn thing to do. Last weekend I went up to Stewart Field to see Bob -boy – I really had a wonderful time. This is the first weekend I haven't seen him since Xmas. I think Ryan, Marty and I will be going in to New York tomorrow. Anywhere away from here. Right now I think I'll drown my sorrows in drink starting at 10 a.m. tomorrow morning when we hit the Great White Way. I'm jesting of course! Ha!!!

You asked me if had heard from Dick. I have not only heard from him but seen the "salty sea scout" 2 weekends ago. He's stationed in Brooklyn at present. I think his 10 day furlough starts today or tomorrow. He really looks swell. That Sunday Dick, Bob and I were home, both of them came over – you should hear Walton play boogie-woogie - he's a solid sender. Last weekend he came home and so did Meg. They got together for quite a while. Pater and Meg had a little spat. Bolan would kill me if she knew I was shooting off my mouth like this, of course. I know she won't ever hear of it – naturally – you're sooooo dependable, honey!!!! By the way, mother was asking for you the other day.

We just came up from playing a few thousand hands of bridge – not much to do with our time, you know.

So, H.S. is still giving you a break. I'd love to see a letter she wrote to you and the letter you wrote back – no question, they are priceless.

I guess I must have told you about our new teacher. Dr. Remer. He sure is a pip. We usually have a spot of coffee before classes – need to!!! I swear that man knows more jokes – like, definition of a French breakfast. A roll in bed with a little honey. Strictly Remer!!!

My brother has about three more weeks to go before he gets his wings. Can't wait. The other night he and his instructor were in a crack-up. They were coming in for a landing and somehow turned over going 85 mph. I nearly died when I heard that.

Well, peaches, s'all for the time being. I expect to hear from you again real soon!

Lotsa love,
Peaches

How you coming with my grass skirt?
Hi, Charlie – I'm Peaches's suitemate and had to say hello before she put
this in the mail – I've seen you're picture! That's the reason I had to put
in a word – Marines are the favorites now and forever! – I won't say be
good – just take it easy. Kay Galbraith (the gal next door).

Charlie Darling old beau

How's every little thing? Well, Peaches is out cold on the floor, she still
can't understand why she should send a letter to you air mail. I just beat
her to a pulp trying to make her put six cents on it—that's a lot of bull!!!

Have you run into my little brother Don? He must be around in your
vicinity. He wants to get a look at the chocolate babies too!

Your Peaches and I really have a good time up here raising the roof,
smoking in bed and drinking beer in the johns, more darn fun.

Mary Jo is getting all excited about putting on all air mail stamps so
she wants me to hurry—so's that!

Good luck to you and don't drink too much south sea island moonshine.

     Love,
      Sally Jane

       4th Bn. 15th Marines
       Sixth Marine Division
       San Francisco, Cal.
       February 17, 1945

Dear Don,

I was very glad to get your letter tonight. I thought it was from Betty
at first. Your writing has really improved. I guess you'll be quite a guy
when I see you next. Maybe we can get a couple of dates and have a time
for ourselves. We could bring Betty and her boyfriend, too. I suppose they
would get in the bag and ruin the party.

I'm sorry to hear that Dad can't get many cigarettes but we aren't
allowed to send them home. I wouldn't want to try 'cause the brig isn't
the nicest place to be in. Besides, you know I wouldn't do a thing like that.

I'm sending home some of my extra gear. My sea bag is so full of crap
now I can hardly move it. There is also an old club in the package. I found
it back in the boon docks. The handle is wired up because it's cracked. You'll
be able to glue it pretty easily. Don't hit Betty with it.

About trapping. If I were you I'd quit for this year and get ready for
next year. Get all your trays together and boil them and then put them in

a good dry place. It's too late to make any money now, and the skunks and muskrats are breeding now. You wouldn't want to catch the mothers cause next year there won't be any. Next fall I'll tell you just where you can get them. Most all of the other trappers will be in the service so you'll have an open field. So forget about trapping for now. Concentrate on your school work, and keep the letters coming to me.

Love,

Charlie

232 Mountain Drive

West Hartford, Conn.

February 17, 1945

Dear Charlie,

Today is my 20th birthday and I feel very good and happy that I have had such a nice 20 years with so many nice friends. If my dad were here, my life would really be complete .It's probably difficult for people to understand how a girl could feel as I do about my dad, but when I was younger he used to talk about how things would be when I got older, and how much fun we would have. He used to kid me about the boyfriends I'd have. Maybe it's better this way 'cause he might not be able to help me choose the right one.

Charlie, dear, you mustn't be disgusted with Benny. It really isn't like you to tell me not to think too much about him. We've been going together for 3 years now and have been happy. We couldn't be happy if we were just tied to each other. We're so young and would be bored to tears with just each other. Love is partly understanding and tolerance, and those virtues have to be acquired. What could be better than acquiring them now?

The etching of the chapel is lovely. I love little churches. They're much easier to pray in. During Lent I'm going to early mass and trying to do extra things. I pray for you every day – I don't think I ever told you that – and I hope it helps you to fulfill lots of your dreams.

I think I'll leave you here, my pet, because this might depress you and I don't want that. I'll write you a silly, goofy letter in a couple days.

Affectionately,

Helena

By the way, did you get the dictionary I sent?
I'm enclosing another "Blondie" cartoon. I gave up cigarettes but am inclined to enjoy Ben's pipe, with the same general results.

65 Arthur Street
New Britain, Conn.
February 18, 1945

Dear Charlesie Warlsie,

Here I am all charged up again. Received a letter from you this past week but have yet to read it. You see, it arrived here at home and Mother sent it to Brooklyn. In the meantime, I was on my way home. I'll answer your note when I get back.

Believe it or not, I'm home on a 7 day leave. I report back to Brooklyn on Tuesday morning. I have no idea when I'll be home again. I should be shoving off any day now. I left Brooklyn Tuesday last and spent two days in New York City. I arrived home Thursday with a couple of fellas who are stationed on the same ship as I. These two fellas stayed until Sat. nite. I've got a "sorry story" to tell you — it concerns Ginger (swinger) Dillon — Wheeeee! You see I was trying to think up a couple of dates for these two fellas. I finally got Ginger and Irene Dawson — anywho, I went into the Stanley Works to see Ginger about the date. I walked up to her, asked her about the date, got it all fixed up and asked her what time she wanted to be picked up. As it happens we've had quite a bit of snow and you can imagine what a time I'd have trying to get up So. Mountain Drive. I asked Ginger the condition of the road and she replied, "Oh, you needn't worry — I've been ploughed out!" I said, "What did you say, you've been ploughed out? I don't want to go out with you then!" Laff!! I thought my pants would never dry. The kid that went out with her said that he could have gone the limit with her but he wasn't prepared. I think that we should add Ginger to our "pisser list." But you should see her sister.

Since I wrote you last I've been out twice with that Staten Island girl (alias Southern Iceland). Her name is Alice Olsen and she's a blonde. I swear that the day I get a crush on a girl other than a blonde I'll smash my own cherry with a sledge hammer. Course, I could start raving about her in my usual manner. But you could perhaps tell me what I'm going to say before I start.

I walked into the Drug Store Friday and saw "Morry" the Horrible. You can just imagine him in his inimitable blaze manner. The greeting "How are ya, Swabby?" No further conversation. I remember when you came home from Harvard, Charlie, you said, "Gosh, Dick, I feel sorry for Morry." Well, I felt the same way, I didn't feel sorry that he wasn't in the Service, but I just felt sorry for him as a "man." Funny thing though, I guess that he'll always get by.

479

Friday, I went to the N.B. Halls of Learning to see some of the old clan. The Ethiopian Kid(is –it- a –nose- or- a- rose) Sala, James, Schmidt, Guilford, McCauley – they're all still there.

This must be an age of regeneration or something. Remember Gladys Hummer? Well, she's taking up nursing at N.B.G.H. I'll bet for every needle she throws, she'll expect a "meat" needle in exchange What's this world coming to?

When I get back to Brooklyn my days will be limited. At present I'm not living on the ship. Perhaps I'll start this when I return Tuesday. It seems so strange trying to convince myself that I will be leaving the country soon.

Now how are things with you, you ole turd you? I was speaking to Benny and he says that you're on Guadalcanal. You certainly get around, don't you? I can imagine the bull session you and I are going to have one of these days.

I'll write you again soon, Chas. The address on the envelope is one I'm not sure of at present. Perhaps in my next letter I'll be able to give you a definite address.

Til I hear from you next, keep it in your pants and if you can't, think of me on the fifth – if you get that far. S'all for now!!

As ever,

Dick

17 Anise Street
New Britain, Conn.
February 19, 1945

Dear Brother,

Hiiiiii, kid, how are you? (Just call me Benjamin). I received a letter from you today and Saturday Mother received three letters.

I'm enclosing a few snapshots of the snow. I took a few more but they didn't come out. I'm also sending a picture of Benny's brother George and his girl, Polly Jones. It was in The Red And Gold, and I thought you'd get a kick out of it. It reminds me so much of Benjamin. His girl is sort of nice, but ahem, a little on the wide side.

School is the same as usual and next week we get our week vacation. Boy, I can't wait.

I'm glad you got so many Valentines from all your girlfriends. It was nice of Launa to send you two of them.. This is a short letter, but nothing else to write. More tomorrow.

Love and kisses,
Betty

PS. *Did you send a lot of Valentines to the Gooks?*

17 Anise Street
New Britain, Conn.
February 23, 1945

Dear Brother,

I wish you'd make up your mind on whether you're going to start school again or not. You'll be so used to staying in bed you'll never want to start studying again.

Donny's out in the kitchen moaning. He got a piece of onion. You'd think he's going out or something tonight. Maybe with Charlotte?? I still kid him about her.

Well, we got out of school this Friday for a whole week. I'm so happy. Friday there's going to be a "Band Concert." I guess that I'll go.

Donny brought your sword to school for a George Washington play. He just told me now. He said go ahead and tell him. G'wan I don't care. Like heck he doesn't, he's all excited.

Lent starts tomorrow and I'm giving up candy. You should just give up. (Ha, ha!).

You shouldn't say that about your tan coat. You know you love it. (The dog's been sleeping on it.) Well, I guess that's all for now.

Love,

Betty

P.S. In English we're having Short Stories and of course I have to read them. I don't mind reading so much now. Perhaps I'll start reading a novel one of these days.

The other night (Saturday) Danny Bray, K. Neubauer and Bielert were down to the Stanley Hotel. There were two guys down there and they wanted to know what kind of a sailor Danny was, 'cause he was home so often and why Kenny wasn't in the army. They had an argument over it and they went out in a dark alley and had a brawl. Kenny was all scratched up and bloody so I can imagine how Bray and Bielert looked. They must have had some fight.

That's all the "Bloody" news for now.

Sis

17 Anise Street
New Britain, Conn.

March 20, 1945

Dear Brother,

I received my necklace and bracelet today and gosh they're pretty. Thanks a lot. They remind me of something the Egyptians wore. I'll wear them to school tomorrow and see how the girls like them.

I also received a letter from you today. You said you haven't heard from Dickey. Well, he was home this weekend. He was suppose to come over here yesterday afternoon, but he didn't. I saw him downtown Saturday and he said he received a letter from you about two days before. I guess you'll hear from him shortly.

I'm glad you received your shoes. Were the shoes so big you had to put cardboard in them? I got width B and you told me to get C.

I thought Mother told you we had received the $90 money order. We have it all spent already. (hah, hah).

We started American Poetry in English today. I'm glad we finally got something I enjoy.

I guess you are pretty fickle when you haven't heard from H.S. Cheryl in two weeks. I think you're losing your touch. (G' Wan!)

Our Sodality gave a dance Friday and it really charged me. Most of the girls in the So-duality are about thirteen or fourteen so all the little boys were there. I had more darn fun. The boys came up to my knees. I sat and talked with Father Webb practically all night, I almost broke out when the kids started to play, "Going to Jerusalem." (More fun for the kids).

Elise Glabau (Aud's sister) got married two weeks ago. She married a soldier and the name will slay you. Salvatore Scapelletti. But I know him and he's really swell. Elise has been going with him for about two years now. He went to Yale, too. It's just the name that sounds so awful.

Aud Glabau goes with a kid named Francis Wesaly. His nickname is "Wiesel." She certainly picks some pips. Now take me for instance, I can't stand the crazy kids in High School. I think they're all a bunch of jerks. And I'm not fooling either.

I guess that's all for now and thanks again for the necklace and bracelet.

Love & Kisses, xxxxx

Betty

P.S. I took a few pictures of the snow etc. If they come out I'll send them to you. O.K? I've saved that film for about a year so they had better come out.

-SEVEN-

OKINAWA 1945

Loaf Hill, seen from the north. This unpretentious elevation formed one leg of a triangular system which protected the left flank of the Shuri Line.

> *4th Bn. 15th Marines*
> *Sixth Marine Division*
> *San Francisco, Cal.*
> *April 1, 1945*

Dear Folks,

I still can't say much or anything in fact about where I am or what I am doing etc. All I can tell you is that I'm fine and the food is pretty good.

I haven't received any mail in over two weeks now, but I should get some soon now that we are on land.

You know what I would like for my birthday. It's a little early, I know, but it will take that long to get here. I want, and really need, a Colt 32 automatic like the one Dad traded. You can get a holster easy enough at Hadfields or Maniers and one of Dad's friends should be able to get him some ammunition. In fact, I think I could get it out here if I had to. See what you can do as soon as possible. Maybe you could use this as a request. Well, that's all for now. Don't worry about me 'cause I'm alright.

> *Love,*
> *Charlie*

> *4th Bn. 15th Marines*
> *Sixth Marine Division*
> *San Francisco, Cal.*
> *April 14, 1945*

Dear Folks,

The censorship has been partially lifted and I can tell you a few things. I'm on Okinawa. Dad probably read about my Division being here in the paper.

We've been eating rations, of course, but they aren't bad. We cook over an open fire in our helmets. At first we were allowed to kill the chickens and pigs around, but we aren't allowed to do that any more. I've seen several good Japs (dead ones) but we've been quite lucky.

I got my first mail on the island yesterday. Two letters from Launa. I'll probably get quite a load of mail soon. Then I'll be able to write a lot more.

I'm enclosing some Jap money. Some of it is invasion money that I bought before hitting the island. The rest is the McCoy. Save all the junk I send home 'cause I'll want it for souvenirs after the war. I bought two hand-carved really nice war clubs before I left for here. Also, a grass skirt. I'll send it home when I get out of combat.

Well, that's the scoop for today. Write soon and I'll write again tomorrow.

Love,

Charlie

P.S. Excuse the messy writing. I hope you can read it.

P.S.S. Tough – I won't send the money home till this operation is over. Things is tough all over. D– the censor!

4th Bn. 15th Marines

Sixth Marine Division

San Francisco, Cal.

April 15, 1945

Dear Mom,

A whole load of mail finally got here yesterday but there was only one letter from you. There will be a lot more in today, I guess. The letter from you was dated the 15th of March.

Yesterday we heard that the war in Germany was over and that Russia had declared war on Japan and that the Russians were twenty miles inside Manchuria. We almost went mad with joy. Then last night we heard the news and it didn't say a thing about it. It may still be true 'cause we are a whole day behind. We didn't hear about the President dying till last Friday.

Everyone out here felt pretty bad about the President's death. It sure was a shame.

We haven't had too much medical work to do so far. Our outfit has been extra lucky so far. The days are fine but at night the Japs raise hell and we do most of our firing at night. Last night I was nearly asleep. I was all wrapped up in a blanket and poncho just as snug as a bug in a rug. Then all our guns opened up and I nearly dug twelve more feet into the ground. Fun!

The people here are all about four feet high. Most of them are peasants. You should see the rice fields here. The farms are just as neat and not a weed in them.

I have a little Jap money and some coins but I can't send them home yet. Maybe if we ever get out of this combat zone I'll be able to.

I was sorry to hear about Jane dying. She certainly was a good hearted soul.

What is Tommy's rate? He's a sergeant but what kind? He's been lucky to be home so much. He was only overseas about six months, wasn't he?

485

I owe Aunt Anna a letter but I haven't time to write now. Tell her that I was asking for her, and that I'll write when I can.

Love to all,

Charlie

4th Bn. 15th Marines

Sixth Marine Division

San Francisco, Cal.

April 17, 1945 (V-Mail)

Dear Mom & Dad,

 This is the Okinawa kid again. I still haven't got a heck of a lot to tell you.

 I'm still fine and the Nips aren't giving us too much trouble. We've been pretty lucky so far on that score.

 I still haven't received any mail from you yet, but I will soon.

 I guess you know more about the campaign here than I do.

 We just know about our immediate vicinity.

 I'm not losing any weight and I'm getting enough to eat.

 I hope that this gets to you soon and that you won't worry about me.

Love,

Charlie

4th Bn. 15th Marines

Sixth Marine Division

San Francisco, Cal.

April 20, 1945

Dear lil' sister,

 How's the working girl? I can picture you working in Birnbaum's! "Turn on the green light, Lizzie, the lady wants a green dress. Dot's good goods. It looks wery well on you."

 I'm enclosing a little Jap money. I'll send stuff home from time to time as soon as I am able. You and Donny can show the stuff around but I wish you'd keep track of the stuff for me. I've got a flag and some coins, too, but, as I said before, I can't send that stuff home yet.

 Ernie Pyle was killed a short distance from where I am. It's not the same island tho. We were suppose to hit that island but a few Japs are in the way—we'll get rid of them soon. Do you want me to send you some Jap ears or a quart of Jap blood? Donny is probably all excited now.

 You should see the kids here, they are just as cute as hell (the big ones are nice, too— Ga' Wan!).No kidding, all the little girls look like Imogene in Dixie Dugan. The boys can say "Gung Ho" and we tried to get some to

486

sing "Shoo-Shoo, Baby" but all they could sing was the "Shoo-Shoo" part. We give them sugar etc. More fun!

Did I tell you that I heard from Cheryl? She says that we should be friends and a lot of other crap. So like a big-hearted kid, I wrote her a dehydrated letter. I told her I was too busy etc. Here we go again –

Launa has been writing almost every day. God bless the child. She said that she saw you downtown and that you were getting awfully cute. So, I told her she must have the wrong person. Ga' Wan! How about some pictures? Well, little Darlin', that's all for now. Write soon.

Love and kisses,

Cha Lee Yung (The Okinawa kid)

4*th* Bn. 15*th* Marines

Sixth Marine Division

San Francisco, Cal.

April 24, 1945

Dear Folks,

I'm sorry that I haven't written lately but I just couldn't find time.

I'll have more time to myself from now on, however. We are setting up a permanent camp now.

All the fighting has ceased up at our end of the island. That is most of it. There are a few scattered pockets behind our lines. We advanced north so fast that we didn't have time to wipe them all out. The doggies are still fluffing off at their end of the island. The Marines took three-quarters of it and the Army can't even secure one quarter of it. Iwo Jima was secured in twenty-one days and that was a darn sight tougher. They've been at it now for twenty-four days.

We have a pretty nice tent for ourselves here. We looted three civilian houses and got a lot of mats, desks, chairs tables etc. Most all of the houses have been destroyed by artillery or burning.

Some mail came in yesterday but I only got one. That was from Launa. I should have a lot of back mail coming in. Well, that's all for now, write soon.

Love,

Charlie

4*th* Bn. 15*th* Marines

Sixth Marine Division

San Francisco, Cal.

April 26, 1945

Dear Folks,

I haven't written in the last three or four days so I guess it's time that I did.

I haven't had any mail in about a week now. Very little mail has been coming in.

Our part of the island is secure now, so there isn't any need of you worrying.

Our sick bay is all set up. We have quite a bit of Jap gear. We use Jap peroxide and adhesive tape.

I have a few nice Jap thermometers for souvenirs. We can't send anything home, however.

I should get some mail tomorrow and then I'll write some long letters. But just now I can't think of a darn thing to tell you. I'm sort of anxious to get an answer to my first letters written on this island. If you see any clippings on the Sixth Marine Division send them on to me.

Bye for now. I'll write again tomorrow.

All my love,
Charlie

4th Bn. 15th Marines
Sixth Marine Division
San Francisco, Cal.
April 28, 1945

Dear Mom, Dad and the little tots –

This is my nightly quickie. I've been busy as heck for the last few days .I haven't received any mail for a week now but there is supposed to be some in tonight. Nothing to write about happens around here. We get up in the morning, work on our sick bay, treat the patients and go to bed at night. I'll be able to write more when I hear from you but until then I'll just have to write brief letters and tell you that I'm alright.

Tell Dad if he can't get me a .32 a .45 will be alright. I won't be able to get any ammunition for a .32 anyway. That's about all for now and please don't worry about me.

Love,
Charlie

4th Bn. 15th Marines
Sixth Marine Division
San Francisco, Cal.
April 29, 1945

Dear Mom,

I just received your letter of March 20 and I don't have to tell you how glad I was to get it. I look forward to your letters and it seems as tho you hardly ever write.

Today is Sunday. I wouldn't even know it if I didn't keep up our daily records. I haven't been to church in over a month and a half now. Time goes by pretty fast in combat.

You will probably get this around Mother's Day. I'm not sure when it is but I think it's somewhere around the second Sunday in May. I haven't any money and so I can't send anything this year. I'm sorry that I wasn't able to send anything at Easter either. Next year I should be home. I sure hope so. I hope that you won't think that I've forgotten.

I get quite a kick out of the cigarette shortage in the States. I've been smoking like a fiend since we started on this campaign. I've quit again but it's about all we have to do.

I went out on a patrol today. A Jap bomber was shot down in our area last night. We hiked all morning and finally found the plane. It was in pretty good shape but the crew was gone. They took the machine guns off of it and went off into the hills. There were two big empty saki (Jap booze) bottles in the plane. I guess they need to be a little boozed up to come over us. We've been knocking them down right and left.

As you know, by the newspapers, the Marines have taken ¾ of this island and the doggies haven't even started to take their ¼. That's why the Marines hate the doggies so.

I have a letter to Betty to answer. I'll do that tomorrow. The days go by so quickly around here. I wish that the months went by just as fast.

Launa has been writing pretty regularly, and I got a letter from Helena, too. She said that Benjamin was on a shake down cruise. Well, Mom, I guess I've covered about everything. I'll write to Sis tomorrow. I hope that you've been hearing from me.

Love,

Charlie

4th Bn. 15th Marines
Sixth Marine Division
San Francisco, Cal.
2 May 1945

Dear Folks,

What a day! It's been raining for the past two days. There isn't much to do today tho.

There hasn't been any mail in the battalion for about five days now. Sooner or later we are bound to get some.

The rain is good in a way. When it's cloudy the Jap bombers can't come over. When they do come over, they have to fly pretty high 'cause our AA fire is pretty accurate.

The gooks here are getting braver every day. There is one here from Montana. That is, he spent a lot of time there. The other day an officer said, "Get those gooks out of our area." And old Dick Montana said, "They not gooks, you gooks." That major really got mad.

That's all for now, write soon.

Love,

Charlie

4ᵗʰ Bn. 15ᵗʰ Marines
Sixth Marine Division
San Francisco, Cal.
May 6, 1945

Dear Folks,

We had a mail call last night but I didn't get any from home. I got two from Launa and two from Tony DiAngelo. Both of them were pretty old.

We've left the north end of the island and are now relieving the yellow doggies. (Thirty-five days and the doggies still haven't taken Naha!).What an outfit they are!

All the NCO's were issued jungle hammocks to sleep in. The only trouble is they are off the ground. Every time the shrapnel starts dropping we have to roll out.

The Nips come over every morning about three o'clock. Then the fun starts. The search lights open up, the forties, fifties and nineties start thumping. Most of the time they get away but we've shot plenty down. It's just like the Fourth of July only more so. Flares and tracers really light up the area.

Al G. is in Luzon. He said he was just cut a little. He said it will take fifty notarized, authenticated letters to make his family believe that he is in one piece. He said he was thinking of sending them a picture of him in the nude.

Today is Sunday again but all the days are alike here. We are up pretty high now in a pine grove The weather is a lot like spring at home. Well, that's all for now, write soon.

Love,

Charlie

4th Bn. 15th Marines
Sixth Marine Division
San Francisco, Cal.
8 May 1945

Dear Folks,

It's the Okinawa kid again, bringing you the news from the Pacific.

No mail for about four days now. The last mail I got was two from Al G. and two from Launa. I guess I told you about those.

I haven't been out of my hammock all day. I just got out for breakfast and supper. It's been raining all day. It started last night. Everything is so damn muddy. When the mud gets to be about ten feet thick, orders will come to move up to the front. It happens every time we displace. I guess we've had about one good day for displacing in ten. That's what makes life so interesting!

They say that all hostilities have ceased in Europe. We don't believe anything we hear anymore. It really doesn't make much difference, anyway.

I went to Mass Sunday afternoon. First time I've been in a long time. The priest wore dungarees, leggings and field shoes. He just had the stole on.

I've got to go to chow now. I'm starved. I heard we were having creamed (canned) turkey for chow. I'll write again tomorrow.

All my love,

Charlie

4th Bn. 15th Marines
Sixth Marine Division
San Francisco, Cal.
13 May 1945

Dear Dad,

I just received your letter of May 1st. I received one from Launa and Betty, too. I haven't received any mail written from April 20th – May 1st so you can see how fouled up everything is.

I'll have to sort of give you the word on one point. I can't have you think we are fluffing off, you know. We had it fairly easy when we were in the north but now we are in the south. The doggies had forty days to take

491

Naha and didn't gain a yard. We moved up to the front two days ago and expect to take Naha today. Hot stuff, huh? Our artillery outfit is nearest to the front. We can watch the battle with field glasses.

Yesterday I went up to the front lines to get a good look. It was pretty gruesome. We've had heavy casualties so far. Dead were lying all over the place. Most of them were Jap, however.

About five planes came over last night to bomb the fleet. We have a good view of the harbor from where we are. We shot down three of them. One of them crash dived into one of our ships. I can't tell you what kind it was, tho.

I guess a .45 would be better than a .32. Send me one as soon as you can, huh? I could have used it yesterday. A carbine is rather awkward for exploring caves and tombs.

I picked up a Jap helmet, belt, cartridge case and bayonet yesterday. Donny should be glad to hear that. I don't know when I'll be able to send the stuff home.

All in all I'm having quite a time. By the time you get this the Marines will probably have secured the south end of this island, too.

Tell Mom to write and I hope that you will answer this right away. I really look forward to your letters so don't disappoint me.

Your loving son,
Charlie

4th Bn. 15th Marines
Sixth Marine Division
San Francisco, Cal.
May 14, 1945

Dear Mom,

I got four letters last night. One from you and Benjamin and two from Launa. Your letter was dated 10th of April. That was almost a month ago.

There is quite a lot of excitement going on around here. We should take Naha today or tomorrow. Our casualties have been pretty heavy. There are a lot of dead Japs lying around. We don't bury them unless they are in our immediate area. They stink something awful.

It isn't as bad as I thought it would be. We caught several mortar shells in our area last night and I slept through the whole thing. A foxhole is as safe as can be. We have a big tomb in back of us and nothing would get us in there.

From the sound of Benjamin's letter, he's still in the States. The lucky fish.

So you're still rock gardening, huh? I can hardly wait to get home and do some work around the yard. We will have to put the garden up in back in shape again. I think I'll buy some rhododendron plants next time. Stolen ones don't seem to take too well. Did that rose bush and all that mountain laurel die, too? I thought for sure some of that stuff would live. How about the hedges up there and the lilacs? Tell me all about them.

The weather here has been beautiful. Just like it is at home. We aren't up with the pines now, but sort of on a plain near an airstrip. You probably have seen lots of maps in the paper. I guess we must be about a mile and a half from Naha. That town will be one big hole in the ground when we get through. That's about all for now, Mom. I owe Betty a letter so I'll write to her tomorrow. Bye for now –

All my love,
Charlie

4th Bn. 15th Marines
Sixth Marine Division
San Francisco, Cal.
May 16, 1945

Dear Mom,

I received your letter with the pictures in it last night. The letter got here in eight days which is really fast.

I sent the pictures back in a letter to Betty yesterday. I hope that she won't take the letter serious. They were terrible. Why did you ever let her get that coat. It looked like something Madame Queen would wear. Those shoulders and that neck! How old is she now, twenty-seven or twenty-eight? I kidded her about that, too.

I'm glad to hear that you went to Confession. Did Pa go to church on Easter like he said? He didn't mention going in his letters. You'd better get him on the ball.

I got a letter from Helena yesterday. She said Benjamin was on his shake down cruise. He's another Stateside commando.

I don't know how long it will take to secure this rock but I hope it's soon. I want to get the hell out of here. It isn't bad but it's so monotonous and dreary. Every day it get rougher. This will be worse than Iwo Jima soon, if it isn't now. There are lots of flies, too. They are especially thick because of the bodies.

Last night was pretty quiet. Our guns fired all night but the Japs only returned a few shells early this morning.

493

We will go to a rest area when we get through here. Maybe we will be there by the time you get this letter but I doubt it. The days go by awfully fast and the months lag. If I don't catch another operation next spring, I should be home for Easter. Launa keeps telling me that that isn't too long. I guess it isn't. Meanwhile, I'll keep marking the calendar.

Cheryl hasn't written in over a month. I'm tempted to write but I'd better not. I wrote her a V-Mail since I've been here. She's probably waiting for me to write.

I guess I told you I got a letter from Benjamin. I answered it yesterday. I haven't heard from Dick in quite some time. He must be evacuating wounded from Europe.

Donny hasn't written in quite some time. Has he forgotten how? Tell him if he has forgotten how to write, he can draw pictures. That's all for now. Write soon and whatever you do don't worry about me. There's no need at all.

All my love,
Charlie

4th Bn. 15th Marines
Sixth Marine Division
San Francisco, Cal.
May 18, 1945

Dear Bunny head –

First I'll apologize for the pencil writing. But I ain't got no udder ting to write youse wit , so it's got to be done, see. Pardon me, but my New Britain accent slips out once in a while. You could send me a pen for my birthday. Just the pen, not the pencil. If you sent it airmail it would get here pretty rapidly (Just hinting, you know).

It's hotter than heck here today. The nights get nice and cool. We have to wear our jackets. We sleep with our clothes on.

The funniest thing happened last night. A Jap plane flew over and we heard the bombs swishing down. The cave is about three feet from where we sleep (it's too stuffy to sleep in). Anywho, the doctor couldn't find the entrance and one fellow looked into a mirror that we have near the cave and he thought he saw a Jap in the cave. I was in the cave before they even landed. We nearly died laughing. Ya –

You don't know how lucky I am to be with the artillery. Every night we lay down a smoke screen to evacuate the wounded. Last night we lost one of our best Lieutenants. He was on the FO (forward observer) team.

494

The infantry has it really rough. I saw my friend from med. bn. He's with the infantry. We got a gallon of coke syrup from the Red Cross the other day. We mix it with water. Horse ----but good! I'll have to tell you that joke when I get back. You'll fill your scivvie drawers laughing.

You said you were getting some good records. I hope you'll get Rum &Coca Cola (the record, stop drooling!) by the A. Sisters. That record sends me (but I'm too smart to go.) We hear it on the Tokyo broadcast once in a while. By the time I get home, you will probably be doing a lot of new dances (the pogo hop etc.). Does Wart do the lindy or black-bottom yet? Mary Hennessey and I were experts at the "Farmers Shuffle". Well, bobby socks, I'll have to leave you now. I have a few pieces I must lux.

Your big brudder,

Blood and guts

How do you like the enclosed cartoon?. In case you don't know what "Joe" is, it's coffee.   Yours again,

C.

4ᵗʰ Bn. 15ᵗʰ Marines

Sixth Marine Division

San Francisco, Cal.

May 20, 1945

Dear Kids,

I wasn't going to write today but seeing as how I went to Communion this morning and am feeling pretty good I thought that I'd give you all a break. I was burned up yesterday 'cause I didn't get any mail.

We had church services right in back of our guns this morning. Very picturesque – every time they fired I nearly dived into a foxhole. More fun!

I hope that you are saving some clippings on the Okinawa campaign for me. You don't have to save any about the doggies , just the 6ᵗʰ Marine Div. and all the pictures you can find.

The priest gave us some cards to send home. He wants us to let the folks back home know that we are all good lil' boys?!?

The weather has been lousy yesterday and today. It looks like it's going to clear, however. Boy, how I dread the rain.

We've been on this rock fifty days today. I don't know when we'll get off. We've been see-sawing on Sugar Loaf and Chocolate Drop (sounds like one of Betty's boyfriends) hill for almost two weeks now. There isn't a damn thing left on either one of them except charred rock, shell holes and corpses.

It's raining again! Yipes! Half the sky is clear so I guess it's just a shower.

I'm going up to see if I can see Elon this afternoon. His regiment is resting only about a half mile behind us. He really leads a rugged life in the infantry.

I've enclosed some more Jap money. I don't know whether I sent any of this type home. I'm going to send some cartoons, too, if I can find them. Bye for now, and write real soon.

Love to all,
Charlie

4th Bn. 15th Marines
Sixth Marine Division
San Francisco, Cal.
21May1945

Dear lil' Sister,

I received a letter from you yesterday dated the 19th of April. A little late but better late than never I guess.

I was pretty mad because you didn't "blow any smoke up my behind." That means flatter me. All you said was "It's swell that you got a new rate." Period. Do you think they hand these out in chow line?

You should have been here last night. We had more fun. More fun than the time I backed the car over your foot. About ten-thirty last night the Japs made first, a bonsai charge and then a counter attack. We were pushed back at first but then we laid in a terrific artillery barrage. In less than half an hour we laid in over fifteen hundred xxxxxx (still nervous) rounds. Those one hundred and fives of ours are really good. Anyway, after the barrage the infantry recaptured Sugar Loaf (for the umpteenth time) and made more gains. Hot Dawg –

I hit the sack at about 12:30 and didn't wake up until eight this morning. I slept like a log. I had my shoes on (clothes, too) and my pogo stick was waiting outside ready for a take off at any moment.

It's our fifty-first day today on this rock. If our losses continue as they have been, we'll have to be relieved in a week or so. That's about all for now. I'll write again tomorrow.

Love etc.
Charlie

4th Bn. 15th Marines
Sixth Marine Division

San Francisco, Cal.
22 May1945

Dear Donny,

I received your letter, one from Mother and four from Launa yesterday. I was beginning to think that you had forgotten how to write.

I know that you are excited about souvenirs. So far I have a Jap bayonet, helmet, belt and flag. It's kind of hard to lay all that stuff around and we can't send it home yet. As soon as we get into Naha I may be able to pick up a rifle. Now there is more of our equipment lying around than there is Jap. Every time we find a Jap or American rifle near the front, it has to be broken 'cause if the Japs push us back they will be able to use them. As it is they are using some of our machine guns and ammunition that they took on Sugar Loaf Hill. When the doggies retreated (before the Marines came down here) they left their equipment, dead, and wounded. The doggies fight different from the Marines. When the doggies encounter mortar fire, they stop and dig in. Then the Nips can keep them pinned down and kill a lot of them at the same time. That method is all right if there is a motorized Division like they had in Europe, but out here they can't make gains that way. The Marines keep on going and take the ground. In the end the casualties are the same but the doggies are still in the same place with nothing gained. That 27th Army Division really fouled everything up. The Marines think more of the 7th and 77th Army Divisions.

Well, Hugo, I have to close now. Write soon.

Love,

Charlie

4th Bn. 15th Marines
Sixth Marine Division
San Francisco, Cal.
23 May1945

Dear Sis,

I just received your letter dated the eighth of May. Mail seems to be getting better. Those pictures of Donny were good even though they were sort of hazy. (I still can't tell when they are upside down).

You said that the Sixth Marine Division wasn't mentioned much on the radio. It had better be now. It's about time they blew a little smoke our way.

You said I have to see a band meet when I get home. I'll only see it if you're performing. The only bands I want to hear are Dance bands and *football bands. Dig, dig, dig, well ah reet! Some day we'll go to the Falcon's Hall and get our rocks off. We'll either double-date or go ourselves. Launa goes big for the polka and shuffle! That's too far off to think of tho.*

I was sorry to hear about Prince getting hurt. If I were home I could have put the stitches in for only a few dollars. – Ga Wan –should I send Prince some flowers or would he prefer a Jap arm or leg to chew on?

It's been raining all day and everything is muddy. I never knew mud could be so lousy. I told one of the fellows that it rained during your vacation and he said, 'Ask her if she had to sleep out in it." I informed him that our house was partially covered with a straw roof. We do have fun !Gotta scram now. Write soon, little Darlin'.

Love,

Charlie

4ᵗʰ Bn. 15ᵗʰ Marines
Sixth Marine Division
San Francisco, Cal.
25 May1945

Dear Folksies,

How's every little thing this morning? It's raining here. It rained for three days and cleared up yesterday. We thought we were in for a week or two of nice weather, but this morning it started in again. Everything is muddy, even me.

I've got a couple of cartoons that are pretty good. They are a little muddy but think nothing of it.

We had some air action last night for the first time in over a week. I was in and out of my fox hole eleventeen times. Every time I'd get in I'd hear someone say, "Here he comes again. They've got him in the search lights!" Then I'd have to get out and watch. They were around for about an hour but I don't think we shot any down. We threw everything but our 105's at them but no dice. They were pretty high. You can't imagine the fireworks from the tracers.

The damp weather gets me down. They say it's good for making love and sleeping. I have a new Time Magazine and another book to read.

There isn't anything else to write about. I'll write again tomorrow if I hear from you.

Love,

Charlie

4ᵗʰ Bn. 15ᵗʰ Marines

Sixth Marine Division
San Francisco, Cal.
29 May1945

Dear Folks,

First of all I'll apologize for not writing in the last few days. There really isn't any excuse for it. I guess it was because of the rain. As you probably know from the radio, it's been raining for six days now. Everything is muddy. It's over three feet deep on the roads. Tracked vehicles can just about get through.

There hasn't been much mail in the battalion. We haven't had a mail call in about five days. I think that's due to the mud, too.

There haven't been many planes over here lately. On the shortwave broadcast from the States every night, we hear about all the planes being shot down but I haven't seen many.

The Twenty-Seventh army division is coming into the line again. They say that they want to redeem themselves. They will probably grab the credit for Naha and Shuri, too. That's the dogfaces for you. Old General Buckner got relieved. We got a kick out of that.

This is a short letter but I can't think of anything else to write about. I wish we'd go to our rest area soon. This is getting dull.

Well, folks, I'll close for now. Write soon 'cause you know how I look forward to your letters.

Love to all,
Charlie

4ᵗʰ Bn. 15ᵗʰ Marines
Sixth Marine Division
San Francisco, Cal.
June 1, 1945

Dearest Mom,

I received your letter and two from Sis last night. I'll answer yours today and hers tomorrow.

The rain has stopped and the mud is drying up. It will take a couple of weeks of sunshine to do a good job. The mud is hip-deep in most places. The roads are worst of all.

I have a Nip rifle. It's kind of beat up but I've been working on it for the past two days steadily. I'll tell Pa about it when I hear from him.

The day I went up after the Nip rifle I missed dinner. They just had some C-ration stew. When I came back that night everyone had dysentery but me. So I laughed at them. I hope I never get that stuff.

That land mine Merton stepped on must have been a dud. We call all duds "Uncle Dudley."

I've been on this rock for sixty-two days now. I hope we get relieved soon.

Why don't you send me packages? Not home made stuff 'cause that smashes. Send things like sardines, smoked cheese, dill pickles, olives, anchovies —pickled or canned — herring, canned peppers etc. We never get anything good like that to eat. I'll bet I haven't received ten packages since I've been overseas. I ought to rate one a week anyway. What's wrong with you people, aren't you patriotic? How about sending me some of the things I mentioned, huh?

There isn't much more to say. We may get some mail in tonight. I hope so. Bye for now and don't worry about me.

All my love,
Charlie

4th Bn. 15th Marines
Sixth Marine Division
San Francisco, Cal.
4 June 1945

Dear Dad,

I received your letter dated the twenty-first of March along with one from Betty last night. I also received a few birthday cards.

There is no reason at all for worrying about me. The only caves we ever go in have had the once over with a flame thrower.

I have a .31 caliber Jap rifle. It was pretty beat up and rusty when I found it . I sanded it down with emery cloth and blued it with some no. 30 oil and a blow torch. I'm not going to try to fix the stock. It is bolt action and very similar to our 03's. The bore is very good. I've been getting my rocks off firing it. I'd rather carry that than my carbine. It's lighter than the 03. I'll send it home when I get back to a rest camp.

Forty-fives are scarcer than hen's teeth. They are taken off bodies before they hit the ground. I had a Thompson sub-machine gun for a while. I turned it in 'cause it was heavy and I couldn't think of anyway to get it home. It was a .45 caliber. Just the thing for deer hunting. When it's fired it *keeps going up. It was a nice toy(?). There are also lots of BAR's (Browning Automatic Rifles) lying around but they weigh eighteen pounds.*

We are expecting a typhoon later on this afternoon. About an hour ago the sky really darkened and it's been pouring ever since. If it doesn't stop soon we will never secure this rock.

I'm sorry I mentioned going into caves. I should have known better. We feel just as safe here as we would back home. We've been here so long – it seems like always. It's sixty-five days today. That's about all for now, Dad, write soon.

Love,

Charlie

4ᵗʰ Bn. 15ᵗʰ Marines
Sixth Marine Division
San Francisco, Cal.
8 June1945

Dear Mom,

I received your letter and Donny's last night. I can't find the letter now, so I'll have to answer it from memory.

I got a letter from Cheryl last night. It was the first one in a long time. She told me that she was learning to drive and that she would have the car quite often. That did it! I wrote a long encouraging letter to her this morning. She will probably call you up. I hope that she doesn't start writing too often. Once a week is about how often I like to hear from her.

I received Betty's card and one from Kitty last night. Both of them were awfully nice. Thank Kitty for me. I don't know what her address is. I always get a card from Kitty on all the holidays.

The picture I sent was of some Jap corpsmen. I found it in one of these gook houses. I just thought that I'd enclose it.

You asked me how we took care of our casualties. I'll explain it the best I can. Each battery has two corpsmen – when there is a casualty in the battery they treat him and take him to the battalion aid station (that is what I am with). We give them plasma etc. and evacuate them to the Division field hospital. If they are bad the Division field hospital evacuates them by air or hospital ship to base hospitals on other islands. It is just a long chain. We haven't the room or facilities to keep casualties here. We have been pretty lucky. I'd say we had about ten percent casualties. That is low.

We are in a new position now. We moved up yesterday. We are on a high cliff overlooking all of Naha. I don't think we will move again until

501

we leave the island. Our guns can reach any part of the island now. That is where the Japs are. I guess that this is all for now, Mom. I'll write to Donny tomorrow.

Love,
Charlie

4th Bn. 15th Marines
Sixth Marine Division
San Francisco, Cal.
11 June1945

Dear Don,

I received your letter enclosed with Mother's the other day. I've been rather busy and this is the first chance I've had to answer.

The weather has been very nice here lately. I think it may rain tonight, however. The sky looks pretty dark.

I found a Belgian shot gun yesterday. It belonged to a Japanese naval officer. It's a twelve gauge and very light. You and I will be able to go duck hunting when I get home. I also found a seventeen jewel combination pocket and stop watch. It has no crystal on it though. I'll send it home when I can and have it fixed up. I also have a Jap mess gear. Everyone is souvenir happy around here. It makes the days go by much faster. I worked all day cleaning my shot gun. I'm short a trigger guard but that doesn't really matter.

You should be out of school by the time you get this. You will probably be sorry and miss it very much. Let's see – you are going into the third grade now, aren't you? I'm just kidding. I know you are going into the eighth grade. I'll bet that Betty will stay back again. She has been in high school for six years now, hasn't she? Some one told me that all the bobby sox kids thought she was a teacher.

You'll have to excuse all the scratches in this letter. It's getting dark now and I can hardly see. You'd better tell that family of ours to start writing. I haven't had a letter for the past three mail calls. Bye for now.

Your loving brother,
Charlie

4th Bn. 15th Marines
Sixth Marine Division
San Francisco, Cal.
12 June1945

502

Dear Mom,

I haven't much to say but you said you wanted me to write even if it was just a few lines.

We have to move up again tomorrow at four o'clock. Cripes, are we mad. This is a swell spot we are in and we've only been here a few days. I'm pretty positive this will be the last move before we leave the island. It had better be! We were supposed to take the peninsula near Naha and then secure. But the Army is stuck again and the Marines have to take their sector. Our division (twenty thousand men) has had eleven thousand casualties. We are all out of replacements. Two of our own corpsmen had to go to the infantry. We drew straws to see who would go. Our battalion is short four corpsmen now. We will get our replacements when we get back to our rest camp.

I have a Jap army, navy and marine blanket. The army is grey, the marine green, and the navy white with a blue cross in the corner. The white one is sort of dirty, but it can be dry cleaned when I send it home. They make nice souvenirs and beach blankets.

I washed all my clothes today. I hope they will be dry before we leave in the morning. I'm going down to the mountain spring to take a bath now. I'll write again tomorrow.

> *Love,*
> *Charlie*
>
> *4ᵗʰ Bn. 15ᵗʰ Marines*
> *Sixth Marine Division*
> *San Francisco, Cal.*
> *18 June1945*

Dear Mom,

I just received a letter from you, one from Kitty and one from Benny. I have Kitty's address now so I'll drop her a line tomorrow. She sent me a lot of clippings.

I got a kick out of Freddy losing his sea bag. I never heard of such a thing. I suppose he wrote and asked Aunt Anna for money to buy new clothes. Send me his address, will you? I haven't heard from him in a long time.

I found a nice silk Jap flag today. I also found a silver opium pipe. It has Jap writing on it. I'm going to trade off my shot gun for two flags tomorrow. When I get aboard ship, I'll be able to trade the flags for most anything. The shot gun is too much trouble. It rusts most every night and I have to clean it every morning. It's made in Belgium anyway. I don't know how I'll lug all my junk around as it is. If anyone ever stole my souvenirs, I'd crack up for sure.

I traded some Jap money for some pictures of Jap dead. They are too gruesome to send thru the mail. The censor would never pass them. More tomorrow. Write!

Love,
Charlie

4th Bn. 15th Marines
Sixth Marine Division
San Francisco, Cal.
20 June1945

Dear Betty,

It's me again. I wasn't going to write today, but we just had a mail call and there was a letter from you. So I thought I'd give you a break.

The campaign is about over but casualties are still walking in and people are still getting killed. We expect it to be over by Friday at the latest.

I guess when you get this the news of General Buckner's death will be old. In a way it is a good thing he died 'cause he would have had to answer a lot of questions later on. He fouled up this campaign in a big way. There hasn't been an announcement of the casualties yet, but it will be a terrific figure when it is announced.

You'd better not put that navy hammock up. I'll need that for shipping my navy gear around when I get back into the navy. You'd probably kill yourself getting into it anywho.

I wrote to Joe Rizzo today. I didn't know he was home until Mary Hennessey told me. I also answered Charlie Farmer's letter.

I have a little box of saki (Jap booze) dishes to send home. They have Jap military pictures on. They are like little cups. When I visit the girls around home, I'll give them a few souvenirs. They are really pretty nice. I have the box all packed and ready to go. We won't be able to send packages for a few days yet – till the island is secure. The box will get home next fall if someone doesn't steal it en route.

You said Mother wanted to know what I did all day. Well, it's like this: sometimes we go to parties, dances, horse races etc. No kidding, I couldn't tell you what I do all day 'cause every day is different. Some days we go for supplies in the jeep, we clean our rifles, treat patients, hunt souvenirs etc. - anything to kill time. This month has just flown by. If they would *only start feeding us. It looks like rain again. That's all we need. I don't care how much it rains as long as it doesn't hold us up. I can't wait to get off this lousy rock. Gotta go now. Write soon, little Darlin'.*

Love,
Charlie

4th Bn. 15th Marines
Sixth Marine Division
San Francisco, Cal.
23 June 1945

Dear Mom,

I just received your letter dated the 14th of June. It was the first letter for me in three days.

I've been busy for the past two days. I've been fixing up a sword I found. It had a wood handle, so I took it off and am working on a bone handle. It has a good blade.

This island is secure now. There are still plenty snipers around. One fellow was guarding a bunch of prisoners and was shot right through the heart. Civilians have been pouring out of the hills all week. Lots of them are wounded and the rest of them are in rags and look like a bunch of animals. Boy, they look terrible!

You asked me what we have been eating. Powdered eggs, canned meatloaf, dehydrated potatoes and canned hash of all kinds. We had fresh eggs one morning. I wish they could put up fresh milk somehow. I've never seen milk once since I've been overseas. I don't think I've lost much weight though.

Stillwell is in charge of the Tenth Army now. The Sixth Marine Division is part of the Tenth Army, you know. If we stay in the Tenth Army, we will probably go to China after three or four months in a rest camp. I'd much rather go to China than Japan.

The weather here has been pretty nice so far. I hope it stays that way.

There isn't much more to write about. Everything seems so quiet now that our guns have been secured. Those one hundred and five howitzers of ours really make a bang. The guns are ready to go aboard ship. Now all we need is a ship.

I've been out in the sun all day and am so tired I can hardly write. Bye for now.

Love,
Charlie

Connecticut College
New London, Conn.
June 23, 1945

Hello, Darling –

I was very surprised to hear from you again. As I understand it you were rather sick of "fanning the flame" or some such stuff. I'm glad to hear that I'm sill wonderful and that you're still in love with me. I don't want to be crude, dearest, but it did rather reek of a snow job. But don't let it worry you – all this junk about honesty being the best policy only leads to woe. You're the one that taught me that, darling. So carry on –

It seems so good to be writing to you again. It didn't quite seem possible that it was going to be all over – especially while there was a gorgeous moon. I think that when I'm a stodgy old married woman of 45 with four children, full moons will always remind me of you.

Everyone is saying the war will be over by Xmas – but I don't dare believe it. Japan is certainly taking an awful pounding right now though. So, of course, rumors of surrender are all over. They must know they haven't got a chance, and it would save so many lives if they would only quit now. But I guess that would be too much to hope for.

I read "Forever Amber" too, and I agree with you – it stank. It was sort of a take off on "Gone With The Wind" only a little more crude. I started skipping pages about half way through and I never did finish it. After a while that stuff gets a little monotonous. Wasn't "Valley of Decision" wonderful? I read it last summer. They've made a move of it with Greer Garson.

Enough idle chatter. I'll write tomorrow.

Love,

Launa

17 Anise Street
New Britain, Conn.
June 27, 1945

Dear Charlie,

Well, here I am again. Today it's nice out but awfully windy.

We receive mail regularly from you which is very good. Mother answered one of your letters yesterday.

Donny's complaining now because he's 37 cents short for his papers. Here's where Mother starts dishing out with the moola. He's some pip. For almost three days now he's been making a big airplane model. He has two bridge tables in the living-room, which he's making it on. I remember when you used to buy models but never finished them. Donny is really pretty good at it though.

Last night our Sodality gave our play again at the Polish Orphanage. We had more fun and horsed it up but good. The kids laughed and that's all that's necessary.

After the play I went to another dance at the golf course given by the Army detachment from the Newington home. It was some fun and they had a neat floor show with tap dancers, singers, comedians etc. Three other girls and myself were invited by some Lieutenants that were at the last dance. They had a buffet lunch, too. I guess I'm just stepping out with society, that's all!

Tonite I'm going to a dance at St. John's Church. The high school kids from our parish and St. John's are giving it, but St. John's have a hall and we haven't. First at 7:30 there is going to be a hot dog (weenie) roast and then dancing. Also two kids from each parish are going to be chosen to go to the shore for a day with Father Webb and Father O'Meara. We are going to have a drawing to see who wins.

Sunday all the CYO (Catholic Youth Organizations) got together and gave an outing at Stanley Quarter park. The priests played the boys in a game of baseball and the priests won. All the new priests are young and lots of fun.

I was just trying to think where you are now that the battle of Okinawa is over. I hope you will be at a rest base pretty soon. It was also good to hear that you're getting better food for a change.

I'm enclosing a couple of pictures that are lulus. I wasn't going to send them but I already told you that I had a film. The cameras are crazy old things and they don't take great pictures, but here's a couple of the ones that can be seen a little. No! I'm not doing an act!

Well, I have to go out and practice now for a spell. Bye now —
Love and kisses,
Betty
P.S. I'm only working half days for a while. Then maybe I won't work at all!

91 West Street
New Britain, Conn.
June 27, 1945

My dearest sweet Peaches,

You don't know how glad I was to hear from you. I guess you had a good reason for not answering my letters sooner. I didn't even know where in sam hill you were. From all reports – I guess there is quite a little monkey business going on out there.

Thanks so much for the "lettuce." I am going out and buy a grass skirt with it. Cripes – that "yen" really and truly stinks – excuse my expressive vocabulary but that is the only word I know to describe the odor.

My sister left this morning for Mexico – the lucky so and so! Just when I got back from taking Mother and Alice to the station – the Herald called. So I had to give them the information and I haven't the faintest idea if it's right. I don't know if 10 or 1000 girls are going on the trip. They also wanted her picture. When I saw it on the front page, I nearly had a stroke. I'll probably catch hell.

So Walton is carrying the torch again – I feel sorry for him. I hate to see a wonderful guy like him waste his time on anything so futile, 'cause right now Meg is all wrapped up in Pater. But you can't tell. This is strictly between you and me!!! Pater is still home. He got a 10 day extension. That makes 25 days he has been home. Some people have all the luck. I shouldn't sound so bitter though – 'cause his father is still very ill.

This Monday I start working at last. I should have started two weeks ago but that clown Dr. Benjamin got all balled up. I can't complain because I've done nothing but loaf since I got home!

You must know Louie DiPinto – he was that short, fat Italian kid – went around with Randy Lynch, Schmitz and the T.S, mob. Known for his cream convertible! Meg and I used to flip for pennies with him – more fun!!!

This afternoon Betty Logan, Barb M, and I went to see "Back to Bataan." Very good! That is about all we do – is take in flickers.

Well, sweetie, you sound pretty well down and out – but don't worry, you'll be home doing the farmer's shuffle before you know it. Lets make it a standing date to make the rounds of the bars when you get home. Mother is still laughing about that "Cha Lee" business. S'all this trip – write again real soon.

Oceans of love,
Mary Jo

4ᵗʰ Bn. 15ᵗʰ Marines
Sixth Marine Division
San Francisco, Cal.

27 June1945

Dear little (devil) Darlin'—

This is about the first letter I've written in three days. I've been waiting for a letter to answer. I received two from you today and my morale soared two hundred degrees. I damn near died laughing at your letter, in fact, my scivvies are still on the line.

The weather is still beautiful. It's rather windy at times but after the heat on the Canal anything is better. In a way, I'm going to hate going to Guam. They say the heat is terrific, too. Have you seen the picture of Guamanian girls in Life Magazine? Ga-Wan!

I wrote to Launa breaking things off over two weeks ago. She hasn't received the letter yet and I've been receiving letters (nice ones) apologizing for her not being able to write during her exam period. The crap will hit the fan when she gets the letter. I feel like and want to write to her but I'm not going to. Not for a few months anyway. I've got a lot of time to do out here. (Sounds like a prison only more so.) Keep the letters flowing, little Darlin'.

Your loving brother,
Charlie

4ʰ Bn. 15ᵗʰ Marines
Sixth Marine Division
San Francisco, Cal.
28 June1945

Dear Sis,

I wrote to you yesterday, but I still owe you a letter so this is it. We had a mail call today but I didn't score. You lose eighteen points, so there!

What a chow we had! (Not a chow dog, goop). Dehydrated cabbage (made in the pot we washed the baby's ankle in) and greasy canned corned beef. My stomach feels as though it has the blue goofuss. Did I ever tell you about the time Ray and I ate the dehydrated cereal? One night we were starved. All there was to eat was this box of cereal. You are supposed to add water and let it stand for twenty minutes. We added water but didn't wait. In about an hour I was thinking about sending home for a maternity dress, and Ray was sure he was going to have twins. We do have fun! Don't get excited, our stomachs receded shortly.

"Roger" means alright or okay. You should hear some of the code names that come over our radio. Have to get back to work now.

Love and kisses,
Charlie

509

4ᵗʰ Bn. 15ᵗʰ Marines
Sixth Marine Division
San Francisco, Cal.
30 June1945

Dear Sis,

I just received your letter and one from Aunt Anna. I was awfully glad to get both of them. You had the clipping in it about the battle being over. More smoke up our brow!

Did I tell you about the book I just finished reading? It was "The Valley of Decision." It was really a fine story. Now I'm reading "Arrowsmith." It is another good book. I'm next on the "Forever Amber" list, so as you can see my literary life has taken a turn for the best. Before long I'll be able to speak English again.

Saturday night and no place to go. When I get home, I'm going to go out every night for at least ten years. Tell me something – is the White Horse still on the corner of North St. and Hartford Ave.? We will have to see a lot of that place. The Blue Palace, too, and the Chicken Shack (how will I ever forget that place, after all the times we've been there?)

I'm not going to blow too much smoke your way over your report card. Eng, Biology and Latin were alright but the rest!! Do you know that I never went to Safe Driving and got an A (Rita Leonard used to check names and gave me the test beforehand.)

Last night there was a movie on the island. It was about five miles from our camp. About ninety of us went in one truck. It reminded me of Ziegler's car when it was loaded. I wasn't sitting on Lil's lap, however.

I just sent home a Jap officer's jacket so don't get too excited. There is something else nicer in the package for you. I hope the things don't get all mildew and moldy. There is a black kimono in one. Do I look sharp in it. Slicker than owl spit! Don't let Prince sleep on it.

I guess that's about all for now. Write soon and have fun.

Love,
Charlie

17 Anise Street
New Britain, Conn.
July 2, 1945

Dear Son,

Never a dull moment around here, Betty's getting ready to go up and get a permanent. She's a busy girl. Irene was over last night and she played *the piano while Donny played his guitar. We almost died laughing. He isn't doing so bad – if he would only practice.*

Chas. Farmer didn't pass this year. Fan felt pretty bad. I didn't tell Donny or he would tease him. Donny beat up Roger Paulson the other day. He had him by the neck when Pa came by with the truck or he might have choked him. Was Donny mad. He said if Dad didn't come along he would have killed Roger. More fun.

Jane Rawlings is going to live in Florida. John is still there – he was promoted again. They always say to tell Charlie we're asking for him.

Violet Carlson said she put a four leaf clover in your card – did you find it?

Pa said he is going to take piano lessons. We are having our piano tuned next week. I see where you and Betty will have to learn to sing or play some instrument. Well, that's all for now. Take care of yourself.

Love,

Mother

1st Bn. 15th Marines
Sixth Marine Division
San Francisco, Cal.
July 2, 1945

Dear Mom,

This is going to be one of those short sweet letters. I've been busy all morning, washing clothes etc. I've got about a million things to do.

My address has been changed. That is the main reason for this note. It's the First Bn. 15th Marines c/o FPO San Francisco. Just the same as before only the First Bn. instead of the 4th. It's the same outfit only they re-shuffled the batteries. That's about all for now. I'll write the next chance I get.

Love,

Charlie

P.S. *If you see Cheryl (the dear child) notify her of the change. I'd write but she owes me a letter. No time anyway.*

USS Mercy
FPO San Fran. Cal.
July 3, 1945

Dear Charlie –

I received your June 15th letter yesterday. I had been waiting anxiously for it to arrive, and it was really a treat hearing from you again. I'm happy to hear that you are safe and in good spirits.

511

I feel the same as you do, Chas. I've so much that I want to get off my mind. I'd give anything for one of those "nite" walks we used to take. When we get that opportunity again, we certainly will have a variety of experiences and opinions to express. It's really something to look forward to.

Of course, you know by now we paid you a visit at the time of the writing of the letter which I received yesterday. I'm surprised that you didn't mention anything about it in your letter. I imagine that it takes time for things like that to get around. We pulled in with my having great expectations of seeing you. After awhile I realized it was almost impossible as the island hadn't been secured and I couldn't get ashore. We stayed about four or five days and then pushed off with a load of patients. I was busy almost night and day during the run. I inquired amongst quite a few patients about the location of your outfit. Many of them hardly knew just about where you were. I was told you were in a comparatively safe place and I was satisfied. I feel certain that we'll meet some day soon. We'll be pulling in and out of these Pacific ports all the time. If you hear that we're in port, don't hesitate a minute to come aboard.

At present we are in dry-dock having our bottom scraped and painted. It's at the point when you'll be resting soon. How long we'll stay here I don't know. Won't be long though.

Your "Sea stories" are quite amazing. I had a chance to talk to a number of patients and they told me stories that were very similar to yours. Just to think that we were young, innocent kids a couple of years ago just graduating from high school, makes this whole mess seem like a dream. I can't figure out yet whether the experience of war to this generation will be of any value to it. I guess that only time will tell.

As you say, big doings are in the making. I guess no one knows when or where it will come off, but it's bound to break soon. I doubt that you'll be in on the next push. I know one thing, and that is that we'll be in and out of them from here on in unless something. . . . Enuf of dis luffink, let's fock!

I get mail in bunches every time I hit port. My main correspondents are now at home, Fleurette, and you. I get occasional letters from others if I have the energy to write. Fleurette, for some reason, has been writing quite frequently. I know what she's after – and it's not green with envy. That lil old girl had better watch out or I'm liable to "stick her" when I get home. Acres and acres and it's all mine – I haven't heard from Mary in a long time. Meg is writing quite regularly. She's been working in N.B.G.H.

I'm not going to break hers when I get home, Charlie, I'm just going to push it aside. Wheeeee!

I went out with "Frenchy" Valin when I was home last Feb. I knew that she was engaged and so did she – I think – although she didn't act much like it.

You should have quite a vocabulary by the time I see you again. When we get back to the States together we ought to take Meg and Mary out again and bellow with, "For Christ's sake, pass that f---in joe." I think they would defecate rather than draw small stores.

Remember those really crazy letters that we used to write each other? Gosh, that was a hell of a lot of fun. You know, I've forgotten all of our old lines. We sure were a bunch of pissers in our youth. Speaking of youth, I am out of my teens. I want to thank you for having remembered me. You were one of the few that did. I really appreciate it.

Well, my "hot potato," that's all for now. If I don't hear from you before too long, I'll write you. Till then, Charlie, take care and God Bless You.

Always,

Dick

51 Forest St.
Oakwood, Conn.
July 3, 1945

Dearest Chas,

I got another of your letters the other day and it was swell to hear from you again. I couldn't imagine why you hadn't written sooner though because since it seems all of a month ago since I had written to you, but in your letter you said you had just gotten mine. So that explained it. I guess it must have gotten lost on the way, but as you did get it, we really shouldn't find fault, even though it was a month late.

Here it is the night before the 4th of July and things are beginning to sound like a miniature battle-field already. The kids are really going to go to town with firework from the sound of things around the neighborhood. I don't blame them though, even though I've given my little toy gun away and don't have any more sky rockets to shoot off myself. I still get a kick out of watching them. Gee, I can remember Dad coming home with an arm full of sparklers and what have you a couple of years ago, and if he didn't have every color of the rainbow, I used to raise the roof off the house. I suppose things like that don't interest you anymore either, do they – after seeing things explode every day like you do, the fun sort of wears off. That's about the only thing we never saw together, isn't it? I don't ever remember seeing fireworks together, do you?

I hope it doesn't rain tomorrow though. Mother, Dad and I are taking Helena, her mom and Joyce to Candlewood Lake for the day. Remember I told you my Uncle has a cottage down there. You know, it's been two years since I've been swimming in anything bigger than a bathtub. I'm afraid I might sink. Maybe I'd better bring my little water wings, uh? Helen's going, too, of course. Joyce doesn't have to worry, she can swim and dive beautifully. 'Member the time we saw her in the water carnival at Beachland pool? I'll never forget the way you grabbed me by the legs when you discovered me standing up on the bleachers. What I could never figure out is how did you ever grab the right ones – boy, with all those girls there you might have made a mistake and what a mess you'd have been in!! Guess it was your lucky night.

It's really a beautiful night. The moon is so lovely. Wonder if it's like that where you are today.

In your letter you said how awful all the mud was. At that time there was so much rain it was even bad around here. Have things gotten any better since then? I hope so, it's bad enough to be there let alone having two ft. deep mud around.

Can you tell me whether you are at the same place? And whether or not things are getting any better? From what the papers say it looks brighter, but you can't really tell unless you're there. You did sound encouraging though when you said you might be home around Christmas time. Oh, Charlie, it will be wonderful having you home again. Do you think we'll both be glad to re-acquaint ourselves with one another again? I don't think we'll have much trouble, we can't when you think of all the fun we used to have together – gee, we could laugh at practically anything if we were together long enough. Why we even laughed at the scolding my father gave us about the fire place. Every time I go down cellar after wood I laugh to myself about that. I'll never forget the expression on your face. You were both petrified and bewildered.

I looked around New Britain for some film today, but it's still as scarce as ever. If I can I'll get some tomorrow. I want to so I can send you some pictures of us. I've been trying to get some film since last Christmas for you – guess there just isn't any.

What about you? Gee, I'd love a picture of you. Have you changed much – gained any weight?

Oh by the way, Chas, Joyce got a nice letter from Freddy today, it's been ages since they've written but it looks like the spirit might be revived. I hope so because we can all have fun together when you get back. We'll have to go to Meriden Tower sometime, too. Hope it's warmer than the last time we were there. Remember, Heathcliff dear, you nearly froze.

No, Charles, I don't have my dog anymore. In fact, we gave her away last fall – She was much too big and lively for the neighborhood. Mother says she's going to give me a couple of them for a wedding present then she won't have to be cleaning up after them, but I just laughed and said, "silly girl." I'll be busy myself then.

About my job. I have been on the new one just about 2 mos. and although it's nerve wracking as heck – what with telephones ringing and bills to be collected and tel. to be disconnected for non-payment etc. I still like it. I can't wait for you to come into the office – wait till you see how impressive my desk looks and how businesslike I have to look. It really kills me at times, but I've got to maintain my dignity (that's what they keep telling me at the office anyway).

Well, Chas honey, I'd better close so I can start to get ready for bed. We're supposed to pick Helen up at 8:00 tomorrow morning. That's a crime to have to get up at 7:00 on my day off.

There's loads more that I have to tell you but I'll save it till next time, O.K.?

Write awfully soon because I'll be waiting to hear from you again.

Take care, Charlie, and may this letter find you well and happy. Do write soon and often, too. Until next time.

All my love,
Cheryl

17 Anise Street
New Britain, Conn.
July 9, 1945

Dear Son,

It's a long time since I wrote you, and you might have already said plenty about not getting any mail from me but to tell the truth I just don't know what to say. Betty and Mother write a couple times a week and to put in my two cents doesn't make sense at all.

The last time I wrote was before I went on a fishing trip to Vt. on June 6. To begin with the fishing was lousy. They had a freshet about the time we got there and the lake (Champlain) was about 6 ft. higher than it had been in 20 years. We caught a few Northern Pike, some Wall Eyes and Perch. Buck and Wally Miller and a couple of guy's from Fafnir's went along. We drank up a lot of whisky and beer, had a good place to sleep and eat, what more could a body want.

Since I got back I went to work in earnest and am again tired of the grind, maybe I'll take a week off about a month from now. There is still plenty of work around but nothing to spend money on. I tried to buy a pair of summer pants today, Mother and I went in about half a dozen stores and I finally got a pair for $3.95 that used to cost about a buck and a half a few years ago.

We have a nice garden this year and no kidding it's clean and free of weeds, sort of take pride in it. We have enough vegetables for a boarding house. Last week we bought a couple of broilers and a quarter of a pig from a farmer. We split the pork three ways and we drew cards for the ham and I won. It cost me $9.50 for 13 lbs. of fresh ham so you can imagine what a piece of meat is worth. You can't get anything in the stores and you would wonder where the hell everything disappeared to. You can't even buy soap, only one bar at a time. This is not griping only filling in lines to let you know how things are. Don't worry, we get plenty to eat. I'm just as fat as ever, an even 200.

We expected to get 100 chicks from Montgomery Ward last week but so far they haven't arrived. I cleaned out the chicken coop last week, took Donny and I three days. It is as clean as the club house now, white washed and all.

We got a letter from you today, addressed to Mother. It was rather short, dated July 2nd with your new address. I'm glad that the island is now secured and that you will get a rest for a while and maybe the war will be over before you get into combat again. Them Japs will fold up I think after they get a good pounding over the next few months.

Tommy is home for good, he bought his civvies last week and was over with Shirley a couple of times already. He doesn't feel so hot after having a serious operation on his spine. He was over to the college this afternoon seeing about a teaching job for the fall opening of schools. He also expects to go housekeeping as soon as he can get located with a job. He might work out of town and said that wherever he lands a job that's where he's going to settle down.

Things around here are okay. It's hotter than heck most of the time. It rained a little this afternoon but now it is 7 p.m. and the sun is out nice and bright.

I don't know whether you remember the Jackson boy that lived on the corner of Hillcrest Ave. and Foxon Place. Well, he was killed in an air accident in California yesterday, He completed 87 missions over in Europe.

Donny is still grinding away on the guitar and he's getting along pretty good, so Mr. Tata tells him. We had the piano tuned up yesterday, wondered why the keys were sticking and wouldn't play. When the guy took it apart he found pencils, matches, cherrystones and marbles underneath the keys, the thing was all fouled up. I think I'll take a few lesson so when you get back we'll greet you with a tune, we'll have to get Betty to sing for us, she's still swinging the baton and does a lot of practicing.

I've got to go to Plainville tonight to see some wallpaper on a job I'm supposed to start next week. I hope this will find you in the best of health, so bye for now – everything is okay on the home front.

Your Pop

From the letters you have sent in the past, you seem to be collecting quite a number of souvenirs. How the heck do you expect to bring home all that junk? You should start sending it along while the sending is good so you won't have so much to carry around. Send me a Jap pistol if you can lay your hands on one. If it's a good one and in perfect condition ship it home and I'll pay you whatever you have to lay out for it.

So long for now and take it easy and stay away from those geishas.

232 Mountain Drive
West Hartford, Conn.
July 10, 1945

Dear Charlie,

It's a very long time since I've written, isn't it? I think of you every day it seems, but just can't seem to write. Tonight my mom scolded me and told me I'd better get busy at the morale building or she'd disown me.

I'd better start anew instead of trying to answer your last letter, except for two things. You asked me if you had ever sent me a poem by Edgar Guest. You didn't and I'd, of course, be very pleased to receive it. And then I must mention that horrible mix-up we got in over whether or not I knew you were on Okinawa. Way back eons ago you wrote from there and said you were happy to see pine trees there. Remember? Then I wrote and said I didn't know there were pine trees anywhere in the S.P. and I didn't mention Okinawa. And in your last letter you retorted, "Don't you know I'm on Okinawa?" Mon Dieu! I was going crazy. I'm awfully glad the

517

island finally fell, but now God only knows where you'll be and we just can't go through that again. I promise to be more cooperative next time.

There isn't much news. I've been swimming and picnicking a few times, trying to be gay. The return of fellows from ETO has made many girls happy, but simply decreases my zest for living. All my men are in the South Pacific.

Last Saturday a friend and I went bicycling and were out from 9:30 a.m. till 4. We were rather silly to stay out so long but most of the time was spent climbing up Avon Mountain. Oh my aching back! It was very high. We had fun though and in Farmington we found a rippling brook and took off our shoes and let the water trickle over our toes. We picked some forget-me-nots and pinks and we both wanted to send them in letters but the sun shriveled them all up.

When we have our picnic next spring, we can pick some. Of course, picking wild flowers may not be within your scope, but you can rest and I'll do the gathering.

I've just finished reading a last year's best seller, "Tap Roots." It's one of those Civil War novels and was very good. I'm now ready to start studying Nancy's psychology book. I think it should be interesting and no doubt will be of immeasurable help some time.

Have you heard from Ben? I keep hoping you might be able to see him some time. It's been about a year since you met in Little Rock, isn't it?

Remember the Shakespeare sonnet I was going to send you? I'm enclosing it with this. I think I have tried your patience long enough.

Affectionately,

Helena

P.S. By the way, darlin', did you get my birthday card and box?

-EIGHT-

GUAM 1945

R & R— REST and recreation. What a laugh. Even after Okinawa, Guam was the pits. Tropical heat, stifling humidity, insects. A dust cloud kicked up by military traffic over dirt roads hung permanently over the camp. On the Canal our tent was in a grove fifty feet from the sea; here, I drove my jeep to the coast ten miles from camp for a swim. A week after we got set up, replacement drafts from the States began arriving to fill our depleted ranks—not that we were going anywhere soon. Having just lost five thousand guys on Okinawa, it would be six months or more before the division was ready for combat. What we didn't know was that the United States had already scheduled a nuclear attack that would bring the empire of Japan to its knees.

In mid-August the announcement of the Jap capitulation came over the radio shortly after we had turned in for the night. No one was in the least excited.

"Big deal," one guy said from beneath his mosquito net. "Don't turn on the light."

Another quipped, "What the fuck does that make me, town marshal?"

The next morning at muster we learned our outfit was to represent the corps at the formal surrender of Japan and later rejoin the rest of the division, which was being sent to China for occupation duty. On August 30, a beautifully bright summer day, our transport, along with the battleship *Missouri*, cruisers, destroyers, and service vessels boldly entered the formidable Tokyo Bay. Picture-perfect snow-capped Mount Fujiyama rose ahead under blue skies. White sheets draped enemy coastal guns looking down on us from the heavily fortified hills bordering the bay. No Americans were yet on shore. Finally, the order came to load our weapons. We were going in. Some ten minutes later, the order was rescinded. At four o'clock, we docked at the Yokosuka Naval Base and filed down the gangway, our weapons unloaded. In compliance with the terms of surrender, all enemy small arms and swords were neatly stacked on the concrete apron outside of the three story barracks that had been prepared for our use. Neither side fired a shot.

Sixth Marine Division
San Francisco, Cal.
5 July 1945

Dear Folks,

Well, I'm at our rest camp at last. What a place! It will be a month before we get the camp in shape. The climate is pretty good though and there aren't any flies or mosquitoes. It will be a nice place when it's finished. The ocean is miles away so I don't think there will be much swimming.

I received the candy Mother sent and also a box of assorted stuff from Helena. I got about fifty letters, I guess. I don't know when I will get them all answered.

Today is Sunday but I didn't get to go to church. There was too much to do. It feels good to sleep on a cot with a mattress and to wear khakis again. All the tents have wooden decks and we have showers. There are a couple movies about a mile away but in a week or so we will have our own screen.

Both of the packages I got were in excellent condition. I think it takes about six weeks for packages. I've got to go to supper now. I'll write again tomorrow when I have more time. Write soon.

Love,
Charlie

P.S. Thanks again for the candy.

1st Bn. 15th Marines
Sixth Marine Division
San Francisco, Cal.
July 17, 1945

Hello little Darlin',

I have quite a few letters of yours to answer. I'll start with this one of July 1st,

That job of taking the boss's pin head child to the movies must have been awfully hard. Where did you ever learn to do that? Why I always thought you were afraid to buy tickets! Ga Wan!

In your letter you said that the car was fouled up again! I thought that Dad just got it out of the garage. Maybe they forgot to put the motor back in – did Pa look? Sometimes he thinks it would run (walk, anyway) without a motor. You all ought to take the motor out and put Donny in and let him push. Princie wouldn't be any good at it 'cause he may see a cat and besides he told me in his last letter that he would much rather drive.

521

Those pictures were a riot. If you write so much on yours I would have written "not a match" and sent it back. I like the one of you and Donny best. The one of Donny alone was good, too. In all the pictures I get of Mother she looks so worried. I don't know why she should worry. Prince can take care of himself now and I'm better off here than I would be at Shirley's house. Ga Wan! It must be you and Donny, huh?

I almost swallowed my bridge when I heard Donny was going to Nathan Hale. Mon Dieu! When I think of the smooching parties we had in Betty Jane Barbor's cellar etc. I bless myself and ask the Lord to spare our little Poopsie! But we did have more fun than a barrel of monkeys (more like apes, I think),

You asked my how many feet Ray dug in the dirt. Well I'll tell you – he hasn't come up yet, but I'll ask him when he does.

This is supposed to be a rest camp but it won't be for a month yet. We really have a lot of work to do. We have electric lights in our tent now. I was so thrilled that I sat up all night just turning them off and on.

I wrote Shirley a nice sweet letter this morning. Poor child – loves me like a fatha – the fatha away the beetta. She loves me for herself, not for myself.

Last night I saw "The Picture of Dorian Grey." I would have liked it better in an enclosed theater. There was an awfully lot of dialogue and it was a dark picture (not Negroes, you clown).

I've answered two of your letters and have a whole pile of others to answer (all fan mail, of course). That girl in Deep River writes a couple times a week. She must be a beast! She said she would send a picture, however.

Are you sure you can't get any 620 film? Other fellows get film.

In coming to our rest area we brought with us a small "vic"—found in a Jap house with about ten good state-side records—"I'm Beginning To See The Light"(I love it), "Sentimental Journey", "What Makes the Sun Set?"(Frankie!),"Without A Song", "Night And Day", "Star Dust" and a few others. Well, angel puss, I've got to get on with my correspondence. Bye –bye now.

Your luffink brudder,
Charlie

17 Anise Street
New Britain, Conn.
July 20, 1945

Dear Charlie,

We received a letter from you Monday and are very glad to hear that you're at a rest base. (I don't suppose you can tell us where you are.) But at least you're there so that's the main thing. Are you getting enough to eat?

Also Monday we received your other gear with the dishes, mess gear and etc. in it. I guess you didn't pack the dishes very good because a few of them were broken. But they really are pretty. It's funny how they put the rising sun on practically everything they make. Donny got a kick out of the Jap caps. He looks like a real Jap with the coat and cap on. I brought my kimono in to show the girls at work and they all thought it was swell and they all wanted you to send one for them. I said I was very sorry but you've moved to a new base. Hah. Mr. Birnbaum saw it and asked if it was something they were going to have on sale Wednesday. We all laughed like heck. He doesn't know anything from a hole in the wall anyway.

Yesterday our store had a picnic at Stanley Pool but I didn't go 'cause I had my baton lesson to take, but I bet they had a swell time.

Mother is going to Hartford shopping with Lala this morning. Perhaps they'll do a little shoplifting, too.

I'm glad that you received the candy Mother sent and that it wasn't spoiled. I thought it would take a little longer than it did.

Gosh I bet it feels good for you to be able to take showers again. You practically lived in the shower when you were home. I guess that's all for now. Write soon and tell me everything that's going on at the base.

Love and kisses, xxxxx

Betty

1ˢᵗ Bn. 15ᵗʰ Marines
Sixth Marine Division
San Francisco, Cal.`
21 July 1945

Dear Dad,

I received you letter yesterday and, as usual, I was very glad to hear from you.

First I'll start with some bad news. My second class rate got bounced back. It was no fault of mine. There is a compliment in the regiment and (censored) copped the rates for his men and the battalions got screwed. Raymond (he was first class) and I really got a raw deal. I was thinking about asking for a transfer. (censored) yet. He's from Hartford, too! It burns me up just thinking about it. We worked so damned hard, too.

I wish I thought that the Japs would fold up in a few months. After seeing the way they were dug in on Okinawa I think the super-forts would have to fly underground to get them. They are just like animals.

Do you know how much Jap pistols are? They run anywhere from two hundred and fifty dollars up. Money isn't worth much out here. I don't know how I'll send all my junk home. I'll be able to send about three hundred dollars home next week. We are getting paid then.

Life here is sort of boring but there is a lot of work to do. The days go by rather quickly but the months drag. I'm afraid I'll be out here for another year. I've got to close now so I can go to the movie. Don't wait so long to write next time.

Your loving son,
Charlie

Connecticut College
New London, Conn.
July 24, 1945

Dearest Goop,

I forgot to mail this today so I tore it open and decided to add to it. I read it over and it sounds awfully nasty – I really don't feel that way. I was just blowing my top again – you'd think I'd learn not to put it on paper, wouldn't you?

What made me to decide to write again? First a full moon, and second "f." A combination of the two was too much for me. Disregarding all the crap I wrote before – I did miss hearing from you. But it's funny – I know you're still thinking about me – and I think of you just as often as when I hear from you. 'Nuff of this.

Min had her baby – it was a boy. 7 pounds 15 ounces. So she's very happy. John was in England when it was born – the baby is named after him. Funny how time changes things, huh?

Fido died about the beginning of June. He was old and I guess his heart just gave out. I miss him awfully. He was a pest, but it's so quiet without him. So-o you won't have any percolator to tear you to pieces when you come home.

I'm 140 pages behind in my lesson so I'd better quit. Why don't you come home and talk to me, hmmmm?

Launa

1ˢᵗ Bn. 15ᵗʰ Marines
Sixth Marine Division

524

San Francisco, Cal.
26 July 1945

Dearest Mom,

It's been quite a while since I wrote to you last but I've had so much to do.

I have a new pen. I bought it at our PX (post exchange) for five dollars. It's a darn good one. A Sheaffer! It would cost about ten dollars in the States. I'll probably lose it soon but I'll try not to. I had to wait in line for over two hours. It's the first time I've seen pens for sale since I've been overseas.

Tell the Farmers I will write when I get a chance. There is so darn much to do. I will be all caught up next week. I just received a letter from Betty. I will answer her tomorrow.

The weather here is still awfully warm. It gets pretty dusty too. Got to go now—

Here I am again. We had a pretty good supper for a change – Roast (shoe leather) beef, potatoes, carrots and peas and chocolate cake. Lots better than usual.

This writing isn't very good for a new pen, is it? It's me, not the pen. I've got to take a shower as soon as I get through writing.

I think that I will go to the movies tonight. I have some work I could do but I don't see why I should kill myself for them. Not after the raw deal they played on Ray and me.

I wish that we would go on another campaign. The time goes by so fast on an operation. I should be home after the next one. I'd better be. I resign!

Well, Mom, as I said before there is nothing much to write about. Tomorrow I'll get some money orders and send my shekels home. Bye for now.

Love,
Charlie

Connecticut College
New London, Conn.
July 27, 1945

Hello, Dearest,

I'm in a state of perfect comfort – with a gripe against no one – with the exception of the Japs who are the cause of you being so far away. I just took a shower and I'm sprawled out on the bed smoking a cigarette and listening to the radio. Oh such bliss. What more could I ask for—except maybe to have you around to argue with. But I don't feel particularly like arguing — well we'd better drop that.

I got another letter today — you said you were waiting to write until you heard from me. That means I won't be getting much mail from you — 'cause after you'd decided we'd better stop writing I stopped naturally. So I suppose you won't get any mail from me — then you'll get mad again. It's a vicious circle. You know we don't actually get along at all. I can't understand how it's lasted this long — on and off. It must be six years or so — but let's don't think about that — it makes me feel old.

You've told me about that picture "Devotion" about six times — it must be really good. I've never even heard of it.

I certainly hope you can get back to Harvard if that's what you want. That's a beautiful place — and a darn good college. Are you still going to major in economics? I never had any before this summer but I like it a lot. It's something practical — something that's going on today — not something dead and buried.

We were all furious at the picture Life painted of Conn. They made the place look like a country club. No, darling — there's no man shortage — not in quantity. But on the whole, the quality is pretty low grade.

I thought I'd die laughing at the buckets of hot and cold water. Is it that bad? Actually that's just about right — one day I'm likely to hate you and the next I'm madly in love with you. You figure it out 'cause at this point I'm half asleep. Goodnight, darling —

My love always,
Launa

1ˢᵗ Bn. 15ᵗʰ Marines
Sixth Marine Division
San Francisco, Cal.
27 July 1945

Dear Mom,

This is going to be another quickie. It seems as tho I'm always in a hurry now.

I drew three hundred and forty dollars in back pay. I'll send three hundred of it home. It will be better for me to send one hundred at a time. It will be safer, too. I've spent about twenty already. I don't know on what. I have a pen and a lighter is all. The rest went on little things.

Today is another scorcher. If only there were a place to swim here. We are about twelve miles from a good swim place. The bugle just blew for chow and I'm starved. I may write to Sis later on this afternoon. Bye for now.
All my love,
Charlie

1ˢᵗ Bn. 15ᵗʰ Marines
Sixth Marine Division
San Francisco, Cal.
28 July 1945

Dear Mom,

It's me again. I'm enclosing the second money order for one hundred dollars. I'll send the last one some time tomorrow. I sure hope that they get there.

It is awfully hot and dusty here today. Especially dusty. Our camp is right near a road and every time a truck or jeep goes by we get an awful cloud of coral dust. Things will be a lot better as soon as they get a system and start wetting down the roads.

Last night I saw a stage show. It was a concert of some sort. There was an opera singer from the Chicago Opera Company, a nice looking violinist, a baritone and a piano player. We probably would have thrown our shoes at them in the States, but they went over pretty good out here. The show we saw last week was much better.

From what you keep telling me about the Farmers, I'll bet their place looks pretty good. Have you any plans for remodeling our kitchen or front porch yet? I know that we talked about it every year. I guess that materials are pretty scarce.

The food here is about semi-crappy. We have fresh eggs about three times a week now and yesterday we had fresh turkey for the second time.

There were a lot of peace rumors around. I guess that the ultimatum sent to the Japs started them. I don't think they will quit for a long time yet. I sure wish they would surrender. I'm ready to go home at any time. I think that I will drop the Farmers a line. I owe them a letter anyway. Bye for now –
Your loving son,
Charlie

1ˢᵗ Bn. 15ᵗʰ Marines
Sixth Marine Division
San Francisco, Cal.
28 July 1945

Dear Sis,

When there is a fire mission on, it sounds like this; "Quickmatch, (that's us) this is Pipin. I hear you loud and clear, how do you hear me? Over." Then we say, "Pipin, this is Quickmatch, I hear you loud and clear – Roger and out." This goes on for hours. I'll imitate them when I get home. It's a riot.

I wish these mosquitoes would give me something. I'd go home anyway. Would you like me with my head all swollen or my leg as big as a tree trunk? Cheryl would!

I've run out of things to say. I keep telling them they should send me home, but they can't see it. There are too many dogfaces at home now anywho. I should be home early next summer. That isn't so long. Like hell it isn't! Maybe I'll build a little raft and go over the hill.

I'll get any package you send. Insure them tho. It only costs three cents to insure a five dollar package and insuring it means safe handling. Wrap it WELL and I'll get it. Don't put any sweets in it. Stick to the list I sent, I could go for some right now. I'm not foolin'— I'm droolin'.

I'm going to start holding my breath for those pictures. So if you don't want me to turn blue or green, you'd better send them – quick like a bunny (rare –bit).

Everything is so quiet here, now. We have very little to do. I've been reading "The Valley of Decision." It's really a fine story and I'm enjoying it. It has been made into a movie. Maybe I'll see it when I get to Guam. I'd like to. That's about all for now. I'll write again as soon as I hear from you. You'd better carry a black jack or brass knuckles if you go out with those New London sailors. On second thought, I think just a plain old ordinary lead pipe will do. Have fun!

Love,

Charlie

1ˢᵗ Bn. 15ᵗʰ Marines
Sixth Marine Division
FPO San Francisco, Cal.
29 July 1945

Dear Mom,

Today it rained all afternoon. So everyone slept. The tent next to ours had a radio so we had good music for a change. I really enjoyed lying down and doing nothing all afternoon.

528

There was a mail call today but I didn't get any mail. I didn't get any yesterday either. What's the matter, are you all starting to dope off?

Last night I saw a pretty good movie. It was "Rhapsody In Blue." There was a lot of music in it. Musical pictures always go over big out here. Tonight they are showing "Meet Me In St. Louis" with Judy Garland and Margaret O'Brien. It should be very good.

Last night I heard the "Hit Parade." It has been ages since I heard that program. This afternoon I heard Kate Smith's program. There isn't any advertising on the programs we hear or in the magazines either. We get the "Sat. Eve. Post," "Time," "Look," "Life," "New Yorker" and a few others.

Cigarettes are getting scarce here. On the campaign there were cartons thrown away. People only smoked "Luckies" and "Camels." Now people are smoking "Old Golds."

I am enclosing my third and last money order. I hope you have received the other two by this time.

The rain has stopped now and it's clearing up. We had chicken for dinner. It was pretty good. For supper we had cold meat and cheese. That's the standard Saturday night supper in all the services, I guess.

The battalion across the road from us had an epidemic of food poisoning. Not too serious but they have been evacuating men to the hospital all afternoon. I don't think any of the fellows in our outfit will get it. They say it was the chicken they had for dinner. It's a good thing that we have different mess halls. Well, Mom, I think I'll take a shower before I go to the movies. Bye for now and write soon.

> *Love and kisses,*
> *Charlie*
>
> *1st Bn. 15th Marines*
> *Sixth Marine Division*
> *FPO San Francisco, Cal.*
> *31 July 1945*

Dear little Mono—

I received your letter this afternoon and was very glad to get it. The only mail I've received in the past five days is your letter and one from Marietta. I'm due for a whole flock of mail this week, however.

I'm glad you received the boxes I sent. Did you get the both of them or just one? Ray's package got home quite some time ago. I was sorry to hear the kimonos weren't very good. I had to carry them around for a long time before I could mail them. Were all the pieces of lacquer ware broken? I hope you didn't put them in hot water. I don't think they are used for rice. Okinawa is famous for its red lacquer ware. Let me know if you get the both boxes. How does that blue kimono fit you? You should see me in the black one! H—S-! Zootie!

There is a radio in the tent next to ours and we hear music all day. How do you like the song "I'm Beginning To See The Light?" I think it is pretty smooth. You had better start saving shoe coupons 'cause you'll have to teach me how to dance all over again. "Blue Palace" and "White Horse Tavern" here we come! Corn Pecking! If I don't stop thinking about going home, I'll be building a wear-ever pogo stick and taking off. You might see me come bounding over Swanson's hill at any time. "Out of the sticks in '46" is my motto.

When you were traveling with the Douglases (sounds like you were with a carnival, well freaks anyway!),you should have taken a ride over to see me. What's the matter with you – are you getting one way or something?

You said that beaches weren't what they used to be. How could they be with me out here? Tell me something – have you ever found out why they build the shore so near the ocean? Do you think it's 'cause they have so much sand there? –I wonder??

What was Greer Garson doing in New Britain? You said, and I quote, "I saw the picture 'Valley Of Decision' with Greer Garson." I didn't even know you knew her. You never tell me nothing – Ga Wan – ya Clown! It was a good book but I missed the picture. I had a chance to see it. The pictures are never as good as the books, however.

Now I am reading "Leave Her To Heaven." It is a fair novel but nothing to write home about (then what the hell am I writing home about it for? I'll bite, tell me!) It was written by the same fellow that wrote "The Strange Woman." That wasn't very good either.

I should write to Cheryl now, but I don't feel quite in the mood to. "Never do today what you can do tomorrow" is the motto of the tropics.

I'm on my fourth page now and still going strong. I don't know why I write long letters to you – you only write about a page and a half to me. Don't tell me that you don't know any more words. I guess I'm just big and easy – yeh, either that or a ham sandwich.

You said that you hadn't heard from me yet. By the time you get this you should have received a whole pile of letters from me. From now on I'm only going to write when I get a letter. So just write as often as you want to hear from me. It's too damn hard to start a letter when I haven't got one to answer.

The chow here has been pretty good lately. The chow here at best is horse crap, of course, but it's better than field rations. We had ice cream yesterday and cherry pie tonight.

I read a short book the other night called "The Feather Merchants." It was written by a soldier about civilians. Laugh – I've got eleven pairs of scivvie drawers on the line! I don't think civilians would find it funny at all. You have to be a service man. It was a riot, however.

This is absolutely the last page. I've about run out of things to say anyway. Write soon, little Darling 'cause your letters are wonderful - my morale sends you his love and says for you to write more often too. He says that you really, really charge him.

Love,

Charlie

P.S. This is much too long to read over so you'll have to correct it yourself.

Connecticut College
New London, Conn.
August 5, 1945

Darling –

I got your letter this morning so things are much better. It's funny how one letter can fix everything up, isn't it? By the way, Stinky, it was a very sweet letter – I've been feeling wonderful all day.

I think it's a swell idea for us not to fight anymore. It seems as if we've gone from one battle into another for the past six months. I keep telling myself I won't fight with you anymore, but we always seem to end up that way. The kids kid me about it no end – if I say you're mad at me they always …(missing page).

I'm over my quota – this is the fourth page. See what one letter can do to me? And besides, I'm 5 chapters behind in Ec. This was supposed to be my night to catch up.

Everyone is so certain that the war is going to be over in a month at the most now that Russia is in and we have the new bomb. But as you said, I'm afraid to believe it. Rumors are flying everywhere of course – but we've been lapping up rumors for the last year or so. So I guess all we can do is wait and hope.

As you can see I could go on endlessly –but I've already gone one page too far so I'd better quit. Goodnight, darling.

My love always,

Launa

P.S. Have you heard "There's No You"? Nice, mmmmm?

Connecticut College
New London, Conn.
August 6, 1945

Hello, Goop —

What're you trying to do — play hard to get? You intrigue me. And after I've given you the best years of my life would you desert me now? You dog! Have you no honor, sir? Could it be that that undying puddle of purple passion is dying? Alas! Here I sit — a lonely maiden in her ivory tower waiting breathlessly for a message (airmail) from her long departed lover. I'm getting pale and wan — no appetite - can't sleep. People have died from such and unrequited passion as mine. I shall probably keel over one of these days — clutching a withered camellia. My dying word will no doubt be "Glurg!" — or something equally romantic and memorable. And all this will be on your conscience — now will you send me a postcard??

Everybody is quite excited about the new atomic bomb. We just heard about it this afternoon. It's supposed to do more damage than a thousand heavy bombers and it only weighs 400 lbs. When you hear them talk about it on the radio, it sounds like something you'd read in Flash Gordon. Can you imagine what those will do to Japan? Everyone's hoping that this will force them to quit — God I hope so.

Summer school goes along about the same as usual — except that I've got a new teacher. But he looks just like the "Deacon" — so right away, of course, I can't stand him. But I'll overlook it and give him a chance.

You don't deserve any more than 3 pages, m' love. And I won't tell you I miss you and would like to see you and miss like heck not hearing from you or any of that stuff just 'cause you're so nasty! But why don't you write, huh?

Love always,
Launa

475 Glen Street
New Britain, Conn.
August 7, 1945

Dearest Nephew,

Many thanks for trying to get information on the Katz boy's death. I had Uncle Pete show the parts of your letter so they'd know we had written to you as they requested.

Well I'm sure glad you're at a rest camp getting the rest you're entitled to after going through all that you did.

532

Well Tom has been operated on and came home the 2nd of July. He's coming along o.k. and has got a job beginning Sept. 10th teaching Industrial Arts in Suffield. I think he's doing alright for himself in the short time he's been home.

Tag got home on the 2nd of August on a 15 day leave which can mean anything. At present he's in Vermont with his wife having a good time fishing.

What do you think of your brother working on the tobacco fields? He's working to buy fishing tackle. I saw the souvenirs you sent home. Donny put on the uniform, pulled out his ears and if he didn't look like a Jap. Uncle Pete and I got a great kick out of him. So many of those little dishes got broke, all the prettiest ones of course, what are they used for? I'd like one of those red ones if you have one to spare with a cover. Your father said he was going to wear one of the kimonos like your mother, how about it? Well anyway, we sure did have a great laugh so you'll know you made us all happy by sending them home. Bob is going to try to get into Teachers College this fall. I hope he succeeds.

Saw your mother today. Tommy took me over. Oh, yes, he bought a car as he will have to commute back and forth as rents are pretty scarce. After he gets working, he'll have a chance to look for one. Well, pal, I'll close hoping you are able to read this writing. Write when you can. Love and best wishes from all.

As ever.

Aunt Anna

P.S. Saw Uncle Bernie and he wants to be remembered to you.

17 Anise Street
New Britain, Conn.
August 8, 1945

Dear Charlie,

Well, how are you today? I'll explain this stationery. I'm at the canteen for a little visit. One of the girls I work with is a hostess and she told me to drop in and see her. It's quite dead in here tonight except for the phonograph going full blast.

We sent a package out to you yesterday. You can only send five pounds so there really isn't much in there. You won't get it for about two months anyway. We will send another one out soon.

533

I was supposed to go to the shore with Jeanne this year but they aren't going. Something came up and they couldn't get the cottage so I'm going to back yard beach. I really don't care though.

Freddy is home on a nine-day leave and was over to see us last nite for a while. He's stationed in Norfolk, Virginia, and he thinks he's going to New York when he gets back.

Sunday we went down to the lake to Menousek's cottage. There are a lot of people down there this year. A lady wanted to lease her cottage out for the whole year at $240 and Dad wanted to take it but mother objected. So that was the end.

Dad bought a $50 out-board motor today. So I guess he'll take us out motoring on the lake pretty soon.

Donny is still struggling with his guitar lessons and I was trying to teach him to sing while he plays. It was really funny. Daddy was saying, "Sing, don't talk!!!" (Fun for the kids),

I work half days and now we have Mondays off so I don't mind it at all.

Tommy was discharged, so he's now running around looking for a teaching job. He can't get used to being a civilian. Shirley works and he sits around on his fanny all day. Only kidding, but it's true!! I think he deserves to be sitting around. He can't be doing any lifting and etc. for a while because of his back. I guess that's all for now.

Love & Kisses,

Betty

P.S. Have you any idea when you're leaving or where you're going? Just curious?

17 Anise Street
New Britain, Conn.
August 9, 1945

Dear Charlie,

How's my big brother today? We haven't heard from you in over a week now and figure you've been transferred to a new base or something. We hope to hear from you soon.

Monday I went to Soundview for the day with the Douglases. We had a swell time. You see, they couldn't get a cottage near the shore, so Mr. Douglas is taking us to different places during the week. Yesterday we went to the town of Hadlyme to see the Gillette Castle on the Connecticut River. I don't know whether you've ever heard of it before but William Gillette

534

was a playwright and actor. He built a beautiful big castle on the Conn. River. It's the most beautiful thing I've ever seen. There's an admission fee of 30 cents to go thru it, but it really was worth it. We even went up to the tower. There is a ferryboat to take the cars across the river to the castle and back but we just took it back, because Mrs. Douglas was afraid of it.

Today we were suppose to go to Ocean Beach, but the weather wasn't so good. It rained hard last night and looks like rain again.

I'm enclosing The Servicemen's News and also a clipping that I meant to send you a long time ago. Donny just went fishing over by the Stanley Pool. That kid is just crazy about fishing. Our garden is coming along good. I guess that Mother will do a lot of canning this year.

I guess that's about all for now.

> *Love & Kisses,*
> *Betty*

> *Connecticut College*
> *New London, Conn.*
> *August 10, 1945*

Macushla –

No, I'm not insulting you darling. That's a very endearing term – wish, of course. It looks silly on paper but I love the way it sounds. Silly, huh?

I'm going mad with all the stories of surrender. Everybody on the radio is speculating as to whether the surrender terms will be accepted or not. I wish they'd shut up until it's definite. That would be so much easier on the nerves. But it is going to be over soon. I can't believe it, can you? Maybe by the time you get this it will be all over. Can you imagine peace after so long? We've been wishing for it for so long – oh, I'll shut up. It isn't certain yet – I'm as bad as everybody else, I guess. It's just that is seems so very close now.

Marvin says to tell you that you owe him 6 cents for the nice fat letter I got today. Charges will be pressed when you appear on the doorstep –O.K? You seemed to be feeling quite high when you wrote—it must have been more than "one sweet letter" from me that did it. It sounded good though – your other letters sounded kind of blue. Not that I blame you – it must get damn monotonous. But it can't be much longer ––there I go again. It's the only thing I can think of.

To get on to our literary discussion, you're not so far ahead of me in reading. I read "Leave Her To Heaven" – it was rather fascinating in a horrible sort of way. I never did get to "Strange Woman" – it looked kind of trashy – how was it? And as for "Barefoot Boy With Cheek"—I loved it. A sad-sack sailor gave it to me last winter for a birthday present. I had to read the good parts to the whole second floor of course. The romantic gal who was always hungry took the cake. The poor fellow was in the process of whispering sweet nothings to her and all she could talk about was a pot of beans. Jeez – romantic, huh?

You asked me why "Forever Amber" was so popular. For the same reason that you and I both went out of our way to read it. I wouldn't have missed it for the world after all the talk I'd heard about it – just human nature I guess.

I'm over my quota again. On paper I'm quite a windbag.

Stop rubbing it in by asking me to come out and see you. That would be quite gay, wouldn't it? I thought I'd die laughing at the conflagration that's going to take place next spring. Trying to scare me? Maybe I should warn you, I don't scare easily. But would you advise me to buy a muzzle or a straitjacket or something. But couldn't you manage it for Xmas or summer vacation instead of just before final exams? I'm afraid you'll be an awful hunk of distraction – do you want me to flunk out entirely?

Seriously, for the first time your coming home doesn't seem like something in another world. It won't be too long – so I guess all I can do is wait – but very impatiently. I refuse to start another page. Goodnight, Macushla.

My love always,
Launa

17 Anise Street
New Britain, Conn.
August 10,1945

Dear Charlie –

Well, Kid, how the heck are you? I'm sorry I haven't written lately but honestly I've been awfully busy working. For the past two weeks I've been working full time. Today isn't so busy so I thought I'd write to you while I was at the desk.

Gee, I thought when you got to a rest base you'd be a little more content but from your letters you seem a little disgusted with things. I'm glad that you can see some movies now anyway. You said you were going to see "Meet Me In St. Louis." Well how did you like it? I thought it was swell.

Well last night we went up to see Donny and Conway at the farm in Broadbrook. Mr. & Mrs. Narosky came with us to see Conway. Boy they certainly are having the time of their lives. Donny was all excited 'cause he just got paid for the three days he worked and he got 15.60. That's certainly is good pay for a kid eleven years old. Ah, and then I have a nice time, too, when we go up to see Donny, 'cause Aunt Lizzy has a son Albert and what a swell fellow he is. He has a Victrola and lots of records so we danced practically all night long. Henrietta (Conway's sister) has quite a crush on Al, but he wouldn't even look her way. So she's mad as heck 'cause we have so much fun together. Al's a member of the "crash crew" at Bradley Field and he works there every other day. On the other days he works helping his father on the farm. We have a date for Saturday nite (if I can get out of work at six) or if not, Monday nite. Don't you think that's nice that he's coming all the way from Broadbrook to see me?

Sunday we went down to Clinton to Tryon's cottage. In the morning Daddy, Bob Tryon, Chester and I went clamming at Niantic. I guess we got almost a bushel of clams. They were good, too! We stayed at Tryons Sunday nite and came home early Monday morning.

Mrs. Blum, Mr. Birnbaum's daughter, wanted to take me to Cape Cod with them this week on a vacation to look after Richard but Si (Mrs. Blum's brother and another boss) wouldn't let me go 'cause there were too many soldiers there at the Cape. Of course, that wouldn't bother me at all. Well I guess that's all for now.

Love and kisses, xxxxx
Betty

16 Anise Street
New Britain, Conn.
August 10, 1945

Hi Charlie –

You must think it's about time I wrote but you know me. I got a kick out of your letter and I sure feel sorry for you and the boys. There is no such thing as lack of nookie here – the girls here are all suffering from the want of it.

I was just reading the paper about the atomic bomb, it sure is a swell thing. There was only one thing wrong and that is that it didn't blow all the G.D. Japs to hell. We think now that the war may end soon with Russia going in to the fight, why didn't they do that right away.

Our boys are away for a weeks vacation and your brother is away working on the tobacco farm with some friends of Kitty's. Your mother says he may last a week.

We expect to take a picture of our house and then we will send you a snapshot. It isn't much different but we have filled it in a little bit more and the grass is coming along good. We also had a door cut through the dining room and that is swell, now I can step out without the neighbors seeing me. The weather here isn't so hot, its really been cool and the gardens are very late. There is no more to say now but please don't mind my spelling or writing, this is the first time I wrote in a hell of a time. We think of you daily so do a good job and come home soon before you're too old to enjoy it. As ever,

Fan your neighbors,

Chas, Fan, Chas and Don Farmer

P.S. It just came over the radio that the Japs are about to give up. Isn't that swell? Oh, boy, it won't be long now.

Connecticut College
New London, Conn.
August 11, 1945

Hello, Darling –

The war's over – at least I think it is. The same thing is happening as before with Germany. Everyone is thinking it's over before it's official – it makes it kind of anti-climax when it does come.

Just heard on the radio that a broadcast had been picked up from Chunking – the Japs have rejected the surrender terms and hostilities will continue. That settles that I guess. It's so damn stupid – I hope they blow them all to hell. It seems so awful for people to be killed now when the end is so near. Let's not get morbid.

I read in the paper that they were shooting off guns and ringing sirens on Okinawa to celebrate the surrender. Why do they get everybody so excited before they're sure? I guess I'd better wait till tomorrow to finish this – you couldn't exactly call this my sunniest mood.

Hi Stinky –

It's a hot lazy Sunday afternoon – so I decided to write some more and see if I can't wake up. We spent all last night and all this morning listening to the radio. It's amazing how much talking they can do and tell you absolutely nothing. Everybody's just waiting I guess. The papers say we should know one way or the other today.

Let's change the subject – how are you? And what do you do all day? You never tell me – except that you are building a dispensary. Or am I too young to know? And by the way, how's my friend Cheryl? You haven't mentioned her lately – or have you given up trying to raise my blood pressure? And whatever happened to the girl you were in love with – the one that was going to be a nun? I'm way behind on what goes on in your life.

Fri. Aug 17

Hello Jughead –

This letter is sort of on the installment plan – I guess I quit before because the suspense was getting me down. But it's over – the war is all over! At first I really couldn't believe it – but I'm so happy now I feel that I'm going to explode or something. Such celebrating I've never seen in my life. The news came at 7 so the kids came over and we went out to see if we could make as much noise as everybody else. People were dancing in the streets – one man was standing on a street corner with a pail of ice, cases of soda, and heaven knows how much liquor – free to anyone going by. I can't begin to tell you what it was like. I've never seen so many happy people in my life. We even traveled on to New London – and even there it was rowdy (well, not very!) – just a lot of people having a good time. We did up all the so-called night clubs of course – and pulled in at 4 in the morning. I still haven't quite recovered. We went to church the next morning – there was a very nice service. I can't tell you how glad I am – it hasn't quite sunk in yet, I guess. I'd better stop writing or this letter never will be finished. But it won't be next spring when I'll see you – will you be home before Xmas? What the heck would they need the Marines to occupy Japan for – can't the little army boys do that by themselves? Anyway, tell 'em you're needed at home to bolster female morale – essential and all that stuff.

This letter is a hodge-podge anyway, so I won't drag it out. See you soon, Macushla –

(O.K. so it won't be so soon – but it sounds good, doesn't it?)

Love always,
Launa

17 Anise Street
New Britain, Conn.
August 12, 1945

Dear Charlie –

Well, how are you this nice hot day? Daddy is just leaving for the rifle range. I guess he's going to go with Buck Miller.

Boy, isn't the war news swell! I guess the war will be over in a few days how. Perhaps by the time you get this letter, it will be over already. (I hope).

Last night Al came down from Broadbrook and we went out. We went to see "Out Of This World" with Eddie Bracken and it was funny as all heck. After the movies we went out to Gabers for a little dancing. Dad said that's what he used to call it, too! Al has a nice little grey coupe. I guess it takes about an hour to get to New Britain from Broadbrook. He's going to come down next week again. (Love that man!)

Barbara F. came home from her two weeks vacation at the shore yesterday, so today we are going to go somewhere. We'll perhaps end up at the Newington Theater – that's where we go when we don't know what to do.

I received two letters from you Thursday and in one of them about five lines were censored.

Gee, I'm certainly glad you and Launa are back on the beam. It's about time. Cripes, you know you love her, so I don't see why in the heck you're always arguing. What's the story anywho??

You asked me how long it takes to get your letters. Well it only takes a week – eight days at the most. That really is a short time too.

Well, I guess you better hurry up and come home 'cause I bought a snazzy new black and aqua evening gown so we can do some stepping out. You can leave Launa home and take me out. O.K? But if she insists on going, I'll get one of the boys and we'll make it a foursome. How's that sound?

I guess we aren't the only ones that have beer parties, huh? I bet you got all stinko, too. You ol' souse.

Those drawings were very good I must say. I never knew you had such talent.

We only received two of your packages. I think that one of the cardboard ones got lost or maybe it will come later. (I hope so.) That's all the news for now.

Love & Kisses, xxxxx
Betty

17 Anise Street
New Britain, Conn.
August 14, 1945
VJ Day

Dear Charlie –

Boy oh Boy, today is VJ Day and everyone is so excited. At seven o'clock when the end of the war was announced, the horns started tooting, firecrackers, guns and everything were shooting off. Here it is 10 'clock and the racket is still going on. Dad had one of his guns out and was shooting into the hill. Prince and Butch were so excited they were running around like chickens with their heads cut off.

Dad just came into the room and said to tell you that he and mother are at Neubauer's and that Princey is in the kitchen lying down!! That's a hot one all right!! He's feeling a little wuzzy already. Mother was so happy but still she was crying a little – you know how sentimental she is – she said she felt sorry for all the mothers whose boys would never be home.

Some kids just called up and told me to come downtown. They said that there's a big celebration, but I'd just as soon sit home and I'll still be just as well off. Right?

I guess this is one of the happiest days of my life, but the happiest one will be the day that you come home for good. How long do you think it will be before you can come home? I figured it will be at least 3 or four months!! What do you think? But the main thing is you won't have to go out and fight anymore.

I guess I won't have to work now for a couple of days and that will be just fine.

Perhaps tomorrow we are going to take a ride up to Broad Brook to see Donny – then I'll be able to see Al, too – honestly, I've never met anyone I liked better than I do him. (sh-sh it's a secret).Well that's all for now. Write and tell me what happened around where you are today.

Love and kisses, XXXXX
Betty

-NINE-

JAPAN 1945

The Daibutsu Kamakura

TOKYO BAY, SEPTEMBER 2, 1945. Under cloudy skies, Admiral Nimitz, Generals Wainwright and MacArthur, and a host of top US officials met with representatives of the emperor of Japan on board the battleship *Missouri*. A formal treaty was ratified, and the war was officially over. Our outfit was then assigned shore patrol duty in the area about the naval base at Yokosuka. A sightseeing tour of Tokyo included a visit to the shrine of the Great Buddha, or Daibutsu, and several parks. For me, far more impressive were the factories dug deep into the hillsides about the capital. Similar to Okinawa, but on a much more elaborate scale, mile after mile of illuminated caves revealed command posts, communication centers, ammunition dumps, food storage facilities, medical clinics, and machine shops of every kind—all organized and orchestrated for that final showdown. God bless the atomic bomb. A conventional invasion of mainland Japan would have easily cost us a million dead. And who would have been right in the vanguard, but the Sixth Marine Division.

17 Anise Street
New Britain, Conn
August 15, 1945

Dear Brother,

Here I am again. I haven't mailed this letter so I thought I'd add a little more today.

Well, this morning mother, me and the Farmers went to church. I guess you know it's the Feast of the Assumption today.

Tessie came down for dinner and after she took mother, me and Mrs. Newbauer up to Broadbrook. We just came home a few minutes ago. Mother and the others left me at the farm where Donny is and they went on to Somers to see some of Tessie's relations etc. Al and I went to Crystal Lake. That's about 10 miles from Broadbrook and it's neat up there. We didn't go swimming but just sat on the beach and then walked around for a while. Al wanted to take a canoe out but I, of course, didn't feel like it. (I was afraid he might tip the boat over.) G 'Wan!!! So I guess it was about 5:30 when we left the lake. The gas rationing is off now so Al filled his tank right up to the top. He wanted to ride all day but we didn't have the time. He said he will perhaps be down Sunday (can't wait).

543

We have quite a lot of people out in the kitchen still celebrating V-J Day ,drinking the old cider etc. Gosh, I can't still hardly believe that it's true about the whole darn war being over. It said in the paper tonite that 7,000,000 men in the service will be returned to civilian life within the next 12 months. I hope you come home quicker than that. Well, I'll say goodbye for a while. Bundles of love,

Your little sister,
Betty xxxxx

17 Anise Street
New Britain, Conn.
August 17, 1945

Dear Son,

We got a letter from you dated Aug. 8th yesterday and one to Betty this morning of August 10th. I noted in both of them the lack of mail you are getting from home. And also how your morale is dragging all over the island. It seems that nobody has anything to write about. Betty writes about twice a week, me once a month and Mother about, I couldn't say, all I hear is always, Betty write Sonny a letter. It seems we all depend on Betty although I wrote you a letter about two weeks ago and you should have it by now.

The war as you know was declared over on Tuesday 7 P.M. Two days were declared holidays, and boy what a commotion around here. It was a zoo. Looting package stores and taverns closed when the report came over the radio. Otherwise everybody got stinking. We had our share of it over to the Neubauers till three in the morning. I took Wednesday off but went back to work Thursday. Gas went off the ration list with all canned goods (as though you are interested in these things). All except the GAS, just think all you want to gallivant around the country. The papers say that there will be about five million out of work by Nov. The Aircraft up in Hartford is shut down for a couple of weeks and I heard today that they are going to lay off about 20 thousand in their plants in Conn. As for myself, I'm not worrying, I have plenty of work, in fact too much.

(Back to the war again). When the announcement came over the radio that the war was over, all the sirens and shop whistles started tooting. Cars kept blowing their horns and someone started shooting. Eddy Neubauer came over and we got out the Johnson and ran off about twenty shots rapid fire into the back of the chicken coop, what a racket. Eddy told me that he *is going to have the empty shells chromium plated and give them to you when you get home.*

Mother, Mrs. Neubauer and Tessie went over to the tobacco farm to see Donny Wednesday. He likes the job so well he doesn't care about coming home. The reason $5.20 per day for eight hours work. He's a capitalist now. We might take a ride up there tonight with some people who have a kid up there.

Albert DePinto has been working for me for a couple of weeks and he has already taken his physical and expects to get drafted and go away on the 27th of this month. The country has gone nuts if they take him now that the shooting is all over. He's 28 and has a kid. I didn't know if you ever knew he was married.

We're all glad that it's over, what a relief. Mother would have gone cuckoo if anything happened to you—she was worried almost sick when you were over at Okinawa. I didn't feel like working anymore myself and I figured every time I came home from work that there would be some sort of telegram or notice how you were bumped off.

From my way of thinking about your chances of getting home early, I believe that the boys who have seen action or went through a campaign will be the first ones to get back and I really think you will be home before Christmas, although you will not get anything definite about it until around Nov. They're still drafting the kids and the ones that have been over for a year or so I think will be shipped back soon. Boy, am I an arm chair strategist. Well, let's hope so anyway and don't let the gremlins get the best of you. The war is over now and it's only a matter of time in getting back. When the shooting was going on, your life wasn't worth a plugged nickel, you were liable to get bumped off any minute when in action or anywhere near the front. So just sit back and wait like they do in sing-sing, just keep marking off the days on the calendar and the day will soon come before you know it.

Everybody at home is o.k. and I hope this finds you in the best of health.

I saw Buck Miller last Saturday and he asked me if I wanted to go in on buying a farm up in Vt. They have one in mind for a deer hunting camp. It consists of 75 acres of land, a farm house in good shape and a couple of barns and a darn good place for hunting and fishing. Walter Mller, Ernest Nyquist, the guy who runs the East St. Bus Line, are going to be the partners. They're buying the whole caboodle for 600 bucks. Cheap.(Six Hundred).

So when you get back we'll have a place to go in the fall. This is no kidding, we're all going up to the place to look it over, maybe this weekend. It's about 20 miles from White River Junction, Vermont. Maybe there's good skiing up there in the winter. Well, so long for now and don't get down in the dumps just because you don't get a letter every day of the week.

Your Pop

Connecticut College
New London, Conn.
August 19, 1945

Dear Charlie,

Just a quick note for now. It's fun to fight while you're around 'cause it never lasts long. But by mail it lasts too long. I'll honestly try to write more often—and when I don't, please don't write and tell me I'm a slut —o.k?

I'm sorry I went off on a tangent about the snow job. I know it wasn't — it just sounded like one at the time. It's o.k. from everybody else but I couldn't stand it from you. Do you know what I mean? You're sort of a special case — very special.

About your demotion — it doesn't seem to bother you too much — at least it shouldn't. As for me, I'd be perfectly happy if they demoted you right back to a lousy civilian. Hmmmm — what a pleasant thought. Why don't you work on that?

By the way, you made some crack about me thinking you were a jerk. I think you were in one of those indigo moods, darling. You know better, don't you? I think I know you as well as I know anyone — and I think I know the very nicest side of you. Your letters are not stupid either, Dope. How many times do I have to tell you I'd rather read a letter from you than anyone I know. I'd better shut up — I think you just like to hear how wonderful you are.

Am I forgiven? Take care, darling. It won't be long now.

Love,

Launa

1ˢᵗ Bn. 15ᵗʰ Marines
Sixth Marine Division
San Francisco, Cal.
August 19, 1945

Dear Mom and Dad,

I received both of your letters a few days ago. Seeing that I haven't very much to say, I thought I'd answer them together.

I was shocked nearly to death when I heard about Donny working on that tobacco farm. I think it's terrible. He's only twelve and living independent like that won't do him any good. Pa said he was going to let Donny keep all the money. That will ruin him. Once he starts having money, he will want more and more. He will realize what he can do with it. He will be wanting to quit school before he gets out of Nathan Hale. I saw it happen to all the kids who started working early. Mick started working more and more in the drug store and in no time he quit. Think of what it will do to a twelve year old! Mrs. Walton had about the best idea. Dick used to earn money and he handed it all over to her. She banked it and gave him about a dollar a week. When he got out of H.S. he had over fifteen hundred dollars in the bank to go to college with or to buy a car or whatever he wanted. If you had made me do something like that, I would have been a lot better off. I think that both of you have always been too good and easy with us kids anyway. Whenever we wanted anything, all we had to do was yell for a week or so. I hope Donny will get on the ball and prepare for college. It's the only thing that I hope I will be able to do after this thing is over. If Mother started him saving, he would take an interest in it when he had about a hundred dollars. And make it his alone and in his name. Maybe we can make our little Poopsie president some day, and then we will all be in like Flynn. I really worry about little Wart on that farm. Cripes, next thing I know Betty will have a job in Wallingford at Tillies! Just kidding, of course – I often hear Pa joke of the place.

I found out that Irene M. handed out a lot of bull crap. Don't believe a thing she said.

There's nothing I can tell you other than to read the newspapers and listen to the radio.

I don't think I'll be home this year but maybe the first part of next. I hope so. I also hope that this surrender is on the level. The Japs seem to be stalling.

I can hardly wait till I get home. That's all I ever think about. There should be lots of gasoline and chow by the first of next year.

Under this new point system, I should get out in about twenty years with no questions asked. I've got my hopes pinned on getting out next May. My record book says my enlistment is up then. I'll just have to keep my fingers crossed till then. Those chickens you bought should be good by then.

Oh, I almost forgot. My second class goes into effect the first of September. H.S! Did we pull off a shrewd deal on the ones that screwed us! I'll tell you all about it someday. It's a long story.

The chow is really good now. I guess sea life must really agree with me. Chicken and ice cream for chow today. I'm going to get in line now. Bye and write soon.

Love to all,
Charlie

1ˢᵗ Bn. 15ᵗʰ Marines
Sixth Marine Division
San Francisco, Cal.
31 August 1945
Japan

Dear Folks,

Look where I am! Hot dawg – I certainly get around, don't I?

I wrote to you last when I was aboard ship. I suppose you got that letter by now. I wasn't allowed to say much.

We left Guam over two weeks ago but didn't get here till yesterday. We met the fleet out at sea and drifted around until the way was clear of mines. It was quite exciting to see Mount Fujiyama.

We are living in a Jap naval barracks. They had bunks for us but the mattresses and blankets were full of lice and fleas. We burned all the mattresses and blankets and used our own.

Today it is raining but it doesn't matter 'cause the streets are gravel and there isn't any mud around here. The climate here is a lot like that in the States.

I haven't been in to Tokyo yet, but they say it is almost as bad as Naha. Most of the people here have taken off into the boon-docks.

No mail has caught up with us, yet. We should get some in a day or so. I'm not going to write to anyone until I get some mail.

How about some size 620 film!? You ought to be able to get some somewhere. You seem to be able to get it for the other camera. I'd like to take some pictures while I'm here.

I don't think there is much chance of getting home before next spring. They will undoubtedly send all the doggies home first. I guess that's all for now. I'll write again soon.

Love,
Charlie

USS Mercy
FPO San Fran. Cal.
Sept. 3, 1945

Volume I. Read this first.

Dear Charlie –

This letter should be about a volume long.

Volume II. Written on the nite of Sept. 3 along with Volume I. Don't ask me how long a volume is. No, it's not a new name for "it." Sounds interesting tho'. "Volumes and volumes of ass and it's all mine."

First of all, ya ole turd, it's the same old story – my taking a "helluva" long time to write. To bring you up to date, after we returned from Okinawa we dropped our load of patients at Guam. The next day we hit Saipan and six days later returned to Guam. Ask me why and I'll slug ya! Believe it or not on July 1ˢᵗ I was over the damn side scraping the barnacles off the bottom of this "banana barge." I'll never forget that as long as I love and live. "A Birthday Under Her Belly." That's the name of the book I'm going to write about that day. Author: "Ima Scraper." We left Guam on July 5ᵗʰ and rendezvoused (Hey, does any of youse know how to speak French?) with the 3ʳᵈ and 5ᵗʰ Fleets for the next 45 days. This was the period of time which the leveling off of Japan was taking place. On August 14ᵗʰ, the day that Japan accepted our terms, we were ordered back to Guam to unload patients and load stores. That urinated us off because we figured we weren't going to get a chance to go into Tokyo. We hit Guam on August 18ᵗʰ in the morning, unloaded our patients and started loading stores. We left Guam the next day at 1:00 p.m. During this time I tried to locate you, but with no luck. I had no means of transportation, and I learned that if you were anywhere you were quite a distance away – past Agana or some "faunced up" place. I was only hoping and praying that you'd get word that we were in and that you'd make a visit – but no luck. If I had a liberty I might have been able to find you, but as it was I was on a stores working party and that made things more difficult. What really "angered my anus" was that we had no mail waiting for us at Guam. It wasn't until 10 days later that we got some. On August 28ᵗʰ we got our first mail call in 54 days. This brought me two, letters that is, from you dated July 29 and Aug. 5ᵗʰ. I don't know whether this was your latest mail as it gave no mention of what you had done since Okinawa. On the 28ᵗʰ we anchored in Sagami Bay. On the 30ᵗʰ we "dropped the hook" in Tokyo Bay just off Yokohama and moved north just outside Tokyo on Sept. 1ˢᵗ. Yesterday, with the aid of a telescope, I saw some of the ceremony of the signing of the peace. For all I know, you may be part of the occupying forces and saw all this yourself. I doubt it tho'. We left the Bay tonite and are heading for a point 30 miles from Nagoya to pick up prisoners of war. We were to do the same at Tokyo but the need seems to be greater at Maisaka and that's where we're going. We arrive at 600 a.m. tomorrow. That about brings us up to date, "lamby pie."

Your manuscript of the 29th really "tickled my toy." I'll do my best to make a reply.

You're getting a "helluva" good selection of movies. "Rhapsody in Blue" must have been good. Our latest double feature was "Tom Mixes Cement" and "Pangs of Passion." For adults only. "All that meat and dehydrated potatoes."

Just think, Charlie, the last time I wrote we were still at war. Now the world is at peace once again. I needn't give a discourse on this atomic bomb. We both undoubtedly have our ideas about it. Now our thoughts are turning toward the return to civilian life and the beginning of a new era. I've learned so very, very much about life since I've been in the service. It's an education in itself. I've learned where I'm weak and strong — more or less — and that's a good thing to know. You know, I just can't wait till you and I get together and start comparing notes, sea stories, experiences, opinions. Gosh, that'll be wonderful. I can just see us atop the hill overlooking our fair city (Stanley Manor) talking things over. What different things we'll talk about and how different we'll talk about them. We'll have very different philosophies to compare.

Old "Joe the mailman" says 4 sheets to an envelope, so I'll close this temporarily and start a new letter. I'll number the volumes.

As ever,
Dick

"Charlesie"

Here I am again with another ejaculation. On the fifth to you.

About books — I've slowed down a great deal in my reading lately. My latest book is "Green Light" which is very good. I finished "The Way of all Flesh," "Windswept," and "Three Musketeers", no less, not long ago. I think I'll read "Keys of the Kingdom." I read that book "Lost Weekend" last May when I was in sick bay with "pussy" fever. Talk about weird characters — that screwball of an author is "faunced in the cladestow." I'll try to locate the "Feather Merchants" and give you my opinion of it.

About women. To begin with, I have had very little mail—to be precise 2 mail calls in two months, so I don't know who remembers me or who doesn't. Anywho, in those two "calls" I received a total of ten letters from Fleurette. The woman is all but coming right out and asking for it. She's been *sending me these bathing suit pictures, etc. Golly damn! Has that woman filled out! I believe that it can be "promoted." She's probably got her virginity tucked away in a strong box, but who am I to deny the girl of anything? Who knows? I haven't heard from Meg in a long time – the same for Mary. That blonde in Staten Island has slowed up writing me, and that one and only in California hasn't written in four months. You know, Charlie, when I get back I'm really going to get around. None of this one woman stuff. I'll be out for a good time and one other thing. Damnation, what a little overseas duty does to a guy! I'm sure that you'll do the same but may not feel the same. I've learned a lot about a lot of women lately. I've learned their wants, their crazy ideas etc. I'm more or less prepared to take care of things. When I remember that night with Caroline and Ginger, I kick myself in the pants – once for being so slow and again for "shooting the moon."*

As for your feline situation, perhaps it's because I haven't received your letters in succession that I don't know what's going on. Launa is still the love of your life, I guess. It's funny, but I don't believe that I could ever feel about a girl the way you feel about her. If they call that love, I don't want too much of it. I feel that love is something sacred and beautiful. Your affair has been filled with some ecstatic moments, I guess, but it has also been filled with periods of doubt and bewilderment. Of course, love wouldn't be very good if you never were in doubt. However, you've been taunted and led to despair too long. It seems that I should let it go on for a while and then end it. But perhaps doubt, bewilderment, despair build for an everlasting love. I don't know.

What you say about Meg and Mary has crossed my mind a number of times lately. I believe that if treated properly it could be "processed." My feeling for Meg is so changed! I consider her very much of a character now. She's something of an experiment. We should have great times with them when we return some day. Remember? Beckley's Beer Garden ....the swim and my jump without a parachute....Meg and Mary undressing in the car....Old Black Magic...." Do you always wipe it off, Charlie? I feel that I've always played perpetually for safety. I can't understand how I got that feeling of the want of security in me. I've always been that way. I've never taken too many chances in life with realization that if I were caught I would be reprimanded for it. I guess that you'd more or less call me cautious with an instinctive desire to make an attempt.

You never did send me the Edgar Guest poem which you picked up in Naha. What were you thinking – ya clown. And, Charlie, I notice you're back to PhM 3/c. What's the story?

Sept. 5, 1945

Well, my lil' lamb, since I wrote last yours truly has worked his "beauteous butt" off for once. Yesterday, we picked up prisoners of war from Musaka. We processed 900 of them, returned about 250 and transferred about 650. They came from Narumi, Yakasaki, Yatsushima. Most of the men were o.k. except for malnourishment. They were principally from Corregidor, Bataan, Luzon, Java, Hong Kong, Singapore etc. We started processing the men about 1200 noon yesterday and we didn't stop till 400 a.m. today. I got only about a couple hours sleep but I feel fine. Of course, I can't begin to tell some of the stories that were told. I talked to one Marine photographer who is doing a few assignments here. He claimed to have been on Okinawa, so I asked about your Division etc. He told me that he had just left the 15th Marines a few days ago and that you are in the Tokyo area in all probability. I'll be damned – if I can ever locate you it will be a miracle.

Now that censorship regulations have been lifted at least for us, we may be able to get together.

My latest book is "Boston Adventure." It has started out o.k. I remember your mentioning it to me. That's all, Charlie, take care of yourself wherever you are. Think of me on the fifth and don't "faunce your cladistow."

As ever your friend,
Dick

1st Bn. 15th Marines
Sixth Marine Division
FPO San Francisco, Cal.
6 September 1945

Dear Dad,

At last my mail caught up with me. I received over thirty letters last night. Boy, did I knock myself out reading them all. Your letter dated the 17th of Aug. was among them. There were several from Mom and Betty, too.

All the letters were about the war being over. No one out here got very excited. We were more excited about coming here. The war won't be over for us until we get home. Most of the fellows did not think much about not having to go on another operation. In combat, they don't have working parties and it isn't G.I. at all.

I don't think the Marines will be home for quite some time. The Army always comes first and goes first. I'm still counting on next spring, however.

I hope that you get that place in White River Junction. That is right in the heart of ski country. I told Benjamin that you might get a place up there. We ought to be able to help fix up the joint. All we do in the Marine Corps is improvise.

The base is pretty good. The people around live like animals, however. They take a leak along the streets and their homes are just shacks. They are very small and look like apes. There hasn't been any trouble, yet and they seem to be willing to cooperate with the Americans.

That's about all for now. I have a lot of other letters to answer so I'll close.

Love,
Charlie

1ˢᵗ Bn. 15ᵗʰ Marines
Sixth Marine Division
San Francisco, Cal
6 September 1945

Dear Sis,

I have a whole sit pot of letters from you all to answer so I might as well give you a break and start answering.

All I heard in your letters was, "Al this and Al that." I thought it was Al Pep at first, but the last letter I read explained that he was a shoveller. I'll bet he's good at doing the Farmer's Shuffle.

You should see the pictures I got from Launa! Whit Wheeeee! I'd send them to you, but I haven't stopped drooling yet. Boy, did they knock me out. I was ready to leap on a life-raft and take off. Nothing like getting prepared. I'll probably be jet propelled by the time I get to see her again. Will close on that high note and write a longer letter as soon as I catch up with some of this correspondence.

Love,
Charlie

1ˢᵗ Bn. 15ᵗʰ Marines
Sixth Marine Division
San Francisco, Cal.
10 September 1945
Japan

Dear Mom,

It's me again. There isn't much to write about but I have some time so I thought I'd write. The censorship has stopped so I can say what I want.

553

This is really quite a place. Tomorrow we are going to be able to go on liberty. I can hardly wait – everyone is getting ready – shinning shoes etc. This is the first civilized base we've been near in a long time – way over a year. Guadalcanal was much nicer than Guam. I hated Guam. It was hot all the time and there wasn't anything to do.

As this is a nice camp, we will only be here a short time. In fact, we have already started thinking about packing up. No one knows for sure as to where we are headed but it seems to be China. I'll be oriental before I get out of here. Just so long as we don't go to Guam I'll be happy.

We have an early and a late movie. I slept all afternoon (we had a big party last night and were up all night) so I'm going to the nine o'clock show. Just like the States – two shows. Some Tarzan is on and I know it won't be so hot but I have nothing else to do.

I received your letter from Boston and don't have to tell you how worried I am. Now it's my turn to worry about you. The sooner that goiter is removed the better. When do you think they will be able to take you? When did you first find out about it?

Aunt Anna wrote and said she would like one of those red lacquer dishes with the cover. I can't get any more here, so will you give her one?

We haven't had any mail lately (last three days) but will probably get some tomorrow.

I had a letter from Joe Rizzo the other day. He is stationed in New Mexico. He doesn't care for it at all. He said he'd rather be in England or France.

All that Nip money that we collected on Okinawa is good here. I have over three hundred yen. Tomorrow is pay day but I am only going to draw three hundred and seventy-five yen. The value of the yen is fifteen to one American dollar. Three hundred and seventy five yen is equivalent to twenty five American shekels

I didn't think I had much to write about but I'm on my third page.

Is Freddy still in New Hampshire? I haven't heard from him in ages.

I guess that is about all for tonight. I'll write again soon and let you know what the town is like. Bye –

Love,

Charlie

P.S. Did Pa buy that place in Vermont yet?

1st Bn. 15th Marines
Sixth Marine Division

San Francisco, Cal.
12 September 1945

Dear Sis,

This is going to be short and sweet. I've been traipsing the streets of Yokosuka all day and my feet are killing me. There is nothing much to write about. The town is dirty and the shops are closed. It was good to get out even though we only had four hours.

We are moving again! Cripes, that burns me up. We have a nice N.C.O. club with Jap waiters etc. Strictly a B.T.O's life.

I don't know where the hell we are going. We are supposed to be ready to leave by the day after tomorrow. It seems that we are going to Guam and will meet the rest of the Sixth Division (There are only a few battalions here) and then shove off for China. My eyes are getting slanted from being over here so long.

Tell Mom that she'd had better take it easy and you'd better try to stay home at least fifteen minutes a day to help her. Every time I hear from you, you are either coming from or going to Broad Brook. Just kidding, of course.

Every nut you go out with reminds you of me!? That was long ago. (Oh yeah!) New Britsky will think an atomic bomb landed when I get home. That's if I don't die of nervous prostration first.

Tonight I saw "Thrill of a Romance." The sound was too deep and little Suzan Dorsey (T.D.'s daughter) sounded like Lauren Bacall when she sang. That did it!

Some Jap program is on now and my head is so heavy it is lying on the table. I'll write a goofier letter tomorrow, Darlin'.

Love,

Charlie

USS Mercy
FPO San Fran. Cal.
September 13, 1945

Dear Charlsie,

The saga continues. *Look over your stay in the Navy, and you'll discover your opportunities, successes, failures, advantages, disadvantages. It all adds up. I'm a bit digressive, but that's the way I feel as the moment, so bear with me.*

You mentioned that you remembered reading something about life being lived in the past and not in the present or future. You remember it undoubtedly from "King's Row."

I agree with you that one way to enjoy life is to let it pass by. Another thing – I read in The Readers Digest recently about a woman who had been set out into the world at the age of 10 and got along quite well. She believed that "maturity was an artificial conception. To begin life at the age of 15 or 20 is too late. It is out of proportion to the average length of life." She goes on to say, "Children, if not properly handled, would run grave risks at the age of 10. If all 10 yr. olds were treated as adults, we would be better off. As things stand, the risks are not appreciably greater than are normal anyway. In any case, something might happen and one day must happen. The world is a dangerous if fascinating place to live in and to pray perpetually for safety is as ridiculous as dodging lightening in a thunder storm. We have in life, finally, only one real concern, to live – live dangerously since we must, but at any rate all the time that fate allows us." Looking back on this letter, I don't know what put me in this mood. Enuff of dis luffink, let's ……

As ever,
Dick

17 Anise Street
New Britain, Conn.
September 14, 1945

Dear Son,

We got a couple letters from you yesterday, one to Betty and one to me. I note that you are at Yokosuka Bay. We looked it up on the map and know just about where you are located. I always had the idea that you were in Japan as we didn't get a letter from you in over three weeks.

Also got the shot gun and stuffed packed in the paper box, shells, helmet, bayonet etc. The gun is not so hot but maybe you can use the regular shells in it. I wouldn't try the express shells in it as it's liable to burst. We'll have to get a trigger guard somewhere or I could make one. The Samurai sword is quite ducky. We'll fix the handle for you, also the saber should be glued up. Last night I went out to the chicken run and lopped the head off a rooster with the sword. One swing bowled it over.

We read a lot in the papers about the occupation and articles written by different correspondents in Yokosuka Bay, it must be quite near Tokyo. From what the papers say there will be little if any trouble with the Japs— they're washed up and know it, I only hope you are able to get some sort of furlough or release in the next few months. I believe by the end of next spring they will ship most men out of Japan. There wouldn't be any need *for keeping 5,000 men there for occupation. Well, it's a good thing you came out with your whole skin so when you get down in the dumps just think of all those kids who will never come home. It could have been a lot worse.*

Everything at home is O.K. It is fall now and the leaves are beginning to fall. I went picking mushrooms yesterday up in West Hartford where we used to go, didn't get any though. Betty is in her last year in High and Donny is finally in Nathan Hale and still peddling papers. He worked a month at the farm and brought home 75.00. Believe it or not, he handed me the dough. We're putting it in the bank for him and I told him last week that for every dollar he puts in the bank from his paper route money, I will give him a buck towards his account. He likes the idea and has agreed to 50 cents spending money a week. Don't worry about the kid being spoiled, He's a good kid and doing very nicely, He's been playing commando with Charles Farmer all morning, wearing the Jap helmet covered with green grass with the ammunition pouch and bayonet in his belt. What a time they are having, running around the house and shooting machine guns at each other.

This afternoon Mother, Tessie and Donny took a trip to Lake Pocatapaug to see the Peplaus. I'm staying home with Betty for a while. This morning I listened to the Auburn and believe it or not, there isn't a squeak or a rattle in the car, better than new. (I'm saving it for you when you get home.)We'll keep the old bus until we can get a new one but I don't think they will be available for at least another year.

There is still plenty of work in my business of painting. Albert DePinto is working for me now and we get along real good. Have been busy right along and haven't had time to go up to Vt. to see that camp I told you about—the other fellows haven't had the time either.

See if you can get hold of a scope for a rifle, a real good one. There maybe plenty around where you are, or a real good rifle, one that hasn't shown a lot of use and can be made into a sporting rifle for deer. A lot of these rifles are being shipped by the men from Germany. The Ziegler kids sent home a couple of dandy German rifles that are the nerts.

Well, this is all for now. I hope this finds you in the best of health.

Love from the whole family,
Your Pop

1st Bn. 15th Marines
Sixth Marine Division
San Francisco, Cal.

14 September 1945
Last night in Japan.

Dear Mom,

We are all ready to move again. We've just finished packing. I just took my chest of personal gear over to the truck. Everyone thinks we are going on to Guam and then to China. Boy, I hope that we don't stay on Guam.

I received the package today. Everything in it was fine except the canned hot dogs. That's one of the chief overseas dishes. I mailed a lot of crap home today. I looked all over town for something for Betty's birthday. All I could find was a little set of boxes – one fits on top of the other. She will be able to use it on her dresser. Put the other stuff away so that it won't get lost. Especially the opium pipe and corps book.

I got a letter from Mick yesterday. He is stationed in Maine. He said that he thought he would be sent out here again in December or January.

Yesterday I went sightseeing in Yokohama and Tokyo. Yokohama is burned out but there is a lot of Tokyo left. We visited the royal shrines, the Emperor's palace and lots of other places. It is a beautiful city and has some nice boulevards and highways. It's a lot like New York and the trains are still running. How I wish I had some 620 film. I don't see why you can't get some when you get it for your camera. See if you can find some, huh?

I owe Launa a letter, so I'd better write and keep peace. We haven't had a fight in months so we are due for one.

I lost my Nip rifle or rather someone swiped it over a week ago. Today, however, I got hold of a brand new 30 caliber and a good 25 caliber. I don't know how I'll ever get them home. I'll probably have to tote them all the way. I'll get them home if it kills me.

Those souvenirs from Guam should get home soon. The sword I sent home was all in pieces. If Dad could get Eddy Newbauer to have it plated and fixed up, I'd really appreciate it.

I've got to go out now. Someone just yelled "mail call." Bye and write soon.

Your loving son,
Charlie

P.S. What about that place in Vermont?

-TEN-

HOMEWARD BOUND 1945

65 Arthur Street
New Britain, Conn.
September 15, 1945

Hi, Charles,

Received your letter this morning and sure was glad to hear from you again. I wasn't surprised that you're in Japan as I saw all the Marines in the Sixth Division in a newsreel but I didn't see you. I just wish all you kids were heading home. Dickey was also there in Japan, I guess he is picking up the prisoners of war. He was there when the peace was signed. He said he will never forget it, and that he will have plenty to talk about when he gets home. I think that will be soon—after he loads up this last time. They said they would have all the wounded men home in 90 days.

Dickey wrote and said he was at sea 54 days and didn't receive any mail and that it was getting under his skin. Then the 54th day he got mail, he said he received two from you. His last letter was August 30th and I haven't heard from him again. I hope he is on his way home.

My husband wants to thank you for saying hello to him. He sends his regards and hopes you will be home soon.

It's funny you boys are so close yet your paths don't cross. I wish you would meet—that would be wonderful.

He wrote and told me he anesthetized a person. He said it was quite an experience for him which he will never forget. The good part about it was that he performed the operation under difficult circumstances. He said the patient had good veins for injection. The nurse surprised him and said, "Let Walton take over." He almost fell through the deck.

Well, Charles that's all. Things are still the same here, wish you luck and speedy return.

As ever,
Mrs. Richard Walton

Connecticut College
New London, Conn.
September 16, 1945

Darling –

Are you furious? I suppose you have a right to be – it's weeks since I've written. But somehow I just couldn't – I can't explain it. You seemed so awfully far away and when I started to write, I felt as though I were writing to a stranger. It's been almost a month since I heard from you – and *it isn't easy to keep writing when you aren't getting any answers. But I've been feeling on top of the world since your two letters came yesterday – I'd about given up hope.*

So you're in Japan. At first I kept hoping you wouldn't get stuck in the occupation forces – so you could come home sooner. But I guess they wouldn't be sending you home anyway so it's much better to be moving around and seeing things. They won't just stick you there and forget all about you for a year or so, will they? Please!!

Seriously, do you have any idea when you'll be home? I'm dreaming of a white Christmas – but I don't like dreaming alone, darling. It'll be two years by then – isn't that long enough? As the song says, "How long can a girl go on dreaming?"

Your letters were both so long that it'll take me ages to answer them. Better do it on the installment plan. First of all – are you sure it was me you were dancing with to "Put Your Arms Around Me, Honey?" From the way your letter reads the brazen hussy must have kissed you. I'm innocent – so help me. I'm the shy retiring type, remember?

By the way, you said a long time ago that you'd grown. How tall are you anyway? I know you're taller than I am – and I'm five seven, so where does that put you?

I was glad to see that you and my old friend Cheryl are still on the best of terms. As I recall Phoebe thought she was very sweet when she met her, too. I guess maybe it's just me – she isn't bad. I don't even remember what I used to dislike her for. She made me awfully mad for some reason – and just about that time you stepped into the picture, which of course only led to more woe. At first I started fooling around with you just to see her fume (in her sweet way of course) and look what all that led to. I think maybe you were just trying to make her jealous – how about that? Honestly, doesn't that seem centuries ago? I feel old when I think of it. And here we are – still battling it out – fun though, hmmmm? But just to conclude the discussion, I would like to bump into her some day. Doesn't she live in Hartford? What fun!

I just read another paragraph of your letter – you said Cheryl was too selfish. Is that a backhanded crack at me, darling? Don't bother to say no – I admit it. But aren't you a rather self-centered creature yourself, Stinky? That makes us about even. I'm not insulting you – so don't blow your top. Just being truthful – terrible habit.

Speaking of being truthful – you started telling me how faithful you'd been to me (by the way, I'm flattered) in relation to the next paragraph about the geisha girls I suppose. Yes, I'm broadminded – I guess – I think. People have been trying to explain the ways of the world to me – so I guess geisha girls are all right. That's what they tell me anyway. Oh, now I'm in over my head again. I guess maybe that's something a person has to decide for himself. I wish to heck they'd send you home – I liked you the way you were very much.

My mind is beginning to get befuddled I guess, so I'd better quit. This letter is almost as long as yours – and I'll save the other one to answer tomorrow. Goodnight, my darling.

Yours,

Launa

P.S. I'll be back at school Sept. 20th. Address letters there – O.K?

Jinsen, Korea
Sept. 17, 1945

Dear Charlie,

Look where the hell you are! I'd swap places with you anytime. I got one liberty since I left Pearl Harbor—that was about three days ago. I walked about three hours and went back to the ship. All red light districts were closed and guarded by MP's. We couldn't eat or drink anything and weren't allowed to carry money. I say "up their asses everyone." A thing that surprised me though was Jap soldiers (probably officers) allowed to walk the streets armed with side arms and sword. I heard the civilians would kill them if we took the arms away, for my dough let them if they want to.

White River Junction! It's right up there where I want to be. You've got the right idea with the wine, women and skiing. Boy! I need some dissipation but good. The only thing that keeps me from going mad is thinking about what a lot of fun I'll have with the thousand dollars I'll have saved when I get home.

Scuttlebutt rides high about getting home and getting discharged.

a)   *One fellow, a radio technician, has bet $225 that we'll be in the States by Jan. 1st 1946. I think he saw a secret dispatch in the coding room or something of that nature to bet all that.*

b)   *All the officers seem pretty optimistic about getting back.*

c)   *The Guam and Alaska (CB's) are going back in about a month and we are acting as a screen for them right now.*

562

d) *We've lost forty men (discharged) already and in a month or so we should lose at least that many more.*

In my opinion mid-winter or early spring we'll be in the good old U.S.A. We can't get replacements out here so we'll have to go back pretty soon.

I've got pretty good duty right now as far as work goes. I have a radioman's job and whale watch boat duty one day out of four, the rest of the time I crap out and see movies or write letters. Of course we have our technician work – cleaning equipment and studying new gear now that we'll lose a few techs in a month or so. But on the whole I have it pretty easy. I should put in for 1st, but being second is too much fun.

I hope to be discharged by next summer. Our Captain says we'll be out by then. I now have 22.5 points – what about you?

Helen is getting sweeter and sweeter every day. I think she's pretty darn wonderful. If I were getting married tomorrow, I'd marry her without blinking an eyelash. But from the tone of her letters we're as good as married. I don't plan to get married for years yet. No kidding, Charlie, I can see a noose tighten around my neck. All I have to do is take it off though, but it fits I think and it's not uncomfortable so I'm letting it stay there but keeping it open till I get back to the States where I'll get my proper perspective. You get pissed off at me every time I mention something about Helen. What do you think I should do this time, if anything?

I've been thinking a lot about college next fall also. I know if I don't go next year I'll never go. So I applied for all the information I could get from the University of Vermont (co-ed to be sure) with plenty of skiing in Burlington, Middlebury, Dartmouth and the University of Conn. (co-ed also). Another good deal is Syracuse University (co-ed) with all hands living in private hotels, where the house lady turns her back to everything as long as she gets her rent. I'm writing for info from them today. Plenty of skiing there, too.

I'll be writing a book soon if I don't run out of words. I've thought about Cornell up in Ithaca, N.Y. Plenty of snow and women there also.

When I read the catalogs I'm going to get, I'll have a better idea of where I'd like to go, then I'll have to start worrying about getting in. Anyway, I am planning.

I haven't told my Dad about my plans to go into business with him yet, but I'm going to be sure before I build up his hopes. Write soon and tell me more of your plans.

As ever,
Ben

Connecticut College
New London, Conn
September 19, 1945

Hi, Stinky –

    This is going to be kind of short 'cause I'm dead tired. I spent most of the day packing and lugging suitcases around trying to get back to school. But I made it – and I'm back at the old grind again. I only had 9 days vacation from summer school so I can't say I'm especially enthusiastic about being back. It really isn't bad though – I'm afraid I'm getting to like the old place.

    We've got a beautiful room – with a beautiful view of the ocean. And the moon is here again – shinning on the water. So you know my feeble mind is wondering where it shouldn't ought never to go. Couldn't you move at least a couple of thousand miles closer? It might help. It really seems a shame to waste all that moonlight. I could go on for hours – but as you say it's like beating your head against a stonewall, hmmmm?

    Meg and I are rooming together again, of course. We get along too well to split up. You'd like her – she isn't dashing or exotic – just a real sweet kid (not the Cheryl kind of sweet either). When I get in the dumps, she always feels happy – she sort of keeps me from driving myself mad.

    I got a letter from you yesterday, the one you wrote after you'd been out on the binge– are you sure you were over it when you wrote? The letter was a scream! You said something to the effect that all they had to mix drinks with there were dining cars !?! and where were you on the party – it sounded like a night club – do they have them there? And can the females dance? And why don't you come home and dance with me anyway? And why don't I stop day dreaming?

    Pris Jones isn't coming back for the winter – she's going back to Syracuse. I saw some of the girls that used to live with her and they told me.

    I get quite a charge our of reading about the people over there. You don't tell me half enough about what it's like. I thought that Japan was quite modern. That women wore heels and short skirts. Do they all wear those thing-a-ma-bobs like ski pants?

    They're playing "There Is No You" – ain't it the truth, darling. It must be the moon so just take me with a grain of salt. Could be I'm quite highly seasoned anyway.

    I think maybe this is all my brain can stand of this stuff. And probably about all you can take. I'll quit and write again soon. See how much encouragement I get from just three letters? Aren't you afraid that I'll be one of those clinging women that you can't get rid of? Well, don't worry too hard, darling, and write soon.

My love always,
Launa

17 Anise Street
New Britain, Conn.
September 23, 1945

Dear Son,

It's weeks since I have written to you so I must get busy. Well everything is o.k. with us. Pa had a bum leg, he must have caught cold in it. He couldn't straighten it out. But he took a hot bath and put a heating pad on it and went to work this morning.

I've been busy canning but I'm all thru now. I've been waiting to hear from Boston but they say it takes a couple of months. They are so busy up there.

Well, Betty got thru in Birnbaum's. She has quite a lot of homework.

Donny is getting used to Nathan Hale. I have quite a job getting him out in the morning. He takes his bike so he makes it on time.

Freddy was home for over Sunday. He is in Portsmouth, New Hampshire. I told him to write to you. He has a new girl from Bristol. She goes to college in S. Carolina. He is pretty sweet on her. He wants to give her a diamond.

Cheryl called and said she was sick so write and tell her how sorry you were to hear it. She said she can't wait until you get home. She said she doesn't go anywhere.

I washed that white blanket you sent home and it turned out beautiful. Betty said how she is going to put it on her bed. I told her she will think of a Jap being in her bed.

Donny got a big kick out of the swords. Donny and Pa went up to the chicken coop and cut a couple of the chickens heads off with it. Pa said it was too bad you couldn't get a good gun.

Well, I hope you get home for Xmas. The paper said how they were going to send a lot home from across.

I was just over to see Fannie- she is sick again and looks terrible. Charlie Farmer was home sick last week. Joe Nealon is in the hospital but Nellie said he felt better. He wants to come home.

565

I washed this morning and when I had all the clothes out my line broke – was I mad.

Tommy and Shirley were here Sat. They are looking for a rent in Suffield. Tag expects to be discharged soon. Well, I want the mail man to take this so I will close. Take care of yourself.

Love,

Mother

Excuse this pen– it's all I could find around here.

At sea

September 24, 1945

Dear Mom,

We are supposed to dock tomorrow but I'm not sure that we will get off this boat. I think they will take the mail off so I will put this in the box tonight.

What a trip this has been! Before we left we ran into a typhoon so we anchored in Tokyo Bay till it blew over. We just got the end of it so it wasn't very rough. Yesterday our generator went on the blink and we were stranded six hundred miles from Guam. We were towed for a while – our generator was fixed this morning so we are now going full speed ahead. It would have been something if the war had been on. We would have been a dead duck if there were any subs in the area.

The food here is really good. The ships always have fresh fruit and fresh meat every day. We have ice cream every other day. I'll be getting fat – wouldn't that be something?

Have you heard from Boston yet? I hope that you are taking your medicine regularly. If I was home you would. You'd better have that goiter taken care of so we can do a lot of running around when I get home.

I received a role of 620 film from Jane. So if we go to China I'll have my picture taken with some of those oriental dolls. I'd like to send one to Cheryl.

The transport I am on is known as an APA (Amphibious Personnel Attack, I think), There are only six hundred troop aboard so we all have two bunks. One for our gear, and one to sleep in. It's a good size ship – it carries a crew of over five hundred swabbies.

There is enough reading material around to keep us busy – if it weren't for that we wouldn't have a thing to do. The sea air really gives me an appetite, so I'm always one of the first when chow is called. At dinner I usually run the line twice.

The funniest thing happened yesterday. I was sprawled out under a Higgins boat reading and they fired the five inch gun over my head (on the next deck), I almost jumped overboard. Then all the anti-aircraft guns opened up and I thought for sure some Jap hadn't got the word. They were just burning up ammunition, however. It was like the Fourth of July with all the guns firing. I guess that is the last gun play we will see in the war. I'll not complain if it's the last I ever see.

Everyone seems to think we will stop at Guam for six hours, take on supplies, and head for China. That is all unofficial. We won't know anything till tomorrow. I hope we don't unload all our gear and stay. I told you before, I think Guam is about the worse spot in the Pacific.

Betty and Donny must be sick of school by now. How do you keep up with Betty and her boyfriends? Every time I get a letter she is raving about another one. It was Red Shine last time, and some Lali before that.

Maybe we will receive some mail when we dock tomorrow. Then I'll be able to write on the way to China. I didn't think I'd have much to write but I'm on my third page. I've almost run out of things to say.

Did I tell you that I received your picture and the ones of Betty, Tommy and Shirley ? I thought the one of you was the best. Pretty soon it will be time to mail Xmas packages so I am going to tell you what I want now. I want a photo album with some of those corner hinges to put the pictures in. I have almost forty pictures now and want something to keep them in. Everyone has a photo collection and every once in a while we will haul out our pictures and show them around. So see if you can find some kind of an album, huh?

I've really run out of things to say now. I'll write again the day after tomorrow if we get off the ship. If you don't hear from me for about another two weeks you will know that I am off to China. Lately I've been covering more ground than Mrs. Roosevelt ever thought of.

Give my love to all and be a good li'l mother and take care of yourself.
Your loving son,
Charlie

P.S. Have you come across any 620 film yet?
P.S.S. Don't forget to keep on writing, even when you don't hear from me.
P.S. S. S. One of the fellows just came up and said, "Hey, Doc, do you think they will send me home with the piles?" I said, "I don't see how they could send you home without them!"—I'm so clever –yeah—.

1ˢᵗ Bn. 15ᵗʰ Marines
Sixth Marine Division
San Francisco, Cal.
25 September 1945
Guam

Dear Mom,

Well, here I am again. I got here yesterday and am sick of this place already.

When I was coming into the harbor, I saw Dick's ship. I'm going to go down and see if he is still there tomorrow. I would like to go today but there is too much work to be done.

I received a letter from Betty yesterday and about five more from other people. I'll answer the one from Sis tomorrow.

No one knows what we will do or where we are going or if we're staying. The Fourth Marine Regiment and only one battalion of the Fifteenth Regiment (that's us) went to Japan. The rest of the Division stayed here. The Fourth stayed in Japan and we came back. All the Sixth is leaving for China today and what we will do no one knows. I don't think we are going to China but what we will do here I can't imagine. What a mess.

It rained here yesterday and this morning. Everything is muddy this morning. It really isn't as bad as it seems here. We have good tents – the chow will be better if we are the only outfit that stays here and we have shower facilities.

I owe Launa a letter so I'll close now. This is kind of short but there isn't anything to write. Bye now and take good care of yourself.

Love,
Charlie

1ˢᵗ Bn. 15ᵗʰ Marines
Sixth Marine Division
San Francisco, Cal.
28 September 1945
Guam

Dear Betty,

I've really been gallivanting around today. This morning I built a box and shipped two Jap rifles home. I was really glad to get rid of them. I've been carrying them since Okinawa.

I took a role of film today. I mailed the role of film home. It was on 120 film so have the pictures enlarged so that they are about the size of the pictures you take. Have five sets made for me. I've been promising people pictures for ages. I sent the roll airmail so you should get it right away. I'm dying to see how they come out, so have them developed and send them back airmail.

This afternoon another fellow and I went to the Third Division and saw a lot of friends that we knew in the States. I saw them when I was on Guam the last time, too.

Hardly any mail at all has been coming into this battalion. It will take a week or so before it starts coming in regularly. It's awfully hard to write a letter without one to answer. That's a hint for you to write more often.

I'm waiting for those pictures to come back already. Still keep looking for 620 film for me tho. One of the fellows has a new camera and has lent me his old one till we leave.

The latest rumor is that we will be here for around thirty days. No one knows where we will go tho. China probably. There isn't much more to say. Write soon, huh —

Love,
Charlie

1ˢᵗ Bn. 15ᵗʰ Marines
Sixth Marine Division
San Francisco, Cal.
30 September 1945
Guam

Dear Mom,

Here I am again. This is going to be a short letter again 'cause I haven't a letter to answer. It seems like ages since I last heard from you.

I sent a roll of film home and asked to have five sets sent me. If you haven't had the roll developed yet, only have four made for me. That will be plenty.

This afternoon two of the corpsmen and I took the jeep and went sight seeing. We went up in the mountains and down near the bay. It was something to do.

I got two swell letters today. It was the first mail I received in ages. One from Dick and another from Launa. Launa is back in college again. She said that she was trying to will me home for Xmas. I wish she could but I don't think there is a chance.

I haven't seen any good movies lately. Our movie theater starts tomorrow. We ought to have some good movies then.

Now that I've told you what I've been up to, how about what you've been doing? Have you heard anything from Boston yet? Let me know when you do. Well, I'll close now. Write soon.

Love,
Charlie

17 Anise Street
New Britain, Conn.
October 2, 1945

Dear Son,

Rec'd your letter yesterday and so did Betty. It was just a week since we heard from you.

So, you are stationed on Guam. Do you think you will stay there? That place is pretty well built up. It's too bad you couldn't have stayed in Tokyo a little longer so you could see more of the place. I really think you will be home soon. I hope.

Well there isn't much to talk about. I was sick last week with the grip but I'm all right now.

Shirley and Tommy were here. They went house keeping in Windsor Locks, that's just 5 miles from where Tom teaches. He likes it very much. Shirley isn't working. She was laid off. But she is collecting social security $22.50 a week. Bobby is going to Teachers College and he likes it. He came over for dinner yesterday. He was all painted up with one pants leg rolled up, an apron on and a big sign with his name on. Did he look funny. He was being initiated. He said he had to crawl on his hands and knees all the way down the hall and bark like a dog. He also had to scrub the hall with a toothbrush. He said he would be over today.

Tag expects to be discharged this week. He is going back to work for the Gas Co. Freddy is still in New Hampshire.

One of Betty's boy friends joined the Navy and he doesn't like it at all. She got a kick out of you calling him Red Shine- his name is Bob. You were right when you told her Albert was too old for her. I told her that myself. But she hasn't seen him lately. She thinks these other kids are too silly. I'm glad you told her they're only kids like herself and I would rather have them act silly instead of being serious. She is too young to think about a steady boy friend.

It's a good thing Donny doesn't care about the girls. He is always kidding Betty. Boy, does he get a kick out of those swords. He had the Jap uniform on and the hat and sword—did he look funny.

I think he likes school a little better now. He is interested in shop electrical work.

Lala was just here. It's 11 a.m. now and I must finish this before the mailman comes. Kenneth is going pretty steady with some girl that works down at the Dairy. She is a Swede and they don't like that very much. He wanted to buy her a watch for Xmas. So it must be serious. He seems to stick to his job all right. Well, I guess I'll close and start dinner for Bobby will be here. Take care of yourself.

Love,

Mother

Conn. College

New London, Conn.

October 4, 1945

Hello, Darling,

I'm about to fall on my face I'm so tired – but I have to wait up for Meg to come in so I thought I might as well write to you. My mind couldn't possibly stay on economics for more than 2 minutes.

I got another letter today – although I didn't expect it. So I'd better get on the ball – I'm a little behind as usual.

When you started telling me about your longing for pajamas I decided it was time you came home. If you'll come home I'll buy you 2 doz. pairs – how about it? I must be going mad.

You said you were having some pictures taken. Please, please can't I have some? No kidding sometimes I really don't know what you look like in spite of this practically life-size face that stares at me all day from the desk. A snap shot would be a little more real. Seven out of the eight would almost satisfy – does that sound familiar?

Evidently you're happy at the idea of going to China – there's no accounting for taste. To me it just seems a couple of thousand miles further away – and in the wrong direction.

I'm awfully tired. If you were here we could probably stay up and talk for hours – but pushing a pen is rather a poor substitute. I sometimes wish I could talk to you – for only an hour or so. It would make things much easier, wouldn't it? It was always so easy to talk to you. But there's no sense

571

in crying in the soup — there is bound to be an end to this farce sometime soon. Write soon and take care of yourself, darling.

Love,

Launa

1ˢᵗ Bn. 15ᵗʰ Marines
Sixth Marine Division
San Francisco, Cal.
4 October 1945
Guam

Dear Mom,

I just received your later dated 24ᵗʰ September. I was very glad to get it 'cause it's been ages since I heard from any of you.

I'm glad that my sword got home. But tell Donny to leave it alone. If anything happens to it, I'll cut his head off. Tell him that. I think I will anyway if he doesn't write soon. If you ever knew what I did to get that. I almost lost my behind that day. So keep all of my souvenirs locked up and together. My hair almost turned white when you told me he had it in the chicken coop. The handle on it is bone and needs a lot of work done on it anyway. That's a genuine Samurai sword.

I've been feeling irritable as hell lately. It's been raining all week and there isn't much to do. If I sound crabby in this letter blame it on the weather.

I was sorry to hear that Pa was sick. Tell him to take better care of himself.

The fifteenth of this month our battalion is starting a school. I signed up for a course in plane geometry and trigonometry. I hope we are still here.

I sent some pictures of a Buddha that I saw in Japan home. I also sent a certificate about me landing in Japan. I want to frame them when I get home. I hope they won't get wrinkled or torn on the way. I'll have enough junk to start a pawnshop after the war. I'll sort it out when I get back.

Tell Pa I sent two good guns home for him. They should get there in about six weeks if they get there at all.

I'm glad that blanket turned out nice. I didn't think it would. I would have picked up a few more if I had known they were any good.

I won't be home for Xmas, that's for sure. They haven't even taken the fellows with the points yet. If I'm not home by next summer I'll marry some gook and have you all come out and see me.

Cheryl owes me a letter, so I'm not going to write. I don't want to lead her on. I'm not anxious to see her anyway. When she told you that she didn't go anywhere, you should have told her that you weren't the Chaplain. I don't go out dancing myself. (Don't get around much anymore).

What the hell's wrong with the people on Anise Street? From the sound of your letter they must all be sick.

There is a laundry on this island. Hallelujah! They don't press the clothes but they do a good job of washing them.

I saw a movie last night that was a howl. The name of it was "Murder He Says" with Marjorie Maine. It was the kind of movie you'd get a charge out of. See it if you get a chance. It's about a mountaineer family of cutthroats. I laughed till I was sick. You should see Marjorie Maine swing a whip. I guess that's about all for today, Mom. Write soon and let me know as soon as you hear anything from Boston.

Your loving son,
Charlie Jr.

USS Mercy
FPO San Fran. Cal.
October 5, 1945

Dear Charlie,

I shouldn't be writing this to you now because it is too late, for one thing, and I'm about "creaming" with inward excitement. I know that I'm going to leave things out that I'd like to tell you, but I'll give it a try and tell you everything that's left unsaid in another letter.

First of all, amid the clamor and clang of a crowd of wild receptionists the Mercy pulled into San Francisco with a load of POW's from Japan. I experienced quite a thrill in seeing the Golden Gate — even tho I'm only to be here for a short while. We arrived only a few hours ago at 7:20 p.m. to be exact. We started on the long trip from Yokohama on Sept. 19th. On Sept. 20 we hit Guam and left on the 24th. Pearl Harbor was made on Oct. 2nd and here we are in the States on the 7th. As the scuttlebutt goes we'll be heading west again in 10 days. Whatever is going to happen in 10 days tho remains to be seen. We may be back to Guam again shortly, but most indications point to "Pearl" and then back to here again. Everything is all "faunced up" in short.

I probably won't get liberty until Tuesday. We disembark our patients in the morning and the Hospital Corpsmen should be free of their duties for a while. There are 160 of us aboard, so with the exception of a few men

573

for sick bay duty I may get liberty tomorrow. I want to call home first and then that little girl whom I met in Los Angeles a year ago. It'll be more damn fun!

I received three letters from you since I wrote last. Your D-Day letter which I received in Guam just before we left and two tonight dated Sept. 4th and Oct. 2nd. Sunuva Bitch! That's the first thing I could think of to say when I received your note saying that we missed each by only a few hours in Guam again. Damn it. Don't we live right? I thought for sure you'd be in Japan for months or even years. That's nothing to wish upon a man, but that's what I figured. Every time I think of it I have an immature menopause and orchiditis sets in. I had just better not think of it anymore, as it'll only build up my low blood pressure. Just let me cool off for a while and then I'll start again.

I received two letters from Mary in the last 5 days. She's at Columbia U. taking a dental hygiene course. She's as lovable as ever and sounds all sexed up. In both of her letters she reminded me our (all four) future date at Beckley's. She couldn't say enough about it. I also got a note from "Hot Pants." Her unmentionables are sizzling with steam. With Pater away and Danny Kelly, Jim Donnelly, and Brian Green at home, she says, 'For about two weeks we had quite a time. They've gone back now'. (My heart bleeds for the lil' girl). She goes on to say, and this is one for Dorothy Dix, 'Maybe coming home is in the near future for you now. (sounds hungry, doesn't she?) I hope it's soon, Dick (getting familiar by calling me "Dick"). Take care and get home quick! I have "nuthin" to do.' Crap! Same old Meg! The old girl is certainly going to be surprised in the change of yours truly when I anchor. So much for the "die with a hard on column."

Those snaps of Launa are terrific! I see what you see in her! Or maybe you haven't seen it yet. I've showed them to all the boys in surgery and am returning them in this note. Remember our agreement of changing mates on honeymoon nite? Wheeeee! Don't care if I do die. I'm too much up in the air to talk seriously about anything or anyone so I'll just ramble on!

We have over 100 men that are being sent from this ship to separation centers for discharge tomorrow. Discharge! What a laugh – is it a sandwich or a disease. Every time I even think of getting out, I realize something, and start singing the sour milk song, "Bum-tity, Bum-tity, Bum-tity Bum!" I have about 21 points accumulated! Ha, ha! What the hell good would it do me?

I am reading "So Little Time" by John Marquand. I just finished a book called, "Psychology You Can Use." Our N.P. doctor would appreciate me now.

Your D-Day letter really took the cake. I first read it through without smiling or even thinking about laughing. The second time I about flew into a "fucking" fit of laughter. Each time I read it, it grew more funny. I read your whole anecdote to all the fellows in surgery, ardent listeners as they were – no one dared walk away from the little circle for fear of stitching one another.

It's way past lights out, and I'm writing you from the Chief of Surgery's office. He's probably plastered on the beach. If we have an emergency tonight, I'll probably have to do it alone. If the MAA makes rounds in here, I'll probably be doing extra duty for the next month.

I'll close now. I'll write you just before we pull out of here, so that you will know just where I am going. Write soon, ya old turd. Take care.

As ever,

Dick alias the Cherry

1ˢᵗ Bn. 15ᵗʰ Marines
Sixth Marine Division
San Francisco, Cal.
9 October 1945
Guam

Dear Mom,

Today is really nice. The sun is out for the first time in a week and the mud is drying up fast. It will be awfully hot in an hour or so but now it's nice.

I should be mad at all of you. I can see that none of your are breaking your arm writing. We had a mail call last night and I didn't get one letter. Some guys got ten or eleven. Maybe I should have asked them for one. Maybe we will have some more mail today. I hope so.

Yesterday I started on my fifteenth month overseas. The time has been going by rather quick lately but it's beginning to drag again.

Last night I saw a USO show down at the air field. It wasn't too good but it's the first show I've seen since the last time we were here. I get just as much of a kick out of the audience as I do out of the actors. You should hear them yell if they don't like an act. They do everything but throw their shoes at the actors. There are always a lot of dogs around and when they start barking everyone yells shut-up, and you can't hear anything. It usually ends up with everyone laughing. It's going to be dull going to a movie at home—if I ever find time to go to one.

Have you heard from Boston yet? Don't forget to let me know when you do.

I have some work to do now, so I'll close. I'll write tomorrow or as soon as I hear from you. Take care of yourself.

Love,
Charlie Jr.

1ˢᵗ Bn. 15ᵗʰ Marines
Sixth Marine Division
San Francisco , Cal.
10 October 1945
Guam

Dear Mom and Dad,

It's me again with the daily scuttle-butt. I ought to wait till I hear from you before I write but if I do that you will never hear from me.

Last night I saw another U.S.O. show. I'm getting to be a regular playboy with all these shows. It was the best show I ever saw out here. There was a good comedian, two singers (women) and a tall and a short girl that did acrobatics. They were really funny. I'll bet that those actors never got such a big reception in their life. There was one big fat girl, who easily weighed 200 lbs. The guys clapped so much for her, and she really ate it up. She would have sung all night if she could have. Then there was a cute dancer that danced till she damn near fainted and still everyone hollered for more. What a time!

On the way back from the show we met a gook kid about fourteen years old. He said – come on over to my Aunt's house and we will have steak and chicken- so we went with him. We went in the house and I thought I was downtown on Saturday night. His Aunt's (the old bag) name was Dolores and she looked like one. She was five feet tall and five feet wide. She was singing like mad, and believe it or not she sang, "You Are My Sunshine." The gooks are crazy about American songs. It seemed like there were hundreds of Marines, Seabees and Doggies in that house. Everyone was in the bag or getting that way. It seems that this kid was sending everyone there. We had a lot of good laughs. What a joint. That's about all for now. Write soon.

Love,
Charlie

Conn. College
New London, Conn.
October 11, 1945

Hello, Darling,

I wrote you a three page letter two days ago – but I made the mistake of reading it the next day so it was torn up. I didn't mean half the things I was saying – I wonder if I do that in all my letters? It will only lead to bloodshed!

I got a letter from you yesterday and got all agitated about it. It was about going into the Maritime Service – you wanted my opinion – as usual it's quite emphatic. The only reason this appeals to you, as far as I can see, is because you'd be able to get married – you'd have enough money to support a wife – and kiddies too, I suppose. Please don't take it, Charlie. In the first place I'm afraid that the idea of getting married is what's influencing you. I have no intention of getting married for at least 4 or 5 years to you or anyone else – even if I did decide I loved you. It seems to me you're giving up freedom for a little security – and you're too young to worry about having a steady income all the time. If you were 30 or 35 I might see the point. Please make up your mind as if there weren't any me, would you?

You're only 20, Charlie, and doesn't it seem foolish to be thinking of tying yourself down with a wife and kids? And a job like that doesn't give you any freedom – if you want to dash to New York or go on a binge, it's just too bad.

I guess this all sounds pretty trite – like your trying to give advice to your sister. But it's just that I don't want you to go into something that you'll be sorry for later – just so we'll be able to get married – when you know the outcome of that is as shaky as it is. It's silly to plan your life around that. Do you follow me at all?

Anyway, it would be better if you went to college and waited awhile before thinking about getting married. To be realistic about it all, you can't even be sure you've met the right girl yet. You forget, you've been out of civilization quite a awhile – maybe you haven't seen the latest models.

This is a lousy letter – I sound like Dorothy Dix – but you asked me so I told you. And now I'm exhausted – with two hours of psychology ahead of me. Think it over before you do anything, huh? Goodnight, Charlie.

My love always,
Launa

1ˢᵗ Bn. 15ᵗʰ Marines

Sixth Marine Division
FPO 926 San Francisco, Cal.
13 October 1945
Guam

Dear Mom and Dad,

I still haven't heard from you in quite some time but I believe the mail shortage was due to the storm on Okinawa. Okinawa was the mail separation center.

The day before yesterday I got a nice long letter from Launa. She said that my mail was all mixed up, too. It will get settled when you start writing FPO 926 on the address.

I wish I would hear from you about those pictures I sent home to be developed. I hope that you are still looking for film, too. Everyone else seems to get it. I'd like to take some more pictures here. It's a shame that I couldn't take some in Japan, Okinawa, and Guadalcanal.

I'll be getting paid next week. I have two hundred and fifty dollars on the books. Then I'll have a couple hundred dollars when I hit the States next spring. Boy, I'll need it.

I haven't seen any good shows or movies lately. There are a few good movies coming, however.

What ever happened to the place in Vermont Pa was going to buy? I hope that wasn't a pipe dream like remodeling the house every year.

The time has been going by pretty fast but I don't know why. There isn't anything to do here and all the days are alike. I've got a little work to do so I'll close now. Write soon.

Your loving son,
Charlie Jr.

17 Anise Street
New Britain, Conn.
October 14, 1945

Dear Charlie,

Mother and I received a letter from you Friday.

We got your pictures Friday, but only 6 of the eight came out and still they aren't too good. Mother thinks you look awfully thin but I don't. You never were a "potsick" anyway!! I'm sending you some of the pictures in this letter and the rest Mother will send. O.K??

We also received your certificate and the pictures of Buddha, they were very interesting. I'll get a frame for the certificate and frame it for you.

Mother still has a little cold left but she'll be o.k. in a few days.

Yesterday I went to Stamford with the Band and Cheerleaders. We went up on three chartered buses at 9 o'clock in the morning. It was more fun! We sang and yelled all the way up and back. We won the game and the score was 14 to 13. It was exciting and Stamford was mad as heck!! There were police and S.P. guarding the whole place so no riots would start. There were a few rowdies that started flinging things but they were quieted down. One fellow threw a rock through the bus window after the game but no one was hurt. We got home about 8:30.

Friday I was in the fashion show at our Carnival. It was really beautiful and not just because I was in it either. There was a large platform with a long pier extending from it with all palms around. They had Al Gentile's orchestra to play when the models came out on the platform. I modeled some pretty sharp outfits – one was a green coat trimmed with Persian lamb and a hat ($30.00) to match. Then I had a sleek black dress with blue sequins and a black hat. For the gown I wore a black and white one and boy was it snazzy. I was a little scared when I went out at first but after I loved it!! (Fun!)

Last night was the last night of our Carnival. Sophie Lincoln won the $200 door prize. Wasn't she lucky? She almost dropped dead when they called her number. Donny won a cake last night, yep he took the cake.

I'm still slaving away doing my homework. English kills me and so does Miss Connor. We're studying Lincoln now and it stinks.

I don't think I told you before but Daddy bought us a set of Americana Encyclopedias. Isn't that neat? They haven't come yet but they should next week. It's too bad that we didn't have them long ago. I think they cost about $150. Remember the salesman that came here about three years ago and stayed about four hours trying to sell Dad some books, and this one only asked him and Dad said he'd buy them. I can't wait till we get them. Maybe now I'll be smart in school! Well, so long for now.

Love and kisses,

Betty

P.S. My friend Bob still writes to me every day.

17 Anise Street
New Britain, Conn.
October 17, 1945

Dear Charlie,

How are you? There's not much to say so I'll not write much.

One of the teachers from Nathan Hale was asking about you, Miss Noonan, the science teacher.

I'm enclosing a picture of me and don't think I wear the Jap stuff around the house. I don't. I had Prince out for a walk in the woods this afternoon but he doesn't mind at all.

Speaking of woods I intend to do a little trapping this year. Last year you told me when trapping season came around you would tell me where a few good places for trapping were so I would like to know.

All that darn sister of ours does all day long is holler – holler – holler. As soon as she squeals on me once more, boy oh boy, what I got against her.

We got checked the other day in school and I weigh 103 lbs and am 5 feet 2 inches. Think of that when you said you'll cut my head off for not writing.

I went to St. Francis carnival last night and I won a chocolate cake.

We didn't receive the guns you sent home but I suppose we will any day now. By the way which one or are they both Japanese? There's not much more to say so I'll sign off here.

Little Wart
Donnie

1ˢᵗ Bn. 15ᵗʰ Marines
Sixth Marine Division
FPO 926 San Francisco, Cal.
21 October 1945
Guam

Dear Mom and Dad,

I can't remember when I wrote last but I think it was a few days ago.

There hasn't been any mail for the outfit all week. I can't imagine where the hold up is.

I drew a little over two hundred dollars the other day. I'll enclose one money order in this and another in the next letter.

There isn't much to write about here. All we do is play cards and go to the movies at night. This morning I went to church and it was a wedding mass. A couple of Guamanians took the leap. There were many gooks in church and it was like a state-side wedding. The bride had all the trimmings and the groom wore a carnation. I think he is a steward's mate in the Navy.

It's been rather warm lately. Yesterday we went swimming. I'll close now, chow-time. I wonder what's on the "ulcer gulch" menu today. Probably creamed field shoes! Write soon.

Love,

Charlie

1st Bn. 15th Marines
Sixth Marine Division
FPO 926 San Francisco, Cal.
22 October 1945
Guam

Dear Don,

I received your letter written on the 15th yesterday. It took just one week to get here and that's very good time.

Those pictures of you were swell. I wish that mine had come out as clear. I'm getting some back tomorrow. I had a couple taken with my war paint on. If they come out I'll send the negatives home to be printed.

Guess where I went today? To school! We have a little converted mess hall and we have classes three times a week. I'm taking a course in geometry and trigonometry, I didn't learn much when I went to Nathan Hale or High School. I was too interested in extra curricular activities (that means ra-ra affairs). I hope that you will get good grades.

You can say hello to Miss Noonan for me. You'll have to take me to N.H. when I get back so that I can visit all the teachers. Maybe they will give me the scoop on you, so you had better get on the ball.

Both of the rifles I sent home are Nip. One is a .25 caliber and the other is a .31. I have some ammo for the .31 but I didn't want to send it through the mail.

I'm enclosing a very rough map of where, I believe, you will be able to trap some muskrats. We got most of ours in the part of the brook marked with X's. We used to lay out our traps at night and take them up in the morning. They can get stolen rather easily there, so be careful. You have to stake in your traps good, too, 'cause the brook might rise overnight and you won't be able to get your traps until next spring.

There isn't much doing out here. It rained all day.

There are an awful lot of replacements coming in from the States. Most of them are all about sixteen or seventeen. They are really getting sucked in. The poor dopes! I'm glad that you aren't old enough to join.

The high point men are supposed to leave our outfit this week. I'm still counting on next Easter. Boy, will we have a time. Whit whew!

This is a messy letter. I hope that you won't have too much difficulty reading it. Bye for now and study hard.

Your loving brother,
Charlie

1ˢᵗ Bn. 15ᵗʰ Marines
Sixth Marine Division
FPO 926 San Francisco, Cal.
23 October 1945
Guam

Dear Mom,

I just got through washing all my clothes. What a job! It's a swell day, however, and they will be dry in a few hours.

I'm enclosing my other money order. You should have the first one by now.

The mail situation has been terrible lately. In the last two weeks there was just one mail call. That was the day I got a letter from Betty and Donny. I answered Donny's yesterday and will answer Sis's tomorrow.

From the looks of things we will be here for a long time. We just found out that we were supposed to stay in Japan with the Fourth Marines but someone fouled-up the detail and here we are.

We would all go nuts if we didn't have our jeep to run around in. We are always using it to go someplace.

I hope that you found a photo album for me. My pictures are piling up. And don't forget to send some of those corner stickers. An album about the size of the one we have home would be nice. I'll be able to take good care of it, now that we won't be moving around.

Have you heard from Boston, yet? Let me know as soon as you do. Write soon.

Love,
Charlie Jr.

1ˢᵗ Bn. 15ᵗʰ Marines
Sixth Marine Division
FPO 926 San Francisco, Cal.
25 October 1945
Guam

Dear Sis,

As per usual, I haven't much to say but I have a letter of yours to answer, and as I haven't written in a few days it seems like a good idea.

I got a letter from Mother the other day. It looks like I'm going to have to continue starving. I was hoping for some packages with chow in them. I've only told you about ten-thousand times the things I want. Any kind of canned fish, except salmon—tuna, potato sticks, fruit cake (not homemade 'cause it spoils – bought cake is plenty good out here). I've lost about thirty lbs (well ten anyway) since we got back here. All we have is canned hash or canned sausage and powdered milk. We have never had fresh vegetables and have had fresh meat twice. We can usually chisel a loaf of bread at night if we can find something to smear on it. Canned peppers would be swell. This is the last time I'm going to ask for anything, so if you don't want to send anything don't keep asking me what I want or keep saying you don't know what to send. Just try not eating for a month and then go into a grocery store. Capish?!

As I've said a hundred or more times before, nothing happens here that I could write about. All the days are the same.

I haven't seen any good movies lately. Yes, I did, too. The other night I saw B. Davis in "The Corn Is Green." It was rather deep but I liked it a lot.

The classes we have here help pass the time. We have them three times a week.

That's about all, little Darlin' – Write soon.

Your starving brother,

Charlie

P.S. If you don't send me some chow, I'll look like I was in a Jap concentration camp when I get home. You'd like that, wouldn't ya, Betty? Ga' wan!

17 Anise Street
New Britain, Conn.
October 25, 1945

Dear Son,

Just a few lines to let you know we are still living. The first thing that I must tell you is that Betty got your 10.00 dollars about 8 a.m. and was she surprised. She's been sick with the diarrhea for the last three days and she's pretty well washed out. She thought the truant officer was after her when the car drove up this morning with the special delivery. She is lying on the couch listening to the radio.

583

She had a nice birthday. Aunt Lena sent her $5.00 and Kitty and Tessie were down last nite and Aunt Anna and they all brought her something. Too bad she had to be sick.

Pa isn't working today. He took a couple of days off on account of rain. He just bought Betty some medicine to check the runs. Freddy was home last week, but we didn't see him. I heard from Boston, I have to go up the 14th of Nov. Aunt Anna wants to go up for a check-up. She thinks she may have some gland trouble. If she goes, Shirley is going to drive us up. They can stay at May and Sam's house and come back the next day.

Pa is going hunting the 2nd of Nov. and he will be back the 10th.

Well, Pa is going up to the P.O. to mail out some valves, so I will close and I will write again in a few days.

Love,
Mother

1st Bn. 15th Marines
Sixth Marine Division
FPO 926 San Francisco, Cal.
26 October 1945
Guam

Dear Brother,

We received two letters from you today, one for mother and the other for me. You sure are doing a lot of traveling around. Perhaps by the time you get this, you'll be in a new place.

Thanks for the brotherly lecture on Al. I haven't seen him now in two weeks so I guess it's o.k. You acted as though he's an old man but gosh he really isn't. He likes a lot of fun just like me but let's forget about him for a while. O.K??

I guess I told you that Bob Shine (Not Red Shine) joined the Navy and he writes to me most every day. He's a swell kid and I really miss him. He was down to see me practically every night and even Mother misses him now. He positively despises the Navy and can't wait until he gets home and that won't be until about next Xmas. Right now his company is restricted for three weeks 'cause someone stole $40.00 from a wallet. I'm going to send him some writing paper tonight 'cause he says he can't even go far enough to buy any. (maybe he just wants me to send him some).

Saturday I was supposed to go to Holyoke, Mass. with the Cheerleaders and Band but Friday I went over to Drum Corps and Mr. Bonner told me our Corps was going to Waterbury to a Drum meet. Boy, was I burnt up and I even cried when I got home. We went up to Waterbury in three cars and we had lots of fun after all. We had to march in a long parade through Waterbury center but I loved every minute of it. At every corner there was somebody taking pictures with flash-bulb cameras. At night there was a dance and I met a bunch of nice fellows from the Hartford Corps. One especially was really super. His name was Fran Reynolds – nice and tall with brown wavy hair. I guess being a majorette is really fun even though you get nervous at times and shame a Corps that sounds like hell. We've really had a lot of trouble with the St. Francis Corps. Kids quit and new kids come in. The shortest girl is about 3 feet and the tallest 6 feet. Sometimes I get so mad at them I could scream. At present we are supposed to have 25 members but only 16 showed up yesterday. Well, we'll just keep struggling along.

I'm sending you a few clippings I thought would interest you.

How do you like our new John Campbell Park? I'll bet you never thought that little square would be anything. We had a real nice dedication Sunday. The N.B. High band was there and the place was crowded. That's all for now.

Love and kisses, xxxxx
Betty

17 Anise Street
New Britain, Conn.
October 30, 1945

Dear Son,

This is going to be a short letter because I want to go downtown this A.M. I want to put your money orders in the bank. We rec'd one of them yesterday in the morning and one in the afternoon.

We also rec'd a box from you with Betty's boxes and other things. The four wooden dishes were broken and the hand on the statue was broken off, but I can get some glue and we can fix that. What's the statue suppose to be? Betty got a kick out of that Jap medical book.

Now we have to wait for the guns to get here. That's what Donny is interested in.

Well, Pa and Tag are getting all set to go hunting Friday nite. They went target practicing Sunday afternoon with Buck Miller and Walter.

Tommy, Pete, Bobby and Shirley went rabbit hunting Sat. morning and they got 12 rabbits. They gave us two of them. We will have them for supper tonite.

Did I tell you Bill Ziegler was married to an Iowa girl? They have a baby boy and came to N.B. and had the baby baptized Sunday. We were

585

invited. Betty and I and Lala went up. Not a drink in the place so we didn't stay. Good thing Dad and Ed Neubauer didn't go up.

Spudy's wife had a baby boy last Sat. She is out in Texas with him. He took up flying. He will have to stay in for another year to finish his training.

Oh, yes, Donny got your letter yesterday. I am going to look for a photo album this morning. Well, I will close. I will write again this week.

Love,

Mother

17 Anise Street
New Britain, Conn.
November 2, 1945

Dear Charlie,

Here I am again and I guess it's about a week since I've written to you. We received your box you sent home and thanks a lot for the lacquer boxes. They're really pretty, but I can't quite figure out how they are supposed to go.

That Jap medical book was really interesting but I couldn't read it! (peculiar, isn't it?)

Tonight there's a rally over at the high school given by the Athletic Association. I'm going with Barbara and some other kids. We have a swell time at those crazy dances.

Tomorrow there's going to be another "Band Meet" in Thompsonville. Our Corps isn't going, but I may go up anyway.

Mother just came back from Mr. Westermans with a beautiful bouquet of chrysanthemums. I never saw anything as pretty. They are all different colors, purple and yellow and orange. He has a whole yard full of them.

My English is just awful. I wish I had any teacher but Miss Connor. The kids that have Miss Adams like her a lot. Cripes, she doesn't even speak English. Oh, well —

We got our Encyclopedias a few days ago and they sure are swell. We also got four volumes of World War II. The books are all bound in a red color. Dad is going to have to buy us some kind of a bookcase to keep them in.

Tonight Dad leaves for Maine. Now I'll be able to play the records without him shutting the Victrola off on me. Tag is all excited about going and he couldn't wait until today came.

Well, that's all for now — there really isn't much to say.

Love and kisses, xxxxx

Betty

1ˢᵗ Bn. 15ᵗʰ Marines

Sixth Marine Division
FPO 926 San Francisco, Cal.
22 November 1945
Guam- Thanksgiving Day.

Dear Dad,

I received your letter of November 10 yesterday. I was really glad to get it 'cause I hadn't heard from you in about ten days. I was beginning to worry about you all.

I'm sorry that you didn't get a deer in Maine. You'd better get one next year or Mom will begin to think all of you go up there to have the two-legged variety. You said you don't care about going up there anymore, but I'll bet you'll be all set next year. I'd go myself if I could use a sub Thompson. They are the nuts. I had one on Okinawa, but when we got back here I had to turn it in. The Army has a new machine gun that is very small – it's called a "grease gun." Maybe you've seen pictures of them.

This morning I had to take a fellow to the hospital for an X-ray. I ate chow there. They had a big turkey dinner. Tonight our outfit is having a big turkey dinner, so I'll have had two before the day is over. Boy, what a chow hound I am!

I've got my gear all ready to go. We are going to the Transient Center to await transportation to China. I'll write at the transient center and when I'm aboard ship.

You should have seen me smoking a cigar last night. We were having a friendly game of pinochle and one of the fellows threw a handful of "White Owls" on the table. So we all bit off the ends and started puffing. I damn near fell off the chair before I came to the end of it. What a time – I didn't get sick though.

I don't know when I'll get mail again. I hope we will get mail at the transient center.

I'm about finished now. There isn't anything else to write. I hope that Mother is home when this gets there. Bye for now.

Love to all,
Charlie Jr.

1st Bn. 15th Marines
Sixth Marine Division
FPO 926 San Francisco, Cal.
25 November 1945
Guam

Dear Folks,

Well, I'm settled in my new home. This place isn't as bad as I thought it would be. We have tents with wooden decks and the chow is fair.

At this place the HAs are on mess duty, the PhM 3rds are on guard duty, the PhM 1sts are in charge of the details and the second class do nothing. What a life! I usually get up about ten, wash and then stroll around the area till chow time. After chow I take a sun bath and read till shower time. After the shower I have supper and go to the movie. Rough life in the field!

I expect to be leaving for Tien Sen, China, to join the Sixth Division as soon as I can get transportation.

I've met hundreds of corpsmen that I used to know. It's embarrassing sometimes 'cause I never remember their names. Lots of fellows I knew in corps school are here and most all of the fellows I came overseas with are here. I met one of the fellows that I did duty with in Memphis. He just came overseas. I don't envy him 'cause he will never get home. I expect to be home for Easter.

I went to mass this morning like a good lil' boy. They have a nice chapel here.

I don't know when I'll start getting mail gain. Just when I start getting mail it's always time to shove off. Tough – I lose.

I'll have to close now. It's almost dinner time and I have to put on my dungarees. We aren't allowed to go to chow in shorts.

Bye now – I'll write tomorrow even if I don't hear from you.

Love to all,

Charlie

-ELEVEN-

NEW BRITAIN, CONNECTICUT 2013

SUMMER DREW TO A close and with it my own private world on the third floor. On the day after Labor Day, I transcribed the last of the correspondence, a letter of mine from Guam. My task was over, finished. Strangely bereft, I regarded the empty box and searched about for any letter I might have missed. Nothing. That was it. How did it happen that I had lost contact with the writers of all those letters after the war? Where were they now? My parents, of course, were gone—my mother at eighty-five, my father at seventy-four. Both had enjoyed full, happy lives. Sadly, my brother, also seventy-four, had died recently from a pernicious blood disorder, leaving behind a wife and five grown children. I was still close to my sister, Betty, and kept in touch with Benny Navikas. But what of Launa, Dick, Helen, Mary Jo, Meg, Cheryl, and all those who had stepped back into my life through their letters over the past three months? That bubble world had now receded into the murky recesses of the past. In a melancholic funk, I lost interest in gardening, reading, and even writing. Unable to shake this depression, I moped about the house and took solitary walks in Stanley Park. Despite the brilliant spectacle of fall foliage, I stood on the little wooden bridge next to the spillway, unable to get the letters out of my mind. Circe, God love her, attempted to give me my space but could not hide her concern.

"Darling, it's only normal for you to feel let down. All summer you've been holed up on the third floor in a fever of excitement. That last letter from Guam wraps up things so very nicely. You should be very proud."

"Then why do I feel like such a shit? All those guys and gals—we wrote every day. We were so close. And then after that last letter from Guam, a dead silence. Where are they now? What are they up to? Why do I feel so depressed?"

"You must be positive," Circe said thoughtfully. "Look, Betty is just around the corner, and we often see Benny. You know, sometimes it gives me the shivers when I think of the letters. I wasn't acquainted with your folks or any of your friends before we discovered them. Now I feel that I know them like family. It truly amazes me. You were all so young, so innocent, and so in love. But all that was in the distant past. What you need now is some kind of closure."

"Easier said than done. What do we do, look for another cache of letters? I'd give anything to see some of the letters I wrote to Launa and Dick. Perhaps those epistles are out in cyberspace. Do you think we should have my computer service track them down?"

"Now you're being facetious. The answer is right at your fingertips. Sit down at the computer and start punching in the names of those old friends. I know you, darling. You won't have a moment's peace until you do. By the way, speaking of peace, in that last letter from Guam you were about to be sent to China. Did you ever get there?"

"One ordeal I was spared," I said. "And a night in the transient center on Guam I will never forget. A week or so after we got back from Japan, a bunch of us were hanging out in the slop shoot awaiting orders to join the division in China. Suddenly there came an announcement over the PA speaker. Our outfit was being shipped stateside. The band then struck up *Sentimental Journey*, and I was on my way. A week later I boarded the *USS Cowpens*, a carrier converted into a troop ship that took us to San Francisco. I was home for Christmas. In April my discharge came through, and that fall I enrolled at the state teachers college near my home. I wanted to write and assumed one English program was much like the next. The head of the department, Dr. Fowler, a nice old gent, set me straight. As long as I wasn't going to teach, he suggested I apply to a liberal arts school. I worked my butt off for grades and the following year transferred to Columbia."

"And it was at Columbia that you started writing about the war," Circe replied with genuine interest. "Were you always interested in writing?"

I chuckled. "For that answer, we have to go back to my sixth-grade teacher, a real character I'll never forget. She used to read us Keats's *Grecian Urn* every morning. Anyway, one day she was asking us what we planned to do in the future. I told her I'd like to write, but didn't know what to write about. She assured me that one day I would find a subject."

"How right she was. Darling, I know that Okinawa was the last battle in the war, but why was it so different from the other islands? What made you want to write about it?"

"Several things. For starters, the Sixth Marine Division was newly formed and untried. D-day was April 1, which also happened to be April Fools' Day, the day of the full moon, and Easter Sunday. After what had happened on Tarawa and Iwo, we expected a real bloodbath. But the landing was unopposed, not a Jap in sight. In just eighty-two days, we captured a major airfield, secured the northern three quarters of the island, went south, took the capital Naha, and mopped up the holdouts at the end of the rock. Okinawa was not only the largest amphibious invasion of the Pacific campaign, but also the last major operation of the war. More people died during that campaign than all those killed in the bombings of Hiroshima and Nagasaki. Our casualties totaled more than 38,000. Of these, 12,000 died or went missing. The Japs lost more than 107,000 dead. We'll never know how many Okinawan conscripts and civilians perished, but the number is well over 100,000. These were ground losses. We hear more about navy losses because the press found the kamikaze attacks more dramatic—like the staged flag raising on Iwo. But the battle in Naha Bay was certainly bloody. Thirty-four allied ships sent to the bottom, four hundred others damaged. On top of this, the fleet had lost 763 aircraft."

"So your sixth grade teacher was right," Circe said. "You did find your subject. And you had a ringside seat."

"More than that. The navy considered corpsmen as marines, and the marines considered us still navy. That gave us a lot of freedom. In the sickbay there was no difference between a private and an officer. You should have heard some of our bull sessions."

"I can imagine. You know, you were there the entire time, yet you say little of the fighting in your letters. I find that sort of, well, strange."

"Censorship, my love. We were under a tight news blackout. We didn't know what was going on in Europe or Asia. I was on Guadalcanal eight months and couldn't mention the name of the island. Okinawa was different, but do you think the folks back home wanted to hear about the stench of rotting corpses on the battleground, the flies and the maggots? "

Circe shuddered. "I guess not. So at Columbia that you seriously begin writing."

"Right, while I was getting my BA. In my junior year I met and married Marcie. We lived in the city and stayed on until I got an MA. I still had time coming under the GI Bill, so we went up to Yale to work on a PhD. That's where Marcie was diagnosed with thyroid cancer. I had to put my writing on hold and found a job teaching high school English. After two years of surgery and atomic iodine, my wife miraculously made a full recovery and was eager to adopt a child. More miraculously, before this could happen, we had three of our own. By 1967 I had a full-time teaching job and was running a general store. To get out of the rat race and back to my writing, I signed a three-year contract to teach at Athens College in Greece. Everyone thought we were nuts. But it turned out to be the right move. I managed to finish my war novel and later on published two bestsellers . And then ... and ...

"You lost Marcie," Circe said quietly. "And I had lost George." She hesitated and added with a smile, "But look how lucky we were to find each other. And then Hydra. Now there, my love, is a story with a happy ending."

"I only wish the letters ended that way. So much is left up in the air. One moment I think it would be kind of nice to find out what happened to Launa, Helen, Cheryl, and Dick. The next moment, I feel I don't want to know if it means getting into something unpleasant."

"Like the death of your cousin Freddy. I suspected as much when you told me of his father's suicide."

"You've lost me, sweetie. My uncle Herman died forty or so years earlier. Freddy was only a little kid. What are you saying?"

Circe smiled ruefully. "Nothing escapes kids, no matter how young they are. When I was doing my counseling, we always said, 'Wait till they hit fifty.'"

"Meaning?"

"Damaged goods. Gifted students who have been traumatized as youngsters. Victims of sexual, alcohol, or drug abuse; one-parent home; no-parent home; parents home but not really there. Miraculously, some of these boys, and girls, manage to overcome their background and wind up with scholarships at major universities."

"More power to them. It had to be in the genes. I always ..."

Circe put her finger on my lips. "Just let me finish before you jump to any conclusions. Sometime in midlife—it could be at forty or fifty—those early demons resurface. Life becomes unbearable. These victims become abusers themselves or turn to drugs and alcohol. Many commit suicide."

I winced. "Jesus, the profile does fit my cousin. Freddy came out of the war a first-rate electrician. Got married, started a business. On one or two occasions I lent him money and he always paid me back. You couldn't meet a nicer guy. But he never seemed to have any direction. When we were kids, I would say, 'Let's go hunting, or fishing, or to this or that movie.' He would agree at once. He never came up with an idea of his own. Then, like you say, he hit forty or so and everything began to go downhill. He started drinking, lost his business, and his wife left him. One winter night he froze to death on a park bench over in Middletown. I had to identify his body. It was a blessing Freddy never had kids."

"Your cousin wasn't the only one," Circe said quietly. "Didn't you tell me that your friend Lucy lost her mother at a young age?"

"By golly, you're right." I was struck by my wife's observation. "Lucy was brought up by her father and the apple of his eye. The two were more like a couple than father and daughter. She could do no wrong. Cussing, sassing back, smoking, drinking—her father thought she was cute. But then when we were in high school, he remarried. The new wife was a nice lady, but Lucy hated her. She couldn't wait to get into art school and out of the house. The real friction started when Lucy flunked out and moved back home. I don't think Lucy ever worked. Over the years I'd drop in to see her, and we'd talk about old times. The tension in that house was thick enough to cut with a knife. Then her father died. Heart attack. He was cleaning their pool. The stepmother then threw Lucy out of the house. I believe her father left her a small inheritance, enough to live on, anyway. And you're right. She was in her mid-forties when she died two or three years later—that damn cancer again. Lucy always claimed she was an artist, but I never did see any of her work."

At Circe's urgings, the following morning I sat down again at the computer. I punched in the name Joe Rizzo, and I came up with a phone number in Bristol. I called his home and got his wife, Pam, whom I'd never met. I learned Joe had died in 2002, after being inducted into the Purple Heart Hall of Honor. The couple had two sons. We lived only a few miles apart and didn't know it. Such a shame.

To get a line on those who might still be in the area, I turned to my sister. Like me, Betty was born in New Britain. And while I left home after high school and never looked back, Betty remained in our old hometown. After attending local public schools, she graduated from the nearby state teachers college, taught elementary school, married, raised two daughters, and became a widow, all in New Britain. If there was something Betty did not know about the place, one of a gaggle of friends, who had been with her since grade school, surely would. Through Betty and her network I learned Merton Savage, Mick Leary, Joe Donnelly, and Roger Whipple were deceased.

On a more positive note, Betty came up with phone numbers for Tony DiAngelo and Seymour Cohen. Both still resided in New Britain. Danny Bray, Betty learned from his sister, was living in Jupiter, Florida. It was great talking to these guys and renewing old friendships. Hoping to get a line on Dick Walton, I quizzed Seymour, who was also a doctor. He told me that Dick had gone to Yale School of Medicine after Duke, something I had known, and that he had later practiced in Vernon, Connecticut. He hadn't heard from Dick in years and thought he might have moved out of the state.

"Keep on checking," my sister urged. "You never know who is going to turn up. The other night I was playing bridge with my group, and Greta Allen mentioned that her sister-in-law Mary is living down in Branford on the shoreline. She usually goes to Florida early in September, but you might be able to catch her before she leaves."

"Allen … Mary Allen … it rings a bell but—"

"Mary Jo Hennessey. Allen was her married name. Her husband died and she remarried. Her name is now Parsons, or something like that. I'll get her number for you from Greta."

When I called and asked to speak to Peaches, Mary Jo sounded a bit frail but was still the cheerful, giggly girl with a wild sense of humor I remembered from high school. Recently widowed for the second time, she had two daughters living nearby and divided her time between Palm Beach and Branford. On the down side, all those years in the sun on the golf course, cocktails, and smoking had taken their toll. Her legs, she chuckled, now had crocodile skin, and she was on oxygen for emphysema. She had read my last novel on Native Americans in our area and wanted to get in touch but believed I was still living in Greece.

"Haven't heard from her or of her in years," she said when I asked about Meg. "Not a word since the murder."

"Murder?" I chuckled, in the belief that this was another of her jokes. "Mary Jo, who did you knock off?"

"Not funny, you clown. But then again, some people might think so. No one was surprised. That's for certain."

"Mary Jo, who are you talking about?" I asked, realizing she was serious. "What murder?"

"Morry Blair, who else?"

"No, not the Spook!" I exclaimed in disbelief. "When? Where? What happened?"

"Oh, years ago, the early seventies. Down in Miami. No one knows exactly what happened. The case has never been solved. But you can bet your last dollar it was something shady. As I said, no one was surprised. Morry was always up to no good."

"And Meg? How did she take all this?"

"I believe they were divorced at the time, or at least separated. She stayed on in Florida with her sister and died a few years ago. That Meg was something else."

"She certainly was. No flies on that one, my mother would say. I wonder if Dick Walton knows all this. He was certainly stuck on her at one time."

"How could he not know? It was in all the papers for days."

"Well, I didn't know. But then I was teaching in Greece at the time. My wife had cancer, the three kids were...."

"Tell me about it," Mary Jo scoffed. "I had two husbands to contend with and two kids to bring up. But you know, Charlie," she added on a bright note, "I've been blessed. Both husbands were fine men, and I couldn't have better daughters. I have a lovely home here and another in Florida." She laughed, and added, "Money. That's the secret of the good life today. Fortunately, I've always had plenty. If it weren't for this damn oxygen tank, I'd be out on the golf course instead of sitting in a chair all day bored out of my skull. I don't know whether I'm lucky or not, but my mind is still sharper than ever."

"It sure is," I agreed. "Mary Jo, you sound great. Now let me tell you what my wife recently discovered in our attic."

She was delighted to hear about the letters and eager to read them, especially those of hers pertaining to Meg and Dick. And she was alert; emphysema had in no way impaired her memory. Unfortunately, however, she had kept none of my letters.

"My God, how could I?" She giggled. "If either of my husbands saw some of the stuff I'd written, they would have divorced me on the spot. I can't wait to read them. What devils we were, especially you and Dick. And that Meg!"

"I'm sure you can help me," I said. "There are so many blanks you can fill in, people and events I can only partially recall. Why don't I drive down to the shore and show you some letters? You can meet my wife at the same time."

"Sorry, Peaches, but we will have to postpone our date until I return in the spring. Not that I'm playing hard to get," she giggled, "but my doctor in Florida has been trying out some new therapy on my legs, and I have to get back." She laughed again. "Today, if the medicine doesn't get you, the doctors will. Anyway, we depart tomorrow. This afternoon my daughter is running me up to Middletown to have my hair done."

"Middletown?" I chuckled. "I'm glad it's your hair. There for a moment I thought you were about to commit yourself to the state nuthouse."

Mary Jo chuckled. "Peaches, you are the same old clown. But do you know something," she added, her tone suddenly serious, "I'm ready to go. I've had a long life and, as I've said, two swell husbands, two great kids. Other than those letters, I can't think of a thing to keep me around." In the next breath, she laughed again. "You know, Charlie, I often think it was our humor more than anything else that got us through those war years. Middletown. I'd forgotten the asylum was there. Actually, it's a pleasant town on the river. Do you know it?"

"Danny Bray went to Wesleyan there. And a girl I used to write to had a brother who lived there. Nice-looking gal. A shame she was going with my friend Benny at the time. You must remember Ben Navikas."

"Of course I do. He was in your class but broke his leg and wound up graduating with us. His girlfriend's name wouldn't be French, by any chance, would it?"

I nearly dropped the phone. "French!" I all but shouted. "That's the girl I was talking about. I often dated her cousin Cheryl. We wrote all during the war. What can you tell me?"

597

"Not much really. But this past July, I met a woman at the hairdresser's by that name. She claimed she had an aunt who once lived in West Hartford."

"That's Helen. Something tells me Helen passed away some time ago. But if my mind isn't playing tricks, she did have a brother Larry in Middletown in the insurance business, I think."

"There you go, Peaches." Mary Jo laughed. "Didn't I tell you my memory was still in good shape? Now send me off a copy of those letters."

At the New Britain library I found a number in the Middletown yellow pages for the French Insurance Company and made my call. Larry was no longer with the firm. His son Tom had taken over the business and would get back to me. Two hours later I was talking to Tom, a pleasant-sounding guy, who assured me that I had the correct family. His parents, Larry and Marion, whom I knew only through Helen, had been living in Florida but recently moved back to Middletown for medical reasons. The best news was about Helen. Alive and well, his aunt was now living in Maine just outside of Portland. He believed Cheryl had moved out to California several years ago, but was uncertain. Helen would know.

I left a message on Helen's answering machine. She got back to me that evening, excitedly telling me she recognized my name the moment she saw it on her machine. Rumors of her demise, she laughed, had circulated years ago when a woman of the same name died in a neighboring town. Like any eighty-five-year-old she had her health problems but was managing very well on her own. She had a son and three grandchildren. After the death of her husband a few years back, she had moved into an independent-living facility. She still drove but avoided the national highway, confining herself to town and her cottage on a nearby lake. Her cousin Cheryl had married the boy next door after the war and moved out to California. She had four children, three with PhDs. The fourth, an entrepreneur, had made a fortune in a sports industry. Her husband died of a brain embolism at the age of fifty, and Cheryl married a second time. Sadly, Cheryl herself had passed on five years ago.

"What did I tell you," Circe said, after reading a copy of Cheryl's obit that Helen had sent. "Two more accounted for. Now we have the Walton fellow and…."

"I know, I know, Launa Darcy," I said uneasily. Launa had been foremost in my mind since the discovery of her letters in the attic. Something, however, held me back. Anxious as I was to contact her, I was not yet prepared to make that approach. "For now let's focus on Dick. He has to be somewhere here in Connecticut."

Wrack my brain as I might, I had no recollection of any contact with Dick after the war. What I did have among the letters was a 1955 Christmas card that had a photo of Dick with a toddler on his shoulder. I assumed this was his son. Signed "Dick," the envelope bore no return address. After further browsing on the Internet I came upon a 1984 *New York Times* article announcing the marriage of Melanie Strauss to Eugene Blair Walton, the son of Dr. and Mrs. Richard Walton of Vernon, Connecticut. The groom had graduated from the Choate School and Duke University and later served in the Peace Corps. The groom's father, the article concluded, was a surgeon in private practice in Hartford, Connecticut.

Eureka! There it was. A phone call to Choate put me in contact with a most helpful gal by the name of Mickey, who gave me a phone number in Sacramento, California. Soon I was speaking with Melanie Walton, who sadly informed me that her father-in-law, Dick, had died in July 1992. An e-mail to her husband explaining my quest brought a prompt reply.

Sacramento, CA.
January 6, 2011

Dear Charles,

Thank you very much for tracking me down! It's very exciting to learn of a connection with my father that goes back so far.

I know that you spent some time talking to Melanie yesterday, but I will give you a quick story:

When you last heard from my Dad in 1955, he was likely still a surgical resident at Yale. (I say "likely," because I do not remember exactly when he finished medical school or his residency.) He went on to have a very successful career as a general surgeon in Vernon. He continued his association with Yale as a clinic professor throughout his career. He also served as the President of the Connecticut State Medical Society. He retired around 1989 and moved to North Carolina to enjoy his lifelong passion of golf. Sadly, he died in 1992 from prostate cancer. My Dad loved golf, music, plays, and the Red Sox. My Mom was a nurse, but took many years off from her career to raise her family of five children. She returned to work in the mid-1970's in the hospital that my Dad practiced and retired about the same time as my Dad. My Mom died three years ago.

Thank you again for reaching out to me. A day does not go by where I do not think about my parents. They were very devoted to each other and to their family, and they had a very happy life together. I would love to hear more about you and about any stories or recollections that you may have about my Dad.

Best Regards,
Gene Walton

"What a damn shame," I said, deeply moved after reading the letter to Circe. "Only sixty-seven. Prostate cancer. And Dick was a doctor. Such a pity that we never got together. He was such a great guy, so alive. I can't believe that he's gone."

"It is sad, very sad," Circe agreed. "But after the war each of you had a direction and pursued your own dream. I'm sure he thought of you often. His letters tell me how close you were. Like brothers."

A day or so later, I awoke with severe back pain and found myself unable to mount the steps to the third floor. After sitting glued before the computer all summer, I had irritated an old herniated disk. On powerful painkillers, I spent the next month hobbling about with a cane until I finally found the right doctor, who cleared up my problem with an epidural. My first social venture out of the house was to a surprise birthday luncheon for my sister at the home of her neighbors, Dr. and Emma James. Talking with Dr. James, I was surprised to learn that he had been in the high school class of 1946, just a year behind me. After serving as a medic in the Philippines during the war, he attended dental school and practiced in New Britain until his retirement a few years ago. He remembered Morry Blair but could shed no light on what happened to the guy down in Florida, saying he was always something of an unsavory character. We talked about Dick Walton, and I told him of my collection of letters. He remembered Meg Bolan and Mary Jo as "two attractive livewires" in his class. He confirmed Meg had passed away years ago. Casually, he remarked that Mary Jo had died only a week ago.

Taken aback, I believed he was experiencing one of those senior moments that frequently afflict the elderly. "Are you sure? I talked to her a month ago before she went to Florida, and she was fine. There wasn't anything in the paper. Where did you get the news?"

"AOL," he replied. "I never bother with newspapers any longer."

I had my doubts, but Doc James had it right. The very next day the Hartford Courant had a lengthy obituary on Mary Jo Hennessy Allen Parsons. It mentioned no cause of death, only that Mary Jo had passed away peacefully at age eighty-six. A call to her daughter Sally, a registered nurse, was more informative. She believed her mother had been the victim of an overdose of radiation. Before leaving Florida this past spring, she had undergone a series of treatments for melanoma lesions on her legs.

"Crocodile skin," I said to Circe. "That's what Mary Jo called it. And she never complained. She joked about it. Poor Peaches. Another one of the old gang gone. I was counting on her to fill in some of the blanks for me. She will be sorely missed."

I phoned Helen to tell her the sad news. We had been e-mailing and phoning regularly since we first got back in touch, but because of the long drive to Maine had not yet met face to face. Helen had never met Mary Jo, but felt as though she knew her after reading the Peaches letters.

"She sounds like fun," Helen said after offering her condolences. "I wish I could have met her. Eighty-six? Younger than you and I, Charles, but take heart. My brother is ninety-five and doing fine. His wife is a few years younger and has been slipping into confusion. But what can you say after a person has had such a long and good life?" she added with a chuckle. "Like us. You never know. Not many tough old birds left."

The fine October weather continued into the first week of November. In keeping with my doctor's regimen that I walk at least a mile each day, Circe and I began a daily trek to Betty's house, where we usually had lunch. Extending our walk home after one such jaunt, I pointed out to Circe the old the skating pond, the wooden bridge, and the spillway in the park, landmarks that she had been reading about in the letters. All were remarkably unchanged after over half a century. A few blocks away from the park, however, I was in for quite a surprise. The sign on the corner read *Arthur Street*, but the Walton house was gone, along with Valin house and every other residential dwelling on the street. In their stead stood a multistory dormitory and a series of academic buildings, all now incorporated into the bordering university campus. Was my mind playing tricks? To assure myself that I was not a little addled, we walked over to the former Darcy residence on nearby Arthur Court. The short cul-de-sac that I recalled had two houses on either side and the Darcy property across the far end. All had fallen into a state of total disrepair. In keeping with cracked sidewalks and potholes in the street, battered pickup trucks and junk cars littered the neglected grounds. None of the houses had been painted in years. Broken windows and several doors stood open to the weather. It appeared squatters were living in the old Darcy house, but there was no one around to ask.

"Jesus, Circe, the place is a junkyard!" I exclaimed as we left the court. "Have you ever in your life seen such a mess? And just around the corner from the university. Talk about urban blight. You can't believe what a nice neighborhood that was. So many memories. The hours I spent under the streetlight down at the end! I just hope Launa hasn't seen it."

"Hardly likely," Circe replied. "How long ago did she move from New Britain?"

"Sixty years or so, if you can believe it. I have the idea she is living somewhere nearby, probably in the West Hartford area. She must come back to New Britain to visit old friends. I really would like to see her again. But then how would I approach her after all these years? A phone call? Just appear on her doorstep? And what would her husband say? I wonder if she had those sons she wrote about in her letters. I know she's out there someplace. It would be so neat to meet up and talk over old times."

"I wouldn't get too wound up or be overly optimistic," Circe cautioned, shaking her head. "I'm sorry, darling, but from what I've gathered from her letters and from what you've told me, I'm afraid you may be disappointed like you were with Dick Walton."

"Oh, come on, love. Look, I found Helen, and I can find Launa. My vibes tell me she is out there waiting for her old boyfriend to give her a buzz."

"After so many years? When was the last time you had news of her?"

"It had to be 1949. Benny ran into her while shopping in West Hartford. He told me she had recently married that guy from Fox's."

"And what about you? When was the last time you two actually saw each other?"

I felt the blood rush to my face. "The day she dumped me," I said bluntly, after some reflection. "A day I'll never forget. It's like it happened yesterday. I ... I ... oh, Jesus, I really don't want to discuss this."

"But we should discuss it – unless, of course, you don't want to know what happened to her."

I again fell silent. "The spring of 1947," I began slowly, measuring my words. "West Hartford. Her parents had recently bought a house there. I drove up thinking it would be the happiest day of my life. It turned out to be the worst." I paused, unsure whether or not I wanted to continue.

"You were at the teachers college at the time, weren't you?" Circe prompted. "The year after the war."

I nodded. "I had finished the year and been accepted at Columbia. I was on cloud nine. Launa was graduating; I had the GI Bill and money in the bank for an engagement ring. I saw us setting up our home in New York. In her letters Launa wrote about going there to work after graduation. She also talked about becoming a doctor. What could be more perfect? In my excitement, I called New London to tell her I was coming down with great news. She wasn't there, so I talked to her roommate, Gabby, a flirty screwball. To make a long story short, she told me that Launa was in West Hartford with her folks, something to do with a job after graduation - a marketing fellowship at Fox's, one of the premier department stores in the country. It seems her mother had gotten her an interview, and Launa had a callback that day."

"So what did you do?" Circe asked when I again fell silent.

I looked at my wife. "I didn't know what the hell was going on. Especially when Gabby told me some older guy named Fred had been driving down weekends to see Launa. I was curious but not jealous. Since the ninth grade there had been only one guy in Launa's life, and that was yours truly. To get to the bottom of things, I drove up to West Hartford. I remember it was around four o'clock on a Saturday afternoon. I had thought about calling first, but I didn't want any static from her parents. They were always off doing their own thing and never around all the time I was going with Launa, so

I had never met them. Anyway, I found the house without difficulty. Surprisingly, it wasn't one of those West Hartford mansions I had expected, but a cheap-looking two-bedroom Cape with a single-car garage. Launa answered the door. Quite surprised to see me, she nervously glanced about and turned her cheek when I attempted to kiss her. She was pale and had dark circles beneath her eyes. I sensed at once something was not right. But she assured me everything was fine. "Phoebe is here," she continued in a voice hardly above a whisper. "Marvin is playing golf. As soon as he gets back, they're off to a cocktail party at the Statler."

"Great, I thought to myself in the belief that we would have the evening to ourselves as she led me into a spartanly furnished living room. I can still see it clearly: only a sofa and two easy chairs, no rug on the floor, no picture on the wall or a decoration. Nothing to indicated a home. We sat on the sofa, and talked about Fox's. She had gotten the fellowship in marketing, supposedly a good deal that paid well. She hadn't said anything to me earlier because she wanted to be sure of the job. Launa was like that. To be honest, I didn't give a damn about the Fox's fellowship. I then told her I had been accepted at Columbia, and she was genuinely delighted. I took her hand and was just about to pop the big question when this woman suddenly sauntered into the room. My eyes popped out of my head as Launa introduced Phoebe. The woman was more than beautiful, she was stunning. Hair, eyes, lips, skin, all exquisitely made-up. And tall, five ten or so. She wore a floor-length brocade shift and sandals. A cigarette in one hand, a drink in the other, she settled into a chair opposite us and showed no intention of leaving. Speechless, I stared at her. Even though Launa never wore makeup, the resemblance between the two was uncanny. They could have been sisters rather than mother and daughter."

Circe smiled ruefully. "The way Miss Phoebe would have preferred it, I'm sure. According to several studies, women and men with extraordinary good looks apparently often feel a sense of entitlement to the bounties of this earth."

"This one certainly did. With her looks, she would have made a splash wherever she and the husband went. Or so I thought until Launa introduced us and the woman opened her mouth. One moment she was all sugar and cream, a real charmer. The next moment she was coarse and tough. Street smart, know what I mean? She said her sister Minnie – the Miss O'Hare that Launa had lived with that year in New Britain – had told her all about me. She knew about Harvard and said that it was too bad I didn't have the brains to stay there."

"What a ghastly thing to say," Circe said. "The woman must...."

"Wait, there's more. You haven't heard the half of it. When Launa tried to smooth things over, saying I'd been accepted at Columbia, her mother made a snotty remark about 'Jew York' and asked what I intended to study. I told her liberal arts. And that I wanted to write. She scoffed and said writers today were starving to death. By this time, I was beginning to like the woman less and less. It was obvious she wanted me out of there. At the same time I felt trapped, like a rabbit in a python cage. I was being toyed with before the fatal strike, which wasn't long in coming. Taking a drag on her cigarette, she cagily asked Launa if she had told me about Fred."

"The older fellow?" Circe asked. "The one who had been running down to New London to see her?"

"Right. I looked at Launa, and she turned away, avoiding my eyes. She said there was nothing to tell."

"What on earth was her mother up to?"

"The bitch said Fred had been driving down to New London to see her daughter and that a week ago he had presented her with a two carat diamond. The ring was at the jeweler's being sized."

"My God, what did you say?"

"I don't know. Something stupid like, *Six or six and a half. Why didn't he ask me?* I was at a total loss. My whole world was crumbling about me."

"And Launa? What was her reaction?"

"She told me that she hadn't said yes yet."

"And her mother?"

"Words I'll never forget. 'You'll say yes when the time comes,' she threatened Launa. She then went on about Fred being a big shot at Fox's who'd be running the company some day."

"You must have been mortified."

"More than that. Love, hate, rage. I looked at Launa. Never had I loved her more than at that moment, or hated anyone more than I did her mother. If I had a knife, a pistol, a weapon of any kind, I would have happily dispatched her on the spot."

"And Launa? The poor girl must have been horribly upset. What did she say?"

"Not a word. She had tears in her eyes, and a look that I've never forgotten. It told me that she loved me. It also told me that not only would she not cross that smug bitch sitting across from us, but that she couldn't. And that was it. The rest of that afternoon is a blank. I don't remember leaving or the drive home. I was in shock."

"And Launa? How did you feel about her?"

"No different. Of course, I was heartsick. At the same time, I had to admit the python had a point. I was twenty-one. What did I have to offer? Not even the proverbial pot. Launa was finishing college and ready to settle down. I had years of schooling ahead of me, and no guarantee of when I would be making a buck. Living on a government handout in a cheap flat wasn't all that attractive."

"That wouldn't have mattered, not if she loved you." Circe paused and then asked, "Was this the last time you two saw each other?"

"The very last. But I still didn't believe we were through. I had hope until I heard she was married. By that time I was at Columbia and had turned my life around. Like I said, I met Marcie and we got married in my junior year. But that's another story."

"And so Launa faded into the background?"

"More or less, you can say that. But I could never put that final meeting in West Hartford behind me. That look in Launa's eyes still haunts me."

Circe smiled and held my hand. "Well, that's understandable. You had been in love with the girl since you were in the ninth grade. Any breakup was bound to be traumatic. But that, my darling, was in the far, far past. Now, in the present, do you have any idea how we should go about our search for Launa?"

"I have as a matter of fact," I replied smugly. "I've been thinking about this a lot lately. I know exactly where we are going to start, and it's not on the Internet. Tomorrow we'll be taking a little ride."

The next morning I was all set to visit Connecticut College, a two-hour drive from New Britain. I phoned the alumni office to check on their hours. The clerk seemed reluctant to divulge any information other than the fact that a Launa Darcy had graduated in the class of 1947. No, the school did not have her current address. And no, the school did not have a married name. Full stop.

"That was a downer," I said, turning to Circe. "Did the dingbat think I was some kind of a nut stalking an eighty-five-year-old woman?"

Back to square one, I read through the letters for a clue but came up empty-handed. And suddenly there was a bolt from the blue. Briarly Hall! Launa had been enrolled in the prep school the fall after she had been shipped out of New Britain.

The alumni secretary at Briarly was pleasant, even eager to assist me. The school had nothing current, but their old records did show a married name of Henry and an address in North Granby, Connecticut.

Circe was skeptical. "I hope you know what you're doing, Charlie. I'm still afraid you may be in for a disappointment."

"Not this time, love. My vibes tell me we're on the right track. Think positive. Isn't that what you keep telling me?"

On this high note, I punched my information into the computer and struck pay dirt. *Edward Henry.* There he was in East Granby.

Scarcely able to contain myself, and without any forethought as to what I would say, I dialed the number on the screen . My heart racing, I looked at Circe while listening to the phone ring.

A woman picked up.

I took a deep breath and swallowed hard. Somehow, I managed to give my name and ask for Launa Henry.

"I'm Renee, her daughter-in-law."

Words failed me. "I ... I ..." I stammered. "I'm an old friend of Launa's ... from New Britain ... the ninth grade ... we ..."

"Hang on a second, you want to talk to my husband."

"Hey, Ed!" I heard her shout. "Pick up the phone. An old boyfriend of Launa's is on the line."

"Ed Henry," said a brusque, businesslike voice. "What's this about my mother?"

"We wrote during the war," I said. "I was with the marines out in ..."

The tone brightened. "No shit! I was a marine sergeant in Nam. *Semper Fi.* Once a Jarhead, always a Jarhead. How can I help you, old buddy?"

"Ed, Mr. Young called about Launa," Renee broke in. "A girl couldn't have wished for a better mother-in-law."

"And she was a great mom," Ed added. "The best."

Was a great mom. The starch went out of me. Every fiber in my body shrieked *no, no, no..* Contrary to Circe's ambivalent outlook, I had been certain all along that I would find Launa alive and well as I did Helena and Mary Jo.

"Launa passed away in 1989," Renee resumed. "It seems like yesterday. We all miss her. Not a day ..."

"But ... but ... so young ..." I faltered, struggling to reconcile myself to what I was hearing.

"A blessing, in a way," Fred rejoined. "Diabetes and lung cancer. No picnic, let me tell you."

"It was more than that, Ed," Renee said quietly. "After your dad died there was all that business with Phoebe. She made your mother's life hell. Don't you remember that last Mother's Day? Launa was tired. She wanted to go. She just didn't want to live through that holiday."

"It was a long time ago," Ed said. "Water over the dam. But you're right about Mother's Day. My mother got her wish and died on the day before the holiday."

Numbed by what I had heard, I managed to express my condolences and ended our conversation with the understanding that we would talk again.

"Only sixty-three," I said to Circe. "Launa has been gone for twenty-two years, nearly a quarter of a century."

"And all that time you believed she was living. What else did they have to say?"

"The daughter-in-law said something about Mother's Day. I have a feeling that there's more here than meets the eye. I'll have to talk to Ed again."

At Circe's suggestion, we set up a timetable to get a clearer indication of Launa's life. We added bits and pieces of information gleaned from the Indian Lake letters of 1940 and those written to me during the war from 1943 to 1945.

Subsequent calls to Ed and Renee revealed the dates of Launa's marriage and the birth of her son, but there was no mention of Phoebe or Marvin. As in my case, her son had gone back to school after his hitch in the marines and was now an engineer working for the state. His father, Ed Sr., died in 1975 at the age of fifty-six.

He had gone into the hospital for a routine hernia operation and sometime during the night fallen out of bed. He wasn't discovered until hours later and died of a ruptured pancreas.

"My God, 1975!" I exclaimed to Circe. A chill ran down my spine. " Marcie died that same year. Launa and I were both in the same boat. But she had no brothers or sisters. She was on her own with a son to support. Why didn't I hear about it? Someone should have known. Benny, even my sister."

"I don't know about that," Circe said thoughtfully. "Not if she had left New Britain and was living in West Hartford under the name of Henry. Perhaps her parents helped her out. Check with Ed the next time you talk to him."

Ed laughed cynically when I broached the subject. "Are you kidding? Phoebe was never around when we needed her. We had a big house, and as long as my father was alive, he served as a buffer. He wouldn't take any shit from Phoebe. But then after he died, and Marvin a short time later, Phoebe moved in and took over. All she did was bitch and find fault. I begged my mother to put her in a home, but she wouldn't hear of it. I finally joined the corps just to get away from all the screaming and hollering."

"Poor Launa," I said to Circe after reporting my conversation with Ed. "Everything seems to go downhill after the death of her husband. Even the mighty Fox's went into decline and ultimately folded. But Launa was no shrinking violet. Ed said she was something of a liberated woman, a feminist long before the movement got underway. Perhaps this is why she never remarried."

"Somehow that doesn't surprise me. It fits her history of prior neglect," Circe said, shaking her head. "But think of her mother, the woman who defied the gods. A classic narcissist, she could have stepped out of a Greek tragedy. She had absolutely no concern for the welfare of others, not even her own daughter. From the time of her birth, that child was emotionally abandoned, shunted aside to live with a relative or enrolled in a boarding school. And when she developed into a beautiful young woman, the mother was right there to manipulate her into a marriage for gain that was to prove futile. And fatal. "

"You're right, love. It is like a Greek tragedy. How did you figure this all out?"

"It doesn't take much imagination when you look back through the letters and from what we've been told by the Henrys. Here you have the beautiful Phoebe—I hesitate to use the word mother—and her obsession with dwelling among the rich and famous. What do we know about her husband?"

" Pussy-whipped, in Ed's book, a real wimp. What you would expect from someone married to Phoebe. But Marvin was also debonair and a smooth talker. The perfect host, for years he managed hotels and resorts in Florida and New England."

"Managed," Circe said, nodding. "Obviously the man was enamored with Phoebe, just as you were with her daughter. And how did he go about impressing this beauty who saw only dollar signs? Was she led to believe he was the owner of this ... this ..."

"Inn. The White Horse. Launa stayed there before she went to college. Pretty ritzy, I would say."

"Precisely. And exactly what Phoebe was seeking, life among the elite. We may never know, but I'd venture she may have believed she was marrying the owner. You can imagine the ire when she learned her husband was one step above the waiters and chambermaids."

"So why didn't she up and leave the guy? She was still a looker."

"This is all speculation on my part, but she may have been pregnant. The word *abortion* was vilified then. And didn't you say the family was Irish Catholic?"

"I really can't see that stopping Phoebe," I said, fascinated by Circe's spin. "Somehow, I can't feel sorry for her. So what did the bitch do, according to your theory?"

"The woman was no stay-at-home mom. She cut her losses and made the best of a bad deal. She neglected the child, stuck with her husband, and continued to mingle with the hoi polloi."

"The pregnancy angle could be valid. Fred said his grandmother was always whining about the difficult delivery she had with Launa. Okay, so Phoebe settled for second best. Always the bridesmaid, never the bride. Old Marvin might also have had a weakness for the bottle, according to Ed. Seems his wife kept him on the straight and narrow."

Circe shook her head. "Not for his good, you can be sure. But for hers."

"Poor bastard. Who wouldn't drink living with the python? Launa, however, seems to have gotten along with her dad, even though he, too, was absent a good part of the time."

"Perhaps, but the two were no match for Phoebe. She ruled the roost with an iron fist. The husband could take it; the daughter could not. The poor girl never had a chance."

I looked at Circe skeptically. "How can you be so sure? A lot of psychiatry today has turned out to be pure hogwash."

Circe smiled knowingly. "Then think of it as common sense. Look again at the letters. Launa never had a real interest in other men, just you. She cared for you dearly, but it wasn't love. Because of her damaged psyche, the kind of love you were seeking from her was impossible. Launa was bright. We get this again and again in her letters. As long as Phoebe was alive, she believed, hoped she might be the recipient of that love from her mother which would restore the missing element."

"You could be right," I had to admit. "According to Ed, Launa's health wasn't too good at the time. She finally realized she couldn't take care of the demanding Phoebe and put her in a nursing home. Launa stopped in at the nursing home every day to see that the bitter old crone was getting proper treatment. And she managed to hold down a job in an insurance firm."

"Launa was a good person. It must have been somewhat of a relief for her when Phoebe was finally gone. Such a burden all those years. What else did Ed have to say?"

"What else was there to say? That said it all. I don't know how much Launa drank, but she was a heavy smoker. Between diabetes, lung cancer, and Phoebe, she was worn out. Mother's Day was the final irony. She could no longer face up to the charade."

Circe brushed the tears from her eyes. "You're right. The poor dear finally understood what her mother had done to her life and just gave up."

Or perhaps, I thought to myself the next day, the true tragedy lay in the fact that Launa had understood her plight from the very beginning. At my desk on the third floor, I leafed through the letters a final time before putting them back into the box for storage.

You're about the only thing in my life I can count on. Remind me to tell you about my life sometime – it's quite a hellish mess. You really know very little about me when it comes right down to it, m'love.

Speaking of New York, I'm going to take an apartment there after I graduate. Sounds quite gay, don't you think?

Min is going to have a baby. Whoever would have thought that of Miss O'Hare! But I think it's wonderful – and I hope it's a boy.

The latest news about the Darcy family is that Dad is thinking of leasing an apartment by the year in West Harford. That entails selling the house in New Britain…which is about the only home I ever had. When I finally do get a home, "I ain't ever gonna roam, law'd."

A Christmas without a tree, indifferent parents whose only interest was moving up the social scale, a preference for sons over daughters, the stark West Hartford house. The red flags were all up. Why hadn't I seen them and taken some action? Circe, who could be more objective, pointed out that Launa's psyche had been scarred long before I came on to the scene. Blindsided by love, I saw in Launa only the beauty I wished to behold. And now she was gone as were my parents, brother, Dick, and all those who had played such a critical role in my past. I looked again at the pair of silver lapel pins, which would hold little interest for anyone alive today. Should I take them over to the park and drop them into the spillway to blend with the elements? Were they even mine to dispose of? I didn't think so. Somewhat regretfully, I arranged the tokens in their case and then set it into the box with the letters of the rightful owners, those two kids who had pledged their love to each other in another world long, long ago. That world had now vanished. Still, it would not surprise me if a pair of wraith-like figures were to appear on that wooden bridge in the park on the night of the next full moon.

ABOUT THE AUTHOR

Charles Young was born in New Britain, Connecticut. He finished high school in 1943 and entered a naval program at Harvard University. After serving in the US Navy and the US Marine Corps during World War II, he attended Central Connecticut University for a year before transferring to Columbia University where he received a BA and an MA. He then spent a year in a PhD program at Yale University. In 1967 he moved to Athens, Greece, with his wife Marcie and their three children, Tina, Fay, and Charles. There he taught at Athens College. In 1978, following the death of his wife, he moved to the island of Hydra, pursued his writing and taught at the National Maritime Academy. Two of his novels, *The Last Man On Earth* and *Clouds Over Hydra*, became bestsellers. Other novels are *Luck Of The Draw*, *Potassett*, and *The Hydra Chronicle*. Young and his second wife, Mary, divide their time between Hydra, Greece, and Madison, Connecticut.

CPSIA information can be obtained at www.ICGtesting.com
Printed in the USA
LVOW08*1150120114

369094LV00002B/94/P